D1502287

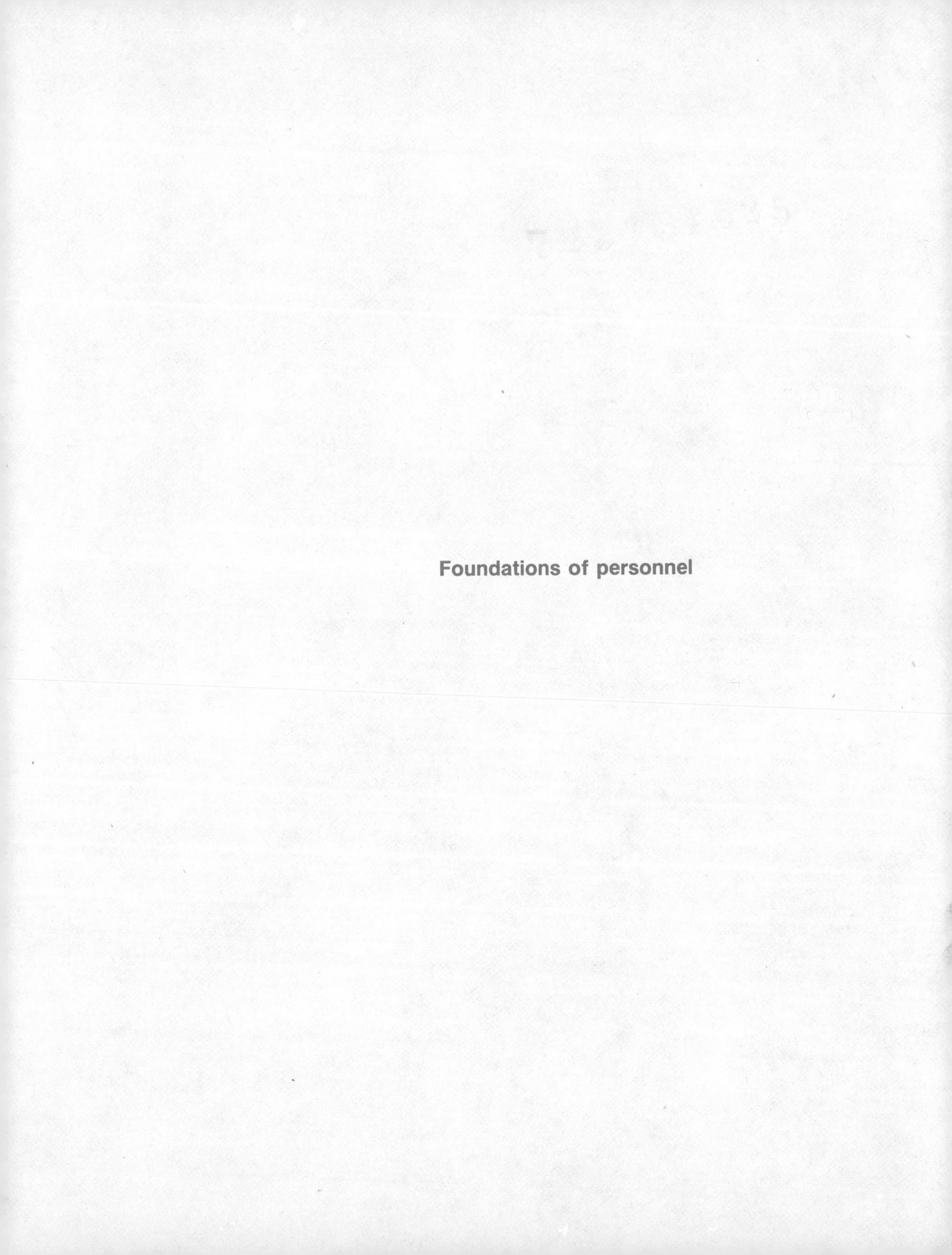

Foundations of personnel

Foundations of personnel

William F. Glueck
The University of Georgia

1979

BUSINESS PUBLICATIONS, INC. Dallas, Texas 75243
Irwin-Dorsey Limited Georgetown, Ontario L7G 4B3

Principal photography by James W. Morgenthaler.

ISBN 0-256-02202-X
Library of Congress Catalog Card No. 78–70016

Printed in the United States of America

1 2 3 4 5 6 7 8 9 0 K 6 5 4 3 2 1 0 9

This book is dedicated to my parents
ALICE BUXSEL GLUECK
and
FRANK CHARLES GLUECK
for all their help over the years.

Preface

Experienced managers tell us constantly that their most significant problems at work are "people" problems. And these problems are increasing because of an important influence of government regulation and legislation. The goal of this book is to introduce you to the functions of personnel and their impact on the entire enterprise. It will help the reader become a more effective employee in the personnel aspects of his/her job on many levels: entry, supervisor, middle manager, or executive.

Let's discuss briefly how the book has been written.

1. Each chapter begins with a list of behavioral objectives and a chapter outline.

2. Each chapter is held together by a case which is introduced early in the chapter, added to during the chapter, and concluded at the end of the chapter.

3. Each chapter begins with a diagnostic model and an analysis of how the individual and environmental factors affecting the personnel function influence the topic of the chapter.

4. Next, early in each chapter, the roles the personnel manager or personnel specialist and the operating managers play in the personnel function are described, as are the strategic decisions top managers make to lead to personnel effectiveness. This ties in with the emphasis in Chapter 1 on how personnel relates to top managers' strategic decisions.

5. The introduction also includes definitions of the activities and why they are performed.

6. A large number of pictures and illustrations are used to enhance learning. (Photos used to illustrate cases, unless indicated otherwise, were posed and do not represent real persons or situations.)

7. Each chapter concludes with recommendations for the most effective way to use personnel in different organizations since the personnel function is not performed the same way in all organizations. The mechanism used to do this is seven model organizations. These seven differ systematically by size (number of employees), complexity of products or services, and volatility of organization (degree to which the products/services change over time). Examples of the model organizations are given from business, government, and hospitals. The reader is invited to focus on the organization where she or he has worked or wants to work. Thus the reader can get an idea of how personnel management is practiced.

8. This book is based on a large number of research references. No footnotes

clutter the pages, however. A short reference list is provided at the end of the book.

An important emphasis of this book is cost/benefits analysis of the personnel function. In each personnel area, an attempt has been made to try to evaluate its usefulness in terms of cost and benefits to the employer. Since personnel must compete for resources against requests for new machinery, more advertising, and new buildings, the expenditures and investments in the organization's people must be justified.

The chapter summary, conclusions, and recommendations include a summary of the major points, often in the form of propositions and recommendations for use in the seven model organizations.

The topics covered emphasize the most vital areas in personnel today.

- First the book deals with factors in the individual and in the work environment that influence people at work. This portion draws heavily on the most recent and relevant findings of the behavioral sciences and other disciplines.
- Then there follows a chapter on communications, designed to emphasize how communications are critical to effective human resource management.
- The challenges of personnel management are discussed—planning for employment, recruitment, selection, and so on. I have tried very hard to put emphasis on the most significant and relevant topics in personnel today, including equal employment opportunity, health and safety, compensation and benefits (including pensions), and career development.

Some newer topics include: personnel specialization and professionalization, including ASPA's Accreditation Program (Chapter 1); a complete discussion of the labor force data (Chapter 4); the section on job analysis and job specifications (Chapter 4); and a complete section on working conditions including four-day weeks and flexitime.

An appendix to the recruiting chapter (Chapter 5) develops a strategy for the reader on how to find a job, and one to the selection chapter (Chapter 6) describes effective interviewing techniques. The latter chapter combines selection techniques for all employees, including managerial and professional. The performance evaluation chapter (Chapter 8) integrates evaluation of all employees, including managers.

Significant treatment of organizational development, transactional analysis, and behavioral modeling training is given in Chapter 10. Compensation has been split into two chapters and includes strong coverage of pay surveys and compensation issues such as salaries for everyone, pay secrecy, security in pay, and size of pay raises (Chapters 11 and 12). The pension chapter includes current questions such as the solvency of social security, ERISA, and ERISA's impact (Chapter 14). The health and safety chapter has given careful attention to the current problems in Workers' Compensation and OSHA (Chapter 15). The EEO chapter (Chapter 16) provides a complete summary of the legal status of EEO, as well as effective programs to deal with EEO problems. The labor chapter (Chapter 17) includes current changes in the laws and regulations of collective bargaining in all three sectors in the United States—private (business), public (government), and nonprofit (such as education and health).

The book contrasts personnel practices in the different sectors and whenever personnel practices differ significantly among them the differences are described. Important differences exist, for example, in labor relations, equal employment opportunities, health and safety, selection, compensation, and other areas.

Another book published by Business Publications, Inc., that can expand your understanding of personnel is William F. Glueck, *Cases and Exercises in Personnel,* revised edition (1978). This book is composed entirely of cases, incident cases, role-playing exercises, in-basket exercises, and experimental and field exercises. The book also includes cases and exercises for student application of personnel concepts to real life situations.

A third book published by Business Publications is *Workbook and Study Guide in Personnel* by William F. Glueck, Jerry Wall, and David Gray (1979). The book consists of sample test questions, homework exercises, field exercises, short cases and similar materials designed to help the student test his or her knowledge and provide the instructor with the ability to have in class or out of class work done to enhance personnel learning.

A fourth book published by Business Publications is *Personnel: A Book of Readings* by William F. Glueck (1979). This volume provides the opportunity for students and instructors to discuss significant research, conceptual materials, and position papers vital to an understanding of personnel today.

Foundations of Personnel has been written with the purpose of informing and exciting you about the importance and challenges of personnel. I hope it has achieved its purpose.

Acknowledgments

A book is always the product of many people. As the dedication page indicates, I want to acknowledge the love of learning I received from my parents.

But there are many people I wish to thank for their help on this book. The reviewers of this book were very helpful. They included Thomas H. Stone, University of Iowa; Ken Van Voorhis, University of South Florida; M. Gene Newport, University of Alabama-Birmingham; John A. Belt, Wichita State University; Cary D. Thorp, Jr., University of Nebraska; Herbert Heneman, Jr., University of Minnesota; David W. Belcher, San Diego State University; Walter Newsom, Mississippi State University; Jerry Wall, Western Illinois University; and Harish Jain, McMaster University;

I would like to thank the persons who gave me permission to reprint their material. This is especially true for those allowing me to reprint their cases.

My colleagues at the University of Georgia contributed ideas and useful criticism. Especially helpful were James Ledvinka, who helped greatly in the EEO area and James Lahiff, who helped in the selection area. I wish to thank James W. Morgenthaler for the fine job that he did in taking the photos which enhance the text. I also wish to thank Norman Miller for all his help. I am also most grateful for the very supportive climate at the University of Georgia. This is due to the efforts of Richard Huseman, Chairman, Department of Management, and Dean William Flewellen, Jr. They have helped me in more ways than they realize.

Very *special* thanks goes to Jean M. Miller, my administrative assistant. Jean helps in hundreds of ways and is crucial to the success of this book.

Finally, I wish to thank my wife, Nancy, who has been very helpful in many ways and was especially helpful on this book. She receives the *most special* thanks.

February 1979 WILLIAM F. GLUECK

Contents

part three
RECRUITMENT, SELECTION, AND ORIENTATION, 114

part four
PERFORMANCE EVALUATION AND DEVELOPMENT OF PERSONNEL, 198

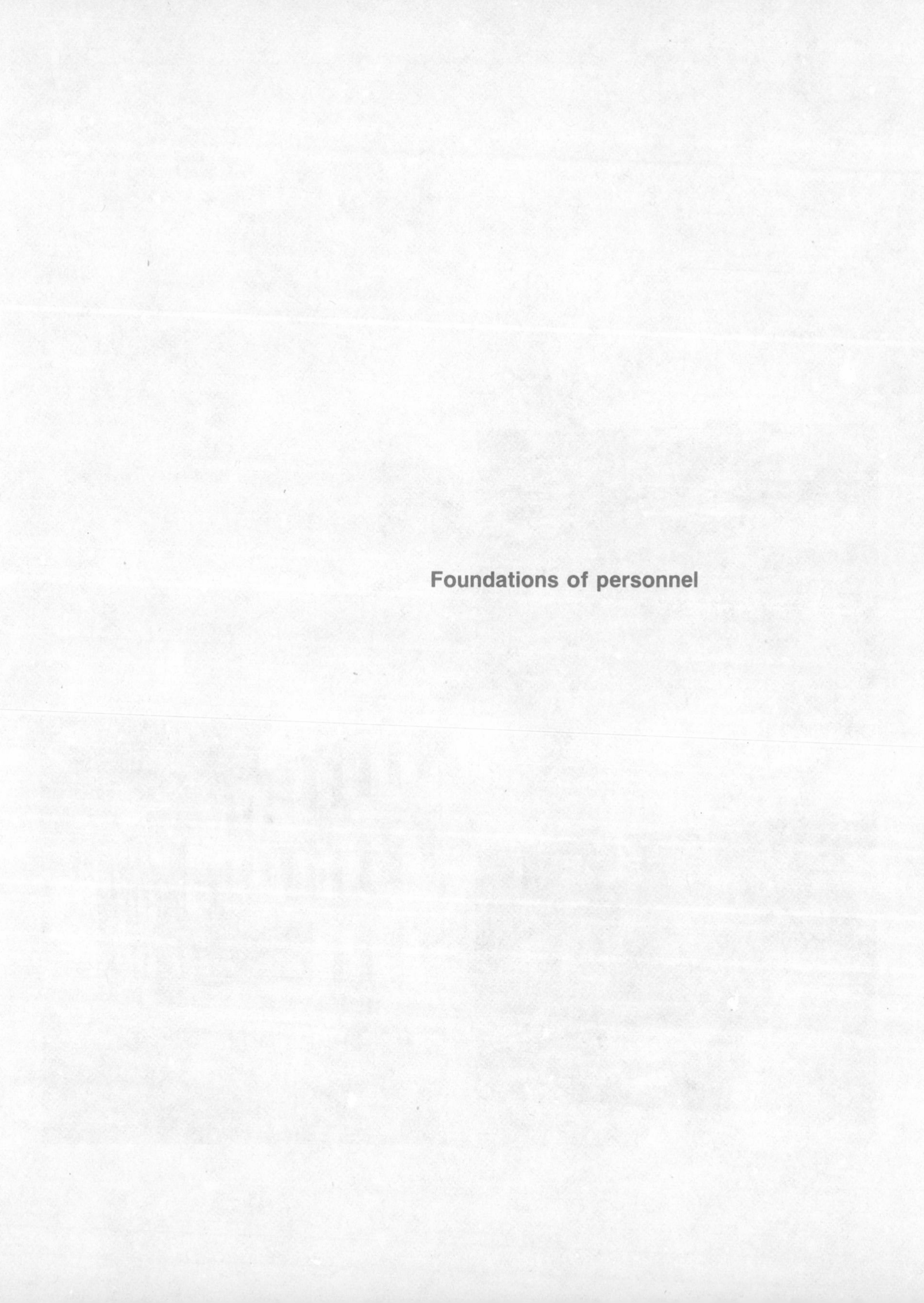

Foundations of personnel

HUTCHINS, COX,
STROUD & PIERSON
NSURANCE - REAL ESTATE
"SINCE 1890"

FEDERAL BUILDING

part one

Introduction to personnel

Personnel is that aspect of management which is concerned with the effective management of people at work. Personnel examines what is, can be, or should be done to make people both more productive and more satisfied with their working lives.

This book has been written for all those interested in personnel: employees, supervisors, managers, and other administrators. Its goal is to help develop more effective managers and staff specialists who work directly in people management functions. Their function is called personnel, employee relations, or human resources management.

Part One consists of three chapters. Chapter 1 is an introduction to personnel. The diagnostic approach to personnel is introduced in Chapter 2, which also reviews what is generally known about people and how this knowledge affects their effectiveness at work. The ways managers use knowledge of environmental factors, such as the work setting, government regulations, and union restrictions, to influence the performance of people at work are also discussed in Chapter 2. Chapter 3 describes communication and its relationship to personnel.

1

An introduction to personnel

Chapter objectives

- To tell you what personnel is and why it is worth studying.
- To show that personnel work is performed by operating managers, personnel specialists, and sometimes by both groups working together.
- To introduce you to the world of the personnel manager.
- To outline how this book will describe personnel management.

Chapter outline

John Traswell is a successful executive. He works for a firm producing popular music recordings. Up until now, he has held production and operations positions. He has been offered an executive position in the company's personnel department.

John

John earned a degree in business administration ten years ago. He remembers some coverage of personnel in a management course he took 12 years ago. But he hasn't had formal training in it. His company gave him some time to think about the personnel position. While doing so, he started gathering clippings and noting other references to personnel activities. Some items he noted provided this information:

- In 1978, the United Mine Workers union shut down the unionized mines with a strike. Soon the coal stopped flowing to power companies. People had to cut the temperatures in their homes; workplaces such as factories had to close. Federal marshals were sent to the coalfields to enforce a Taft-Hartley injunction and to prevent violence. President Carter began to question the feasibility of shifting from petroleum to coal to meet our energy needs.
- In recent years the United States has experienced raging inflation. When this happens the average person's paycheck drops. This has led to demands for pay increases, as it has at John's company. If these pay increases are granted without increases in productivity, prices go up. This leads to more inflation, more demands for higher pay, and so on.
- Managers have always tried to reduce costs, especially in times of inflation and recession. Often cost cutting has focused on better financial management and similar items. But payroll costs are the largest single item at John's firm and in the budgets of most enterprises. So when the squeeze comes, more and more enterprises turn to layoffs in an effort to develop greater personnel effectiveness.
- Numerous persons are always unemployed. Many economists believe this is because the minimum wage is scheduled to be $2.90 in 1979 and $3.35 in 1981.
- In 1977, the U.S. government passed the largest tax increase in its history. Were these taxes needed to fight a war? No. They were needed to try to prevent the bankruptcy of the social security systems. A major reason for the increase was that inflation had cut the value of social security benefits. But studies indicate that the increase in social security taxes has caused more unemployment and more inflation.
- In 1977, the value of U.S. private pension plans was $350 billion. If their growth continues at the current rate, private pension funds will equal $700 billion in 1985. That's more than all stocks and bonds in the stock market were valued at in 1975.
- Cummins Engine Company has been studying the impact of the Employment Retirement and Income Security Act (ERISA.) In 1970, the firm set aside $2 million a year for its pension plan. Soon it had to set aside $10 million, and by 1995 it was expected the cost would be $42 million per year. What do you think these increases do to the prices of their products?
- From 1974 to 1975, General Motors spent $29 million and invested 11 million years to implement federal government safety regulations as specified by the Occupational Safety and Health Act (OSHA). GM was inspected 614 times and received 258 citations. But GM had no reduction in accidents during this period.
- Many enterprises are being sued for employment discrimination by women and minorities. These include the city of Chicago, the U.S. Army, Chase Manhattan Bank, and United Airlines. These enterprises know what EEOC and OFCCP mean. Women, minorities, and the handicapped are increasingly seeking more jobs and better jobs than they have had in the past.
- Employers are complaining that one of their biggest problems today is trying to get a fair day's work from employees who are drunk or spaced out on drugs on the job. This is one of John's problems with his employees at work.

As John thought about these news stories and his experiences at work, he realized that personnel is an important job. In fact, maybe it was too challenging for him. He wondered if he should take the personnel job at his firm. (We will learn his decision at the end of the chapter.)

John's situation and the news stories associated with his job choice decision are all related to the personnel job. They should help bring home to you the relevance and impact of personnel today, whether you are an employee, a supervisor or operating manager, a taxpayer, or a personnel specialist, or you are studying to be an employee, manager, or personnel manager. This book is designed to make you knowledgeable about these and many other significant management challenges. It will help you become a more effective manager of people and personnel issues.

For any enterprise to operate effectively, it must have money, materials, supplies, equipment, ideas about the services or products to offer those who might use its outputs, and people to run the enterprise. *The effective management of people at work—the function of personnel—is the subject of this book.*

People are the most important resource in the enterprise, since people make the decisions concerning all other organizational resources. People operate the machines, borrow the money, and come up with the ideas which give the enterprise its purpose.

In spite of its importance, however, the personnel function has been misunderstood, undermanaged, or mismanaged in many enterprises. The material in this book, supplemented with practical experience, should make the task of managing people at work easier and should produce better results.

In this book, "personnel" is the term used for the personnel or people function of an organization. Some enterprises call this function manpower management, human resources management, or employee relations, or they use other terms which are virtually the same as personnel. For simplicity's sake, the term "personnel" will be used here.

> Personnel is that function of all enterprises which provides for effective utilization of human resources to achieve both the objectives of the enterprise and the satisfaction and development of the employees.

Personnel consists of numerous activities, including:

- Employee planning.
- Employee recruitment, selection, and orientation.
- Career development and counseling, performance evaluation, and training and development.
- Compensation and protection.
- Safety and health.
- Equal employment opportunity programs.
- Labor relations.
- Discipline, control, and evaluation of the personnel function.

These activities are the subjects of the various chapters in the book. They also appear as elements in the diagnostic model of the personnel function which is employed throughout. (This model is described in Chapter 2.) These also are the topics of the news stories John Traswell was noting at the beginning of this chapter. Three things should be stressed about personnel at the outset. Personnel is:

Future oriented. Effective personnel management is *future* oriented. It is concerned with helping an enterprise achieve its objectives in the future by providing for competent, well-motivated employees.

Action oriented. Effective personnel management is *action* oriented. Personnel is not focused on record keeping, written procedures, or rules; rather, it emphasizes the solution of employment problems to help achieve organizational objectives and facilitate employee development and satisfaction.

Individuality oriented. Whenever possible personnel treats each employee as an *individual* and offers the services and programs to meet the individual's needs. McDonald's, the fast-food chain, has gone so far as to give its chief personnel executive the title of Vice President of Individuality.

PERSONNEL AND ORGANIZATIONAL EFFECTIVENESS

Personnel activities can help in many ways to ensure that the enterprise will survive and prosper. The following case example illustrates how oversight of the personnel function can detract from the effectiveness of the enterprise.

> Ted Byers is the president of a firm with 225 employees, called Services Unlimited, which offers maintenance and repair services to enterprises in its area on a contract or fee basis. The firm is reasonably successful. Ted, who has always been mechanically inclined, is a registered professional engineer in Illinois. He graduated with honors in mechanical engineering from Purdue University ten years ago. He worked for a similar firm in Chicago, then started his own service company there.
>
> Helen Brooks is in charge of financial and accounting activities, and Ed Webber contacts the accounts and sells SU's services. Ted handles purchasing and oversees the operations of the equipment himself, but whenever he is working on an important mechanical problem or bidding a job he is likely to be interrupted. It may be a dispute between supervisor and worker; or someone quits; or an employee wants a raise or is dissatisfied with the holiday schedule.

It should be fairly obvious that Ted has organized to take care of his money, marketing, and machinery problems, but he is disinclined to deal with people problems. Yet a closer analysis of his firm would show that these problems are limiting his growth and his satisfaction with SU. What Ted needs is some help on personnel management.

Successful firms recognize that the human resource deserves attention because it is a significant factor in top management's strategic decisions, which guide the organization in its future operations. People do the work and create the ideas that allow the enterprise to survive. Even the most capital-intensive enterprises need people to run them.

Managers analyze the objectives, examine the environment for opportunities and threats, evaluate the strengths and weaknesses of the organization, and make strategic decisions based on these analyses. Personnel considerations are a significant part of these decisions in several ways. For one thing, people limit or enhance the strengths and weaknesses of the enterprise: A construction firm with too few engineers could not get the contract it seeks, for example. Current changes in the environment often are related to human resources, such as shifts in the composition, education, and work attitudes of employees; demands for more liberalized work organizations; and increased expectations of what the personnel function should provide.

One problem top management has in making strategic planning decisions regarding people is that all other resources are evaluated in terms of money. At present, people are not. There has been a movement toward human resource accounting, which would place dollar values on the human assets of the enterprise. Up to the present, however, it has been talked about by professors but rarely implemented.

OBJECTIVES OF THE PERSONNEL FUNCTION

The contributions personnel makes to organizational effectiveness are reflected in the objectives pursued by personnel specialists and departments. These include the following:

Objectives of the personnel function:

1. To help the enterprise reach its goals.
2. To use the work force efficiently.
3. To provide the enterprise with well-trained and well-motivated employees.
4. To increase to the fullest the employee's job satisfaction and self-actualization.
5. To develop and maintain a quality of work life which makes employment in the enterprise a desirable personal and social situation.
6. To communicate personnel and managerial policies to all concerned.
7. To help maintain ethical policies and behavior.
8. To manage change to the mutual advantage of individuals, groups, the enterprise, and the public.

• To Help the Enterprise Reach Its Goals

This is how David Babcock, chairman of the board and chief executive officer of the May Company and formerly its personnel vice president, expresses the first purpose of personnel: "Personnel, like other subunits of the enterprise, exists to achieve the goals of the enterprise first and foremost. If it does not serve that purpose, personnel (or any other subunit) will wither and die." But this goal is a bit general. Personnel's goals can be stated more specifically.

• To Use the Work Force Efficiently

Clyde Benedict, the chief personnel officer for Integon Corporation, stated this purpose somewhat differently. He says the purpose is: "To make people strengths productive, to benefit customers, stockholders, and employees." I believe this is the purpose Walt Disney had in mind when he said his greatest accomplishment was to build the Disney organization with its people.

Personnel can use important measures to determine whether it is achieving this goal. These include:

Low costs of labor. A unit's labor costs are considered in relation to the enterprise's past history and its competitors.

Low absenteeism and turnover costs. Absenteeism and turnover costs are considered relative to past experience of the enterprise and its competitors, and considering the phase in which the business cycle is.

Low scrap rates. In general, personnel is interested in setting organizational standards and policies to control personnel costs and keep close watch on the financial impact of human resource needs on the enterprise.

Chapter 19 discusses in some detail how personnel departments perform this auditing and planning function.

• To Provide the Enterprise with Well-Trained and Well-Motivated Employees

This is the effectiveness measure for personnel. David Babcock, of the May Company, phrases this purpose as "building and protecting the most valuable asset of the enterprise: people." Pehr Gyllenhammar, president of the Volvo Company in Sweden, has phrased it this way:

> For many years it has been said that capital is the bottleneck for a developing industry. I don't think this any longer holds true. I think it's the work force and the company's inability to recruit and maintain a good work force that does constitute the bottleneck for production. I don't know of any major project backed by good ideas, vigor, and enthusiasm that has been stopped by a shortage of cash. I do know of industries whose growth has been partly stopped or hampered because they can't maintain an efficient and enthusiastic labor force, and I think this will hold true even more in the future. . . .

So the personnel effectiveness measure—its chief effectiveness measure, anyway—is to provide the right people at the right phase of production and at the right time for the enterprise.

• To Increase to the Fullest the Employee's Job Satisfaction and Self-Actualization

Thus far, the emphasis has been on the enterprise's needs. But unlike computers or cash balances, employees have feelings of their own. For employees to be most productive, they must feel that the job is right for their abilities and that they are being treated equitably. For many, if not most, employees, the job is a major source of their personal identity. Most of us spend the majority of our waking hours at work and getting to and from work. Thus our identity can well be tied to our job. The job provides for most of our financial sustenance, too.

I am not saying that satisfied employees are *automatically* more productive. That is not true, although many of you probably believe that. Unsatisfied employees do *tend* to quit more often, to be absent more frequently, and to produce lower quality work than satisfied workers do. Nevertheless, both satisfied and dissatisfied employees may perform equally in quantitative terms, such as processing the same number of insurance claims per hour. How to measure satisfaction and how satisfaction and performance are related is discussed in more detail in Chapter 19.

- To Develop and Maintain a Quality of Work Life Which Makes Employment in the Enterprise a Desirable Personal and Social Situation

This purpose is closely related to the one above. Quality of work life is a somewhat general concept. Generally speaking, it refers to several aspects of the job experience. These include: management and supervisory style, freedom and autonomy to make decisions on the job, satisfactory physical surroundings at work, job safety, satisfactory working hours, and meaningful jobs. Not everyone believes that a high quality of life is provided at all work places. Jack Golodner, of the AFL–CIO unions for professional employees, has said:

> The satisfactions that come from the job have disappeared. The professional is working in an environment that is more and more dehumanized. He's working in greater and greater masses. You can go to the aerospace industry and see the way an engineer works, in row on row of engineers. He's just one of hundreds of thousands. And in the universities there's less of a one-to-one relationship with the policymakers, so the faculty member feels less and less important. It's no different from what happened to the blue-collar worker who once was a craftsman with dignity, an individual.

- To Communicate Personnel and Managerial Policies to All Concerned

Clyde Benedict of Integon put it this way: It is personnel's responsibility "to communicate in the fullest possible sense both in tapping ideas, opinions and feelings of customers, noncustomers, regulators, and other external publics as well as in understanding the views of internal human resources. The other facet of this responsibility is communicating managerial decisions to relevant publics in their own language."

Closely related to communication within the enterprise is representation of the enterprise to external units important to it and to personnel and negotiation with these units. The external units most likely to be involved are trade unions and local, state, and federal government bodies which pass laws and issue regulations affecting personnel. The personnel department must also communicate effectively with other top management people to justify its existence and increase its impact on the enterprise.

- To Help Maintain Ethical Policies and Behavior

David Babcock of the May Company feels it is vital for personnel to help communicate and monitor to see that the firm's ethical code is more than a piece of paper. Personnel should develop incentives which reward ethical practices, not the opposite. Clyde Benedict put it this way. "Personnel's purpose is to practice morality in management in preparing people for change; dealing with dissent and conflict; holding high standards of productivity; building acceptance of standards that determine progression; and adhering to the spirit and letter of high professional conduct."

- To Manage Change to the Mutual Advantage of Individuals, Groups, the Enterprise, and the Public

David Babcock of the May Company calls this keeping attuned to the times—the social and economic changes affecting working conditions. This relates to both employee satisfaction and organizational efficiency and effectiveness.

These eight objectives for personnel represent the most significant and most widely accepted ones. There are others and other ways of stating them. But these can serve as the guiding purposes for the personnel function in all enterprises and for all those performing personnel duties. Effective personnel departments set specific, measurable objectives to be accomplished within specified time limits. Chapter 19 discusses how this is done. And each chapter from 4 onward discusses cost/benefit analyses to determine whether the measurable objectives have been met.

The impact of personnel on organizational effectiveness and strategic management can be illustrated further by three more examples:

Managers in the coal mining business must deal with the United Mine Workers. Internal union problems in 1977 when the union split over election of its president spilled over to the workplace. This partially explains the long coal strike of 1978. These factors limited management's ability to increase coal output.

Eaton Corporation had a problem with its productivity rate which made it less competitive. One way it solved this problem was by placing all employees on salaries.

To be competitive and survive in a labor-intensive industry, the enterprise must find the lowest cost labor it can. For example, recently Zenith Corporation laid off 25 percent of its employees to move part of its production to Taiwan and Mexico. Zenith's management claimed they had to do this to survive.

Thus it can be said that personnel activities are essential for the survival of any enterprise. All enterprises utilize personnel work to ensure the necessary human resources are available when needed. In addition, an enterprise will survive and prosper to the extent that it includes personnel inputs in its strategic decisions and implements these decisions with effective personnel policies and programs.

WHO PERFORMS PERSONNEL ACTIVITIES?

In most organizations two groups perform personnel activities: personnel managers and specialists, and operating managers. Who performs personnel duties has changed over time. In all enterprises, operating managers (supervisors, department heads, vice presidents) are involved in personnel, since they are responsible for effective utilization of *all* the resources at their disposal. The human resource is a very special kind of resource. If it is improperly managed, its effectiveness declines more quickly than with other resources. And in all but the most capital-intensive enterprises, the people investment has more effect on organizational effectiveness than other resources, such as money, materials, and equipment.

Therefore, operating managers must spend some of their time as managers of people. In the same way an operating manager is personally responsible if a machine breaks down and production drops, he or she must see to the training, performance, and satisfaction of employees. Studies of how managers use their time indicate that they spend much of their day with other people. Supervisors spend a majority of their time with subordinates. Middle managers spend most of their time with people but less time with employees than supervisors do, and top managers spend less time with employees (about 20 percent) than middle managers do.

In smaller organizations, only operating managers are involved in personnel work. They have many responsibilities: scheduling work, supervising equipment maintenance, and doing personnel work such as hiring and paying people. As the organization increases in size, the operating manager's work is divided up and some of it becomes specialized. Personnel is one such function. Usually the manager of a unit first assigns an assistant to coordinate certain personnel matters. Personnel specialists are employed in enterprises with about 100–150 employees, and a personnel department is created when the number of employees reaches 200–500, depending on the nature of the enterprise.

The interaction of operating and personnel managers

With two sets of managers (operating managers and personnel specialists) making personnel decisions, there can be conflict. This is partly because operating and personnel managers differ on who has authority for what decisions. In addition to role conflict, there may be systemic differences between operating and personnel managers. They have different orientations, called line and staff, which have different objectives.

John and Mary Miner argue that operating and personnel managers also have different motivations, if not personalities. Measured by the Miner sentence completion test, personnel managers are less assertive, less competitive, less interested in administrative detail, and have less positive attitudes toward authority than operating managers do.

The conflict between personnel people and operating managers is most manifest where the decisions must be joint efforts, as on such issues as discipline, physical working conditions, termination, transfer, promotion, and employment planning. Research indicates that operating managers and personnel specialists differ on how much authority personnel should have over job design, labor relations, organization planning, and certain rewards, such as bonuses and promotions.

A personnel and operating manager in consultation

One way to work out actual or potential conflict of this type so that the employee is not caught in the middle is to try to assign the responsibility for some personnel decisions exclusively to operating managers and for others exclusively to personnel specialists. Some observers feel that this is what is happening, and personnel is gaining more power at the expense of the operating managers. Others feel the trend is dysfunctional.

Another approach is to train both sets of managers in how to get along together and how to make joint decisions better. This training is more effective if the enterprise has a career pattern that rotates its managers through both operating and staff positions such as those in personnel. This rotation helps each group understand the other's problems.

To summarize, both personnel specialists and operating managers perform personnel work, and personnel decisions may involve both types of managers. Beginning with Part Two, these interrelationships are explained for each chapter's topic.

The role of the personnel manager or specialist

Certain facts are known about the professional in personnel work. In 1977, there were about 235,000 people employed in personnel work in the United States.

About 60 percent of these work in the private sector, 30 percent in the public sector, and the remaining 10 percent in the third sector (health, education, the arts, libraries, voluntary organizations, and so on). There has been about a 5 percent growth in personnel positions each year since 1970.

When an enterprise creates specialized positions for the personnel function, the primary responsibility for accomplishing the personnel objectives described above is assigned to the personnel managers. But the chief executive is still responsible for the accomplishment of personnel objectives. At all levels in the enterprise, personnel and operating executives must work together to help achieve personnel objectives. The chief personnel executive must market the personnel function within the organization, to employees and operating executives alike.

The ideal personnel executive is knowledgeable of personnel activities and of the enterprise's purpose and operations. Ideally, he or she has had some experience as an operating manager, as well as experience in personnel. The ideal personnel manager has superior interpersonal skills and is creative. It is vital that operating management perceive the personnel manager as a manager first, interested in achieving enterprise goals, and as a specialist adviser in personnel matters secondarily. This makes the personnel executive one of the management team and gives the personnel function a better chance to be effective.

To summarize this section on the role of the personnel manager, the career histories and job descriptions of several personnel leaders are presented here.

Robert L. Berra, Vice President—Personnel for the Monsanto Company, gives these views of the Personnel Department there:

> The scope of the personnel function has expanded considerably in recent years, due both to greater understanding of its contribution internally and to externalities (government legislation, the rise of dissent, etc.) which have had their impact on all organizations. There has, therefore, been an increase in the amount of specialized services rendered to the line. At the same time, the basic personnel contribution of helping the line do its job better has also increased measurably because of the increasing complexity of interpersonal relationships in our present environment.
>
> At Monsanto we believe that the Personnel Department exists primarily to enable those who create, make, and sell to do their jobs better. We try very hard to keep from doing it for them. At Monsanto, nothing has higher priority than the creation of an environment in which each individual has the maximum opportunity to realize his full potential.
>
> We are blessed with exceptional personnel people at Monsanto. We have an excellent mix of seasoned professionals and bright, enthusiastic young people who are honing their professional skills. We are also fortunate to have a significant number of exceptional beginners in the feeder system. Monsanto has traditionally given much attention to its people and, consequently, has considered the Personnel Department as a working partner. However, to who much is given, much is expected, and we are constantly challenged to provide policies which anticipate rather than respond to opportunities.
>
> I see the future of the personnel function as being very bright. One of the reasons is that our background and training lend themselves to both planning and problem solving in an era where both are essential. More importantly, the future of personnel will be determined primarily by the caliber of people that will be attracted to it. When I review the progress of the professionals who have chosen to work in personnel at Monsanto, as I do on an annual basis, I feel good. We seem now to be attracting more than our share of the best and the brightest. The future should take care of itself.

Robert L. Berra
Monsanto Company

Biography

Robert L. Berra, whose title is Vice President–Personnel for the Monsanto Company, joined that organization as assistant training manager at the former Plastics Division in 1951. Berra was graduated from St. Louis University with a BS in commerce and finance. Subsequently he received his MBA degree from the Harvard Graduate School of Business. He has done graduate work in psychology at Washington University, St. Louis.

After holding various positions with Monsanto, Berra became assistant director of the Corporate Personnel Department in June 1967. From October 1970, until June 1974, Berra held the title of Corporate Vice President of Personnel and Public Relations at Foremost-McKesson, Inc. He rejoined Monsanto Company as Vice President–Personnel in June of 1974.

Berra is the author of several articles in the area of management and motivation. He has served as guest lecturer at Harvard Graduate School of Business, Washington University, St. Louis University, Southern Illinois University, and the University of South Carolina.

Job description

Robert L. Berra is responsible for the worldwide direction of the corporate personnel function for Monsanto Company. His areas of responsibility include manpower planning and development, labor and employe relations, salary administration and benefits, professional recruitment and university relations, and corporate headquarters site administration. Berra exercises functional direction of the personnel relations activities in all companies, divisions, and departments of the corporation. He reports to the vice chairman and directly supervises four directors with a total group size of 350–75 employees.

Eileen DeCoursey
Johns-Mansville
Corporation

Biography

Eileen M. DeCoursey was named to the position of Vice President, Employee Relations for Johns-Manville Corporation upon joining J-M in 1975. Before that, she served as vice president and executive assistant to the chairman of Squibb Corporation, a position which included extensive work in personnel planning, employee benefits, compensation and personnel policies. DeCoursey has served as a personnel assistant (Warner-Lambert), a research associate (Handy Associate), junior account executive (Johnson & Higgins), employee relations supervisor (Time, Inc.), and manager of employee benefits (Bristol-Myers). She is a native of Livingston, New Jersey, and received her BS degree from New Jersey State.

Job description

As Vice President, Employee Relations, of Johns-Manville Corporation, Eileen DeCoursey's responsibilities involve the design and development of corporatewide personnel policies, procedures, and programs. These include recruiting, compensation, benefits, affirmative action, management development, and training.

Eileen DeCoursey, Vice President, Employee Relations, for Johns-Manville Corporation says:

> The future of personnel is secure. I think it's going to be the most exciting game in town. And hopefully we are going to attract the best and brightest talent available.
>
> I expect it will become a regular stepping stone to general management such as sales and finance. We are going through enormous changes as we head into "a post-industrial" society. And the impact on employees, as well as our entire way of doing business, will be greater than anything since the design of the assembly line.
>
> Knowledgeable, prepared employee relations professionals must be able to anticipate the changes before they occur so we are in a position to support and assist the transition—not merely to record its happening.

John Blodger, Director of Employee Relations for Bendix Corporation's Electronics and Engine Control Systems Group, says:

> Personnel has come a long way from its initial responsibilities of hiring employees, labor relations, and company picnic planning. Today, the corporation and its employees have high expectations of the personnel professional. This expectation level carries with it a new requirement for individuals occupying positions in the personnel function. Problems of a changing work ethic and the ever-increasing statutory requirements place today's personnel professional at the apex of the man-

John D. Blodger
Bendix Corporation

Biography

John D. Blodger's titles is Group Director of Employee Relations for the Bendix Corporation, Electronics and Engine Control Systems Group, located at Newport News, Virginia. Prior to moving to Newport News, he was Director of Employee Relations for the Communications Division of the Bendix Corporation in Baltimore. Blodger is a graduate of Wayne State University and has acquired BS and MBA degrees. Before joining Bendix, he held a broad range of personnel assignments for several major corporations.

Blodger has been active with the American Society of Personnel Administrators for many years and has held the offices of district director, board member at large, and national treasurer. He is president-elect for 1978 and will assume the presidency in 1979. He is also active in the Industrial Relations Research Association and was formerly a member of the Personnel Association of Greater Baltimore, Inc.

Job description

John Blodger, the Group Director of Employee Relations for Bendix (Electronics and Engine Control Systems Group, Newport News, Virginia), is responsible for total employee relations, the safety and security of a two plant division with employment of 900 salaried and hourly employees, grievance processing through arbitration, wage and salary administration, employee benefits, management development and training programs, and recruitment for both hourly and salaried employees.

agement team. EEO, ERISA, OSHA, organizational development, and management development require specialization and a professional approach to problem solving. Understanding the profit-and-loss concept and the contribution that personnel can make to the bottom line will be the key to bringing these expectations to reality.

Personnel's place in management

How important is personnel in the top management hierarchy? In the past, the answer clearly was: not very important. That is changing. Recent articles have proclaimed that "Personnel is the fast track to the top" and "Personnel directors are the new corporate heros." In fact, personnel is advancing rapidly as a vital force in top management. At some firms, such as RCA, United Parcel Service, and Brown and Williamson Tobacco, the top personnel executive is on the board of directors.

A number of presidents and chief operating officers of large firms were promoted to these positions after substantial personnel experience. Examples include the top executives of Colonial Stores, Cummins Engine Company, Delta Airlines, Eli Lilly, and the May Company.

Ernest F. Boyce
Colonial Stores

Ernest F. Boyce, Chairman and Chief Executive Officer of Colonial Stores, Incorporated, since 1967, joined the firm in 1964 as Vice President/Industrial Relations. Prior to joining Colonial, he was vice president and a director of a major drug chain. Boyce is an alumnus of Boston University and the Harvard Business School. He is a director of the Fulton National Corporation, Coastal States Corporation, Associated Distributors, the Better Business Bureau, Marist College, the Atlanta YMCA, and the Atlanta Rotary Club, a trustee of the Phoenix Society, and vice chairman of the board of St. Joseph's Infirmary.

James Alan Henderson
Cummins Engine
Company, Inc.

James Alan Henderson is President and Chief Operating Officer of Cummins Engine Company, Inc., Columbus, Indiana. He is a graduate of Princeton University and received his MBA degree from Harvard Business School. Henderson has been in his present position since February 1977. Prior to this, his experience included various executive-level positions, including Vice President of Personnel at Cummins. He was a member of the faculty at Harvard Business School for one year and is co-author of a textbook in the field of collective bargaining, *Creative Collective Bargaining.*

William Thomas Beebe
Delta Airlines

William Thomas Beebe, Chairman of the Board of Delta Airlines, is a graduate of the University of Minnesota, where he majored in business administration. Beebee has been in the airlines industry since he joined Chicago and Southern Air Lines on February 20, 1947, in charge of all personnel and labor relations. Prior to joining C & S, he had extensive personnel and labor relations experience with General Electric, United Aircraft Corporation, and, during the war, at the Navy-owned Pratt and Whitney Aircraft Company. After the merger of Delta and C & S in 1953, he served as personnel director of the combined company. After a series of promotions, Beebe was elected to his present position in November 1971.

Richard D. Wood
Eli Lilly & Company

Richard D. Wood became Chairman of the Board of Directors and Chief Executive Officer of Eli Lilly and Company on April 1, 1973. Wood earned a BS degree in engineering from Purdue University and was granted an MBA by the Wharton School of Finance and Commerce at the University of Pennsylvania. He held various positions after joining Eli Lilly in 1950. He was named Executive Director of Industrial Relations in 1969 and served in that capacity until he was elected Executive Vice President in 1971. In addition to serving as Chairman of the Executive Committee, Wood is a member of the boards of Eli Lilly International Corporation, Elizabeth Arden, Inc., IVAC Corporation, and Elanco Products Company.

David E. Babcock
The May Department
Stores Company

David E. Babcock, Chairman of the Board and Chief Executive Officer of the May Department Stores Company, is widely known for his work in personnel and management development in the retail industry. He is the first executive with this background to head a major American retail corporation. During World War II he served in the U.S. Army, attaining the rank of major and serving as personnel director of the Hampton Roads Port of Embarkation. Prior to joining May, Babcock was with the Dayton Hudson Corporation as personnel director, vice president, and a member of the board of directors. Since joining May early in 1967 as Vice President, Organization Planning and Development, he has held various executive positions. He became Chairman of the Board and Chief Executive Officer in 1976.

But let's not get carried away. This is a developing pattern. It is likely to mean in the long run that personnel executives will have a good chance of moving up to the top jobs—as those in marketing, financial, operations, and other positions did in the past. Thus this trend means that many managements recognize the *potential* significance of personnel in enterprise effectiveness.

The fact is that for personnel to contribute its part to the success of an enterprise, the personnel executive must be first rate, and the operating top management must be supportive of personnel. Ed Carlson was when he was the chief executive of United Airlines, and as are many other chief operating officers today. Personnel success requires operating managers who appreciate the value of the personnel function and support it.

Having discussed the role, of the top personnel manager, it should be mentioned that the appendix to this chapter describes personnel careers leading to this goal.

PERSONNEL DEPARTMENT OPERATIONS

Through the years the makeup of personnel departments and how they operate have both changed over time. Personnel units vary by size and sector, but most enterprises keep them small. A recent study found that in the largest headquarters unit there were 150 people.

The number of personnel specialists in relation to the number of operating employees, or the personnel ratio, varies in different industries. The national average, according to one study is one personnel specialist per 200 employees.

Some industries, such as construction, agriculture, retail and wholesale trade, and services, have fewer personnel specialists than the average. Others, such as public utilities, durable goods manufacturing, banking, insurance, and government, have an above-average ratio.

In the largest recent study of the personnel function, the American Society of Personnel Administrators and Prentice-Hall surveyed 1,400 personnel executives and found both personnel staffs and budgets to be growing. Based on this study, Exhibit 1–1 indicates current size and personnel ratio variations.

EXHIBIT 1–1
Size of personnel staff

Industry—number reporting	*Personnel staff ratio**	*Number on personnel staff†*
Manufacturing (under 500 persons)—217	1:96	1–12 (300)
Manufacturing (500–999)—136	1:116	1–20 (800)
Manufacturing (1,000—4,999)—142	1:130	2–90 (4,900)
Manufacturing (over 5,000)—26	1:352	7–126 (22,000)
Research and development—15	1:102	1–60 (5,000)
Public utilities—30	1:154	1–110 (22,339)
Hospitals—108	1:180	1–28 (4,000)
Retail stores—47	1:228	1–31 (5,800)
Banks—104	1:98	1–72 (9,000)
Insurance companies—101	1:101	1–142 (30,000)
Transportation and distribution—24	1:272	1–75 (26,000)
Government agencies—41	1:272	2–104 (68,000)
Education—34	1:161	1–46 (11,300)
Nonprofit organizations—28	1:76	1–12 (1,955)
Other firms—328	1:194	1–120 (35,000)

* Average number of employees on payroll for each person on personnel staff.

† Smallest and largest personnel staff reported for each industry; numbers in parentheses refer to number of employees on payroll for firms reporting largest personnel staffs. (Firms represented here do not necessarily have the lowest or highest *ratio* of personnel staffers, relative to total work force.)

Source: "The Personnel Executive's Job," *Personnel Management: Policies and Practices,* December 14, 1976, published by Prentice-Hall, Inc., Englewood Cliffs, N.J. Reprinted with permission.

How personnel departments allocate their time will be demonstrated in the chapters to follow. An idea of what proportions are devoted to what types of activities can be given here, however. The greatest amount of time (33 percent) is spent in staffing (recruiting, selection, orientation, evaluation, discipline). Next comes compensation and benefits (28.5 percent), and then training and development (11 percent) and labor relations (10 percent). The other activities take 5 percent or less of a personnel unit's time.

One major function of the personnel executive is the development of personnel objectives, procedures, and budgets. As indicated above, the objectives of an enterprise are the ends it seeks to achieve: its reason for existence. Eight of the objectives the personnel function seeks to achieve were also given above. But most of these objectives were stated in very general terms.

To help the enterprise achieve these objectives, more specific statements are developed in all larger, most middle-sized, and some smaller enterprises. Often through the use of management by objectives programs, the general objective is made more specific.

For example, two of the personnel objectives were:

- To provide the enterprise with well trained and well motivated employees and
- To increase to the fullest the employee's job satisfaction and self-actualization.

Let's focus on the second of these objectives for a moment. How is this objective achieved for the enterprise's managers? First, the measurement of these factors can be made specific by designing an attitude survey (see Chapter 3). This survey asks the managers in a scientific manner how satisfied they are and how self-actualized they feel.

The specific objective may be to have 90 percent of the managers check the "very satisfied" answer on the survey. The key issue, though, is to determine what factors increase the satisfaction and self-actualization of the managers. Once these are determined, the enterprise must be geared to increase them in order to heighten managers' satisfaction. In effect, what the enterprise does is to develop plans to increase these factors. These plans are called (1) policies and (2) procedures/rules. Exhibit 1–2 illustrates the relationship between the objectives and plans, indicating that the objectives are the most general factor. For example, job satisfaction for managers is an objective. An enterprise makes an objective more specific by developing policies.

A policy is a general guide to decision making. It provides general guidance for employees in an important decision area.

Policies are developed for areas where problems have developed in the past or in potential problem areas which management considers important enough

EXHIBIT 1–2
Relationship among objectives, policies, and rules

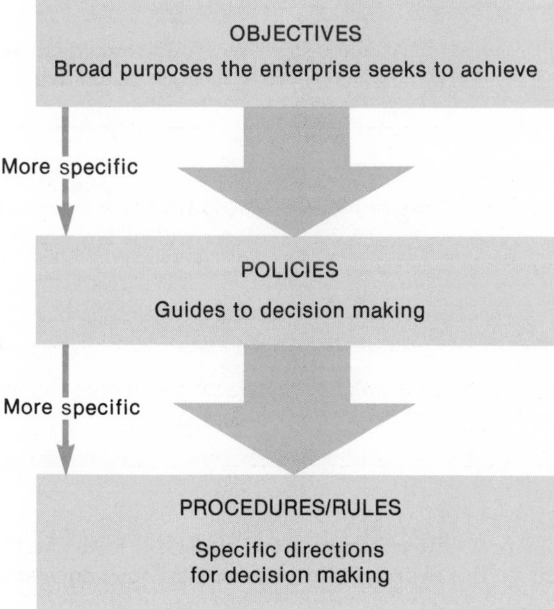

to warrant policy development. Policies free managers from having to make decisions in areas in which they have less competence or on matters with which they do not wish to become involved. This assures some consistency in behavior and allows managers to concentrate on decisions in which they have the most experience and knowledge.

After the broadest policies are developed, some enterprises develop procedures and rules. These are more specific plans which limit the choices of managers and employees, as Exhibit 1–2 shows. Procedures and rules are developed for the same reasons as policies.

> A procedure or rule is a specific direction to action. It tells a manager how to do a particular activity. In larger enterprises, procedures are collected and put into manuals, usually called standard operating procedures (SOPs).

Enterprises must be careful to balance off the need for consistent decision making which flows from a well-developed set of policies and procedures without overdoing it. Some enterprises in effect eliminate managerial initiative by trying to develop policies and procedures for everything. Procedures should be developed only for the most vital areas.

Many readers have difficulty understanding the difference between policies and procedures. An example of the differences can be given by returning to the objective of managerial satisfaction.

As you will learn in later chapters, one factor which often leads to employee and managerial satisfaction is the pattern of promoting present employees to higher positions which become open, rather than hiring from the outside for these openings. This allows present employees to see a good future for themselves. Thus, to help achieve the objective of managerial job satisfaction, an enterprise might develop a promotion policy which specifies that higher management positions will be filled by promoting present employees.

> **Promotion policy.** As the enterprise grows, managers will be promoted from within. Normally, the enterprise will hire only supervisory managers from the outside.

To help assure the other objective—providing the enterprise with well-trained managers—the enterprise might develop a policy for selecting managers according to certain qualifications.

> **Managerial selection policy.** In selecting potential supervisory managers, the enterprise will normally hire college graduates.

How would procedures differ from these policies? Let's look at three procedures that make the managerial selection policy more specific.

> **Procedure 1.** Only graduates of business and engineering schools should be hired for managerial jobs.
> **Procedure 2.** All potential managers should have a full-day site visit and be interviewed by at least four supervisory and middle managerial personnel.
> **Procedure 3.** Preference should be given to veterans in hiring supervisory managers.

Finally, managers assume that their objectives are achieved by developing budgets. Budgets are financial plans allocating funds, equipment, and so on to programs, units, and people. Often money speaks louder than words such as policies and procedures. So the personnel executive makes sure her or his objectives are achieved by budgeting funds in the same way that objectives, policies, procedures, and rules are stated.

Another major facet of personnel operations is how the functions are organized or arranged.

Organizational arrangements

The chief personnel executive reports to the top manager of most enterprises or, in the larger ones, may report to an executive vice president. Exhibit 1–3 shows one way personnel could be organized in a large business. In some larger firms, personnel is divided into two departments, personnel and labor relations. In medium-sized and smaller enterprises, however, personnel and other functions such as public relations may be part of a single department.

Thirty percent of all personnel administrators work for local, state, and federal governments. Exhibit 1–4 is an example of personnel organization in a

EXHIBIT 1–3
Personnel department in a large business

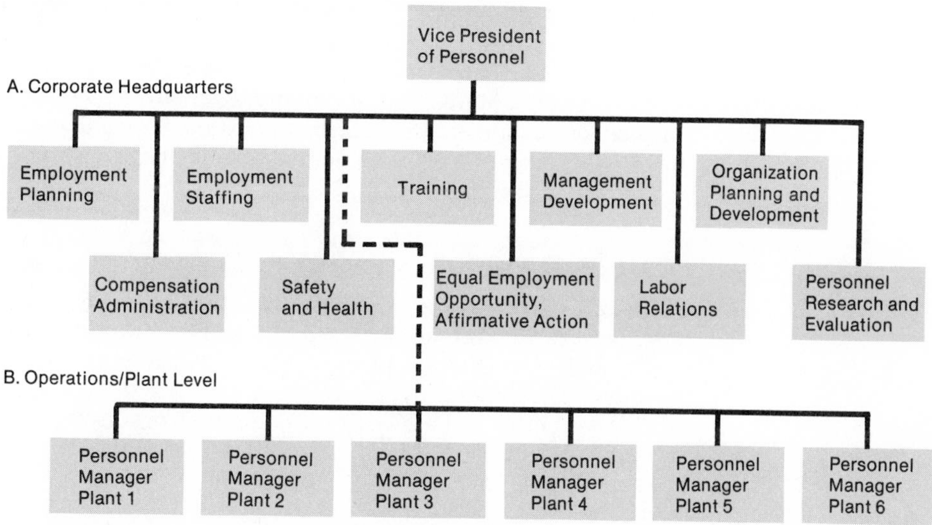

EXHIBIT 1–4
Personnel organization in a U.S. state government

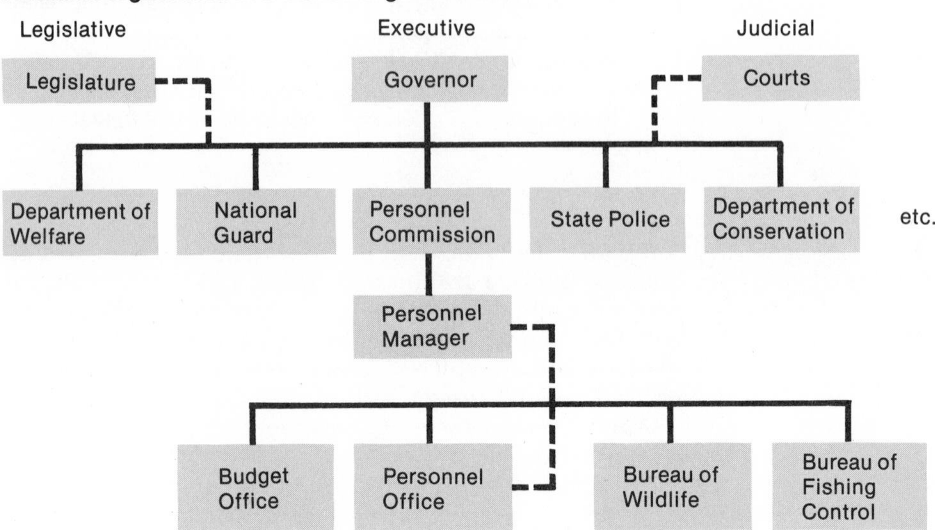

"typical" state government. The legislature and the governor set policy for departments, subject to review by the courts, and appoint a personnel commission which is headed by a personnel officer. This central personnel unit is a policy-making body which serves a policy, advisory, and regulatory purpose which is similar to that of the home office personnel unit of a business. At the federal government level, this personnel commission is called the Civil Service Commission.

In the third sector, such as hospitals and universities, personnel typically is a unit in the business office, as shown in Exhibit 1–5. More will be said about differences in personnel work in these three settings in Chapter 2.

Personnel specialists are usually located at the headquarters of an enterprise, but larger organizations may divide the personnel function. Usually the largest group is at headquarters, but personnel advisors are also stationed at unit levels (for example, a plant) and divisional levels. In this case, the headquarters unit consists of specialists or experts on certain topics and advisers to top management, while the unit-level personnel people are generalists who serve as advisers to operating managers at that level.

PLAN OF THE BOOK

The material on the personnel function presented in this book is organized to suggest solutions to real-life problems. The chapters (and many of the sections) begin with a case study from a real organization which describes a personnel problem being faced today. The method by which the problem is solved is a personnel activity. This activity is defined precisely. Then who performs this activity is discussed. The interrelationship between operating and personnel managers and the role of top management in the activity are described and analyzed.

EXHIBIT 1–5
Organization of a county hospital

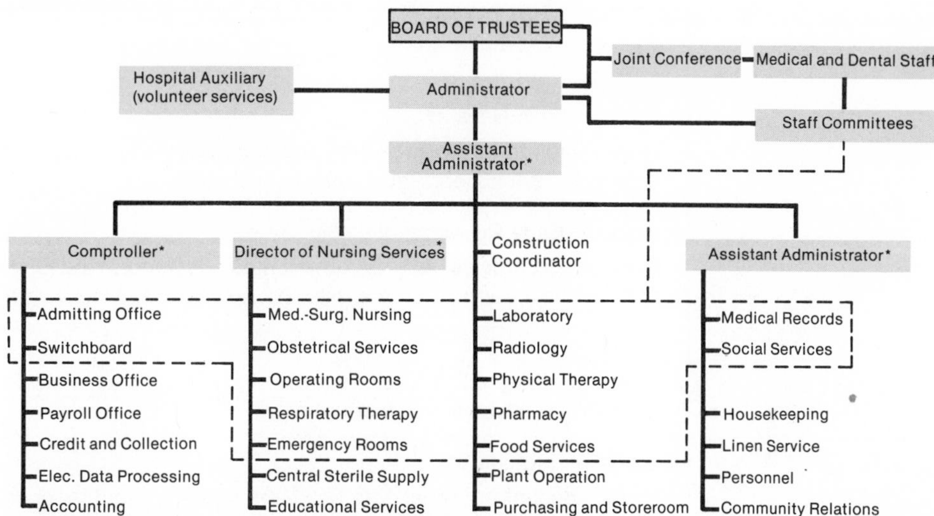

This chart reflects the "line" responsibility and authority in the hospital organization. It should be understood, however, that a great part of the work of the hospital is accomplished through informal interaction between the identified services and functions. These "functional" working relationships are encouraged. Where there is difference in understanding or when changes in procedure are required, the "line" organization should be carefully observed.

* Area directors.

In each chapter (or group of chapters, where an activity is described in more than one), the extent to which the activity has been developed is analyzed. Some personnel activities (or functions) are quite well established, while others are just emerging. The activity being considered is assigned to one of four stages through which personnel activities seem to evolve. The stage at which an activity is currently located can be assessed by examining the literature on the topic—articles, books, and speeches presented at association meetings—and plotting how far along the activity has come, as shown in Exhibit 1–6.

Currently it is most likely that included in Stage I would be the personnel activities of career development and overall organization and management development schemes. In Stage II would be systematic evaluation of the total personnel function and formal orientation. Typical activities in Stage III would be performance evaluation and informal management development. Stage IV functions would include many employment and compensation activities. It appears that historically the personnel function begins by focusing on blue-collar employees and then adds white-collar and clerical workers. Only fully developed personnel departments focus on management and professional employees as well.

The chapters also include a diagnostic analysis of the activity being discussed. It is my view that personnel activities are affected by many different factors, such as the types of people employed, organized labor, and government, and the solution of personnel problems depends on consideration of all these factors. This idea will be thoroughly examined in Chapter 2.

EXHIBIT 1–6
Stages of development of a personnel activity

	Almost Unknown
Stage I: New, New In this stage the experts or originators are exhorting specialists to adopt the function. Panaceas are promised.	↓
Stage II: Early Development In this stage, articles describe how companies perform the function and how happy they are with the results.	↓
Stage III: Conflict The doubts begin. The articles warn: it didn't work for us. Multiple organization studies are undertaken.	↓
Stage IV: Maturity A great deal of empirical data has been gathered, and theories and explanations for the conflict in Stage III are established.	*Well Known*

For each personnel activity, suggestions are given for the techniques, tools, and approaches available to solve the problem, with an evaluation of when each tool is most useful and tips on how to use them well.

The various personnel activities are evaluated with a cost/benefit approach. Since personnel must compete with requests for other resources, such as machinery, advertising, and buildings, the expenditures and investments in the organization's people must be justifiable in cost/benefit terms.

The chapter summary, conclusion, and recommendation sections review the major points in each chapter, and many chapters give them in proposition form. For example, in Chapter 4, the first proposition:

Proposition 4.1. The more volatile the organization's environment, the more likely is the effective organization to forecast the demand for labor formally at each unit and to sum the demand at headquarters.

The recommendations for application of the activity are in the form of suggestions for its use in various types of organizations. Since personnel functions are not performed the same way in all organizations, recommendations are given for the most effective way to handle each problem in seven model organizations which differ systematically by size (number of employees), complexity of products or services, and stability or volatility (degree to which the organization's products or services change over time). If you place your focal organization (where you have worked or want to work) on this scale, you can get an idea of how the personnel challenge would best be handled there. The seven model organizations are defined in Exhibit 1–7.

EXHIBIT 1–7

Seven model organizations in which various personnel practices might be used

1. Large size, low complexity, high stability.
   Examples: Social security agencies, copper smelter, tuberculosis hospital in the 1930s.
2. Medium size, low complexity, high stability.
   Examples: gym shoe manufacturer, Department of Commerce, state of Indiana.
3. Small size, low complexity, high stability.
   Examples: wooden pencil manufacturer, small exterminator.
4. Medium size, moderate complexity, moderate stability.
   Examples: food manufacturer, Memphis city welfare agency.
5. Large size, high complexity, low stability.
   Examples: Mattel Toy Corporation, innovative community general hospital.
6. Medium size, high complexity, low stability.
   Examples: U.S. Office of Economic Opportunity agencies in 1968, fashion clothing manufacturer, innovative multiple-purpose hospital.
7. Small size, high complexity, low stability.
   Examples: Peace Corps in 1961, early OEO agencies, elite psychiatric hospital, small media conglomerate.

SUMMARY

This chapter and all others in the text conclude with a list of statements summarizing the most important concepts covered in the chapter. You can use this list to review your understanding of the personnel process and the personnel manager's job.

In introducing you to the field of personnel, this chapter has defined personnel as that function of all enterprises which provides for effective utilization of human resources to achieve both the objectives of the enterprise and the satisfaction and development of the employees. It has described some of the characteristics of today's personnel managers and a number of approaches to the organization and operation of personnel units. The chapter concludes with a brief description of how the material in this book is organized and the devices we have used to present it. An appendix to the chapter describes careers in personnel and personnel professionalism, including the literature on the topic and accreditation procedures.

The statements below highlight the material covered:

1. Personnel is future and action oriented and focuses on satisfying the needs of individuals at work.
2. Personnel is a necessary function. Effectively performed, it can make the crucial difference between successful and unsuccessful enterprises.
3. One of the challenges faced in personnel is that many decisions require inputs from both operating managers and personnel specialists.
4. This dual purpose can lead to conflict, or it can result in more effective personnel decisions.

Personnel is one of the most challenging and exciting functions in an enterprise today. This book has been written to help you face these challenges more effectively. Chapter 2 introduces important variables in personnel effectiveness and the environment of personnel.

APPENDIX: CAREERS IN PERSONNEL

This appendix discusses what a personnel career is like, describes personnel specialists' positions, and suggests ways personnel specialists can achieve greater professionalism.

Personnel careers

Let us begin this section by discussing what current personnel professionals are like. At present 75 percent of personnel managers are men. Women personnel managers are usually found in medium-sized and smaller organizations. Most personnel managers have college degrees. Those who have attended college in recent years have usually majored in business, economics, psychology, or engineering. Their experience is primarily in personnel work, especially the younger managers.

Personnel specialists have been moving toward greater specialization, if not actual professionalism. College training includes courses such as personnel management, compensation administration, personnel problems, labor law and legislation, and collective bargaining. Those who want to become more specialized may join an association like the American Society for Personnel Administrators, attend meetings, read professional journals, or seek ASPA accreditation.

Personnel specialists generally are paid as other graduates of business schools are at the supervisory and middle-management levels. At top-management levels, they sometimes are paid slightly less than operating vice presidents. Current salaries of personnel specialists and executives are published yearly by the ASPA in its *Salary Survey.*

A typical career ladder for a personnel professional is given in Exhibit 1A–1. A personnel professional can enter personnel in several types of positions. One way is to become a personnel manager for a small unit of a large enterprise. In this position the personnel professional implements headquarters personnel policies at that level and works with local operating managers to help achieve unit goals as well as personnel objectives. This is a very challenging position. The other route is to become a specialized personnel professional. Typically, this position is in a large enterprise, and the duties are associated with a single personnel function. Examples of this type of position include interviewer and recruiter (employment), and compensation, labor relations, and training and development specialists.

As positions open up, the personnel professional can usually move up in the hierarchy. Or the specialist at a large enterprise can move to a smaller enterprise as the chief personnel executive. Typically, a person with a college degree and personnel training will not remain in the bottom two levels of these positions for long.

EXHIBIT 1A–1
Sample career patterns of personnel professionals

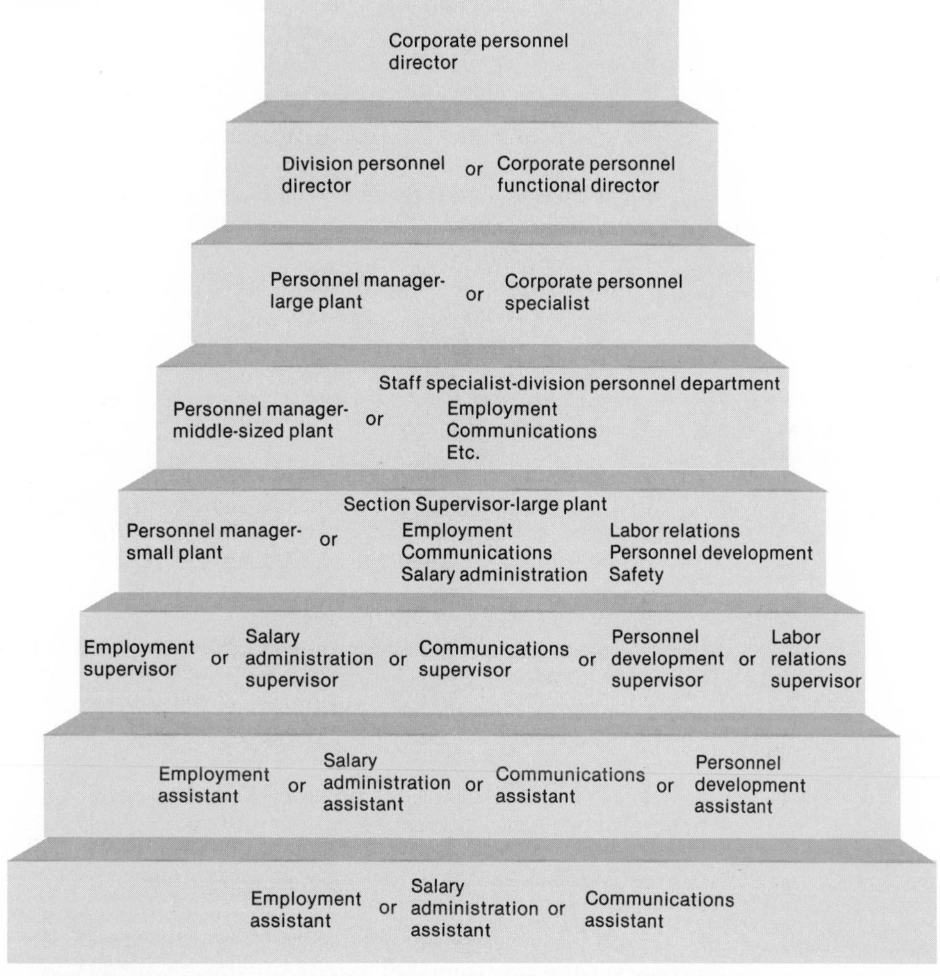

Source: H. H. Mitchell, "Selecting and Developing Personnel Professionals." Reprinted with permission *Personnel Journal* copyright July 1970.

What the personnel specialist does to professionalize

The personnel specialist can advance his or her knowledge of the field by reading specialized journals. These include:

1. Professional journals:
   American Federationist
   Administrative Management
   Employment Benefit Plan Review

Labor Law Journal
Monthly Labor Review
The Personnel Administrator
Personnel
Personnel Journal
Public Personnel Management

2. Scholarly journals. The following is a list of publications written for scholars and executives interested in personnel. Reading these requires more technical training than the journals listed above.
Human Relations
Human Organization
Human Resources Management
Industrial Relations
Industrial and Labor Relations Review
Journal of Applied Psychology
Organizational Behavior and Human Performance
Personnel Psychology

3. Abstracts and services. For those wishing to study specialized areas of literature or to get a total overview, *Personnel Management Abstracts* lists most articles in the field and abstracts many of them. *Psychological Abstracts,* especially the "Industrial and Organizational Psychology" section, can suggest leads. And the *Annual Review of Psychology* often has chapters summarizing the latest trends in personnel.

In addition, several companies offer personnel information services. The best known of these are the Bureau of National Affairs (BNA), Commerce Clearing House (CCH), and Prentice-Hall Services.

Accreditation. One move to increase the professionalism of personnel executives is the American Society of Personnel Administrators Accreditation Program. ASPA has set up the ASPA Accreditation Institute (AAI) to offer personnel executives the opportunity to be accredited as specialists (in a functional area such as employment, placement and personnel planning, or training and development) or generalists (multiple specialisties). Specialists can qualify as accredited personnel specialists or the more advanced accredited personnel diplomates. For generalists, the basic accreditation is accredited personnel manager and the advanced level is accredited executive in personnel. Accreditation requires passing three-hour examinations developed by the Psychological Corporation of New York.

It is difficult to predict the potential impact of accreditation on personnel work at this time. The ASPA survey of 1,400 personnel executives published in 1977 found that 4.6 percent had applied for ASPA accreditation and 20 percent planned to apply. Ten percent said they would not apply, and the rest were unsure.

John Traswell is almost up to D-day—decision day—about his new job offer in personnel. He's talked the situation over with Harry Grosnikle, the vice president of personnel. He's now convinced that personnel has a future at the firm. He's found out that more and more line and operating executives like himself are spending part of their career in personnel. Harry has pointed out that personnel needs executives with operating experience like John's. When the operating experience is combined with training in personnel, it makes a good combination for building the personnel team.

John

John realizes that personnel is an important job with major responsibilities. He knows it is a challenging job. Other executives tell him personnel experience can be great for his career. John has discussed the change with his wife, Grace. She has had experience in a personnel position with her job at a bank, and she is encouraging him to proceed.

After much thought, John decides to accept the personnel position. His next challenge is to learn more about the key problems in personnel and how to solve them. This is your job now, too.

QUESTIONS

1. What is personnel? What activities make up the personnel function?
2. Why do all enterprises engage in personnel work?
3. How do top management's strategic decisions interact with personnel?
4. Personnel is a means to help achieve the enterprise's objectives. Comment.
5. Describe the interaction of personnel and operating managers in making personnel decisions.
6. What industries and sectors employ the most personnel specialists? The least?
7. Describe typical organizational arrangements for personnel units.
8. What are the four stages of development of a personnel activity? How does this concept help you understand personnel work?
9. Describe the seven model organizations in which personnel practices might be used. How does this help you understand personnel work?
10. What is a personnel career like?

REFERENCES

References for all chapters are given at the end of the book.

2

A diagnostic approach to personnel

Chapter objectives

- To introduce the concept of a diagnostic approach to personnel.
- To show how managers use their knowledge of environmental and organizational factors to improve their personnel decisions.
- To show how managers use their knowledge of human behavior to make better personnel decisions.
- To demonstrate how the task to be performed, the work group, and the leader influence personnel decisions.
- To help you be a more effective manager of personnel activities.

Chapter outline

I. An Introduction to the Diagnostic Approach to Personnel Decisions
II. Nature of the Employee and the Personnel Function
   A. Abilities of employees
   B. Employee attitudes and preferences
   C. Motivation of employees
   D. Personality and personnel
III. Environment of the Organization and the Personnel Function
   A. Unions and their requirements in personnel
   B. Government requirements and regulations
   C. Economic conditions
   D. The work sector of the organization
IV. Organizational Factors and the Personnel Function
   A. Goals of controlling interests
   B. Organization style
   C. The nature of the task
   D. The work group
   E. Leader's style and experience
V. How to Use the Diagnostic Model
VI. Summary, Conclusions, and Recommendations
VII. Appendix: A Look at the Composition of the Labor Force

Martha Winston is the newly appointed manager of the National Pancake House in a major city which is known for its beach area. Officially, the restaurant is known as unit 827. National is a large chain. Martha believes that if she does a good job of managing 827, she has an excellent chance to be promoted at National. She is also thinking about opening up her own restaurant someday.

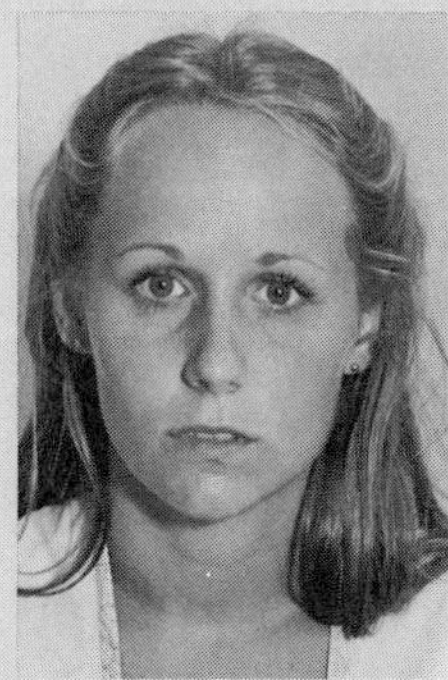

Martha

Martha entered National's management training program after completing college at a small liberal arts school which is well known in her part of the country. The focus of the training program was technical. Martha learned all about the equipment a typical National restaurant has. She also learned about National's finance and accounting system, theft control, and advertising. She was taught a great deal about National's goals for the firm and for unit 827. The topics included sales goals, financial return goals, cleanliness goals, customer service goals, and so on.

She has been at 827 three weeks now and is adjusting pretty well. She is not reaching all the goals National set up for her yet, but she feels she will do so in time. She often wishes the training program had taught her more about the people part of the success equation. Her college courses were not much help to her on this, either.

This problem was in her mind as she sat in her office one morning staring at her paperwork over a cup of coffee. She was thinking of the two cooks on duty, Lenny and Harry. Lenny Melvina is about 24. He's been with National as a cook for almost six years. He finished high school locally. It's the only job he's ever had. He arrives on time, works hard, and leaves on time. He's never absent except for perhaps one day a year for illness. This is what his personnel file shows.

Lenny

Everyone likes Lenny: the other help, his managers, the customers. It's easy to see why. He does his job well and in a friendly manner. For example, today Martha watched Lenny deal with a customer. National has a policy that second helpings are free. A girl, about 13, came up to Lenny and asked for seconds. He asked her in a friendly manner how many more pancakes she wanted. She said: "Oh, I don't know, one or two."

Instead of having her wait at the serving line, he suggested that she be seated and he'd bring her the pancakes. He delivered a plate with three pancakes on it which looked like this:

The customer and her family were very pleased with his effort to please her and give them a little joke too. They told Martha they'd come back again.

The other cook is Harry Bennis. Harry is about 19. He didn't finish high school. He's worked at National for two years. Harry is tolerated rather than liked. Most of his co-workers tend to ignore him. He

Harry

rarely says anything beyond the minimum to co-workers, bosses, and customers. He is often late or absent. In about 1 case in 10, his food is sent back. He's not surly but not too pleasant either. He's not bad enough to fire, but not good enough to be pleased with.

Martha wonders why there are these differences in Lenny and Harry. And what, if anything, she can do about it. It affects her now because she must hire a new cook. Business at 827 has been growing faster than usual, even for this busy season. So the staff needs to be expanded to include at least one new cook. Martha wonders how she can be sure to choose a person like Lenny, not another Harry.

And it's raise time. She doesn't have enough money to give everyone a raise. But it's more complicated than that. To hire the new cook she may have to pay close to what she pays Lenny, because few people are out of work at present. Yet company policy says you must pay senior people like Lenny more. And as if things weren't complicated enough, the pay must be above the government minimum wage.

Many of the employees at 827 told Martha they wanted more pay because the job wasn't too pleasant: the stove was hot, and you had to deal with the public. What should she do?

To help her make an intelligent, effective decision, she went to visit a friend of hers, Amy Adams, who had taken personnel courses at the university. She spent an afternoon with Martha explaining how to deal with the three personnel problems Martha faced (employee satisfaction and performance, selection, and pay) by understanding how three sets of factors affect personnel and organizational effectiveness. These are:

- The nature of the employee.
- The environment of the employing organization.
- The organization, task, work group, and leadership.

AN INTRODUCTION TO THE DIAGNOSTIC APPROACH TO PERSONNEL DECISIONS

One way to look at the three factors and how they relate is to develop a model of the personnel situation: a diagnostic model. There are many factors which could be included in such a model to help you understand the personnel setting. The model used throughout this book is a diagnostic model, presented as Exhibit 2–1. The model is rather complex because understanding what goes on at work is a complicated process. It is divided into two sectors which influence personnel practices and therefore affect organizational effectiveness and personal satisfaction and productivity.

The most important sector is the immediate environment in which personnel activities take place. I call this Zone I. The main factors in the immediate environment include:

The nature of the employee. The employee is an individual with abilities and attitudes he or she was born with or has learned. The origin of these influences is shown in Zone II.

The nature of the task. The task is the job done by the individual and the work group.

The work group. The set of people with whom the individual interacts to accomplish the task is called the work group.

The leader. The person responsible for the productivity of the individual employees and the work group is called the leader.

The organization. This is the employer. Each organization has it own way of setting up an administrative structure which is influenced by its goals.

Other factors which are important to an understanding of the personnel situa-

EXHIBIT 2–1
The diagnostic model: Factors affecting personnel activities and organizational effectiveness

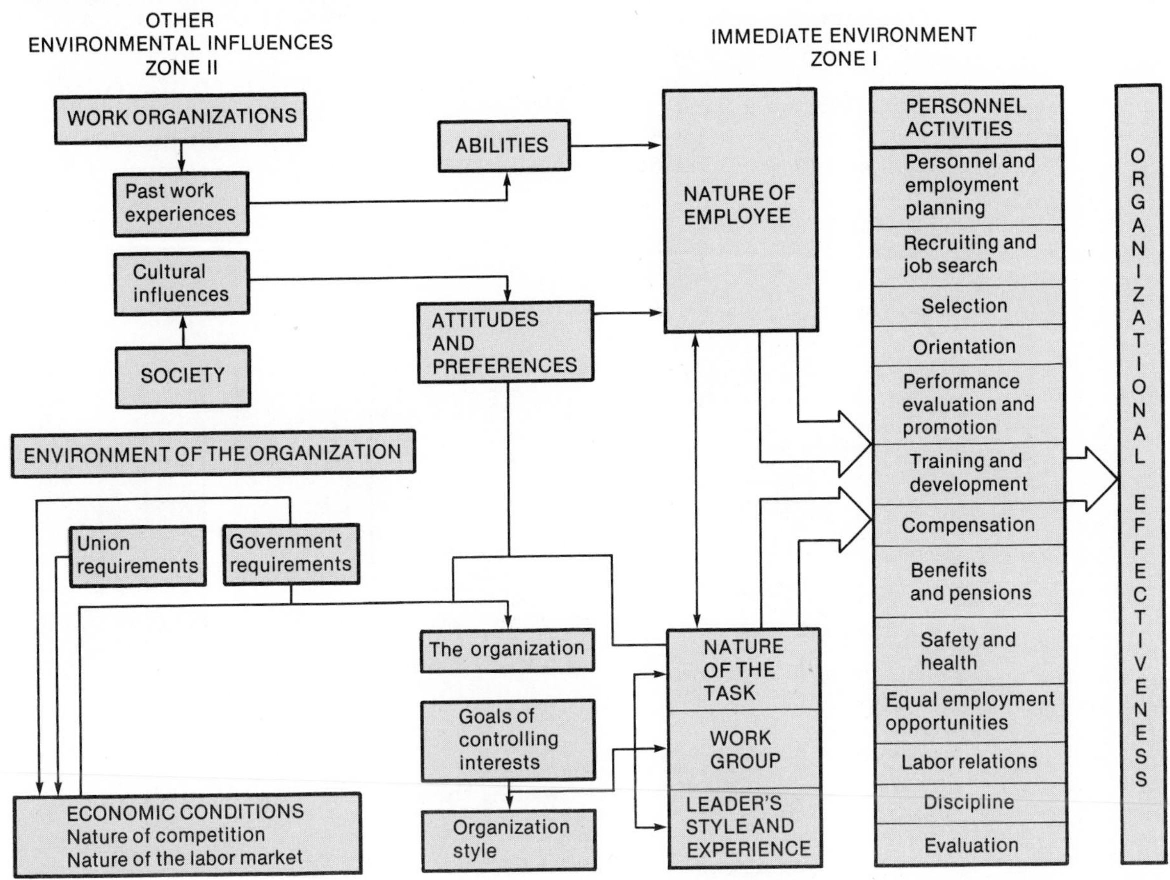

tion are included in Zone II, called other environmental influences. But these factors are not as important as those in Zone I. The factors in Zone II are:

Background factors influencing the employee. Each employee comes to a job with a set of abilities, attitudes, and preferences. The employee has developed these from past work experiences and from society and its cultural influences on how to look at work. The employee also is influenced by the kind of school attended and the family he or she was reared in.

Environmental factors. Three major factors in the environment affect working conditions: the presence or absence of a union; government regulations or laws; and what the economy is like at present.

What this chapter will do is summarize *briefly* what you need to know about each of these factors. Then a few words will be said about how to use the diagnostic model to be a more effective manager or personnel manager. Then how Martha dealt with her problem will be described.

NATURE OF THE EMPLOYEE AND THE PERSONNEL FUNCTION

Although Zones I and II were described separately, considering parts of them together will give you a better understanding of the employee factor in personnel. Exhibit 2–2 is the slice of the model we'll look at first. In this part we are trying to add something to Martha's understanding of why Lenny and Harry behave differently on the job at the National Pancake House. People differ in many characteristics. Lenny and Harry differ in their abilities and their attitudes and preferences. They differ in their total beings (their personalities), too.

EXHIBIT 2–2
Nature of the employee and personnel

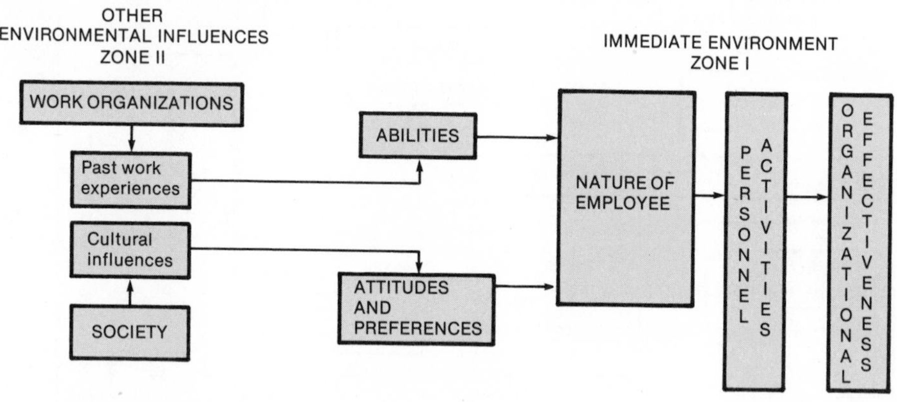

Abilities of employees

Some employee differences affecting the personnel process are due to differences in abilities.

Abilities are skills which humans possess.

Abilities can be classified as mechanical, motor coordination, mental, or creative. Some studies report differences in abilities according to sex or race, but it is not clear whether these differences are due to genetics or learning factors.

According to many psychologists, some of these differences in ability are caused by genetic factors which are rarely subject to change through training. Examples of these differences are finger dexterity and response time. Other abilities, such as interpersonal skills and leadership, are much more easily subjected to change. Humans learn abilities at home, at school, and at work. And their present inventories of abilities are at least partly a consequence of past learning.

Because people differ in abilities, the extent to which employees can be trained in a specific skill varies. In most cases, an aptitude can be developed into an ability by training and experience. But in others it makes more sense to place people who have certain abilities in jobs requiring these abilities. Everyone will not have all the abilities necessary to do these jobs, and a manager does not always have the time or money needed to train people who do not have them.

Managers always seek high levels of performance from employees. Performance can be improved by application of the following formula:

Performance = Ability × Motivation.

Usually, managers overemphasize the ability side of the equation. That is, they are too quick to attribute employee failure to lack of ability. More frequently, the problem is one of motivation. A person somewhat lacking in ability can make up for it with greater motivation which leads to harder work.

To see what the manager can do with knowledge of employee ability differences, consider the example of Harry at National Pancake. Could he lack the abilities to do the job? If it appears that Harry's problem is in fact ability, Martha would have at least two options. One is training, whereby Harry's aptitudes would be developed into the ability needed for the job. The other is placement, whereby Harry could be transferred to another job, such as busboy or cashier.

Do you think Harry's problem is an ability problem?

Employee attitudes and preferences

An attitude is a characteristic and usually long-lasting way of thinking, feeling, and behaving toward an object, idea, person, or group of persons.

A preference is a type of attitude which evaluates an object, idea, or person in a positive or negative way.

For the personnel function, the most relevant attitude is the person's attitude toward work and the place of work in his or her life. People are motivated by powerful emotional forces, and work provides an opportunity for the expression of both aggressive and pleasure-seeking drives. Freud said that a person with the most successful personality development knows how to heighten his or her capacity for obtaining pleasure from mental and intellectual work.

Besides offering a way to channel energy, work also provides the person with income, a justification for existence, and the opportunity to achieve self-esteem and self-worth. How much energy is directed to work is related to how much is directed to family, interpersonal relations, and recreation. And this is partly a consequence of a person's attitudes toward the worth of work in life.

Historically, cultures and individuals have had two fundamentally opposed attitudes towards work.

Instrumental attitude. Work is a means to another end, and usually an unpleasant means. We work so we can reach the goals we seek and to pay our bills.

Work ethic attitude. Work is a satisfying end in itself. By performing work, we can find satisfying, even pleasurable, results and self-fulfillment.

The instrumental attitude has been the predominant one for most workers throughout history. It even prevailed in the United States in the 1800s, when some historians believe the work ethic was strongest. Although the most predominant attitude is the instrumental one, individuals in the work force have varying views of work. These attitudes probably differ with age, sex, race, education, and experience, but there is some tendency for blue-collar and clerical employees to hold instrumental attitudes and for professional, technical, and managerial employees to hold work ethic attitudes.

Which work attitude do you believe Lenny and Harry have?

Attitudes and preferences develop from past experiences in the home, school, and at work. Some psychologists believe that cognitive concepts and attitudes also can be transmitted genetically. Most people move back and forth along the continuum between instrumental and work ethic attitudes over their lifetimes, however. This is probably due to changes in their environments.

How does understanding work attitudes and preferences help managers understand people at work so their effectiveness can be improved? The attitude toward work that an employee holds—instrumental or work ethic—affects most aspects of the personnel process. Many personnel programs (job enlargement, compensation, leadership, and participation programs) are designed to shift employees from instrumental to work ethic attitudes. The assumption is that the behavior changes will result in better quality and increased production, as later chapters will make clear.

Because attitudes can influence behavior, they can also affect performance. But performance is also influenced by learning, perception, abilities, and motivation.

Motivation of employees

> Motivation is that set of attitudes which predisposes a person to act in a specific goal-directed way. Motivation is thus an inner state which energizes, channels, and sustains human behavior to achieve goals.

Work motivation is concerned with those attitudes that channel the person's behavior toward work and away from recreation or other life activity areas. The motivation to work is likely to change as other life activities change.

A number of theories have attempted to explain work motivation. These are shown on the continuum in Exhibit 2–3. The theories differ in their assumptions about how rational the human is and how much behavior is directed by the conscious and the unconscious mind. All of these theories have received some research support, but none has been overwhelmingly substantiated. The extreme theories are *not* likely to achieve full acceptance. At present there is no comprehensive theory of motivation which weighs both the rational and the emotional/instinctual motives.

At the left side of Exhibit 2–3 would be ranged those who explain the motivation of behavior as responses to external stimuli (behaviorism) or to unconscious, possibly unknown, motives. Psychoanalytic theory deemphasizes the rationality of the person, and behaviorism treats the person as easily programmable. At the other extreme is expectancy theory, which sees the person as a rational, pleasure-seeking, but also predictable being. In between is a set of theories which, intentionally or not, portray the person as a semirational, semiemotional being.

In my judgment, only a theory which integrates the conscious/rational and unconscious/emotional bases of motivation will provide adequate understanding of human motivation, and no such theory exists today.

What will a knowledge of motivation do to help a manager be a more effective manager of people? As with work attitudes, a manager who can determine what the work motivations of the employees are will make more effective personnel decisions. For employees who appear to be work oriented and well motivated toward work, incentive compensation systems will likely lead to more production

EXHIBIT 2–3
Views of the nature of the human being and motivation theories

The human acts instinctively (the unconscious)	*The human is a mix of instinctual and rational*	*The human acts rationally (the conscious)*
Psychoanalytic theory	Maslow's hierarchy of needs theory	Consistency theory
Behaviorism theory	McClelland/Atkinson's needs theory	Equity theory
Behavior modification theory	Herzberg's two-factor theory	Expectancy theory

and better quality work. For those who are consciously motivated to do a better job at work, performance evaluation techniques like management by objectives make sense. Managers who can determine which employees are motivated to work harder can select the employees they want. If they know (or can find out) that present employees would respond to security motives, in personnel policies like promotion from within, seniority-based personnel systems, and only extremely rare terminations make sense.

Personality and personnel

Personality is the characteristic way a person thinks and behaves in adjusting to his or her environment. It includes the person's traits, values, motives, genetic blueprint, attitudes, emotional reactivity, abilities, self-image, and intelligence. It also includes the person's visible behavior patterns.

Each employee has developed a unique personality. Because of this, it is highly unlikely that a single set of personnel activities or leadership approaches will be equally successful for *all* employees. The behavioral sciences have found that:

1. The employee, as a person, is both rational and intuitive-emotional in makeup and behavior. Therefore, his or her choices and behavior are a consequence of rational (conscious) and emotional (unconscious) influences. A few choices and some behavior are entirely influenced by one or the other, but most behavior is influenced by both.

2. A person acts in response to her or his internal inclinations and choices and environmental influences. Kurt Lewin explained it this way:

$$\text{Behavior} = f(P, E)$$

or

Behavior is a function of the person and the environment.

At times one or the other predominates, but most behavior is influenced by both.

3. Each individual is unique. He or she acts and thinks in a certain way because of

- The personality the person develops.
- The abilities the person has or learns.
- The attitudes and preferences the person has or develops.
- The motives the person has or develops.

This section has refreshed your memory on some relevant concepts from the behavioral sciences. They indicate that the nature of the employee has a great influence on some personnel decisions, as shown in Exhibit 2–2. The effective manager realizes that the employee's nature is a crucial variable in personnel activities and organizational effectiveness. The implications of this knowledge of human behavior for the various personnel activities to be considered in this book will be described in chapters to come.

ENVIRONMENT OF THE ORGANIZATION AND THE PERSONNEL FUNCTION

The second set of factors affecting personnel are those in the environment outside the organization. Exhibit 2–4 extracts that slice of Exhibit 2–1's total diagnostic model.

At the National Pancake House, Martha's personnel problems are aggravated by the environmental factors. Remember that Martha is faced with a tight labor market (few people who are unemployed) and government wage legislation. She need not cope with a union, however. Let's look at the environmental factors.

Unions and their requirements in personnel

> Mary Agular had been a supervisor at the John Madison Life Insurance Company. At that firm, she could hire her employees, usually with only slight coordination with the personnel department. She could hire them on the basis of merit and promote the best ones when they were ready.
>
> When Mary took a new job with Consolidated Electronics, she found that promotion was determined by seniority and that her employees griped about having to pay union dues. She was warned to watch her step by fellow supervisors—to live by the rules, or a grievance would be filed. Pay raises were to follow a schedule, and everyone in a seniority group was to get the same raise. A number of other working conditions were spelled out in the union contract, and there was a steward in her unit who was, in effect, a countervailing force to her leadership. All these conditions existed because CE's employees belonged to the union.

This case makes the point that the presence of a union directly affects most aspects of personnel—recruiting, selection, performance evaluation, promotion, compensation, and benefits, among others. These effects will be discussed in the rest of the chapters in the book. Chapter 17 focuses directly on relations with labor unions.

EXHIBIT 2–4
Environment of the organization and personnel

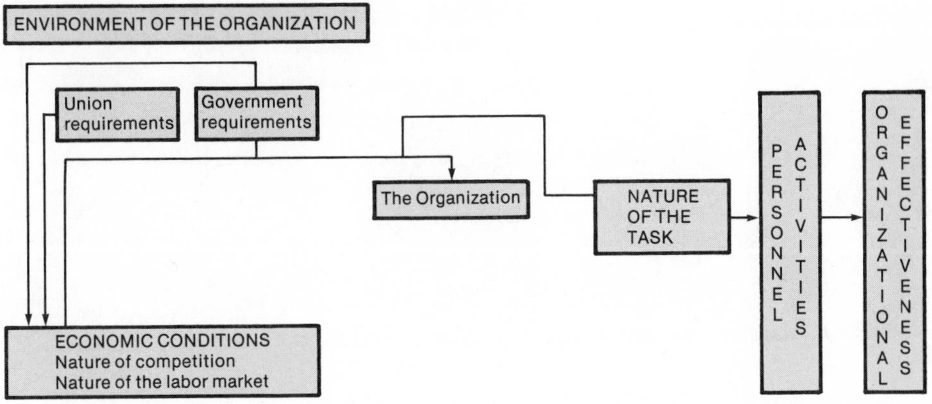

Unions differ just as people differ. There are cooperative unions and combative unions. Those familiar with union history are aware of the kind of toughness a James Hoffa or John L. Lewis can bring to the employment scene. The union leadership of the Air Line Pilots Association, State, Local and Municipal Workers, and others is not so well known, because they have different bargaining styles and philosophies.

At one time, unions were concentrated in a few sectors of the economy, such as mining and manufacturing, and were influential in only a few sections of the United States, primarily the highly industrialized area. But the fastest growing sectors for unions in the United States today are in the third and public sectors. No longer is it useful to think of the unionized employee as a blue-collar factory worker. Today engineers, nurses, teachers, secretaries, salesmen, college professors, and even physicians belong to unions. In sum, unions can be a significant factor in the personnel process.

Government requirements and regulations

The second environmental influence is government law and regulations. These affect the private and third sectors directly. Many federal regulations limit the flexibility of other jurisdictions such as cities and states.

The government regulates and influences some aspects of personnel more directly than others. The major areas of legislation and regulation include:

Equal employment opportunity and human rights legislation, which affects recruiting, selection, evaluation, and promotion directly, and employment planning, orientation, career planning, training and development indirectly.

Compensation regulation, which affects pay, hours of work, unemployment, and similar conditions.

Benefits regulation, which affects pension plans and retirement.

Workers compensation and safety laws, which affect health and safety.

Labor relations laws and regulations, which affect the conduct of collective bargaining.

FRANK AND ERNEST

Government regulation is increasing substantially in 1940, the U.S. Department of Labor administered 18 regulatory programs. In 1975, it administered 134. And that's just *one* government agency affecting managers and the personnel functions.

John Dunlop lists a number of the problems government regulation imposes on management. All of these make the operating and personnel managers' jobs more difficult:

- Regulation encourages simplistic thinking on complicated issues. Small enterprises are treated like large ones. Different industries are regulated the same.
- Designing and administering regulations is an incredibly complex task. This leads to very slow decision making.
- Regulation does not encourage mutual accommodation but rather leads to complicated legal manuevering.
- Many regulations are out of date and serve little social purpose, yet they are not eliminated.
- There is increasing evidence of regulatory overlap and contradictions between different regulatory agencies.

To cope with increasing governmental control, management has tried to influence the passage of relevant legislation and the way it is administered. Managements have sued to determine the constitutionality of many of the laws. When such efforts fail to influence the process as management prefers, it has learned to adapt its personnel policies.

In sum, there are almost no personnel decisions today that are unaffected by government. In what ways and to what degree governments affect the personnel function will be discussed in each chapter, beginning with Chapter 4.

Economic conditions

As was shown in Exhibit 2–4, two aspects of economic conditions affect personnel: the nature of competition, and the nature of the labor market.

The nature of competition. The nature of competition is mainly measured by the degree of competition. The degree of competition affects all three personnel sectors. In industry, competition is considered high when there are many producers competing for the customers' business. The result usually is price pressures. A similar condition can exist in the third sector. When there are more dormitory rooms than there are students at universities, competitive pressures operate on tuition charges, extra services offered, and so on. This can happen in hospitals too. In the public sector, competition for budget increases for an agency, when the total budget (in real dollars) is stable or declining, can be fierce.

The greater the competitive pressure, the less able the organization is to offer additional inducements to employees such as higher pay or benefits. Effective organizations under economic pressure can compete for good employees by offering nonmonetary rewards. For example, they can provide greater job satisfaction through more socializing opportunities, better recognition systems for ego needs, or job placement, which can facilitate personal fulfillment or self-actualization. Sometimes the pressure to produce acts against these possibilities, however.

If there is less competitive pressure, the enterprise has greater flexibility in the variety of personnel programs it can offer. For example, as director of the MBA program at Michigan State University, I interviewed two engineers from a defense contractor in Detroit, 90 miles away, who wanted to enter the program. When it was pointed out there was no night program, they said they could come during the day. This was astonishing. In pressing further, it was found that they had done nothing for the company for two years except to bring in the coffee and do odds and ends. The company was on a cost-plus contract; thus it could "stockpile" them *in case* they were needed and could still recoup their salaries *plus* their built-in profit percentage. Obviously there was no economic or competitive pressure in this situation. And the company could afford to be very generous in pay, benefits, and so on. Contrast this with the competitive food industry, in which five cents on a $10 case of vegetables could lose the order. These firms have to watch their pennies which translates into concern over the costs of large wage increases and excessive fringe benefits. Thus competitive pressures directly and indirectly affect personnel activities.

The nature of the labor market. The labor market also directly affects the personnel function. When there are more workers than jobs, employers find recruiting costs minimal. Employees apply readily, and selection is less difficult; the employer may be able to choose from five or more qualified applicants for each position. Work attitudes tend to be work ethic oriented. Martha Winston had significant personnel problems because this was not the case. When the work ethic predominates in employee attitudes, output rises and performance evaluation can be a motivating experience. A surplus of labor also can reduce employee pressures for compensation and benefit increases. Disciplinary problems, absenteeism, and turnover are likely to decrease, and equal employment opportunity goals may be easier to fill.

The employer must be aware of several labor markets. The primary concern is with the local labor market, from which most blue- and white-collar employees are drawn. Managerial, professional, and technical employees may be recruited from a regional or even national market.

It is quite possible that the local labor market is different from the regional or national markets. For example, in 1976 there was about 7 percent unemployment nationwide, but in Detroit 14 percent of the workers were unemployed. Recruiting blue-collar workers in Detroit was twice or three times as easy as it was in Dallas that year.

If the national and local labor markets differ significantly, there will be some exchange between them. Thus, if Detroit's unemployment rate consistently stays high, those among the unemployed who are younger, have the knowledge of jobs elsewhere, and have the money and motivation to move will do so. This movement tends to increase the labor supply in areas with shortages. There also are international labor markets; when illegal aliens come to the United States to seek work, this changes the labor market balance. It was estimated that there were over 8,000,000 illegal aliens working in the United States in 1975. Currently, some British executives are trying to emigrate to the United States to leave an economy they feel has little future.

In addition to geographic differences in labor markets, there are markets organized by skills and age cohorts. If you are seeking an accountant, it is not much help if the labor market as a whole has a surplus but accountants are scarce. The supply of labor with a particular skill is related to many factors: the number of persons of work age; the attractiveness of the job in pay, benefits, and psychological rewards; the availability of training institutes; and so on. With regard to age, for example, in 1976 the U.S. Department of Labor predicted that by 1990, workers aged 25–54 will rise by 22.4 million, while those in the teenage years will decline by almost 2,000,000. An appendix to this chapter examines in more detail the current composition of the labor force in the United States.

In sum, the personnel function is affected fundamentally by the state of the labor market in the enterprise's location in the region, nation, and world, and for the kinds of employees the enterprise seeks.

The work sector of the organization

The diagnostic model presented in the exhibits above does not contain an element noting the work sector in which the organization is located. This was done so that the model could remain relatively simple.

About 60 percent of professional personnel specialists work in the *private sector,* consisting of businesses owned by individuals, families, and stockholders. The *public sector* is that part of the economy which is owned and operated by a government. In the United States, 30 percent of all employees work in this sector. Many economists define the other institutions in society that are neither government nor profit oriented as the *third sector.* Examples of these institutions are museums, symphony orchestras, private schools and colleges, not-for-profit hospitals and nursing homes, voluntary organizations like churches, and social clubs. About 10 percent of personnel specialists and employees work in the third sector.

In general, private- and third-sector personnel work are structured similarly. Hospitals have different conflicts than most businesses, though. The presence of three hierarchies—the physicians, the administrators, and the board of trustees (representing the public)—can lead to conflicts. Pressures from third-party payees such as Blue Cross or Medicare can lead to other conflicts. Hospitals employ professional groups which zealously guard their "rights," and this also leads to conflict. Structurally, however, personnel work in the private and third sectors is similar, but organizational differences mean that personnel jobs vary.

Personnel in the public sector is *fundamentally different* from the other two sectors because it varies *structurally*. And the public manager faces a different world. In fact, a manager who moves from the private or third sector to the public sector will find the personnel role much more complicated.

The diagnostic model was developed primarily for the private and third sectors. Exhibit 2–5 adjusts the environment portion of the diagnostic model to the public sector setting.

People management in the public sector generally is much more laden with conflict. Politicians, the general public, pressure groups, and reporters look over the shoulders of the public manager and public personnel manager much more than in a private business or in the third sector.

Like all managers, the one in the public sector must seek resources from a hierarchy. But the public hierarchy can include a split between the executive branch (president, governor, city manager) and the legislative branch (Congress, the state legislature, the city council). These forces may choose to have a political fight over any program.

Then there is the press or the communications media, whose business it is to expose "useless, inefficient bureaucrats." They are helped by out-of-power politicians who feed them information to discredit those in office. In addition to these complications, the legal and regulatory restrictions are much greater in the public sector, so there is less flexibility and less room for initiative. Also, public employee unions may lobby for their demands directly with politicians. The unions can often deliver more votes than the public personnel managers can.

In addition to these complications, most public managers must also deal with a central personnel bureau such as the Civil Service Commission. A special problem faced by public managers has always been the appointment to public positions of persons because of political reasons. Formerly, politicians always saw to it that their party workers were employed between elections in government jobs; this is usually called the spoils system. In an attempt to assure that public jobs are assigned on the basis of merit, not political pull, civil service or equivalent central personnel bureaus were established which set personnel policies to govern public employment. Civil Service standardized examinations are now required as part of the selection process for many public-sector jobs.

EXHIBIT 2–5

The environment of the public sector in the diagnostic model

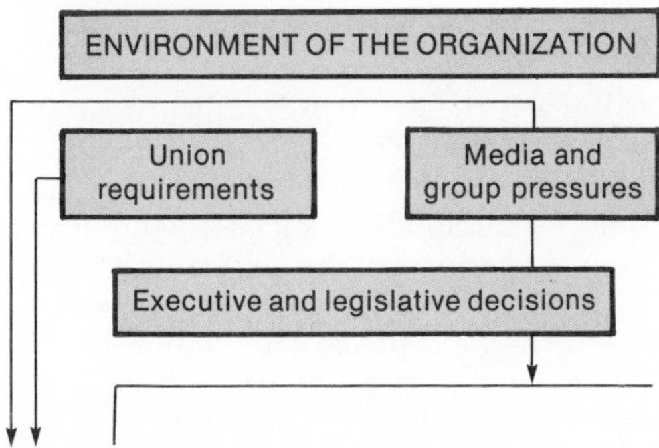

This system was intended to establish merit as the criterion for public employment, but it also increases the system's rigidity and entrenches bureaucracy.

The differences among public-, and private-, and third-sector personnel activities are largely in the structure of the personnel function and the environment of the public manager's job. The personnel function does vary by sector, and these differences will be discussed where they are significant.

In sum, the personnel process is affected by the external environment, especially union requirements, government regulations, economic conditions, and the work sector of the organization.

ORGANIZATIONAL FACTORS AND THE PERSONNEL FUNCTION

The final set of factors affecting personnel is related to the employing enterprise or organization. Exhibit 2–6 highlights the major organizational factors:

- Goals of controlling interests.
- Organization style.
- Nature of the task.
- Work group.
- Leader's style and experience.

Let's examine how each of these factors affects the personnel process.

EXHIBIT 2–6
Organizational factors and personnel

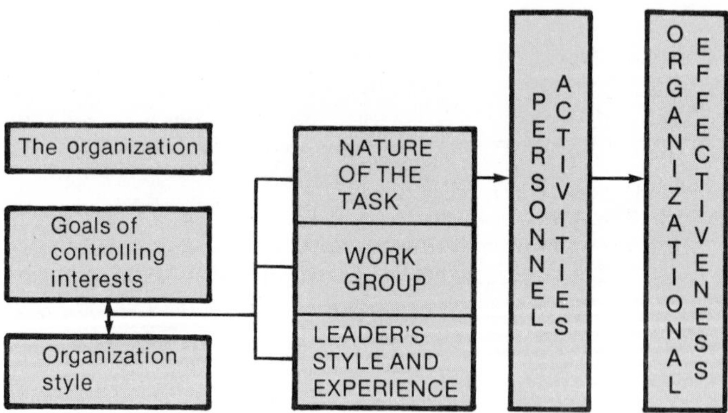

Goals of controlling interests

As shown in Exhibit 2–6, the first two organizational factors (goals and organizational style) are interrelated. The goals of controlling interests differ within and between sectors. All sectors probably include organizations that have goals which include employee satisfaction, survival, and adaptability to change. The differences arise in how *important* the controlling interests rate goals like employee satisfaction relative to other goals. In some organizations, profit is so much more important than employee satisfaction that personnel activities are not well developed. In this case, employee rewards such as pay and benefits are not high. In other organizations, personnel-related goals are highly regarded by the controlling interests. Thus, how much the personnel functions is valued and how it is implemented is affected by these goals.

Organization style

Modern organization theory has provided for many ways to organize. At one extreme is the *conservative-bureaucratic approach.* In this approach, the organization usually centralizes decision making, designs specialized jobs, departmentalizes by function, has standardized policies, uses small spans of control, has clearly defined objectives, and encourages communication through the chain of command.

The opposite extreme—the *liberal-participative approach*—uses decentralized decision making. It enlarges jobs, departmentalizes by product, uses few detailed policies, has large spans of control, and encourages all kinds of communication.

Obviously there are many ways to organize which fall *between* these extreme styles. The two extremes are reflections of fundamentally different managerial philosophies about the nature of the person, the role of work in life, and the most effective ways to supervise. These basic beliefs about how employees are to be treated translate into ideas about the kinds of personnel programs that should be made available to employees.

Most work organizations will fall between these two extremes. Conservative organizations, for example, are likely to prefer more formalized personnel policies, tighter controls on personnel, more directly job-related training, compensation policies tied to stimulus-response motivation theories, and so on. It seems reasonable to hypothesize that truly liberal and truly conservative organizations would have different personnel policies. Of course, most organizations are made up of some units that are liberal and some that are conservative in outlook, so personnel policies would also vary along these dimensions. In these ways, the organization style of the enterprise influences the personnel process.

The nature of the task

The closest organizational factors to the personnel interface are the task, the work group, and the leader. Many experts believe that the task to be performed is one of the two most vital factors affecting personnel. They describe personnel as the effective matching of the nature of the task with the nature of the employee performing the task.

There are perhaps unlimited similarities and differences among jobs which attract or repel possible workers and influence the meaning of work for them. Some of the most significant are:

Degree of physical exertion required. Contrast the job of ditch digger with that of bookkeeper. In general, work involving less physical exertion is preferred by most employees.

Degree of environmental unpleasantness. Contrast the work of a coal miner with a bank teller. In general, employees prefer physically pleasant and safe conditions.

Physical location of work. Some jobs require outside work, others inside. Contrast the job of a telephone lineman in the winter of 1977 or 1976 in Minnesota with that of a disc jockey. Some jobs require the employee to stay in one place. Others permit moving about. Contrast the job of an employee on an assembly line with that of a traveling salesman. There are individual differences in preference for physical location.

Time dimension of work. Some jobs call for long hours of less taxing work, others for shorter periods of intense effort. In some jobs the work is continuous, in others intermittent.

Human interaction on the job. Contrast the position of a radar operator in an isolated location who rarely sees anyone else with that of a receptionist in a busy city hall. Sometimes human interaction results in conflict. Most jobs have some built-in conflict, but some have much more than others. Labor negotiator is a good example of a conflict-laden position, as are troubleshooter and product manager. Less conflict would be expected in jobs such as placement officer in a university, lab technician in a hospital, statistician in a state highway department, or market researcher.

Degree of variety in the task. Contrast the job of a troubleshooter for the president with that of an assembly-line operator in an auto factory. Those with work ethic attitudes tend to prefer variety.

Degree of autonomy. The amount of freedom and responsibility a person has on the job is said to be the degree of autonomy provided for in the work. Contrast the autonomy of a college professor with that of a fee clerk in the college bursar's office.

Task identity. The degree of wholeness, in a job—the feeling of completing a whole job versus a small piece of a job—is its task identity. Contrast again the job of an auto assembler with that of a tax accountant.

Task differences and job design. Because jobs are not created by nature, engineers and personnel specialists can create jobs with varying amounts of the characteristics described above. There are four approaches to those aspects of job design that affect variety, autonomy, task identity and similar job factors. The first is called *work simplification* which leads to very specialized jobs. In the work simplification approach, the complete job (such as making a car) is broken down into small subparts, usually consisting of a few operations. This is done because:

- Less well-trained and less well-paid employees can do these jobs.
- More workers are available for hire, since there are more unskilled than skilled workers.
- By repeating the same operations over and over, the employee gets better at it.
- Many small jobs can be performed simultaneously, so that the complete operation can be done more quickly.

The second approach to job design is *job rotation.* In job rotation, the employees take turns at several work-simplified jobs. Job rotation provides more flexible work assignments, makes it easier to staff the more unpleasant jobs (or heavier jobs), and reduces the boredom and monotony of the work-simplified jobs.

The third approach is *job enlargement,* the opposite of work simplification. If the work-simplified job consisted of three operations, the job enlargement approach expands this until a meaningful subunit (or subprocess) is completed by one person. The theory is that "whole" jobs reduce boredom (by providing more variety) and give more meaning to work.

The fourth approach is *job enrichment.* Job enrichment increases the responsibility of the employees and gives them more autonomy. Job enrichment is said to provide more meaning to work for many employees.

Obviously, there can be a combination of several of these strategies. For example, a likely combination is job enrichment and job enlargement.

The relationship between job design and effective performance is complex. Effective job design *can contribute* to performance and employee satisfaction, but there *is no universally good design of work.* Individual differences, interpersonal relationships, organizational climate, and style and technology affect the relative effectiveness of the four approaches to job design.

How do these task factors affect personnel decisions? They obviously affect recruiting and selection, since the employee will probably be more satisfied and productive if his or her preferences are met. As mentioned above, few jobs match these preferences exactly. There are too many preferences. For jobs that few people prefer because the work is difficult, dirty, or in smoky or hot environments, the manager must provide additional incentives such as more pay, shorter hours, or priority in vacations. Or the manager may try to find employees who can handle the conditions better; for example, deaf people may be hired to work in a noisy environment.

For each personnel decision discussed in the chapters to follow, the task factors that are most salient to each activity will be described.

The work group

A work group is a set of two or more people who see themselves as a group, who are interdependent with one another for the accomplishment of a purpose, and who communicate and interact with one another on a more or less continuous basis. In many cases (but not always), they work closely together physically.

An effective group is one whose:

- Members function and act as a team.
- Members participate fully in group discussions.
- Group goals are clearly developed.
- Resources are adequate to accomplish group goals.
- Members furnish many useful suggestions leading to goal achievement.

Most effective work groups are small (research indicates that 7 to 14 members is a good range), and their members have eye contact and work closely together. Effective groups also generally have stability of membership, and their members are similar in backgrounds. Their membership is composed of persons who depend on the group to satisfy their needs.

A group which is effective as a work unit will help achieve the goals of the enterprise. Thus it is in the manager's interest to make the groups effective. This also is in the interests of employees, because effective groups serve their members' social needs.

While the effective group generally supports management and the organization's goals, it also can work against them. This usually is so when the group perceives the organization's goals as being in conflict with its own. If the work group is effective and works with management, the manager's job is easier, and objectives are more likely to be achieved. If the group is working against the manager, an effort must be made to change the group's norms and behavior by use of the manager's leadership, discipline, and reward powers, or by the transfer of some group members.

Work groups are directly related to the success of personnel activities. If they oppose personnel programs, they can ruin them. Examples of programs which can be successes or failures depending on work-group support or resistance include incentive compensation, profit sharing, safety, and labor relations. Operational and personnel managers who desire success in such programs should build work-group participation into the design and implementation of personnel activities.

Leader's style and experience

The experience and leadership style of the operating manager or leader directly affect personnel activities because many, if not most, personnel programs must be implemented at the work-unit level. Thus the operating manager–leader is a crucial link in the personnel function. To illustrate how the experience and style of operating management influences the personnel function, consider the following case situation.

The Acme Manufacturing Company has just completed its evaluation of personnel procedures (see Chapter 19). At Acme, thus process includes sending the supervisors reports on the previous period's personnel indicators such as accident rates, turnover (number of persons quitting), amount of absenteeism from the job, and quality reports (number of items that had to be remanufactured because of poor quality). Supervisors were also provided with results of the company attitude survey. Each supervisor was given the average response for all employees in the company for each item on the survey, and the average response for the employees in the supervisor's unit. Those items that differed significantly from the company's average response were circled.

In unit 1 the supervisor is Jenny Argo, who has been a supervisor for less than a year. Her unit's absenteeism, turnover, accident rate, and quality were more than 10 percent worse than the company average. The attitude survey indicated that Jenny's employees were significantly more dissatisfied with Jenny's leadership style, style of communicating, amount of communication, and willingness to discuss work problems with employees.

In unit 2 the supervisor is Claudia Wagner. Claudia has been supervisor for five years. Her unit's absenteeism, turnover, accident rate and quality were 3 percent worse than the company average. The attitude survey indicated about average evaluations of Claudia's supervisory skills.

Jenny

Claudia

The day the reports came out, Jenny and Claudia had lunch together and discussed the reports.

Claudia: I'm really upset. Those results tell me I'm doing something wrong. I plan to invite Mary Jane Uyalde from the Personnel Department down. I must be doing something wrong. Maybe my weekly employee meetings are being conducted wrong.

Jenny: What weekly meeting?

Claudia: I have a meeting on Friday afternoon about coffee break time and we kick around suggestions on how to get the job done better. My gang tells me when I'm leaning too hard on them and about their work problems.

Jenny: What a waste of time! You're the supervisor. Why do you give up your authority to the girls like that?

Claudia: I don't give up anything. We help each other. Besides, my results are three times better than yours. Why should I listen to your advice?

Jenny: Don't worry about results. Mine aren't bad. And if it gets any worse, I plan to knock some heads and kick some butts around. That'll shape them up.

This case example is designed to point out that the way supervisory and personnel decisions are made varies with the leadership style of the managers. Jenny is inexperienced as a leader. She is not concerned about some rather poor results in personnel. She seems to assume that tough disciplinary measures will solve whatever is causing the problems. Claudia is more experienced. She is seeking all the help she can get from the personnel specialist and her employees to get at the causes of her problem. Claudia's problem is much less severe. But Claudia sees her problem as serious. Jenny does not.

In addition to differences in experience, there are differences in the leadership style of the two leaders in this example. They see the role of the leader differently. They also perceive the relationship between themselves as leaders and their work group differently.

Jenny follows a conservative leadership style. She sees the role of the leader as making the decisions for the work group. She sees communication between herself and the work group primarily as one-way communication downward: from her to the employees. Jenny sees herself as having more formal authority than the employees and having the power to discipline and apply sanctions to the employees if they don't perform well. Note that she didn't discuss her ability to reward positively those who are doing well, but she did discuss "kicking butts." Conservative leaders structure the whole job situation and take full responsibility for all aspects of it.

Claudia follows a middle-of-the-road leadership style. She sees the role of the leader as making the decisions after she discusses various aspects with the work group. Claudia's communication patterns go two ways, as evidenced by her group meetings. Claudia takes responsibility for results but seeks the help of the work group and of the personnel department. Claudia is willing to share her authority with her work group and with personnel. She appears willing to take both positive and negative approaches to rewards.

There is another leadership style, the liberal style, which was not illustrated in the case. In the liberal style, the work group, with the leader as a member, has authority to make decisions, is responsible for communications, decides on rewards, and so on.

Of course, leadership style is a complicated topic. Many management experts believe that most styles can be effective, given the right match of leader, employees, and task situation. It should be clear that the experience and preferred leadership style of the operating manager–leader will influence how personnel decisions are made and how personnel programs are communicated and implemented.

HOW TO USE THE DIAGNOSTIC MODEL

You've now had a chance to learn something about the diagnostic model: this book's way of organizing the important factors affecting personnel. It is complicated because the world of work and people is complicated. The model tells you that three sets of factors influence the personnel situation.

Factors influencing personnel:

Nature of the employee—what the employee's abilities, attitudes/preferences, motives, etc. are.

Nature of the environment—how the union, government, and economy affect the personnel situation.

Organizational factors—goals and organization style, tasks to be done, work group, and leaders' experiences and styles.

I contend that when managers consider a personnel situation, they are more effective if they think about the three sets of factors influencing personnel before they make a decision. Chapters 4–19 tell you *how* each of these factors affects a specific personnel decision, such as the selection and pay decisions Martha Winston is considering at the National Pancake House.

Have you been wondering why the model is called a diagnostic model? The term "diagnostic" is used because the model decision maker on which it is based is the physician. An effective physician examines all the evidence bearing on a case. The physician gets as much objective data as he or she can from laboratory tests, observes the patient's medical history, and asks what the symptoms are. Then he or she makes a judgment of the most probable cause of the symptoms and prescribes the treatment most likely to reduce the pain and eliminate the cause. If the treatment does not work, the doctor assumes that the next most probable cause is at work and attempts to treat it, and so on.

Managers concerned with personnel should adopt a similar model. First they need to analyze the personnel problem—or the person with a problem—by looking at all the data at hand. Then they decide which causes are operating and how the problem can be solved. They do not give up if the most probable cause does not seem to be operating. Rather, they proceed down the list of causes until the underlying source of the problem is found.

Suppose, for example, a manager notices from the weekly production reports that productivity in the department has been declining over the past few weeks.

There could be a number of reasons for this decline. Perhaps the equipment in the department has become defective and is not working properly. Or the materials and supplies have been of a comparatively lower quality. Or the cause might be the employees. Perhaps some of the more highly skilled employees have been promoted, transferred to other departments, or quit, and their replacements lack the necessary skills and experience to perform the work effectively. Or, perhaps the problem is one of poor employee morale.

In investigating the problem, the diagnostic manager may find that turnover in the department has been quite high, that absenteeism has been increasing, and that there have been more complaints and grievances. All of these are symptoms of low employee satisfaction. If the manager concludes that the most likely cause of poor production in the department is the low satisfaction of employees, a solution for this problem will be sought. The manager may consider such prescriptions as providing better working conditions, increasing pay and other financial benefits, improving communication between supervisor and employees, redesigning the jobs to make them more interesting and challenging, or modifying the manager's own leadership style.

If, after treating the morale problem, productivity is still low, the manager will turn to the next most probable cause of this production problem and continue down the list of causes until the right one is found and corrected.

You, too, can use the data about the employee, environment, and organization factors to become an effective diagnostic manager.

SUMMARY, CONCLUSIONS, AND RECOMMENDATIONS

The main objective of this chapter has been to introduce you to the diagnostic model of personnel management. Chapter 2 briefly reviews some applicable findings from the social sciences to show you how they apply to personnel decisions. It also examines two other aspects of the environment of the personnel function: the physical location of the enterprise in a labor market, and the work sector in which it is located. This book has been written with the assumption that effective personnel management will result if the manager or specialist follows a diagnostic approach.

A summary of the major points covered in this chapter follows:

1. Good personnel relations contribute to organizational effectiveness, along with such functions as financial management, operations management, marketing, and client relations activities.
2. The diagnostic approach suggests that before you choose a personnel program you should examine the nature of the employees, the environmental influences on the organizations, and organizational factors. Personnel decisions are made with these factors as moderating variables, and personnel activities are influenced by them.
3. Abilities are skills which humans possess.
4. An attitude is a characteristic and usually long-lasting way of thinking, feeling, and behaving, and a preference is a type of attitude which evaluates an object, idea, or persons in a positive or negative way.
5. Motivation, the inner state which energizes, channels, and sustains human behavior to achieve goals, is an important concept in developing personnel practices.
6. Various factors in the environment, such as unionization of employees,

government regulations, and competitive pressures, also exert strong influences on the personnel function.

7. The work sector in which the organization is operating—public, private or third—determines the complexity and bureacratic level of the personnel function.
8. Organization factors, including the goals of controlling interests, organization style, the nature of the task, make-up of the work group, and leader's style and experience, must all be taken into account to maximize the effectiveness of the personnel function.
9. The status of the labor market also can facilitate or be detrimental to a company's personnel efforts.
10. U.S. locations are different from Canadian, European from Venezuelan, for example. Thus, personnel must adapt to the cultural environment of work.

The appendix to this chapter discusses the labor force and the physical location of the organization in some detail. Chapter 3 turns to another behavioral process that is vital to an effective personnel function: communications.

APPENDIX: A LOOK AT THE COMPOSITION OF THE LABOR FORCE

In 1979, the U.S. population was approximately 221 million and the labor force comprised about 93 million persons. These figures indicate that about 62 percent of all males 16 years and over were employed. This ranges from about 47 percent for males 16–17 to 25 percent for males over 65; the largest percentage of employed males was about 96 percent of all males 25–44 years of age. Female employment participation was 47 percent, but this is growing. About 34 percent of girls 16–17 were employed. The highest proportion was about 54 percent of women 45–54, and only 9 percent of women over 65 were employed. From 1947 to 1975, the female population increased 52 percent, but the percentage of women working increased 123 percent.

The U.S. labor force is also becoming composed of more single and fewer married persons. One third of all workers are single, and 90 percent of the recent growth in the labor force has been in single workers.

More participation in the labor force has become possible as the life span of the population has lengthened. In the United States, the typical man now lives about 67 years, and the typical woman about 72 years.

In general, the contribution of the U.S. labor force has been growing as productivity has increased. The most productive workers are in (and are expected to be in) the agriculture, forestry, and fishing industries, followed by transportation, communication, public utilities, mining, finance, insurance, and real estate. In the lower productivity category are workers in merchandising, manufacturing, and construction. The least productive workers are in services.

The percentage of the labor force employed by manufacturing, construction, mining, and agriculture has stabilized or declined. It is estimated that by 1980 two times as many persons (60,000,000) will be employed in service industries such as transportation, utilities, trade, financial, general services, and government as in the stabilized industries (30,000,000). As far as types of workers are concerned, by 1980 it is predicted that farm workers will represent about 2 to 3 percent; service workers, about 12 percent; blue-collar workers, 33 percent;

and the rest—over 50 percent—will be white-collar workers (professional and technical, clerical, sales, and managers). Blue-collar workers, especially unskilled workers, are declining in relative importance. One of the fastest growing segments of employment is state and local government workers. From 1950 to 1975, total employment was up 44 percent, while state and local government employment increased by 193 percent.

A closer look at some groups of employees in the labor force

The recent emphasis on equal employment opportunity programs makes analysis of subgroups in the population of special interest. We will look at some statistics on them and will examine the case of temporary and part-time employees, many of whom come from these groups.

Women in the labor force. In recent years, about 40 percent of the full-time U.S. work force has been women. The number of married women in the labor force has increased 205 percent since 1947, at the same time that the number of male married employees has increased by 27 percent. In the midseventies, 52 percent of married women with children aged 6–17 held full-time jobs, and 35 percent of married women with children aged six or under worked. Fifty-one percent of black children and 37 percent of white children 18 and under had mothers in the labor force.

Although it is alleged that everyone has equal job opportunities, it is difficult to argue with the facts of discrimination against women in the workplace. Typically, women hold the lower status, low-pay jobs. For example, one recent study of 163 companies found that 31 percent had 50 percent or more women employees, and 82 percent employed at least 19 percent women. If discrimination were not practiced, at least half of the companies with 50 percent women workers should have a majority of women in higher status, higher paying jobs. This study found, however, that less than 10 percent of the high-pay, high-status jobs were held by women. Similar conditions exist in the public and third sectors.

Minorities in the labor force. The situation for women's employment is similar for racial and ethnic minorities in the United States. Large numbers of minority peoples, such as Hispanic Americans, blacks, and American Indians, are employed in low-skill, low-pay jobs, and few are in high-status, high-pay jobs.

Historically, the most recent immigrant group took the lowest level jobs offered. This was true of the Irish, Polish, Yugoslavs, and Jews. One difference between the immigrant groups and other minorities is that most of the minority groups were living in the United States long before the immigrants arrived—the Indians from the beginning, as were many of the Hispanics in the Southwest, and the blacks since the mid 1700s. They have not advanced to the degree that the immigrants have, however. The Indians were kept on reservations, and the Hispanics remained in the areas that once belonged to the Mexican Republic (except for the Cuban and Puerto Rican immigrants, who came much later). Most blacks remained in Southern agriculture until relatively recently. These minorities represent 11 to 12 percent of the U.S. population. They have been less well educated than the majority, although recent programs have attempted to improve this situation. Movement to better paying, higher status jobs has been a problem for racial and ethnic minorities, as it has for women.

The older employee. The age discrimination legislation defines an older employee as one between the ages of 40 and 70. About 21 percent of the labor force currently is in this category. This portion of the labor force is protected by law because some employers hold negative stereotypes about older workers.

Probably one of the most difficult employment problems today is the older employee who loses his job through no fault of his own. Employers assume that because he is older he is less qualified and less able to adapt. And benefits plans (which may amount to one third of base compensation) are set up in such a way that it costs more to employ older people.

One of the first things to remember about the aging process is that each person ages at a different rate. As we grow older, we lose some of our faculties. But this process is going on all our lives. Rarely is a swimmer better than in his midteens, for example. The key, then, is to match employees with jobs. Older workers may be less efficient on some jobs requiring quick physical response rates. But this is more important for a race driver or airline pilot than for a stock analyst or social worker.

Most studies indicate that even for jobs requiring physical work, employees over 45 have no more accidents than younger employees do. They also have the same or lower rates of absenteeism, at least until age 55. The worst accident rate observed in one study was for employees under 35. When total performance is considered (speed, accuracy, judgment, loyalty, etc.), the older employee has been found to be at least as effective as the younger one. Yet our society tends to assume that the older employee is less effective.

Handicapped workers in the labor force. There are more than 6.5 million handicapped workers in the United States. Studies of handicapped persons indicate that they are of all age groups, of both sexes, and in many occupations. About 56 percent have been disabled by disease, 30 percent by accident, and 14 percent by congenital diseases. In the latter category, the largest group of people have lost the use of arms or legs, or have back problems. The next largest number are amputees and blind (or partially blind) employees.

Many handicapped persons have had difficulty finding employment of any kind because employers and fellow workers believe that they could not do the job or would cause an excessive number of accidents.

Few people use all their faculties on a job, and there are many jobs for those who do not have all their faculties. As far as my own "abilities" at carpentry are concerned, a builder is probably better off with a one-legged carpenter. When the handicapped are properly matched to jobs, studies show that two thirds of the physically handicapped produce at the same rate as nonhandicapped workers, 24 percent perform at higher levels, and only 10 percent performs at a lower rate. Absenteeism and turnover are normally lower for the handicapped, for two reasons. The handicapped have had their abilities matched to their jobs better, and most handicapped workers seem better adjusted to working and have more favorable attitudes toward work. Thus they are better motivated to do a good job. Most studies indicate that handicapped persons have fewer accidents than nonhandicapped persons.

Of course, some handicapped people are physically or psychologically unable to work. Some who are marginally employable can work in training jobs at sheltered workshops and organizations such as Goodwill Industries. But for those able to work, it is most important that the handicapped be treated as normally as other workers. They will respond better to fair treatment than to paternalism. They want a chance.

It is in the interest of the nation's economy and society that the handicapped be transformed from economic liabilities to assets. It is even more important to the handicapped individuals to be able to attain employment and thus economic and psychological independence.

Veterans in the labor force. Veterans are former servicemen released from active duty by the military. They are not easily recognized as special employees by employers, but they do have a readjustment to make to civilian life. The government has attempted to ease reentry to civilian life of Vietnam veterans with several programs.

About one fourth of all returning veterans have resumed their interrupted educational careers. But the great majority have entered the civilian labor market, many seeking their first full-time jobs. As of January 1, 1977, there were 558,000 Vietnam veterans aged 20–34 unemployed in this country. The unemployment rate for veterans was 8.6 percent, while the average unemployment rate was 7.8 percent. In the 20–24 age bracket, veterans' unemployment was 18 percent.

Congress has provided specific reentry adjustments for veterans, usually referred to as reemployment rights. In addition to reemployment, Congress has enacted laws making it easier for veterans to enter the federal career service. These include a preference system of points added to test scores for veterans, the Veterans Readjustment Appointment, waivers of physical requirements, the restriction of certain jobs to veterans, preference for retention in case of reduction of force, and similar procedures. The Veterans' Administration also assists veterans who are seeking employment through job marts and apprenticeship training programs. Priority for referral to appropriate training programs and job openings is given to eligible veterans, with first consideration to the disabled veteran. Other federal benefits have also become available to veterans operating their own businesses through the Small Business Administration. Similarly, unemployment compensation for veterans provides a weekly income for a limited period of time, varying with state laws. And in 1977, the Carter administration proposed a $1.3 billion program of economic stimuli designed to get Vietnam-era veterans back to work.

Personnel programs designed to improve the conditions of these parts of the labor force are discussed in all chapters from Chapter 4 onward. They are also the focus of Chapter 16, on equal employment opportunity programs.

Part-time and temporary help employees. The labor force members considered so far have been full-time employees: those who regularly work about 40 hours weekly. But the labor market includes another group: part-time employees, who regularly (and usually voluntarily) are employed for less than the normal work week. A person who is working part time because she or he cannot get a full-time job is involuntarily a part-time employee. The focus in this section is on the *voluntary* part-time employee.

The government lists 10,500,000 part-time employees, of whom 3,500,000 classified themselves as involuntary in 1976. But there are many more part-time employees who, because of the nature of their employment, never are listed in these statistics. One estimate in 1975 was that there actually were about 15,000,000 part-time employees in the United States. In fact, part-time employment is growing faster than full-time employment.

Most part-timers are drawn from these segments of the population: women, students, retired and older persons, the physically and mentally handicapped, and moonlighters. Most part-time work is in the service industries, especially education, health care, personal services (for example, beauty shops), business services such as advertising, and entertainment and recreation. The second most frequent location of part-time industry is in retail and wholesale trade, and next is manufacturing. Very few part-time jobs exist in mining, construction, transportation, public utilities, finance, and insurance.

In addition, many enterprises lease employees from service companies for custodial, security, maintenance and food service jobs. The advantages of leasing these employees are lower recruiting and selection costs, less compensation (because benefits are fewer), and lower turnover and training costs. Leasing employees may be prohibited by the union contract, however, and the enterprise has less control over the quality of work.

There are many advantages in part-time work for employers. These include flexibility in scheduling, lower total compensation costs (direct and indirect), and stabilization of employment. Some plants have been set up entirely for part-timers.

Employees like part-time work because it fits their hours, or they want to work less than full time. Some women work out job-sharing plans; for example, one woman works mornings while the other does housework and cares for the children; in the afternoons, the roles are reversed.

There are disadvantages, too. Part-time work may require additional training and record-keeping expenses and can increase supervisory burdens. Some studies indicate that the performance levels of part-timers (especially student part-timers) are lower. Unions sometimes oppose the use of part-timers, viewing them as substitutes for additional full-time employees. The implications of part-time employees for the personnel function will be discussed in the chapters on selection, orientation, training, compensation, benefits, and pensions.

The labor force and physical location of the enterprise

The location of the enterprise influences the kinds of people it hires and the personnel activities conducted in it. If a hospital, plant, university, or government bureau is located in a rural area, certain conditions are more likely than if it is located in an urban area. For example, the work force in a rural area might be more willing to accept conservative organization styles. Recruiting and selection in rural areas will be different in that there may be fewer applicants. Yet the enterprise may find a larger proportion of hireable workers ingrained with the work ethic. It also may be harder to schedule overtime if workers are supplementing farm incomes with an eight-hour shift at a factory. There may be fewer minority "problems," but it also may be difficult to recruit professional/technical personnel, who have shown a preference to work near continuing education and cultural opportunities. While pay may be lower in rural areas, so are costs of living.

An urban location might be advantageous for recruiting and holding professional workers. Urban locations provide a bigger labor force but generally call for higher wages. The late shifts may be a problem here, too, but for different reasons. Workers may not feel safe late at night in the parking lots or going home.

Thus geographic location influences the kinds of workers available to staff the enterprise. The location or setting is extremely significant for companies operating in other countries. The employees may speak a different language, abide by the Napoleonic legal code, practice different religions, have different work attitudes and so on. Let's consider some of the major differences between home-based and other-country enterprises.

Educational factors. Examples include the number of skilled employees available, attitudes toward education, and literacy level. Educational deficiencies in some countries can lead to a scarcity of qualified employees, as well as a lack of educational facilities to upgrade potential employees.

Behavioral factors. Societies differ in factors such as attitudes toward wealth, the desirability of profits, managerial role, and authority.

Legal-political factors. Laws and political structures differ and can encourage or discourage private enterprise. Nations also differ in degree of political stability. Some countries are very nationalistic (even xenophobic). Such countries can require local ownership of enterprises or, if they are so inclined, expropriate foreign concerns.

Economic factors. Economics differ in basic structure, inflation rate, ownership constraints, and the like.

The nations of the world can be divided into three economic categories: fully developed, developing, and less developed. The fully developed nations include the United States and Canada, Australia, Israel, Japan, South Africa, and most European countries (the United Kingdom, West Germany, France, the U.S.S.R., Belgium, Luxembourg, the Netherlands, Switzerland, Italy, Sweden, Denmark, Norway, Finland). In these countries American and Canadian managers will find fewer differences in educational, behavioral, economic, and legal-political factors than they are likely to encounter in developing or less developed countries.

The developing nations are those that are well along in economic development but cannot yet be said to be fully developed. Examples include Brazil, Mexico, Argentina, Venezuela, Spain, Nigeria, Saudi Arabia, Iran, India, and eastern Europe. These countries provide more constraints in all four factors than developed countries do.

Third-World nations—the less developed countries—are the most difficult to work in because of significant constraints in all four factors. The remaining 90 or so countries in the world are in this group. A sample list would include Egypt, Bolivia, and Upper Volta.

To be successful abroad, personnel managers must learn all they can about the countries in which they will be working. There are many sources of this kind of information. Knowledge of differences among nations in educational, behavioral, legal-political and economic factors is essential for managerial success abroad. It is equally important (and more difficult) for the enterprise to obtain managers with proper attitudes toward other countries and their cultures. A manager with the wrong set of attitudes may try to transfer North American ways of doing things directly to the host country, without considering the constraints in these four factors. The more significant the differences, the more likely they are to cause problems for the unperceptive manager.

Effective managers who work abroad must adapt their personnel practices to conditions in the host country and learn to understand the new culture. A whole new field is developing for human resource planning in multinational enterprises. There are significant challenges in such personnel activities. Just as the tools of management science do not work on very unstable problems, so leadership styles and personnel activities that work for educated, achievement-oriented employees may not do so for uneducated nonachievers. A liberal-style manager in the United States may have to become a middle-of-the-road manager in Egypt.

In sum, the physical location of the enterprise (rural or urban, or at home or abroad, for example) can have significant impact on how personnel tools are used and which activities are conducted.

Martha picked up her cup of coffee and thought: Amy helped me a lot. But it is my job to figure out what to do. She wonders what factors could cause the differences between Lenny and Harry. It could be personality differences. Lenny is an outgoing person, and Harry tends to be introverted. There are some differences in abilities. Lenny is more agile. He uses his hands well. Harry seems a bit clumsier. And Lenny is more experienced—he's been on the job four more years than Harry.

Lenny and Harry have the same leader and work group. They do the same task at the same time. The environment is the same. These couldn't cause the differences.

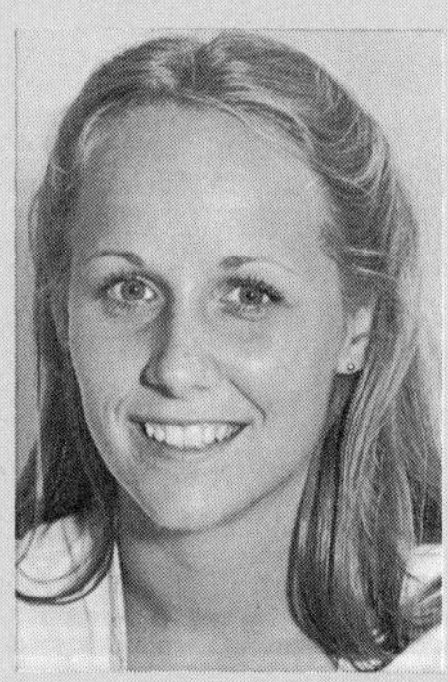

Martha

This narrows the option down to motivation and attitude differences. Was there a good match of interests and abilities with the job? Martha decided to discuss the issues informally with Harry. Later that day, she invited Harry to have a soft drink with her.

Martha: Harry, this is the first chance I've had to chat with you for very long. How do you like it at National by now?

Harry: It's O.K. It's a job.

Martha: Is there anything we can do to make it better than just a job for you?

Harry: Not really. Jobs are jobs. They are all the same.

Martha: All of them? Did you ever have a dream about what you wanted to do?

Harry: Sure. I've always wanted to be a disc jockey, but I hated school. So I quit. Then I got married and I'm locked in. I can't go back to school and make it.

Martha: I didn't know you wanted to go back to school. I'm sure you could go to night school.

Harry: I might be ready for that now.

Martha: If I can help by scheduling you differently, let me know. Everyone should get all the schooling they can. And who knows? You could go on to be assistant manager here—or even a disc jockey.

After talking with Martha, Harry did go back to school. His work improved, as did his willingness to be friendlier with co-workers and customers. Martha's chats became more frequent with all the employees, including Harry. Harry did graduate from high school and now is an assistant manager for National. He's very happy in his job.

Harry

What about Lenny? He's chief cook at 827. He's had several opportunities to become assistant manager, but he loves his work and has refused to be transferred. As Lenny put it, "I've found my niche. I do my job, then go to the beach. No worries. And I get to talk to lots of nice people."

What about the new cook? The pay issue had to be settled first. Martha contacted the home office, emphasizing that business had been steadily increasing at 827. When she told them that she needed more money to hire an extra cook to handle the increased business, they gave her more, but not enough to completely satisfy everyone.

Instead of hiding this fact from the rest of her employees, Martha explained the situation and asked them for their suggestions. Their solution was to help her recruit a cook with some experience, but one who would not demand so high a salary that their raises would be eliminated. All of the employees asked their friends for leads to fill the vacancy. Martha called guidance counselors at schools and the state employment service.

Within a week, Martha had hired Fran, a friend of Harry's. Lenny, Harry, and all the other employees liked her very much, and she worked out well as the third cook. Besides that, employee satisfaction improved all around. Not only could Martha pay Fran what she expected as a beginning wage, but all the other employees got a slight increase in pay, too.

QUESTIONS

1. What is the diagnostic approach to personnel functions? Why is it important?
2. What are abilities? Attitudes and preferences? Motivation? How do these affect personnel activities?
3. Discuss briefly why employees differ in abilities, attitudes and preferences, personality, and motivation. Of what significance are these differences to personnel decisions?
4. Personnel activities are not much affected by a union. Do you agree or disagree?
5. Does the degree of competition affect the personnel function? How?
6. How does the state of the labor market affect the personnel function? Please be specific!
7. The personnel function is essentially the same in the private, public, and third sectors. Comment.
8. In what ways do the goals of controlling interests affect personnel?
9. In what ways does an organization's style affect personnel?
10. How do tasks differ? How does this affect the manager interested in personnel?
11. What is an effective group? How does it affect personnel activities?
12. How do leadership styles and leader experience affect personnel?

3

Communication and personnel

Chapter objectives

- To make you aware of the significance of communications to managerial effectiveness.
- To understand how communication and the personnel function are interrelated.
- To help you understand how communication takes place.
- To improve your communication skills as a manager.
- To introduce the most effective communication media.
- To illustrate the channels of communication.

Chapter outline

Edward W. Sparrow Hospital is a medium-sized (250-bed) community general hospital in a West Coast city of 750,000. Sparrow employs 610 persons. It is not affiliated with a university and therefore is not a teaching hospital. Nor is it affiliated with a church.

Sparrow Hospital was built in the 1920s. It is located in the downtown area and has inadequate parking, as does the neighborhood. About six years ago, a major new hospital, St. Joseph's, was built in the area. Its facilities are excellent, and it has a good location. When these 400 beds were added to the city's existing hospital facilities, the regional medical planning commission predicted there would be problems. The area would have 100 beds too many. They were right.

As the city's oldest facility, Sparrow was hurt the most by St. Joseph's. Many of the leading physicians on staff transferred their primary affiliation to St. Joseph's. They placed most of their patients there and began to use Sparrow only when they couldn't get a patient into St. Joseph's. Sparrow's percentage of occupancy (patient census) dropped from about 89 to 69 percent. Deficits mounted. The board of trustees was worried. But Thomas Ventner, the hospital administrator, didn't seem to notice. He was 59 years old and was happily contemplating retirement after 20-some years of service at Sparrow. As things deteriorated and Tom did not seem to be doing much to prevent further deterioration of the hospital's patient census, the board pressured him to consider early retirement. Finally he did retire, about a year ago.

The board hired Marjorie Perdita as the new hospital administrator. She had faced a similar situation in a hospital in the East and had coped with it. She had done as well as any of the other candidates they were considering.

Marjorie

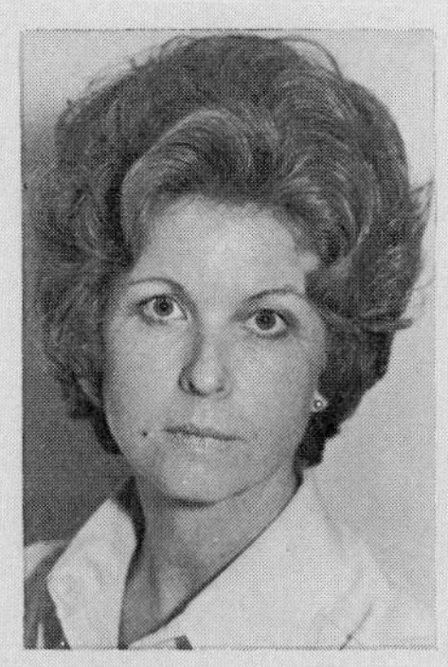

It is Monday morning. After being on the job for enough time to get her bearings, Administrator Perdita has begun to take steps to slow down and if possible reverse the slide. She has had some redecorating done. She has contracted for more parking. She has phased out some expensive, infrequently used wards such as obstetrics and added some new services. This has brought the patent census up to 72 percent.

The deficits are still large, however. Marjorie has proposed further reductions in personnel to the board. This should cut costs and generate funds for further modernization and the hoped-for attraction of more medical staff. The employees are already jittery, since there have been some recent layoffs. They know things are not going well.

There were inadequate communications at the time of the last layoffs. To prevent this happening again, Marjorie asks the hospital's personnel administrator, Edmund Farrell, to visit her.

INTRODUCTION TO COMMUNICATIONS

This chapter is designed to help you deal with communications problems like those at Sparrow Hospital. Communication is an important managerial function for operating and personnel managers. Did you know that studies of how managers spend their time indicates that at least half of it is devoted to communicating? Some studies show that up to 90 percent of managerial time is spent in communication. To get just about any task performed one must communicate with others.

In fact, Chester Barnard, probably one of the best businessmen and management theorists the United States has ever produced, implied that communication is the key job of management. He said:

> The coordination of efforts essential to a system of cooperation requires an organized system of communication. Such a system of communication implies centers or points

> of interconnection and can only operate as these centers are occupied by persons who are called executives. It might be said that the function of executives is to serve as channels of communications. . . .

Did you know that:

- Effective communication leads to more effective performance.

For example, Fred Allen, Chairman and chief operating officer of Pitney Bowes, attributes a substantial portion of the company's enviable performance record to its effective communication program. He said: "While our results cannot be attributed solely to our communications program, it clearly deserves much of the credit."

- Effective communication provides the information necessary for an enterprise to adjust to a changing world.

To reduce the uncertainty in our changing world, we need effective communications. To solve managerial problems, we need the information and advice of others which the communication process provides.

- Effective communication is essential if we expect employees and units to achieve enterprise goals.

Both planning and control functions of management require effective communications. Perhaps that's why Barnard sees communications as the heart of a manager's job.

Though you may realize the importance of communication to managers, a brief chapter on it in this book on personnel is still needed. The reason is that whether you become an operating manager or personnel manager, you *cannot* be effective in the personnel function without a fundamental understanding of skills in communication. For example, consider four of the personnel functions shown in Exhibit 2–1, which introduced the diagnostic model of personnel in Chapter 2:

Recruiting. To recruit potential employees effectively, the recruiter must "talk" to the prospect and convince him or her: "Our enterprise is a good place to work, and this job is right for you." This can be done in a one-on-one discussion, in written form, or over the phone.

Training. To train a person well, the trainer must convey information to a trainee and motivate the trainee to want to learn the material.

Performance evaluation. To do performance evaluation effectively, the evaluator must assess an employee's record and convince him or her that past successes will continue in the future. The evaluator also tries to motivate the employee to improve any weaknesses.

Labor relations. And to make labor relations work, each side must convey to the other the position it has on an issue and why this position is held.

It is clear that these personnel functions include more than communication skills. It is also clear that without effective communications, they would not be fulfilled.

Communication is also discussed in this book because many enterprises expect personnel departments to function as advisers to operating managers on employee communications. Personnel departments are asked to help develop communication skills in the enterprise's managers. Sometimes they are asked to supplement personal, face-to-face communications between managers and employees with written communications to employees, as will be seen later in the chapter.

Communications is not listed as a separate personnel activity in Exhibit 2–1 because it underlies almost all personnel activities. Nevertheless, it is a significant enough skill.

HOW COMMUNICATION TAKES PLACE

Exhibit 3–1 models the communication process. First the sender has the idea for the message, its purpose (1, thinking). Then the sender encodes the message into the form in which it will be transmitted: words, bodily movements such as gestures, or other symbols such as writing (2, encoding). Next the message is sent verbally by a medium—in person, on the phone—or in writing (3, transmitting). Then a channel, formal or informal, is chosen. After these three steps, the sender has completed the initial phase of communication.

Then the receiver must decode the message. This is affected by how the receiver perceives the symbols and nonverbal behavior of the sender (4 and 5, perceiving and decoding). Finally comes understanding (6).

EXHIBIT 3–1
A communication model

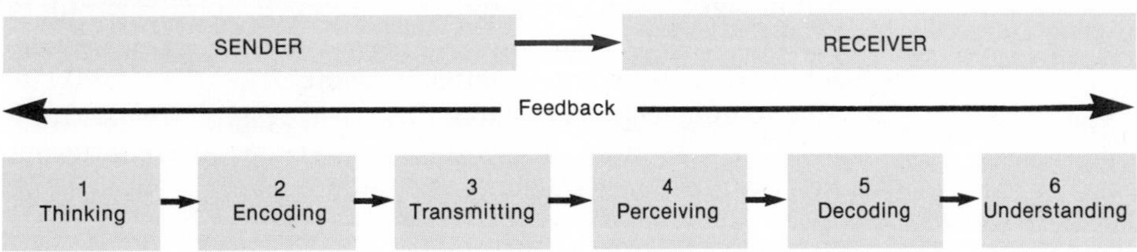

Another important element to consider is feedback. In the process of person-to-person communication, cues are sent between the sender and receiver which affect the process of communication at the time of the communication.

EFFECTIVE COMMUNICATION

Communication is effective if each step in the communication process is completed. It can break down if *any step* is incomplete or blocked by barriers to effective communication. To avoid miscommunicating or not communicating at all, here are seven pieces of advice to follow. These apply to whatever medium or media of communication you choose to use.

1. Effectively think through what the message is before preparing the message.

A person cannot communicate effectively unless she or he has thought through, logically and thoroughly, what is to be said. This prevents unclear messages. And receivers are not likely to receive the communication accurately unless the sender appears to know what he or she is talking about. Whatever Marjorie decides to say, she must be sure just what the message is before she encodes it.

2. Encode the message in words that are meaningful to the receiver.

The effective communicator realizes that the message must be attuned to the needs of the receiver. This means that the sender realizes that the receiver's perception may be different from the sender's because of differences in age, emotional makeup, background, personality, or education, and other differences. Therefore the words or other symbols used must be words or symbols the receiver is familiar with. Words not in the receiver's vocabulary should not be used. Words that have different emotional impact to the receiver than to the sender should not be used. Mostly, the message must be encoded so that it will tap the motives and needs of the receiver. And the message should be presented in an interesting manner.

For example, it would probably be a mistake for Marjorie to consider sending a message that focuses entirely on the hospital's problems. The message must also include her concern for the employees' welfare and how the employees' job security will be protected. It would also be a mistake to use technical budget and managerial words like "fiscal necessity" in talking with maintenance or laundry personnel, for example. There are more suitable words that are more meaningful to them, such as "going broke."

3. Encode the complete message.

One of the most frequent sources of miscommunication is when the sender condenses or overly shortens the message. As a result, an incomplete message is sent. Obviously the sender must not make the message too long, or the interest level of the receiver will be lost. But the sender must be sure to encode all *crucial* elements of the message if she or he wishes to communicate effectively.

4. Transmit the message with sincerity, using reinforcing verbal and nonverbal symbols, and minimizing status differentials between sender and receiver.

It is vital that the sender is sincere and appears to be sincere in what he or she is communicating. The receiver must perceive that the sender *believes* what is being said. Thus the sender's verbal and nonverbal behavior must reinforce each other and not be contradictory. For example, the sender must look like he is sincere and sure of the message. Nervous gestures or refusal to look the receiver in the eye is likely to contradict sincere words.

In sum, the sender must be trustworthy in communications. If in the past the sender lied or gave incomplete or incorrect information, then proper encoding and nonverbal behavior probably will not offset the receiver's lack of trust in the sender.

The sender must also try to avoid misperceptions in the message arising from status differences with the receiver. For example, if the president of a firm is trying to communicate to a janitor, it probably is useful for the president to get up from behind the desk and talk to the janitor side by side while both are comfortably seated.

Presentation of the message should be interesting, short, and to the point. The message should be delivered with variation in voice and with the receiver, not the sender, in mind. Do you think the restaurant patron in the cartoon, shown on the following page, has the waitress in mind as he orders his food? This is no way to communicate a desire for good service.

5. The receiver should be trained to listen effectively and be encouraged to provide feedback and ask questions to clarify items in the message which are not understood.

If suggestions 1–4 are used by the sender, the receiver will probably understand most of the message. The semantics problem will be overcome. The receiver is also likely to perceive that the sender is desirous of communicating. If, in addition, the sender asks for questions or encourages feedback in verbal and nonverbal behavior, this will encourage the receiver to comment or ask for clarification of points that are unclear.

Listening is a skill which can be developed. So is the observation of nonverbal communication. Listening training is not provided as frequently as it should be, however. But the receiver should be trained in effective listening to avoid the problem of selective perception: hearing what he or she wants to hear rather than what was said.

6. Communication is more effective if it is provided at the right time with the right media and through the right channels.

"Let me see if I have it correctly, sir. To hell with the appetizer. A chopped sirloin that damn well better be rare. No goddam relish tray. Who cares which salad dressing, since they all taste like sludge?"

Drawing by Stevenson; © 1973 The New Yorker Magazine, Inc.

Effective communciations require selection of appropriate media and channels (see the sections below). Timing is vital to effective communications. If Marjorie tries to discuss the important hospital problems facing her five minutes before quitting time, this would probably be a mistake. Another mistake would be to give an employee bad news about his job the day his father dies. And it is very unwise to discuss what must be done in December in March and then not bring the subject up again before December.

The message should be sent in time for the employee to be able to complete a task on schedule. It should be sent when there are few interruptions and when there is adequate time for interaction and discussion. The time should be one when the employee appears receptive to the message. Of course, emergencies do not always schedule themselves when we would want them to. But, if possible, the time chosen to send a message should be carefully scheduled.

Another problem to avoid is communication overload. Research has found that human beings can absorb only so much communication and information in a given period of time. If too many messages are sent, later messages will be misinterpreted or not understood, due to the receiver's inattention or fatigue. The sender should try to pace the communications to avoid overload. The receiver should take steps such as having others take messages, using a telephone recorder, or restricting incoming messages when he or she feels overloaded temporarily.

> 7. The sender should develop a feedback and control system to assure that the message was received and understood.

Messages can get lost if they are sent in written form. A telephone message left with someone else also may never reach the receiver. Messages sent through several levels of an organization may be lost or misinterpreted. It is vital, when other than face-to-face communication is used, that checks be made to see if important messages have been received. If face-to-face communication is used, a supportive communications climate should be developed to encourage receivers to ask for clarifications and give feedback. In this way, the sender is reassured that the intended message has been received.

If these seven pieces of advice are heeded, it is more certain that distortions of the sender and receiver will be overcome and that the communication channel and timing will be appropriate. If this is so, Step 6 in the communication model, understanding, should result.

It is Tuesday morning. Further analysis of the budget deficits has convinced Marjorie Perdita that the ideal number of employees for the hospital is about 410, given its current patient census. (Of course, she is hopeful of raising the occupancy rate.) Her talk with Edmund has given her some ideas about communicating regarding layoffs. The message, if she decides to send it, is clear. But she's wondering whether the message should be given verbally or in writing, and who should deliver it.

As she thinks about the issue, she searches for an alternative to laying off 200 people. After all, most of the staff has been with Sparrow many years. The productivity rate is generally good. It isn't the hospital staff's fault that there are too many hospitals in town now. In fact, from what she could find out and from what Edmund had found out for her, most of the staff has been working extra hard to make the hospital a friendlier, cleaner place. This was helping to raise the occupancy rate even a little more than her other measures had already done.

One alternative to laying off 200 people would be to put a freeze on pay and benefits and lay off fewer people. Then attrition would take care of some of the costs. But how do you tell people that in these inflationary times there would be no pay and benefit raises for the foreseeable future? Marjorie wondered how to communicate these facts without throwing the staff into a panic, lowering morale, and causing other problems. She decided to ask Edmund to come by for a consultation on this.

COMMUNICATION MEDIA

The Sparrow Hospital situation brings us to the issue of how the message is sent (the medium) and the channel it travels. Marjorie (or any communicator) could choose to send her message through one or more of four media: oral-personal, oral-mechanical, audiovisual, or written.

Oral-personal messages. In oral-personal messages, the sender is in face-to-face communication with an individual, a small group, or a mass audience. The message is conveyed verbally. Oral-personal messages are the most frequently used form of communication in the workplace.

Oral-mechanical messages. The sender conveys the message verbally over the telephone or leaves the message on a telephone recorder or tape recorder.

Audiovisual messages. The sender could also convey the message to the receiver with sound movies, TV cassettes, or similar mechanisms.

Written messages. The sender conveys the message by the written word. Typical examples include memos, letters, notices on bulletin boards, newsletters, news sheets, house organs, payroll stuffers, and similar means. Written messages are much less frequently used in small and medium-sized organizations than oral messages. In general, it is more difficult to get speedy and accurate feedback from written communications. And in oral-personal communication, the verbal message can be reinforced by nonverbal messages.

We communicate nonverbally by touch, use of the body, distance from the receiver, eye contact, and facial expression. In general, eye contact and facial expression convey the type of emotion the sender is feeling at the time of communication. Intensity of emotion comes across from the distance between the sender and receiver, the postures, and the gestures used to communicate. For example, a warm handshake can reinforce a "Hello, how are you?" A smile conveys a different message than does a frown. Verbal communication is not only the words we use but how we say them—the pitch, quality, volume, speed, and rhythm of speech. Talking too fast prevents nonverbal behavior from reinforcing verbal statements. Variety in pitch of voice can raise interest. The greater the volume of the voice, the more emphasis. All these verbal and nonverbal cues can reinforce or contradict the message.

Which media for which messages?

If you want a simple answer, research indicates that the best way to communicate important messages is to send the message orally first and then confirm it in writing. Employees prefer this pattern, and studies of accuracy and amount of message remembered indicate this is the best approach. These studies also indicate that oral-only messages are next most effective, followed by written only. The least effective media are bulletin board only and grapevine only.

These studies did not consider the efficiency of the messages, however. It is much more costly in time to communicate twice than once. Most enterprises use oral followed by written means for the most important messages, oral alone for the next most important, written alone for routine messages, and grapevine and bulletin boards to supplement these media. This policy considers the costs of communication. It also emphasizes the most important communications and probably prevents communication overloads.

CHANNELS OF COMMUNICATION

A communication channel is the route through which messages pass. It is the linkage of personnel who pass the messages on.

There are two kinds of channels: formal and informal. The *formal channel* usually consists of the vertical chain of command: the employee's superiors upwards and subordinates downwards, as established by the enterprise. A great deal, if not most, written communication follows the formal channels. Much of the oral communication also follows the formal channels. Because of the bulk of messages following formal channels, these channels can be slow.

Informal channels bypass the formal channels. The best known of these are the grapevine and open-door policies. In enterprises with open-door policies, people are encouraged to bring information to those outside the formal channels if it is important enough, or if the problem involves someone in the chain of command. Sometimes this is encouraged by managers who create occasions to receive informal messages. This is done in a number of ways: at social events, by eating at employee cafeterias, or by visiting with employees, for example.

The grapevine is the informal channel of persons who exchange information regularly outside the formal channels of communication.

Grapevines develop because they are fast, efficient, and generally accurate, especially if details of the message received are pursued through formal channels. And grapevines fulfill employees' social needs. Studies indicate that effective managers are part of the grapevine and use it to transmit messages.

Both formal and informal channels are used by effective managers. The formal channels are used for all routine and most nonroutine messages. Informal channels are very helpful in nonroutine message transmission.

A grapevine in operation

It is Tuesday at 4 P.M. Before Marjorie could set up an appointment with Edmund, he called her and said he wanted to see her; that it was urgent.

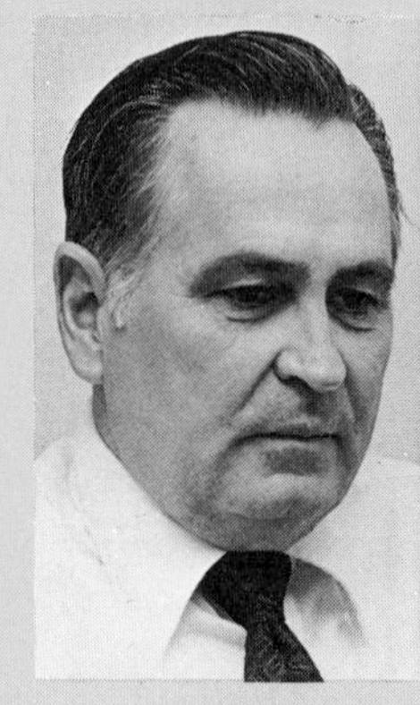

Edmund

Edmund: I've just heard through the grapevine that there have been union organizers around getting some employees to sign registration cards. From what I hear, a fair number are signing. Marjorie, they are scared. They think by joining the union they can save their jobs and do better financially. You know what a problem hospitals that have unionized have had. If at all possible, we want to do what we can to keep us as a working family here—not the them and us that happens with unions in the place.

Marjorie: You don't have to convince me about unions. We had them at the last hospital where I worked, and things got more complicated. It couldn't have come at a worse time. Well, you and I are going to sit down right now and figure out this communication, pay, union, layoff problem. We need to act now!

At Sparrow Hospital, it is apparent that Marjorie is used to having the personnel department serve communication purposes. That is not unusual. In fact, personnel departments serve many communication roles, as I pointed out earlier.

THE PERSONNEL DEPARTMENT AND COMMUNICATIONS

Thus far we have considered how any manager can communicate more effectively. Since this book is on personnel, however, you want to know how the personnel department is involved in communications for internal purposes and how it is involved in improving the communication activities of the enterprise. Personnel aids communications in six ways.

The personnel manager and communications:

1. The personnel executive communicates to superiors, subordinates, and peers, as all other managers do.
2. Personnel communicates personnel policies to the enterprise.
3. Personnel provides communication training for the enterprise's employees and executives.
4. The personnel department helps operating managers prepare their communications.
5. The personnel department may become a spokesperson for operating management.
6. The personnel department seeks information for communicating to operating management.

The personnel executive as a communicator and manager

Like any other executive, personnel managers spend most of their time communicating with superiors, subordinates, and peers. Effective personnel executives use skills as persuasive communicators to help superiors to protect and increase the unit's budget. They express the personnel viewpoint on issues that arise in top management. They assure that the personnel aspects of strategic management problems are considered. You saw this happen as Edmund consulted with Marjorie about efforts to unionize employees. Personnel executives also bring to top management's attention factors in the environment which are likely to affect personnel and the enterprise, such as new laws or regulations or proposals for them. Major changes in personnel policies and labor market conditions are other examples of environmental changes which will affect personnel and the enterprise.

Since personnel executives are also managers of people in personnel departments, they have all the usual managerial duties requiring communication: resource allocations, goal setting, organizational changes, control devices, promotions, raises, and so on. Personnel executives should set a good example for other managers on how to run a department, especially as regards effective communication.

Personnel executives also communicate with their peers in finance, operations, marketing, accounting, and legal departments to accomplish enterprise goals. Peer relationships are often the most difficult, and personnel executives need to pay special care to communicating with their equals.

The previous sections in the chapter were designed to help personnel executives to be effective communicators in their managerial roles. Now we will look at the personnel executive as a communicator.

Personnel as a communicator of policies

One of the most frequent ways the personnel department utilizes its communications skills is to inform executives and employees in the enterprise about

Sample policies communication

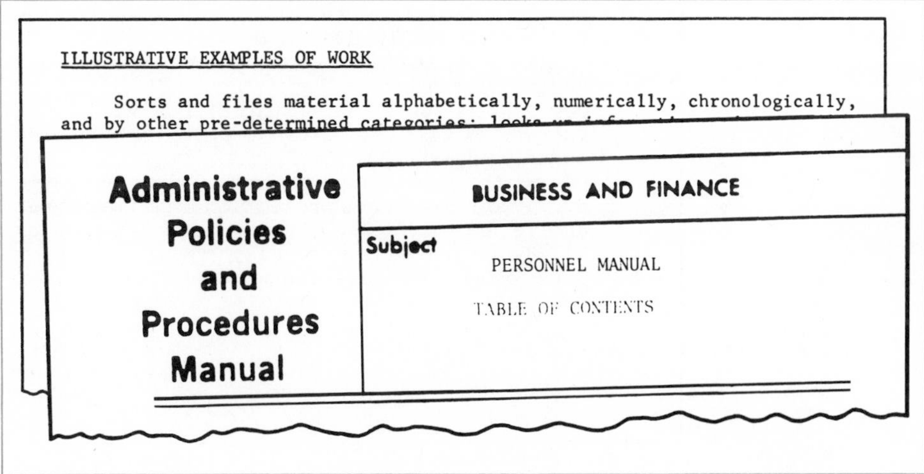

personnel policies. This occasion arises when laws and regulations change or when management changes its personnel policies or wishes to reemphasize them and in similar circumstances. The goal is to change or reinforce employee behavior to agree with set policies. For this to happen, employees must understand the policy and support it with their behavior.

This is personnel's chance to use the seven pieces of advice about effective communication offered above and to choose the correct channels and media. If personnel cannot communicate well and set an example for the enterprise, how can accountants, engineers, or production managers be expected to do so?

Exhibit 3–2 is an example of a communication about employee benefits. Do you think it uses the seven suggestions for effective communication? I asked a

EXHIBIT 3–2
Example of a benefit communication

PERSONNEL SERVICES DIVISION

June 2, 1978

TO: Employees of University with Plan "A" Family Coverage
SUBJECT: Change in Group Health Insurance Program

The Board of Regents has announced a major policy change in the State's participation in the cost of employee health insurance to be effective July 1, 1978. This change results from action taken by the State this year to provide health insurance benefit funding on a consistent basis for all State employees. Under the new funding formula established by the State, the University will pay 70% of the total premium cost for an employee's health insurance coverage, up to a maximum premium rate established by the Board of Regents, and the employee must pay 30% of the total premium cost. This funding formula will apply regardless of the employee's selected level of protection (individual or family).

According to our records, you are insured for Plan "A" family health insurance coverage. The total monthly premium for this coverage is $66.00 per month. Effective July 1, 1978 the University will pay 70% of this total premium rate or $46.20 per month, and you will pay 30% of this total premium rate or $19.80 per month. This change will result in a reduction in your cost for health insurance protection from its present level of $30.76 per month. Your payroll deduction for health insurance will be reduced automatically with no action required on your part to initiate this change.

Yours truly,

Director
Personnel Services Division

number of employees what they believed the message was. Most said that their costs had increased. How could that be? They didn't read it all. It was too technical. The heading should have said something like "Health Insurance Premiums Cut." The first emphasis should have been the employee savings and last the reason *why* the cut came. Do you agree?

Personnel as a communications trainer

Another communication task personnel frequently undertakes is to train managers and employees in effective communication skills. Chapters 9 and 10 will discuss this function in more detail. In general, personnel trainers present material on effective communications similar to that discussed above. A series of exercises and evaluation procedures then is used to reinforce the content training. This training is designed to improve communications in the enterprise and thus to help it achieve its goals.

Personnel as a communications resource for operating management

Operating managers may seek personnel's aid in preparing written or audiovisual messages to transmit to the employees in their departments. In this role, personnel serves as technical advisor to the manager-communicator. Its advice focuses on more effective methods to get the message across to the receivers. If the enterprise is large enough to have its own public relations or communications unit, these specialists may serve this role rather than the personnel specialist.

Personnel as a spokesperson for management

In many large enterprises, operating management asks personnel to develop material to convey to employees information on company policies, points of view, news, and so on. The typical media used for these messages are handbooks, newspapers, house organs, newsletters, and bulletin boards. The first step in making these messages effective is to determine what information is needed by employees. This can be done by a communication analysis or an audit to check the speed and accuracy of communications, or the enterprise may ask the employees what they need to know. For example, Paula Cowan studied blue Cross employees and found that they were confused about the enterprise's organization and ignorant of its basic policies. Attitude surveys (see below) also can be used to determine communication needs.

What can personnel departments do to improve communications on such matters? One way is to publish employee handbooks to be distributed at orientation sessions of new employees which are conducted by personnel. They can also be used to retrain employees when communication needs analyses indicate employee knowledge is lacking. These handbooks typically include the following:

EMPLOYEE HANDBOOK CONTENTS

Data about the enterprise
- Goals of the enterprise
- History of the enterprise
- Organization structure

Data about pay and benefits
- Earnings and salary review policies
- Pay relative to other employers
- Benefits and services available, including insurance, time off with pay, pensions, etc.

Company policies and rules on working conditions
- Hours of work
- Prohibitions in the workplace
- What behavior will lead to termination and termination policies

Promotion policies

Safety and health policies and rules

Union contract provisions

Equal employment opportunity policies and procedures

Your future career opportunities with the enterprise

For these handbooks to be of much use, the seven suggestions for effective communication must be followed. Studies such as Keith Davis's indicate that there are semantic and readability problems with many handbooks. That is, the handbook is written at too high or too technical a level for the employees to understand them. Some enterprises publish several handbooks at different reading levels.

In addition to handbooks, many large enterprises publish house organs of various kinds. These include newsletters, magazines, and newspapers. These kinds of publications usually are insured monthly. In a house organ, both good news and bad, and both employee and organizational news should be included. The organization news may describe current accomplishments with regard to goals, major trends in the environment affecting them, top-management positions on various issues, news about new benefit plans and the opening of new offices, and so on. Personal news could include items on marriages, retirements, births, and awards, as well as pictures of the unit's winning sports teams and smiling general managers handing checks to Red Cross leaders, for example.

These can be effective, but they also can cost a great deal of money. Readership has been shown by surveys to vary from 10 to 67 percent. Thomas Kindre found that some house organs cost about $20 per employee each year. There is little direct, systematic evidence about the impact of these publications, but there is some indirect evidence that they are effective to some extent.

Some underground newspapers serve as counterbalances to the house organs. But they mainly complain about company practices and indicate the failure of formal channels to find out what employees really have to say. Examples of these publications are *The Met Lifer* (Metropolitan Life Insurance company), *Standard Oiler* (Standard Oil Company—California), and *AT&T* (Pacific Telephone and Telegraph). *The Wall Street Journal* reports that when an employee wrote a critical letter to the editor of the house organ at Metropolitan Life, it didn't publish it. The letter did appear in *The Met Lifer,* however.

As with handbooks, the reading level of the house organ should be appropriate for the audience. The topics should be of interest to the reader, and the publication costs should be kept low. In view of the evidence that oral communication is more effective and the lack of evidence of significant benefits from house organs, enterprises should be cautious about starting them. Cost/benefit studies should be undertaken to determine if they should be continued. Less regularly used media such as newsheets, letters to employees' homes, payroll stuffers, and hot lines probably make more sense. They can be issued as needed, and their costs are lower.

Personnel as an information seeker

Earlier in the chapter, we discussed how managers use formal and informal channels to gather information and communicate with employees. Formally, 78 percent of enterprises report using the chain of command, whereby supervisors communicate downward and gather information. Forty percent report holding formal meetings to gather information. Informally, 86 percent of executives report they try to gather information from informal discussions with employees, and 59 percent use the grapevine to gather information as well as distribute it.

Personnel is asked to gather information to help the enterprise achieve its goals. But management and the personnel department should attempt to gather this information only if it wants to hear what the employees have to say and are willing to do something about the results. Otherwise, doing so raises employee expectations and may hurt management's feelings. Studies consistently show that management underestimates employees' negative feelings, and the further the management is from the employees, the worse are management's predictions. So for the effort to be worthwhile, top management—in fact, all levels of management—must support the effort and be willing to receive the feedback and do something about it.

There are a number of data sources and approaches the personnel department can use. Among those discussed in other chapters are:

- Data which arise from counseling encounters and which are used ethically (for more details, see Chapter 7).
- Suggestions systems—combination information and reward systems (for more details, see Chapter 12).
- Grievance and complaint procedures (see Chapters 17 and 18 for more details).
- Exit interviews with employees leaving the enterprise (for more details, see Chapter 19).

Two additional approaches the personnel department can take to data gathering and upward communication are to utilize the attitude survey and the department's information systems.

Attitude surveys. About 30 percent of enterprises (mostly the larger and medium-sized ones) conduct regular, formal information-seeking experiences called attitude surveys. They usually are conducted on a yearly basis. The enter-

EXHIBIT 3–3
Typical topics in attitude surveys

Attitudes toward working conditions and the job	*Attitudes toward compensation and rewards*	*Attitudes toward supervisor*	*Attitudes toward the employer*
Physical working conditions Work scheduling and planning Work assignments and worker abilities Job demands Job security Hours of work Safety on the job Interpersonal relations at work Adequacy of training by employer	Salaries Benefits Promotions Status and recognition	Communication abilities Qualifications and abilities Supervisory style	Personnel policies Communications General reputation in community Reputation nationally Attitudes toward future unionization

prise itself can design the surveys, but approaches developed by consultants and similar services are also available. The survey develops a snapshot view of employee attitudes by unit and total organization. Typical topics surveyed are given in Exhibit 3–3.

One vital factor in the usefulness of attitude surveys is maintaining confidentiality of the data provided by employees. To assure reliability and validity of the data as far as possible, it has become typical to assure anonymity by questioning groups of employees together. Often the information is gathered by an outside consultant such as a university professor. Studies indicate that about 75 percent of attitude surveys use outside consultants for administration and analysis.

A typical survey is handled as follows. The personnel department contacts a consultant to administer the survey. The consultant first works with personnel in developing the data-gathering approach. Design of these questionnaires or interview schedules is an important technical project. It should be done by professionals in personnel or psychology. Typically, the consultant works with the personnel department and a sample of operating managers and employees in developing the survey. Finally, the consultant gathers the data and processes it or sends it to a computer service center for processing. No one from the employing organization sees the actual data or questionnaires completed by the employees.

In preparation for the attitude survey, employees receive a letter explaining the purpose of the study (such as to improve working conditions). The letter also explains the safeguards for the employees that will be provided, such as the use of consultants. If a questionnaire is used, the employees complete them in homogeneous groups: exempt or nonexempt, for example.

The two principal methods used to gather data are interviews and questionnaires. Sometimes both are used by an enterprise. Surveys indicate that almost two thirds of employers use questionnaires alone, less than 10 percent use only interviews, and the rest use a combination of both. Yet the best study done on the subject (by F. Berrien and W. Angoff) indicates that information is more reliable and complete if interviews are used. Usually the interviews follow the structured approach (see Chapter 6 for more details). If questionnaires are used,

EXHIBIT 3–4
Excerpt from attitude questionnaire

1. Considering the present cost of living, my pay is

Excellent	Good	Fair	Poor	Very poor
☐	☐	☐	☐	☐

2. Considering everything, my working hours are

Very poor	Poor	Fair	Good	Excellent
☐	☐	☐	☐	☐

3. The spirit of cooperation among employees in my department is

Excellent	Good	Fair	Poor	Very poor
☐	☐	☐	☐	☐

three approaches are followed: yes, no, or don't-know answers; open-ended essay questions; or structured questions with multiple-choice answers. An example of the latter is given in Exhibit 3–4.

After the data are gathered, they are analyzed. Present responses are compared to past ones to see if the trends are positive or negative. Responses from different subunits are compared to see if some are more favorable than others.

Overall indications lead to management actions of one type or another. Policies are revised, enforced, or created, and the results are communicated to the employees. Without some feedback and action, the survey is ritualistic and not useful, as both managers and personnel researchers have found. For example, when I was administering an attitude survey at one company, an employee took me aside and asked me why I was wasting my time doing that. When asked what he meant, he said: "This is just a farce. All they want is to be told how good they are. Last year on the survey, they asked the office people if they'd like to join a union. We never heard another word about that question, and it's not on this year's survey. The grapevine has it the majority said 'Yes' and it scared the *#&* out of management."

If Sparrow Hospital had been using attitude surveys, Edmund might have received some clues as to whether the employees are likely to want a union and how they feel about their pay and benefits. If for example, most Sparrow employees are very satisfied with their pay, giving up a pay raise this year may be less of a problem than if they are mostly dissatisfied.

Personnel information systems and data bases. The second data-gathering approach personnel can take is to gather information from its information system. The information system exists as a memory or recall aid to managers and employees; as objective documentation for solving personnel problems or meeting legal requirements; and as a data resource for analysis and planning for the future. The personnel information system is a part of what Von Court Hare calls the communications–management information system or Preston LeBreton calls the administrative intelligence–information system.

The information system serves the purpose of helping make other personnel activities such as employment planning more effective. How can a firm plan its future needs for employees if it has no readily accessible records of its current employees? How can an enterprise develop a recruiting plan to replace those

A computerized information system

retiring if it doesn't know how many people will retire, and from which positions? The system also provides data that management needs to plan the future of the enterprise, as we will see in Chapter 4.

To be efficient and effective, the personnel information system must keep the correct data up to date in an easily accessible form. This goal is better achieved if the users of the data (both operating managers and personnel specialists) have an input in the design of the system and help determine the form the reports and other outputs will take. The criterion the system is measured by is how well it provides accurate, reliable data that is timely, complete, and useful; that management needs to know; and that does not duplicate data in an interfacing information system.

Typically, the data kept include personal information on employees, including characteristics, work experience, and education. The system also can include records on recruiting, compensation, performance evaluation, length of service/layoff, union membership, attitude/morale, benefit plan, safety, and similar items. These data are kept for legal and memory recall reasons. But they are perhaps even more useful in analyzing present problems and anticipating future problems. Some examples of analyses from data on the information system include:

- Age distribution and retirement analyses.
- Description of applicant pool.
- Identification of best and worst selection practices.

- Recruitment budget specifications.
- EEO analyses and reports.
- Prediction of success in finding specific work skills at desired salaries.
- Analysis of time span required to fill open position.
- Recruitment sources evaluation.
- Employee profiles for promotion, reassignment, or special assignment.
- Planning for college recruitment, availability of special skills, etc.
- Individual comparisons of salary growth rates.
- Evaluation of appraisal practices.
- Statistical analysis of absenteeism, tardiness, etc.
- Analysis of benefits expenditures and return from investment on these.
- Patterns of safety hazards.
- Reports on career movement patterns.
- OSHA reports and analyses.
- Evaluations of environmental factors affecting employee attitudes, turnover, productivity, etc.

SUMMARY

Chapter 3 makes it clear why communications is the most important skill a personnel manager (or any manager, for that matter) can develop. Guidelines for effective communication and how personnel helps the enterprise achieve its goals by facilitating communication are given in the statements below:

1. Up to 90 percent of managerial time is spent in communication.
2. Effective communication leads to more effective performance, provides information necessary for an enterprise to adjust to a changing world, and is essential if we expect employees and units to achieve enterprise goals.
3. You *cannot* be effective in the personnel function without a fundamental understanding of communication and skills in communicating.
4. Communication takes place in the following manner:
   a. The sender has the idea for the message (thinking).
   b. The sender encodes the message.
   c. The message is transmitted verbally or in writing.
   d. A channel is chosen (formal or informal).
   e. The receiver decodes the message.
   f. Understanding and feedback take place between the receiver and sender.
5. Several points to remember to make communication effective include:
   a. Think through the message before preparing it.
   b. Make sure the words you use are meaningful to the receiver and that the message is clear.
   c. Be sincere in your transmission and reinforce your message with appropriate verbal and nonverbal symbols and cues.
   d. Be a good listener and encourage questions to help clarify your message.
   e. Make sure you choose the right time and place for your communication.
   f. Develop a feedback and control system to assure that the message has been received and understood.

6. The media to use in communicating effectively are classified as oral-personal, oral-mechanical, audiovisual, or written.
7. Research indicates that the best way to communicate important messages is to send the message orally first, then confirm it in writing.
8. Nevertheless, each medium has appropriate uses, depending on the purpose of the message, its importance, and its timing.
9. Channels for communication are the routes through which the messages pass. They are formal or informal.
   a. Formal channels usually consist of a vertical chain of command; most written communications follow this channel.
   b. The grapevine is the informal channel used to exchange information regularly outside the formal channels. This is helpful for transmitting nonroutine messages.
10. Personnel managers aid communications in six ways:
   a. The personnel executive communicates to superiors, subordinates, and peers, like all other managers.
   b. Personnel communicates personnel policies to the enterprise.
   c. Personnel provides communication training for the enterprise.
   d. Personnel helps other managers prepare their communications.
   e. Personnel may become a spokesperson for operating management.
   f. Personnel seeks information for communication to operating management.

The next chapter outlines personnel's role in employment planning.

As Marjorie and Edmund got down to details of their hospital administration and personnel communication problems, Marjorie asked, "What do you recommend, Edmund?"

Edmund: We have two issues: a personnel policy issue and a communication issue. I suggest that we compromise the policy issue. I suggest that we try to reduce the payroll by about 100 people over the next year by attrition and early retirements. We can try to reduce the costs for the other 100 by a freeze on pay and benefits for a year and by increasing the patient census by about as much as we did in your first year here.

Marjorie: I believe I can sell the board on that. We have some surplus left from the old days. The trustees know what kind of employees we have. They don't want to hurt them. And I'll do my best to visit with some of the doctors who have left. I understand not all of them are happy at St. Joseph's. I believe we can do some things here to fit their needs and woo them and their patients back.

But do you think the employees will buy that? How do you think we ought to communicate this?

Edmund: I believe this calls for some face-to-face meetings with the employees. We should tell them the truth. They probably think things are worse than they are. If we appeal to their loyalty, most will cooperate. You and I should address them personally and follow up with personal letters to all affected. I believe we in personnel should visit with all those who could take early retirement and explain the options. Obviously, we won't pressure them.

Marjorie: How do we deal with the union issue?

Edmund: I believe we should tell the employees the facts and say nothing about a union. If we do, they may feel we are acting because of the union threat. That's not so. It came at the same time, that's all.

Marjorie: OK. That's what we'll do.

Edmund

Marjorie got on the phone and got the trustees to support the plan. Both Marjorie and Edmund worked late that night preparing their talks. Marjorie was to explain the overall problems and how the hospital needed the employees' help. Edmund would describe the nitty gritty—where attrition and early retirement were more necessary (maintenance, laundry, housekeeping, business office) and less necessary (nursing, pharmacy, labs). Then both would ask for help. Edmund would also describe the early retirement seminars offered during working hours.

The talks were delivered in each department. Employees were urged to ask questions, and they did. Marjorie was especially well received when she stressed how she had increased the patient census and all the steps she was taking to increase it even more next year. She also thanked the employees for their help and positive attitudes in a difficult period. The employees appreciated the trustees' and the staff's positions. As several employees put it: "We'll help you. At most workplaces, they'd just lay you off. Here at Sparrow, they treat you like a human being. You're doing the best with circumstances beyond your control."

Six months later, Sparrow was somewhat out of the woods, although not completely. Marjorie's efforts had increased the census to 78 percent occupancy. Costs had been cut in supplies and other areas. Early retirement was taken by 25 employees, and normal attrition eliminated another 63. The union was unable to get enough registration cards to authorize an election.

Marjorie

Marjorie and Edmund communicated orally and in writing with employees about the status of things. They encouraged the supervisors to reinforce these messages. And Marjorie prepared to face the trustees with a continued deficit, a much smaller one, however. At that point Marjorie was considering asking for more debt to improve the physical facilities and a slight increase in prices, so as to give employees a raise, however small, in the coming year.

QUESTIONS

1. How much time do managers spend communicating? According to the text, why is effective communication necessary? Give several reasons.
2. Briefly describe the communication process.
3. What are the seven steps a manager should take to avoid miscommunication?
4. What is communication overload? What can one do to avoid communication overload?
5. List the four methods of communication. When and where is each one most effective for the manager?
6. Describe the nonverbal cues which enhance a communication. What do they convey to the receiver?

7. What is a communication channel? A formal channel? An informal channel?
8. In what ways can a personnel manager aid communications? Name at least 5.
9. What data does a good personnel handbook include?
10. Outline the information-gathering process the personnel department should follow, and how an attitude survey is conducted. What purpose does this survey serve?

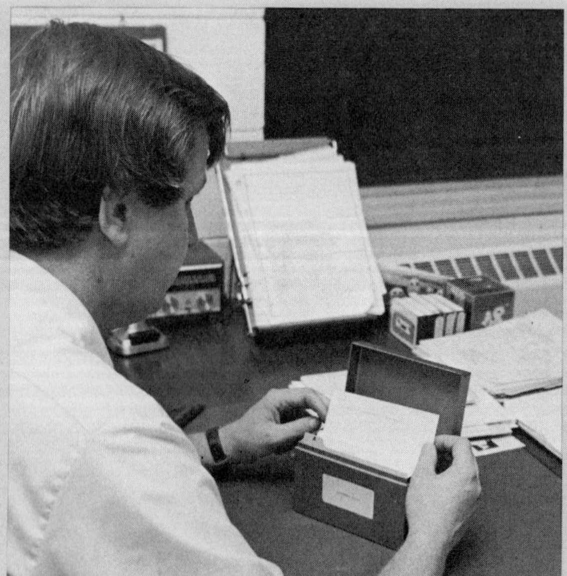

part two

Planning and personnel

Part Two's subject matter is so important that although only one chapter is devoted to the topic, it is set off in its own section. This is so because personnel and employment planning must come first before other personnel activities can be performed efficiently.

The subjects in Chapter 4 include determining the current supply of employees in the enterprise and matching it with the forecast of the demand. Then the action decisions which must be taken are discussed. These include what must be done when there are shortages and surpluses. Important factors affecting employment planning, such as job analysis and the employment of women, minorities, the handicapped, and veterans, are discussed, as are such new working conditions as scheduling by flexitime and the four-day week.

4

Personnel and employment planning

Chapter objectives

- To show what personnel and employment planning is and why effective enterprises perform it.
- To demonstrate how managers forecast demand for and analyze the supply of employees in the enterprise.
- To indicate how job analysis affects personnel and employment planning.
- To show how various work schedules, such as shift work, flexitime, and compressed work weeks, affect the supply of employees and their satisfaction and effectiveness.
- To indicate how to analyze the supply of employees for EEO implications, and action decisions such as layoffs, demotions, and terminations.

Chapter outline

I. Introduction to Personnel and Employment Planning
   A. Reasons for personnel and employment planning
   B. Who performs the planning?
II. A Diagnostic Approach to Personnel and Employment Planning
III. Forecasting Future Demand for Employees
   A. Employment forecasting techniques
   B. Preparing the forecast
IV. Job Information and Personnel Planning
   A. Job analysis
   B. Job descriptions and specifications
V. Analysis of the Supply of Present Employees
   A. Designing skills inventory systems
   B. Maintaining the skills inventory
VI. Work Schedules and the Supply of Employees
   A. Shift work
   B. Compressed work weeks
   C. Flexitime (flexible hours)
VII. Action Decisions in Personnel and Employment Planning
   A. Analyzing the composition of the work force
   B. Action decisions with no variance in supply and demand
   C. Action decisions with a shortage of employees
   D. Action decisions in surplus conditions
VIII. Summary, Conclusions, and Recommendations
   A. Employment planning systems for model organizations

"What do you mean we're going to lose the government contract?" asked the company president, Ted Sloane.

"We're going to lose it," said the personnel vice president, Anne Wilson. "We don't have trained personnel to meet the contract specifications. We have to furnish records to show that we have an adequate number of employees with the right technical qualifications who meet the government's equal employment opportunity goals. I don't have those kinds of records available at a moment's notice. You know I asked you to let me set up a personnel planning information system, and we never got around to it."

* * *

"John, should I schedule a trip to visit State University next month, like last year?" asked Maggie Smith, the company's employee recruiter. John, the personnel manager, agreed she should. When Maggie asked "How many people should I recruit, and what types?" John said, "I guess like last year. Let's see how many good ones you turn up. Then we'll decide if we have enough slots for them."

Experiences like those described above, which are common, are evidence that many managers fail to plan for human resource needs. They never know what their needs are because they neglect personnel and employment planning (called manpower planning by some).

Personnel and employment planning is the process which helps to provide adequate human resources to achieve future organizational objectives. It includes forecasting future needs for employees of various types; comparing these needs with the present work force; and determining the numbers and types of employees to be recruited or phased out of the organization's employment group.

INTRODUCTION TO PERSONNEL AND EMPLOYMENT PLANNING

Exhibit 4–1 models the personnel and employment planning process. As the model indicates, top management examines the environment, analyzes the strategic advantages of the enterprise, and sets its objectives for the coming period. Then it makes strategic and operating decisions to achieve the objectives of the enterprise. The personnel capabilities of the enterprise are among the factors analyzed in the strategic management process. An example of a strategic decision is General Electric's decision to sell its computer business. This meant that General Electric's supply of employees was cut when the business was sold to another company.

Once the strategy is set, personnel does its part to assure its success and to achieve the enterprise's objectives. It does this by comparing the present supply of human resources with projected demand for them. This comparison leads to action decisions: add employees, cut employees, or reallocate employees internally.

Reasons for personnel and employment planning

All organizations perform personnel planning, informally or formally. The formal employment techniques are described in this chapter because the informal methods are increasingly unsatisfactory for organizations requiring skilled labor in a fast-changing labor market. It is important to point out that most

EXHIBIT 4–1
The personnel and employment planning process

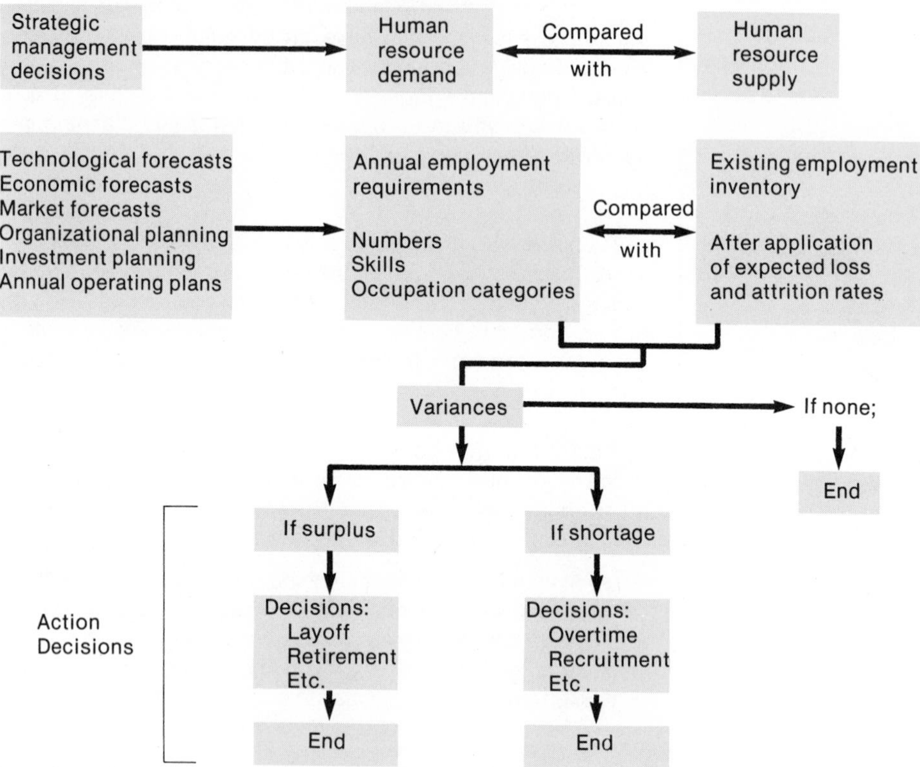

enterprises do more talking about formal employment planning than performing it. The military is a significant user of planning, but only a minority of other enterprises use it. Therefore, personnel and employment planning is in Stage II of development, or early development (see Exhibit 1–6).

The major reasons for formal employment planning are to achieve:

- More effective and efficient use of human resources.
- More satisfied and better developed employees.
- More effective equal employment opportunity planning.

More effective and efficient use of people at work. Employment planning should precede all other personnel activities. For example, how could you schedule recruiting if you did not know how many people you needed? How could you select effectively if you did not know the kinds of persons needed for job openings? Careful analysis of all personnel activities shows that their effectiveness and efficiency, which result in increased productivity, depend on employment planning.

More satisfied and better developed employees. Employees who work for enterprises that use good employment planning systems have a better chance to participate in planning their own careers and to share in training and development experiences. Thus they are likely to feel their talents are important to the employer, and they have a better chance to use their talents in the kinds of jobs that use these talents. This often leads to greater employee satisfaction and its consequences: lower absenteeism, lower turnover, fewer accidents, and higher quality of work.

More effective EEO planning. As will be pointed out frequently in this book, government has increased its demands for equal employment opportunities. Personnel information systems help enterprises to formally plan employment distribution. Then it is easier to complete the required government reports and respond satisfactorily to EEO demands.

In sum, effective employment planning assures that the personnel function will be built on a foundation of good planning.

Who performs the planning?

Effectiveness in personnel activities requires the efforts and cooperation of personnel and operating managers. The activities described in this chapter are outlined in Exhibit 4–2, which shows which planning activities are performed by operating and by personnel managers.

EXHIBIT 4–2

Personnel and employment planning activities performed by personnel and operating managers

Personnel and employment planning activities	*Operating manager (OM)*	*Personnel manager (PM)*
Strategic management decisions	Performed by OM with inputs from PM	Provides information inputs for OM
Forecasting employment demands		Performed by PM, based on strategic management decisions
Job analysis	Provides information inputs for PM	Performed by PM with information inputs from OM
Analysis of supply of employees	Provides information inputs for PM	Performed by PM with information inputs from OM
Work scheduling decisions	Joint responsibility	Joint responsibility
Action decision: Analyzing the composition of the work force		Performed by PM
Action decision: Shortage of employees	Provides information inputs for PM	Performed by PM with information inputs from OM
Action decision: Surplus of employees	Policy decisions by OM with inputs from PM	Implementation decisions by PM

A DIAGNOSTIC APPROACH TO PERSONNEL AND EMPLOYMENT PLANNING

Exhibit 4–3 highlights the factors in the diagnostic model that are most important to employment planning. One of the most significant factors affecting personnel planning is the goals of the controlling interests in the organization. If planning and effective utilization of human resources is not a significant goal for the enterprise, employment planning will not be performed formally, or it will be done in a slipshod way. If the goals of top management include stable growth, employment planning will be less important than if the goals include rapid expansion, diversification, or other factors with a significant impact on future employment needs.

Government policies are another important factor in personnel planning. Requirements for equal employment opportunity and promotion call for more personnel planning for women and other employees in minority groups and special

EXHIBIT 4–3

Factors affecting personnel and employment planning and organizational effectiveness

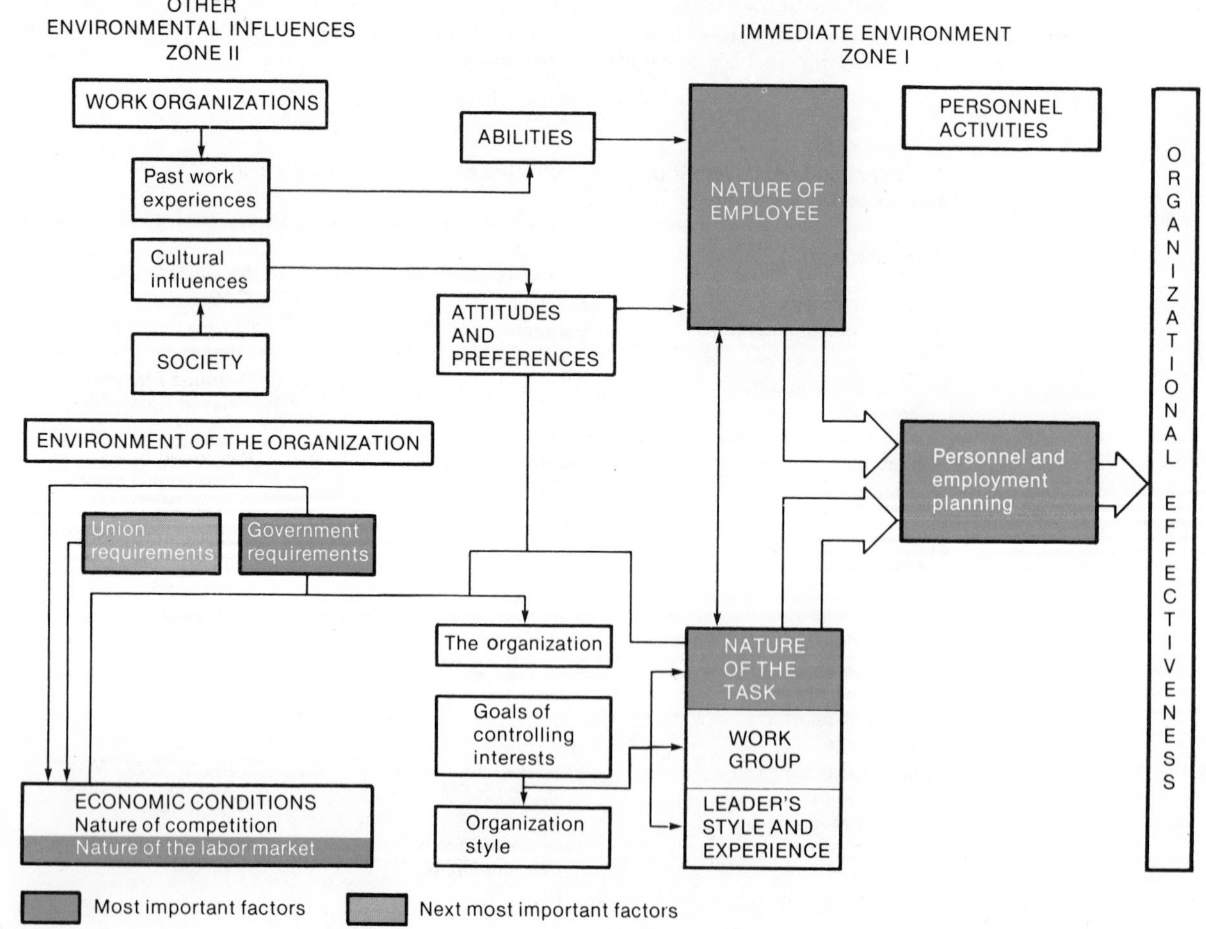

categories. Another example is the recent change by the government raising the age of mandatory retirement. (See Chapter 14 for details.)

The conditions in the labor market also have a significant impact on the amount and type of employment planning done in an enterprise: When there is 14 percent unemployment an employer has more hiring flexibility than when there is 2 percent unemployment in the relevant sector.

To a lesser extent than the government, unions may restrict the ability to hire and promote employees, so they are a factor in employment planning. The sections on methods of personnel planning show how these factors affect whether employment planning takes place, and if it does, how often, how far ahead, and in what ways.

The types of persons employed and the tasks they do also determine the kind of planning necessary. Needs for unskilled employees do not have to be planned two years ahead; but computer sales persons, for example, need years of training before coming on track.

FORECASTING FUTURE DEMAND FOR EMPLOYEES

Scene: Board meeting at the Acme Publishing Company.

George Slone (chairman and chief executive): Exhibit A is our planned budget and our objectives for next year. I'd appreciate your comments.

Martha Kemp (outside director): George, I note that overall, you are projecting a modest growth trend for next year. You also have had a series of increased worker productivity projects going to cut employee costs. Just how many people will you employ next year to reach your sales and profit objectives?"

George: That's a good question. Martha. I don't know exactly. John, what's the answer?

John Arturo (vice president, personnel): That's hard to say. It depends on lots of factors.

Martha: Frankly, John, that's not much of an answer. I can look at the figures in this exhibit and see how much money we need. The marketing people tell me how many units they are going to sell. Why can't you tell me how many people we'll need to get the job done—our people-cost figure?

John could have answered Martha's question if Acme's personnel department had developed an effective employee forecasting system—the first element of the employment planning system.

The employment requirements of an enterprise flow from the strategic decisions made by its top managers. Simply put, the top managers combine economic, technological and market forecasts with investment planning to help personnel calculate the number of employees needed by skill and occupational categories.

Employment forecasting techniques

Essentially there are three organizational approaches to employment forecasting. The headquarters can forecast the total demand (top-down approach);

the units can forecast their own demand (bottom-up approach), or there can be a combination of the other two.

Four forecasting techniques will be described here: three-top-down techniques—expert estimate, trend projection, and modeling—and the bottom-up unit-forecasting technique.

The expert-estimate technique. The least sophisticated approach to employment planning is for an "expert" to forecast the employment needs based on her or his own experience and intuition. The personnel manager may do this by thinking about past employment levels and questioning future needs, which is a quite informal system. The expert-estimate technique can be more effective if the experts use the Delphi technique.

The Delphi technique is a set of procedures originally developed by the Rand Corporation in the late 1940s. Its purpose is to obtain the most reliable consensus of opinion of a group of experts. Basically, the Delphi consists of intensive questioning of each expert, through a series of questionnaires, to get the data desired. The procedures are designed to avoid direct meetings between the experts in order to maximize independent thinking.

A person who serves as intermediary in the questioning sends out the questionnaires to the experts and asks them to give, for example, their best estimates of employment needs for the coming year. The intermediary prepares a summary of the results, calculating the average response and the most extreme answers. Then the experts are asked to estimate the number again. Usually the questionnaires and responses tend to narrow down over these rounds. The average number is then used as the forecast.

A forecast by a single expert is the most frequently used approach to forecasting employment. It works well in small and middle-sized enterprises which are in stable environments. The Delphi technique improves these estimates in larger and more volatile enterprises. Expert estimate is an inexpensive way to forecast.

The trend-projection technique. The second technique is to develop a forecast based on a past relationship between a factor related to employment and employment itself. For example, in many businesses, sales levels are related to employment needs. So the personnel planner can develop a table or graph showing past relationships between sales and employment. Exhibit 4–4 gives an example of a trend-projection forecast for a hypothetical company, Rugby Sporting Goods Company. Note that as Rugby's sales increased, so did the firm's employment needs. But the increases were not linear. In late 1975, Rugby instituted a productivity plan which led to 3 percent increased productivity per year. As Rugby forecasted employee needs, it adjusted them for expected productivity gains for 1979 and 1980.

Trend projection is a frequently used technique. But it is not as widely used as expert estimate or unit demand. It is also an inexpensive way to forecast employment needs.

Modeling and multiple-predictive techniques. The third top-down approach to prediction of demand uses the most sophisticated forecasting and modeling techniques. Trend projections are based on relating a single factor (such as sales) to employment. The more advanced approaches relate many factors to employment, such as sales, gross national product, and discretionary income. Or they mathematically model the enterprise and simulate, using such methods as Markov models and analytical formulations. Only larger enterprises with

EXHIBIT 4–4
Sample trend-protection employment forecast for Rugby Sporting Goods Company

Year	*Sales*	*Employee census*	*Employee forecast adjusted for annual productivity rate increase of 3 percent*
Actual data			
1975	100,000,000	5,000	5,000
1976	120,000,000	6,000	5,825
1977	140,000,000	7,000	6,598
1978	160,000,000	8,000	7,321
	Sales forecast	*Employee forecast*	
Forecast			
1979	180,000,000	9,000	7,996
1980	200,000,000	10,000	8,626

corporate staff capacities can use this approach. These are the most costly approaches to employment forecasting because of the cost of computer time and salaries of highly paid experts to design the models.

The unit demand forecasting technique. The unit forecast is a bottom-up approach to forecasting demand. Headquarters sums these unit forecasts, and the result becomes the employment forecast. The unit manager analyzes the unit's person-by-person, job-by-job needs in the present as well as the future.

By analyzing present and future requirements on the job, and the skills of the incumbents, this method focuses on quality of workers. Often it is initiated by a letter or a phone call.

Bill Foster (vice president, personnel): John, Bill Foster here. We're trying to get our forecast for employment needs together for next year so that we can get it into the budget. Will you get your net needs for next budget year to me by the end of the week? Use Form EP–1—it has a place for present employees in each of your units, less retirements, plus new employees needed for new business. Thanks!

John Jones (manager, division 1): Bill, I'll get right on it.

Usually the manager would start with a list of the jobs in the unit by name. This list would also record the number of jobholders for each job. The manager evaluates both the numbers and skills of the present personnel. Consideration is given to the effects of expected losses through retirement, promotion, or other reasons. Whether those losses will require replacement and what the projected growth needs will be are questions the manager must answer and project into his or her calculations in determining net employment needs.

The manager's evaluation based on the present number of employees has two assumptions built into it: that the best use has been made of the available personnel, and that demand for the product or service of the unit will be the same for next year as this. With regard to the first assumption, the manager can examine the job design and work load of each employee, using such techniques as time and motion studies. The manager may also attempt to judge the productivity of the employees in the unit by comparing the cost per product or service produced with those of similar units in the organization and others. Past productivity rates can be compared with present ones, after adjusting for changes in the job, or subjective evaluations can be made of the productivity of certain employees compared to others. In addition, it may be necessary to base employment needs on workforce analysis, with adjustments for current data on absenteeism and turnover.

The unit analyzes its product or service demand by projecting trends. Using methods similar to the trend technique for the organization, the unit determines if it may need more employees because of a change in product or service demand. Finally, the unit manager prepares an estimate of total employment needs and plans for how the unit can fulfill these needs.

Preparing the forecast

A personnel executive at headquarters who is responsible for employment demand forecast will improve the estimates by checking with personnel and operating executives in the field. If the units forecast their own needs, the personnel executive sums their estimates, and this becomes the forecast. What happens if both the bottom-up and top-down approaches are used, and the forecasts conflict? In all probability, the manager reconciles the two totals by averaging them or examining more closely the major variances between the two. The Delphi technique could be used to do this. One or several forecasts can be used to produce a single employment forecast.

JOB INFORMATION AND PERSONNEL PLANNING

In the employment-demand forecasting aspect of employment planning, the bottom-up or unit-forecasting method calls for each unit to determine the number of people needed to accomplish the unit's objectives. The basic building block of this forecast is the number of jobs to be filled. The number of jobs in a unit can be reduced by more efficient job design, as discussed in Chapter 2. Closely related to job design are job information procedures. Information about jobs involves three processes: job analysis, job description, and job specifications.

Job analysis is the process by which a job analyzer gathers data about a job. These data include: activities; the tools and equipment used; job-related items such as materials used, products made, services rendered; work performance; working conditions; and requirements necessary to do the job, such as knowledge, skills, experience, and personal attributes.

Job description is a written statement which details the duties and responsibilities of a job.

Job specification is a written statement which lists the qualifications a person needs to perform the job effectively.

Job analysis

Job analysis is performed for many reasons: to provide information for the preparation of job descriptions and specifications; to help in the hiring, orientation, and training of employees; as an aid in job evaluation for pay purposes;

for collective bargaining reasons; for safety purposes; and as a requirement in equal employment opportunity planning and analysis.

Job analysis can use one or many of the following seven methods:

1. Examination of previous job analyses or job descriptions of the position or other records.
2. Observation of the job and the job occupant.
3. Interviews of job occupants or supervisors by a single analyst or a group of them.
4. Structured or open-ended questionnaires to be completed by job occupants or supervisors.
5. Self-recording of data and observations, in a log or diary kept by the job occupant.
6. Recording of job activities on film or with audio means.
7. Analyzing equipment design information from blueprints and design data.

Methods 1, 4, and 7 are the quickest but may develop less reliable data than other methods. Methods 2, 3, 5, and 6 are more accurate but more costly. As far as observation and other data-gathering techniques are concerned, it has been found that proper work-sampling techniques add to the quality of the data's reliability and validity.

After the data are gathered, they are recorded on a job analysis schedule such as that shown in Exhibit 4–5. The Department of Labor's *Handbook for Analyzing Jobs* has guidelines for analyzing jobs and 298 work fields as related to the *Dictionary of Occupational Titles.* This approach emphasizes systematic verbal description of the functions performed on the job.

Job descriptions and specifications

After job analysis is complete, the enterprise can prepare its job descriptions and job specifications. A good source of reference to use for writing job descriptions and job specifications is *The Dictionary of Occupational Titles.* In its latest form, it contains almost 40,000 titles and almost 25,000 actual job descriptions. More than half of these are in production and transportation, followed by professional, technical, managerial, and unclassified positions. Many enterprises use these as guides and sometimes simply copy them from the dictionary.

Exhibit 4–6 is an example of a job description (one of many types). The job is summarized in a general description. Then the major work duties are listed. To serve any purpose, the job description must be kept up to date. It must also be complete. Finally, the job description must be behaviorally based. That is, it should be based on job objectives.

Exhibit 4–7 is an example of job specifications for the same job described in Exhibit 4–6. The job specification clarifies the skills and experience necessary to perform the job effectively. Preferably, the number of months or years of experience is specified, as well as the specific education or training required. On specifications for positions requiring physical effort, the degree of effort required is specified; for example, the amount of weight to be lifted. Where appropriate, the responsibility section also includes the quantities of assets and equipment to be supervised. Finally, for many jobs, job conditions, such as the degree of environmental unpleasantness (heat, dust, etc.), are given.

Since job specifications can have a significant impact on selection of employees, it is vital to avoid employment discrimination at this point in the personnel

EXHIBIT 4–5

Excerpts from U.S. Training and Employment Service job analysis schedule for a dough mixer

JOB: DOUGH MIXER (BAKERY PRODUCTS INDUSTRY)

4. Job Summary:

   Operates mixing machine to mix ingredients for straight and sponge (yeast) doughs according to established formulas, directs other workers in fermentation of dough, and cuts dough into pieces with hand cutter.

15. Description of Tasks:
    1. Dumps ingredients into mixing machine: Examines production schedule to determine type of bread to be produced, such as rye, whole wheat, or white. Refers to formula card for quantities and types of ingredients required, such as flour, water, milk, vitamin solutions, and shortening. Weighs out, measures, and dumps ingredients into mixing machine.
    2. Operates mixing machine: Turns valves and other hand controls to set mixing time according to type of dough being mixed. Presses button to start agitator blades in machine. Observes gauges and dials on equipment continuously to verify temperature of dough and mixing time. Feels dough for desired consistency. Adds water or flour to mix measuring vessels and adjusts mixing time and controls to obtain desired elasticity in mix.
    3. Directs other workers in fermentation of dough: Prepares fermentation schedule according to type of dough being raised. Sprays portable dough *trough* with lubricant to prevent adherence of mixed dough to trough. Directs *dough-mixer helper* in positioning trough beneath door of mixer to catch dough when mixing cycle is complete. Pushes, or directs other workers to push, troughs of dough into fermentation room.
    4. Cuts dough: Dumps fermentated dough onto worktable. Manually kneads dough to eliminate gases formed by yeast. Cuts dough into pieces with hand cutter. Places cut dough on proofing rack and covers with cloth.
    5. Performs miscellaneous duties: Records on work sheet number of batches mixed during work shift. Informs *bake shop foreman* when repairs or major adjustments are required for machines and equipment.

process. The specifications must avoid violating the equal employment opportunity laws described in Chapter 16. Avoid sex stereotyping in job titles. The jobs should be labeled nonsexually. The jobs are for flight attendants, not stewardesses, and for postal carriers, not mailmen. The specifications should list only qualifications which studies have shown are absolute minimums for effective performance. Graduation from college should not be specified unless the enterprise has no present employee or applicant who could perform the job effectively but who did not graduate from college. Lengthy experience requirements (for example, ten years) also should be avoided, unless no one with less experience ever could perform the job effectively.

Job specifications must be guided by the experience of the enterprise, ***not the opinions*** of its personnel or operating officers.

EXHIBIT 4–6
Job description of a personnel manager

JOB TITLE: PERSONNEL MANAGER

Department: Personnel
Date: Jan. 1, 1979

General Description of the Job

Performs responsible administrative work managing personnel activities of a large state agency or institution. Work involves responsibility for the planning and administration of a personnel program which includes recruitment, examination, selection, evaluation, appointment, promotion, transfer, and recommended change of status of agency employees, and a system of communication for disseminating necessary information to workers. Works under general supervision, exercising initiative and independent judgment in the performance of assigned tasks.

Duties of the Job

Participates in overall planning and policy making to provide effective and uniform personnel services.

Communicates policy through organization levels by bulletin, meetings, and personal contact.

Interviews applicants, evaluates qualifications, classifies applications.

Recruits and screens applicants to fill vacancies and reviews applications of qualified persons.

Confers with supervisors on personnel matters, including placement problems, retention or release of probationary employees, transfers, demotions, and dismissals of permanent employees.

Supervises administration of tests.

Initiates personnel training activities and coordinates these activities with work of officials and supervisors.

Establishes effective service rating system, trains unit supervisors in making employee evaluations.

Maintains employee personnel files.

Supervises a group of employees directly and through subordinates.

Performs related work as assigned.

ANALYSIS OF THE SUPPLY OF PRESENT EMPLOYEES

After a manager has projected the employment needs of the enterprise, the next step in employment planning is to determine the availability of those presently at work in it: the supply of employees.

On the basis of strategic management decisions, the personnel manager compares the demand for people needed to achieve the enterprise's objectives with the present supply of people to determine the need to hire, lay off, promote, or train. These are the action decisions. The major tool of analysis used to analyze employment supply is the skills inventory. In some enterprises, a separate skills

EXHIBIT 4–7
Job specifications for personnel manager

General Qualification Requirements

Experience and training
Should have considerable experience in personnel administration. Four years is a minimum.

Education
Graduation from a four-year college or university, with major work in personnel or business administration.

Knowledge, skills, and abilities
Considerable knowledge of principles and practices of personnel administration; selection and assignment of personnel; job evaluation.

Responsibility
Supervises a department of three personnel professionals and one clerical employee.

inventory, called a management inventory, is developed just for the managerial employees.

Marjorie Lancer is vice president, personnel, of a medium-sized firm. One of the division vice presidents, Howard Cantobello, calls her on the phone and says, after some small talk, "Marge, we've decided to enter the Latin American market and we need a person who has ten years' experience, and a degree in industrial engineering and who can speak Spanish. Before I go outside, why not check to see if we have a person like that who might be interested in a job in our division. We can make it worthwhile financially, and the sky's the limit on promotions." Marjorie agrees to see what she can do.

This is one example of the uses to which a skills inventory can be put in the enterprise. There are many others. If the firm has a computerized skills inventory, Marjorie can give Howard an answer quickly. If there is no such inventory, she will have to call or write a lot of people and ask about many prospects.

Good skills inventories enable organizations to determine quickly and expeditiously what kinds of people with specific skills are presently available, whenever they decide to expand to accept new contracts or change their strategies. It is also useful in planning for training, management development, promotion, transfer, and related personnel activities.

A skills inventory in its simplest form is a list of the names, certain characteristics, and skills of the people working for the organization. It provides a way to acquire these data and makes them available where needed in an efficient manner.

For a small organization, it is relatively easy to know how many employees there are, what they do, and what they can do. A mom-and-pop grocery store may employ only the owners and have two part-time helpers to "plan" for. When they see that one part-time employee is going to graduate in June, they know they need to replace him. Sources of supply could include their own children, converting their other part-time helper into a full-time assistant, or the school's employment office.

It is quite a different situation with a school system employing hundreds at numerous locations, or such mammoth organizations as the Air Force or IBM. These kinds of organizations must know how many full-time and peripheral employees they have working for them, and where. They must know what skills prospective employees would need to replace people who quit, retire, or are fired, or to add them for new functions or more work.

The methods for handling such a challenge range from simple records on 3″ × 5″ cards to sophisticated statistical and mathematical techniques such as simulation and Markov chain analysis. But the basic tool for assessing the supply of people and talents available within the organization is the skills inventory. Skills inventory tools can range from simple pieces of paper, forms, and 3″ × 5″ cards to sophisticated computer information systems. The degree of sophistication necessary is related to the size, complexity, and volatility of the organization.

In smaller manual systems of skills inventories, the data are entered on cards, the more advanced having notches or loops which can be "pulled" by the use of long metal bars (Cardex). Thus, if an organization wants to get a list of employees speaking French fluently, it pulls all the cards notched at a particular place or with loop 15 on the card. If there are multiple criteria, this subset is then checked for the next characteristic. This can also be done with summary overlays: All those with certain characteristics are punched onto cards, several of these summary cards are laid atop one another, and only those still visible on the last overlay fit the criteria for selection.

At the other extreme are very complex and sophisticated systems. Enterprises such as IBM, RCA, the U.S. Civil Service Commission and others have computerized inventories that allow them to plan employees' careers and define their business and other facts like this.

Designing skills inventory systems

Once the decision is made to have a skills inventory system, the challenge is what data the system should contain. An organization can only retrieve what is designed into the system.

The list of data coded into skills inventories is almost endless, and it must be tailored to the needs of each organization. Some of the more common items include: name, employee number, present location, date of birth, date of employment, job classification or code, prior experience, history of work experience in the organization, specific skills and knowledge, education, field of education (formal education and courses taken since leaving school), knowledge of a foreign language, health, professional qualifications, publications, licenses, patents, hobbies, a supervisory evaluation of the employee's capabilities, and salary/salary range. Items often omitted, but becoming increasingly important, are the employee's own stated career goals and objectives, including geographical preferences and intended retirement date.

Skills inventory data serve to identify employees for specific assignments which will fulfill not only organizational objectives but individual ones as well.

EXHIBIT 4–8
Skills inventory summary card

NAME	DIV.	DEPT.	CLOCK	GROUP	SERIAL NO.	

QUALIFICATIONS INVENTORY SUMMARY CARD

I. A. EXPERIENCE CODES — YRS.

1. ______ ___
2. ______ ___
3. ______ ___
4. ______ ___
5. ______ ___
6. ______ ___

II. FOREIGN LANGUAGE CODES

1. ______
2. ______
3. ______
4. ______
5. ______

III. A. EDUCATION

DEGREE CODES	MAJOR CODES	YEAR OF DEGREE	COLLEGE CODES
1.			
2.			
3.			
4.			

I. B. UNCODED EXPERIENCE — YRS.

______ ___
______ ___

III. B. YEARS OF COLLEGE

CIRCLE EQUIVALENT TO FULL YEARS OF COLLEGE COMPLETED

0, 1, 2, 3, 4, 5, 6, 7, 7+

Source: W. Barnes, Identifying Manpower Potential (New York: AMACOM, a division of American Management Associations, 1963).

Exhibit 4–8 is an example of the summarization of data from the forms used on a skills inventory, either computerized or manual. These summary cards provide the data that are used in assessing and analyzing the supply of people working for the organization.

Maintaining the skills inventory

While designing the system is the most difficult part of developing a skills inventory, planning for the gathering, maintaining, handling, and updating of data is also important. The two principal methods for gathering data are the interview and the questionnaire. Each method has unique costs and benefits. The questionnaire is faster and less expensive when many employees are involved. But inaccuracies are usually greater. People often do not spend enough time on a questionnaire. There are those who contend, therefore, that the trained interviewer can complete the reports more quickly and accurately, and this in the long run more than offsets the costs of the interviewer.

A procedure for keeping the files updated also must be planned. The method used depends on the frequency of change and the uses of the data. For some organizations, an annual update is adequate. In others, where changes are made often and use is frequent, shorter update periods may be necessary. Some organizations make provisions for monthly updating of changeable data and annual checks for less changeable data. One way to do this is to include updating forms in payroll envelopes.

Finally, a decision whether to store the data manually or on the computer must be made. This decision is based on costs of the computer and frequency of use of the data. The computer also provides the possibility of using comparative analyses of employment on a time series basis and other sophisticated studies.

Skills inventories are useful only if management uses the data in making significant decisions. Top management's support is necessary here. Before a manager uses the skills inventory for help in selection decisions, he or she must be trained to avoid system abuse. Examples of these are:

- Making requests simply on the basis that "it would be nice to know."
- Making requests for searches which are not backed up by bona fide requisitions that have been budgeted.
- Specifying too many characteristics for a desired employee so that no one fits all the characteristics.

As an example of the third type of abuse, consider the following request of a skills inventory system:

> Wanted—A person with the following qualifications: BS in business, experience in finance and marketing, with at least two years with the company and making less than $14,000 per year.

Assume 1,000 employees. The chance of finding a person with all these characteristics is the product of the percent of probability in each category. Thus if twenty percent of the 1,000 have a BS in business; 10 percent have experience in finance; 10 percent have experience in marketing; 70 percent have two years or more seniority; and 50 percent make more than $14,000, the chance of finding such a person is .20 × .10 × .10 × .70 × .50, or .0007, or less than one chance in a thousand. Those who set requirements must recognize that being overly specific reduces the chance of finding any suitable employee.

WORK SCHEDULES AND THE SUPPLY OF EMPLOYEES

When people work and how long they work affects the analysis of employee needs and the supply of employees. For example, eight hours of work can be performed by one full-time employee or two part-time employees; ten hours of work can be performed by one employee on overtime or one full-time and one part-time employee.

Hours of work also affect the facilities the employer must provide. When schools are used for two shifts a day, this reduces the need for added buildings. Factories can run two regular-time shifts per week if one shift works four 10-hour days and the other works three 12-hour days.

Of course, the hours employees work is not entirely up to the discretion of employers; the government limits the number of working hours. It also requires overtime to be paid beyond the normal working hours (see Chapter 11).

Several trends in employment and working hours have the potential for significant impact on the personnel function in the future. One is the use of more part-time workers employed on a regular basis. This practice will be explored in Chapter 5, and the impact of part-time employment will be discussed in subsequent chapters. Another is the management of shift work, moonlighting, and overtime.

Shift work

One way to increase output is to schedule a second shift or minishift, in addition to the regular day shift. An enterprise might also add a night shift, if power costs are cheaper then. There is a trend in this direction.

When shift work is used, there are two approaches to scheduling it: to assign people to shifts, or to rotate them through shifts. Most employees prefer not to rotate their work schedules, but if rotation is used, they would rather have changes every several days rather than at week-long or month-long intervals. Second and third shift work generally affects employees adversely. It interferes with time-oriented bodily functions, such as digestion, sleeping, and elimination. Rotating shift work particularly affects personal and family lives and social participation adversely.

There are some advantages to second and third shift work for employees. Usually the pay is better. There are free daytime hours, and often there is less responsibility and supervision. Studies have found that shift workers take such shifts because they provide the only jobs available, and they afford higher pay. About one-third of shift workers prefer shift work, and younger men and women with prior shift-work experience adjust most easily to it.

Enterprises adopt second and third shifts to use their equipment and facilities more efficiently and to get the work out. Are these shifts really efficient, from a human resource point of view? One study found that the day shift was 3 percent more productive than second shifts overall, but there were marked individual productivity differences between employees on the two shifts.

Compressed work weeks

Terry and Vicki Shea and their two sons are walking down Padre Island's beach on a Friday morning. Why isn't Terry working? Because United Services Auto Insurance, where Terry is employed as director of research, operates on a four-day week, Monday through Thursday. The company works four ten-hour days, with a half hour off for lunch. In fact, Terry tends to work a half day on two of the four Fridays each month to catch up on his work.

Ralph and Cindee Hurlburt also work four-day weeks. Ralph works for Armour in a meat-packing plant as blue-collar worker. He works from 6:30 A.M. to 5 P.M., with a 30-minute lunch hour. He shovels five tons of ground beef a day from a machine to a metal hopper. Ralph says he's ready to drop when the day is over, goes to bed each night at 8:00 and has developed a bad arm from the strain. He's paid $4.06 per hour. Cindee stands for ten hours per day carrying trays of meat and loading them in a 50-degree plant. She earns $3.73 per hour. And what do Ralph and Cindee do on their extra day off? They moonlight to earn extra money. (From *The Wall Street Journal,* February 16, 1977.)

* * *

The Norgen Company in Denver, a capital-intensive manufacturer of accessory equipment for pneumatic machinery, adopted the four-day week seven years ago. It did so to compete for skilled labor when it could not compete on the basis of pay, and to keep a union out. Initially, employees and customers were unhappy with the change; working mothers particularly did not like the schedule. But over the long run, absenteeism and turnover were reduced. Productivity did not decline because losses from fatigue were offset by savings from fewer clean-up and start-up periods, fewer breaks, and three fewer holidays each year. Accidents did not increase. The management believes the experiment is a success partly because the job is boring, in a noisy atmosphere and employees like an extra day away from the job, especially in an area like Denver. (From *The Wall Street Journal,* February 17, 1977.)

A compressed work week is the scheduling of the normal 40 hours of weekly work in less than five days. The typical compressed work week follows a four-day, 40-hour schedule. Less frequently a three-day, 36-hour weekly schedule is used. Usually, in a four-day week, the work days are Tuesday through Friday or Monday through Thursday.

Is compressed work-week scheduling a widespread practice? In the United States, about 10,000 enterprises, involving about 744,000 employees, use it. In fact, the number of employees on compressed work weeks declined by 35,000 from 1975 to 1976, and many more employees (1,115,000) work seven-day weeks than compressed work weeks. In most cases, the management initiates the plan, but some unions, such as the UAW, seem to favor it.

Is the compressed work week a good idea? The answer is not clear. Some negative studies indicate that positive results are realized early in the experiment, and then they decline. Although it is too early to say for sure, it appears that individual and job differences explain many of the contradictions in the research findings. In general, older employees find a compressed work week where the work is physically or mentally taxing undesirable, and many younger single employees find it interferes with their social lives. Working mothers with younger children also tend to be unhappy with it. Thus middle-aged people

"Well, I for one hope we don't go to a four-day work week . . . I would never get used to saying, 'Thank God it's Thursday.' "

Reprinted by permission of The Wall Street Journal.

may be most likely to accept compressed work weeks. Another factor is the task involved. In general, heavy physical or taxing mental work probably is not suitable for a compressed work-week schedule.

It appears that the compressed work week has limited applicability. Work loads which result in fatigue, preferences of many employees, and customer demands limit its usefulness. It tends to lead to more moonlighting; those who are most likely to moonlight currently are those who are working conpressed work weeks. Statistics now indicate a decline in its use. Flexitime is likely to be the more popular scheduling system in the future.

Flexitime (flexible hours)

Flexitime gives each employee some freedom in selecting the hours he or she chooses to work. The State Street Bank in Boston is typical of enterprises which have recently installed flexitime. The employees work a five-day week but can vary their starting times, as long as they work their full hours over the week. The plan for State Street's typical work week is shown in Exhibit 4–9. All employees work from 11:00 to 2:00, since these are the hours with peak work loads and communications. This is also the time meetings take place and employees work together. A survey of the results of the bank's introduction of flexitime has indicated that the majority of employees are satisfied with this type of work scheduling.

> Flexitime is an arrangement of working hours which provides for all workers to be present for a specified period in the morning and afternoon (core time), but the rest of the required hours may be completed at their discretion within a specified period.

In Europe, flexitime is quite widespread and is increasing as use of the compressed work week declines. About 5,000,000 Europeans work on flexitime schedules. In the United States more employees are now on flexitime than in compressed work-week plans. About 3,500,000 workers *officially* have flexitime. Most management and professional employees have unofficial flexitime, of course. About 13 percent of all private-sector employers with 50 employees or more use flexitime. The trend is accelerating.

Enterprises using flexitime in the United States include General Motors, Control Data, Wards, NCR, Nestlé, American Airlines, First National Bank of Boston, Blue Cross–Blue Shield of California, Exxon, Pacific Gas and Electric, Hewlett Packard, Smith Kline, John Hancock Life, Continental Telephone, the Social Security Administration, and Defense Supply Company.

Does flexitime make sense? There has been less research on flexitime than on the compressed work week because it is newer, and the research that has

EXHIBIT 4–9
Typical work schedule at State Street Bank

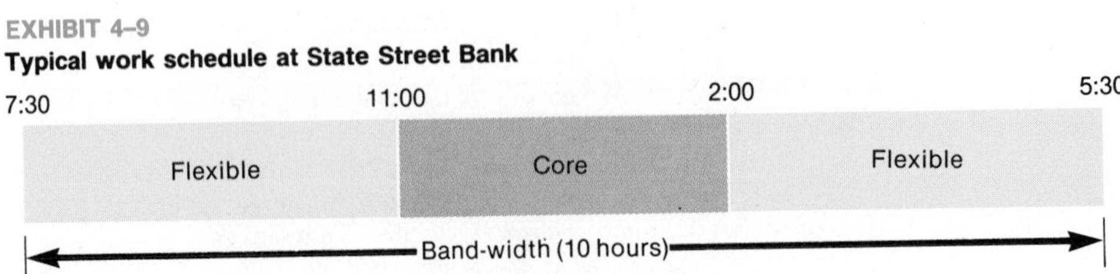

been done is less scientific and sophisticated. In a summary of the research, I found that there are no studies showing negative results. This can be because flexitime is still in Stage 1 of development or because it is a useful method. Its future appears bright because it has fewer serious disadvantages and because it is easier to implement than the compressed work week.

Flexitime affects the supply of labor to the extent that it can lead to more productivity per employee and can lower the need for employees. Because it provides for longer operating hours, there is a possibility of using minishifts with part-time or temporary employees.

ACTION DECISIONS IN PERSONNEL AND EMPLOYMENT PLANNING

There are several managerial decisions to be made once demand for people has been forecast and compared to supply. Exhibit 4–10 presents a more detailed outline of the action decisions. Another action decision which is not shown in the figure is increasingly important today: analyzing the work force to comply with government equal employment opportunity programs. We will discuss this problem first.

Analyzing the composition of the work force

The extent to which the work force of an enterprise approximates the composition of the total work force for the area is an essential consideration in programs enacted by the federal and state governments of the United States to protect members of certain groups from being discriminated against in employ-

EXHIBIT 4–10
Employment planning action decisions

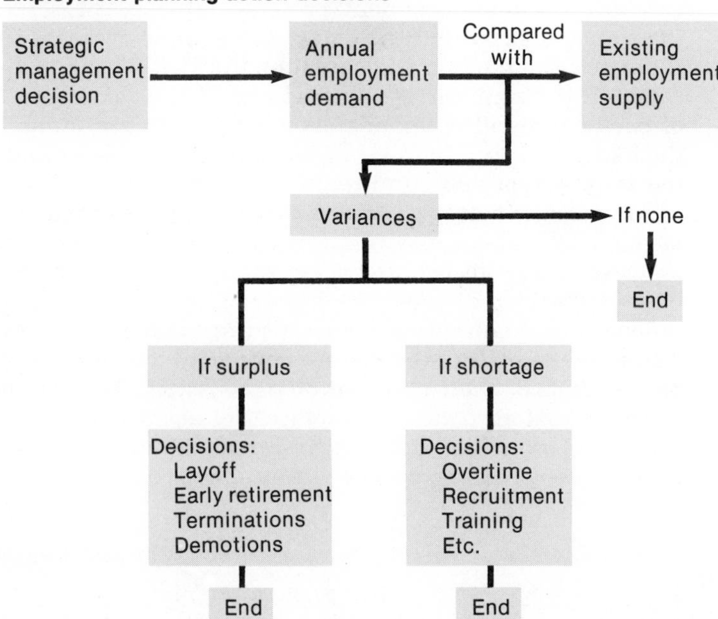

Employment planning conference

ment opportunities. Government agencies enforce these laws. In the United States, these agencies are the Equal Employment Opportunities Commission and the Office of Federal Contract Compliance, at the federal level, and state fair employment practices commissions.

The makeup of the present labor force in the United States and some discrepancies between the ideal of equal employment opportunity and the reality of these opportunities for certain groups was described in Chapter 2, and Chapter 16 will discuss the equal employment opportunity programs set up by employers to make the ideal more of a reality.

The enterprise must keep records of the distribution of employees by categories, levels (top management, professional, operatives, etc.), and pay groups. If the statistics show that the enterprise's employment patterns are substantially different from the overall population in its geographic area and by employment category, the employer is vulnerable to EEO legal action. This brings the threat of back-pay liability, mandatory hiring goals for women and minorities, and the like. Many socially responsible employers have voluntarily tried to improve the employment opportunities of these groups.

Antidiscriminatory programs enforced by government or promoted by popular opinion make it essential for the employer to examine the distribution of employees in protected categories (race, sex, etc.) at all levels to see if the enterprise has *in fact* discriminated against any group in its hiring and promotion practices. The enterprise cannot discriminate against any group (including, of course, white males, who are not ordinarily considered a minority group) solely on the basis of their personal characteristics. The purpose of this analysis is to assure that all potential employees of equal ability have an equal chance at hiring and promotion and other rewards. The specific programs used for analysis of these items will be discussed throughout the book.

Action decisions with no variance in supply and demand

It is possible for the enterprise, after matching the demand for employees with the supply at hand, to find that previous planning has been so excellent that the demand is matched exactly with the supply. In this case employment planning has served its purpose well in helping the enterprise to meet its objectives.

An exact match is rare. More frequently the total supply is correct, but there are variances in subgroups. These data become inputs to facilitate decisions about training, promotion, demotion, and similar decisions. Thus Exhibit 4–10 shows "end" if there are no variances, but the process may not end. It may require additional personnel decisions.

Action decisions with a shortage of employees

When employment specialists comparing demand to supply find the supply of workers is less than the demand, several possibilities are open to the enterprise. If the shortage is small and employees are willing to work overtime, it can be filled with present employees. If the shortage is of higher skilled employees, training and promotions of present employees, together with recruitment of lower skilled employees, are a possibility. This decision can also include recalling previously laid-off employees. Outside the enterprise, additional employees, either part time or full time, can be hired, or some of the work can be contracted out to other enterprises.

Action decisions in surplus conditions

When comparison of employee demand and supply indicates a surplus, the alternative solutions include attrition, early retirements, demotions, layoffs, and terminations. Surplus employee decisions are some of the most difficult decisions managers must make, because the employees who are considered surplus are seldom responsible for the conditions leading to the surplus. A shortage of a raw material such as fuel, or a poorly designed or marketed product can cause an enterprise to have a surplus of employees.

As a first approach to deal with a surplus most enterprises avoid layoffs and terminations by such means as attrition, early retirement, work creation, and work sharing. Many enterprises can reduce their work force simply by not replacing those who retire or quit (attrition). Sometimes this approach is accelerated by encouraging employees close to retirement to leave early (see Chapter 14), but this can amount to layoffs of older employees if the enterprise is not careful. Another approach is for the enterprise to give surplus employees jobs such as painting the plant or extra maintenance chores to keep them on the payroll. In the mid-seventies recessions, firms such as Kimberly Clark, Toyo Kogyo, Dow Chemical, Lockheed, American Shipbuilding, Aerojet General, and Raytheon used this approach.

Another variation of this approach is work sharing. Instead of attempting to decide whom to layoff, the enterprise asks all employees to work less than normal hours and thus share the work. Many unions favor this approach. In recent recessions, many firms have given the employees a voice in how to deal with surplus conditions, and some groups of employees have elected work sharing.

If there is a surplus of employees at higher levels, demotion may be used to reduce the work force. After World War II, as the Army reduced its size it had too many higher level officers to staff the number of positions left. So many officers were demoted to their "permanent" rank, not the one they held in 1945. The numerous ways demotion can be handled include: lowered job status with the same salary or lowered salary; the same status with lower compensation; being bypassed in seniority for promotion; changing to a less desirable job; the same formal status, but with decreased span of control; being excluded from a general salary increase; insertion of positions above the person in the hierarchy; moving to a staff position; elimination of the position and reassignment; and transfer out of direct line for promotion. Demotions are very difficult for employees to accept, and valued employees may leave because of them.

In managing a surplus through layoffs, employers take the surplus employees off the payroll "temporarily" to reduce the surplus. Some employers may feel more willing to accept this method because unemployment compensation plans are now available (see Chapter 11). If the layoff is likely to be semipermanent or permanent, it is in effect a termination and results usually in the payment of severance pay as well as unemployment compensation.

When the enterprise is getting close to the point where layoffs are necessary, employees know business is down, and the workplace buzzes with rumors. Remember how the employees reacted when Sparrow Hospital (Chapter 3) was faced with more layoffs. Managers should make layoff decisions as early as possible to give employees ample notice. This is especially important when there will be mass layoffs, as in the auto industry in the midseventies.

Employees can get bitter at layoff time. For example, Ford Motor Company experienced sabotage in the midst of the layoffs in the midseventies. Fear affects productivity and employee satisfaction, and most employers will try to avoid layoffs if at all possible.

How does a manager decide whom to lay off? Two criteria have been used: merit and seniority. In the past the most senior employee was laid off last. A second approach now is to lay off those with lower merit ratings. Merit means that those who do the job the best are kept; those who perform poorly are laid off. Chapter 8 explains how management assigns merit ratings. If merit ratings are not precise, unions may fight their exclusive use as a reason for laying off particular employees.

Using seniority as the only criterion may mean that recently hired minorities and women are laid off first. This pits minority rights against seniority rights, and the courts have been hard pressed to resolve the conflict. In a case with important implications for seniority systems, the U.S. Supreme Court decided that minority applicants who are discriminatorily rejected by an employer and later hired must be given seniority credit from the date of that rejection. Such seniority credits represent a breach in the tradition of seniority rights, but they do not apply to most minorities and women hired under EEO plans, for by and large they never were discriminately rejected. In short, federal EEO policies have not endangered seniority very much. While seniority has lost some judicial skirmishes to EEO, it remains the principal criterion of employment rights for hourly employees.

The final approach used to reduce employment surpluses is termination. Most employers use it as a last resort. Anyone who has watched Willy Loman in *Death of a Salesman* or the star of Neil Simon's *Prisoner of Second Avenue* knows why. Termination is usually very painful to both the employer and the employee. EEO requirements apply to terminations as well as layoffs. When terminations take place, many employers engage in outplacement: a serious attempt by the enterprise to help terminated employees find suitable jobs.

SUMMARY, CONCLUSIONS, AND RECOMMENDATIONS

This chapter has pointed out the significant factors in the diagnostic model that affect personnel and employment planning. It began by emphasizing that this personnel activity is an integral aspect of strategic planning by top management. This personnel function assures the enterprise success in maintaining its personnel capacities by comparing the present supply of human resources with the projected demand for them. In summary:

1. The major reasons for formal employment planning are to achieve:
   a. More effective and efficient use of human resources.
   b. More satisfied and better developed employees.
   c. More effective equal employment opportunity planning.
2. The personnel and employment planning process is a joint responsibility of personnel and operating managers, with each performing specific functions in the process.
3. Four forecasting techniques used to determine work-force needs described in the chapter are: expert-estimate, trend-projection, modeling, and unit-forecasting techniques.
4. To provide realistic job information and to streamline efficient job design, three processes used are:
   a. Job analysis—gathering data on a job.
   b. Job description—a written statement detailing duties and responsibilities of the job.
   c. Job specifications—a written statement listing the qualifications a person needs to perform a job effectively.
5. The next step in the planning process is to determine the availability of those presently employed by the enterprise who can fill projected vacancies. The skills inventory can serve this purpose.
6. Work schedules, such as shift work, compressed work weeks, or flexitime, can be used by the enterprise to adjust present employee availability to new employee needs.
7. Action decisions in a shortage of employees depend on the magnitude of the shortage: overtime, retraining of lower skilled employees, hiring additional employees, or subcontracting some of the work.
8. Action decisions in surplus conditions include attrition, early retirement, demotions, layoffs, and terminations.
9. Effective enterprises will analyze the supply/demand match of employees in advance so as to take necessary steps to reschedule, recruit, or lay off employees. They will analyze work-force composition to determine that it meets legal constraints.

To supplement the statements above, this chapter introduces the use of summary propositions to highlight some of the major points that have been made about various personnel activities and to tie these to earlier material. They serve as recommendations as well as a concise form of summary.

Proposition 4.1. The more volatile the organization's environment, the more likely is the effective organization to forecast the demand for labor formally at each unit and to sum the demand at headquarters.

Proposition 4.2. The more complex the product and services offered by the organization, the more likely is the effective organization to forecast the demand for labor formally at each unit level and to sum the demand at headquarters.

Proposition 4.3. The larger the organization, the more stable its environment, and the less complex its product-service line, the more likely is the effective organization to use modeling or multiple-predictive techniques to forecast its employment demand.

Proposition 4.4. The more volatile the organization's environment, the less likely are detailed formal job analysis, description, and specification systems to be efficient.

Proposition 4.5. The more volatile the organization's environment, the more likely is the effective organization to use more sophisticated and computerized skills inventories.

Proposition 4.6. The more complex the products and services offered by the organization, the more likely is the effective organization to use more sophisticated and computerized skills inventories.

Proposition 4.7. The more geographically dispersed the organization's members, the more likely is the effective organization to use more sophisticated and computerized skills inventories.

Proposition 4.8. Compressed work weeks are likely to be preferred by employees with instrumental work values whose jobs do not require heavy physical or taxing mental work and who are middle-aged.

Proposition 4.9. Flexitime systems are likely to be successful in work that does not require significant interdependence, with supportive middle management and unions, and where significant outlays for buffer stocks and utility costs are not required.

Proposition 4.10. If shift work is required, it is more likely to be successful if the employees are assigned to a shift permanently with the right to bid for better shifts, and if there are reasonable shift differentials in pay and other rewards.

Employment planning systems for model organizations

Another feature of this text which is introduced in this chapter is a summary of the possible uses of each personnel activity in the seven model organizations identified in Chapter 1 (Exhibit 1–7). The recommendations for employment planning in these model organizations are given in Exhibit 4–11. The exhibit outlines the major activities of personnel and employment planning that are most useful for various types of enterprises.

Personnel and employment planning can be an integral part of the personnel process. It is most directly related to recruitment, selection, training, and promotion. By matching employment supply and demand, the organization can know how many persons of what type it needs to fill positions from within (by promotion or training) and how many it must acquire from outside (by recruitment and selection).

EXHIBIT 4–11
Recommendations on personnel and employment planning for model organizations

	Analysis of supply (skills inventory)		*Method of demand analysis*				*Level where employment is analyzed*		
Type of organization	*Manual*	*Computerized*	*Expert*	*Trend*	*Model/ multiple*	*Unit*	*HQ*	*Unit*	*Both*
1. Large size, low complexity, high stability		X			X	X	X		
2. Medium size, low complexity, high stability	X				X	X	X		
3. Small size, low complexity, high stability	X			X			X		
4. Medium size, moderate complexity, moderate stability	X			X		X		X	
5. Large size, high complexity, low stability		X		X		X			X
6. Medium size, high complexity, low stability	X			X		X		X	
7. Small size, high complexity, low stability	X		X					X	

Part Three, to follow, is devoted to recruitment, selection, and orientation—filling employment needs from outside the organization when personnel and employment planning decisions show this need and orienting new employees to the job.

QUESTIONS

1. What is personnel and employment planning? How does it relate to other personnel activities?
2. What techniques are used for forecasting future employment needs?
3. Describe how you would choose a forecasting technique for several kinds of enterprises, such as a small manufacturer of ashtrays, a large steel company, or a moderate-sized general hospital.
4. Contrast job descriptions, job specifications, and job analysis.
5. How does job analysis relate to other personnel activities?
6. How is analysis of employment supply related to demand analysis?
7. What is a skills inventory? Discuss how to design an effective skills inventory.
8. Compressed work weeks are the wave of the future—the way most of us will have our work scheduled. Comment.
9. What is flexitime? Discuss the probable future of flexitime.
10. Why should an enterprise analyze the composition of its work force? How?
11. What action decisions can be made when there is a worker shortage? Which is best?
12. What action decisions can be made when there is a worker surplus? Which is best?

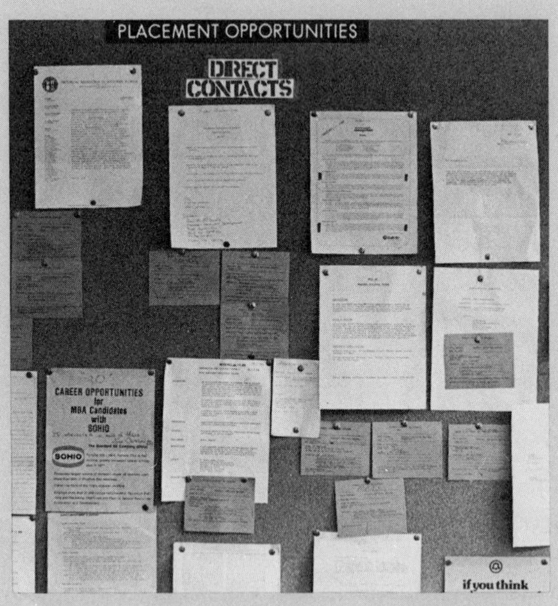
PLACEMENT OPPORTUNITIES
DIRECT CONTACTS
CAREER OPPORTUNITIES for MBA Candidates with SOHIO
SOHIO
if you think

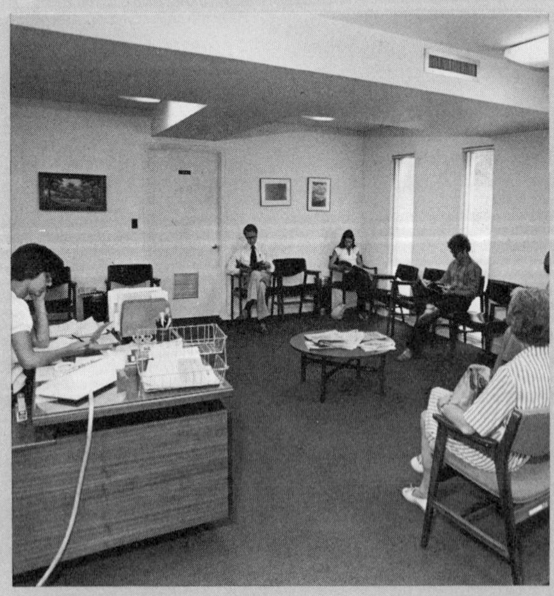

part three

Recruitment, selection, and orientation

Part Three is concerned with recruitment, selection, orientation of employees and career development. Given the data provided by personnel and employment planning—how many people are needed, of what type, and when and where—the organization sets out to acquire the persons needed in the most effective way.

Chapter 5 discusses recruiting, or attracting good personnel to the enterprise. Recruitment results in a list of potential employees for each position, from which the enterprise selects the most qualified people available. This chapter also includes a section on effective ways to find a job. Chapter 6 shows how organizations select the best recruits from among those who apply for open positions. The final chapter of this part, Chapter 7, is concerned with orienting new employees to their jobs.

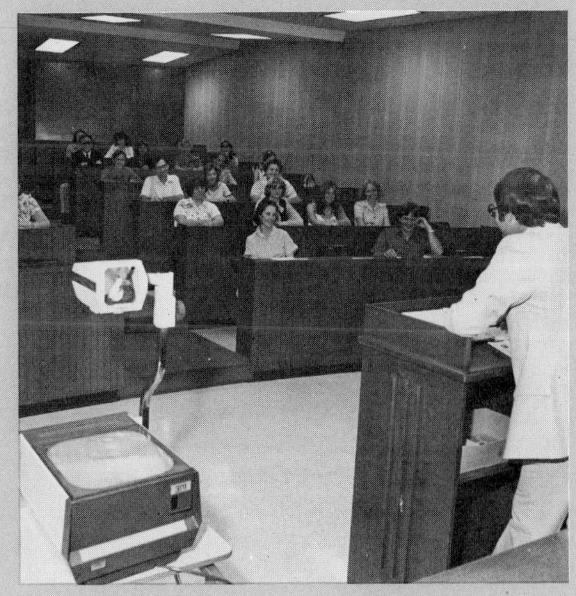

5

Recruiting and job search

Chapter objectives

- To learn how to develop an effective recruiting program for an enterprise.
- To describe the recruiting process: who does it, how they do it, and where they seek recruits.
- To show you how to find a job for yourself.

Chapter outline

I. A Diagnostic Approach to Recruitment
   A. External influences
II. Interactions of the Recruit and the Organization
   A. The organization's view of recruiting
   B. The potential employee's view of recruiting
   C. Job search and finding a job
III. Who Does the Recruiting?
IV. Sources of Recruits
   A. Job posting and bidding
   B. Inside moonlighting and employees' friends
   C. External sources
V. Methods of Recruiting
   A. Media advertisements
   B. Use of recruiters
   C. Computer matching services
   D. Special-event recruiting
   E. Summer internships
VI. College Recruiting
   A. The effective college recruiter
VII. Cost/Benefit Analysis of Recruiting
VIII. Summary, Conclusions, and Recommendations

The mission of the military is to defend the country against its enemies. In performing this duty, the military's "employees" may be injured, perhaps incapacitated for life; many also may die. The military's "executives" expect unquestioning obedience, and military personnel must live in the same area where they work, in communities that may consist almost entirely of military staff. The employer provides for many of their social and off-work facilities—recreational, religious, social, shopping.

Everyone does not find this way of life appealing. Each year, thousands of military personnel retire or leave the service. Now Congress has mandated a volunteer military force. If the economy provides many positions with more attractive rewards, how does the military attract enough applicants to offer them jobs?

* * *

Mary Buggins is about to graduate from pharmacy school. She wants to work in or around the Los Angeles area because its an exciting place to live, and she believes it will offer her a secure future in her chosen profession. Now she needs a job, but how does she find one? The college has a placement office, and there are the help-wanted ads to check. Or she could walk into pharmacies that appeal to her and ask for a job, or run an ad in the situations-wanted column, or go to an employment agency. Which method is the best for Mary?

These two examples illustrate problems faced by organizations and individuals which the recruiting process can help solve. This chapter describes effective ways to recruit the people needed to offset shortages in human resources which become apparent as a result of personnel employment planning.

Recruiting is that set of activities an enterprise uses to attract job candidates who have the abilities and attitudes needed to help the enterprise achieve its objectives.

Job search is the set of activities a person undertakes to seek and find a position which will provide him or her with sustenance and other rewards.

Recruiting is related directly to a number of other personnel activities, as shown in Exhibit 5–1.

Personnel and employment planning determines the number of employees needed, and all subsequent personnel activities (such as selection, orientation, development, compensation) cannot be effective unless good employees have been recruited. The Prentice-Hall/ASPA survey of 1,400 personnel executives

EXHIBIT 5–1
Recruiting and other personnel activities

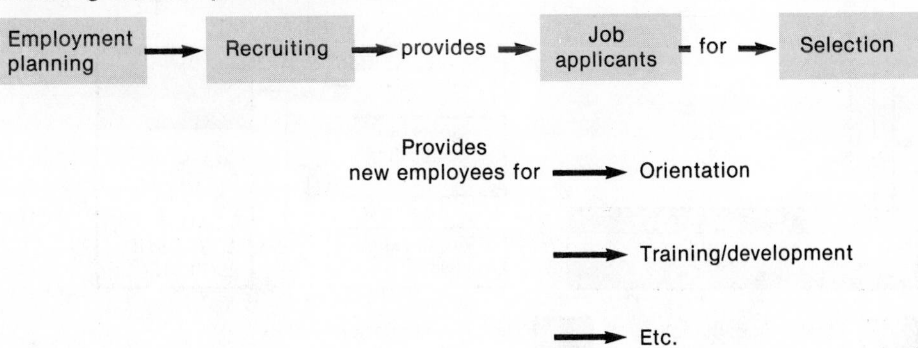

found that they rated recruiting/selection as their most important function in a nonunionized firm. Recruiting can be costly. For example, it has been estimated that recruiting cost the following percentages of the first-year salary of various specialists and managers: senior engineer, 68 percent; accountant, 61 percent; secretary, 51 percent; supervisor, 40 percent; middle manager, 33 percent; and top manager, 25 percent. Thus for a $60,000-a-year executive, recruiting can cost $15,000; recruiting engineers can cost $11,900. Yet recruiting is not a well-developed personnel function; it is at Stage II or possibly Stage III (see Exhibit 1–6 in Chapter 1).

A DIAGNOSTIC APPROACH TO RECRUITMENT

Exhibit 5–2 examines how the recruiting process is affected by various factors in the environment. The recruiting process begins with an attempt to find em-

EXHIBIT 5–2

Factors affecting recruitment of employees and organizational effectiveness

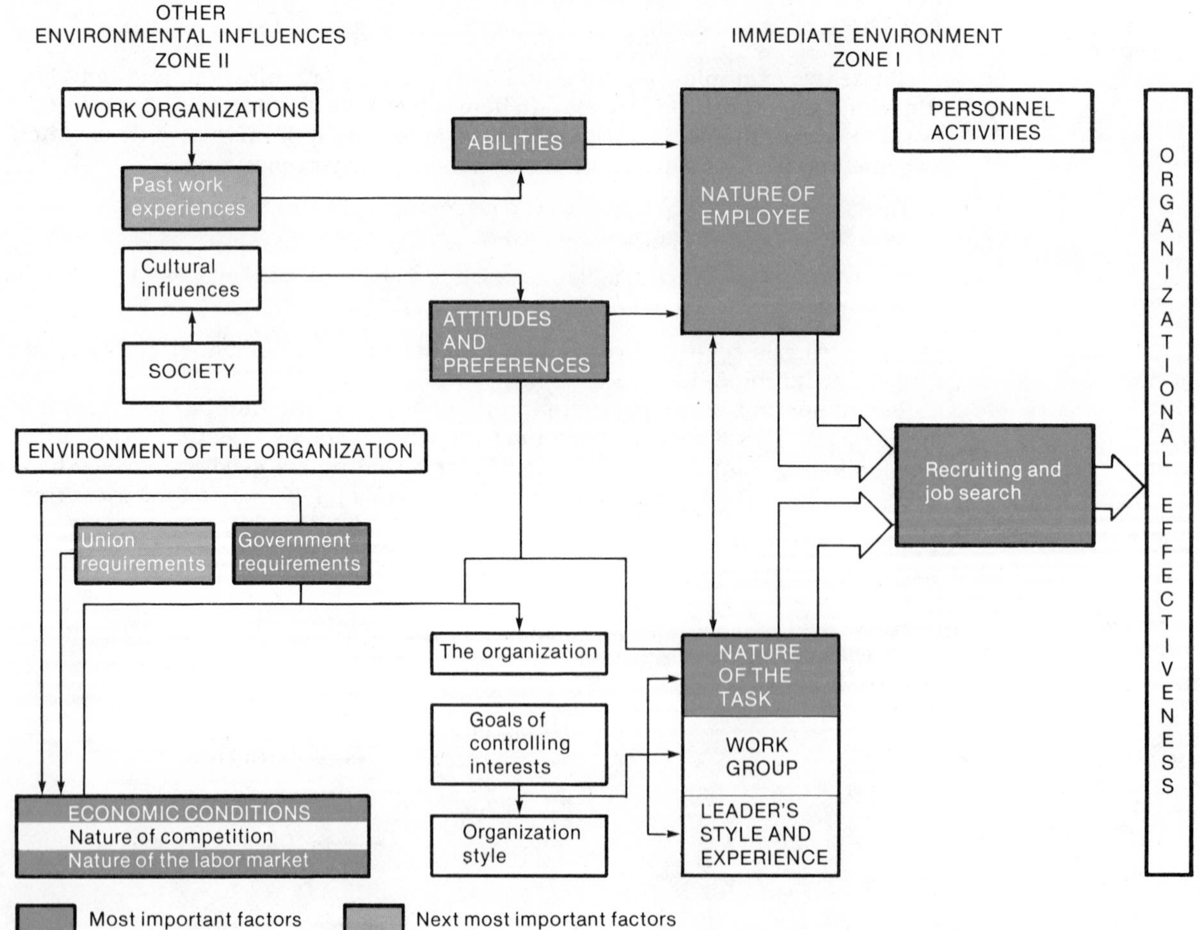

ployees with the abilities and attitudes desired by the enterprise and to match them with the tasks to be performed. Whether potential employees will respond to the recruiting effort depends on the attitudes they have developed toward those tasks and the enterprise, on the basis of their past social and working experiences. Their perception of the task will also be affected by the work climate in the enterprise.

How difficult the recruiting job is depends on a number of factors: external influences such as government and union restrictions and the labor market, plus the employer's requirements and candidates' preferences. External factors are discussed in this section, and the important interaction of the organization as a recruiter and the employee as a recruit is examined in the next section.

External influences

Government and union restrictions. Government regulations prohibiting discrimination in hiring and employment have a direct impact on recruiting practices. As will be described in more detail in Chapter 16, government agencies can and do review the following information about recruiting to see if an enterprise has violated the law:

- The list of recruitment sources (such as employment agencies, civic organizations, schools) for each job category.
- Recruiting advertising.
- Estimates of the firm's employment needs for the coming year.
- Statistics on the number of applicants processed by category (sex, race, etc.) and by job category or level.

The government may require an enterprise to use EEO programs to recruit qualified employees who are not well represented in the present work force. For example, a firm with no female managers may be required to recruit at women's colleges offering degrees likely to lead to management positions with the enterprise.

Exhibit 5–3 provides a guide to what recruiters can and cannot legally do or ask in recruiting interviews. Other personal characteristics recruiters need to be wary of, because they may discriminate or do not relate directly to performance, are birthplace; use of second names or aliases; religious affiliation; citizenship; membership in clubs, societies, and lodges; and social security numbers. In some states, it is illegal to ask about the type of military discharge and past police records. Many public organizations must be careful to follow state or local statutes on recruiting.

Obviously, these government restrictions affect who can be recruited, how, and where. In addition, some union contracts restrict recruiting to union hiring halls (as will be discussed in Chapter 6). This restriction does not apply for many employers, but where it does the recruiting function is turned over to the union, at least for those employees who are unionized.

Labor market conditions. The second external environmental factor affecting recruiting is labor market conditions (these were described in some detail in Chapter 2). The labor market affects recruiting in this way: If there is a surplus of labor at recruiting time, even informal attempts at recruiting will probably attract more than enough applicants. But when full employment is nearly

EXHIBIT 5–3
Dos and don'ts in recruiting interviews

Subject	*Can do or ask*	*Cannot do or ask*
Sex	Notice appearance.	Make comments or notes unless sex is a bona fide occupational qualification.
Marital status	Ask status after hiring, for insurance purposes.	Are you married? Single? Divorced? Engaged? Are you living with anyone? Do you see your ex-spouse?
Children	Ask numbers and ages of children after hiring, for insurance purposes.	Do you have children at home? How old? Who cares for them? Do you plan more children?
Physical data	Explain manual labor, lifting, other requirements of the job. Show how it is performed. Require physical exam.	How tall are you? How heavy?
Criminal record	If security clearance is necessary, can be done prior to employment.	Have you ever been arrested, convicted, or spent time in jail?
Military status	Are you a veteran? Why not? Any job-related experience?	What type of discharge do you have? What branch did you serve in?
Age	Age after hiring. Are you over 18?	How old are you? Estimate age.
Housing	If you have no phone, how can we reach you?	Do you own your home? Do you rent? Do you live in an apartment or a house?

Source: *Business Week,* May 26, 1975, p. 77.

reached in an area, skillful and prolonged recruiting may be necessary to attract any applicants that fulfill the expectations of the enterprise.

The employer can find out about the current employment picture in several ways. The federal Department of Labor issues employment reports, and state divisions of employment security and labor usually can provide information on local employment conditions. There are also sources of information about specific types of employees. Craft unions and professional associations keep track of employment conditions as they affect their members. Current college recruiting efforts are analyzed by the Conference Board, A. C. Nielsen, and the Endicott Report, which appears in *The Journal of College Placement.* Various personnel journals and *The Wall Street Journal* also regularly report on employment conditions.

Other sources provide summary data such as indexes of employment. One of the most interesting indexes is that of the Conference Board, which keeps track of help-wanted advertising in 52 major newspapers across the nation, using 1967 as a base year of 100. Local conditions are more important than national conditions, unless the employer is recruiting nationwide.

INTERACTIONS OF THE RECRUIT AND THE ORGANIZATION

After considering how external factors such as government, unions, and labor market conditions restrict the options of an enterprise to recruit (and an applicant to be recruited), the next step in understanding the recruiting process is to consider the interaction of the applicants and the enterprise in recruiting.

In Exhibit 5–2 (the diagnostic model for recruitment and selection), the nature of the organization and the goals of the managers are highlighted, as is the nature of the task. The techniques used and sources of recruits vary with the job. As far as the applicants are concerned, their abilities, attitudes, and past work experience affect how they go about seeking a job.

The recruiting process consists of the matching of the employer's desired qualifications with the applicant's qualifications. The employer offers a job with associated rewards; he is looking for certain characteristics in a potential employee. The recruit has abilities and attitudes to offer and is looking for a kind of job that meets his minimum expectations. A match is made when sufficient overlap exists between these two sets of expectations. The recruiting process usually requires some modifications and compromises on both sides.

The organization's view of recruiting

Three aspects affect recruiting from the organization's viewpoint: the recruiting requirements set, organization policies and procedures, and the organizational image.

Requirements for recruits. Organizations specify the requirements they consider ideal in applicants for positions. The employer easily can have unrealistic expectations of potential employees: They might expect applicants who stand first in their class, are president of all extracurricular activities, have worked their way through school, have Johnny Carson's ability to charm, are good looking, have ten years' experience (at age 21), and are willing to work long hours for almost no money. Or, to meet federal requirements, they might specify a black woman, but one who is in the upper 10 percent of her graduating class and has an undergraduate degree in engineering and an MBA.

As contrasted with this unrealistic approach, the effective enterprise examines the specifications that are absolutely necessary for the job. Then it uses these as its beginning expectations for recruits (see the section on job analysis, job description, and job specifications in Chapter 4).

Organization policies and practices. In some organizations personnel policies and practices affect recruiting and who is recruited. One of the most important of these is promotion from within. For all practical purposes, this policy means that many organizations only recruit from outside the organization at the initial hiring level. They feel this is fair to present loyal employees and assures them a secure future and a fair chance at promotion, and most employees favor this approach. Some employers also feel this practice helps protect trade secrets. The techniques used for internal recruiting will be discussed below.

Is promotion from within always a good policy? No. An enterprise may grow so stable that it is set in its ways. The business does not compete effectively, or the government bureau will not adjust to legislative requirements. In such cases, promotion from within may be detrimental, and new employees from outside might be helpful.

Other recruiting policies can also affect recruiting. Certain organizations have always hired more than their fair share of the handicapped, or veterans, or ex-convicts, for example, and they may look to these sources first. Others may be involved in nepotism to favor relatives. All these policies affect who is recruited.

Organizational image. The image of the employer generally held by the public also affects recruitment. There are differences in attracting engineers, systems analysts, tool and die makers, marketing researchers, cost accountants, and employment specialists, for such diverse enterprises and situations as:

NASA at the height of the space program, when men were walking on the moon.

The U.S. Army attempting to recruit volunteers just after Vietnam was completely taken over by Hanoi.

St. John's hospital—the best known, best equipped hospital in town.

Harvard University trying to recruit faculty members to teach and students to attend its MBA program.

A small soap company, trying to hire salespersons, which must compete with Procter and Gamble for recruits.

IBM trying to recruit research scientists for its lab.

As you can imagine, the good or bad, well-known or unknown images of these enterprises will affect how they are viewed by the public and job recruits. The enterprise's image is complex, but it probably is based on what the enterprise does and whether it is perceived as providing a good place to work. The larger the enterprise, the more likely it is to have a well-developed image. A firm that produces a product or service the potential employee knows about or uses is also more likely to have an image for the applicant. The probability is that a potential employee will have a clearer image of a chewing gum company than a manufacturer of subassemblies for a cyclotron.

The enterprise's image is affected by the industry it is in. These images change. In the past, petroleum had a positive image. The ecology movement has changed that.

How does this image affect recruiting? Job applicants seldom can have interviews with all the organizations that have job openings of interest to them. Because there are time and energy limits to the job search, they do some preliminary screening. One of these screens is the image the applicants have of the enterprise, which can attract or repel them. They don't accept interviews with bad-image enterprises unless they have to.

In sum, the ideal job specifications preferred by an enterprise may have to

"Now, I hope you don't have the idea that working for I.T.T. is all intrigue and adventure."

Drawing by C. Barsotti; © 1973 The New Yorker Magazine, Inc.

be adjusted to meet the realities of the labor market, government or union restrictions, the limitations of its policies and practices, and its image. If an inadequate number of quality personnel apply, the enterprise may have to either adjust the job to fit the best applicant or increase its recruiting efforts.

The potential employee's view of recruiting

Exhibit 5–2 highlighted several factors relevant to how a recruit looks for a job. The applicant has abilities, attitudes, and preferences based on past work experiences and influences by parents, teachers, and others. These factors affect recruits two ways: how they set their job preferences, and how they go about seeking a job. Understanding these is vital to effective recruiting by organizations.

Preferences of recruits for organizations and jobs. Just as enterprises have ideal specifications for recruits, so do recruits have a set of preferences for a job. Mary Buggins's preference for work in Los Angeles is an example. A student leaving college may want a job in San Diego because of its climate, paying $25,000 a year and with little or no responsibility or supervision. This recruit is as unlikely to get *all* his expectations fulfilled as the enterprise is. The recruit also faces the limits of the labor market (good or bad from the recruit's point of view, which is usually the opposite of the enterprise's), government and union restrictions, and the limits of organizational policies and practices. The recruit must anticipate compromises just as the enterprise does.

From the individual's point of view, organization choice is a two-step process. First, the individual makes an occupational choice—probably in high school or just after. Then she or he makes a choice of the organization to work for within the occupation chosen.

What factors affect the organization-choice decision? A number of researchers have found that more educated persons know the labor market better, have higher expectations of work, and find organizations that pay more and provide more stable employment. Although much of the research suggests that this decision is fairly rational, the more careful studies indicate that the decision is also influenced by unconscious processes, chance, and luck. Whether one seeks a job at all or how hard one looks depends partly on the availability of unemployment insurance (see Chapter 11).

Some studies have indicated that the organizational choice tends to be correlated with single factors. One study found blue-collar workers went after the highest paying jobs; another found workers trying to match multiple needs with multiple job characteristics, such as high pay and preferred job type; and a third found the approach varied by personality differences.

Job search and finding a job

Exhibit 5–4 outlines the pattern followed by effective job searchers. Examine Step 1: Realize that your first job choice is part of your career objectives. Do you see this job as the first of a chain of jobs with this company? Or is this just a job to get experience before you start your own business? More is said about this and Steps 5 and 6 in Chapter 7.

Step 2 is fulfilled by reading newspapers and professional publications in the area where you'd like to live, and describing the jobs you'd like to have. College placement offices have job information, as do professional associations,

EXHIBIT 5–4
Career decision strategy

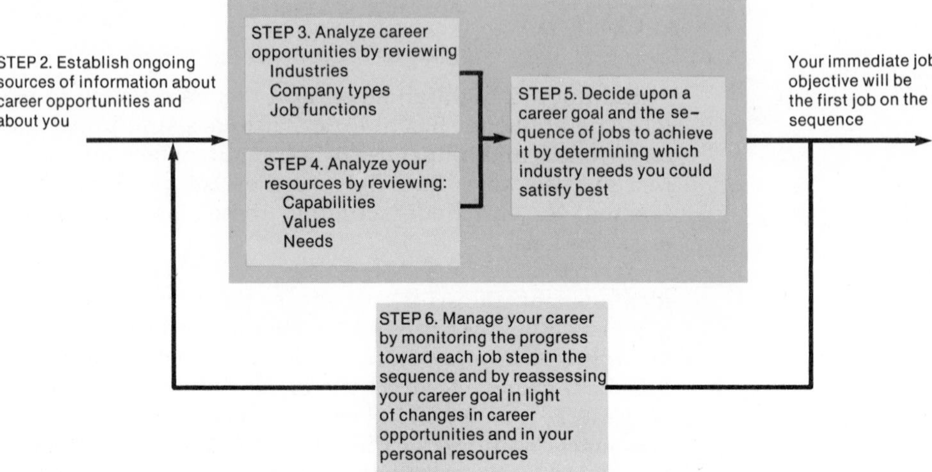

Source: B. Greco, *How to Get a Job That's Right for You* (Homewood, Ill.: Dow Jones-Irwin, 1975. © 1975 by Dow Jones–Irwin, Inc.).

employment agencies, and search firms. Personal contacts also are a good source of information.

The data from Step 2 allow you to complete Step 3 with regard to industry. With regard to company type and job function, you need to analyze the answers to certain kinds of questions about potential employers.

Questions about employers:

1. Do I have a size preference: small, medium, or large, or no size preference?
2. Do I have a sector preference (private, not for profit, public sector)?
3. What kinds of industries interest me? This is usually based on interests in company products or services. Do I prefer mechanical objects or counseling people? This is a crucial question.
4. Have I checked to make sure that the sector or product or service has a good future and will lead to growth in opportunity?

At this point, you may have determined, for example, that what you really want is a job near home, in a small firm in the toy industry, that you can buy out some day. Answers to these questions will help you narrow the list of potential employers to a reasonable size.

As far as Step 4 is concerned, there are several questions you need to answer about your values and needs. Questions of this type are almost unlimited. What you must do first is rank them in importance so you know the tradeoffs between them. You *will not* find a job with *all* the characteristics you choose.

Questions about me:

1. How hard do I like to work?
2. Do I like to be my own boss, or would I rather work for someone else?
3. Do I like to work alone, with a few others, or with large groups?
4. Do I like work at an even pace or in bursts of energy?
5. Does location matter? Do I want to work near home? In warmer climates? In ski country? Am I willing to be mobile?
6. How much money do I want? Am I willing to work for less money but in a more interesting job?
7. Do I like to work in one place or many, indoors or outdoors?
8. How much variety do I want in work?

Then you need to analyze what you have to offer that comprises your comparative advantages. These can include education (for example, grades, kinds of courses, skills developed), interpersonal skills, personality traits, and personal contacts.

After completing Steps 3 and 4, you are ready to look for a job. Use all the sources available to you: employment agencies, personal contacts, professional associations, and so on. If you use mail to send resumé's, the letters should be personalized, and telephone follow-up is necessary. Personal contacts should be used wherever possible.

One study of over 200 personnel managers who normally screen applicants for positions found that it is essential for cover letters accompanying resumés to be personally typed, no longer than one page, and truthful. They should include these items, in order of importance:

Position you are seeking.

Specific job objectives.

Your career objectives.

Reason you are seeking employment.

An indication that you know something about the organization.

The same study found that preferred resumés were personally typed, no more than two pages in length, and on high quality paper, etc. The most important items the managers surveyed in this study were looking for on a resumé were, in order: current address; past work experience; college major; job objectives and goals; date of availability for the job; career objectives; permanent address; tenure on previous jobs; colleges and universities attended; specific physical limitations; and job location requirements. Other items they preferred were, in order: overall health status; salary requirements; travel limitations; minor in college; grades in college major; military experience; years in which degrees were awarded; overall grade-point average; membership in organizations; and awards and scholarships.

Successful job seekers prepare for job interviews. Some suggestions for this are given in Chapter 6. As with other skills, practice makes perfect. Practice interviewing before a videotape with a friend role playing the interviewer. You can learn from each other.

Typical questions asked in job interviews:

1. What qualifications do you have that make you feel you will be a success in your field?
2. How much do you know about our company? Its product or service?
3. How did you pay for your college expenses?
4. Why did you choose this particular field of work?
5. What type of position are you most interested in?
6. Why do you want to work for our company?
7. What jobs have you held previously? How did you find them? Why did you leave? What have you learned from these positions that will help you in the job with our company?
8. Have you set a goal for yourself about the salary you expect by age 30? Why? 35? Why?
9. What is most important to you—making money or performing a service for people?
10. Do you have a geographic preference? For example, what size city do you prefer? Are you willing to relocate?
11. What do you see as your major weakness?

Once you have had job interviews, be sure to follow up those that interest you by sending a letter or calling the interviewer. This requires you to write down and remember the interviewer's name and some details of the job being offered.

WHO DOES THE RECRUITING?

Clark Kirby is just entering the office of the vice president of personnel, Lewis Yates. Clark has worked for Gunther Manufacturing for ten years. After a short management training program, Clark had spent almost two years as operating supervisor in a plant. After that, a position had opened up in personnel. Clark had majored in personnel at California State University at Los Angeles and wanted to try it. He had liked personnel and done well at it. He had moved up in the department headquarters in Chicago during the next seven years.

Gunther is a growing firm. For a middle-sized operation, it has one of the fastest growth records in the industry. Now, Gunther is opening up a new plant in the quickly expanding Houston market. The plant's location is in one of Houston's suburbs, 15 miles from downtown.

Lewis has selected Clark to be the Houston plant personnel manager. This was what Clark had been waiting for: a chance to be on his own and to show what he can do for Lewis, who has been very sup-

Clark

portive of his career, and for Gunther. He was very excited as he entered Lewis's office.

Lewis

Lewis greeted him with, "Well, Clark, I hope you realize how much we are counting on you in Houston. Shortly you'll be meeting your new plant manager, Ed Humphrey. You'll be working for him, but responsible to me to see that Gunther's personnel policies are carried out.

"The plant will be staffed initially with the following employees. These are in effect your recruiting quotas:

Managers	38
Professional/technical	10
Clerical	44
Skilled employees	104
Semiskilled employees	400

Also note that you will receive a budget for maximum initial pay for this group shortly.

"You and Ed should work out the details. You are eligible to recruit some employees from the home office and other plants. But excessive raiding is not allowed. Remember too that Gunther has an equal employment opportunity problem. Wherever possible, try to hire qualified minorities and women to help us meet our goal.

"Your own personnel office consists of yourself, one personnel specialist to help you run the employment office, and one clerical employee. Good Luck!"

Clark quickly arranged for a meeting with Ed, his new boss. Ed is about 50 years old. He is a high school graduate who started with Gunther as a blue-collar employee when he was 18 years old. After ten years in various blue-collar positions, Ed became a foreman. Eight years later he was selected as an assistant to the plant manager. After several years in this position, he was made one of the three assistant plant managers at one of Gunther's plants in Chicago. He held that position until being given the position of plant manager at the new Houston plant.

Ed

After introductions, Clark and Ed talked.

Clark: Here are the figures for employees which Lewis gave me. He also said we could recruit some people from Gunther, but not to raid beyond company policy. Also, Lewis said we needed to do an exceptional job recruiting minorities and women because we have an EEO problem. In Houston, that means finding Hispanics, blacks, and women.

Ed: Let's get something straight right off. You work for me now, not Lewis. Here's a list of 20 managers I want to take with me. It's your job to convince them to come to Houston with me. In cases where my help might persuade some to come along, call on me. But I'm very harassed now trying to get machinery ordered, the plant laid out, financing arranged, and so on. Call on me only when you must, you *understand?*

Oh, one more thing. That EEO * # /OX, you can forget that. The Houston plant is going to be the most efficient in the company, or else! And if that means hiring the best workers and they all turn out to be white, that's tough, you get me? Keep me posted on what's happening. Good to have you on board.

EXHIBIT 5–5

The roles of operating and personnel managers in recruitment

Recruiting function	*Operating manager (OM)*	*Personnel manager (PM)*
Set recruiting goals	Set by OM with advice of PM	Advises OM on state of labor market
Decide on sources of recruits and recruiting policies	Policy decision, outside v. inside, set by OM with advice of PM	Advises OM on status of possible inside recruits
Decide on methods of recruiting	OM advises PM on methods of recruiting	PM decides on recruiting methods with advice of OM
College recruiting	OM occasionally recruits at colleges	PM normally recruits at colleges
Cost/benefit studies of recruiting	OM evaluates results of cost/benefit studies and decides accuracy	PM performs cost/benefit studies

A typical employment office

The situation at Gunther illustrates who handles the responsibilities for recruiting employees. The roles of operating and personnel managers in recruiting are shown in Exhibit 5–5.

Personnel and employment planning gives operating managers the data needed to set recruiting quotas. In larger enterprises, sometimes this process is formalized by authorizations. That is, a budget is prepared showing the maximum number of people to be recruited and the maximum salary that can be paid. Lewis gave these items to Clark at Gunther Corporation.

Who does the recruiting? In larger enterprises, the personnel department does it. The branch of the department with this responsibility is called the employment office or department. It is staffed by recruiters, interviewers, and clerical employees. This group also does the preliminary selection, as will be described in Chapter 6. Employment offices are specialized units which provide a place to which applicants can apply. They conduct the recruiting, both at the work site and away from it. A typical employment office is shown.

When applicants appear in person at the work site, the employment office serves a similar purpose. This initial meeting might be called the reception phase of employment. The applicant is greeted, supplied with an application blank, and perhaps given some information on present hiring conditions and the enterprise as a place to work. If the applicant is treated indifferently or rudely at this phase, he or she can form a lasting poor impression of the workplace. The reception phase is a great deal like the initial contact a salesperson makes with a prospective customer. What kind of impression did the prospective employee in the cartoon get?

"We'll be happy to put you on file, Mr. Bannister, but we don't have anything for an underling at the moment."

All applicants are potential employees, as well as clients for the enterprise's services or products. Therefore, it is vital that those who greet and process applicants (in person or by phone) be well trained in communication techniques and interpersonal skills. They should enjoy meeting the public and helping people in stressful conditions, for job seeking can be a difficult experience for many applicants.

In smaller enterprises, multipurpose personnel people do the recruiting, along with their other duties, or operating managers may take time to recruit and interview applicants. Sometimes the enterprise puts together a recruiting committee of operating and personnel managers.

The role of recruiter is very important. The recruiter is usually the first person from the enterprise that an applicant away from the work site meets. Applicants' impressions about the enterprise are based to a large degree on their encounter with the recruiter. Effective recruiter behavior is described later in this chapter as an aspect of college recruiting.

SOURCES OF RECRUITS

Once the enterprise has decided it needs additional employees, it is faced with two recruiting decisions: where to search (sources), and how to notify applicants of the positions (methods). Two sources of applicants could be used: internal (present employees), and external (those not presently affiliated with the enterprise). Exhibit 5–6 lists many of the sources of recruits.

EXHIBIT 5–6
Sources for recruiting various types of employees

Sources	*Blue collar*	*Gray collar*	*White collar*	*Managerial, technical, professional*
Internal				
Job posting and bidding	X	X	X	
Friends of present employees	X	X	X	
Skills inventories	X	X	X	X
External				
Walk-ins, including previous employees	X	X	X	
Agencies				
Temporary help			X	
Private employment agencies			X	
Public employment agencies*	X	X	X	
Executive search firms				X
Educational institutions				
High school	X	X	X	
Vocational/technical	X	X	X	X
College and universities				X
Other				
Unions	X			
Professional associations				X
Military services	X			X
Former employees	X	X	X	X

* Normally called U.S. Employment Service.

Job posting and bidding

If the employee shortage is for higher level employees, and if the enterprise approves of promoting from within, it will use the skills inventories to search for candidates (see Chapter 4). But personnel managers may not be aware of all employees who want to be considered for promotion, so they use an approach called job posting and bidding. In the job-posting system, the enterprise notifies its present employees of openings, using bulletin boards, company publications, and so on. About 25 percent of white-collar firms surveyed used the system, as did most large Minnesota firms. Most firms found the system useful; for example, the Bank of Virginia filled 18 percent of its openings as a result of job posting.

Dahl and Pinto provide a useful set of guidelines for effective job-posting systems:

- Post all permanent promotion and transfer opportunities.
- Post the jobs for about one week prior to recruiting outside the enterprise.
- Clarify eligibility rules. For example, minimum service in the present position might be specified as six months. Seniority may be the decision rule used to choose between several equally qualified applicants.
- List job specifications. Application forms should be available.
- Inform all applicants what happens in the choice.

Inside moonlighting and employees' friends

If the labor shortage is short term or a great amount of additional work is not necessary, the organization can use inside moonlighting. It could offer to pay bonuses of various types to people not on a time payroll. Overtime procedures are already developed for those on time payrolls.

Before going outside to recruit, many enterprises ask present employees to encourage friends or relatives to apply. In his study of the job-search behavior of 1,500 men, Michael Ornstein found that 23 percent of white and 29 percent of black men found their first jobs through friends, and 31 percent of both whites and blacks found their jobs through help of the family. These are *first* jobs; there presently are no data on what percentage of applicants for later jobs use these sources. These data indicate how powerful this source of recruits could be for enterprises, should they use it wisely. Some equal employment opportunity programs prohibit using friends as a major recruiting source, however.

External sources

Exhibit 5–6 also indicates a number of external sources of recruits and which sources supply applicants for various types of jobs. When an enterprise has exhausted internal sources, these sources are used. Studies indicating when each external source is used are not extensive.

The most fruitful of the outside sources is walk-ins. Ornstein found that one third of his sample got their first jobs that way. Private employment agencies place some white-collar employees and serve as a source of recruits for many employers. Counselors in schools and teachers can also help, usually for managerial, professional, technical, and white-collar employees. The state employment security offices, partially using federal funds, have tried to serve more applicants and enterprise needs, but these agencies still provide primarily blue-collar, gray-collar, and only a few white-collar applicants. They try to tie into school counseling services, too. Still most studies, are very critical of the costs and benefits of the public agencies. They do not help employees or applicants as much as they should.

Thus, even though there appear to be many sources from which employees can be recruited, employees use only a few to recruit each type of employee.

Clark decided to use job posting as a method of attracting professional/technical and managerial employees at the Los Angeles office to the new plant in Houston. He also made the personal contacts Ed asked for in recruiting managerial employees, and the skills inventory was used to come up with more applicants. Clark contacted these also. He did not use job posting or the skills inventory for clerical, skilled, or semiskilled employees. He knew that for Gunther, as with most enterprises, these categories of employees rarely wish to move to another location. Most companies don't want to pay transfer costs for these categories of employment, either.

Clark went to Houston and set up the employment office at the new location. He ran an ad in Houston's afternoon paper and placed a job listing with a private employment agency for the personnel specialist and clerk-typist for his office. Then he hired these two employees and set up the office to receive walk-ins. He provided application blanks and policy guidelines on when selection would proceed.

Clark listed the available positions with the U.S. Employment Service. He also contacted private agencies. He selected the private agencies after calling a number of personnel managers in the Houston area in similar businesses and who were also ASPA members. The personnel specialist notified the high schools, vocational-technical schools, and colleges of the positions. The schools selected included all the vocational-technical schools, the junior colleges, and the colleges in the Houston area. Also, all high school guidance counseling departments were notified. Now Clark wonders what other media he ought to use to publicize the positions.

METHODS OF RECRUITING

A number of methods can be used to recruit external applicants; advertising, personal recruiting, computerized matching services, special-event recruiting, and summer internships are discussed here. There is also a separate section on college recruitment of potential managers and professionals.

To decide which method to use, the organization should know which are most likely to attract potential employees. Relatively few studies of the job-seeking helps used by applicants have been made, but Exhibit 5–7 suggests the most likely media for various categories of employees.

Media advertisements

Organizations advertise to acquire recruits. Various media are used, the most common of which are the daily newspaper help-wanted ads. Enterprises also advertise for people in trade and professional publications. Other media used are billboards, subway and bus cards, radio, telephone, and television. Some job-seekers do a reverse twist; they advertise for a situation wanted and reward anyone who tips them off about a job.

An example of an innovative recruiting ad is one used to staff Halls Crown

EXHIBIT 5–7
Methods of recruiting for various types of employees

Method	*Blue collar*	*Gray collar*	*White collar*	*Managerial, professional, technical*
Media advertisements				
Newspaper want ads	X	X	X	X
Professional journals and other media	X	X	X	X
Recruiters				X
Computer matching services				X
Special-event recruiting				X
Summer internships				X
Coop programs	Select highly skilled	Select highly skilled	Select highly skilled	

Shopping Center, in Kansas City, this full-page ad in the Sunday *Kansas City Star* is reproduced in the accompanying box. Note how the ad disassociates the center from seeking clerks and attempts to recruit persons whose interests are likely to affect performance.

THIS IS A WANT AD

What we want is a show of hands from you out there who would be interested in pursuing your personal pastimes . . . and getting paid for it.

For instance: are you a sports nut, a music buff, an antique collector, a candle-dipper, a Canoe Clubber, a shutterbug, a rock hound or a stargazer? If so, a very satisfying career awaits you on our Leisure-Lifestyle Level.

Or, do you have a personal passion for fabrics, jewels, furs, fine art, furniture, designer fashions? We think you could find happiness working on our Gracious-Lifestyle Level.

Or, are you a here-and-now type who loves the passing parade of things that are fun and topical, whether that means horoscopes or exciting new fashions? Then you'd never tire of your job on our New-Lifestyle Level.

Mind you, we're not looking for sales clerks. (If we were, we'd advertise in the Classified Section.) What we're seeking is people with a deep personal interest in all the exciting lifestyle concepts we'll be introducing at Halls Crown Center. The way we have it figured, nobody is better qualified to sell telescopes all day than the guy or gal who spends evenings stargazing. And nobody will be happier with the job.

Even if dealing with customers isn't your thing, come see us if you're interested in quality merchandising and all that goes with it. We need attendants, markers, receivers, packers, wrappers, handlers, finishers, fitters. In short, you can find an especially rewarding career at Halls Crown Center, whether or not you're interested in selling.

Make sense to you? Then come tell us your dream . . . and we'll show you ours.

Apply Now to Our Interviewing Office
Open 8:30 to 5:30, Monday through Friday

Another innovative way to attract prospective employees with particular skills is the use of recorded want ads. These were want ads used by 40 companies recruiting engineers and scientists at a New York City convention. At a special recruiting center, job hunters were able to pick up a telephone and hear a three-minute taped recruiting message which included job description and company contract details.

Help-wanted ads must be carefully prepared. Media must be chosen, coded for media study, and impact analyzed afterwards. If the enterprise's name is not used and a box number is substituted, the impact may not be as great, but if the name is used too many applicants may appear, and screening procedures for too many people can be costly. This is a difficult decision to make in preparing recruitment advertisements.

In addition, the ad must not violate EEO requirements by indicating preferences for a particular racial, religious, national origin, or sex group.

Use of recruiters

Some enterprises use recruiters or scouts who search the schools (as baseball scouts search the ball diamonds) for new talent. Recruiters can be ineffective as screeners of good applicants if they use stereotypes in screening or are more influenced by recent interviews than earlier ones. This will be made clearer in the discussion of college recruiters in this chapter and the problems of interviewing in Chapter 6.

Computer matching services

Systems similar to the computer dating services that flourished a few years ago have been developed to match people desiring jobs and organizations needing people. These amount to extraorganizational skills inventories, and they are a natural use of the computer. The U.S. Employment Service's Job Bank is attempting to fill the need for a nationwide job-matching network to reduce unemployment. In addition to this government service, there are several private-sector systems (GRAD, IRIS, PICS) and the Department of Labor's LINCS.

Little is known about these systems in practice, but they seem to have potential use for specifically qualified jobs. I doubt they will be effective at managerial levels, however.

Special-event recruiting

When the supply of employees available is not large or when the organization is new or not well known, some organizations have successfully used special events to attract potential employees. They may stage open houses, schedule headquarters visits, provide literature, and advertise these events in appropriate media. To attract professionals, organizations may have hospitality suites at professional meetings. Executives also make speeches at association meetings or schools to get the organization's image across. Ford Motor Company conducted symposia on college campuses and sponsored cultural events to attract attention to its qualifications as a good employer.

One of the most interesting approaches is to promote job fairs and native daughter and son days. A group of firms sponsors a meeting or exhibition at which each has a booth to publicize jobs available. Some experts claim recruiting costs have been cut 80 percent using these methods. They may be scheduled on holidays to reach college students home at that time or to give the presently employed a chance to look around. This technique is especially useful for smaller, less well-known employers. It appeals to job seekers who wish to locate in a particular area and those wanting to minimize travel and interview time.

Summer internships

Another approach to recruiting and getting specialized work done that has been tried by many organizations is to hire students during the summer as interns. This approach has been used by businesses (Sherwin-Williams Company, Chase Manhattan Bank, Standard Oil Company of Ohio, Kaiser Aluminum, First National City Bank), government agencies (City of New York), and hospitals. Students in accredited graduate hospital programs, for example, serve a summer period called a preceptorship. Pay is from $100 per week up.

There are a number of purposes for these programs. They allow organizations to get specific projects done, expose them to talented potential employees who may become their "recruiters" at school, and provide trial-run employment to determine if they want to hire particular people full time. *The Wall Street Journal* has reported that some firms are using this technique to help recruit women and blacks.

From the student's point of view, the summer internship means a job with pay, some experience in the world of work, a possible future job, and a chance to use one's talents in a realistic environment. In a way, it is a short form of some co-op college work and study programs.

The organization usually provides supervision and a choice of projects to be done. Some of the projects the City of New York's college interns worked on during one summer were snow emergency planning, complaint handling, attitude survey of lower level employees, and information dissemination.

There are costs to these programs, of course. Sometimes the interns take up a lot of supervisory time, and the work done is not always the best. But the major problem some organizations have encountered concerns the expectations of students. Some students expect everything to be perfect at work. When it is not, they get negative impressions about the organization they have worked for, assuming that it is more messed up than others in the field. Such disillusioned students become *reverse recruiters.* This effect has caused some organizations to drop the programs. Others have done so when they found they were not able to recruit many interns.

COLLEGE RECRUITING

Many of you reading this section will be interested in learning how to improve your chances at getting a job. This section looks at college recruiting from the point of view of the enterprise.

The college recruiting process is similar in some ways to other recruiting, but in college recruiting the enterprise sends an employee, usually called a recruiter, to a campus to interview candidates and describe the enterprise to them. Coinciding with the visit, brochures and other literature about the organization are often distributed. This literature is customarily expensively designed and produced, but much of it is poorly written and includes the wrong materials for recruiting purposes. An enterprise may also run ads to attract students or conduct seminars at which company executives talk about various facets of the organization.

In the typical procedure, those seeking employment register at the college placement service. This placement service is a labor market exchange providing opportunities for students and employers to meet and discuss potential hiring. During the recruiting season (from about mid-October to mid-March), candidates are advised through student newspapers, mailings, bulletin boards, and so forth of scheduled visits. At the placement service, they reserve preliminary interviews with employers they want to see and are given brochures and other literature about the firms. After the preliminary interviews and before leaving the campus, each recruiter invites the chosen candidates to make a site visit at a later date. Those lower on the list are told they are being considered and are called upon if students chosen first decide not to accept employment with the firm.

Students who are invited to the site are given more job information and meet appropriate potential supervisors and other executives. They are entertained and may be given a series of psychological tests as well. The organization bears all expenses. If the organization desires to hire an individual, he or she is given an offer prior to leaving the site or shortly thereafter by mail or phone. Some bargaining may take place on salary and benefits, depending on the current labor market. The candidate then decides whether to accept or reject the offer.

With which companies do the students sign up to interview? They choose those whose work sounds interesting and whose recruiting program is well done and which have a good image. Generally speaking, the more interviews a student has, the greater variety of job offers he or she will get, and often the offers are better as well.

Various persons influence the applicant in job choice: peers, family, wife/husband or companion, and professors. The main influence appears to be the recruiter. You can learn a lot about the job situation by knowing what goes on on the recruiter's side of the desk. Mary Kale, a recruiter for Bethlehem Steel, has a recruiting day like this:

Mary Kale is 28 and has been with Bethlehem for 7 years. She was a metallurgist for two years and has been a recruiter for five. In 1976, she recruited 26 of the 106 persons Bethlehem hired and has a high acceptance rate among her recruits. She is one of the 3,500 full-time recruiters in the United States today.

Two recent weeks are typical of her work life. One week she interviewed for five days at Cornell; she had to drive three hours through a snow squall to get there. The next week, she flew and drove on Sunday to Grove City to interview there Monday. She drove to Youngstown, Ohio, and interviewed there Tuesday, then drove back to Pittsburgh. Wednesday and Thursday she interviewed at Carnegie Mellon and other Pittsburgh schools. Friday was spent in a hotel interviewing.

What's her day like? She eats an early breakfast and begins interviewing at 9 A.M. She interviews candidates for 30 minutes each, takes a 30-minute walk instead of lunch, and resumes interviews until 5:30 P.M. In brief opens periods she tries to line up other candidates, but typically she interviews 54 people a week. After a quick supper, she spends the evening in her hotel room writing reports on the day's recruits, calling recruit prospects for later interviews, and reading the resumés of the next day's prospects.

In each interview, she begins by putting the recruit at ease, then asks the recruit about himself or herself. Next she discusses the job requirements and what the company has to offer, and asks for questions. She sees herself as much as a job counselor as recruiter. She wants to help recruits find a direction for their lives, and also to acquire the best employees for Bethlehem.

So if, when you are interviewed, you suspect the recruiter is tired, usually he or she is. Recruiters do not want prospects to have a stressful experience; rather they see a mutually satisfactory interview as a first step in your organizational choice. The college recruiting process is modeled in Exhibit 5–8. As you

EXHIBIT 5–8
The college recruiting process

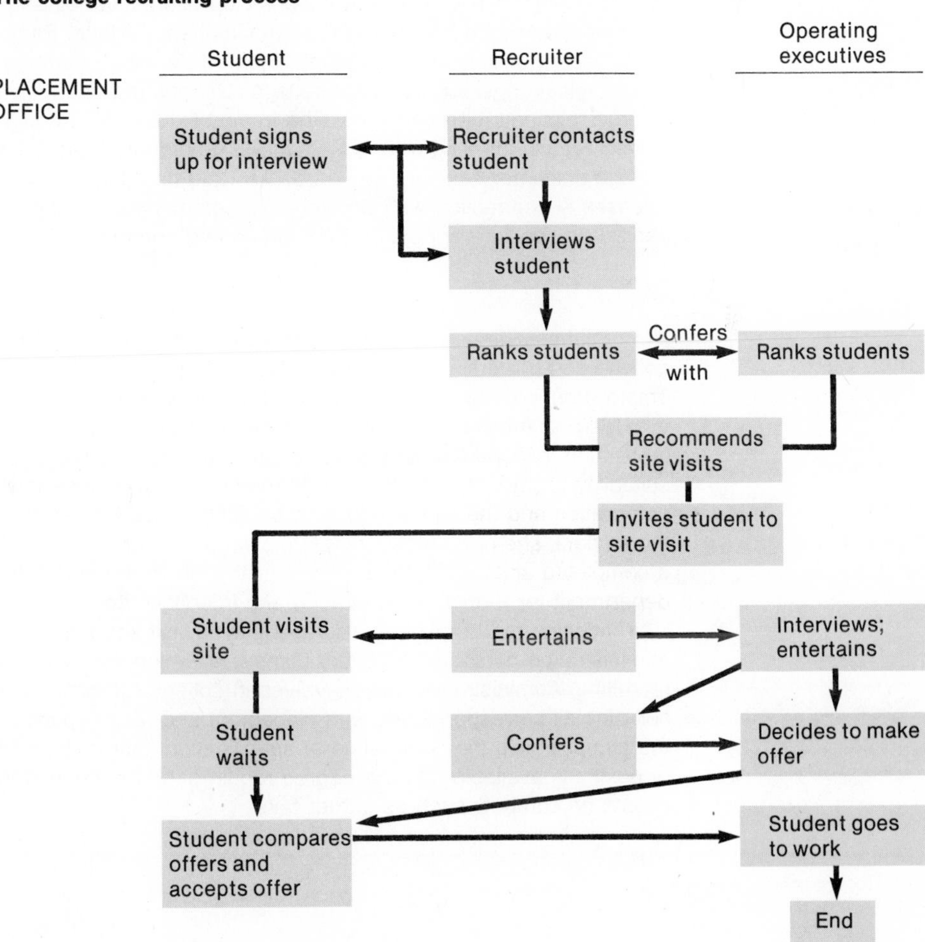

Mary E. Kale
Bethlehem Steel
Corporation

Biography

Mary E. Kale, Senior College Relations Representative for Bethlehem Steel Company, earned a BS in chemistry at Chatham College, Pittsburgh. Before her present position with Bethlehem Steel, Kale was a management trainee, metallurgical engineer, assistant college relations representative, and college relations representative. She travels extensively throughout the United States, meeting with industrial and government leaders as well as college placement officers and students. Kale has done videotaped news releases in connection with Bethlehem's communication effort and has served on specially appointed task forces and committees.

Job description

At Bethlehem Steel Corporation, a recruiter's job consists primarily of visiting college and university campuses to interview graduating seniors for employment with the corporation. During the interview, the recruiter's objective is to learn as much as possible about the candidate's academic qualifications, motivation, experience, and goals, in order to evaluate her or his overall suitability for the jobs available. This requires an in-depth knowledge of the corporation and the types of jobs to be filled. Once the recruiter evaluates the student, she or he must complete a written record of the interview, obtain a completed application form, and refer the file to the appropriate corporate department for further consideration and interview if desired.

In addition to interviewing, representatives visit key faculty and administration personnel on every campus at which the corporation conducts recruiting. Administrative tasks involved in college relations work include handling all correspondence with placement and faculty people concerning the campus visit, the completion of specification sheets describing the types of positions available and the degree required, and coordination of special events on campus, such as career fairs.

can see, effective recruiting requires efforts of both personnel and operating executives.

The effective college recruiter

In college recruiting, generally three elements are involved: the organization, the applicant, and the intervening variable—the recruiter. The recruiter is the filter and the matcher, the one who is actually seen by the applicants and is studied as a representative of the company. The recruiter is not just an employee but is viewed as an example of the kind of person the organization employs and wants in the future.

Students tend to prefer recruiters who are under age 55, with the strongest preference being 35–55 and 25–35 the next highest preference. They also like it if the recruiter has had work experience in their specialities and has some personal knowledge of the university they are visiting. Students also have preferences for specific behavior during the recruiting interview. Characteristics in the recruiter they want most are friendliness, knowledge, personal interest in the applicant, and truthfulness. Secondarily, some applicants (usually average students) prefer enthusiastic and convincing communicators.

Major flaws students have found in typical recruiters are:

Lack of interest in the applicant. They infer this if the recruiter's presentation is mechanical—bureaucratic—programmed. One student reported, "The company might just as well have sent a tape recorder."

Lack of enthusiasm. If the recruiter seems bored, students infer that he or she represents a dull and uninteresting company.

Stress or too-personal interviews. Students resent too many personal questions about their social class, their parents, and so forth. They want to be evaluated for their own accomplishments. They also unanimously reject stress or sarcastic interviewing styles.

Time allocation by recruiters. The final criticism of recruiters has to do with how much time they talk and how much they let applicants talk or ask questions. From the point of view of the applicant, much of the recruiter's time is wasted with a long canned history of the company, number of employees, branches, products, assets, pension plans, and so forth. Many of the questions the recruiter asks applicants are answered on the application blank, anyway.

These findings reemphasize the need for an enterprise engaged in college recruiting to train effective recruiters and to have a well-planned visitation schedule. Too many enterprises do not plan the recruiting interview as well as they do their product sales presentations. The recruiter normally has 30 minutes per interview; he should use them well. The applicant should receive printed material describing the less interesting aspects of information (such as organization history and details of organization operations). The interview period should be divided about equally between the recruiter and the applicant. Students want to hear about the job itself, the work climate, and the kind of person the organization is trying to hire for the job. Then they would like to be able to discuss how they might fit in and to ask a few questions. Too often, the recruiter talks for 25 minutes and almost as an afterthought asks if there are any questions.

It is also important for recruiters to provide realistic expectations of the job. When they do so, there is significantly lower turnover of new employees, and the same number of people apply. Researchers have found that most recruiters give general, glowing descriptions of the company rather than balanced or truthful presentations.

Companies that wish to influence applicants should also review their recruiting literature to make sure it appeals to the most successful students. This literature, plus advertisements and articles in trade publications, is the main nonhuman influence on the organization-choice decision.

COST/BENEFIT ANALYSIS OF RECRUITING

Many aspects of recruitment, such as the effectiveness of recruiters, can be evaluated. Enterprises assign goals to recruiting by types of employees. For example, a goal for a recruiter might be to hire 350 unskilled and semiskilled employees, or 100 technicians, or 100 managerial employees per year. Then the organization can decide who are the best recruiters. They may be those who meet or exceed quotas and those whose recruits stay with the organization and are evaluated well by their superiors.

Sources of recruits also can be evaluated. In college recruiting, the organization can divide the number of job acceptances by the number of campus interviews to compute the cost per hire at each college. Then it drops from the list campuses that are not productive.

The methods of recruiting can be evaluated by various means. Exhibit 5–9 compares the results of a number of these methods. The enterprise can calculate the cost of each method (such as advertising) and divide it by the benefits it yields (acceptances of offers). After the interviews the enterprise can also examine how much accurate job information was provided during the recruitment process.

EXHIBIT 5–9
Yields of recruiting methods by various calculations

Source of recruit	*Yield*	*Total yield (percent)*	*Ratio of acceptance to receipt of resumé*	*Ratio of acceptance to offer*
Write-ins	2,127	34.77%	6.40	58.37
Advertising	1,979	32.35	1.16	38.98
Agencies	856	14.00	1.99	32.07
Direct college placement	465	7.60	1.50	13.21
Internal company	447	7.30	10.07	65.22
Walk-ins	134	2.19	5.97	57.14
Employee referrals	109	1.78	8.26	81.82

Source: Roger Hawk, *The Recruitment Function* (New York: AMACOM, a division of American Management Associations, 1967. All rights reserved.

SUMMARY, CONCLUSIONS, AND RECOMMENDATIONS

This chapter has demonstrated the process whereby enterprises recruit additional employees, suggested the importance of recruiting, and shown who recruits, where, and how. To summarize, the following points are repeated:

1. Recruiting is the set of activities an enterprise uses to attract job candidates who have the abilities and attitudes needed to help the enterprise achieve its objectives.

2. External factors which affect the recruiting process include influences such as government and union restrictions and the state of the labor market.
3. Three aspects affect recruiting from the organization's viewpoint: the recruiting requirements set, organization policies and procedures, and the organizational image.
4. Applicants' abilities, attitudes, and preferences, based on past work experiences and influences by parents, teachers, and others, affect them in two ways: how they set job preferences, and how they go about seeking a job.
5. In larger enterprises the personnel department does the recruiting; in smaller enterprises, multipurpose personnel people or operating managers recruit and interview applicants.
6. Two sources of recruits could be used to fill needs for additional employees: present employees (internal) or those not presently affiliated with the enterprise (external).
   a. Internal sources can be tapped through the use of job posting and bidding; moonlighting by present employees; and seeking recommendations from present employees regarding friends who might fill these vacancies.
   b. External sources include walk-ins, referrals from schools, and state employment offices.
7. Advertising, personal recruiting, computerized matching services, special-event recruiting, and summer internships are methods which can be used to recruit external applicants.
8. The criteria which characterize a successful college recruiter are:
   a. Age is between 35 and 55.
   b. Shows a genuine interest in the applicant.
   c. Is enthusiastic.
   d. Is neither too personal nor too stressful in approach.
   e. Allots enough time for applicant's comments and questions.
9. A better job of recruiting and matching employees to job will mean lower employee turnover and greater employee satisfaction and organizational effectiveness.
10. In larger organizations, recruiting functions are more extensively planned and evaluated.

Likely approaches used by the seven model organizations specified in Exhibit 1–7 (Chapter 1) are summarized in Exhibit 5–10. It should be noted that several of the model organizations employ different categories of employees. For example, a small, violatile hospital and a small, volatile toy company employ different kinds of employees, and the sources of recruits used would vary in such organizations. Only a few of the aspects of recruitment have been summarized in this table.

In addition, a series of propositions about recruiting can serve as suggestions for effective recruiting.

Proposition 5.1. The lower the unemployment in the relevant sector of the labor market, the more likely effective organizations are to use formal recruiting methods and multiple sources.

Proposition 5.2. The less known the organization is to relevant applicants, the harder it must work to recruit in times of lower unemployment.

EXHIBIT 5–10

Recommendation on recruiting practices for model organizations

	Employment conditions affect recruiting		*Importance of image*		*Methods of recruiting*							
Type of organization	*Greatly*	*Little*	*Crucial*	*Not too important*	*Employ-ment agencies*	*News-paper ads*	*Radio com-mercials*	*Present employees*	*Computer matching*	*Special events*	*College recruiting*	*Summer intern ships*
1. Large size, low complexity, high stability	X			X	X	X			X		X	X
2. Medium size, low complexity, high stability		X		X	X	X		X	X		X	
3. Small size, low complexity, high stability	X		X		X	X	X	X		X		
4. Medium size, moderate com-plexity, moderate stability		X	X		X	X	X	X	X	X	X	
5. Large size, high complexity, low stability		X		X	X	X			X		X	X
6. Medium size, high complexity, low stability		X	X		X	X	X	X		X	X	
7. Small size, high complexity, low stability	X		X		X	X	X	X		X		X

Proposition 5.3. The worse the job or organizational image, the harder the organization must work to recruit added employees.

Proposition 5.4. The higher the level of the job, the larger the geographic area from which the organization must recruit.

Proposition 5.5. The worse the job or organizational image and the lower the unemployment, the harder the organization must work to recruit and the more of its preferences it must relax or the more it must improve the employment conditions offered.

Harder work at recruiting means the use of more sources of supply, more media, and larger expenditures for each medium. If times are bad (high unemployment), the reverse of Propositions 5.3 and 5.5 will be true. Chapter 16 describes recruiting methods most appropriate for disadvantaged employees, in response to EEO pressures. Effective selection and hiring of employees is the subject of Chapter 6.

Clark Kirby got prices of ads from all the Houston papers, including suburban papers and ethnic papers. He also discussed the impact and readership of the papers with the personnel managers he'd befriended. On this basis, he chose the major Houston afternoon paper, the leading black newspaper, the leading Hispanic paper, and a suburban paper in an area near the plant.

He also investigated the leading radio stations and selected the one that had the highest rating of the top three and the lowest commercial cost. He chose commuter times to run the radio ads. The advertising approach was innovative.

The pay and working conditions offered at the Houston plant were competitive. After Clark's recruiting campaign, he had the following numbers of applicants:

Managerial positions	68
Professional/technical	10
Clerical	78
Skilled employees	110
Semiskilled employees	720

Clark notified Ed of the results. The next job is to select the best of the applicants for hiring. Clark knows that is no easy job. Effective selection/hiring is the subject of Chapter 6.

QUESTIONS

1. What is recruiting? Job search?
2. How does recruiting relate to other personnel activities?
3. Give some dos and don'ts in recruiting interviews as far as legality is concerned.
4. Describe a model of the recruiting/attraction process. How do enterprise requirements, organizational policies, and organizational pay affect the process?
5. How do career planning and job preferences relate to effective job finding? Outline an approach to specify the job characteristics you want prior to job search.
6. Describe how you plan to get your job when you leave college.
7. Who is responsible for recruiting?
8. What sources of recruits do enterprises use for blue-collar, white-collar, and managerial recruits?
9. Compare and contrast the effectiveness of the methods of recruiting, such as advertising, special events, internships, and others.
10. How do enterprises recruit college students for jobs? What are effective and ineffective recruiters like?

6

Selection of personnel

Chapter objectives

- To help you understand the factors affecting the selection decision.
- To demonstrate what selection criteria are available and how they can be used to make selection more effective.
- To help you understand the selection process and how to use selection tools such as interviews and biodata more effectively.

Chapter outline

Case continued from Chapter 5

Clark

Clark Kirby is satisfied. He and his assistants have recruited 986 applicants for the 596 positions Gunther will have at its Houston plant. But before he gets too satisfied, he realizes that there is a big job ahead of him. Which 596 of the 986 should be hired? And who should do the hiring?

The personnel specialist has done some preliminary screening. Most of the applicants have completed an application blank. But where does he go from here?

Clark has called Ed Humprey, the plant manager, and asked if he wished to be involved in the hiring. Ed said that he only had time to choose his top management team. The rest is up to Clark. Clark reminded Ed that the company didn't want them to hire too many present employees; raiding this would be another Gunther plant. Ed said he knew that and would abide by company policy.

As Clark begins to plan how to make 596 decisions.

Selection is the process by which an enterprise chooses from a list of applicants the person or persons who best meet the selection criteria for the position available, considering current environmental conditions.

This definition emphasizes the effectiveness aspect of selection, but selection decisions must also be efficient. The second purpose of selection is to improve the proportion of successful employees chosen from the applicant list at the least cost. Selection costs can be high. In 1975, it was estimated that it cost enterprises $4,000 to select a top-level executive, $1,500 to select a middle manager, $1,000 for a supervisor, $1,925 for an engineer, $2,250 for an accountant, and $1,800 for a secretary.

The basic objective of selection is to obtain the employees most likely to meet the enterprise's standards of performance. The employees' satisfaction and complete development of their abilities are included in this objective.

A DIAGNOSTIC APPROACH TO THE SELECTION PROCESS

When Clark Kirby sets out to hire 596 employees, the selection process is influenced by many factors. These factors are highlighted in the diagnostic model in Exhibit 6–1. We'll begin by examining the factors in Zone II.

Environmental circumstances influencing selection

The environment of the organization. The nature of the organization doing the selecting affects the process it uses. The private and third sectors use similar methods, but the public sector is different. Traditionally, in the public sector selection has been made on the basis of either political patronage or merit. The patronage system rewards those who have worked to elect public officials with jobs. This was the only method used in the public sector until the civil service reforms of the late 1800s. Patronage is still practiced today. In the private

EXHIBIT 6–1
Factors affecting selection of personnel and organizational effectiveness

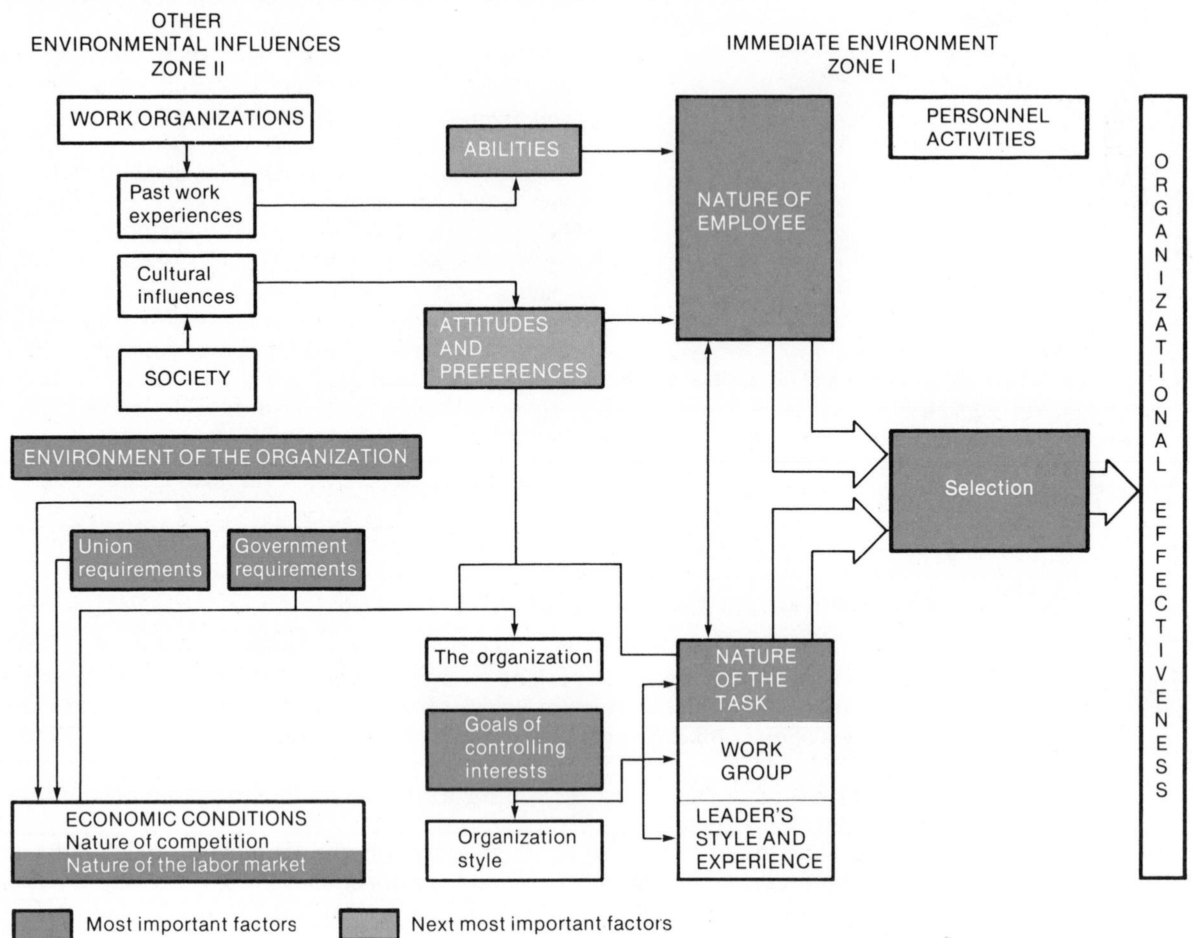

and third sectors friendship with managers or employees can become a factor in the choice, but this is not the same thing as patronage. Pure "merit" selection (choice based on the employee's excellence in abilities and experience) is an idea which systematic personnel selection tries to achieve but seldom does.

Other aspects of the enterprise affecting selection are its size, complexity, and technological volatility. Systematic, reliable, and valid personnel selection techniques are sometimes costly to develop and use. When this is so, only large enterprises can afford to use them. To justify the development of these techniques, there must be stability in the technology and thus the jobs. If the enterprise is complex and has a large number of jobs with only a few occupants, sophisticated techniques to select these jobholders are not cost effective. The extent to which size dictates how many employees there are in each work group also affects the usefulness of the techniques. (Specific recommendations about these factors will be given in the propositions at the end of the chapter.) In sum, the size, complexity, technological volatility, and nature of the enterprise will influence the selection techniques that are cost effective for the enterprise.

Nature of the labor market. The second circumstance affecting the selection decision is the labor market with which the enterprise must deal. If there are many applicants, the selection decision can be complicated. If there is only one applicant, it is relatively easy. The labor market for the enterprise is affected by the labor market in the country as a whole, the region, or the city in which the enterprise is located. It is further affected by the working conditions the organization offers, the job itself, and the organization's image. (These were discussed earlier in the book and will be covered in Chapters 11–14, on compensation and benefits.) For example hospital dieticians trying to hire dishwashers or food preparation helpers do not have much of a selection decision to worry about. The job can be unpleasant, and it is performed at unpopular hours (the breakfast crew might have to arrive at 5:30 A.M.). The work day can be long, the pay is not good, and frequently there are no possibilities for promotion. For such jobs, an applicant who can walk in the door and is found to be free of communicable disease will usually be hired. Rarely are there enough applicants. A civil service specialist who must choose from hundreds of applicants for foreign service postings to European embassies has a much more difficult selection decision to make.

Those who work in personnel analyze this labor market factor by use of the selection ratio:

$$\text{Selection ratio} = \frac{\text{Number of applicants selected}}{\text{Number of applicants available for selection}}$$

Consider Clark Kirby's problem at Gunther. The selection ratios are: managers 38/68, or about 1:2, professional/technical, 10/10, or 1:1; clerical, 44/78, or about 1:2; skilled, 104/110, or about 1:1; semiskilled, 400/720, or almost 1:2. When the selection ratio is 1:1, the selection process is short and unsophisticated. If the selection ratio is 1:2, the process can be quite detailed, as described below. The larger ratio also means the enterprise can be quite selective in its choice. It is more likely that employees who fit the organization's criteria for success will be hired when the ratio is 1:2 than when it is 1:1.

Union requirements. If the enterprise is unionized or partly so, union membership prior to hiring or shortly thereafter is a factor in the selection decision. Sometimes the union contract requires that seniority (experience at the job with the company) be the only criterion, or a major one, in selection. If the union has a hiring hall, the union makes the selection decision for the organization. In many ways, openly and subtly, a union can affect an enterprise's selection process.

Government requirements. The fourth circumstance affecting selection is government. In the United States, governments have passed laws designed to guarantee equal employment opportunity and human rights. These requirements are described in detail in Chapter 16, but we will briefly summarize their impact on selection decisions.

Many state governments prohibit employers from asking prospective employees questions about race, sex, national origin, and the like. Even indirect questions are sometimes prohibited. For example, several states restrict questions having to do with marital and family status, even though they are asked of everybody, because some employers have used such questions to reject women on the basis of their domestic situations. Another troublesome area is credit: the logic is that various minority groups are more likely to have encountered credit problems, so such questions tend to have an adverse impact on members of those groups.

In the United States, the federal government also regulates selection practices. Generally, the important question is whether a practice is likely to have an adverse impact on a prospect because of her or his age, race, sex, religion, or national origin. Members of racial and ethnic groups are less likely to meet educational requirements or to score high on certain standardized ability and aptitude tests. Women are generally less likely to pass weight-lifting tests, and women, Asian Americans, and Hispanic Americans are less likely to meet minimum height requirements.

If selection procedures have unequal impact on prospective employees, they must conform to U.S. regulations such as the Guidelines for Employee Selection Procedures issued by the U.S. Equal Employment Opportunity Commission (EEOC). These guidelines must be followed by virtually all employers with 15 or more employees. Recently a second set of guidelines (known as the Federal Executive Agency Guidelines) was jointly issued by three other agencies. These are applicable to most employers who have federal contracts or receive federal funds (who must also follow the first set of guidelines issued by EEOC). For the most part these guidelines are quite similar, but there are some differences, and the EEOC guidelines are generally more demanding.

Much has been said about how stringent, complex, and unreasonable the federal selection guidelines are. While there is some truth in those complaints, the selection guidelines call for little more than adequate development and validation of selection procedures—the same sort of procedures that have been called for by industrial psychologists for decades.

The immediate environment and selection

You will note that in Zone I of Exhibit 6–1, the goals of controlling interests in the organization, the nature of the employee, and the nature of the task are highlighted. The basic objective of selection—to obtain high-performing employees—may be modified by the operating managers or controlling interests. It is management's responsibility to set selection objectives, such as:

- Employees who will stay with the company many years.
- Employees who have low accident rates.
- Employees who have high quality standards.
- Employees who get along with their co-workers.
- Employees who get along with our customers.

These characteristics can influence the kind of employees selected. They do not always correlate exactly with highest quantitative performance.

Selection seeks to identify the abilities and attitudes of the applicant so that these can be matched up with job requirements. In Chapter 2, we discussed how human beings differ on every possible characteristic: physical, mental, and psychological.

Selection also seeks to identify the nature of the task. From job analysis (described in Chapter 4), job specifications which are up to date and related to behavior are developed. The job specifications are used to define the characteristics (criteria) needed for a person to perform a certain task effectively. The essence of selection is to match the right applicant, who has the right abilities and attitudes, with the right job and its specifications.

One more factor, not shown in Exhibit 6–1, influences the selection decision. This concerns how much time is available to make the selection decision. If there is adequate time, the enterprise may be able to use all the selection tools it normally uses. If there is an emergency, the selection decision may be shortened by dropping one or several of the steps in the selection process.

The selection activity is in Stage IV of development or maturity (see Exhibit 1–6, Chapter 1). It is well developed, and many studies have analyzed the use of the various selection methods.

WHO MAKES SELECTION DECISIONS?

In smaller enterprises with no personnel unit, the operating manager makes selection decisions. In medium-sized and larger enterprises, both operating and personnel managers are involved in selection decisions, as Exhibit 6–2 indicates.

In larger enterprises, the personnel manager in charge of selection is called the employment manager. An example is Audrey Johnson, employee relations manager of the Gillette Company.

Some enterprises also give co-workers a voice in the selection choice. Applicants are interviewed by their co-workers and asked to express their preferences. This procedure is used in university departments where the faculty expresses its preferences on applicants, and at the Lincoln Electric Company in Cleveland, in which the work group recruits and selects replacements or additions.

Generally, more effective selection decisions are made when many people

EXHIBIT 6–2
The role of operating and personnel managers in selection

Selection function	*Operating manager (OM)*	*Personnel manager (PM)*
Choice of selection criteria	Selected by OM	Recommends and implements for selection criteria based on job specifications
Validation of criteria		Performed by PM
Screening interview		Normally performed by personnel
Supervision of application/biodata form		Normally by PM
Employment interview	OM and PM	OM and PM
Testing		Performed by personnel
Background/reference chart		Normally performed by personnel
Physical exam		Normally performed by personnel
Selection/decision	OM decides after considering PM's recommendation	Recommendation by PM to OM

Audrey Johnson
The Gillette Company

Biography

Audrey Johnson, a graduate of the University of Minnesota with an MBA in industrial relations, holds the title of Employee Relations Manager for the Gillette Company, St. Paul, Minnesota. She holds a BA from St. Olaf College and is a graduate of the Harvard-Radcliffe Program in Business Administration. Johnson has had broad personnel experience. Before joining Gillette she worked as a personnel representative at the University of Minnesota. Some of her achievements in her current position include:

Developed and instituted a comprehensive affirmative action plan which successfully stood a federal audit.

Streamlined and systematized employment practices and procedures to ensure their legality and efficiency.

Instituted compensation program with guidelines and controls to ensure uniform and equitable treatment for all employees.

Managed significant benefits changes, including installing a new dental insurance program and offering an HMO option.

Assessed training and development needs for all exempt employees.

Job description

The position of Employee Relations Manager for all personnel administrative functions in the manufacturing center of the Gillette Company, one of the nation's largest personal care manufacturers, involves responsibility for employment, affirmative action, compensation, manpower development and training, benefits, and employee services, along with a complete budget responsibility of $300,000. The employee relations manager also supervises a full-time staff of seven subordinates.

are involved in the decision and when adequate information is furnished to those selecting the candidates. The operating manager and the work group should have more to say about the selection decision than the personnel specialist.

SELECTION CRITERIA

If a selection program is to be successful, the employee characteristics which are believed necessary for effective performance on the job should be stated explicitly in the job specification. The criteria usually can be summarized in several categories: education, experience, physical characteristics, and personal characteristics. Basically, the selection criteria should list the characteristics of present employees who have performed well in the position to be filled. As in personnel and employment planning, however, if the list of characteristics desired is too long, it may not be possible to select anyone. And with no list of criteria, the wrong prospects are likely to be selected. Sometimes, because of limits on what the enterprise can offer or management's objectives, one gets criteria like those in the cartoon.

"What we're really looking for is a not-too-bright young man with no ambition and who is content to stay on the bottom and not louse things up."

Reprinted by permission The Wall Street Journal.

Formal education

An employer selecting among applicants for a job wants to find the person who has the right abilities and attitudes to be successful in the job. These cognitive, motor, physical, and interpersonal attributes are present because of genetic predisposition and because they were learned in the home, at school, on the job, and so on. Most employers attempt to screen for abilities by specifying educational accomplishments. They may seek to achieve their preferences for attitudes similarly.

Employers tend to specify as a criterion the completion of certain amounts of formal education and types of education. For the job of accountant, the employer may list as an educational criterion a bachelor's degree in accounting. The employer may prefer that the degree is from certain institutions, that the grade-point average is higher than some minimum, and that certain honors have been achieved. To be legal, such criteria must relate to past performance of successful accountants at the firm.

Formal education can indicate ability or skills present, and level of accomplishment may indicate the degree of work motivation and intelligence of the applicant. In general, other things being equal, employers tend to prefer more to less education, higher to lower grades, and graduates of more to lesser prestigious schools. But these characteristics must be correlated with job success if the criterion is to be an effective predictor. For example, a group of studies found that two-year nursing programs produce more of the kind of nurses many hospital administrators prefer than four-year programs do. Insurance companies have found the most effective insurance salespersons come from lower prestige schools.

Thus the educational criteria must be validated against job performance. The employer must examine the amount and type of education that correlates with job effectiveness at the enterprise and use it as the selection criterion. This is more effective than relying on preferences, and it is the legal and ethical way to set an educational criterion.

Experience

A second criterion for selection is experience. In general, employers prefer relatively more experience to less, relevant to less relevant experience, and significant to insignificant experience. An employer known to be demanding of its employees would probably choose an applicant who has been successful in the same or a similar job. They equate experience with ability as well as with attitude, reasoning that a prospect who has performed the job before and is applying for a similar job likes the work and will do it well. Since loyalty to the job and the organization are significant, most employers prefer to hire from within, as discussed in Chapter 5.

One way to measure experience within the enterprise is to provide each employee with a seniority rating, which indicates the length of time an employee has been employed. In the military, the date of rank is an equivalent seniority measure. Seniority is measured in various ways: as total time worked for the firm or time worked for the firm on a particular job or in a certain unit. Because some enterprises in the past did not allow certain groups to hold certain jobs, the courts and the EEOC are assigning retroactive and compensatory seniority to some employees.

Physical characteristics

In the past, many employers consciously or unconsciously used physical characteristics (including how an applicant looked) as a selection criterion. Many times this discriminated against ethnic groups and females. The practice is now illegal unless it can be shown that a physical characteristic is directly related to work effectiveness. Studies show that employers were more likely to hire and pay more to taller men, airlines chose stewardesses on the basis of beauty (or their definition of it), and receptionists were often chosen on the same basis. I found one employer who used an "elbow test" as his method of hiring secretaries: He mentally calculated whether, if the woman clasped her hands behind her head, her elbows or her breasts would protrude further. Only those where the elbows lost out were hired, which was hardly relevant to competence for secretarial tasks.

There are some tasks which require certain physical characteristics, usually stamina and strength, which can be tested. Candidates cannot legally be screened out by arbitrary height, weight, and similar requirements. The enterprise should determine the physical characteristics of present successful employees and use an attribute as a criterion *only* when all or most of them have it.

Personal characteristics and personality type

The final criterion category is a catchall called personal characteristics and personality types. One personal characteristic is marital status. Some employers have preferred "stable" married employees, assuming this would lead to lower turnover and higher performance. In 1978, *The Wall Street Journal* pointed out that today this may be reversed. Some firms prefer divorced or single persons because they are more willing to be transferred, to work weekends, and so on. Discrimination in selection based on marital status is illegal in some places, and unless an organization has data to support the relation of this criterion to performance, it makes little sense.

A second personal characteristic is age. It is illegal to discriminate against persons over 40 in the United States, It is not illegal to discriminate against young people, although protecting this group also has been proposed. Any age criterion should be examined by seeing how it relates to present successful employees.

Employers may prefer certain "personality" types for jobs. For example, to use Carl Jung's classification, they may prefer extroverts to introverts. This can be an important characteristic for employees who deal with the public, such as receptionists, salespersons, and caseworkers, but it may not be useful for other jobs, such as actuaries, lab technicians, or keypunch operators. The personality type specified should be based on past experience or be weighted lower than other, more directly relevant criteria.

Whom you know

An informal selection process runs parallel to the formal selection process being described here. For many selection decisions, the formal criteria must be met, but who is selected for the job depends on whom the applicant knows. If the applicant has connections and can get introduced to those doing the hiring, this can have greater impact than somewhat better test socres or references. This informal selection factor is very important in getting hired, as was noted in Chapter 5.

It should be remembered that the selection decision is affected by environmental circumstances and the criteria by which prospective employees for specific tasks are judged. A systematic selection decision is dependent on valid and reliable selection criteria.

Validity and reliability of selection criteria

Before the organization can specify the characteristics to be sought in selection, the success criteria must be defined. Job analysis can indicate that the employee who meets minimum standards for a particular position processes ten claims per hour, for example. This employee also receives an error rating of less than 5 percent and is absent less than six days per year.

The next step is to determine ways of predicting which of the applicants can reach these levels of expectation. Sometimes direct success indicators (such as 10 claims per hour) are available. Other times proxies such as levels of intelligence, the presence of specified abilities, or certain amounts and types of experience are used.

These predictors of success, particularly the more formal mechanisms such as items on a paper-and-pencil test, have two characteristics: reliability and validity. The *reliability* of a selction instrument such as a test is the extent to which the instrument is a *consistent* measure of something. An intelligence test is said to be reliable if the same person's scores do not vary greatly when the test is taken several times. The higher the reliability, the more confidence can be placed in the measurement method. Usually, the instrument is more reliable if it is longer. The instrument used must also be internally consistent to be considered reliable.

Validity in a personnel measurement instrument is the extent to which it is a good predictor of success for the job performance in question. Laurence Siegel contrasts reliability and validity in this way. He points out that the yardstick is a *reliable* measure of space; no matter how many times you carefully measure a basketball player, he will be the same number of feet and inches. But a yardstick has no *validity* as a measure of muscular coordination. Thus a selection device such as a test may be reliable without being valid.

Personnel specialists can compute the validity of a selection instrument several ways. One is to look at presently successful employees, find a factor that is common to them, and designate it as a predictor. This is called *concurrent validity.* A second way is to use an instrument such as a test during the hiring process, then wait until the successful employees are identified and correlate the test or test measures with the successful and unsuccessful employees. This is called *predictive validity.* A third method sometimes used by smaller organizations, because the numbers of persons in similar jobs is too small to use concurrent or predictive methods, is called *synthetic validity.* In this case, elements of several jobs that are similar, rather than a whole job, are used to validate the selection instrument. This method is newer than the other two and is used less frequently.

It should be noted that the criterion used to predict performance or success is a proxy for actual performance. Since good job performance is usually a combination of many things (quality of work, quantity of work, etc.), a criterion such as a supervisor's rating is a proxy for the real measure: job success or performance.

THE SELECTION PROCESS

All organizations make selection decisions, and most make them at least in part informally. The smaller the organization, the more likely it is to take an informal approach to selection decisions. Formal or systematic selection decisions were developed first during World Wars I and II, when employee shortages brought tremendous placement problems and the military had to select and place large numbers of men in many different jobs very quickly and efficiently.

Selection is often thought to be an easy decision. The boss interviews applicants, sizes them up, and lets his or her gut reaction guide the choice. The boss likes one man or woman for the job, and that's it. Selection tools are designed to aid this gut reaction. For most selection decisions, that is all the tools are intended to do; they are designed to increase the proportion of successful employees selected.

The selection decision usually is perceived as a series of steps through which applicants pass. At each step, a few more applicants are screened out by the enterprise, or more applicants accept other job offers and drop from the applicant

EXHIBIT 6–3
Typical selection decision when all possible steps are used (private and third sectors)

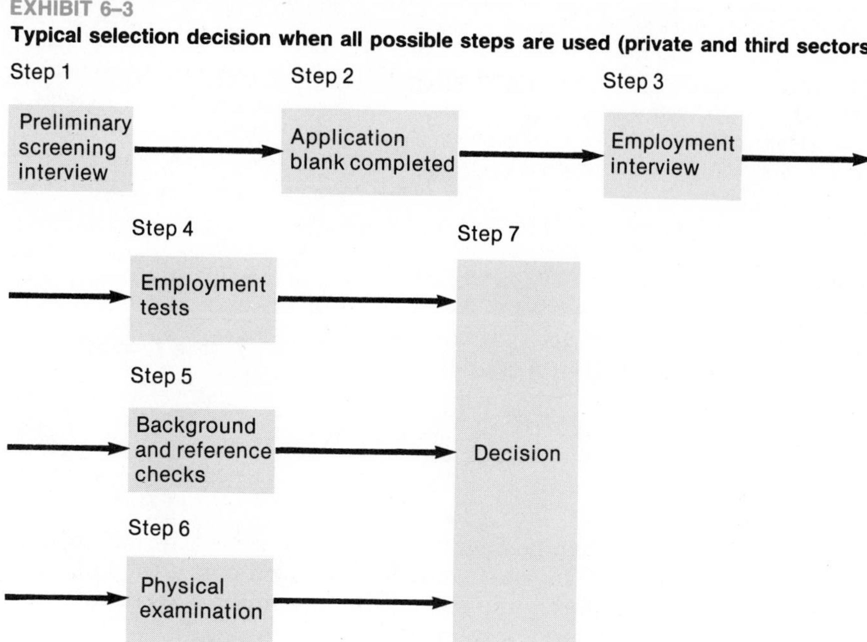

list. Exhibit 6–3 illustrates a typical series of steps for the selection process.

This series is not universally used; for example, government employers test at Step 3 instead of Step 4, as do some private- and third-sector employers. Few organizations use all steps, for they can be time-consuming and expensive, and several steps, such as 4, 5, and 6, may be performed concurrently or at about the same time. Generally speaking, the more important the job, the more each step is likely to be used formally. Almost all employers in the United States use the screening interview, application blank, and interview. Tests are used by a relatively small (and declining) number of employers. Background and reference checks and physical exams are used for some jobs and not others.

Step 1: Preliminary screening interview

Different enterprises can handle Step 1 in various ways, ineffectively or effectively. For some types of jobs, applicants are likely to walk into the employment office or job location. In these cases, a personnel specialist or line manager usually spends a few moments with applicants in what is called the preliminary screening. The organization develops some rough guidelines to be applied in order to reduce the time and expense of actual selection. These guidelines could specify, for example, minimum education or the number of words typed per minute. Only those who meet these criteria are deemed potential employees and are interviewed.

If general appearance and personal characteristics are deemed important, preliminary screening is often done through a brief personal interview in which the personnel specialist or the manager determines key information and forms a general impression of the applicant. On this basis, the successful applicant then moves to the next step in selection, perhaps with the knowledge that lack

Jamie Meadows has just graduated from Martin Luther King High School. She is trying to decide which company to work for. She first goes to the personnel office at James Metal Works. John Walker, a personnel specialist, looks up after about ten minutes. He stays seated.

John: Yes?

Jamie: I've just graduated from high school and am wondering if. . . .

John: (interrupting) Can't you see the sign? Walker goes back to his paper work.

Over in the corner, Jamie notices a small sign that says: "We are not hiring now." Jamie leaves James Metal Works without another word.

Next she goes to Gunther's new employment office, where she is met by Terry Trovers. After her first experience, she approaches Terry somewhat reluctantly.

Jamie: Hello, I'm Jamie Meadows. I just graduated from Martin Luther King High School, and I'm looking for a job.

Terry: Nice to meet you Jamie. Let's sit down over here and talk about you and the jobs we have open right now.

of an essential characteristic has lessened the chances of being seriously considered for the job. In smaller organizations, if the applicant appears to be a likely candidate for the position the preliminary screening can proceed as an employment interview (Step 3).

The employer must be sure that the criteria used in this first step do not violate government antidiscrimination requirements. The EEOC has a publication, *Affirmative Action and Equal Employment: A Guidebook for Employers,* which provides help on this issue (vol. 1, pp. 40–44).

Step 1 is part of the reception portion of recruiting (see Chapter 5). The enterprise has the opportunity to make a good or bad impression on the applicant in this step. James Metal Works made one kind of impression, Gunther Manufacturing another.

Step 2: Completion of application blank/biodata form

Applicants who come to an employment office are asked to complete an application blank after a screening interview. Recruiters often follow a similar procedure. In Gunther's employment office, all applicants who appear qualified, such as Jamie, would do so.

One of the oldest instruments in personnel selection is the application blank. Surveys show that all but the tiniest enterprises have applicants complete an application form or other biodata instrument (such as a biographical data form, biographical information blanks, an individual background survey, or an interview guide). Biodata forms are useful in selection, career planning and counseling, and performance evaluation. They are most likely to meet the EEOC's criticisms of other selection techniques.

Of course, application blanks and biodata forms could be illegal if they include items not relevant to job content. Items on the application blank should be kept to a minimum and should ask primarily for data which the enterprise's biodata studies indicate best predict effective performance. Exhibit 6–4 is an example of an application blank.

Essentially, those advocating the biodata approach argue that past behavior patterns are the best predictor of future behavior patterns. Thus data should be gathered on a person's demographic, experiential, and attitudinal characteristics in a form that lends itself to psychometric evaluation and intrepretation. In constructing the biodata form, a variety of approaches is possible. According to William Owens, the form should be brief; the items should be stated in neutral or pleasant terms; the items should offer all possible answers or categories plus an "escape clause"; and numbered items should add to a scale. Owens argues that sequenced items are preferable to nonsequenced items, and choose-one option items are better than multiple-choice items.

An important biodata substitute or supplement for the application blank is the *biographical information blank* (BIB). The BIB usually has more items than an application blank and includes different kinds of items, relating to such things as attitudes, health, and early life experiences. It uses the multiple-choice answer system. Instead of asking just about education, it might ask:

How old were you when you graduated from the 6th grade?
1. Younger than 10
2. 10–12
3. 13–14
4. 15–16

It also asks opinion questions such as:

How do you feel about being transferred from this city by this company?
1. Would thoroughly enjoy a transfer
2. Would like to experience a transfer
3. Would accept a transfer
4. Would reject a transfer

To use the BIB as a selection tool, the personnel specialist correlates each item on the form with the selection criteria for job success. Those criteria that predict the best for a position are used to help select applicants for that position.

Another variety of biodata form is the *weighted application blank,* an application form designed to be scored as a systematic selection device. The purpose of a weighted application blank is to relate the characteristics of applicants to success on the job. It has been estimated that to develop a weighted blank for a job takes about 100 hours. So it makes sense to develop such blanks only for positions with many jobholders.

The typical approach is to divide present jobholders into two or three categories (in half, high or low; or in thirds, high, middle, or low), based on some success criterion such as performance as measured by production records or supervisor's evaluation, or high versus low turnover. Then the characteristics of high and low performers are examined. On many characteristics for a particular organization and job, there may be no difference by age or education level, but there may be differences on where applicants live and years of experience, for example. A weight is assigned to the degree of differences: for no difference, 0; for some difference, ±1; for a big difference, ±2. Then these weights are totaled for all applicants, and the one with the highest positive score is hired, assuming that the score meets the minimum which past and currently successful employees have attained.

These predictive characteristics vary by job and occupation. For example,

EXHIBIT 6–4
Application blank

EMPLOYMENT APPLICATION
(Please Print Plainly)

DO NOT WRITE IN SPACE BELOW:
Employment Date ________
Department ________
Classification ________
Rate ________

Date ________

NAME ________ (Last, First, Middle Initial) SOCIAL SECURITY NO. ________

PRESENT ADDRESS ________ (No., Street, City, State, Zip) TELEPHONE NO. ________

HOW LONG HAVE YOU LIVED AT ABOVE ADDRESS? ________ ARE YOU A U.S. CITIZEN? ________

PREVIOUS ADDRESS ________ (No., Street, City, State) HOW LONG DID YOU LIVE THERE? ________

DATE OF BIRTH ________ (Mo. Day Yr.) BIRTHPLACE ________ HEIGHT __ft. __in. WEIGHT ____lbs.

The Age Discrimination In Employment Act of 1967 prohibits discrimination on the basis of age with respect to individuals who are at least forty, but less than sixty-five years of age.

DATE OF MARRIAGE ________ NO OF DEPENDENTS INCLUDING YOURSELF ________

NO. OF CHILDREN ________ THEIR AGES ________

DO YOU HAVE ANY PHYSICAL DEFECTS? ____ IF YES, DESCRIBE ________

HAVE YOU HAD A HERNIA OPERATION? ________

HAVE YOU HAD A MAJOR ILLNESS IN THE PAST 5 YEARS? ____ IF YES, DESCRIBE ________

HAVE YOU RECEIVED COMPENSATION FOR INJURIES? ____ IF YES, DESCRIBE ________

POSITION(S) APPLIED FOR ________ RATE OF PAY EXPECTED $____ PER WEEK

WOULD YOU WORK: Full-Time ____ Part-Time ____ Specify days and hours, if part-time ________

WERE YOU PREVIOUSLY EMPLOYED BY US? ____ IF YES, WHEN ________

WERE YOU EVER ARRESTED AND CONVICTED OF AN OFFENSE OTHER THAN A TRAFFIC VIOLATION? ____ IF YES, DESCRIBE IN FULL ____

If you application is considered favorably, on what date will you be available for work? ________ 19____

Nearest person to be notified in case of accident or emergency:

________ Name ________ Address ________ Phone

Are there any other experiences, skills, or qualifications which you feel would especially fit you for work with the Company? ________

(Turn to Next Page)

sometimes the age of the applicant is a good predictor; other times it is not. They may also change over time. Weights need to be recomputed every several years or so, and the weighted application blank must be validated for each job and organization.

Most researchers have found that biodata approaches are reliable. They also find that biodata approaches have very high validity. Studies indicate, however, that although most organizations use application blanks, fewer than a third of the *larger* organizations have utilized weighted application blanks or other biodata approaches. Given the problems with tests, references, and other selec-

EXHIBIT 6–4 *(continued)*

WORK HISTORY

(List your last, or present job first and then others in order back from that one. List all former employment).
Use back page if extra space is necessary.

Name and Address of Company	Started Mo. Yr.	Left Mo. Yr.	Pay At Hire	Pay When Left	What Was Your Job?	Machines Worked On	Why Did You Leave

Have you ever received compensation for any accident or disability? If so, when and for what? Place Employed

EDUCATION

Circle Last Grade Completed:

Grammar 1 2 3 4 5 6 7 8 Location ____

High School 1 2 3 4 School ____ Location ____

College 1 2 3 4 Degree(s) ____ School ____

Major ____ Minor ____

Technical School 1 2 3 4 Course ____ Location ____

Correspondence 1 2 3 4 Course ____ Location ____

GENERAL INFORMATION

Are you registered with Georgia Employment Service? ____ Where? ____

Have you ever been convicted of a crime other than a minor traffic offense? ____

If so, give the details of such conviction. ____

In case of emergency notify: ____
(name) (address) (phone)

I understand that false statements on this application may be considered sufficient cause for dismissal, if and when discovered. I also understand that the use of this blank does not indicate that there are any positions open and does not in any way obligate this company.

I authorize the company to contact my references and former employers, as well as authorize the release of any medical records or information in connection with my physical condition, past or present.

Sign Here ____

tion techniques, the percentage of enterprises using biodata approaches is likely to increase.

Step 3: Employment interview

Employment interviews are part of almost all selection procedures. All studies indicate that over 90 percent of selection decisions involve interviews. And a number of them, indicate that the interview is the *most important aspect* of the selection decision.

Types of interviews. There are three general types of employment interview:

- Structured.
- Semistructured.
- Unstructured.

While all employment interviews are alike in certain respects, each type is also unique in some way. All three include interaction between two or more parties, an applicant and one or more representatives of the potential employer, for a predetermined purpose. This purpose is consideration of an applicant for employment. Information is exchanged, usually through questions and answers. The main differences in employment interviews lie in the interviewer's approach to the process, and the type used depends both on the kind of information desired and the nature of the situation.

In the *structured employment interview,* the interviewer prepares a list of questions in advance and does not deviate from it. In many organizations a standard form is used on which the interviewer notes the applicant's responses to the predetermined questions. Many of the questions asked in a structured interview are forced choice in nature, and the interviewer need only indicate the applicant's response with a check mark on the form.

If the approach is highly structured, the interviewer may also follow a prearranged sequence of questions. In such an interview the interviewer is often little more than a recorder of the interviewee's responses, and little training is required to conduct it. The structured approach is very restrictive, however. The information elicited is narrow and there is little opportunity to adapt to the individual applicant. This approach is equally constraining to the applicant, who is unable to qualify or elaborate on answers to the questions. The Bureau of National Affairs survey found that 19 percent of the companies used a written interview form, while 26 percent employed a standard format for employment interviews. Exhibit 6–5 is an example of a form used for a structured employment interview.

In the *semistructured interview* only the major questions to be asked are prepared in advance, though the interviewer may also prepare some probing questions in areas of inquiry. While this approach calls for greater interviewer preparation, it also allows for more flexibility than the structured approach. The interviewer is free to probe into those areas that seem to merit further investigation. With less structure, however, it is more difficult to replicate these interviews. This approach combines enough structure to facilitate the exchange of factual information with adequate freedom to develop insights.

The *unstructured interview* involves little preparation. The interviewer prepares a list of possible topics to be covered and sometimes does not even do

EXHIBIT 6–5
Patterned interview form—Executive position

Date ______________________ 19 ___

SUMMARY

Rating [1] [2] [3] [4] Comments: ______________________
In making final rating, be sure to consider not only what the applicant can do but also his/her stability, industry, perseverance, loyalty, ability to get along with others, self-reliance, leadership, maturity, motivation, and domestic situation and health.

Interviewer: ______________________ Job considered for: ______________________

Name ______________________ Date of birth ______________________ ; Phone No. ____________
The age discrimination in the employment act and relevant FEP Acts prohibit discrimination with respect to individuals who are at least 40 but less than 65 years of age.

Present address ______________________ City ____________ State ________ How long there? ____________

Were you in the Armed Forces of the U.S.? Yes, branch ____________ (Not to be asked in New Jersey) Dates ________ 19 ___ to ________ 19 ___

________ 19 ___ to ________ 19 ___

If not, why not? ______________________

Where you hospitalized in the service? ______________________

Are you drawing compensation? Yes ___ No ___

Are you employed now? Yes □ No □. (If yes) How soon available? ______________________
What are relationships with present employer?

Why are you applying for this position? ______________________
Is his/her underlying reason a desire for prestige, security, or earnings?

WORK EXPERIENCE. Cover all positions. This information is very important. Interviewer should record last position first. Every month since leaving school should be accounted for. Experience in Armed Forces should be covered as a job (in New Jersey exclude military questions).

LAST OR PRESENT POSITION

Company ______________________ City ____________ From ________ 19 ___ to ________ 19 ___

How was job obtained? ______________________ Whom did you know there? ______________________
Has applicant shown self-reliance in getting jobs?

Nature of work at start ______________________ Starting salary ____________
Will applicant's previous experience be helpful on this job?

In what way did the job change? ______________________
Has applicant made good work progress?

Nature of work at leaving ______________________ Salary at leaving ____________
How much responsibility has applicant had? Any indication of ambition?

Superior ____________ Title ____________ What is he/she like? ______________________
Did applicant get along with superior?

How closely does (or did) he/she supervise you? ________ What authority do (or did) you have? ______________________

Number of people you supervised ____________ What did they do? ______________________
Is applicant a leader?

Responsibility for policy formulation ______________________
Has applicant had management responsibility?

To what extent could you use initiative and judgment? ______________________
Did applicant actively seek responsibility?

that. The overriding advantage of the unstructured type is the freedom it allows the interviewer to adapt to the situation and to the changing stream of applicants. Spontaneity characterizes this approach, but under the control of an untrained interviewer digressions, discontinuity, and eventual frustration for both parties may result.

While the unstructured approach lends itself to the counseling of individuals with problems, it is not limited to guidance. Students frequently encounter personnel recruiters whose sole contribution, other than the opening and closing pleasantries, is "Tell me about yourself." When used by a highly skilled interviewer, the unstructured interview can lead to significant insights which might enable the interviewer to make fine distinctions among applicants. As used by most employment interviewers, however, that is not the case, and it is seldom appropriate for an employment interviewer to relinquish control to such an extent.

Some interviewers try to induce stress into the employment interview process. Generally speaking, this is very dysfunctional to the employment interview process.

A number of studies have examined whether employment interviews are reliable sources of data. Generally speaking, the more structured the interview and the more training the interviewer has, the more reliable the interview.

Interviewing is a skill that can be learned. The following sections describe the purposes and phases of effective interviews.

Purposes of selection interviews. Many employment interviewers perceive their only task as being to screen and select those individuals best suited for employment. While this is unquestionably the *main* function of the employment interview, it is not the only one. A second purpose is public relations: to impress the interviewees with the value of the interviewer's employer.

In addition to the selection and public relations roles, the employment interviewer also must function as an educator. It is the interviewer's responsibility to "educate" the applicants concerning details of the job in question which are not immediately apparent. The interviewer must be able to answer the applicant's questions with honesty and candor. To be effective, the interviewer must remain aware of all three of these functions while conducting the employment interview.

Phases of interviews. There are five distinct phases into which the employment interview may be divided. The phases of the interview suggest the changing nature of the interviewer's strategy as the interview progresses. The phases are: preplanning, clarification of purpose, previewing topics, eliciting and giving information, and closing the interview.

Phase 1: Preplanning. The more informed the interviewer is both on the job in question and on the individual applicant, the more appropriate the interviewer's eventual decision should be. The interviewer should be aware of the duties of the job to be filled. If the job description is unclear or incomplete, the interviewer should get this information from someone presently holding the job or from the person whose job it is to supervise that position.

Thus the interviewer's task is more complex than just getting to know the applicant. The interaction is directed toward the critical requirements, and the interviewer's biases should be less influential than if the task were more general. These critical requirements can usually be limited to four to six. It is such limitation that makes the interviewer's job manageable in a relatively short period of time. By introducing these specifics, the interviewer will be freed from the uncertainties surrounding the global judgments which still characterize many employment interviews.

In addition to becoming familiar with the job, the interviewer must also become somewhat acquainted with the applicant. In general, an application blank is available, and in some cases a resumé and test scores. These should be read in advance. By becoming familiar with the applicant's background in advance, the interviewer avoids the temptation of using the application blank as an outline for the interview. When an interview is tied directly to the application blank, the information elicited usually duplicates what is already a matter of record. Such an approach, in addition to being tedious, is extremely limiting to both participants. The interviewer learns little new information, and the applicant has scant opportunity to elaborate.

When analyzing the application and resumé in advance, the interviewer should look for such things as discrepancies in the information, unexplained gaps in the time periods covered, and other items which raise questions. When planned properly the interview will provide answers to these questions, and it will reveal additional information on the applicant. Sometimes the applicant has already been interviewed by another interviewer, and a report of that interview may be available. In order to maintain objectivity, however, the interviewer should avoid reading this interview report prior to the present interview.

The interviewer should know the time frame within which the interview must be conducted and plan accordingly. The topics to be covered and the time to be budgeted to each of them must be decided. Most employment interviewers attempt to cover work experience, education, and outside interests. Planning should also include how to terminate the interview and what to tell the applicant about the selection process. Enough time also should be budgeted to allow for writing whatever notes and comments are necessary immediately following the interview.

There has been ample research to show that the arrangement of furniture in a setting can either enhance or inhibit communication. A desk may constitute a barrier to communication when placed between interviewer and applicant. Many interviewers who have heeded such findings and restructured their offices accordingly have been pleased with the results. More important than the physical environment, however, is the climate created by the interviewer. The interviewer who provides privacy for the interview and who actively preplans the employment interview is taking a giant step to providing a climate conducive to effective interviewing.

Phase 2: Clarify purpose and enhance relaxation. No survey has ever shown the number of employment interviews conducted in which one or both parties were mistaken as to the job being discussed. Such a survey would probably reveal a high rate of such misunderstandings. In order to avoid such occurrences, even at the risk of belaboring the obvious, the interviewer should make sure that both parties are discussing the same job.

Having accomplished this, the interviewer should establish rapport with the applicant and thereby reduce the tension level. Many interviewers appear to believe that several minutes of chatting about some general topic is a prerequisite for rapport to be established. If the total number of hours devoted annually in interviews to talking about the weather were instead applied to interview preparation, much more information would be exchanged, and better selection decisions would result.

Rather than forcing artificial conversation, the interviewer should allow the applicant a minute or two to become familiar with the surroundings. This can be accomplished by taking a quick reappraisal of the application blank before starting, thus providing a brief respite for the applicant to relax. If this review of the application blank reveals a topic of possible mutual interest to interviewer and applicant, the interviewer can use it to help put the applicant at ease. In the absence of such a topic of mutual interest, however, it is better to launch right into the interview, after allowing adequate time to get comfortably settled. When an interviewer begins an interview by straining to make small talk, the applicant recognizes the artificiality of the attempt. What was originally intended to reduce tension actually can heighten it. Frank and Ernest in the cartoon get right to the point in their opening question, don't they?

Phase 3: Preview the topics. After clarifying the purpose of the interview and attempting to put the applicant at ease, the interviewer can do much to reduce the uncertainty in the interviewer's mind by briefly previewing the topics to be covered in the interview. By simply stating the categories of information of interest and the sequence in which the categories will be covered, the interviewer will be adding some structure which will result in a more confident and trusting applicant and usually in a more productive interview. When the interviewer tells a job seeker that they will be discussing the applicant's background, work experience, formal education, and outside interests, the interviewer is helping the applicant to get organized.

Phase 4: Elicit and give information. Most of the time budgeted for the interview is devoted to this phase. After previewing the topics to be covered, the interviewer should return to the first topic and cover it in as much detail as is deemed necessary. The interviewer implements the strategy determined in the preplanning stage, and the amount of structure becomes obvious. The more structured the interviewer's approach, the more closed questions will be employed, and the more directive will be the techniques of the interviewer.

In most employment interviews, which are of the semistructured type, the interviewer begins each topic with an open-ended question and then proceeds toward a more specific question. This pattern is usually repeated for each topic, while the interviewer is aware of the constraints in the situation.

Although employment interviews are generally perceived as question-and-answer sessions, with the interviewer asking the questions, the interviewer must also encourage questions from the interviewee and be prepared to tell the applicant about the job and the enterprise. It should be the interviewer's task to provide those facts that will help the applicant to make the employment decision.

Phase 5: Close the interview. When approximately 90 percent of the interview has been completed, the interviewer must begin to close the interview. In the remaining minutes the interviewer seeks to answer any remaining questions, to summarize what has been discussed, and to point to the future, indicating what lies ahead for the applicant. The applicant has the right to know whether the interviewer has made a decision and, if so, what it is. It is unethical to allow an applicant to leave an interview not knowing that an adverse decision has already been made. If the applicant is being favorably considered, this also should be made clear, and the remainder of the selection procedure should be explained.

Summary of suggestions for effective interviewing:

1. Work at listening to what and how the applicant communicates to you. Unlike hearing, listening is an active process and requires concentration. Many interviewers plan their next question when they should be listening to the applicant's present response.

2. Be aware of the applicant's nonverbal cues as well as the verbal message. In attempting to get as complete a picture of the applicant as possible, you must not ignore what some consider the most meaningful type of communication, body language.

3. Remain aware of the job requirements throughout the interview. No one is immune to the halo effect, which gives undue weight to one characteristic. You must constantly keep the requirements of the job in mind. Sometimes an applicant possesses some personal mannerism or trait that so attracts or repels the interviewer that the decision is made mostly on the strength of that characteristic, which may be completely irrelevant to the requirements of the job in question.

4. Maintain a balance between open and overly structured questions. Too many of the former, and the interview becomes a meandering conversation; while too many of the latter turn the interview into an interrogation.

5. Wait until you have all of the necessary information before making a decision. Some interviewees start more slowly than others, and what may appear to be disinterest may later prove to have been an initial reserve which dissipates after a few minutes. *Don't evaluate on the basis of a first impression.*

6. Do not ask questions that violate equal employment opportunity laws and regulations (see list in Chapter 5). Focus the interview on the variables identified as crucial criteria for selection.

Step 4: Employment tests

A technique some enterprises use to aid their selection decisions is the employment test. Such a test is a mechanism (either a paper-and-pencil test or a simulation exercise) which attempts to measure certain characteristics of individuals, such as manual dexterity. Psychologists or personnel specialists develop these tests with a procedure that is similar to that described for the weighted application blank. First those most knowledgeable about the job are asked to rank (in order of importance) the abilities and attitudes essential for effective performance in a job. Thus for a secretarial position, the rank might be (A) ability to type, (B) ability to take shorthand, and (C) positive work attitudes. The psychologist prepares items or simulations which it is thought will measure these required characteristics. These are tried out to see if they can in fact separate the qualified from less qualified (on A and B) and easygoing from less easygoing (on C). On such items, psychologists prefer those that about half the applicants will answer with "right" answers and half with the opposite.

The terms or simulations that distinguish the best from the worst are combined into tests. A measure of effectiveness (a criterion) is developed, such as typing x words per minute with y percent errors. All new applicants are given the test. After about two years, those items that prove to have been the best predictors of high performance are kept in the test used for selection, and those found not to be predictive are dropped. This is the validation process.

It is not easy or cheap to validate a test. In a recent study of 2,500 ASPA members, it was found that, on average, a validation study costs $5,000 per job, and some studies cost as much as $20,000. This same study found the use of tests is declining, and they are used most frequently for clerical jobs. About half of the surveyed employers use tests in selection. Middle-sized firms are most likely to use them, followed by larger firms. The smaller firms are least likely to use them. Some industries (transportation and communications, offices, insurance) are more likely to use tests than manufacturers, hospitals, and retailers.

Of the 2,500 personnel managers consulted in this survey, 37.9 percent considered tests "about the same in importance," and 36.5 percent considered them less important than other selection techniques such as the interview and biodata. Less than 20 percent said they disqualified applicants on the basis of test scores alone.

Because of criticisms of the courts and personnel practitioners that tests discriminate against minority employees, separate validity studies may be required for minorities. Because this is expensive, many employers have abandoned the use of tests for minority employees. This criticism applies more to paper-and-pencil tests than performance tests, as Frank Schmidt et al. have shown.

Few organizations have the personnel, time, or money to develop their own tests. Instead, they often purchase and use tests developed elsewhere. The test organization provides a key (or notation) listing which enterprises have used the test in the past and the typical performance of good and bad employees. This is not enough, however; the test must be validated in each organization and for minority and nonminority employee groups before it can be useful.

There are various kinds of tests. The following will be discussed here: work sample performance tests, simulations of performance, paper-and-pencil tests, personality and temperament inventories, and others.

Job sample performance tests. A job sample performance test is an experience that involves actually doing a sample of the work the job involves in a controlled situation. Examples of performance tests include:

Employees running a miniature punch press at a Philadelphia quartermaster depot.

A standard driving course as performance test for forklift operators at the quartermaster depot.

The auditions used by symphony orchestras for hiring purposes. For example, when symphony orchestras select new musicians, the selection panel listens to them play the same piece of music with the same instrument. The applicants are hidden behind a screen at the time.

Standardized typing tests. The applicants are asked to type some work. The speed and accuracy are then computed.

Variations of these performance tests exist in many enterprises. The applicants are asked to run the machines they would run if they got the job, and quality and quantity of output are recorded.

Job sample tests tend to have the highest validities and reliabilities of all tests because they systematically measure behavior directly related to the job. This is not surprising. Imagine that you are an artist who is applying for graduate work in art. You typically must take the Graduate Record Exam, a paper-and-pencil test designed to measure verbal and mathematical "ability." You also must present 12 paintings, drawings, and watercolors (a portfolio) to the Art Department. Which of these selection devices appears likely to be the most reliable and valid measure of your painting ability? Or recall that when you took your driving test, you took two: a paper-and-pencil test, and, when you drove the car, a performance test. Which better tested your driving ability: the paper-and-pencil test, or that tension-filled drive, including the thrilling attempt at parallel parking? A similar principle applies to job selection. Which would be a better predictor of the forklift operator's job performance: the standardized test, in which the applicant drives the truck down and around piles of goods, or a paper-and-pencil test of driving knowledge, intelligence, or whatever?

Reliability and validity figures for all the standardized tests discussed here are available from the test developers. Many are reviewed in regular summaries such as *Annual Review of Psychology.*

Performance simulations. A performance simulation is a non-paper-and-pencil experience designed to determine abilities related to job performance. For example, suppose job analysis indicates that successful job occupants of a specific job require highly developed mechanical or clerical abilities. A number of simulations are available to measure these abilities. The simulation is not direct performance of part of the job, but it comes close to that through simulation. You may have learned to drive by performing first on simulation machines; it was not the same as on-the-street driving, but it was closer than reading about it or observing other drivers.

There are many of these simulation tests. Here are some:

Revised Minnesota Paper Form Board Test. Exhibit 6–6 is an excerpt from the MPFB, which is a test of space visualization. It is used for various jobs. For example, to be a draftsman requires the ability to see things in their relation to space. The applicant must select the item (A–E) which best represents what a group of shapes will look like when assembled.

Psychomotor ability simulations. There are a number of tests which measure such psychomotor abilities as choice reaction time, speed of limb movement, and finger dexterity. One of these is the O'Connor Finger and Tweezer Dexterity Test (see Exhibit 6–7). The person being tested picks up pins with the tweezer and row by row inserts them in the holes across the board, or inserts the pins with the hand normally used. These tests are used for positions with high manual requirements for success, such as assemblers of radio or TV components and watches.

Clerical abilities. Exhibit 6–8 is the first page of the Minnesota Clerical Test. It is a typical test for clerical abilities. This simulation requires the applicants to check numbers and names, skills frequently used in clerical tasks.

EXHIBIT 6–6
Excerpt from Revised Minnesota Paper Form Board Test

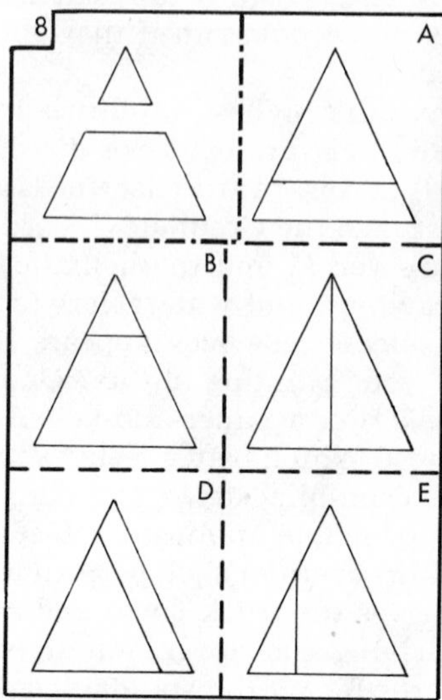

EXHIBIT 6–7
O'Connor Finger and Tweezer Dexterity Test equipment

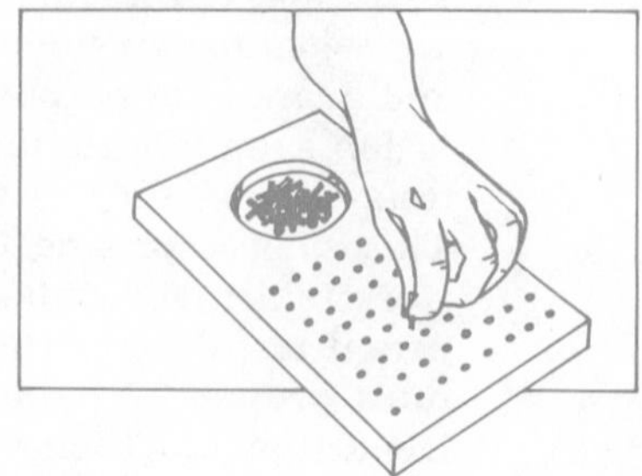

Paper-and-pencil tests. In the third group of tests are paper-and-pencil tests designed to measure general intelligence and aptitudes. Many employers assume that mental abilities are an important component of performance for many jobs. Intelligence and mental ability tests attempt to sample intellectual mental development or skills.

Some examples of paper-and-pencil tests are:

Otis Quick Scoring Mental Ability Test. This test samples several intellectual functions, including vocabulary, arithmetic skills, reasoning, and perception, totaling them to one score. It includes items such as the following:

(a) Which one of the five things below is soft?
(1) glass (2) stone (3) cotton (4) iron (5) ice
(b) A robin is a kind of:
(6) plant (7) bird (8) worm (9) fish (10) flower
(c) Which one of the five numbers below is larger than 55?
(11) 53 (12) 48 (13) 29 (14) 57 (15) 16

Wechsler Adult Intelligence Scale. The Wechsler is a comprehensive paper-and-pencil test of 14 sections grouped into two scores. The verbal score includes general information, arithmetic, similarities, vocabulary, and other items. The

EXHIBIT 6–8

MINNESOTA CLERICAL TEST
(formerly the Minnesota Vocational Test for Clerical Workers)
by Dorothy M. Andrew, Donald G. Patterson, and Howard P. Longstaff

Name ______	Date ______
TEST 1—Number Comparison	TEST 2—Name Comparison
Number Right ______	Number Right ______
Number Wrong ______	Number Wrong ______
Score = R − W ______	Score = R − W ______
Percentile Rating ______	Percentile Rating ______
Norms Used ______	Norms Used ______

INSTRUCTIONS

On the inside pages there are two tests. One of the tests consists of pairs of names and the other of pairs of numbers. If the two names or the two numbers of a pair are exactly the same make a check mark (√) on the line between them: if they are different, make no mark on that line. When the examiner says "Stop!" draw a line under the last pair at which you have looked.

SAMPLES done correctly of pairs of NUMBERS

79542 ___ 79524
1234567 _√_ 1234567

SAMPLES done correctly of pairs of NAMES

John C. Linder ___ John C. Lender
Investors Syndicate _√_ Investors Syndicate

This is a test for speed and accuracy. Work as fast as you can without making mistakes. Do not turn this page until you are told to begin.

performance score includes picture completion, picture arrangement, object assembly, and similar items.

Wonderlic Personnel Test. The Wonderlic is a shortened form of the Otis test using a variety of perceptual, verbal and arithmetical items which provide a total score. Other well-known tests include the Differential Aptitude Test, the SRA Primary Mental Abilities Test, and multiple aptitude tests.

The above three tests are administered to individuals and are paper-and-pencil tests similar to those taken in school. There are also tests of mental ability designed to be administered to groups, including the following example:

California Test of Mental Maturity (adult level). This test is administered to groups and scored by machine. Scores are developed from a series of short tests on spatial relationships, verbal concepts, logic and reasoning, numerical reasoning, memory, and others. These scores are converted to IQ equivalents, and profiles are developed for analyzing performance.

The reliability and validity of paper-and-pencil tests have been studied extensively. In general, they are not as reliable as performance tests or other selection devices such as biodata forms or structured interviews.

Personality inventories and temperament tests. The least reliable of the employment tests are those instruments that attempt to measure a person's personality or temperament. The most frequently used inventory is the Minnesota Multiphasic Personality Inventory. Other paper-and-pencil inventories are the

Why does a fireman wear red suspenders?

A. ☐ *The red goes well with the blue uniform.*
B. ☐ *They can be used to repair a leaky hose.*
C. ☐ *To hold up his pants.*

Drawing by D. Fradon; © 1974 The New Yorker Magazine, Inc.

California Psychological Inventory, the Minnesota Counseling Inventory, the Manifest Anxiety Scale, and the Edwards Personal Preference Schedule.

A different approach, not as direct as the self-reporting inventory, utilizes projective techniques to present vague stimuli, the reactions to which provide data on which psychologists base their assessment and interpretation of a personality. The stimuli are purposely vague in order to reach the unconscious aspects of the personality. Many techniques are used. The most common are the Rorschach Inkblot Test and the Thematic Apperception Test.

Most of these instruments were developed for use by psychiatrists and psychologists in counseling and mental health work, rather than in selection. Because of employee resistance, ethical problems in some questions, and lower reliability and validities, use of the inventories and temperament tests is likely to continue to decline in the future.

The polygraph. Another method currently used by some employers to test employees is the polygraph, sometimes erroneously called a lie detector. This is an instrument that records changes in breathing, blood pressure, pulse, and skin response associated with sweating of palms, and plots these reactions on paper. The person being questioned with a polygraph attached is asked a series of questions. Some are neutral, to achieve a normal response, others stressful, to indicate a response made under pressure. Thus the applicant may be asked: "Is your name Pajanowski?" Then, "Have you ever stolen from an employer?"

Although originally developed for police work, the great majority of polygraph tests today are used to check data during personnel selection. Approximately one fifth of American businesses use the polygraph today. It is understandable why organizations need to determine certain facts about potential employees. On-the-job crime has increased tremendously, and it is estimated that dishonest employees cost employers about $5 billion per year. A good reference check may cost $100; a polygraph test only $25. Some employers offer applicants a choice: Take a polygraph test now, making it possible to make an immediate selection decision, or await the results of a reference check and run the risk of losing the job. Local, state, and federal agencies have begun to use the polygraph, especially for security, police, fire, and health positions.

There are many objections to the use of the polygraph in personnel selection. One is that this device is an invasion of the applicants' privacy and thus a violation of the Fourth Amendment to the Constitution. Second, it is believed that its use could lead to self-incrimination, a violation of the Fifth Amendment. A third objection is that it insults the dignity of the applicant. One study cites cases of applicants being asked questions about their sex lives, for example.

As severe as these objections are, *the most serious question is whether the polygraph is reliable and can get the truth.* The fact is that the polygraph records *physiological* changes in response to stress, not lying or even the conditions necessarily accompanying lying. Many cases have come to light in which persons who lie easily have beaten the polygraph, and it has been shown that the polygraph brands as liars people who respond emotionally to questions. There is significant evidence that polygraphs are neither reliable nor valid. This is the conclusion reached following recent studies by a congressional committee and the Pentagon which made a thorough analysis of all the available data. Compounding this deficiency, one expert has estimated that 80 percent of 1,500 polygraph practitioners are not sufficiently trained to interpret the results of the tests, even if they were reliable and valid.

Such criticisms have led to the banning of the polygraph for employee selection in many jurisdictions. Arbitrators have held against forcing employees to take such tests, and polygraph evidence is not admissible in court unless both sides agree. As a result of congressional hearings, the federal government has severely reduced the use of polygraphs. In spite of these criticisms, however, it appears that the use of the polygraph in selection is increasing.

Summary: Selection, validation, and uses of tests. Suggestions on the effective selection and use of tests include the following suggested by Wilson:

- Test results should be weighed in the context of the applicant's employment history.
- Make sure the test is right for the job in question.
- Be aware of the differences in what the various tests try to measure.
- Use tests that have both general and specific norms.
- Have as high a selection ratio as possible.
- Try the test on present employees before adopting it.
- Seek advice of consultants in test selection.

Organizations which need to process rather large numbers of applicants for jobs have developed job tests or groups of tests called test batteries which allow them to keep records on the usefulness of these tests in hiring. A well-known example is the civil service examinations given by U.S. governmental agencies for many positions.

Step 5: Reference checks and recommendations

If you have ever applied for a job, at some point you were asked to provide a list of references of past supervisors and others. In general, you picked people who could evaluate you effectively and fairly for your new employer—people who know and express your good and bad points equally, like your mother, lover, best friend, and other objective references, right?

For years, as part of the selection process, applicants have been required to submit references or recommendation letters. These indicate past behavior and how well the applicant did at her or his last job. Studies indicate that this has been a common practice for white-collar jobs.

For a letter of recommendation to be useful, it must meet certain conditions:

- The writer must know the applicant's performance level and be competent to assess it.
- The writer must communicate the evaluation effectively to the potential employer.
- The writer must be truthful.

If the applicant chooses the references, the first two conditions may not be met. With regard to the third, many people are reluctant to put in writing what

they really think of the applicant, since he or she may see it. As a result, the person writing the reference either glosses over shortcomings or overemphasizes the applicant's good points. Because of these and other shortcomings, studies of the validity of written references have not been comforting to those using them in selection.

Clemm Kessler and Georgia Gibbs propose a method for potentially improving the validity of letters of reference as a selection tool. In their approach, letters of reference are required only for jobs which have had job analysis performed to develop job specifications (see Chapter 4). A panel of judges (three to six persons) familiar with the job ranks the specifications for relative importance. Then a reference letter is drafted asking the respondent to rate the applicant on the job specifications, which are listed randomly. A sample reference letter for the position of employment interviewer is given as Exhibit 6–9. The references must be familiar with the applicant's past employment. The rankings of the panel and the references are correlated, and the greater the correlation, the more likely is the applicant to be hired.

Congress has passed the Privacy Act of 1974 and the Buckley Amendment. These allow applicants to view letters of reference in their files. The laws apply to public-sector employees and students. But private- and third-sector employers are afraid that the laws will soon apply to them, so many of them will now give out only minimal data: dates of employment, job title, and so on. If this becomes a common practice, reference letters will not be very useful.

When there is need to verify biodata, a more acceptable alternative for a letter might be a phone call to the applicant's previous supervisors. The organization can contact certain persons in order to cross-check opinions or to probe further on doubtful points. Most studies indicate that few employers feel written references alone are a reliable source of data. A majority of enterprises combine telephone checks, written letters of reference, and data obtained from the employment interview. Items checked most frequently are previous employment and educational background (in that order).

Although little data for reliability exists, it appears to be very useful to find out how the applicant performed on previous jobs. This can be the most relevant information for predicting future work behavior. Reference checks would seem in order for the most crucial jobs at any time. Costs of these checks vary from a few cents for a few quick telephone calls to several hundred dollars for a thorough field investigation. It is not known whether privacy legislation is affecting telephone reference checks in the way it has written letters of reference.

Step 6: Physical examinations

Some organizations require that those most likely to be selected for a position complete a medical questionnaire or take a physical examination. The reasons for such a requirement include the following:

- In case of later workers' compensation claims, physical condition at the time of hiring should be known.
- It is important to prevent the hiring of those with serious communicable diseases. This is especially so in hospitals, but it applies in other organizations as well.
- It may be necessary to determine whether the applicant is physically capable of performing the job in question.

EXHIBIT 6–9

Sample reference letter for applicant for employment interviewer positions

Dear ________________

Mr. ________________ is applying for a position with our company and has supplied your name as a reference. We would appreciate it if you would take a few moments to give us your opinions about him.

Listed below is a series of items that may describe skills, abilities, knowledge, or personal characteristics of the applicant to a greater or lesser degree. Will you please look at this list and rank them from most to least like the applicant by placing the appropriate letter in the space below. If you do not have an opinion about a specific item, skip it and rank what you can, beginning with Space 1.

A. Has the ability to develop scheduled and nonscheduled interview formats for various jobs.
B. Can conduct an interview using the nondirective approach
C. Has a neat appearance (clothes clean, in good condition)
D. Makes checks to see if people understand his meaning when he speaks to them.
E. Makes checks to see if he understands people when they speak to him.

1. ______ (Most characteristic of the applicant)
2. ______
3. ______
4. ______
5. ______ (Least characteristic of the applicant)

Now, on the rating scale below, please indicate with a check in the appropriate space the degree to which the applicant possesses the last ranked skill, ability, knowledge or personal characteristic. If he is very high in the characteristic, give a rating of 5; if he is very low, give him a rating of 1. Place your check in between the two extremes if you consider that a more appropriate rating.

Very low |__1__|__2__|__3__|__4__|__5__| Very high

Comments about the applicant:

Source: Clemm C. Kessler, III, and Georgia J. Gibbs, "Getting the Most from Application Blanks and References," *Personnel,* January–February 1975. Reprinted by permission of AMAÇOM, a division of American Management Associations. All rights reserved.

These purposes can be served by the completion of a medical questionnaire, a physical examination, or a work physiology analysis. Richard Chase has discussed the latter technique, which is neither a physical examination to determine whether or not the applicant is in good health nor a psychomotor test. Commonly used for selection of manual workers who will be doing hard labor, it attempts to determine, by physiological indices (heart rate and oxygen consumption), the true fatigue engendered by the work. This is analyzed through simulated job performance. First, the analyst measures applicants and obtains baseline information on these indices while they are seated. Then data are gathered while they are working. The data are analyzed and the workers are ranked; those with the lowest heart rate and oxygen consumption should be hired (all other factors being equal).

Physical examinations have *not* been shown to be very reliable as a predicator of future medical problems. This is at least partially so because of the state of the art of medicine. Different physicians emphasize different factors in the exam, based on their training and specialties. There is some evidence that correlating the presence of certain past medical problems (as learned from the completion of a medical questionnaire) can be as reliable as a physical exam performed by a physician and is probably less costly.

SELECTION OF MANAGERS

The selection process and the tools used vary with the type of employee being hired. The preceding section focused on blue-, gray-, and white-collar employees, but the general process is similar for the managerial employee.

Before a manager is hired, the job is studied. Then the criteria are selected, based on the characteristics of effective managers in the organization at present and likely future needs. *Each enterprise* must do this, since the managerial task differs by level, function, industry, and in other ways. Studies of successful managers across these groups have concluded that many (not all) successful executives have intelligence, drive, good judgment, and managerial skills. Most of the studies avoid the real-world problems like the following. Candidate A scores high on intelligence and motivation, low on verbal skills, and moderate on hard work. Candidate B scores moderate on intelligence, high on motivation, moderate on verbal skills, and high on hard work. Both have good success records. Which one would you choose? The tradeoffs must be assessed for particular jobs and particular organizations.

One recruiter told me this:

> I've read the studies about high intelligence, test scores, and so on in managerial selection. But I've found I've got to look at the job. For example, our most successful *sales managers* are those who grew up on a farm where they learned to work hard on their own. They went to the nearest state college (all they could afford) and majored in business. They got good to better than average grades. They might have done better gradewise if they hadn't had to work their way through school. Our best *accounting managers,* however, did not have that background.

The message is that these studies can indicate the likely predictors of success *in general,* but executive success must be analyzed in each organization. Each of the factors mentioned must be correlated with success measured several ways, to see which works for the organization. However, the focus of selection must be on *behavior,* not just on scores on tests or general impressions.

Once the criteria of managerial success are known, the selection tools to be used are chosen. In general, tests are not frequently used in managerial selection. Reference checks have been a major source of data on managerial applicants, but the legal problems with this tool also apply for executives. Biodata and curriculum vitae analysis is a major tool used for managerial selection. As John Campbell et al. put it, "Very often, a carefully developed typical behavior inventory based on biographical information has proved to be the single best predictor of future job behavior . . . biographic information has proved particularly useful for assessing managerial effectiveness."

The most frequently used selection tool for managers is the interview. More often than not, it is used in conjunction with the other methods. But if only one method is used by an organization, it is likely to be the personal interview.

Studies indicate that more successful managers are hired using judgments derived in employment interviews than decisions based on test scores. This is no doubt so because these judgments can be based on factorially complex behavior, and typical executive performance is behaviorally complex. The interview is likely to continue to be the most used selection method because organizations want to hire managers they feel they can trust and feel comfortable with.

Assessment centers

One very promising method used for managerial selection that is not used for employee selection is the assessment center. It uses multiple selection methods and has many purposes, but the major one is managerial selection and evaluation. They have been used by Sears, J. C. Penny, General Electric, IBM, AT&T, and Sohio, among other companies. Originated by Henry Murray, they were used by the OSS and the British War Office to select spies in World War II.

There are, of course, a variety of approaches to any technique, including the assessment center. Essentially, this is a multiple peer-superior rating method using many inputs of data. The assessment center is described in some detail in Chapter 9. It is an expensive mechanism. Although it is new, evaluation studies so far strongly support the use of assessment center procedures as the most effective method of managerial selection.

THE SELECTION DECISION

These are three types of approaches to the selection decision.

Approaches to selection decisions:

Random choice or chance approaches. Examples of this approach include choosing the third applicant interviewed or putting names in a hat and drawing one out.

Emotional-clinical approach. The manager unconsciously picks the applicant who was most likeable in the interviews.

Systematic-quasirational. The chapter focuses on a systemic approach using various selection techniques, while recognizing that unconscious emotional choices are likely to enter into the decision.

Some studies have been done to contrast and evaluate the various selection techniques. Lawrence Jauch proposes an interesting combination of the systematic and clinical approaches to the selection decision which is inexpensive and realistic enough for the average manager to use. He calls it the paired-comparison method, in which a matrix of the candidates and the criteria is developed, as shown in Exhibit 6–10. Each interviewer compares each candidate to the others on each criterion (I–VII) and ranks them relative to each other (VIII–X). These ranks than are summed or weighted according to the decision maker's evaluation of the opinion of each interviewer.

EXHIBIT 6–10
Selection decision matrix for paired-comparison technique

Criteria \ Candidates	*A–Mr. Black*	*B–Mr. White*	*C–Ms. Neutral*	*D–Mrs. Other*
I. *Education*	College grad.	High school grad.	High school grad.	2 years college
II. *Test scores*	130	110	115	120
III. *Experience*	None	5 years	8 years	2 years
IV. *Job knowledge*	Above average	Excellent	Excellent	Average
V. *Past performance*	Excellent	Average	Above average	Above average
VI. *Desire*	Above average	Average	High	Above average
VII. *Stability*	Low	Average	High	Below average
VIII. *Interviewer 1*	1	3.5	2	3.5
IX. *Interviewer 2*	2	3	1	4
X. *Interviewer 3*	2	4	3	1

"Systemizing the Selection Decision," by Lawrence Jauch. Reprinted with permission *Personnel Journal* copyright © November 1976.

A method similar to Jauch's might be used to try to reconcile differences of opinion on selection between personnel specialists and operating managers. If that does not work it appears reasonable that the operating manager who will supervise the applicant should prevail, since this is the manager who must deal with an unsuitable or ineffective employee.

COST/BENEFIT ANALYSIS FOR THE SELECTION DECISION

One way to evaluate which selection techniques should be used is to consider the probabilities that particular methods will select successful candidates and the costs of these methods. The seven steps in the selection procedure and their probable costs are:

Method	*Cost*
1. Preliminary screening interview	Negligible
2. Application blank/biodata	Negligible
3. Employment interview	Time used × cost per hour

4. Employment tests .... $5–$1,000
5. Background and reference checks..... $100
6. Physical examination.................. $25
7. Decision..............................

Each of these steps can be regarded as a hurdle which will select out the least qualified candidates. Steps 1, 2, and 3 probably will be used in most cases. The questionable ones are 4, 5, and 6 for many persons, and Step 6 may not be appropriate. As for Step 5, the checks need not be used for many jobs which do not involve much responsibility. Each selection technique can be evaluated in terms of costs and benefits.

Costs of training and selecting personnel may have tradeoff features which can be calculated. One final comment about the selection decision. The greater the number of sources of data into the decision, the more probable it is that it will be a good decision. Tests alone will not suffice. Interviews supplemented by background checks and some test results are better. Costs and time constraints however, are obviously crucial.

SUMMARY, CONCLUSIONS, AND RECOMMENDATIONS

Chapter 6 was designed to help you make more effective selection decisions. The basic objective of selection is to obtain the employees most likely to meet the enterprise's standards of performance and who will be satisfied and developed on the job. To do this, the following statements summarize this chapter's conclusions.

1. Selection is influenced by environmental characteristics: whether the enterprise is public or private, labor market conditions and the selection ratio, union requirements, and legal restrictions on selection.
2. Reasonable criteria for the choice must be set prior to selection.
3. The selection process can include up to six steps:
   a. Preliminary screening interview.
   b. Completion of application blank/biodata form.
   c. Employment interview.
   d. Employment tests.
   e. Reference checks and recommendation letters.
   f. Physical examinations.
4. For more important positions (measured by higher pay and responsibility), the selection decision is more likely to be formalized and to use more selection techniques.
5. The effective organization prefers to select persons already in the organization over outside candidates.
6. More effective selection decisions are made if both personnel managers and the future supervisors of potential employees are involved in the selection decision.
7. Using a greater number of accepted methods to gather data for selection decisions increases the number of successful candidates selected.
8. Larger organizations are more likely to use sophisticated selection techniques.
9. For more measurable jobs, tests can be used in the selection decision more effectively.

10. For lower jobs in the hierarchy, tests can be used more effectively in the selection decision.
11. Even if the most able applicant is chosen, there is no guarantee of successful performance on the job.

Exhibit 6–11 summarizes the recommendations for use of the various selection methods in the model organizations (see Exhibit 1–7). While selection appears to be a universally used personnel activity, the techniques adopted are likely to be based on the types of personnel selected rather than the type of organization doing the selection.

EXHIBIT 6–11
Recommendations on selection methods for model organizations

Type of organization	*Screening interview*	*Application blank, biodata*	*Employment interview*	*Performance and ability tests**	*Telephoned background reference check†*	*Physical exam*
1. Large size, low complexity, high stability	X	X	X	X	X	Hospital
2. Medium size, low complexity, high stability	X	X	X	X	X	
3. Small size, low complexity, high stability	X	X				
4. Medium size, moderate complexity, moderate stability	X	X	X	X	X	
5. Large size, high complexity, low stability	X	X	X	X	X	Hospital
6. Medium size, high complexity, low stability	X	X	X			
7. Small size, high complexity, low stability	X	X	X			Hospital

* Usually for blue- and white-collar positions.
† Usually for white-collar and managerial positions.

The following propositions are based on the conclusions of this chapter:

Proposition 6.1. The larger the organization, the more likely is it for selection to follow a systematic-semirational procedure which involves most selection steps or techniques.

Proposition 6.2. The more complex and volatile the organization, the less likely is it to use techniques of selection which do not require extensive validation (such as interviews) effectively.

Chapter 7 describes orientation programs, the next personnel activity, after selection, to affect employees.

If you were Clark Kirby, how would you select the 596 people? You should know that at present, Gunther is not unionized. You remember (don't you?) that Lewis wants you to seriously consider EEO criteria in selection, and Ed doesn't want you to. And these are the two persons you want to please with your decisions.

You wouldn't have enough time to make all the selection decisions yourself. The personnel specialist can help. But this won't be enough either if you are to follow all six steps of selection. Yet Gunther will not authorize additional help to select the people. As Clark, how will you proceed? (Plan your strategy before you turn the page to see what Clark did.)

This is what Clark Kirby did. He didn't have the resources or time to hire all 596. Besides, he believed that operating managers should participate in decisions. So his strategy was to hire the managers first. Then he had the managers help screen and hire the clerical and semiskilled employees.

As far as selection objectives were concerned, Clark accepted the home office's objectives. These were to hire those employees who were most likely to be effective and satisfied. He accepted the job specifications for the most similar positions he could find in the Chicago plant. These specifications listed minimum requirements in education and experience for managers and professional/technical employees. For clerical employees, the emphasis was on minimum experience, plus performance simulation test scores. For skilled employees, the job specifications included minimum experience and test scores on performance simulation tests. This was also true for semiskilled employees.

Clark decided that because of time pressures and the nature of the job differences, he would use the following selection process.

Managers: screening interview, application blank, interview, reference check.

Professional/technical: screening interview, application blank, interview, reference check.

Clerical: screening interview, application blank, interview, tests.

Skilled: screening interview, application blank, tests and interviews for marginal applicants.

Semiskilled: screening interview, application blank, tests and interviews for marginal applicants.

Clark and Ed would hire the managers. Clark would hire the professionals. While these groups were being hired, the personnel specialist would administer the tests to the clerical employees and supervise the reference checking process on the managers and professionals. The personnel specialist would hire the clerical employees. But the managers and professionals would be involved in hiring the clerical personnel to be under their direct supervision.

Then Clark and the personnel specialist would administer the tests to skilled and semiskilled employees. Clark would hire the clearly well-qualified semiskilled employees, except in marginal cases. These would receive a review and, interview by the managers to whom they would report. A similar process would be used to hire the semiskilled employees. Since there were few choices among professional/technical and skilled employees, it was more efficient not to involve the new managers too.

Several problems developed. Clark and Ed had no trouble agreeing on 20 managerial candidates. But in 18 additional cases, Clark felt he had found better candidates. Ed wanted more Chicago people he knew. Lewis, reflecting the position of Chicago managers, objected. Clark found many more qualified minority and female managerial candidates than Ed wanted to accept. They compromised. Ed gave up half his choices to Clark, and Clark did likewise.

There were also problems in the skilled professional categories. These people generally wanted more pay than the budget called for. And the last 20 percent hired were somewhat below minimum specifications. Clark appealed for more budget, given these conditions. The home office gave him half of what he needed. He had to generate the other half by paying less for the bottom 20 percent of the semiskilled and clerical employees. Clark alerted Ed to the probable competence problem. He promised Ed that he'd begin developing a list of qualified applicants in these categories in case they were needed.

In sum, Clark hired the people needed within the adjusted budget, on time, and generally with the required specifications. He was able to make a contribution to equal employment opportunity objectives by hiring somewhat more minorities and women than the total population, less than he could have and less then Lewis wanted, but more than Ed wanted. All were qualified. No reverse discrimination took place.

Compare your solution with Clark's. In what ways was his better? Yours better?

QUESTIONS

1. What is personnel selection? Who makes these decisions? What factors influence personnel selection? How?
2. What is a selection ratio? How does it apply to personnel selection?
3. Who sets selection criteria? How are they developed? Why are they used?
4. Which selection criteria are most important? When?
5. Describe a typical selection process for a manual laborer; top executive; typist.
6. How are biodata forms used in selection? How effective are they? Are they reliable and valid? How frequently are they used?
7. What is an employment interview? How often is it used? What are three types of interview styles? Which are the most reliable?
8. What is a test? A performance test? A simulation? A paper-and-pencil test? Tests are increasing in use in the United States. Comment.
9. When would you use reference checks? For which jobs? How would you do the checks?
10. How does the process of selecting a manager differ from selecting a typist? How is it similar?
11. The systematic-quasirational selection decision is best. Comment.

Chapter objectives

- To demonstrate the importance of effective orientation for employee satisfaction and performance.
- To show how new employees can be oriented effectively.
- To illustrate the effective assignment of new employees.

Chapter outline

I. A Diagnostic Approach to Orientation
II. The Purposes of Orientation
III. Who Orients New Employees?
IV. How Orientation Programs Work
V. Orienting Management Trainees
   A. Formal management training programs
VI. Assignment, Placement, and Orientation Follow-Up
VII. Cost/Benefit Analysis of Orientation Programs
VIII. Summary, Conclusions, and Recommendations

7

Orientation of personnel

Art

Art Johnson was so glad when he got the job at the Coca-Cola bottling works. Art really needed the job; he had been out of work six weeks now, and his wife, Betty, was busy with their two-month-old daughter. Art wanted to do a good job; he wanted to keep the job and get ahead with the company. He certainly hoped they explained how to do the job and what he was expected to get done in a good day's work.

* * *

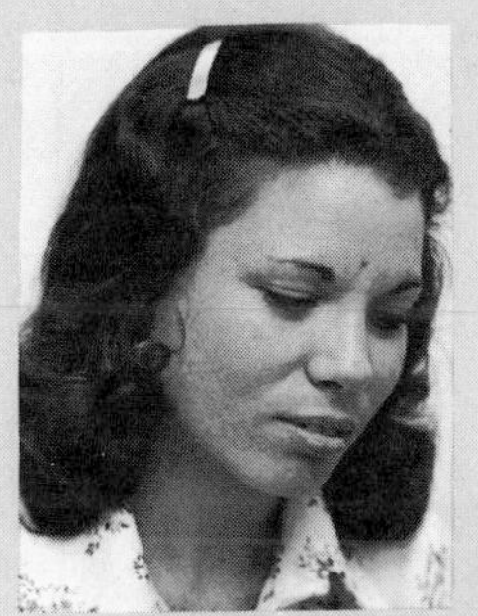

Gigi

Gigi Martinez reported to her first day's job at the department store. She didn't know whether to go back to personnel or where, but she went to the personnel department. She told the receptionist she had been hired as a new sales associate. The receptionist told Gigi to sit down and they'd get to her in a while. She sat there an hour. Finally, the personnel interviewer noticed her and said, "Gigi, what are you doing here? You're supposed to be in Men's Clothing."

Mumbling that no one told her, she rushed out and eventually found Men's Clothing. She approached several sales associates and finally found the department manager. He began: "So you're the new one. A bad start—late your first day. Well, get to work. If you need any help ask for it."

* * *

Sam

Sam Lavalle reported to personnel as the notice of employment said to do. After about six of the new employees were there, orientation began. Miss Wentworth welcomed them to the company and then the "paper blitz" took place. In the next 30 minutes, she gave them a lot of paper—work rules, benefits booklets, pay forms to fill out, and so on. His head was swimming. Then Sam got a slip telling him to report to his new supervisor, Andrew Villanueva, in Room 810. Andrew took him around the facility for three minutes and then pointed out Sam's new workbench and wished him good luck.

Art is an example of the attitude of many if not most new employees—ready to go to work and wanting so much to succeed. Art's case describes the orientation challenge. Gigi is an example of what happens to too many new employees: no help at all. Sam is an example of what most employees encounter: a formal orientation program that is adequate but not all it could be.

Orientation is the personnel activity which introduces new employees to the enterprise and to their tasks, superiors, and work groups.

Orientation has not been studied a great deal. Little scientific research has been done on whether the programs are adequate. Some experts view orientation as a kind of training. Training is discussed in Chapter 9. But I think orientation is so important it deserves a chapter of its own. In terms of the stages of development of personnel functions discussed earlier and shown in Exhibit 1–6 (Chapter 1), it is a Stage II function.

A DIAGNOSTIC APPROACH TO ORIENTATION

Exhibit 7–1 highlights the environmental factors in the diagnostic model that are most important to effective orientation programs: the nature of the employee, and the nature of the task, the work group, and the leadership. The nature of the employee and the task are critical factors; for example, managers are given more detailed orientation programs than other employees. The orientation program focuses on introducing the new employee to the task, the work group, and the supervisor-leader. During orientation the work policies of the

EXHIBIT 7–1
Factors affecting orientation and organizational effectiveness

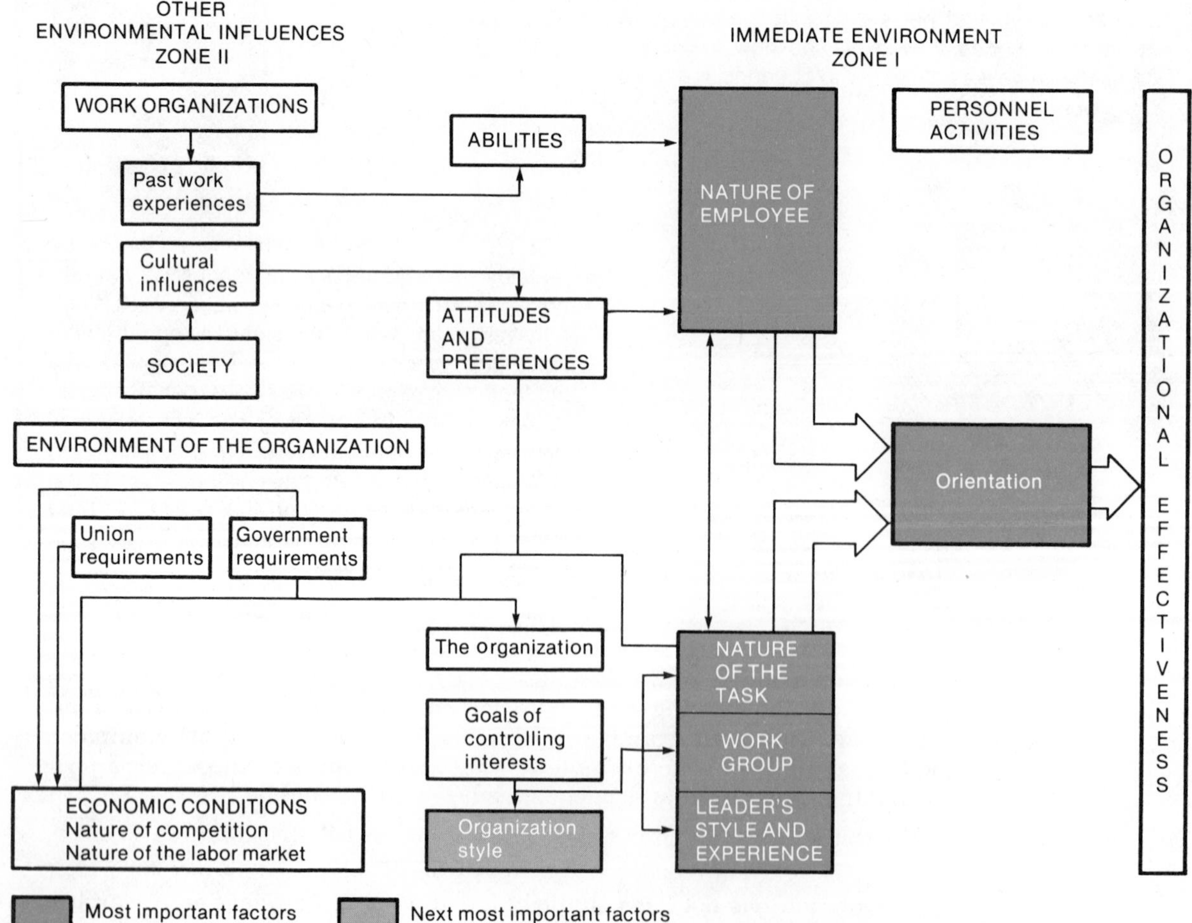

organization, the job conditions, and the people the employee will work with to get the job done are discussed.

The style the enterprise uses to orient new employees is affected by the organization and its climate. What I called conservative-bureaucratic organizations in Chapter 2 will orient employees quite differently than liberal-participative organizations will. The diagnostic manager adapts the orientation program to the individual and gives it a different emphasis for a person with 20 years' experience in the industry than for a new employee who is just out of high school and from a disadvantaged background.

Part-time employees are likely to receive much shorter and less elaborate orientations. It is probable that orientation will be done by the personnel specialist, who will get them on the payroll, explain pay and hours, and turn them over to a supervisor. The supervisor is likely to explain her or his expectations for work, introduce new employees around, show them the job, and encourage them to ask for help.

THE PURPOSES OF ORIENTATION

Effectively done, orientation serves a number of purposes. In general, the orientation process is similar to what sociologists call socialization. The principal purposes of orientation are:

To reduce the start-up costs for a new employee. The new employee does not know the job, how the organization works, or whom to see to get the job done. This means that for a while, the new employee is less efficient than the experienced employee, and additional costs are involved in getting the new employee started. These start-up costs have been estimated for various positions as follows: top manager, to $2,000; middle manager, $1,000; supervisor, $1,000; senior engineer, $900; accountant, $750; and secretary, $400. Effective orientation reduces these start-up costs and enables the new employee to reach standards sooner.

To reduce the amount of anxiety and hazing a new employee experiences. Anxiety in this case means fear of failure on the job. This is a normal fear of the unknown focused on the ability to do the job. This anxiety can be made worse by hazing of the new employee.

Hazing takes place when experienced employees "kid" the new employee. For example, experienced employees may ask the new worker, "How many toys are you producing per hour?" When she answers, she is told, "You'll never last. The last one who did that few was no longer here after two days."

Such hazing serves several purposes. It lets the recruit know he has a lot to learn and thus is dependent on the others for his job, and it is "fun" for the old-timers. But it can cause great anxiety for the recruit. Effective orientation alerts the new person to hazing and reduces anxiety.

To reduce employee turnover. If employees perceive themselves to be ineffective, unwanted, or unneeded and have similar negative feelings, they may seek to deal with them by quitting. Turnover is high during the break-in period, and effective orientation can reduce this costly practice.

To save time for supervisor and co-workers. Improperly oriented employees must still get the job done, and to do so they need help. The most likely people to provide this help are the co-workers and supervisors, who will have to spend time breaking in new employees. Good orientation programs save everyone time.

To develop realistic job expectations, positive attitudes toward the employer, and job satisfaction. In what sociologists call the older professions (law, medicine) or total institutions (the church, prison, the army), the job expectations are clear because they have been developed over long years of training and education. Society has built up a set of attitudes and behaviors that are considered proper for these jobs. For most of the world of work, however, this does not hold true. New employees must learn realistically what the organization expects of them, and their own expectations of the job must be neither too low nor too high. Each worker must incorporate the job and its work values into his or her self-image.

Orientation helps this process. One way to illustrate how orientation serves these purposes is with the story of how Texas Instruments developed its new orientation program (see the box).

Texas Instruments knew that anxieties existing in the early period of work reduced competence and led to dissatisfaction and turnover. The anxiety resulted from awareness on the part of the female assemblers that they must reach the competence level they observed in the experienced employees around them. Many times they did not understand their supervisors' instructions but were afraid to ask further questions and appear stupid. Sometimes this anxiety was compounded by hazing.

Anxiety turned out to be a very important factor in the study at Texas Instruments, which investigated whether an orientation program designed to reduce anxiety would increase competence, heighten satisfaction, and lower turnover. The control group of new recruits was given the traditional orientation program: a typical two-hour briefing on the first day by the personnel department. This included the topics normally covered in orientation (these will be described shortly) and the usual description of the minimum level of performance desired. Then they were introduced to the supervisor, who gave them a short job introduction, and they were off.

The experimental group was given the two-hour orientation the control group received and then six hours of social orientation. Four factors were stressed in the social orientation:

1. They were told that their opportunity to succeed was good. Those being oriented were given facts showing that over 99 percent of the employees achieved company standards. They were shown learning curves of how long it took to achieve various levels of competence. Five or six times during the day it was stressed that all in the group would be successful.

2. They were told to disregard "hall talk." New employees were tipped off about typical hazing. It was suggested that they take it in good humor but ignore it.

3. They were told to take the initiative in communication. It was explained that supervisors were busy and not likely to ask the new worker if she "needed help." Supervisors would be glad to help, but the worker must ask for it, and she would not appear stupid if she did so.

4. They were told to get to know their supervisor. The supervisor was described in important details—what she liked as hobbies, whether she was strict or not, quiet or boisterous, and so forth.

This social orientation had dramatic results. The experimental group had 50 percent less tardiness and absenteeism, and waste was reduced by 80 percent, product costs were cut 15 to 30 percent, training time was cut 50 percent, and training costs cut 66⅔ percent.

WHO ORIENTS NEW EMPLOYEES?

Exhibit 7–2 describes how operating and personnel managers run the orientation program in middle-sized and large enterprises. In smaller enterprises, the operating manager does all the orienting. In some unionized enterprises, union officicals are involved. Personnel also helps train the operating manager for more effective orientation behavior.

EXHIBIT 7–2
Relationship of operating and personnel managers in orientation

Orientation function	*Operating manager (OM)*	*Personnel manager (PM)*
Design the orientation program		PM is consultant with OM
Introduce the new employee to the organization and its history, personnel policies, working conditions and rules. Complete paperwork		PM performs this
Explain the task and job expectations to employee	OM performs this	
Introduce employee to work group and new surroundings. Encourage employees to help new employee	OM performs this	

HOW ORIENTATION PROGRAMS WORK

Orientation programs vary from quite informal, primarily verbal efforts to formal schedules which supplement verbal presentations with written handouts. Formal orientations often include a tour of the facilities or slides, charts, and pictures of them. Usually, they are used when a large number of employees must be oriented.

The formal program usually covers such items as:

- History and general policies of the enterprise.
- Descriptions of the enterprise's sevices or products.
- Organization of the enterprise.
- Safety measures and regulations.
- Personnel policies and practices.
- Compensation, benefits, and employee services provided.
- Daily routine and regulations.

The material can be presented in a variety of forms. For example, in an experiment at Union Electric Company in St. Louis it was found that programmed learning approaches were efficient and effective. The written material may be in the form of handouts and booklets or combined into a single employee handbook (see Chapter 3). The literature and handouts should be examined to see that the reading level is right for the employees in question. Frequently they are too technical or are written at too high a reading level for the employee. A study of the orientations of disadvantaged employees found that initial presentations should be in oral form, followed by written materials, to avoid a feeling of communication overload. The oral, then written, communication pattern should be followed by both personnel people and supervisors.

Guidelines for conducting an employee orientation:

1. Orientation should begin with the most relevant and immediate kinds of information and then proceed to more general policies of the enterprise.
2. The most significant part of orientation is the human side, giving new employees knowledge of what supervisors and co-workers are like, telling them how long it should take to reach standards of effective work, and encouraging them to seek help and advice when needed.
3. New employees should be "sponsored" or directed by an experienced worker or supervisor in the immediate environment who can respond to questions and keep in close touch during the early induction period.
4. New employees should be gradually introduced to the people with whom they will work, rather than given a superficial introduction to all of them on the first day. The object should be to help them get to know their co-workers and supervisors.
5. New employees should be allowed sufficient time to get their feet on the ground before demands on them are increased.

To make sure that the orientation program is complete and works well, larger enterprises prepare checklists of what should be covered. Some are completed by supervisors (see Exhibit 7–3). To make sure the supervisor covers all the important points, some enterprises also prepare an orientation checklist to be filled out by employees (see Exhibit 7–4).

ORIENTING MANAGEMENT TRAINEES

Management trainees are in a special orientation category. Most of these recruits must adjust from college life to work life. Many organizations have prepared rather elaborate orientation programs for potential managers which are called management training programs. There is little doubt that initial experiences with an organization are important predictors of future managerial performance. Research studies make that clear.

Formal management training programs

After recruits have been selected to become managers, there are two distinct approaches to their orientation and placement. The first is to orient them briefly and let them go to work. This is the approach most organizations take with

EXHIBIT 7–3
Supervisor's orientation checklist

Employee's Name:		Discussion completed (please check *each* individual item)
I.	Word of welcome	
II.	Explain overall departmental organization and its relationship to other activities of the company	
III.	Explain employee's individual contribution to the objectives of the department and his starting assignment in broad terms	
IV.	Discuss job content with employee and give him a copy of job description (if available)	
V.	Explain departmental training program(s) and salary increase practices and procedures	
VI.	Discuss where the employee lives and transportation facilities	
VII.	Explain working conditions: a. Hours of work, time sheets b. Use of employee entrance and elevators c. Lunch hours d. Coffee breaks, rest periods e. Personal telephone calls and mail f. Overtime policy and requirements g. Paydays and procedure for being paid h. Lockers i. Other______	
VIII.	Requirements for continuance of employment—explain company standards as to: a. Performance of duties b. Attendance and punctuality c. Handling confidential information d. Behavior e. General appearance f. Wearing of uniforms	
IX.	Introduce new staff member to manager(s) and other supervisors. Special attention should be paid to the person to whom the new employee will be assigned.	
X.	Release employee to immediate supervisor who will: a. Introduce new staff member to fellow workers b. Familiarize the employee with his work place c. Begin on-the-job training	

If not applicable, insert N/A in space provided.

Employee's Signature ______ Supervisor's Signature ______

Date ______ Division ______

Form examined for filing: ______ Date ______ Personnel Department

Source: Joan Holland and Theodore Curtis, "Orientation of New Employees," in Joseph Famularo (ed.), *Handbook of Modern Personnel Administration,* (New York: McGraw-Hill Book Co., 1972), chap. 23.

nonmanagerial employees. The second is to orient and train them in a management training program and then assign them to specific positions. Studies indicate that the most effective management training programs:

Are short (of four to five months' duration, if possible).

Use on-the-job training and minimize classroom teaching.

Encourage high job and training expectations in trainees.

Provide trainees with frequent feedback on their progress or lack of it.

Generally, these qualities are desired by both companies and trainees. Both prefer a minimum of formal classroom work and a maximum of actual work so the company gets productivity sooner and the individual receives rewards sooner. Most of the trainees want to test themselves against the challenge of the real world to see if they can do the job. Training programs that do not allow this and emphasize lectures or mere observation of how departments work will satisfy neither of these objectives.

Perhaps most crucial to an effective management training program is an effective supervisor for the trainee. Too often the trainees are roadblock executives who see themselves as failures because they have not been promoted beyond a certain point. They are likely to haze recruits and give them tough experiences, always supposedly for their own good. Instead, recruits need a good supervisor who understands their problems and wants to get them off to a good start. An example of an effective manager who was an excellent trainer of new employees is given in the accompanying box.

When I was in the food business, I observed one of the best "trainers" in the business. Ray Scheid was also one of the most effective purchasing agents in the food business, the head grocery buyer at the Cincinnati branch of the Kroger Company. Because he was very good at his job, earlier in his career he had been offered many promotions. As is often the case with such promotions, each would have involved a geographic transfer. He liked Cincinnati, and for this and other reasons he preferred to stay in his position there. Scheid liked his job and found it rewarding, but one of his most important rewards was training new managers for Kroger. He often told me of the men he had trained—some of whom later became his bosses. He was as proud of them as if they were his sons. His joy was to teach them all he knew so they could be promoted elsewhere and advance in their careers. He showed no jealousy or desire to be in their shoes. He had had his chances and had chosen a different life. His career was satisfying to him and he lived theirs vicariously. He had all that was needed: technical expertise, a sincere desire to help people learn, and reward when they had learned all he had to teach.

Happy is the trainee whose supervisor is a Ray Scheid instead of a frustrated person who takes out his or her aggression by hazing the trainees.

ASSIGNMENT, PLACEMENT, AND ORIENTATION FOLLOW-UP

The final phase of the orientation program is the assignment of the new employee to the job. At this point, the supervisor is supposed to take over and continue the orientation program. But as the Texas Instruments study demonstrated, supervisors are busy people, and even though they might be well intentioned, they can overlook some of the facts needed by the new employee to do a good job.

One way to assure adequate orientation is to design a feedback system to control the program, or use the management by objectives technique. A form that could be used for this feedback from the trainee is the job information form shown in Exhibit 7–4. The new employee is instructed: "Complete this checklist as well as you can. Then take it to your supervisor, who will go over it with you and give you any additional information you may need." The job information form is signed by employee and supervisor. An appointment set

EXHIBIT 7–4
Orientation follow-up form

JOB INFORMATION

1. The job of my department is to ____________

   My assigned area is ____________

   The most important part of my job is ____________
2. My department head's name is ____________
   His/her office is located ____________
3. I receive my time card from ____________
   Time cards must be turned in on (day) ____________
   to (person) ____________. Pay day for our department is ____________
   If I am out of the hospital on pay day, I can get my pay from ____________ The cashier's office is (where) ____________
4. If I feel ill while at work, I should ____________

   If I become ill while at home, I should notify my supervisor by calling (hosp. phone no.) ____________
   (dept. ext.) ____________ at least one hour before I am expected at work
5. My locker or checkroom is located ____________
6. The hours I am scheduled to work are assigned by ____________

   Any change in my work schedule (days off etc.) is arranged in advance by ____________
   My lunch hour and relief are assigned by ____________
7. Work assignments are given to me by ____________
   I can get help on the job from ____________
8. Some of the things I do on my job are:
   A. ____________
   B. ____________
   C. ____________
   D. ____________
   E. ____________
9. In doing my work I handle the following (check the boxes)

PAPER	☐	EQUIPMENT	☐
SUPPLIES	☐	FOOD	☐
PRODUCTS	☐	PATIENTS	☐

10. If I work with papers:

Papers I handle daily include	They come from	When I finish they are used by

11. If I use equipment, I use ____________

    To keep the equipment in good working order I must ____________
12. If I work with supplies, products or food – the way I handle them is important because ____________
13. My work helps Lenox Hill Hospital give better patient care by ____________
14. When I need supplies, I get them from
    (person) ____________ (place) ____________
    (time) ____________ (day) ____________
15. To keep things running smoothly, I should bring to my supervisor's attention such things as: ____________
16. How well I do my work can be measured by ____________
17. 2 Safety rules that apply in my job are:
    1. ____________
    2. ____________
18. I have had the most difficulty with ____________
19. Things I'd like to know more about are ____________
20. Things I like best about my job are: ____________

SUGGESTIONS I HAVE ____________

Source: Joan Holland and Theodore Curtis, "Orientation of New Employees," in Joseph Famularo (ed.), *Handbook of Modern Personnel Administration,* (New York: McGraw-Hill Book Co., 1972), chap. 23.

up with the orientation group in the first month on the job provides a follow-up opportunity to determine how well the employee is adjusting and permits evaluation of the orientation program (as discussed in the summary section). The form is designed not as a test of knowledge but to help improve the process of orientation.

In general, the placement process is direct: the person is assigned to the job she or he was selected for, often with the supervisor participating in selection. When selection is separated from assignment, various methods of assignment are used: assign the newest recruit to the highest priority position, use a multiple priority system, or adopt a linear programming method. Researchers who studied these three approaches in very large organizations found that the straight priority method was the least effective, linear programming best, and differential priorities about as effective as linear programming. In civil service, the personnel unit supervises the recruiting and selection, but the operating agencies decide on which system of assignment to use and which of the hired persons will be assigned to which jobs.

COST/BENEFIT ANALYSIS OF ORIENTATION PROGRAMS

Evaluating the costs and benefits of orientation programs can follow several approaches. One is to compute the cost per new employee for the orientation program by adding direct and indirect costs:

Direct costs
- Cost of trainers or orientation specialists
- \+ Cost of materials provided
- \+ Cost of space used (if applicable)

Indirect costs
- Cost of time to supervise trainers/orientation specialists
- \+ Cost of supervisors of new employees on the job
- = Orientation costs

After computing these costs, the organization should compare its costs per employee to the costs for comparable organizations. The organization also can compare the costs of running its own program versus contracting it with outside vendors. This is not done often at present.

Trainees can be asked to evaluate the benefits, using an attitude questionnaire. Companies can also experiment (as Texas Instruments did) and measure the differential retention rate and the output rate for a specific orientation program versus no program. The results of two different orientation programs can be compared, and results of attitude surveys and retention rates can be compared with those of other organizations. In all cases, it is easier to compute costs than benefits.

SUMMARY, CONCLUSIONS, AND RECOMMENDATIONS

Orientation programs are an important part of the employment process. The diagnostic manager will recognize that the amount and emphasis of orientation varies with the complexity of the task, the experience of the employee, and the climate in the work group. The manager will adjust the orientation program accordingly, following these basic principles:

1. The principal purposes of orientation include:
   a. To reduce start-up costs for a new employee.
   b. To reduce fear and anxiety of the new employee and hazing from other employees.
   c. To reduce turnover.
   d. To save time for supervisors and co-workers.
   e. To develop realistic job expectations, positive attitudes toward the employer, and job satisfaction.
2. In small enterprises the operating manager does all the orienting; in middle-sized or larger enterprises the operating and personnel managers share this task.
3. A formal orientation program covers:
   a. History, general policies, description of the enterprise's products or services, and organization of the enterprise.
   b. Safety measures and regulations.
   c. Personnel policies and practices.
   d. Compensation, benefits, and employee services provided.
   e. Daily routine and regulations.
4. The shorter the management training and orientation program is, and the closer it is to actual work experience, the more effective it will be.
5. More effective orientation programs include a minimum of technical information and emphasize the social dimensions of the new job (supervisor's expectations, encouragement, climate of work group, etc.).
6. The most crucial factor in an effective management training program is probably an effective supervisor.

Some propositions can be derived about the orientation process and its success or lack of success:

Proposition 7.1. The more a person's first job fits his preferences, the more he will continue to be positively motivated for commitment and performance.

Proposition 7.2. The larger the organization, the more effectively will it use a formal orientation and assignment program.

Proposition 7.3. The more stable the organization, the more effectively will it use a formal orientation and assignment program.

Proposition 7.4. Assignment to and evaluation of orientation programs are likely to be more crucial in larger organizations with more turnover.

Proposition 7.5. In stable, smaller work groups, it soon becomes obvious which of the new employees are "making it" and which need additional help.

Recommendations for use of orientation programs by model organizations are given in Exhibit 7–5.

This chapter completes Part Three of the book. Part Four opens with Chapter 8, which examines performance evaluation of employees once they are on the job.

EXHIBIT 7–5
Recommendations on orientation programs for model organizations

Type of organization	*Informal orientation programs*	*Formal orientation programs*	*Informal placement follow-up*	*Formal placement follow-up*
1. Large size, low complexity, high stability		X		X
2. Medium size, low complexity, high stability		X		X
3. Small size, low complexity high stability	X		X	
4. Medium size, moderate complexity, moderate stability	X		X	
5. Large size, high complexity, low stability		X		X
6. Medium size, high complexity, low stability		X		X
7. Small size, high complexity, low stability	X		X	

Art Johnson was lucky. Even though the Coca Cola Bottling Works was small, it had a well-developed, though informal, orientation program. The personnel manager got Art to complete the required employment forms. Then he chatted with Art about work rules and similar matters. He described Art's new supervisor, Ida Averill, and talked about what the work group was like.

Ida introduced Art around the work group. Then she spent 20 minutes talking about what a good work group it was and what each employee was like. Finally, she talked to Art about what job performance was expected. Then she put Art with Ted Carson. Ted was to be Art's "work buddy" and help train him. Six months later, Art was one of the highest performing employees at the plant, and he loved his job.

* * *

Gigi Martinez was not so lucky. Her first experience at the department store was typical. Her "orientation" consisted of being assigned to a work center and being told, "Well, get to work. If you need help, ask for it." But when she did ask for help, people were too busy. Two weeks later when her boss criticized her in front of others for poor performance, she quit.

* * *

Sam Lavalle got a better start than Gigi. And he made friends with the man at the next workbench, Lionell Narda. When he needed help, Lionell helped. He also filled Sam in on how to get along with his co-workers and with Andrew, the supervisor, who was a bit distant. Six months later, Sam was still at the workbench and performing about average. He seemed to like his work pretty well.

QUESTIONS

1. What are the main purposes of orientation programs? What aspects of orientation seem to be the most neglected?
2. Describe the study of Texas Instruments' orientation program. What does it indicate to you about how to operate an orientation program?
3. Describe a typical orientation program. Which parts of it would you describe as important, very important, or less important? To the employee? To the employer?
4. How important is it to involve the employee's supervisor in the orientation program? Will forms signed by the employee assure the supervisor's participation?
5. How important is an employee's first supervisor to the employee's future at work? Have you experienced a Ray Scheid?
6. How much classroom teaching should there be in a management training program?
7. How can you compute costs and benefits of orientation? Is this an easy process?

part four

Performance evaluation and development of personnel

Part Four is concerned with one of the most vital activities in the personnel function. Chapter 8 focuses on performance evaluation, the most frequently used career counseling aid. Employees can either endure or profit from this experience. Chapters 9 and 10 discuss how the enterprise can improve the abilities and attitudes of employees at work through training and development activities. Chapter 9 discusses how employers can help employees develop meaningful careers for themselves in an enterprise.

8

Performance evaluation and promotion

Chapter objectives

- To demonstrate how to evaluate employees effectively.
- To show why performance evaluation takes place.
- To indicate how often evaluation takes place and who conducts evaluations.
- To help you understand the criteria and tools to use to conduct effective performance evaluations.
- To explain how an effective promotion system operates.

Chapter outline

I. A Diagnostic Approach to Performance Evaluation
II. To Evaluate or Not to Evaluate
III. Reasons for Malfunction or Failure
  A. System design and operating problems
  B. Problems with the evaluator
  C. Employee problems with performance evaluation
IV. Formal Evaluation
  A. Set policies on when, how often, and who evaluates
  B. Gather data on employees
V. Evaluate the Employees: Evaluation Techniques
  A. Individual evaluation methods
  B. Multiple-person evaluation methods
  C. Other methods
  D. Which technique to use
VI. Discuss the Evaluation with the Employee
VII. Make Decisions and File the Evaluation
VIII. Managerial Performance Evaluation
  A. Assessment centers
IX. Promotion Systems
X. Summary, Conclusions, and Recommendations

Felipe

Felipe Hernandez went to work in the maintenance department of Partridge Enterprise, a middle-sized firm, about a year ago. He enjoys being in maintenance, since he has always liked to work with his hands. His supervisor, Ed Smart, is a good maintenance man who helps Felipe when he doesn't understand a problem. But Felipe wishes he knew what Ed thinks of him on the job. Ed never tells Felipe that he does a good job. It seems that Ed chews him out about once a month. Doesn't he think Felipe is trying to do a good job? Doesn't he think he's a good maintenance man?

Knowing the answers to these questions is important to Felipe, because someday he'd like to move up. He hears that Joe is going to retire next year. Joe's job is better and pays more. Felipe wonders if he has a chance to get this job. He also has heard that business is not good right now at some branches. People have been laid off elsewhere. If the crunch hits the New York branch where Felipe works, will he be laid off? He knows seniority is a factor in layoffs. But so is performance. He wishes he knew how he was doing so that he could improve himself, move up, and not get laid off.

This chapter focuses on performance evaluation—the personnel activity designed to satisfy Felipe's needs for performance feedback. It also examines promotion systems.

Performance evaluation is the personnel activity by means of which the enterprise determines the extent to which the employee is performing the job effectively.

Performance evaluation is called by many names, such as performance review, personnel rating, merit rating, performance appraisal, employee appraisal, or employee evaluation. The term used here is performance evaluation.

In many organizations, two evaluation (and promotion) systems exist side by side: the formal and the informal. Supervisors often think about how well employees are doing; this is the informal system. It is influenced by political and interpersonal processes so that employees who are liked better than others have an edge.

Formal performance evaluation is a system set up by the enterprise to *regularly* and *systematically* evaluate employee performance.

This chapter focuses on the formal system for reasons given shortly.

A DIAGNOSTIC APPROACH TO PERFORMANCE EVALUATION

Exhibit 8–1 highlights the relevant factors from the diagnostic model which have significance for performance evaluation and promotion. The first factor is the task performed. A white-collar or supervisory task is more likely to be formally evaluated than some blue-collar tasks. In addition, the performance evaluation technique used will differ with the task being evaluated.

The second factor affecting performance evaluation is the government. Since the passage of antidiscrimination legislation, the government has investigated to determine if enterprises discriminate against protected categories of employees in promotion, pay raises, and other rewards. Performance evaluation is the

EXHIBIT 8–1
Factors affecting performance evaluation and promotion

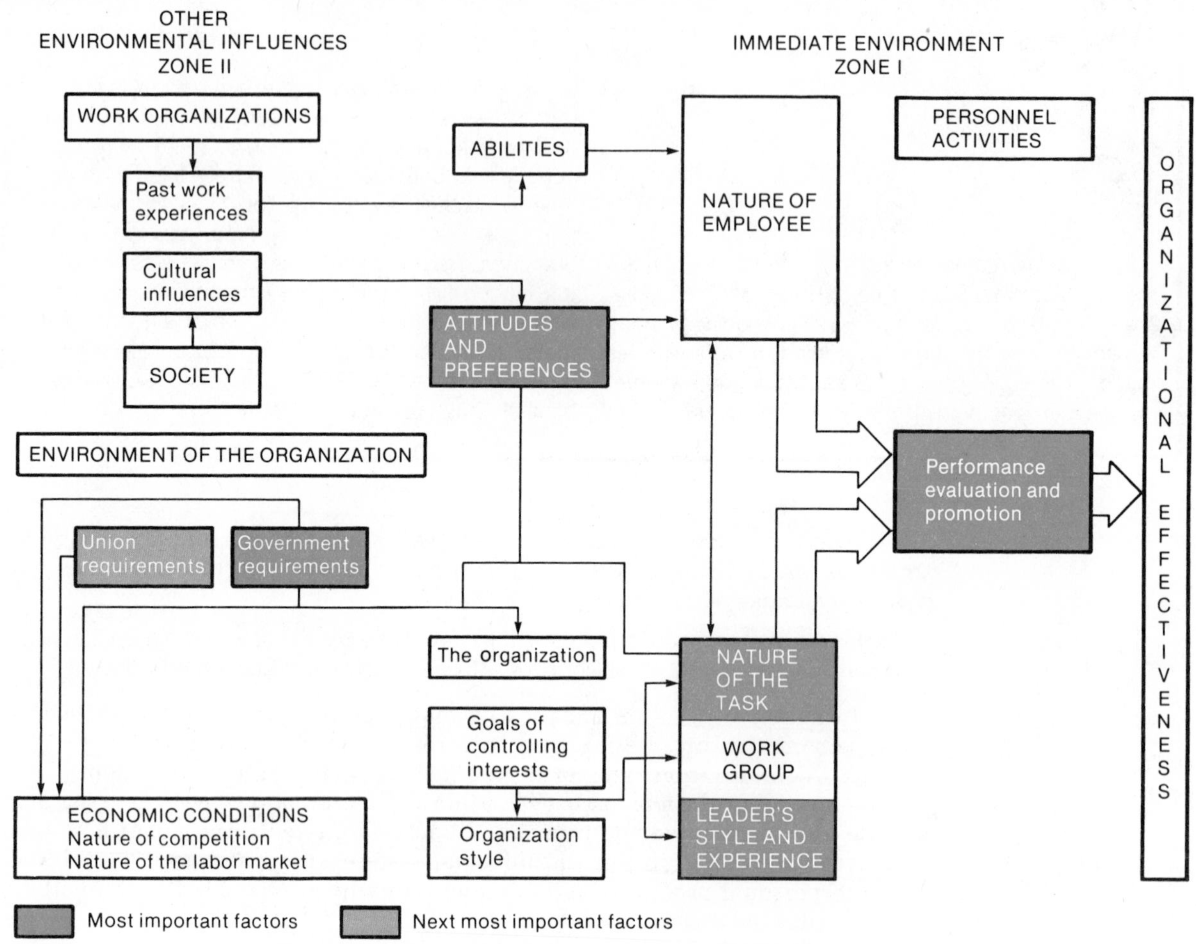

personnel method for allocating these rewards. By inducing enterprises to keep better records to support their decisions, government action has indirectly encouraged better performance evaluation systems. In some cases, enterprises have dropped performance evaluation and rely more strictly on seniority.

What impact has the government had on promotions? One example is the 1973 agreement of American Telephone and Telegraph with the EEOC. AT&T agreed to provide 50,000 higher paying jobs (5,000 of them managerial jobs) for women and 6,000 jobs for minorities (800 managerial jobs). New York Bell, in a response to a State of New York Human Rights Division investigation, agreed to promote women to 57 percent of its supervisory jobs, 46 percent of the middle manager jobs, and 20 percent of its top management jobs.

Recent court cases, such as *Rome* v. *General Motors Corporation* and *Baxter* v. *Savannah Sugar Refining Corporation,* have tended to require enterprises to set up formal performance evaluation systems so that promotions do not discriminate. Other recent cases *(Albemarle Paper Co.* v. *Moody, Wade* v. *Mississippi Cooperative Extension Service)* have indicated that when formal performance evaluation systems are used, they must not be administered or set up in such a way that results discriminate against protected groups.

The third factor influencing performance evaluation is the attitudes and preferences of employees. For many people, especially those whose values fit the work ethic (such as Felipe) evaluations and promotions can be very important. But if this process is badly handled, turnover can increase, morale decline, and productivity drop, as equity and expectancy theory would predict. For employees with instrumental attitudes toward work, performance evaluation is just another process at work. Since work is not too important to them, neither are evaluations. They want a job to get money, and that is it. They might even refuse promotions that involve more responsibility.

The fourth factor that can affect performance evaluation is the leader's (supervisor's) style. Supervisors can use the formal system in a number of ways: fairly or unfairly, in a supportive manner or punitively, positively or negatively. If the supervisor is punitive and negative with an employee who responds to positive reinforcement, performance evaluation can lead to the opposite of the results expected by the enterprise.

Finally, if there is a union present in the enterprise, performance evaluations and the promotion process might be affected. For example, promotion criteria might be written into the contract. Different unions take different positions in support of or opposition to formal performance evaluation. Most oppose the use of nonmeasurable, nonproduction-related factors in performance evaluation. They have good reason to doubt the usefulness of a factor like "initiative" in promotion.

These are the major factors affecting the performance evaluation and promotion process. Now we will briefly examine the case for and against the use of formal performance evaluation.

TO EVALUATE OR NOT TO EVALUATE

Why hasn't Felipe ever been evaluated by his supervisor? In order to answer that question, picture the following scene:

The setting: Office of the executive vice president of Partridge Enterprises. Present are the executive vice president and the vice presidents of the corporation.

Tom Smith (executive vice president): As you know, we're here to make a recommendation to John (the president) on what if anything to do about Mary's suggestion. Mary, why don't you review the issue?

Mary Hartford (vice president, personnel): You all received a copy of my memo to J. B. As you know, when I came here three years ago I felt one of our top priorities in personnel would be to get an evaluation system really running on line here. I want this because performance evaluation is an outstanding motivation technique. After much thought and planning, the results are in my memo. I recommend we institute an MBO type evaluation system from vice presidents through section heads and a graphic rating scale for below that. The MBO would be done quarterly, the rating scale semiannually, and we'd tie rewards such as raises and promotions to the results of the evaluation.

The details are in these memos. We're too big and geographically dispersed now to continue using our informal system.

Tom: Sounds good to me.

Dave Artem (vice president marketing): Me too.

Will Roxer (vice president, finance): Looks fine, Mary.

Fred Fairfax (vice president, manufacturing): Well, it doesn't to me. We had one of these papermill forms systems here ten years ago, and it was a waste of time. It just meant more paper work for us down on the firing line. You staff people sit up here dreaming up more for us to do. We're overburdened now. Besides, I called a few buddies in big firms who have P.E. They say it involves a lot of training of evaluators and it makes half the employees mad when they don't get 100 percent scores on the "grade report." It gets down to a lot of politics when it's all said and done.

If you recommend this, I'll send J. B. a counterproposal and I'll call him to see I get my way, too.

This meeting illustrates many of the arguments pro and con on formal performance evaluation. Let me sum them up for you. Those who favor formal performance evaluation contend that it serves several purposes:

Developmental purposes. It helps determine which employees need more training. It helps evaluate the results of training programs. It helps the employee-supervisor counseling relationship, and it encourages supervisors to observe employee behavior to help employees.

Reward purposes. It helps the enterprise decide who should receive pay raises and promotions. It helps determine who will be laid off. It reinforces the employees' motivation to perform, and so the enterprise's performance increases.

Personnel planning purposes. It serves as a valuable input to skills inventories and personnel planning.

It can be used to validate selection tools.

Performance evaluation will take place in any case, so formal systems are better than informal.

Most enterprises have formal performance evaluation systems, and most of them are satisfied with them.

Those who oppose the formal performance evaluation systems argue that:

They increase paperwork and bureaucracy without benefiting employees much. Operating managers do not use them in reward decisions. (Systems problems)

Managers and employees dislike the evaluation process and are not effective. (Evaluator problems)

Employees who are not evaluated in the top performance category experience a reverse motivation effect: They slow down. (Employee problems)

These problems will be discussed in the next section of the chapter.

On balance, the research indicates that when properly run, a formal performance system achieves its objectives better than no system or only an informal system. That is why most supervisors, office employees, and middle managers experience formal performance evaluation. A majority of blue-collar employees do also.

REASONS FOR MALFUNCTION OR FAILURE

Any system or function can fail or malfunction. Performance evaluation is no exception. Performance evaluation can malfunction because of problems with the system design and operation, the evaluator, or the employee.

System design and operating problems

Performance evaluation systems can fail or malfunction because they are poorly designed. The design can be blamed if the criteria for evaluation are poor, the technique used is cumbersome, or the system is more form than substance. If the criteria used focus on activities instead of output results, or on the person rather than performance, performance evaluation will be hurt. Some evaluation techniques take a long time to do or require extensive written analysis, both of which many managers resist. If this is the problem, another technique can be chosen. Finally, some systems are not on line and running. Some supervisors use the system, but others just fill out the paperwork. Top management's support for performance evaluation can remedy this problem of ritualism.

Let's get back to Felipe and his supervisor, Ed Smart. Now that the vice presidents have had their meeting about performance evaluation, the tentative decision to start up Mary's plan has been passed on to the department heads.

Bob

Ed

Bob Woods (department head): I'm just reviewing your suggested pay and promotions for your unit, Ed. You know I try to delegate as much as I can. But I know some of the people you have set here for big raises and promotions, and I notice some surprising omissions. Since I'm responsible for the whole department, I'd like to review this with you. Understand, I'm not trying to undercut you, Ed.

Ed Smart (supervisor): Oh, I understand, Bob. No problem! Where do you want to start?

Bob: Let me just highspot. I note that Mo Gibbs, who's always been in our high reward group, isn't here, nor is Felipe Hernandez, a good worker. And you do have Joe Berlioz in your high reward group. In the past, he never appeared there. How did you make these recommendations?

Ed: I looked my people over and used my best judgment. That's what you pay me for, isn't it?

Bob: Sure, Ed, but what facts did you use—did you look at the quarterly output printout, their personnel files, or what? How about performance evaluations—Partridge is thinking about a formal system to evaluate employees and help decide who should be promoted and get raises.

Ed: I believe I know my people best. I don't need to go through a lot of paperwork and files to come up with my recommendations.

Too often, a typical manager is like Ed. He knows there is a formal performance evaluation system, but he files it instead of using it. This does no one any good.

Problems with the evaluator

Even if the system is well designed, problems can arise if the evaluators (usually supervisors) are not cooperative and well trained. Supervisors may not be comfortable with the process of evaluation, or what Douglas McGregor called playing God. Often this is because they have not been adequately trained or they have not participated in the design of the program. Inadequate training of evaluators can lead to a series of evaluator problems in performance including:

- The halo effect.
- Standards of evaluation.
- Central tendency.
- Recent behavior bias.
- Personal biases.

The halo effect. The halo effect appears in evaluation when the evaluator tends to assign the same rating or level to each factor being rated for an employee. This results from an overall assessment of the person which totally colors the evaluator's view of the employee.

Standards of evaluation. Problems with evaluation standards arise because of perceptual differences in the meaning of the words used to evaluate employees. Thus *good, adequate, satisfactory,* and *excellent* may mean different things to different evaluators. Some teachers are "easy As," while others almost never give an A. *They* differ in their interpretation of *excellent.* If only one evaluator is used, the evaluation can be distorted. This difficulty arises mostly in graphic rating scales but may also appear with essays, critical incidents, and checklists.

In many systems there is a tendency to rate persons higher than they should be, especially if negative ratings must be explained to employees. This leads to overly lenient evaluations—the performance evaluation equivalent of grade inflation.

Central tendency. Studies have found that some evaluators rate all their personnel within a narrow range. No matter what the actual performance differences between individuals might be, supervisors may rate them all either average or above average. This distorts the results for promotion and compensation decisions. The problem is most likely to be found with graphic rating scales.

Recent-behavior bias. One difficulty with many of the evaluation systems is the time frame of the behavior being evaluated. Evaluators forget more about past behavior than current behavior. Thus many persons are evaluated more on the results of the past several weeks than on six months' average behavior.

Some employees are well aware of this difficulty. If they know the dates of the evaluation, they make it their business to be visible and noticed in many positive ways for several weeks in advance. Many evaluation systems suffer from this difficulty. It can be mitigated by using a technique such as critical incident or management by objectives (MBO) or by irregularly scheduled evaluations.

Personal biases. Various studies have indicated that evaluators' biases can influence their evaluation of employees. If evaluators like certain employees better than others, this can influence the ratings they give. This problem is related to the effects of prejudices against groups of people. Pressures from governmental agencies and managerial values of fairness should lead to equal opportunity and fair performance evaluation. The result should be increased rewards, promotions, and significant careers for all employees, of both sexes and all races, religions, and nationalities. Some evaluation techniques (such as forced choice, field review, performance tests, and MBO) tend to reduce this problem.

Managers should examine the patterns of evaluation and promotion to determine if there might be systematic discrimination at evaluation time and take steps such as supervisory training or discipline to reduce this bias.

Most of the evaluator problems discussed above can be solved by training the evaluator. This training is of two types: how to rate effectively, and how to conduct effective evaluation interviews. The latter is discussed later in this chapter. There is much research to indicate that evaluator training reduces rating errors. In fact, the quality of the evaluator is more important to effective evaluation than the technique used. Training alone will not eliminate all evaluator problems, just as driver training does not eliminate speeding and accidents. But evaluator training, combined with good system design, can make performance evaluation more effective.

Employee problems with performance evaluation

For the evaluation system to work well, the employees must understand it, must feel it is fair, and must be work oriented enough to care about the results. If the system is not explained to the employees so that they understand it, they will not work effectively. One way to foster this understanding is for the employees to participate in system design and be trained to some extent in performance evaluation. Another is the use of self-evaluation systems. With regard to fairness, performance evaluation is in some ways like grading systems in schools. If you have received grades that you thought were unfair and inequitable, that were incorrectly computed or based on the "wrong things" (like attendance alone, for example), you know what your reactions were! Students will say "I got an A" for a course in which they worked hard and were fairly rewarded. They will say *"He* (or she) gave me a D" if they feel it was unfair. Their reactions sometimes are to give up or get angry. Similar responses can come from employees as well. If performance evaluations are incompetent or unfair, the employees may just not listen to them.

Performance evaluation may also be less effective than desired if the employee is not work oriented and sees work only as a means to ends sought off the job. It might be seen only as paperwork, unless the evaluation is so negative that the employee fears termination.

Some critics believe that employees who are rated poorly will not improve their performance but will give up. This is compounded if the technique used is viewed as a zero-sum game—that is, some win and some lose as a result of it. With a system like forced distribution, 90 percent of the people must be told they are not highly regarded, whether they are or not. One study found that 77 percent of General Electric's personnel ranked themselves rather highly.

In forced choice only 10 percent would be rated highly, so 67 to 77 percent of them would find such an evaluation a deflating experience. Some of the performance evaluation tools (forced distribution, ranking, paired comparisons) do not build in an explanation of why the person was ranked as he was. It might be argued that everyone cannot be tops, so the best are rewarded, and the worst will leave. Sometimes quite the contrary happens! Of those who were evaluated poorly at GE, 60 percent lost heart but stayed because they figured they had nowhere else to go.

But this analysis is too simple. In one summary of the research on how a person's expectations of what was going to happen in the evaluation affected his or her reactions to evaluation and behavior afterwards it was found that reaction to positive and negative feedback varied depending on a series of variables: (1) the importance of the task and the motivation to perform it, (2) how highly the employee rates the evaluator, (3) the extent to which the employee has a positive self-image, and (4) the expectancies the employee had prior to the evaluation; for example, did the employee expect a good evaluation or a bad one?

The critics' analysis is based on one theory of the reactions to feedback (self-enhancement/esteem theory). But most research does *not* support this position. Rather, all four conditions listed above affect the likely results of evaluation.

In sum, there are problems with performance evaluation: with the system, the evaluator, and the employee. However, following the suggestions given here can make performance evaluation a useful personnel activity.

Performance evaluation and promotion are personnel activities which are between Stage II and Stage III in development, as defined in Chapter 1 (Exhibit 1–6). There have been studies of evaluation and promotion, as in Stage II, but there is some conflict in the data from the studies, as is true of Stage III functions.

FORMAL EVALUATION

John Partridge, president of Partridge Enterprises, reviewed the proposal from Mary Hartford and Fred Fairfax's complaints. He invited both in for a conference. He was pleased to see the general support for the proposal. But Fred is a key executive, and his support is needed, too.

Fred voiced his opposition, elaborating on the criticisms he had given at the vice presidents' meeting. Then John asked Mary to review the reasons for formal performance evaluation. He approved of the formal approach, and he asked Mary to review briefly how formal performance evaluation would work. She then reviewed the six steps, the alternate approaches Partridge could use, and the one she was recommending.

For formal performance evaluation to be effective, six steps must be taken:

Six steps in formal performance evaluation:

1. Establish performance standards for each position and the criteria for evaluation.
2. Establish performance evaluation policies on when to evaluate, how often to evaluate, and who should evaluate.

3. Have evaluators gather data on employee performance.
4. Have evaluators (and employees in some systems) evaluate employees' performance.
5. Discuss the evaluation with the employee.
6. Make decisions and file the evaluation.

Step 1 was performed when job analysis and work measurement took place (see Chapter 4). But the key issue is: What is and should be evaluated?

The factors on which an employee is evaluated are called the *criteria of the evaluation.* Examples include quality of work, quantity of work, and how well the employee gets along with others at work. One of the major problems is that some systems make *person evaluations* rather than *performance evaluations.*

The criteria used are critical in effective performance evaluation systems. They must be established to keep EEO agencies satisfied, too. After a thorough review of the literature, Patricia Smith listed four characteristics of effective criteria. They must be:

Relevant. Reliable and valid measures of the characteristics being evaluated, and as closely related to job output as possible.

Unbiased. Based on the characteristic, not the person.

Significant. Directly related to enterprise goals.

Practical. Measurable and efficient for the enterprise in question.

Do you think the criterion used in the cartoon, shown on the following page, fits these characteristics?

The evidence is very clear that single performance measures are ineffective because success is multifaceted. Most studies indicate that multiple criteria are necessary to measure performance completely. The multiple criteria are added together statistically or combined into a single multifaceted measure. The criteria choice is not an easy process. One must be careful to evaluate both activities (for example, number of calls a salesperson makes) and results (for example, dollars of sales). A variation is to evaluate both results and how they were accomplished.

Probably a combination of results and activities is desirable for criteria. How do you weight the importance of multiple criteria? For example, if the salesperson is being evaluated on both number of calls and sales dollars and is high on one and low on the other, what is the person's overall rating? Management must weight these criteria.

Michael Kelley studied the evaluation of research scientists, whose job duties are not clear. When the tasks are not clear and performance standards are hard to specify, he found the enterprise responds by asking third persons (such as employee peers and other supervisors) for their opinion of the employee's performance.

The criteria selected depend on the purpose of the evaluation. If the purpose is to improve performance on the job, they should be performance related. If social skills or personality are vital on this or future jobs, these should be stressed.

A BNA study found that for white-collar workers, performance factors such

"Your work is fine, Perkins. It's your aftershave I can't stand."

Drawing by Frascino; © 1973 The New Yorker Magazine, Inc.

as the following were used by these percentages of enterprises surveyed: quality of work (93 percent), quantity of work (90 percent), job knowledge (85 percent), and attendance (79 percent). Personality factors used were initiative (87 percent), cooperation (87 percent), dependability (86 percent), and need for supervision (67 percent). The data for blue-collar workers were parallel: performance factors included quality of work (used by 91 percent), quantity of work (91 percent), attendance (86 percent), and job knowledge (85 percent). Personality factors surveyed were dependability (86 percent), initiative (83 percent), cooperation (83 percent), and need for supervision (77 percent).

This study found that hard-to-measure personality traits are widely used. But the key issue is the weighting of the factors. So perhaps they evaluate the personality factors but do not weight them equally with performance. But perhaps they do.

Whether the evaluation should be based on actual or potential performance depends, it seems to me, on the major purpose of the evaluation for the personnel function. In this respect there are three principal purposes of performance evaluation:

- Improvement of performance.
- Promotion consideration.
- Salary and wage adjustments.

If the main purposes are improved performance or wage adjustment, the emphasis should be on actual performance. If the main purpose is possible promotion, a different emphasis is needed which will assess potential performance on a new job. This is similar to the selection decision, in which past performance on one job must be projected to possible performance on a different one. This is easier to do if the employee has had experience that is relevant to the new job. But the emphasis is different, and assessment of future potential on a different job is more difficult than actual assessment of past performance.

Set policies on when, how often, and who evaluates

When should evaluation be done? There are two basic decisions to be made regarding the timing of performance appraisal: one is when to do it, and the other is how often. In many enterprises performance evaluations are scheduled for arbitrary dates such as the date the person was hired (anniversary date). Or every employee may be evaluated on or near a single calendar date (e.g., May 25). Although the single-day approach is convenient administratively, it probably is not a good idea. It requires managers to spend a lot of time conducting evaluation interviews and completing forms at one time, which may lead them to want to "get it over with" quickly. This probably encourages halo effect ratings, for example. In addition, it may not be related to the normal task cycle of the employee, which can make it difficult for the manager to evaluate performance effectively.

It makes more sense to schedule the evaluation at the completion of a task cycle. For example, tax accountants see the year as April 16 to April 15. Professors consider that the year starts at the beginning of the fall term and terminates after the spring term. For others without clear task cycles based on dates, one way to set the date is by use of the MBO technique, whereby the manager and employee agree upon a task cycle, terminating in evaluation at a specific time. Another approach is to schedule an evaluation when there is a significant change (positive or negative) in an employee's performance.

How often should evaluation be done? The second question concerns how often evaluation should be done. A BNA study found that 74 percent of white-collar and 58 percent of blue-collar employees were evaluated annually, and 25 percent of white-collar and 30 percent of blue-collar employees were evaluated semiannually. About 10 percent were evaluated more often than semiannually.

Psychologists have found that feedback on performance should be given frequently, and the closer the feedback to the action, the more effective it is. For example, it is more effective for a professor to correct an error on a computer program the first time the error appears and show the student how to change it than to wait and flunk the student at the end of the term.

Why, then, do so few firms evaluate frequently? Generally speaking, it is because managers and employees have lots of other things to do. One way to reconcile the ideal with the reality in this respect is for the manager to give frequent feedback to employees informally, and then formally summarize performance at evaluation time. This, of course, is based on the assumption that employees value evaluation and feedback.

As Exhibit 8–2 shows, performance evaluation is another personnel activity which involves both line managers and personnel specialists. For performance evaluation to be more than a yearly paperwork exercise, top management must encourage its use and use it to make reward decisions such as promotions.

EXHIBIT 8–2
Involvement of personnel and operating managers in performance evaluation

Performance evaluation function	*Operating manager (OM)*	*Personnel manager (PM)*
Establish performance standards	Approves the standards	Calculated by PM and engineers
Set policy on when performance evaluation takes place	Approves the policy	Recommends the policy
Set policy on who evaluates	Approves the policy	Recommends the policy
Set policy on criteria of evaluation	Approves the policy	Recommends the policy
Choose the evaluation system	Approves the system	Recommends the system
Train the evaluators		Done by PM
Review employee performance	Done by OM	
Discuss the evaluation with the employee	Done by OM	
File the performance evaluation		Done by PM

Who should evaluate the employee? Exhibit 8–2 indicates that the operating manager (the supervisor) does so. This is true in the huge majority of cases. Other possibilities include:

Rating by a committee of several superiors. The supervisors chosen are those most likely to come in contact with the employee. This approach has the advantages of offsetting bias on the part of one superior alone and adding additional information to the evaluation, especially if it follows a group meeting format.

Rating by the employee's peers (co-workers). In the peer evaluation system the co-workers must know the level of performance of the employee being evaluated. For this system to work, it is preferable for the evaluating peers to trust one another and not be competitive for raises and promotions. This approach may be useful when the tasks of the work unit require frequent working contracts among peers.

Rating by the employee's subordinates. Exxon used this system, and it is used in some universities (students evaluate faculty). It is used more for the developmental aspects of performance evaluation than some of the other methods are.

Rating by someone outside the immediate work situation. This is known as the *field review technique.* In this method a specialized appraiser from outside the job setting, such as a personnel specialist, rates the employee. This is often costly, so it is generally used only for exceptionally important jobs. But it might be used for the entire work force if accusations of prejudice must be countered. A crucial consideration is that the outside evaluator is not likely to have as much data as evaluators in any of the other four approaches and the data developed are from an atypical situation.

Self-evaluation. In this case the employee evaluates herself or himself, with the techniques used by other evaluators or different ones. This approach seems to be used more often for the developmental (as opposed to evaluative) aspects of performance evaluation. It is also used to evaluate an employee who works in physical isolation.

Finally a combination of these approaches can be used. The supervisor's evaluation can be supplemented by a self-evaluation; when evaluation is done jointly, this can be an MBO exercise. The supervisor's results could be supplemented by subordinates' or peers' evaluations.

Evaluation by superiors is the most frequently used method, as noted above. Self-evaluation is used in about 5 percent of evaluations. Peer evaluation is sometimes used by the military and universities but is rarely used elsewhere.

It is probable that evaluation by superiors will continue to be the principal approach used. If the primary purpose of the evaluation is developmental, then the enterprise might consider supplementing it with subordinate evaluations or self-evaluation. If the purpose of the process is reward, then the enterprise might consider adding peer evaluation to superiors' ratings. The field review approach would be used only in special cases. The key to successful performance evaluation appears to be well-trained, carefully selected evaluators who are knowledgeable about the performance of those being evaluated.

Gather data on employees

With regard to gathering data on employees, the evaluators gather information by observation, analysis of data and records, and discussion with the employees. The data they gather are influenced by the criteria used to evaluate, the primary purpose of the evaluation, and the technique used to do the evaluation.

EVALUATE THE EMPLOYEES: EVALUATION TECHNIQUES

A number of techniques for evaluation will be described here. There are several ways to classify these tools. The three categories used here are: individual evaluation methods, multiple-person evaluation methods, and other methods.

Individual evaluation methods

There are five ways to evaluate the person individually. In these systems, employees are evaluated one at a time without *directly* comparing them to other employees.

Graphic rating scale. The most widely used performance evaluation technique is a graphic rating scale. It is also one of the oldest techniques in use. In this technique, the evaluator is presented with a graph such as that shown in Exhibit 8–3 and asked to rate employees on each of the characteristics listed. The number of characteristics rated varies from a few to several dozen.

The ratings can be in a series of boxes as in the exhibit, or they can be on a continuous scale (0–9, or so). In the latter case, the evaluator places a check above descriptive words ranging from *none* to *maximum.* Typically, these ratings are then assigned points. For example, in Exhibit 8–3, *outstanding* may be assigned a score of 4 and *unsatisfactory* a score of 0. Total scores are then computed. In some plans, greater weights may be assigned to more important traits. Evaluators are often asked to explain each rating with a sentence or two.

Two recent modifications of the scale have been designed to make it more effective. One is Fritz Blanz and Edwin Ghiselli's Mixed Standard Scale. Instead

EXHIBIT 8–3
Typical graphic rating scale

Name ____________ Dept. ____________ Date ____________

	Out-standing	*Good*	*Satis-factory*	*Fair*	*Unsatis-factory*
Quantity of work Volume of acceptable work under normal conditions Comments:	☐	☐	☐	☐	☐
Quality of work Thoroughness, neatness and accuracy of work Comments:	☐	☐	☐	☐	☐
Knowledge of job Clear understanding of the facts or factors pertinent to the job Comments:	☐	☐	☐	☐	☐
Personal qualities Personality, appearance, sociability, leadership, integrity Comments:	☐	☐	☐	☐	☐
Cooperation Ability and willingness to work with associates, supervisors, and subordinates toward common goals Comments:	☐	☐	☐	☐	☐
Dependability Conscientious, thorough, accurate, reliable with respect to attendance, lunch periods, reliefs, etc. Comments:	☐	☐	☐	☐	☐
Initiative Earnestness in seeking increased responsibilities. Self-starting, unafraid to proceed alone? Comments:	☐	☐	☐	☐	☐

EXHIBIT 8–4

Standards of performance: Excerpts from U.S. Air Force officers' graphic rating scale

Far below standard rating:

1. Has serious gaps in technical-professional knowledge
   Knows only most rudimentary phases of job
   Lack of knowledge affects productivity
   Requires abnormal amount of checking

2. Reluctant to make decisions on his own
   Decisions are usually not reliable
   Declines to accept responsibility for decisions

3. Fails to plan ahead
   Disorganized and usually unprepared
   Objectives are not met on time

4. Wastes or misuses resources
   No system established for accounting of material
   Causes delay for others by mismanagement

of just rating a trait such as *initiative,* the evaluator is given three statements to describe the trait, such as:

She is a real self-starter. She always takes the initiative and her superior never has to stimulate her. (Best description)
While generally he shows initiative, occasionally his superior has to prod him to get his work done.
He has a tendency to sit around and wait for directions. (Poorest description)

After each description the rater places a check mark (the employee fits the description), a plus sign (the employee is better than the statement), or a minus sign (the employee is poorer than the statement). This results in a seven-point scale, which the authors contend is better than the graphic rating scale.

The second modification is to add operational and benchmark statements to describe different levels of performance. For example, if the employee is evaluated on job knowledge, the form gives a specific example: "What has the employee done to actually demonstrate depth, currency or breadth of job knowledge in the performance of duties? Consider both quality and quantity of work." The performance description statement to guide the rater on this gives these examples of persons deserving that rating (see Exhibit 8–4).

Forced choice. The forced-choice method of evaluation was developed because other methods used at the time led to too many high ratings, which made promotion decisions difficult. In forced choice, the evaluator must choose from a set of descriptive statements about the employee. Typical sets of these statements are given in Exhibit 8–5. The two-, three-, or four-statement items are grouped in a way that the evaluator cannot easily judge which statements apply to the most effective employee.

Typically, personnel specialists prepare the items for the form, and supervisors or other personnel specialists rate the items for applicability. That is, they determine which statements describe effective and ineffective behavior. The supervisor then evaluates the employee. The personnel department adds up the number of statements in each category (for example, effective behavior), and they are summed into an effectiveness index. Forced choice can be used by superiors, peers, subordinates, or a combination of these in evaluating employees.

EXHIBIT 8–5
Forced-choice items used by Exxon, Inc.

MOST		1	MOST
A	Does not anticipate difficulties.		A
B	Grasps explanations quickly.		B
C	Rarely wastes time.		C
D	Easy to talk to.		D
MOST		2	MOST
A	Leader in group activities.		A
B	Wastes time on unimportant things.		B
C	Cool and calm at all times.		C
D	Hard worker.		D

Source: Richard S. Barrett, *Performance Rating.* © 1966 by Richard S. Barrett.

Essay evaluation. In the essay technique of evaluation, the evaluator is asked to describe the strong and weak aspects of the employee's behavior. In some enterprises, the essay technique is the only one used; in others, the essay is combined with another form, such as a graphic rating scale. In this case, the essay summarizes the scale, elaborates on some of the ratings, or discusses added dimensions not on the scale. In both of these approaches the essay can be open ended, but in most cases there are guidelines on the topics to be covered, the purpose of the essay, and so on. The essay method can be used by evaluators who are superiors, peers, or subordinates of the employee to be evaluated.

Management by objectives. Another individual evaluation method in use today is management by objectives (MBO). In this system, the supervisor and employee to be evaluated jointly set objectives in advance for the employee to try to achieve during a specified period. The method encourages, if not requires, them to phrase these objectives primarily in quantitative terms. The evaluation consists of a joint review of the degree of achievement of the objectives. This approach combines the superior and self-evaluation systems.

Exhibit 8–6 is an example of a report developed by a salesperson to show to what extent the objectives were achieved. The employee would also be asked to explain why some were not achieved. Then the objectives for the next period would be agreed upon jointly.

EXHIBIT 8–6
MBO evaluation report for salesperson

Objectives set	*Period objective*	*Accomplishments*	*Variance*
1. Number of sales calls	100	104	+4%
2. Number of new customers contacted	20	18	−10%
3. Number of wholesalers stocking new product 117	30	30	0%
4. Sales of product 12	10,000	9,750	−7.5%
5. Sales of product 17	17,000	18,700	+10%
6. Customer complaints/Service calls	35	11	−33⅓%
7. Number of sales correspondence courses successfully completed	4	2	−50%
8. Number of sales reports in home office within 1 day of end of month	12	10	−20%

Critical incident technique. In this technique, personnel specialists and operating managers prepare lists of statements of very effective and very ineffective behavior for an employee. These are the *critical incidents.* The personnel specialists combine these statements into categories, which vary with the job. For example, W. K. Kircher and Marvin Dunnette described 13 categories they used for evaluating salespersons at the 3M Company. Two of the categories are calling on all accounts and initiating new sales approaches. Another set of categories for evaluating managers generally includes, for example, control of quality, control of people, and organizing activities.

Once the categories are developed and statements of effective and ineffective behavior are provided, the evaluator prepares a log for each employee. During the evaluation period, the evaluator records examples of critical (outstandingly good or bad) behaviors in each of the categories, and the log is used to evaluate the employee at the end of the period. It is also *very useful* for the evaluation interview, since the evaluator can be specific in making positive and negative comments, and it avoids recency bias. The critical incident technique is more likely to be used by superiors than in peer or subordinate evaluations.

Checklists and weighted checklists. Another type of individual evaluation method is the checklist. In its simplest form, the checklist is a set of adjectives or descriptive statements. If the rater believes that the employee possesses a trait listed, the rater checks the item; if not, the rater leaves it blank. A rating score from the checklist equals the number of checks.

A more recent variation is the weighted checklist. Supervisors or personnel specialists familiar with the jobs to be evaluated prepare a large list of descriptive statements about effective and ineffective behavior on jobs, similar to the critical incident process. Judges who have observed behavior on the job sort the statements into piles describing behavior that is scaled from excellent to poor (usually on a 7–11 scale). When there is reasonable agreement on an item (for example, when the standard deviation is small), it is included in the weighted checklist. The weight is the average score of the raters prior to use of the checklist.

The supervisors or other raters receive the checklist without the scores and check the items that apply, as with an unweighted checklist. The employee's evaluation is the sum of the scores (weights) on the items checked. Checklists and weighted checklists can be used by evaluators who are superiors, peers, or subordinates, or by a combination.

Behaviorly anchored rating scales. Another technique which essentially is based on the critical incident approach is the behaviorally anchored rating scale (BARS). This technique is also called the behavioral expectation scale (BES). This is a new, relatively infrequently used technique.

Supervisors give descriptions of actually good and bad performance, and personnel specialists group these into categories (five to ten is typical). As with weighted checklists, the items are evaluated by supervisors (often other than those who submitted the items). A procedure similar to that for weighted checklists is used to verify the evaluations (outstandingly good, for example) with the smallest standard deviation, hopefully around 1.5 on a 7-point scale. These items are then used to construct the BARS.

Exhibit 8–7 is an example of a BARS for a grocery clerk's knowledge and judgment scale. As with this scale, typically the BARS is constructed of six to seven items for each behavioral category.

Recently James Goodale and Ronald Burke have developed an evaluation scale that follows the BARS approach but is not based on specific behavior for a job. The ten dimensions on which all personnel are evaluated are: interpersonal relationships, organizing and planning, reaction to problems, reliability, communicating, adaptability, growth, productivity, quality of work, and teaching. In a sense, this scale is a great deal like a graphic rating scale in that it is used for all employees, but the scale is based on descriptions of behavioral incidents, as in BARS. This approach may prove to be a major step forward for usage of BARS. BARS can be used for evaluation by superiors, peers, or subordinates, or a combination of these.

In the discussion of evaluation approaches and techniques, we have implied that each person is evaluated independent of others, unless the employee is one of the few being evaluated with a multiperson evaluation technique. But

EXHIBIT 8–7

Behaviorally anchored rating scale for evaluating judgment and knowledge of grocery clerks

Performance level	Scale	Behavioral anchor
Extremely good performance	7	–
	–	–By knowing the price of items, this checker would be expected to look for mismarked and unmarked items.
Good performance	6	–
	–	–You can expect this checker to be aware of items that constantly fluctuate in price. –You can expect this checker to know the various sizes of cans—No. 303, No. 2½.
Slightly good performance	5	–
	–	–When in doubt, this checker would ask the other clerk if the item is taxable.
	–	–This checker can be expected to verify with another checker a discrepancy between the shelf and the marked price before ringing up that item.
Neither poor nor good performance	4	–
	–	–When operating the quick check, the lights are flashing, this checker can be expected to check out a customer with 15 items.
Slightly poor performance	3	–
	–	–You could expect this checker to ask the customer the price of an item that he does not know.
	–	–In the daily course of personal relationships, may be expected to linger in long conversations with a customer or another checker.
Poor performance	2	–
	–	–In order to take a break, this checker can be expected to block off the checkstand with people in line.
Extremely poor performance	1	–

Source: L. Fogli, C. L. Hulin, and M. R. Blood, "Development of First-Level Behavioral Job Criteria," *Journal of Applied Psychology*, vol. 55 (1971), pp. 3–8. Copyright 1971 by the American Psychological Association. Reprinted by permission.

this may not be strictly true; the evaluation of one employee can be affected by the evaluations of the others in the work group.

Laboratory research has indicated that when a work group included one employee with poor work attitudes who refused to obey orders, the supervisor evaluated other employees higher. In a study by Ronald Grey and David Kipnis, 59 supervisors of 473 clerical employees were asked to evaluate their employees. The researchers examined how the supervisors evaluated and rewarded them with promotions and pay raises. They found that the presence of employees who were poor in ability and work attitudes (and the proportion of the work group they comprised) affected how the supervisors evaluated *all* the employees. Specifically, when there is one or a small percentage of noncompliant employees, the supervisor gave a *much lower* evaluation to the noncompliant employees and a slightly higher evaluation to the compliant employees. As the percentage of noncompliant employees increased, the supervisors raised the evaluations of the compliant employees *much, much higher.*

Case study research also indicates that some supervisors may perceive pressure not to evaluate all employees at the top of the range. They modify the ratings so they do not seem to have all "excellent" employees. At least some of the time, therefore, evaluators are likely to be influenced in their evaluations of one employee by their evaluations of others in the work group, even when individual evaluation techniques are used.

Multiple-person evaluation methods

The techniques described above are used to evaluate employees one at a time. Three techniques that have been used to evaluate an employee in comparison with other employees being evaluated are discussed in this section.

Ranking. In using the ranking method, the evaluator is asked to rate employees from highest to lowest on some overall criterion. This is very difficult to do if the group of employees being compared numbers over 20. It is also easier to rank the best and worst employees than it is to evaluate the average ones. Simple ranking can be improved by alternative ranking. In this approach the evaluators pick the top and bottom employee first, then select the next highest and next lowest, and move toward the middle.

The ranking method is normally used by superiors evaluating subordinates but could be used by peers as well. It is not normally used for evaluation by subordinates.

Paired comparison. This approach makes the ranking method easier and more reliable. First, the names of the persons to be evaluated are placed on separate sheets (or cards) in a predetermined order, so that each person is compared to all others to be evaluated. The evaluator then checks the person he feels is the better of the two on a criterion for each comparison. Typically the criterion is overall ability to do the present job. The number of times a person is preferred is tallied, and this develops an index of the number of preferences compared to the number being evaluated.

These scores can be converted into standard scores by comparing the scores to the standard deviation and the average of all scores. This method can be used by superiors, peers, subordinates, or some combination of these groups.

Forced distribution. The forced-distribution system is similar to grading on a curve. The evaluator is asked to rate employees in some fixed distribution of categories, such as 10 percent in low, 20 percent in low average, 40 percent in average, 20 percent in high average, and 10 percent in high. One way to do this is to type each employee's name on a card and ask the evaluators to sort the cards into five piles corresponding to the ratings. This should be done twice for the two key criteria of job performance and promotability.

Exhibit 8–8 shows the results of forced-distribution evaluation of 20 employees. One reason forced distribution was developed was to try to alleviate such problems as inflated ratings and central tendency in the graphic rating scale.

A newer variation of forced distribution is the point allocation technique (PAT). In PAT, each rater is given a number of points per employee in the group to be evaluated, and the total points for all employees evaluated cannot exceed the number of points per employee times the number of employees evaluated. The points are allocated on a criterion basis. The forced distribution and

EXHIBIT 8–8
Forced-distribution evaluation of employees in a marketing research unit

High 10%	*Next 20%*	*Middle 40%*	*Next 20%*	*Low 10%*
Leslie Moore	Cinde Lanyon	Max Coggins	Art Willis	Wayne Allison
Tina Little	Sharon Feltman	Tina Holmes	Debbie Salter	Sherry Gruber
	Eddie Dorsey	Julis Jimenex	Tom Booth	
	John Dyer	Lis Amendale	Lance Smith	
		Vince Gaillard		
		Missy Harrington		
		Bill King		
		Shelly Sweat		

PAT are most likely to be used by superiors but could be used by peers or subordinates.

Other methods

Performance tests. One approach to evaluation is to design a job performance test or simulation. Depending on how well the employees do on this, they are promoted or their salaries are adjusted. One such test is used for operating personnel in the Air Force. The assessment center discussed later in the chapter utilizes another.

Field review technique. Unlike many of the approaches discussed above, the field review uses an "objective" outsider as evaluator. The person to be evaluated and the supervisor are questioned orally by an investigator, who usually is from the personnel department. The personnel evaluator probes and questions the supervisor about the employee. This results in an overall rating, such as outstanding, satisfactory, or unsatisfactory.

Which technique to use

Perhaps you now feel saturated with the large number of evaluation techniques. You should know that not all of them are used very often. It is generally recognized that the graphic rating scale is the most widely used technique. Studies indicate that the essay method is also widely used, usually as part of a graphic rating scale form. And checklists are widely used. Studies show that other methods, such as forced choice, critical incident, BARS, performance tests, field review, and MBO, *combined* equal only about 5 percent. Ranking and paired comparison are used by 10 to 13 percent of the employers. MBO is most likely to be used more for managerial, professional, and technical employees, not production and office personnel.

Which technique should be used in a specific instance? The literature on the shortcomings and strengths, reliabilities, and validities of each of these techniques is vast. In essence, there are studies showing that each of the techniques is sometimes good, sometimes poor. The major problems are not with the techniques themselves but *how they are used* and *by whom.* Untrained evaluators or those that have little talent or motivation to evaluate well can destroy or hamper *any* evaluation technique. The evaluator is more critical than the technique in developing effective evaluation systems.

EXHIBIT 8–9

Criteria for choice of performance evaluation techniques

Evaluative Base	*Graphic rating scale*	*Forced choice*	*MBO*	*Essay*	*Critical incidents*	*Weighted checklist*	*BARS*	*Ranking*	*Paired comparison*	*Forced distribution*	*Perfor-mance test*	*Field review*
Developmental cost	Moderate	High	Moderate	Low	Moderate	Moderate	High	Low	Low	Low	High	Moderate
Usage costs	Low	Low	High	High supervisory costs	High	Low	Low	Low	Low	Low	High	High
Ease of use by evaluators	Easy	Moderately difficult	Moderate	Difficult	Difficult	Easy	Easy	Easy	Easy	Easy	Moderately difficult	Easy
Ease of understanding by those evaluated	Easy	Difficult	Moderate	Easy	Easy	Easy	Moderate	Easy	Easy	Easy	Easy	Easy
Useful in promotion decisions	Yes	Yes	Yes	Not easily	Yes	Moderate	Yes	Yes	Yes	Yes	Yes	Yes
Useful in compensa-tion and reward decisions	Yes	Moderate	Yes	Not easily	Yes	Moderate	Yes	Not easily	Not easily	Yes	Yes	Yes
Useful in counseling and development of employees	Moderate	Moderate	Yes	Yes	Yes	Moderate	Yes	No	No	No	Moderate	Yes

Evaluation techniques can be judged on a series of criteria such as costs and purposes. As noted in the discussion of the approaches to evaluation above, at least two major purposes are served by evaluation: counseling and personal development and evaluation for rewards, such as an aid in promotion and decisions. Some evaluation techniques serve one purpose better than others. Some systems cost more to develop and operate than others. Exhibit 8–9 scales the techniques on these criteria to help in the choice.

If the primary purpose of the evaluation is development, for example, then the effective enterprise will use BARS, essay, critical incident, MBO, and field review tools. If the primary purpose of the evaluation is rewards, the effective enterprise will use graphic rating scales, field review, performance tests, forced distribution, MBO, critical incidents, or BARS. And if the primary purpose of the evaluation is developmental and costs are not a concern currently, then field review, MBO, or critical incident methods should be chosen. If the primary purpose is development and costs are a consideration, then BARS or essay methods might be chosen.

What kind of performance evaluation program did Partridge adopt? Mary Hartford described the first part of her proposal to John Partridge after reviewing the criteria, timing, and techniques. She explained that each person would be given specific objectives related to his or her job which were to be achieved. These were the standards for the system and were based on job analysis and work measurement.

For blue-collar and white-collar personnel, they were clear, multiple-purpose standards. They were based primarily on past standards, with some emphasis on future improvement.

The managerial group was to begin to participate in the management by objectives system. They would negotiate with the employees to improve performance. The MBO reviews would be quarterly.

Graphic rating scales would be used semiannually for nonmanagerial employees. The supervisors would choose times for review which matched the work cycle or when major changes in an employee's output were apparent. Personnel would keep track to see that two evaluations took place each year.

Personnel would put on training programs for evaluators and employees to demonstrate how to evaluate effectively and explain the purposes of the system. The evaluators were to be the employees' supervisors.

John thought the suggestions over and approved them. He took the time to explain his reasons to Fred and asked for his support. John also told Mary that when the new system was introduced, he would communicate his full support forcefully to all employees.

DISCUSS THE EVALUATION WITH THE EMPLOYEE

After the evaluator has completed the evaluation, the next thing that should happen is for the evaluation to be discussed with the employee by the evaluator or evaluators in an evaluation interview. Some enterprises use split evaluations to accomplish the dual purposes of evaluations. In evaluation for developmental purposes, the ratings are communicated and appropriate counseling takes place. And in evaluation to determine pay, promotion, and other rewards, the ratings sometimes are not given to the employee. In the usual evaluation, however, the employee acknowledges the evaluation in some way, often by signing a receipt form.

In 97 percent of the enterprises with formal performance evaluation systems,

Norman Maier

Photo courtesy of Houghton Mifflin Company.

the employee receives feedback, normally in the form of an evaluation interview. The evaluator and employee get together for an interview which allows the evaluator to communicate the employee's ratings and to comment on them.

Norman Maier describes three generally used approaches to these interview situations: tell and sell, tell and listen, and problem solving. These are shown in Exhibit 8–10. Research on when each should be used indicates that the tell-and-sell approach is best for new and inexperienced employees, and that the problem-solving approach, which encourages employee participation, is useful for more experienced employees, especially those with work ethic attitudes.

Suggestions for effective evaluation interviews:

1. Superiors and subordinates should prepare for the meeting and be ready to discuss the employee's past performance against the objectives for the period.
2. The superior should put the employee at ease and stress that the interview is not a disciplinary session but a time to review past work, in order to improve the employee's future performance, satisfaction, and personal development.
3. The superior should budget the time so that the employee has approximately half the time to discuss the evaluation and his or her future behavior.
4. The superior should structure the interview as follows:

First, open with *specific positive remarks.* For example, if the employee's quantity of work is good, the superior might say: "John, your work output is excellent. You processed 10 percent more claims than was budgeted."

Second, sandwich performance shortcomings between two positive result discussions. Be specific, and orient the discussion to *performance* comments, *not personal* criticisms. Stress that the purpose of bringing the specific issues up is to alleviate the problems in the *future,* not to criticize the past. Probably no more than one or two important negative points should be brought up at one evaluation. It is difficult for many people to work toward improving more than two points. The handling of negative comments is critical. They should be phrased specifically and be related to *performance,* and it should be apparent to the employee that their purpose is not to criticize but to improve future performance. Many people become very defensive when criticized. Of course, the interviews should be private, between the employee and the evaluator.

Third, conclude with *positive* comments and overall evaluation results.

5. The superior should budget the time for these three aspects of the interview to match the rating. For example, if the employee is an 85 on a scale of 100, 85 percent of the time should be spent on positive comments to *reinforce* this behavior.
6. The final aspect of the interview should focus on *future* objectives and how the superior can help the employee achieve enterprise and personal goals. Properly done, the interviews contribute importantly to the purposes of performance evaluation.

MAKE DECISIONS AND FILE THE EVALUATION

Once the employee and her or his supervisor have discussed the evaluation, the evaluator's superior reviews the evaluation. BNA found that 80 percent of office employees and 76 percent of production employees surveyed had their

EXHIBIT 8–10
Three types of evaluation interviews

Method	*Tell and sell*	*Tell and listen*	*Problem solving*
Role of interviewer	Judge	Judge	Helper
Objective	To communicate evaluation To persuade employee to improve	To communicate evaluation To release defensive feelings	To stimulate growth and development in employee
Assumptions	Employee desires to correct weaknesses if he knows them Any person can improve who so chooses A superior is qualified to evaluate a subordinate	People will change if defensive feelings are removed	Growth can occur without correcting faults Discussing job problems leads to improved performance
Reactions	Defensive behavior suppressed Attempts to cover hostility	Defensive behavior expressed Employee feels accepted	Problem-solving behavior
Skills	Salesmanship Patience	Listening and reflecting feelings Summarizing	Listening and reflecting feelings Reflecting ideas Using exploratory questions Summarizing
Attitude	People profit from criticism and appreciate help	One can respect the feelings of others if one understands them	Discussion develops new ideas and mutual interests
Motivation	Use of positive or negative incentives or both (Extrinsic in that motivation is added to the job itself)	Resistance to change reduced Positive incentive (Extrinsic and some intrinsic motivation)	Increased freedom Increased responsibility (Intrinsic motivation in that interest is inherent in the task)
Gains	Success most probable when employee respects interviewer	Develops favorable attitude to superior which increases probability of success	Almost assured of improvement in some respect
Risks	Loss of loyalty Inhibition of independent judgment Face-saving problems created	Need for change may not be developed	Employee may lack ideas Change may be other than what superior had in mind
Values	Perpetuates existing practices and values	Permits interviewer to change his views in the light of employee's responses Some upward communication	Both learn, since experience and views are pooled Change is facilitated

Source: Reproduced from Norman R. F. Maier, *The Appraisal Interview; Three Basic Approaches* (La Jolla, California: University Associates, 1976). Used with permission.

evaluations reviewed in this manner. Next the personnel department reviews the evaluation and places it on file.

If the employee is unhappy with the evaluation, BNA found that 68 percent of the production employees and 56 percent of the office employees surveyed could appeal it through the union (if they are unionized) or to the evaluator's superior. This is less common in nonbusiness enterprises than businesses. For more data on this, see Chapter 19.

These reviews are designed to prevent situations like Felipe Hernandez's confusion and Ed Smart's failure to give him positive feedback. If the evaluation has been properly done, the employee knows where he or she stands and has received positive feedback on accomplishments and help on shortcomings. This is the developmental aspect of performance evaluation. The reward aspect can include pay raises (see Chapters 11 and 12), and promotions. Let's examine managerial performance evaluation.

MANAGERIAL PERFORMANCE EVALUATION

The evaluation approaches and techniques discussed above apply mainly to performance evaluation for nonmanagerial employees. There are some differences with regard to performance evaluations for managers.

Many, if not most, employers evaluate their managers. A recent BNA survey found that the groups most likely to be evaluated formally are professional/technical employees (76 percent), supervisory managers (76 percent), and middle managers (72 percent). Top managers are formally evaluated in about 50 percent of the enterprises surveyed and informally appraised in another 25 percent.

On what criteria are managers appraised and evaluated? There are many approaches that could be used. One that shows great promise is a system developed by Walter Tornow and Patrick Pinto, who used a management position description questionnaire to identify 13 managerial job factors and to systematically compare and group 433 managerial positions into ten clusters. This kind of approach could lead to systematic evaluation of managerial positions. At present, however, most managers are still evaluated on general factors like managerial skills, personal traits, and capacity.

Typically, the manager is evaluated yearly. The most frequently used techniques, according to a BNA study, include the essay (52 percent), rating scales (45 percent), checklists (26 percent), ranking (13 percent), forced choice (10 percent), and critical incident (8 percent). Many of those in the "other" category (13 percent) use some variation of MBO systems. In 96 percent of the cases, the manager is evaluated by his or her immediate superior. The information is used primarily for reward decisions. In this survey, only 10 percent of the personnel executives rated their management evaluation systems as effective, a discouraging statistic.

Assessment centers

There is one performance evaluation technique that is used primarily for managerial evaluation and selection: the assessment center. Assessment centers were introduced in Chapter 6 on selection.

Joseph Moses et al. define an assessment as "a standardized evaluation of behavior based on multiple inputs." Trained observers using multiple techniques make judgments about behavior, based in part on specially developed assessment simulations. These judgments are pooled at an evaluations meeting at which all relevant data are reported and discussed. The assessors agree on the evaluation of the dimensions and any overall evaluation that is made.

Individuals to be assessed or selected are brought to a facility where, for periods ranging from several days to a week, they are given tests and interviews. They participate in a series of exercises such as management games, leaderless group discussions, in-basket exercises, and mock selection interviews. Assessors are managers whose judgment of people is insightful; they participate in the activities and rate the performance of those being evaluated.

It has been estimated that in 1972 over 100,000 managers passed through assessment centers of such enterprises as AT&T, Sears, J. C. Penney, General Electric, IBM, Sohio, the state of Illinois, and the Internal Revenue Service.

This approach is new, but some evaluations of its usefulness have been done. Most of the research is very positive. Recent literature reviews and analyses, however, have found some problems with them. These problems include overemphasis on interpersonal skills in the evaluations, and examination nerves: the experience of getting nervous and doing poorly on exams. Although assessment centers are new and have shortcomings, they appear to be a very useful mechanism for the evaluation and selection of managers.

PROMOTION SYSTEMS

A promotion is an upward change of position, normally involving greater responsibility and different duties from those of the present position.

For many, promotion does not happen often. Some never experience it in their lifetimes. This is why organizations design reward systems other than promotion—compensation, benefit plans, and so forth. Sometimes what can be called quasipromotions are created to supplement these rewards. The person's title is changed, but the work is not. The older, experienced bookkeeper is promoted to senior bookkeeper, the priest to ArchPriest, the assistant professor to associate professor. Often these are not promotions in the true sense of the word. A promotion usually involves additional or quite different sets of duties and more privileges (added security, admission to clubs, a pension plan, etc.).

The promotion decision is in many ways like the selection decision. The administrator tries to match the best person with the right job. It is different in that, in the promotion decision, the organization has the opportunity to examine performance data. The employer can examine how the employee has done in a job, rather than having to predict how she or he might perform on the job based on test scores, reactions to interviews, or reference letters. It is also different in that the decision is open to greater political pressure. Some candidates for promotion try to influence decision makers by applying their interpersonal skills.

Several criteria have traditionally been used for promotion. Formally, two are most important: merit and seniority. Informally, there is the personality of the candidates and their interpersonal influences.

"And, if for some absurd reason you don't let me get the promotion, please don't let that jerk, Duane Dewlap, get it."

Reprinted by permission The Wall Street Journal.

Seniority, the length of time a person has served, is an important consideration in many promotion decisions. It is calculated on several bases: the organization, the job section, the function performed. Thus, an employee may have ten years' seniority with HEW, five years' seniority in X department (section seniority), and eight years' seniority as a computer programmer (job seniority). This is the required basis for employee promotion in many unionized firms. The unions argue that experience leads to expertise. Unions which take this position resemble Max Weber's bureaucratic model, in which those with the greatest expertise rise to the top. Unions also argue that seniority is a good criterion because it rewards loyalty to the company, is impartial, and is less subject to the biases and favoritism of evaluators.

Management often prefers merit alone, as measured by performance evaluation. They raise the specter of aged incompetents getting all the good jobs if seniority is the sole criterion. The truth lies in between these positions.

In fact, it appears that businesses promote employees on the basis of seniority *and* merit, the relative weight of the criteria varying by the decision and the enterprise. The promotion decisions of managers tend to be informal and based on merit, seniority, and interpersonal attractiveness. EEO and other legal issues may influence some firms to adopt a more formal approach. Performance evaluation ratings are a major indication of merit but hardly the only one considered in promotion decisions.

SUMMARY, CONCLUSIONS, AND RECOMMENDATIONS

Formal performance evaluation of employees is the personnel process by which the enterprise determines how effectively the employee is performing the job. It takes place primarily for white-collar, professional/technical, and managerial employees. It rarely is done for part-time employees, and only about half of all blue-collar employees experience it. Although the data are not entirely clear, it appears that, properly done, performance evaluation is useful for most enterprises and most employees. Promotion is an upward change of position. To summarize the performance evaluation and promotion process, the statements following outline the major points:

1. Factors in the diagnostic model that have significance for performance evaluation and promotion are:
   a. The task performed.
   b. The government.
   c. The attitudes and preferences of the employee.
   d. The leader's or supervisor's style.
   e. The union (if present).
2. The purposes which formal performance evaluation can serve include:
   a. Developmental purposes.
   b. Reward purposes.
   c. Personnel planning purposes.
   d. Validation purposes.
3. Performance evaluation systems can fail or malfunction because of:
   a. Systems design and operating problems.
   b. Problems with the evaluator.
      (1) The halo effect.
      (2) Standards of evaluation.
      (3) Central tendency.
      (4) Recent behavior bias.
      (5) Personal biases.
   c. Employee problems with performance evaluation.
      (1) Employees don't understand the system or its purpose.
      (2) Employees are not work oriented.
      (3) Evaluation may be below the employees' expectations.
4. For formal performance evaluation to be effective, six steps must be taken:
   a. Establish performance standards for each position.
   b. Establish performance evaluation policies on when and how often to evaluate, who should evaluate, the criteria for evaluation, and the evaluation tools to be used.
   c. Have evaluators gather data on employee performance.
   d. Discuss the evaluation with the employee.
   e. Make decisions and file the evaluation.
5. Managerial performance evaluation differs from nonmanagerial performance evaluation in the techniques used and the frequency of evaluations.
6. Criteria which are considered in promotion decisions are both formal and informal:
   a. Formal criteria: Merit and seniority.
   b. Informal criteria: Personality of candidate and interpersonal influences.
7. Properly performed, performance evaluation can contribute to enterprise objectives and employee development and satisfaction.

Based on the above statements, several propositions can be derived regarding the performance evaluation and promotion process:

Proposition 8.1. The larger the enterprise, the more likely it is to have a formal performance evaluation system.

Proposition 8.2. The larger the enterprise, the less volatile it is, and the less complex it is, the more sophisticated will its evaluation tools be.

Proposition 8.3. The larger the organization, the more likely it is to have developed formal promotion systems such as promotable managers' lists and career development plans.

Proposition 8.4. Formal evaluations and promotion systems are recommended for all enterprises, with the possible exception of those that are small, complex, and volatile.

Exhibit 8–11 gives recommendations on the usage of evaluation tools in terms of the ability of the model organizations to use them. It should be obvious from this exhibit that some tools are more universally applicable (essay, critical incident, graphic rating scale, MBO, ranking, paired comparison, forced distribution). Others have fewer applications (performance test, field review, forced choice), and still others are in the middle (assessment centers, weighted checklist).

The next two chapters discuss how the enterprises can improve abilities and attitudes of employees through training and development activities.

Ed Smart was not too happy about having to take time out from his supervisory duties to go to this training session about the new evaluation system. But he'd had some problems with his boss, Bob Woods, over pay and promotions. So even though it sounded like more paperwork and time, he decided to see what they had to say.

The training session began with some short lectures. But most of the session was involved in practice on how to complete the rating forms for several kinds of employees. The supervisors were encouraged to review their employees' files and to jot down notes about employees' good and bad performances. They also practiced the evaluation interviews on each other. Given the ratings, they completed interviews on a very good, an average, and a poor employee.

Other policies were also covered. They learned about the new MBO system and how it was going to work. Still, Ed was a bit skeptical.

About two months later, Ed decided he'd better start the evaluations, since Bob had asked him how they were going. Ed decided to do Felipe Hernandez first. He still was a little worried about how it would go. Felipe had been trained in what to expect. Hope they hadn't built him up too high, Ed thought. In reviewing the files, his notes, and his observations, Ed realized he'd kind of overlooked how well Felipe had come along. Frankly, Ed hadn't been that fond of Puerto Ricans before Felipe had come along, but Felipe had done an excellent job, and so Ed had rated him highly.

Ed called Felipe in for the interview. Ed referred to his notes and started and ended the interview on a positive note. He talked just a little about the shortcomings he'd noticed and offered to help Felipe improve. At the beginning of the interview, Felipe had been nervous. But he beamed at the end.

Ed finished the interview by saying he was recommending Felipe for a good raise at the earliest chance. Over the next few days, Felipe seemed to be especially happy. Maybe it was Ed's imagination, but he seemed to be working a bit harder, too, although he was already a good worker.

That performance evaluation stuff works after all, Ed concluded.

EXHIBIT 8–11

Recommendations on evaluation techniques for model organizations

Type of organization	*Graphic rating scale*	*Forced choice*	*MBO*	*Essay*	*Critical incident*	*Weighted checklist*	*BARS*	*Rank-ing*	*Paired com-parison*	*Forced distri-bution*	*Per-formance test*	*Field review*	*Assess-ment centers*
1. Large size, low complexity, high stability	X	X	X		X	X	X	X	X	X	X	X	X
2. Medium size, low complexity, high stability	X		X	X	X	X	X	X	X	X			X
3. Small size, low complexity, high stability	X		X	X	X			X	X	X			
4. Medium size, moderate complexity, moderate stability	X		X	X	X	X		X	X	X			X
5. Large size, high complexity, low complexity	X		X	X	X			X	X	X		X	X
6. Medium size, high complexity, low stability	X		X	X	X			X	X	X			
7. Small size, high complexity, low stability	X		X	X	X			X	X	X			

QUESTIONS

1. What is performance evaluation?
2. "Performance evaluations cause as many problems as they are designed to solve." Comment. If you agree performance evaluation should take place, explain why.
3. Describe the major problems and malfunctions which can arise for the system, the evaluator, and the employee in performance evaluation.
4. How often should formal performance evaluations take place? Informal ones? How often do they take place?
5. Who usually evaluates employees in enterprises. Who should do so? Under what circumstances? What criteria should be used to evaluate employees? Which ones are used?
6. Compare and contrast performance evaluation techniques. If you were to choose one to be used to evaluate you, which one would it be? Why?
7. What happens after the employee is evaluated? What should happen?
8. Describe how to conduct an effective evaluation interview with a new, inexperienced employee. With an experienced employee.
9. How do managerial evaluations differ from employee evaluations? How are they similar?
10. How are promotion decisions made in business, the military, and the third sector? Which is the best approach?

Chapter objectives

- To define training and examine its purpose.
- To understand who is involved in training and how to manage a training program.
- To help understand the varieties of training programs and methods used by enterprises to improve employee effectiveness and satisfaction.

Chapter outline

I. Introduction to Training and Development
II. A Diagnostic Approach to Training and Development
III. Purposes of Training and Development
IV. Who Is Involved in Training and Development?
V. Managing the Training Program
   A. Determining training needs and objectives
   B. Choosing trainers and trainees
VI. Training and Development Phase
   A. Selection of training content
   B. Training approaches for employees
   C. Training approaches for managers
   D. Which methods and approaches should be used?
VII. Summary, Conclusions, and Recommendations

Training of employees and managers

Harold

Harold Matthews was unhappy. He'd just had an unpleasant visit with his boss, William Custer. Harold is vice president—operations of Young Enterprises, a firm employing about 1,600 persons in the Los Angeles area. The firm manufactures parts for a large aircraft firm nearby.

Since Young Enterprises serves primarily one customer, costs are a major factor in their negotiations. Bill Custer has just told Harold that the new contract is not as good as the last one. Costs will have to be cut. Since labor costs are a high percentage of the total, he must begin to work on these. Purchasing is working on reducing materials costs and Finance is trying to find ways to reduce the cost of capital.

Harold has decided to consult two groups of persons about the cost cutting: personnel and his supervisors. First he calls a meeting of the department heads and key supervisors and prepares his figures. The facts are:

- Their labor costs are rising faster than their competitors' are, and faster than the cost of living.
- These costs are higher any way you measure them: number of employees per unit of output, cost per unit of output, and so on. What's more, the trend is worsening.

At the meeting, Harold explained the facts. Then he asked the supervisors for suggestions. He gave them strong "encouragement" to supervise each employee closely and to make sure that the firm gets a fair day's work for a fair day's pay. Harold took notes of the comments his supervisors made. Some of the better ones were:

Sally Feldman (supervisor): One of my problems is that the people personnel sends me are not up to the output standards of the people I've lost through quits and retirement.

Art Jones (department head): Let's face it, when you look at the records, our recent output isn't up to what we expected when we installed the new machines.

Sam Jacobs (supervisor): The problem is our current crop of employees. They ain't what they used to be!

Harold wondered if they were just passing the buck—or if there was some truth to the complaints. He invited Gwen Meridith, the personnel vice president, in for help.

Gwen

Harold: Gwen, production costs are up and labor efficiency is down. The supervisors are blaming it on the employees. We put new machinery in to get production up. It's up, but not to what it should be, given our investment. What do you think is going on?

Gwen: I suspect that part of what they say has some truth to it. Lately the job market is tight. Last week, I had 20 jobs to fill and only 20 applicants. About half really were somewhat marginal. And let's face it, we put the new machinery in with little preparation of the employees.

Harold: What can we do? We have a serious cost problem.

Gwen: The job market is still tight. I don't see any improvement in the quality of labor in the near future. Sounds like we ought to gear up that training program I've been talking about.

Harold: You prepare something for Bill. Then you and I will go to see him about it.

INTRODUCTION TO TRAINING AND DEVELOPMENT

Harold and Gwen have just described one of the several reasons why training takes place in organizations. Chapter 9 begins a two-chapter segment on training employees and managers (Chapter 9) and their development (Chapter 10). In this introduction, we'll define training and relate it to learning theory and other personnel activities. Next, we'll examine training purposes and the diagnostic approach to training and development. Finally, we'll discuss the management of training programs in enterprises.

Training is the systematic process of altering the behavior of employees in a direction to increase organizational goals.

Management development is the process by which managers gain the experience, skills, and attitudes to become or remain successful leaders in their enterprises.

A formal training program is an effort by the employer to provide opportunities for the employee to acquire job-related skills, attitudes, and knowledge.

Learning is the act by which the individual acquires skills, knowledge, and abilities which result in a relatively permanent change in his or her behavior.

Another way to define training and development is to model it. Irwin Goldstein's model is given in Exhibit 9–1. Each phase of the training and development process will be discussed. This chapter will focus on training programs to improve managerial and employees' abilities. For example, training programs can be geared toward improving typing skills, salesmanship abilities, lathe operation techniques, and so on. Chapter 10 will deal with methods of developing attitudinal change and interpersonal skills in both managers and employees.

Since training is a form of education, some of the findings of learning theory logically might be applicable to training. These principles can be important in the design of both formal and informal training programs. The following is a brief summary of the way learning principles can be applied to job training.

The trainee must be motivated to learn. This motivation involves two factors: awareness of the need to learn, based on the individual's own inadequacy in this regard, and a clear understanding of what needs to be learned. The learner must secure satisfaction from the learning. He/she must see the usefulness of the material in terms of his or her own needs.

The learning must be reinforced. Behavioral psychologists have demonstrated that learners learn best with fairly immediate reinforcement of appropriate behavior. The learner must be rewarded for new behavior in ways that satisfy needs, such as pay, recognition, promotion. Standards of performance should be set for the learner. Benchmarks for learning will provide goals and give a feeling of accomplishment when reached. These standards provide a measure for meaningful feedback.

The training must provide for practice of the material. Learning requires time to assimilate what has been learned, to accept it, to internalize it, and to build confidence in what has been learned. This requires practice and repetition of the material.

The material presented must be meaningful. Appropriate materials for sequential learning (cases, problems, discussion outlines, reading lists) must be provided. The trainer acts as an aid in an efficient learning process.

The learning methods used should be as varied as possible. It is boredom that destroys learning, not fatigue. Any method—whether old-fashioned lecture

EXHIBIT 9–1
Training model

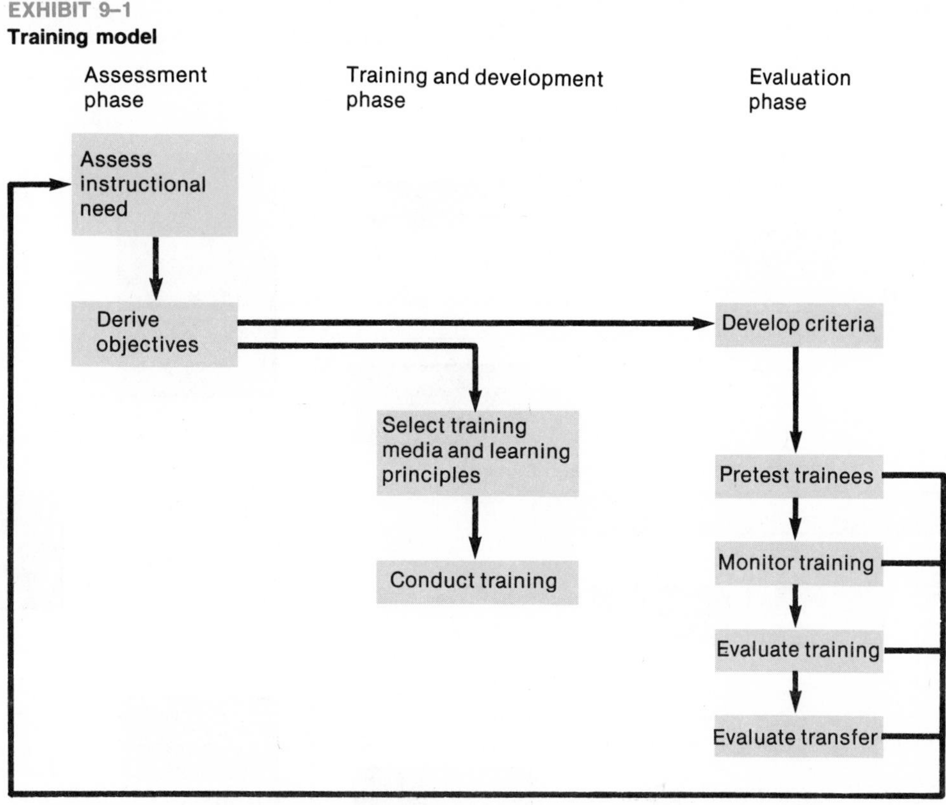

From *Training: Program Development and Evaluation* by I. L. Goldstein. Copyright © 1974 by Wadsworth Publishing Company, Inc. Reprinted by permission of the publisher, Brooks/Cole Publishing Company, Monterey, California.

or programmed learning or the jazziest computer game—will begin to bore some learners if overused.

The material presented must be communicated effectively. Communication must be done in a unified way, and over enough time to allow it to be absorbed (see Chapter 3).

The material taught must transfer to the job situation. The trainer does her or his best to make the training as close to the reality of the job as possible. Thus, when the trainee returns to the job, the training can be applied immediately.

As each aspect of training program design and implementation is discussed, you will see how these learning theory principles are applied.

Training and management development are closely related to many personnel activities. For example, performance evaluation provides the data needed for training. Employment planning decisions may also dictate the need for added training.

Employee training is moderately well developed—a Stage III or possibly Stage IV function in personnel. But management development is a Stage II personnel function. Most people do it, but scientific evaluation of its results is slim.

EXHIBIT 9–2

Factors affecting employee training and development and organizational effectiveness

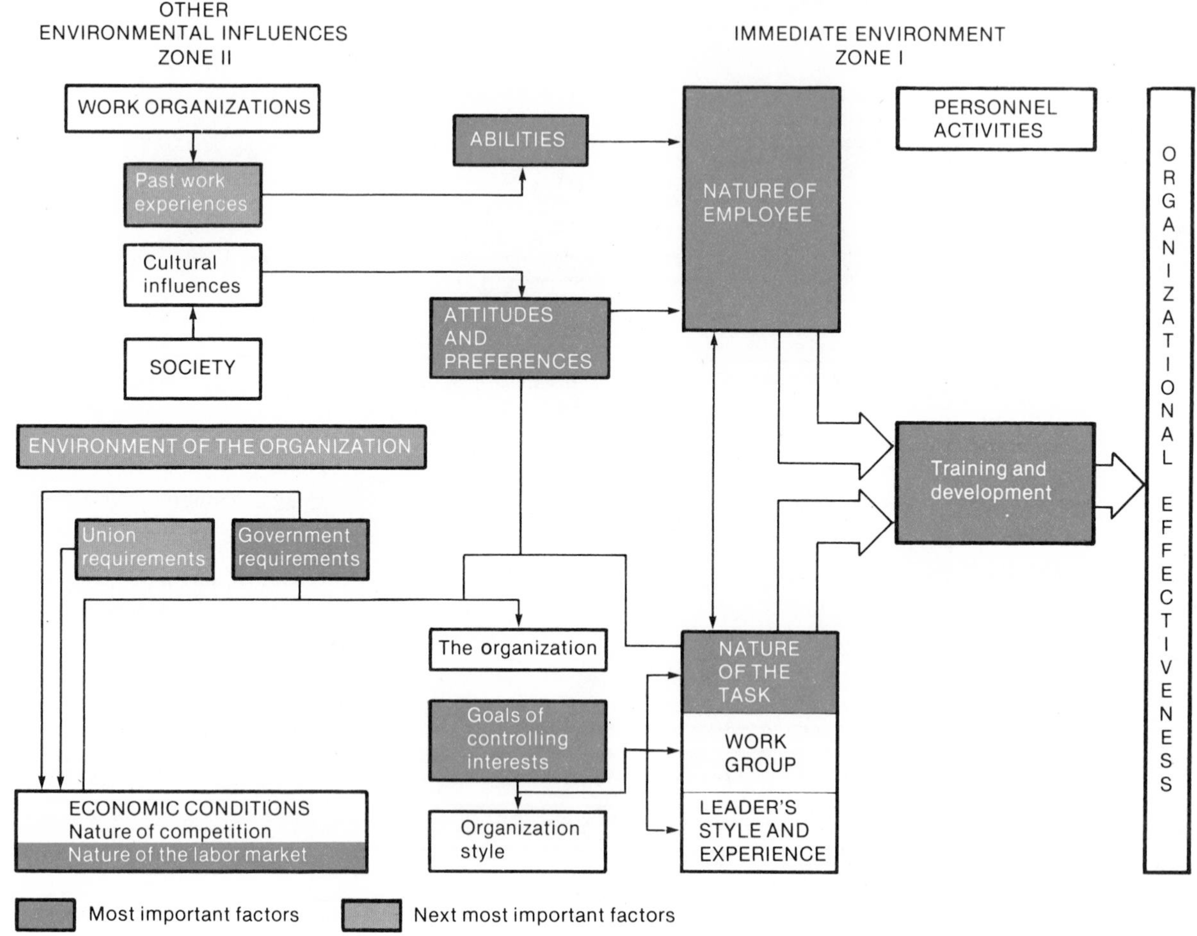

A DIAGNOSTIC APPROACH TO TRAINING AND DEVELOPMENT

Exhibit 9–2 highlights those aspects of the diagnostic model that are especially important to employee training and development. The most important determinants of training are the task to be done and the employees' abilities and attitudes. If the current employees have work ethic attitudes and the skills needed to do the jobs, training may not be too important for the enterprise. More often, because of conditions in the labor market, the enterprise is losing some employees to other enterprises who provide better rewards.

It is also unlikely that the task demands are stable. More frequently, because of volatile technology and market conditions, the jobs are changing, and this requires more training so employees can meet current effectiveness standards. For example, when computers are introduced or new production or operating techniques are instituted, employees must be retrained.

The government also is becoming a vital influence on training. This has been happening in two ways. One is the pressure for equal employment opportunities and human rights (see Chapter 16). If in an enterprise minorities and women work only at the lowest paid, lowest skilled positions, pressure will be applied to upgrade the skills of those who have the potential for upward mobility. This increases the demand for training or retraining.

The second way government influences training is that it provides many training programs. These programs frequently have public policy purposes, such as reduction of unemployment, upgrading the incomes of minority groups, or increasing the competitiveness of underdeveloped regions of the country.

In the United States, the federal government, through the Comprehensive Employment and Training Act (1974) and other manpower legislation, has allocated large sums to the training of potential workers for jobs. The government reimburses training organizations (schools, businesses, unions) or trains the workers itself.

Some unions also are involved in employee training, especially in industries such as construction where the union is larger than the employer. In these cases, the union often does most or all of the training. A large proportion of this type of training occurs in apprenticeship programs.

Finally, the goals of management affect training and development. For example, organization development programs are likely to be chosen by managers who feel that full development of employees is an appropriate enterprise goal.

Employee training is a major undertaking for employers. Almost all large enterprises and most medium-sized ones run their own training programs. They employ 50,000 full-time trainers and spend $100 billion per year on it. Whether an enterprise has a management or professional development program depends a great deal on its size. Smaller enterprises rarely run their own formal development programs; the programs are informal at best. Larger enterprises have elaborate formal programs combining on-the-job with off-the-job development. Others, such as the U.S. military, Exxon, and AT&T, have established large, complex training and development centers for their managers. The Federal Executive Institute at Charlottesville, Virginia, is set up to develop federal government executives, as is the Executive Seminar Center in Berkeley, California, and the U.S. Post Office Center in Norman, Oklahoma.

Formal management development programs exist in almost all large and medium-sized institutions in the United States and many smaller enterprises as well. There has been tremendous growth in this area in the past 30 years, and the trend is still upward. Perhaps as many as 1,000,000 executives per year participate in off-the-job management development exercises.

PURPOSES OF TRAINING AND DEVELOPMENT

There are many reasons why enterprises engage in training and development programs. The most frequently mentioned reasons are:

To improve the quantity of output.

To improve the quality of output.

To lower the costs of waste and equipment maintenance.

To lower the number and costs of accidents.

To lower turnover and absenteeism and increase employees' job satisfaction, since training can improve the employees' self-esteem.

To prevent employee obsolescence.

In effect, training and development help the enterprise to become more efficient and effective and the employee to become more fully developed and satisfied. Given here are the viewpoints of two executives on the purpose of training.

Edgar Speer, chairman and chief executive officer of United States Steel, says:

> We support training and development activities to get results. . . . We're interested in specific things that provide greater rewards to the employee, increased return to the stockholder, and enable reinvestment needs of the business. In other words, [we're interested in] those things which affect the "bottom line." Although you cannot always evaluate training as readily as some other functions, as people improve their performance it is reflected in on-the-job results as well as all aspects of their lives.

William Murray, chairman of the board and chief executive officer of Harris Bank of Chicago, says:

> I readily relate to the fundamentals of good technical training. . . . The training function plays an integral role in the bank by helping upgrade employee performance and the from hire to retire approach provides continuity in the developing process of bank personnel. While we can't measure the absolute results of training programs, our record as an organization indicates we're doing something right.

Remember Harold Matthew's problem at Young Enterprises? The employees are not producing the quality and quantity of output expected, and it appears that training may help reduce costs to make the firm more competitive. Well-trained employees also tend to be more satisfied with their positions and better able to perform their jobs more effectively.

WHO IS INVOLVED IN TRAINING AND DEVELOPMENT?

For training and development to be effective, top management must support it, as Mr. Speer and Mr. Murray do. They provide the budget and psychological

EXHIBIT 9–3
The role of operating and personnel managers in training and development

Training and development function	*Operating manager (OM)*	*Personnel manager (PM)*
Determining training needs and objectives	Approved by OM	Done by PM
Develop training criteria	Approved by OM	Done by PM
Choosing trainer	Jointly chosen: nominated by OM	Jointly chosen: approved by PM
Developing training materials	Approved by OM	Done by PM
Planning and implementing the program		Done by PM
Doing the training	Occasionally done by OM	Normally done by PM
Evaluating the training	OM reviews the results	Done by PM

Milton R. Schieber
Lone Star Industries

Biography

Milton R. Schieber, Manager of Corporate Management Development at Lone Star Industries, Greenwich, Connecticut, and dean of the Lone Star Management Institute, graduated from New York University's School of Commerce. He has pursued graduate studies in psychology and marketing. A graduate of the U.S. Army Command and General Staff College, Schieber is a retired Army colonel, combat commander, and veteran of World War II and Korea.

Prior to joining Lone Star, he served with American Radiator and Standard Sanitary Corporation in various positions. Schieber is a frequent lecturer at industry and professional programs and is noted for his views on management in the real world and objective performance evaluation. He devised and conducts the company's college scholarship and scholarship assistance programs, along with consulting on college and curriculum selection and career planning.

Job description

Devises, creates, plans, develops, conducts, recommends and coordinates management development and training activities for supervisory, managerial and executive personnel of the corporation, thereby contributing to their optimum utilization for their own and the company's advantage. Major programs include managing by objectives, objective performance evaluation, successor identification and training, and manager development programs at all levels.

support. They must indicate to the trainers the training implications of their strategic decisions.

As with other personnel activities, both operating and personnel managers are involved in training. Exhibit 9–3 indicates how. Occasionally more than these two groups are involved. For example, at General Telephone of Florida, the training, labor relations, and public affairs departments combined to prepare video training programs to train managers to handle grievances and arbitration. Community theater actors performed the roles.

In larger enterprises, the personnel manager most involved in the work described in Chapters 9 and 10 is called the training director, or training and development manager. A typical training director is Milton R. Schieber. His work history and the job description for his position, Manager of Corporate Management Development at Lone Star Industries, are given here.

MANAGING THE TRAINING PROGRAM

Young Enterprises does not have a separate training department. So Gwen, with the assistance of Bob McGarrah, the director of training and development, began to think about a training program to help Harold Matthews reach his goal. The program might not have been needed if the job market weren't so tight.

Bob

But since applicants are so scarce, the training program was very important at this point.

Gwen: Bob, what we need is to determine what training programs we should have right now. What do you suggest we do?

Bob: The typical approach is to use organizational analysis, operational analysis, and person analysis. Besides, we need to do some sort of feasibility or cost/benefit analysis to see if the training is worth the effort. This will give us a set of training objectives for a program or set of programs. Then we design the program content and methods around these. After the program is run, we evaluate it.

Gwen: At this point, let's set the objectives and design the program. Then we'll go back to Harold to see if he has any additional suggestions.

Determining training needs and objectives

The first step in managing training is to determine training needs and set objectives for these needs. In effect, the trainers are preparing a training forecast (this is the assessment phase in Exhibit 9–1).

Donald Kirkpatrick says there are four ways to determine the training needs:

By observing the employees to be trained.

By listening to the employees to be trained.

By asking their supervisors about the employees' training needs.

By examining the problems the employees have.

In essence, any gaps between expected and actual results suggest training needs. Active solicitation of suggestions from employees, supervisors, managers, and training committees can also provide training needs ideas.

From the analysis of training needs, the training manager proposes specific training programs to meet specific measurable objectives. These objectives include knowledge, skill, job performance, and output objectives. For example, an objective for clerical training might be "to operate the IBM Selectric typewriter at 60 words per minute with less than two errors per page."

The cost and feasibility assessment is an attempt to determine (before formal evaluation) whether the training costs can be offset by the benefits or whether another approach, such as selection improvements, is more effective.

Determining training needs helps the enterprise achieve several of the learning principles mentioned in the beginning of the chapter:

- If the employee to be trained is involved in assessing training needs, he or she will become more aware of the training needs.
- If specific objectives are set, standards of performance for feedback are designed.

- If the standards are set properly, it is likely that the training program will help transfer results to the job situation.

Although it is obviously desirable to analyze training needs, studies indicate that less than half of larger enterprises (and, one assumes, smaller percentages of medium-sized and smaller enterprises) formally assess training needs and set formal training objectives.

Choosing trainers and trainees

Great care must be exercized in hiring or developing effective instructors or trainers. To some extent, the success of the training program depends upon proper selection of the person who performs the training task. Personal characteristics (the ability to speak well, to write convincingly, to organize the work of others, to be inventive, and to inspire others to greater achievements) are important factors in the selection of trainers.

Although much formal training is performed by professional trainers, often operating supervisors may be the best trainers technically, especially if the training manager helps them prepare the material. Using operating managers as trainers overcomes the frequent criticism that "Training is O.K. in the classroom, but it won't work on the shop floor." The presence of *trained* trainers is a major factor in whether the training program is successful. It will help if these principles of learning are followed:

- Provide for practice of the material.
- Require practice and repetition of the material.
- Communicate the material effectively.

Another planning factor is the selection of trainees who will participate in the programs. In some cases this is obvious; the program may have been designed to train particular new employees in certain skills. In some cases, the training program is designed to help with EEO goals; in others it is to help employees find better jobs elsewhere when layoffs are necessary or to retrain older employees. Techniques similar to selection procedures may be used to select trainees, especially when those who attend the program may be promoted or receive higher wages or salaries as a result. If formal selection techniques are not used, quotas, supervisor nominations, self-nominations, and seniority rules may develop unofficially or officially as selection mechanisms for the programs.

This discussion of trainee selection is normative, however; it implies that enterprises rationally select those employees who need the training and train them. Roger Roderick and Joseph Yaney studied selection of and participation in training programs by 1,247 young males who worked for businesses over a four-year period. Only 1 out of 7 received any formal training during the period. The companies tended to select for further training those men with the best educational backgrounds and from the highest socioeconomic group. This "creaming" meant that those who needed the training the most did not get it, and the gap between the trained and untrained widened. Also because of these selection procedures, blacks received much less training than white males. The companies seemed to select trainees based on the most probable "success ratio" for the training, not those needing the training the most.

TRAINING AND DEVELOPMENT PHASE

After needs and objectives have been determined and trainees and trainers have been selected, the program is run. This is the second phase shown in Exhibit 9–1. This phase includes selection of content and methods to be used and the actual conducting of the training.

Selection of training content

From the analysis of the training needs, the training director derives the content of the training. In the case of Young Enterprises, the company installed new machinery without training the employees in its use. Introduction of new equipment, as in this case, often causes employees' skills to become obsolete, without developing the new skills to cope effectively with the redesigned job.

Since there are well over 35,000 jobs listed in the *Dictionary of Occupational Titles,* the number of skills to be developed can be quite large. For example, in Chapter 3 we discussed how communication skills are a frequent subject of training programs. But all kinds of skills can be taught. The ones *to be* taught are derived from the training needs analyses. They can vary from typing skills improvement, to learning a new computer language, to effective use of a new machine.

Training approaches for employees

Both training for the unskilled and retraining for the obsolete employee follow one of four approaches which combine elements of the *where* and *what* of training. The four principal types of training are apprenticeship, vestibule, on-the-job training, and off-the-job training.

Apprentice training. Apprentice training is a combination of on-the-job and off-the-job training. It requires the cooperation of the employer, trainers at the workplace and in schools (such as vocational schools), government agencies, and the skilled-trade unions.

Governments regulate apprentice training. In the United States, the major law is the Apprenticeship Act of 1937. Typically the government also subsidizes these programs. The U.S. Department of Labor funds apprenticeship programs in the building trades, mining, auto repair, oil, and other fields. In 1976, these were funded for $18,000,000. The department also issues standards and regulations governing these programs. About 30,000 persons are trained yearly by this method.

The apprentice commits herself or himself to a period of training and learning that involves both formal classroom learning and practical on-the-job experience. These periods can vary from two years or so (barber, ironworker, foundryman, baker, meat cutter, engraver) through four or five years (electrician, photoengraver, tool and die maker, plumber, job pressman), up to ten years (steelplate engraver). During this period, the pay is less than that for the master worker.

Research evaluating construction workers trained by the apprenticeship method versus on-the-job training indicates that apprentices are better trained, get promoted sooner, and experience less unemployment later. Thus apprentice training can be effective.

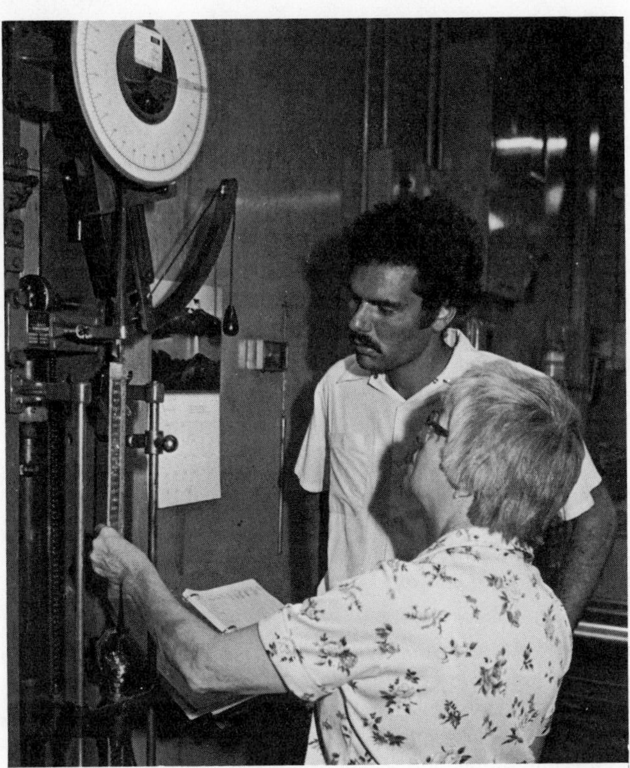

An apprentice training program

Vestibule training. In vestibule training, the trainee learns the job in an environment that simulates the real working environment as closely as possible. An example would be the simulated cockpit of a Boeing 747 used to train airline pilots in operating that specific airplane. A machine operator trainee might run a machine under the supervision of a trainer until he learns how to use it properly. Only then would he be sent to the shop floor. This procedure can be quite expensive if the number of trainees supervised is not large, but it can be effective under certain circumstances. Some employees trained in the vestibule method have adjustment problems when they begin full-time work, since the vestibule area is safer and less hectic.

On-the-job training. Probably the most widely used method of training (formal and informal) is on-the-job training. The employee is placed into the real work situation and shown the job and the tricks of the trade by an experienced employee or the supervisor. Although this program is apparently simple and relatively less costly, if it is not handled properly the costs can be high in damaged machinery, unsatisfied customers, misfiled forms, and poorly taught workers. To prevent these problems, trainers must be carefully selected and trained. The trainee should be placed with a trainer who is similar in background and personality. The trainer should be motivated by training and rewarded for doing it well. The trainer should use effective training techniques in instructing the trainee.

EXHIBIT 9–4
Job instruction training (JIT) methods

First, here's what you *must do* to *get ready* to teach a job:

1. Decide what the learner must be taught in order to do the job efficiently, safely, economically, and intelligently.
2. Have the right tools, equipment, supplies, and material ready.
3. Have the workplace properly arranged, just as the worker will be expected to keep it.

Then, you should *instruct* the learner by the following *four basic steps:*

Step I—*Preparation* (of the learner)

1. Put the learner at *ease.*
2. Find out what he already knows about the job.
3. Get him interested and desirous of learning the job.

Step II—*Presentation* (of the operations and knowledge)

1. *Tell, show, illustrate* and *question* in order to put over the new knowledge and operations.
2. Instruct slowly, clearly, completely, and patiently, one point at a time.
3. Check, question, and repeat.
4. Make sure the learner really knows.

Step III—*Performance try-out*

1. Test learner by having him perform the job.
2. Ask questions beginning with *why, how, when* or *where.*
3. Observe performance, correct errors, and repeat instructions if necessary.
4. Continue until you *know he knows.*

Step IV—*Follow-up*

1. Put him "on his own."
2. Check frequently to be sure he follows instructions.
3. Taper off extra supervision and close follow-up until he is qualified to work with normal supervision.

Remember—If the learner hasn't learned, the teacher hasn't taught.

One approach to systematic on-the-job training is the job instruction training (JIT) system developed during World War II. In this system, the trainers first train the supervisors, who in turn train the employees. Exhibit 9–4 describes the steps of JIT training as given in the War Manpower Commission's bulletin, "Training within Industry Series in 1945." These are the instructions given to supervisors on how to train new or present employees.

Another frequently used on-the-job training technique is job rotation. In this approach, the trainee is taught several positions in succession over a period of time so the trainee can be used in several positions.

On-the-job experiences in management development. There are four approaches to on-the-job management development. These programs are not mutually exclusive; often they are run simultaneously. On-the-job management development is the preferred type from many points of view, especially because of its relevance and immediate transferability to the job.

Approaches to on-the-job management development:

Coaching and counseling in the present position.

Transition to new job experiences while staying at the old job.

Self-improvement programs.

Job rotation and transfer career plans.

Coaching and counseling. One of the best and most frequently used methods of developing new managers is for effective managers to teach them. The coach-superior sets a good example of how to be a manager. He also answers questions and explains why things are done the way they are. It is the coach-superior's obligation to see to it that the manager-trainee makes the proper contacts so that the job can be learned easily and performed in a more adequate way. In some ways, the coach-superior–manager-trainee relationship resembles the buddy system in employee training.

One technique the superior may use is to have decision-making meetings with the trainee at which procedures are agreed upon. If the trainee is to learn, the superior must give him or her enough authority to make decisions and perhaps even make mistakes. This approach not only provides opportunities to learn, it requires effective delegation, which develops a feeling of mutual confidence. Appropriately chosen committee assignments can be used as a form of coaching and counseling

Although most organizations use coaching and counseling as either a formal or an informal management development technique, it is not without its problems. Coaching and counseling fail when inadequate time is set aside for them, the subordinate is allowed to make no mistakes, rivalry develops, or the dependency needs of the subordinate are not recognized or accepted by the superior.

In sum, many experts contend that coaching and counseling, when coupled with planned job rotation through jobs and functions, is an effective technique. It can fit the manager's background and utilizes the principle of learning by doing, which has been proven effective. Finally, the method involves the supervisors, which is essential to successful management development.

Transitory, anticipatory experiences. Another approach to management development is to provide transitory experiences. Once it has been determined that a person will be promoted to a specific job, provision is made for a short period before the promotion in which he learns the new job, performing some of his new duties while still performing most of his old ones. This intermediate position is labeled differently in various organizations as assistant-to, understudy, multiple management, or management apprenticeship.

The main characteristic of this type of program is that it gives a person likely to hold a position in the future partial prior experience. In some approaches, the trainee performs a part of the actual job; thus, an assistant-to does some parts of the job for the incumbent. In multiple management, several decision-making bodies make decisions about the same problem and compare them—a junior board or group's decisions are compared to those of senior management groups. Another variation is to provide trainees with a series of assignments that are part of the new job in order to train them and broaden their experience.

To the extent that transitory experiences simulate the future job and are challenging, and the trainees' supervisors are effective managers themselves, they seem to provide an eminently reasonable approach to management development. Little systematic study has been made of the effectiveness of this approach, however, and it appears to be used less often than coaching or counseling.

Self-improvement programs. The third approach to on-the-job experience is a self-improvement program pursued while on the job. The manager may take a correspondence course or study individually at home to improve job skills, attend local professional association meetings in the evenings or at lunchtime, and take part in annual or quarterly professional meetings.

Transfers and rotation. In the fourth on-the-job approach, trainees are rotated through a series of jobs to broaden their managerial experience. Enterprises that develop programmed career plans which include a mix of functional and geographic transfers are described in Chapter 10.

Advocates of rotation and transfer contend that this approach broadens the manager's background, accelerates the promotion of highly competent individuals, introduces more new ideas into the organization, and increases the effectiveness of the enterprise. But some research evidence questions this. Individual differences affect whether or not the results will be positive, and generalists may not be the most effective managers in many specialized positions.

Geographic transfers are desirable when fundamentally different job situations exist at various places. They allow new ideas to be tried instead of meeting each situation with the comment, "We always do it that way here." As in many other types of development, trained supervisors can make this technique more effective.

In general, because of the perceived relevance of on-the-job experience, it should be provided in management development programs. Because of individual differences in development and rewards by organizations, however, off-the-job development programs should supplement them where expertise is not readily available inside the organization. Exclusively on-the-job programs lead to a narrow perspective and the inhibition of new ideas coming into the organization.

Off-the-job training. Other than apprenticeship, vestibule training, and on-the-job training, all other training is off-the-job training, whether it is done in organization classrooms, vocational schools, or elsewhere. Organizations with the biggest training programs often use off-the-job training. The majority of the 50,000 trainers in the United States and the $100 billion spent on training is in off-the-job training. The most frequently used methods for off-the-job training are the conference/discussion, programmed instruction, computer-assisted, and simulation approaches.

Conference/discussion approach. The most frequently used training method is for a trainer to give a lecture and involve the trainee in a discussion of the material to be learned. The effective classroom presentation supplements the verbal part with audiovisual aids such as blackboards, slides, and mockups. Frequently these lectures are videotaped or audio taped. The method allows the trainer's message to be given in many locations and to be repeated as often as needed for the benefit of the trainees. Videotape recording also allows for self-confrontation, which is especially useful in such programs as sales training and interpersonal relations. The trainee's presentation can be taped and played back for analysis.

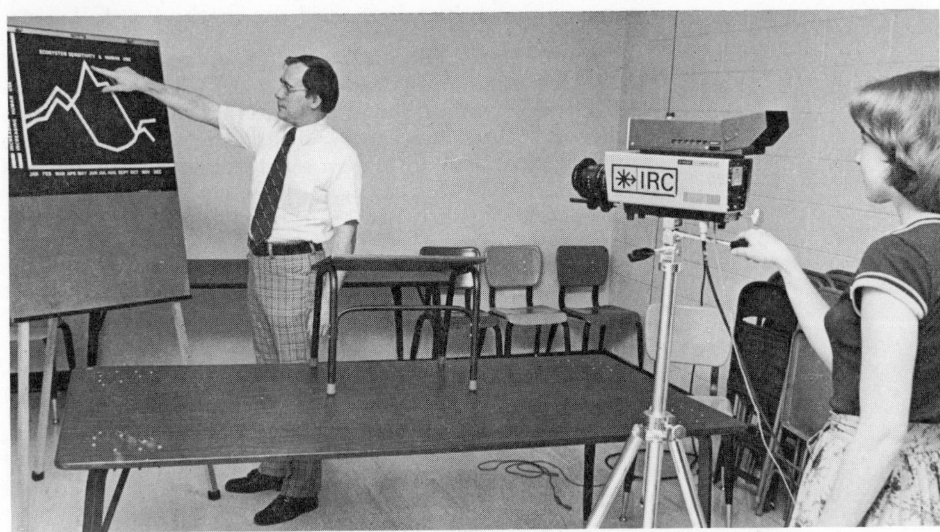

Videotaping a lecture

When properly done, the conference/discussion method is a useful approach to many subjects.

Programmed instruction and computer-assisted instruction. One of the newer methods being used in organizational training is programmed instruction. Material can be presented on teaching machines or in text form, and behaviorist learning principles are followed closely. Programmed instruction is a useful method for self-instruction when the development cost of the materials has been paid by another organization and the materials are available. It might also be a useful method if there are enough trainees to amortize the development cost, if the trainees are likely to be motivated enough to move ahead with this approach, and if the material to be presented is suitable to the method.

Programmed instruction

Leonard Silvern has described the method as follows:

> Programmed instruction is a technique for instructing without the presence or intervention of a human instructor. It is a learner-centered method of instruction, which presents subject-matter to the trainee in small steps or increments, requiring frequent responses from him and immediately informing him of the correctness of his responses. The trainee's responses may be written, oral, or manipulative. A response may be constructed, as in the completion type; it may be selected from among several alternatives, as in the multiple-choice type; or it may assume one or more of a variety of other styles.

Features of programmed instruction, according to Silvern, are:

Instruction is provided without the presence or intervention of a human instructor.

The learner learns at his own rate (conventional group instruction, films, television, and other media and methods that do not allow learner control do not satisfy this criterion).

Instruction is presented in small incremental steps requiring frequent responses by the learner; step size is a function of the subject matter and the characteristics of the learner population.

There is a participative overt interaction, or two-way communication, between the learner and the instructional program.

The learner receives immediate feedback informing him of his progress.

Reinforcement is used to strengthen learning.

The sequence of lessons is carefully controlled and consistent.

The instructional program shapes and controls behavior.

Programmed instruction may have wide application in organizational training programs, especially for programs whose characteristics fit those discussed above. It can also be developed in computer-assisted forms.

Training approaches for managers

Several other methods used to present materials are more frequent in management development programs than in employee training.

The case method. One widely used technique is the case method. A case is a written description of a real decision-making situation. Trainees are asked to study the case to determine problems, analyze them for their significance, propose solutions, choose the best solution, and implement it. More learning takes place if there is interaction between the trainer and trainees and among trainees.

The case method lends itself more to some kinds of material (business policy) than to well-structured material. It is easier to listen to a lecture and be given a formula than to tease the formula out of a case, for example. With proper trainers and good cases, the case method is a very effective device for improving and clarifying rational decision making.

Variations on the case method. One variation of the case method is the incident method. In the incident method, just the bare outlines of the situation are given initially, and the students are assigned a role in which to view the incident. Additional data are available if the students ask the right questions. Each student "solves" the case, and groups based on similiarity of solutions are formed. Each group then formulate a strong statement of position, and the groups debate or role play their solutions. The instructor tells what actually happened in the case and the consequences, and everyone compares their solutions with the results. The final step is for participants to try to apply this knowledge to their own job situations.

Role playing. Role playing is a cross between the case method and attitude development programs (to be described in Chapter 10). Each person being developed is assigned a role in a training situation (such as a case) and asked to play the role and to react to other players' role playing. The player is asked to pretend he or she is a focal person in the situation and to react to the stimuli as that person would. The players are provided with background information on the situation and the players. There are no scripts. Sometimes the role plays are videotaped and reanalyzed as part of the development situation. Often role playing is done in trainee groups of a dozen or so persons.

The success of this method depends on the ability of the players to play the assigned roles believably.

Synectics. One approach which attempts to deal with nonprogrammed decision training and to stimulate creativity in decision making is synectics, or the development of creative capacity. The creative process is the mental activity in a problem-stating, problem-solving situation where artistic or technical inventions are the result. Synectics uses mechanisms to simulate these characteristics through analogies that are direct and personal or symbolic and fantastical. It seeks to make the strange familiar and the familiar strange through creativity.

The in-basket technique. Another method used to develop managerial decision-making abilities is the in-basket technique. The trainee is given a box of

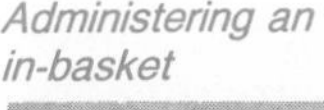

Administering an in-basket

material which includes typical items from a specific manager's mail and a telephone list. Important and pressing matters such as out-of-stock positions, customer complaints, or the demand for a report from a superior are mixed in with routine business matters such as a request to speak at a dinner or a decision on the date of the company picnic four weeks hence. The trainee is analyzed and critiqued on the number of decisions made in the time period allotted, the quality of decisions, and the priorities chosen for making them. One well-known application of the in-basket technique is Charles Kepner and Benjamin Tregoe's Apex Company cases. In general, although expensive, in-baskets are effective training devices.

Management games. Essentially, management games describe the operating characteristics of a company, industry, or enterprise. These descriptions take the form of equations which are manipulated after decisions have been made.

In a typical operation, teams of players are asked to make a series of operating (or top-management) decisions. In business games, for example, the players may be asked to decide on such matters as the price of the product, purchase of materials, production scheduling, funds borrowing, marketing, and R&D expenditures. When each player on the team has made a decision, the interactions of these decisions are computed (manually or by computer) in accordance with the model. For example, if price is linearly related to volume, a decrease in price of X percent will affect the volume, subject to general price levels. Players on the team must reconcile their individual decisions with those of the other team members prior to the final decision. Then each team's decisions compete with those of the other teams. The output is how much profit, market share, and so forth each team has won in the competition. The results are given to the participants, who then make their next decisions.

Games are used to train managers in all sectors. Advantages of games include the integration of several interacting decisions, the ability to experiment with decisions, the provision of feedback experiences on decisions, and the requirement that decisions be made with inadequate data, which usually simulates reality. The main criticisms of most games concern their limitation of novelty or creativity in decision making, the cost of development and administration, the unreality of some of the models, and the disturbing tendency of many participants to look for the key to win the game instead of concentrating on making good decisions. Many participants seem to feel the games are rigged, and a few factors or even a single factor may be the key to winning.

Are games effective training mechanisms? Although games lead to high participant interest and motivation and participant recognition of the interrelationships in decisions, the empirical evidence of effectiveness is mixed.

Which methods and approaches should be used?

This choice is made on the basis of the number of trainees for each program, the relative costs per trainee for each method, the availability of training materials in various forms (including the trainers' capabilities), and the employees' relative efficiency in learning. In general, it is true that the more active the trainee, the greater the motivation to learn. The probability of success is higher in that instance. If there are only a few trainers, individualized programmed instruction may be considered. If none of the trainers is capable of giving certain

EXHIBIT 9–5
Roles of trainees affected by different training methods

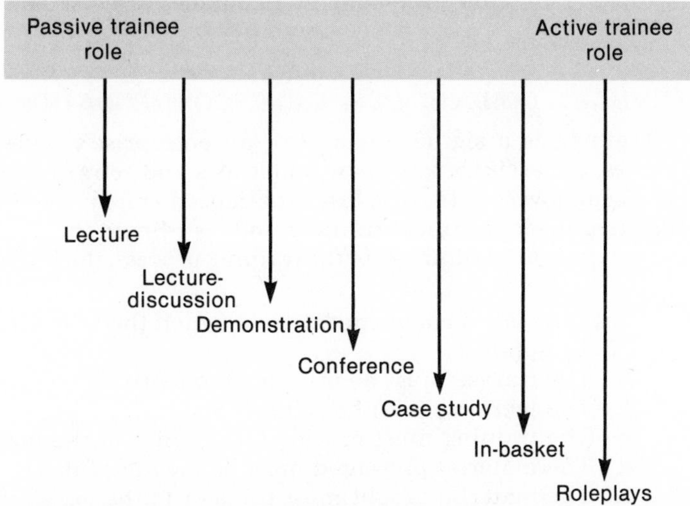

From *Handbook of Creative Learning Exercises,* by Herbert M. Engel. Copyright © 1973 by Gulf Publishing Company, Houston, Texas. Used with permission. All rights reserved.

instruction, outside trainers may be contacted, or movies or videotapes might be used. Finally, the method used should reflect the degree of active participation desired for the program, as illustrated in Exhibit 9–5.

Inevitably, the question as to how effective each form of training is must be answered. There are studies to support the effectiveness of all methods; if a method is appropriate for the particular program in question, it should be used.

Studies have found the following training methods are used by larger companies with advanced personnel practices: 53 percent used the lecture method; 29 percent, the conference method; and 20 percent, programmed instruction. As to the tools available, 67 percent had chalkboards; 63 percent, movies; and almost 50 percent, film clips, flip charts, and slides. More than a third used exhibits and posters, and a few had magnetic boards, closed-circuit TV, and tape recorders. The use of the newer techniques has undoubtedly increased since this study.

Probably the most frequently used methods are lectures and conferences. These are useful to the extent that the trainer is skilled in communication and there are enough trainees to average out the costs per trainee. Methods that frequently supplement the lecture are movies, slides, tapes, and other audiovisual aids.

Another survey found that almost all enterprises used lectures and conferences. Other techniques such as simulation, role playing, and programmed instruction were used by about 15 percent of the companies.

The other approach to making this decision is to evaluate a method or approach after it is used. These evaluations are kept and become an input to future decisions. Evaluation, the last phase of the management of training, is discussed in Chapter 10, after development techniques are discussed.

SUMMARY, CONCLUSIONS, AND RECOMMENDATIONS

Training is a significant part of an enterprise's investment in human resources. Supervisors train new employees and retrain older ones. More experienced employees help train less experienced employees. Personnel training specialists provide technical training and coordinate the overall training effort of the enterprise. To summarize the training process, the following points are listed:

1. Training is a form of education to which the following learning principles can be applied:
   a. The trainee must be motivated to learn.
   b. The learning must be reinforced.
   c. The training must provide for practice of the material.
   d. The material presented must be meaningful.
   e. The material taught must transfer to the job situation.
2. Purposes of training and development include:
   a. To improve the quantity of output.
   b. To improve the quality of output.
   c. To lower the costs of waste and equipment maintenance.
   d. To lower the number and costs of accidents.
   e. To lower turnover and absenteeism and increase employee job satisfaction.
   f. To prevent employee obsolescence.
3. When employee turnover is great, it is more important for the organization to provide formal technical training for employees.
4. Effective organizations design their training programs only after assessing the organization's and individual's training needs and setting training objectives.
5. Effective training programs select trainees on the basis of the trainees' needs as well as organizational objectives.
6. Effective training programs carefully select and develop trainers for the programs.
7. Effective enterprises evaluate training programs against the program objectives (effectiveness measure) and cost/benefit ratios (efficiency measures).
8. Effective management development programs emphasize on-the-job development programs and supplement them with off-the-job experiences and programs.
9. Training approaches for employees are:
   a. Apprenticeship.
   b. Vestibule.
   c. On-the-job training (coaching and counseling; transitory experiences; self-improvement programs; transfers and rotation).
   d. Off-the-job training (conference/discussion; programmed instruction; computer assisted; simulation approaches).
10. In addition to the above, management development programs can include:

EXHIBIT 9–6

Recommendations on management development programs for model organizations

Type of organization	*Formal program*	*Informal program*	*On-the-job programs*	*Off-the-job programs*
1. Large size, low complexity, high stability	X		X	X
2. Medium size, low complexity, high stability		X	X	
3. Small size, low complexity, high stability		X	X	
4. Medium size, moderate complexity, moderate stability		X	X	X
5. Large size, high complexity, low stability	X		X	X
6. Medium size, high complexity, low stability		X	X	
7. Small size, high complexity, low stability		X	X	

a. The case method.
b. Role playing.
c. Synectics.
d. The in-basket technique.
e. Management games.

Since each enterprise' must train a variety of employee groups which have different methods and approaches, the table of recommended training practices for the model organizations will only include management development programs (see Exhibit 9–6).

After Bob and Gwen performed the training needs analysis, he isolated the skills training necessary. The supervisors and employees told him the key need was improved training in the use of the new equipment. He also identified other work-related skills which appeared to decrease employee efficiency.

Then Bob prepared a proposed training program. The training needs analysis had identified the employees who needed the training the most. For trainers, he decided to propose that the manufacturer of the new equipment should provide a trainer. This person would train Bob and several supervisors who appeared to have the greatest potential to run employee training programs. He also proposed that the manufacturer provide a mockup of the machines to use in the training (if available). Lacking that, slides would be used. Then the firm would use several machines for training alone—a semivestibule approach. The cost would be minimal. The manufacturer would provide the training free.

Harold approved the plan, and the training sessions were conducted. Two months after the training was completed, however, there was little change in results. Gwen realized that they had not done as good a job in cost feasibility study as they should have. No formal evaluation of the training had been planned or done.

Gwen and Bob went back to the supervisors to interview them on what had happened. Some of the comments were:

Sandy Feldman (supervisor): I told you people the problem was who you hired. Training bimbos like I got won't help.

Sam Jacobs (supervisor): I thought that training would help. It did a little, for a while. But my problem has become discipline. They know how to do the job—they just don't seem to want to do it.

Harry Samson (supervisor): Maybe the problem was *how* the training was done—I don't know. I see little real results so far.

Bob and Gwen decided to do a formal evaluation of training on the next program. As for what to do now, performance evaluation time was coming up. Maybe the use of rewards for better employees would help. Maybe more and better training would have results. And maybe the labor market had opened up and some terminations and rehirings would be the answer. They'd just have to keep working on it until they could really help Harold and the company. (There will be more about this case in Chapter 10.)

QUESTIONS

1. What is training? Management training and development?
2. Can everyone learn or be trained?
3. What principles of learning affect training? How?
4. What factors in the diagnostic model affect training the most? Why?
5. Why do enterprises perform training? Management development?
6. Who is involved in the planning and operating of formal training in enterprises?
7. How do training managers determine training needs and objectives? Why do they do so (or should they)?
8. What kinds of persons make good trainers?
9. Describe the major training methods. Which are best?
10. What are the major on-the-job management development programs? Which are the best programs? Why?

10

Development of employees and managers

Chapter objectives

- To demonstrate why employers try to develop the attitudes and interpersonal skills of managerial and other employees.
- To help you understand the major techniques used to develop managers and employees and their advantages and shortcomings.
- To discuss what organizational development is and why enterprises engage in it.
- To help you understand the techniques used to make career planning, career development, and career counseling effective.

Chapter outline

I. Introduction to Development
II. Developing Interpersonal Skills and Attitudes
  A. Predecessors to current development programs
  B. Behavior modeling–interaction management
  C. Transactional analysis
  D. Sensitivity training
  E. Management by objectives (MBO) and other programs
III. Career Development
IV. Career Planning and Development by Individuals
  A. Phases in career planning and development
V. Career Development by Organizations
VI. Career Development Counseling
VII. Organizational Development
VIII. Evaluation of Training and Development
IX. Summary, Conclusions, and Recommendations

Case continued from Chapter 9

Later the same year, Gwen Meridith, Young Enterprises's personnel vice president faces another problem. She has received the results of Young's third annual attitude survey from the firm's consultant. (An attitude survey is an instrument to measure employee's feelings about their employer. See Chapters 3 and 19 for more information about them.) Bob McGarrah, the director of training and development is called in to discuss them.

Gwen: Bob, look at the results of the items on training and development. Even though we have not had the desired results on our new training program, Item 17 indicates that the blue- and white-collar employees are very satisfied with our technical training program. So are the managers. Now look at the questions on development. There seems to be serious dissatisfaction there on the part of the employees and managers. With regard to the employee dissatisfaction, this may be related to Item 27. There is a fair amount of dissatisfaction with their supervisors' management styles. Maybe that is why our training program has not given us the desired results! What are your comments?

Bob: Well, Gwen, we haven't done much on nontechnical training here at Young. We have not tried to run off-the-job development programs. We don't do career development. Nor have we ever considered organizational development programs. How do you feel about them?

Gwen: As you know, Bob, my background is labor relations. I have kept up in other areas such as EEO, OSHA, and compensation. But I'm asking for your help on this. I'm not too familiar with these programs. Why don't you get together a report to tell me what's happening in development these days.

Bob prepared a summary of the current trends and happenings in development for managers and employees. The next section covers many of the points Gwen wanted to know about attitude and supervisory-style programs.

INTRODUCTION TO DEVELOPMENT

This chapter completes a two-chapter unit on training and development of managers and employees. Chapter 9 focused primarily on the training of managers and employees to improve their abilities. In addition, training and development also can focus on interpersonal skills and attitudes. It can be argued that effective interpersonal skills are also abilities, but these programs have as their goals the changing of attitudes as well as the development of skills.

Organizations enter into attitude-change and interpersonal skills training programs for many reasons. One is to improve the effectiveness of their employees, especially managers, in their day-to-day work or in specific programs. The latter might be designed to improve meetings and conferences or to help employees adjust their attitudes toward overseas assignments. A second and very important purpose is to help the organization's managers and employees understand themselves better and learn how to cope with modern living.

Some programs designed to affect attitudes are oriented toward the attitudes, interpersonal skills, and organization climate of whole organizational units. These programs, which are called *organization development* (OD), generally take as the ideal what I call in Chapter 2 the liberal organization and leadership style. Some large enterprises also encourage individuals to use these programs to develop careers for themselves with the enterprise.

A number of other programs could be described. The ones that will be emphasized here are:

- Behavioral modeling–interaction management.
- Transactional analysis.

- Sensitivity training.
- Management by objectives.
- Career development.
- Organizational development.

Although the chapter indicates that all employees participate in development programs, most enterprises focus on the development of managerial and professional employees.

DEVELOPING INTERPERSONAL SKILLS AND ATTITUDES

As mentioned in Chapter 9, the diagnostic factors in and purposes of training and development programs are similar. The people involved in development programs are similar to those who supervise training, therefore these sections of Chapter 9 will not be repeated here. It should be pointed out, however, that there is a somewhat greater tendency for firms to hire outside consultants and trainers to oversee development programs than is done for training programs.

Predecessors to current development programs

The earliest programs designed to affect employee and managerial attitudes, called *human relations programs,* were oriented toward individual development. Human relations programs were an outgrowth of the human relations movement, which fostered consideration of the individual in the operation of industry in the 1930s to the 1950s. The rationale of the movement from the enterprise's point of view, was that an employee-centered, liberal supervisory style would lead to more satisfied employees. This in turn would reduce absenteeism, employee turnover, and strikes. Sometimes the style also increased performance. But, as was discussed in Chapter 2, effective performance has multiple causes, and supervisory attitudes and behavior are only one factor influencing it.

The effectiveness of these general human relations programs was measured by direct improvement in objectively measured results, such as a reduction in turnover. They were also called effective if they changed the attitudes of the managers in the direction desired or if the managers participating said the programs were worthwhile. In reviewing the evidence on the effectiveness of human relations programs, John Campbell et al. found that 80 percent of the programs evaluated had significant positive results, as measured by attitudes and opinions about these programs.

Such positive results have encouraged enterprises to continue to conduct interpersonal skills and attitude-change programs. Several of the current programs which apply behavior modification to training and development programs are discussed in this section. A number of the training methods described in Chapter 9 are also used in interpersonal skills and attitude-change programs. Those most frequently used are the case, incident, role-playing, and in-basket techniques.

Behavior modeling–interaction management

A relatively new approach to training in interpersonal skills is behavior modeling, which is also called interaction management or imitating models. The

EXHIBIT 10–1
Model of traditional training program

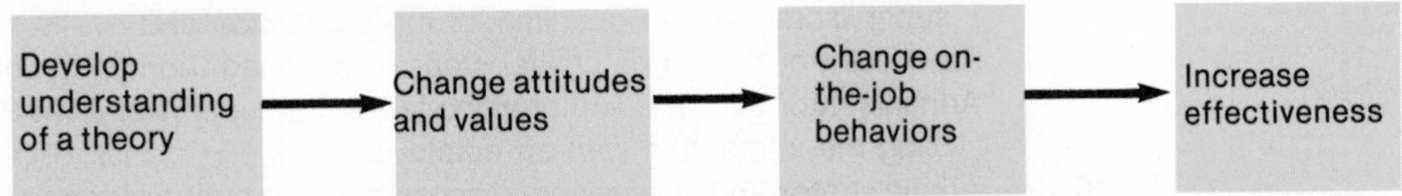

From *Training: Program Development and Evaluation* by I. L. Goldstein. Copyright © 1974 by Wadsworth Publishing Company, Inc. Reprinted by permission of the publisher, Brooks/Cole Publishing Company, Monterey, California.

traditional training model could be as shown in Exhibit 10–1. In behavior modeling, as developed by A. P. Goldstein and M. Sorcher, the development model is as shown in Exhibit 10–2.

The behavior modeling–interaction management (BMIM) approach begins by identifying 19 interpersonal problems that employees, especially managers, face. Typical problems are gaining acceptance as a new supervisor, handling discrimination complaints, delegating responsibility, improving attendance, effective discipline, overcoming resistance to change, setting performance goals, motivating average performance, handling emotional situations, reducing tardiness, and taking corrective action.

There are four steps in the process:

1. Modeling of effective behavior—often by use of films.
2. Role playing.
3. Social reinforcement—trainees and trainers praise effective role plays.
4. Transfer of training to the job.

A typical BMIM training module is shown in Exhibit 10–3. BMIM applies the principles of learning described in Chapter 9 to the development situation. Exhibit 10–4 shows how.

BMIM has been introduced into a number of enterprises, including AT&T, General Electric, IBM, RCA, Boise Cascade, Kaiser Corporation, Olin, B. F. Goodrich, and others. So far, the research evidence is generally positive. In a series of studies, the groups trained in BMIM have outperformed those who received no training or traditional management development training.

BMIM appears to have a bright future.

EXHIBIT 10–2
Model of behavior modeling training program

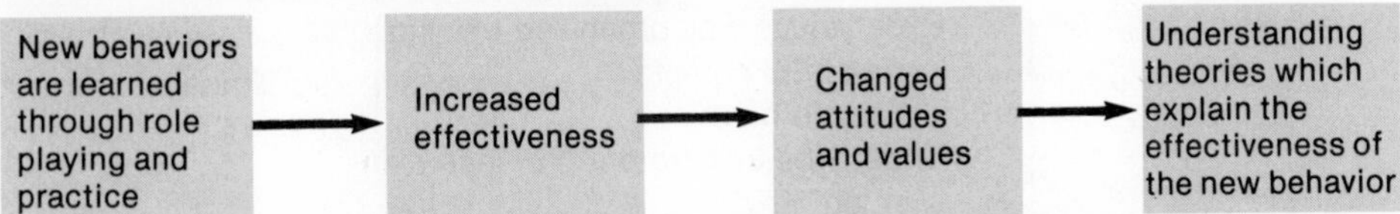

From *Training: Program Development and Evaluation* by I. L. Goldstein. Copyright © 1974 by Wadsworth Publishing Company, Inc. Reprinted by permission of the publisher, Brooks/Cole Publishing Company, Monterey, California.

EXHIBIT 10–3

BMIM module

Administrator announces the interaction skill being considered and the supervisors read an overview of the interaction skill	5 minutes
Administrator describes critical steps in handling the interaction	5 minutes
Administrator shows a film or video tape of a supervisor effectively handling the interaction with an employee	10 minutes
Administrator and supervisors discuss how the supervisor depicted handled the critical steps	5 minutes
Three supervisors take turns in skill practice exercises by handling similar situations with employees. Background information is provided the "supervisor" and "employee" in each skill practice exercise. The handling of the situations is observed by the other supervisors and the administrator using specially prepared Observer Guides. The use of positive reinforcement by the observers helps to build confidence and skill in skill-practicing supervisors	60 minutes
Supervisors write their own interaction situations based on job-related problems, using forms provided in workbooks	10 minutes
Supervisors take turns in skill practice sessions by becoming the "employee" in the participant-written situations, while other supervisors use the interaction skills to handle these situations. These skills practice exercises are also observed and discussed	60 minutes
Supervisors read a summary of the skill module. Using specially designed forms, they plan on-the-job applications of the interaction skills. The administrator hands out a Critical Steps card for supervisors to utilize on the job	10 minutes

Source: William Byham and James Robinson, "Interaction Management: Supervisory Training that Changes Performance," *The Personnel Administrator,* February 1976.

EXHIBIT 10–4

Learning theory principles applied to BMIM (conditions for effective learning)

Learning principles	*BMIM method*
Principles whereby learner:	
Is motivated to improve	
Understands desired skills	Modeling
Actively participates Gets needed practice	Role playing
Gets feedback on performance Is reinforced for appropriate skills	Social reinforcement
Experiences well-organized training Simple to complex Easy to hard	Transfer of training
Undergoes training performance akin to job	

Source: Allen Kraut, "Developing Managerial Skills via Modeling Techniques," *Personnel Psychology* 29 (1976), pp. 325–28.

Transactional analysis

One of the newer development programs is transactional analysis (TA). At present it is rarely used in small companies and occasionally used in medium-sized, large, and very large firms.

Transactional analysis was originally developed by Eric Berne to be used in psychotherapy. Since then, its application has spread to mental counseling, family counseling, and the world of work. TA uses Gestalt therapy and Berne's analysis to help people understand themselves and achieve better self-awareness, responsibility, and genuineness. It focuses on *now* as opposed to the Freudian emphasis on the past. Its goal is to make those who undergo the analysis "winners"—that is, people who respond authentically to others by being credible, genuine, responsive, and trustworthy, who understand themselves and appreciate others and who are self-reliant. "Losers" are not genuine persons and "play games" instead of communicating and behaving honestly.

The analytical technique Berne uses is his description of the personality structure. According to Berne, the personality structure is composed of the Parent, the Adult, and the Child. Although Berne sees differences, I believe his analysis is an adaptation of Freud's superego, ego, and id. But the analysis of interactions, communications, and behavior is much more direct in transactional analysis than in Freudian analysis.

For purposes of transactional analysis, each person's personality has a Parent, Adult, and Child ego state. The Parent tends to be righteous, dogmatic, evaluative, and protective. The Adult is the reasoning ego state. It seeks factual discussion in decisions and interactions. The Child is dependent, selfish, and rebellious. The child desires immediate satisfaction, is emotional, and seeks approval.

When two people interact, they face each other with one of the three ego states predominating. This leads to two possible transactions:

1. *Complementary.* The ego states match. For example, both persons operate in the adult ego state. Exhibit 10–5 exemplifies complementary transactions in a business setting.

EXHIBIT 10–5

Complementary transactions in Parent, Adult and Child ego states

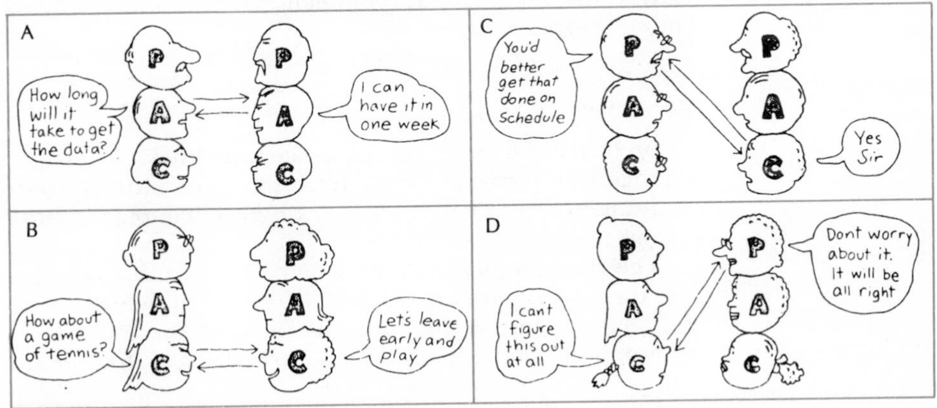

Source: Muriel James, *The OK Boss* (Reading, Mass.: Addison-Wesley Publishing Company, 1975).

EXHIBIT 10–6
Crossed transactions in Parent, Adult, and Child ego states

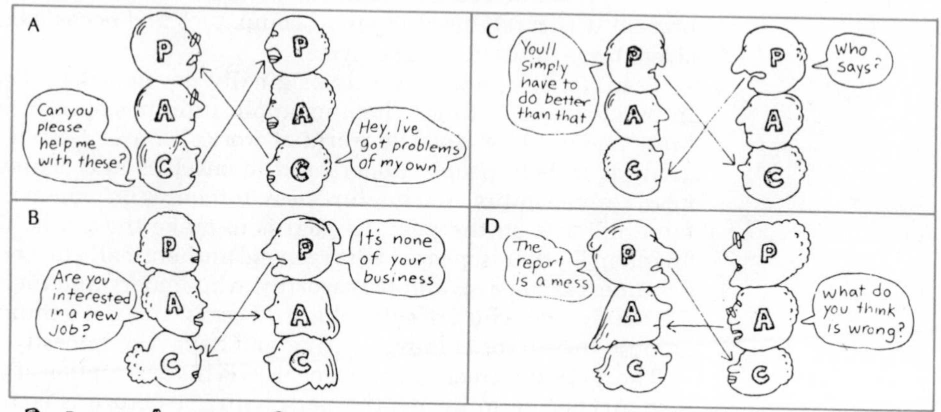

P = Parent; A = Adult; C = Child.

Source: Muriel James, *The OK Boss* (Reading, Mass.: Addison-Wesley Publishing Company, 1975).

2. *Crossed.* The two persons are operating in different ego states that do not parallel each other. Exhibit 10–6 gives examples of these relationships between business associates.

Transactional analysis points out that all interactions involve "stroking." By this, TA people mean any verbal and nonverbal signal of recognition and approval or disapproval. Positive verbal stroking is shown in Exhibit 10–5, A, B, and D; negative verbal strokes are illustrated in Exhibit 10–6, A, B, and C.

Few studies have been done on the effectiveness of the technique, but those who have used it tend to approve of its results, and those who have not are usually dubious. In a study of TA at General Telephone, the researchers found significantly lower turnover in employees supervised by those trained in TA than the control group, and the benefit cost ratio is good. TA should have a significant impact on development programs and organizational development in the future.

Sensitivity training

Probably the most controversial and most investigated form of attitude-change–interpersonal skills training is sensitivity training (ST). Sensitivity training is also called T-group training, encounter-group training, and by other terms.

The many approaches to sensitivity training vary in the degree to which the training is structured, the role of the trainer, the mix of the emotional and rational in the training, and the focus of the training: on the individual, the group, or the total organization. All tend to have these characteristics in common:

There is a permissive atmosphere to encourage free discussion.

There is an unstructured agenda; the members partially determine the subject of the meetings.

The learning takes place by nonlecture methods. Typically the members learn by the experience in the meetings.

Frustration is likely when the meeting seems to wander.

Just as the style of the training varies, so do its objectives. In some, the objectives are personal growth and self-understanding. In other, more structural approaches, some job-centered problems are introduced.

Sensitivity training has been criticized for being expensive, for invading trainees' privacy, for hastening breakdowns, and for lack of carryover into the workplace. Although it was a very popular technique in the 1960s, it seemed to have declined severely by the late 1970s.

The evidence is mixed on whether sensitivity training achieves its objectives. Individual differences influence its effectiveness. George Strauss believes it is most likely to be effective on persons who are open to new ideas prior to ST, have high levels of interpersonal trust, participate most during ST, change most during ST, and have the power to introduce changes at work.

I participated in a ST group in the late 1960s. Based on that experience and a literature review, I believe that ST could be useful to a person whose job requires frequent interaction with others, who also knows little about interpersonal skills, and whose personality is such that self-revelation is not threatening. It can be a powerful mechanism for attitude change and development, but it should be used only on *carefully chosen managers* and for positions that *require sensitive interpersonal skills* for successful execution of the job.

Management by objectives (MBO) and other programs

New training programs aimed at changing managerial interpersonal skills are always appearing. For example, Charles Kepner and Benjamin Tregoe now offer Telos, a program based on a leadership model which utilizes on-line computer feedback. And Robert Blake and Jane Mouton, of Managerial Grid fame, now offer Critiqube.

Sometimes MBO systems and approaches are used in organizational and management development. A survey of ASPA members and personnel professors found that management by objectives is used rather widely in medium-size and larger companies and occasionally in smaller ones. Top and middle managers were widely involved. The MBO programs were rated as moderately successful, and most felt the benefits justified their costs.

It would be impossible to review all the development programs being offered today. This chapter has touched on only a few.

CAREER DEVELOPMENT

Another approach to development of the employee is career development.

A career is a sequence of work-related experiences in which a person participates during the span of his or her work life.

Career development is the personnel activity which helps individuals plan their future careers within the enterprise, in order to help the enterprise achieve its objectives and the employee to achieve maximum self-development.

The need for career development is illustrated in the following situation.

Sally Feldman, one of the supervisors heard from earlier, and Jim Thomsen are having a few drinks after work at The Golden Bough, a bar near Young Enterprises. Sally is having a down day. She shares her feelings with Jim.

Sally: Well another Friday and the week is over. But something's missing.

Jim: What do you mean, Sally?

Sally: I go to work on Monday, Tuesday, every day, and what do I accomplish?

Jim: Sally, you've got a good job. You make good money. You make a contribution to your company. What else do you want?

Sally: I'm not sure. I've been with Young for four years. After a training program, I started on my first job, and now I'm on my second. But what does it lead to? Where am I going? What are my chances of becoming a department head? And why am I going where I'm headed, anyway? The first job didn't have much to do with the second; I get the feeling I got it because it opened up, not because I was needed or that it built anything for me. My brother is a career army officer. He pretty much knows how his life will be spent. I don't.

Jim: My company has a career development plan to help me with that. Doesn't yours?

Sally: No.

Jim: Well, you could develop a career plan for yourself. Would that help?

Sally: Sure, but how do I do that? And besides, would it mean anything if my company isn't involved?

Jim: I'm not sure.

Sally: I've got to get some control of my life so I can see some purpose to it—some sort of plan.

Jim: Yeah. Bartender, I'll have another piña colada.

The next day Sally went to see Gwen Meridith and ask her what Young Enterprises was going to do about career development. She brought along a copy of what Jim Thomsen's company was doing. It was a combination of individual and enterprise development programs something like those described below.

Companies or individuals get involved in career development for five reasons:

- To help achieve employee and organizational goals.
- To help reduce the tendency of some department heads to hoard people, preventing their promotion for fear that their replacements will be less effective.
- To reduce employee obsolescence.
- To reduce turnover and personnel costs, because employees will be more satisfied.
- To help the enterprise meet equal employment opportunity goals by developing needed minority and female employees for potential promotion.

Three people are necessary for effective career development. The most important is the employee. Only the individual employee can tie together her or his family stages, personal life stages, and career stages in order to develop a complete life career plan. There must also be a personnel specialist to help guide and advise employees whose career is being developed. And the employee's operating supervisor can be very helpful in terms of advice, counseling, and sponsorship. This is normally an informal process between the supervisor and the employee, however.

What should the individual employee do to plan a career? Answers to this question are suggested in the following section.

CAREER PLANNING AND DEVELOPMENT BY INDIVIDUALS

A career can lend order and meaning to events and provide a relationship, including work, in which a person is involved. And a career is central to the complete development of an individual's identity. Thus it is important for an employee to plan a career, even if the employer provides little guidance or encouragement.

Phases in career planning and development

Individual career planning and development normally involves four phases:

1. Self-appraisal.
2. Information gathering on occupations.
3. Goal selection.
4. Planning and implementation.

Self-appraisal. First, the individuals must know themselves. They are helped to do this by counseling, guidance, and testing. The Strong Vocational Interest Blank and Kuder Preference Record can help determine interests, and counseling can interpret the results in relation to other aspects of the employees' lives. Feedback from parents and supervisors also helps, and simulations such as John Holland's Self-Directed Search can help employees become more self-aware.

Information gathering on occupations. Gathering information on current job opportunities (see Chapter 5) helps employees in their choices of careers, jobs, and employers.

Goal selection. Employees must set the goals sought in their careers. These goals can be set in quantitative terms, such as:

- Number of persons to be supervised by a specific age (for example, 8,000 by age 30).
- Target salary for number of years or age (for example, to make one's age in salary by age 35: $35,000 per year at age 35).
- To attain a title by a certain age (for example, vice president by age 40).
- Colleague goal: to be working with at least four compatible colleagues by age 25.
- Whether or not to own one's own business.

Due to individual differences, people's objectives will vary. What is important is setting goals precisely. But the individual should not become inflexible. If your goal is to become a millionaire by 35 and if the goal is close at that age, you should be willing to wait until you are 36. The success of career planning depends on how good employees are at assessing their comparative advantages and knowing how the industry in which they work typically moves people along.

The goals listed above were oriented towards men. When women set career goals, some may choose to have several phases, to include a period for child bearing and care. In this case, women's goals may be different from men's. When women seek only work careers, the goals could be very similar. In a family where both husband and wife have careers, the career goals of the two must be developed together so the tradeoffs are clear. Whose career suffers if one is transferred? Or do they both refuse transfers? These potential career goal conflicts must be planned for.

Planning and implementation. The next phase is planning the career to achieve the goals. Regular checkpoints are used to make sure that the goals are achieved on time. Real career success often requires playing "success chess." By the rules for this game, a successful manager:

- Maintains the largest number of job options possible.
- Does not waste time working for an immobile manager.
- Becomes a crucial subordinate to a mobile superior.
- Always favors increased exposure and visibility.
- Is prepared to nominate himself or herself for jobs that come open. This manager defines the corporation as a market of jobs.
- Leaves a company when the career has slowed too much.
- Is ready to quit if necessary.
- Does not let success in a present job preempt the career plan. This could reduce upward mobility.

Employees who have set their personal career goals are in a better position to profit from career development programs offered by the enterprises for which they are working.

CAREER DEVELOPMENT BY ORGANIZATIONS

Some organizations actively help employees build careers for themselves. These enterprises include the Internal Revenue Service, Union Oil, American Telephone and Telegraph, the state of Washington, G. D. Searle, and the Government Accounting Office.

An example of career development by an organization is the approach taken by a major telephone company. The typical career path it uses to develop a general manager is given in Exhibit 10–7. Exhibit 10–8 lists the steps in an actual career for a general manager with this company. In addition to position rotation and on-the-job training, the company provides one- and two-week training programs at the manager's current location. It also offers a college tuition reimbursement plan if the managers choose to further their formal educations.

A second illustration of career development is a program offered by the U.S. Air Force. The Air Force, a large organization, employs hundreds of thousands of employees. It has a very sophisticated employment planning system based on determination of needs and a personnel planning system for determining assignments. In conjunction with these systems, the Air Force has developed a complex career development plan for its cadre of officers. The purpose of career development for the Air Force is to assure that enough highly qualified

EXHIBIT 10–7
Typical career path for general manager in telephone company

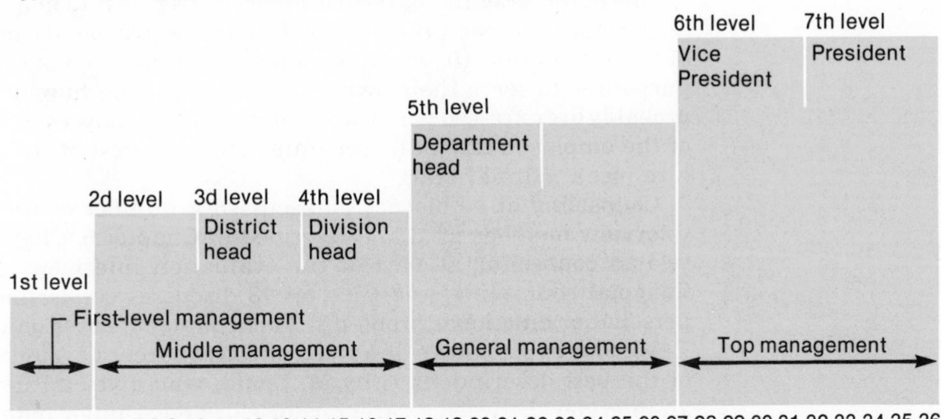

officers are available and that these officers are promoted to responsible positions.

Specific career plans which specify the different kinds of experience and education desirable for each career specialty are also developed. The service develops career progression guides to help in career development. Each career specialty has career management positional experience and on- and off-the-job training. Individuals hired experience assignments that develop them personally and use their particular talents. While in these positions they serve as understudies and are counseled and coached by a superior.

EXHIBIT 10–8
Career path of a general manager in telephone company

Level	*Job title*	*Location*	*Department*	*Years in position*
1st	Staff assistant	Home office	Commercial	2½ years
1st	Manager	District office, small city	Commercial	1½ years
2d	Unit manager	Home office	Commercial	1 year
2d	Data sales manager	Home office	Commercial	2½ years
2d	Rate engineer	District office	Commercial	1½ years
3d	District manager	District office	Commercial	1½ years
3d	College employment representative	Home office	Personnel	1 year
3d	Corporate headquarters	New York	Human resource development	2 years
4th	College relations director	Home office	Personnel	1 year
4th	Division manager	Division office	Commercial	3½ years
5th	Assistant vice president, personnel	Home office	Personnel	5 years

CAREER DEVELOPMENT COUNSELING

One of the essential parts of a supervisor's role is to help subordinates develop as persons and reach their goals. Employees frequently produce more because of such programs. However, work organizations are not schools. Their primary purpose is to serve their owners and clients. The human relations movement probably overstressed personal counseling of employees. Still, the technical skills of the employee cannot be separated from the rest of the person. One does not hire just a pair of hands.

Counseling of employees is discussed a number of times in this book. The interview methods used are described in Chapter 6. Chapter 8 discusses work-related counseling as part of the evaluation interview. Chapter 13 discusses financial counseling, and Chapter 18 discusses counseling of employees with personal or emotional problems. This chapter focuses on career counseling.

Various experts have described effective career development counseling. One of the best descriptions is by M. Gould, who gives an interesting example of an interview between a career counselor and a junior manager whose goal was to become chairman of the board in a brief time. Gould describes how the counselor tried to gather hard data on the employee prior to the interview: how many courses and seminars he had attended, his reading habits (extent and kinds of books), and his civic and professional activities. Gould maintains that this information is an indication of the importance the individual attaches to the need for continuing development.

Then the counselor asked about the employee's career goals and tried to work realism into the discussion of goals. The counselor helped the young manager to see that his career goal was unrealistic, given his current progress and maturation. The interview was directed toward a more attainable goal for that individual.

Another test for realism is the individual's discussion of what he sees as his strong point (characteristics or factors which will help him achieve his goal) and soft spots (those that may impede his progress). Difficulties and successes the individual is experiencing with subordinates, peers, and superiors are also a part of this phase of the conversations. Careful listening has frequently helped to expand this information most usefully. For example, one individual in Gould's study stated, "I think I'm pretty fair in the field of labor relations." In feeding back what he had heard, the counselor was careful to include this comment. The conversation at that point went like this:

COUNSELOR: And you see yourself as only pretty fair in labor relations, right?

EMPLOYEE: No, that's not right.

COUNSELOR: You see yourself as better than fair?

EMPLOYEE: I sure do.

COUNSELOR: Good?

EMPLOYEE: Darned good.

There then followed a fruitful discussion of the risks of understatement—you might be believed! The point was also made that due concern should be shown about image so that what others see and hear is compatible with the individual's true worth.

This is one example of the kind of career counseling possible in a career development program. There are many other possibilities, including midlife career crisis counseling.

ORGANIZATIONAL DEVELOPMENT

Bob

Back to Bob. What was he doing to help Gwen start up a career development program for Young Enterprises?

After presenting potential development and career development plans to Gwen, Bob had prepared a report on current trends in organizational development. Some of the points Bob discussed in his report are given below.

One type of development which overlaps several of the methods already discussed is organizational development (OD), which seeks to change attitudes, values, organization structure, and managerial practices to improve performance. There are a number of variations of organizational development, but some of the more common characteristics are:

- The focus of the development is the total organization, not the individual or a small group of individuals.
- The methods used are group discussions, team-building exercises, confrontation meetings, and intergroup conflict experiences. Thus the primary methodology is *experiential* learning.
- A consultant or change agent is used as a facilitator or catalyst.

Organizational development frequently is conducted by outside consultants in a series of seven phases.

Phases in the OD process:

1. *Initial diagnosis.* The consultant seeks to determine the enterprises' problems.
2. *Data collection.* After the initial diagnosis, the consultant surveys the enterprise extensively to find out the problem and possible solutions.
3. *Feedback and confrontation.* The consultant feeds these findings back to the group and sets priorities for change.
4. *Planning–problem solving.* The problem-solving groups begin to solve the problems chosen for solutions.
5. *Team building.* The consultant uses role play, sensitivity training, and games to strengthen the bonds of the problem-solving groups (teams).
6. *Intergroup development.* The consultant develops bonds between teams to build larger groups.
7. *Follow-up and evaluation.* The consultant analyzes the results against the objectives of OD.

Newton Margulies and Anthony Raia, two well-known experts on OD, have summarized its values, process, and technology (methods), as shown in Exhibit 10–9.

How effective is organizational development? This is hard to say; Strauss notes that "as a rapidly evolving field, OD presents a moving target, making it difficult to define or criticize." Strauss has identified eight common forms of OD, for example. Most of the studies have been done by OD consultants, and most show positive results in terms of employee satisfaction. Strauss points out that since the consultants are in the business of selling OD, it is unlikely that they would report its failures. There have been studies indicating that OD increases productivity or organizational effectiveness, although in all the studies it was only one of several changes taking place at the time.

In sum, it appears plausible that organizational development can help increase productivity and satisfaction. But much more research is needed before we know what kind of OD, in which kind of organizations, and under what conditions.

EVALUATION OF TRAINING AND DEVELOPMENT

In Chapter 9, the problem Gwen Meridith and Harold Matthews faced in deciding whether the training offered was effective. They had not designed a formal evaluation of the training program. This is also an issue in the current development program Gwen is proposing. This section focuses on that issue.

Evaluation of training is the final phase of the training and development program (see Exhibit 9–1 in Chapter 9). Cost/benefit analysis generally is more feasible for training than for many other personnel functions. Costs are relatively easy to compute: they equal direct costs of training (trainer cost, materials cost, and lost productivity, if it is done on company time) and indirect costs (a fair share of administrative overhead of the personnel department).

Essentially, the evaluation should be made by comparing the results (the benefits) with the objectives of the training and development program which were set in the assessment phase. It is easier to evaluate the results of some training programs (e.g., typing) than others (e.g., decision making and leadership). The criteria used to evaluate training and development depend on the objectives of the program and who sets the criteria: management, the trainers, or the trainees. For example, one study found that trainees who were asked to develop their own evaluative criteria chose standards which varied from knowledge of the subject to the amount of socializing allowed during training sessions.

There are three types of criteria for evaluating training: internal, external, and participant reaction. *Internal criteria* are those directly associated with the content of the program. *External criteria* are related more to the ultimate purpose of training—for example, improving the effectiveness of the employee. Possible external criteria include job performance rating, increases in sales volume, or decreases in turnover. *Participant reaction,* or how the subjects feel about the benefits of a specific training or development experience, is commonly used as an internal criterion.

Most experts argue that it is more effective to use multiple criteria to evaluate training. Others contend that a single criterion, such as the extent of transfer of training to on-the-job performance or other aspects of performance, is a satisfactory evaluation approach.

EXHIBIT 10–9

An integrative approach to organizational development

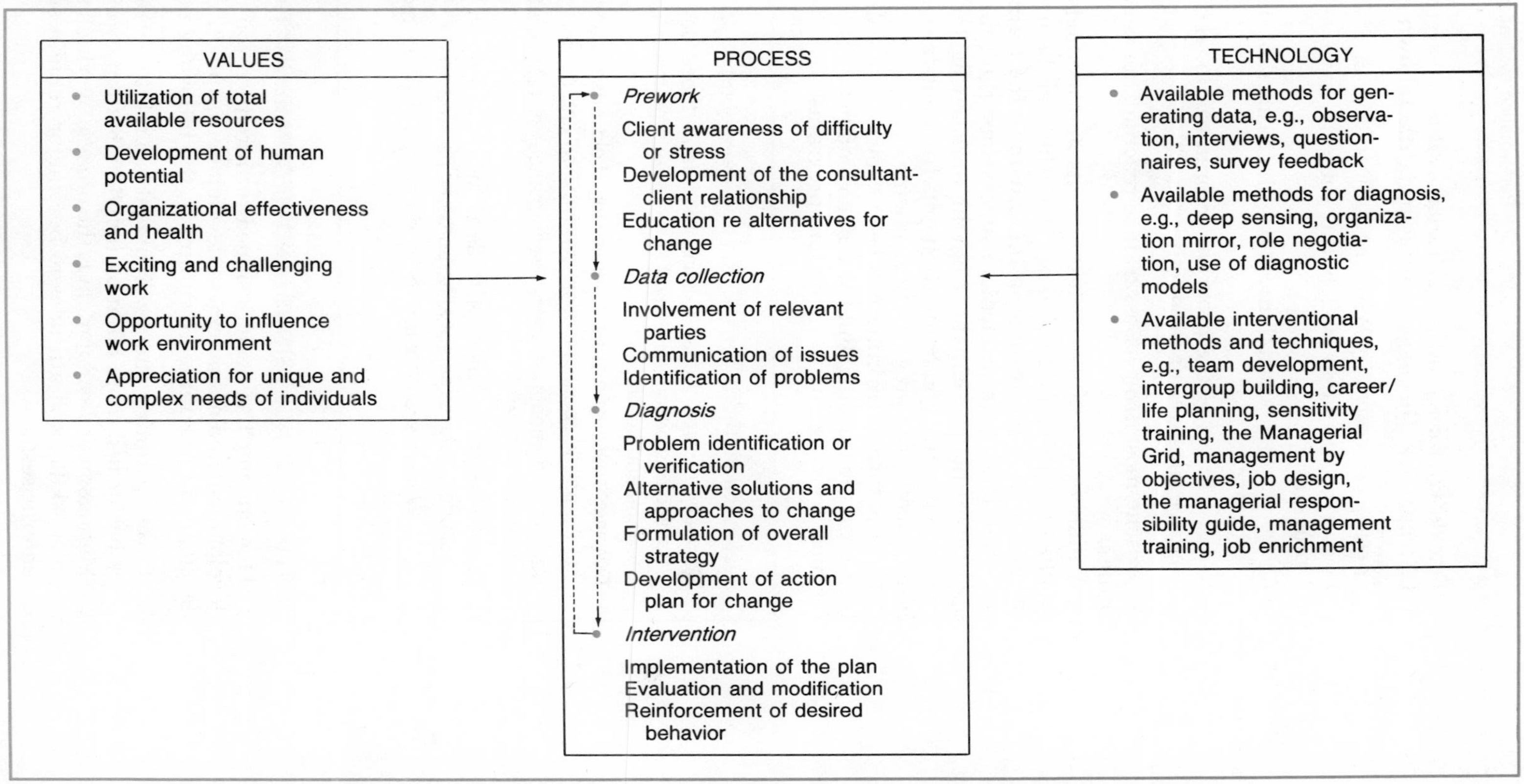

VALUES

- Utilization of total available resources
- Development of human potential
- Organizational effectiveness and health
- Exciting and challenging work
- Opportunity to influence work environment
- Appreciation for unique and complex needs of individuals

PROCESS

Prework

Client awareness of difficulty or stress
Development of the consultant-client relationship
Education re alternatives for change

Data collection

Involvement of relevant parties
Communication of issues
Identification of problems

Diagnosis

Problem identification or verification
Alternative solutions and approaches to change
Formulation of overall strategy
Development of action plan for change

Intervention

Implementation of the plan
Evaluation and modification
Reinforcement of desired behavior

TECHNOLOGY

- Available methods for generating data, e.g., observation, interviews, questionnaires, survey feedback
- Available methods for diagnosis, e.g., deep sensing, organization mirror, role negotiation, use of diagnostic models
- Available interventional methods and techniques, e.g., team development, intergroup building, career/life planning, sensitivity training, the Managerial Grid, management by objectives, job design, the managerial responsibility guide, management training, job enrichment

Source: Newton Margulies and Anthony Raia, *Conceptual Foundations of Organization Development* (New York: McGraw-Hill Book Co., 1978).

One design for a multiple-criterion evaluation system was developed by Donald Kirkpatrick. He suggests measuring the following:

Participant reaction. Whether subjects like or dislike the program.

Learning. Extent to which the subjects have assimilated the training program.

Behavior. An external measure of changes or lack of changes in job behavior.

Results. Effect of the program on organizational dimensions such as employee turnover or productivity.

At present, most firms assess trainee reaction, but very few measure behavioral results.

A number of evaluation instruments and methods can be used to measure results of training (see the box). Data that can be used for evaluation include information on the trainee in the program; the trainee's immediate superiors and superiors above immediate supervisors; the trainee's subordinates (where applicable); nonparticipants from the work setting, including the subject's peers; company records; and nonparticipants from outside the work setting who might be affected by the program (e.g., clients).

In sum, formal training has been shown to be more effective than informal training or no training. But the results tend to be assumed rather than evaluated for most training and development programs.

Evaluation methods for training and development programs:

Company records. Either existing records or those devised for the evaluation of training or development, used to measure production turnover, grievances, absenteeism, and so on.

Observational techniques. Interviewing, field observation, and so on, to evaluate skills, ability, communication, productivity, and so on.

Ratings. Judgments of ability, performance, or ratings of satisfaction with various factors.

Questionnaires. A variety of types to measure decision making, problem solving, attitudes, values, personality, perceptions, and so on.

Tests. Written examinations or performance tests to measure changes in ability or knowledge.

SUMMARY, CONCLUSIONS, AND RECOMMENDATIONS

This chapter has been designed to introduce you to the processes of career development and management development, and the evaluation of training and development programs. In summary, the following points are made:

1. Career planning and development is a relatively new personnel activity and is performed more often by individuals than by enterprises.
2. Management development is the process by which managers gain the experience, skills, and attitudes to become or remain successful leaders in their enterprises.

3. Management and professional development is designed to reduce obsolescence and to increase employee satisfaction and productivity.
4. Methods which can be used to modify employee and managerial attitudes and interpersonal skills include behavior modeling–interaction management, transactional analysis, sensitivity training, MBO, and others.
6. An organizational approach to career development can include specific career plans which specify the different kinds of experience and education desirable for each career specialty.
5. An individual approach to career planning and development follows this pattern:
   a. Self-appraisal.
   b. Information gathering on occupations.
   c. Goal selection.
   d. Planning and implementation.
7. Career development counseling is an essential part of the supervisor's role to help subordinates develop as persons and reach their goals.
8. Organizational development is a technique which overlaps the other methods. It seeks to change attitudes, values, organization structure, and managerial practices to improve performance.
9. The final phase of training and development programs is evaluation.

Several propositions which apply more to the development phase of personnel than to training are listed below:

Proposition 10.1. The more employees identify with the work ethic, the more likely are they to find career development satisfying, and the more likely is it to affect the performance positively.

Proposition 10.2. The more volatile the organization's environment, the more difficult it is to pursue detailed career development plans, and thus the less likely is the function to be found.

Proposition 10.3. The more the enterprise rewards its managers for developing human resources, the more likely is it to offer career development and counseling.

Proposition 10.4. The more volatile the environment of the enterprise or the job, the higher will be the proportion of obsolescent managers in the job.

Proposition 10.5. The older the managerial group, the higher will be the percentage of obsolescent managers.

Proposition 10.6. The larger the organization, the more likely is it to provide formal management development training for its managers, potential managers, and professionals.

Unlike other chapters, Chapter 10 will not have a chart indicating recommendations on career development for model organizations. It is too new a function to make this prediction possible. It is to be expected, however, that large and medium-sized and more stable organizations will develop formal career development programs if top management chooses to support them as part of its personnel strategy.

Chapter 11 begins the discussion of an area of personnel which is important to everyone: compensation.

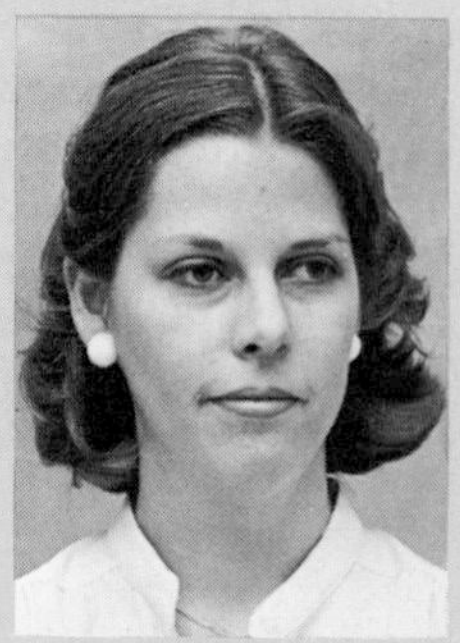
Gwen

After absorbing the material Bob has brought her, Gwen approaches Lester Young, Young Enterprise's president on an informal basis.

Gwen: You know, Les, our last attitude survey indicated major dissatisfaction with our development program at Young. We've been doing some research in our shop about some career, organizational, and other development programs. I'm sure I couldn't work it into this year's budget. But we're only six weeks away from the new budget time. I feel it is very important at this time. As you know, we were not completely satisfied with the training program on the new machinery. In addition, one or two of our supervisors have come in to complain about the lack of a career development program for them. How would you like us to proceed?

Lester: I have heard some talk about OD at a recent American Manufacturers Association meeting. I hear its quite costly. We may have some problems in this area, but we're in no position to make a major investment in development at the present time in view of our earnings situation. Why not work up a modest program for presentation to the budget and goals meeting six weeks from now—no more than 5 percent of your current budget as an increment.

Gwen: Will do, Les.

Gwen and Bob put together a proposal which they viewed as Phase 1. They proposed an individual career development program with some help from personnel for one half of 1 percent of current budget.

After investigating the potential costs of an OD consultant, they felt they should begin to move in the development area. They proposed some beginning funds for planning an OD program, the first phase of which would involve initial diagnosis and small sample data collection. They proposed to set up an experiment using a behavior-modeling program in one unit for supervisory style, with a control group. Evaluation procedures were to be formal. They specified desired outputs: better readings from the attitude survey, some improvements in turnover and absenteeism, and some results in the productivity problem.

Lester and the budget and goals committee accepted the proposal. Phase 1 began, and it was successful. Little by little, the company accepted a development program. The results were encouraging to all—Lester, Gwen, Bob, Harold, and Sally.

QUESTIONS

1. Describe the major development programs designed to improve interpersonal skills and affect attitudes. Describe the ones you'd like to participate in.
2. What is organizational development?
3. Under what conditions is organizational development effective?
4. What is career development?
5. What kinds of enterprises and individuals engage in career planning and career development? Why do they do so?
6. How does career counseling take place?
7. Why should enterprises evaluate training and development? How can they do so?
8. Outline the phases in career planning and development.

9. Give two reasons why organizations enter into attitude-change and interpersonal skills training programs.
10. The predecessor of current development programs was called human relations programs. What was the major emphasis of these programs, and how effective were they?

Lark

part five

Compensation, benefits, and services

Part Five discusses a very important set of personnel activities: compensation, benefits, and services.

Chapter 11 introduces the subject of compensation and pay. It discusses the potential impact of pay on employees and discusses pay level, pay structure, and individual pay determination. Chapter 12 completes this discussion by focusing on incentives and pay schemes, managerial compensation, and several significant policy issues regarding compensation.

Chapter 13 covers all benefits and services except for pensions. The potential impact of benefits and services is considered, and the major benefits that employers provide for employees are discussed.

Chapter 14, the final chapter in Part Five, focuses on retirement policies and a very important benefit: pensions. This is considered separately from the other benefits because of the legal requirements for pensions and their complex nature and high cost.

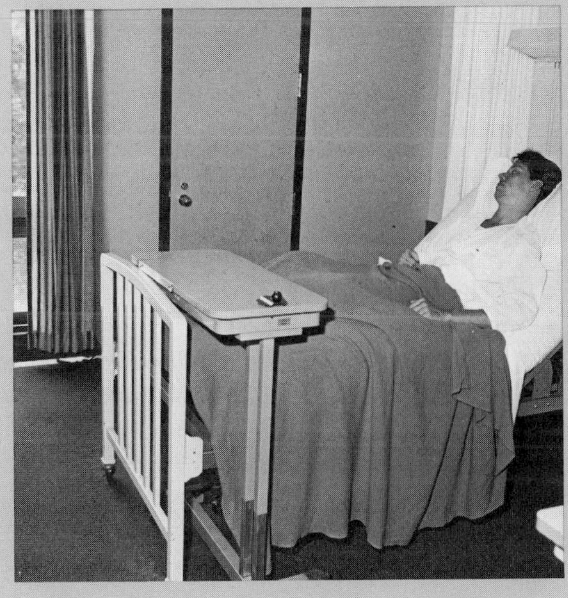

11

An introduction to compensation

Chapter objectives

- To show how employee preferences and motivation affect pay.
- To show how environmental influences and internal factors affect pay levels and policies.
- To discuss pay surveys and how they help management assess its pay status relative to comparable enterprises.
- To show how to evaluate jobs and set up a pay structure.
- To help you understand how individual pay determination is done.

Chapter outline

I. Introduction to Compensation
   A. Objectives of compensation
   B. Compensation decision makers
   C. Compensation decisions
II. A Diagnostic Approach to Compensation
III. Compensation and Employee Satisfaction
IV. Compensation and Employee Performance
   A. Job desirability
V. External Influences on Pay Levels
   A. Government influences
   B. Union influences on compensation
   C. Economic conditions and compensation
   D. Nature of the labor market and compensation
VI. Pay Surveys and Comparable Pay Levels
   A. Who conducts wage surveys?
   B. How pay surveys are conducted and used
VII. Organizational Influences on Pay Levels
   A. Goals of controlling interests and managerial pay strategy
VIII. The Pay-Level Decision
IX. Pay Structures
   A. Job evaluation
   B. Pay classes, rate ranges, and classifications
X. Individual Pay Determination
XI. Summary, Conclusions, and Recommendations

Cardeson National Bank is a small firm which was founded in suburban Pittsburgh ten years ago. For the first year and a half, it operated out of a prefabricated building on a small lot across from the shopping center. Then it built a nice building on the site. Later it added two branch offices in adjoining suburbs. CNB now employs about 150 persons.

Poppa Joe

The founder of the bank and still president is Joseph Paderewski, an entrepreneur who made his first career in construction and building. Poppa Joe, as everyone calls him, is 60 years old. He has spent most of his energies building the bank. He did this by raising the money from the original stockholders, developing a marketing plan to get enough depositors to use CNB, and finding good locations at which to build banks.

Poppa Joe has done almost all the hiring. He's always established the pay rates himself for each employee, based on experience, potential, and how much the employee needs to help support self and family. Recently, Guido Panelli, his executive vice president, has been bringing Poppa Joe some problems he hasn't had time for. Guido has mentioned something about salaries, but Poppa Joe hasn't given it much thought.

Guido

Poppa Joe has always had an open-door policy. Yesterday a teller, Arte Jamison, came in to see him.

Arte Jamison: Poppa Joe, you hired me five years ago. I came in to tell you that I'm quitting. I had to tell Mr. Panelli about this problem a couple of times and nothing happened. So I'm gone. I'm going to work for Pittsburgh National Bank for more money.

Poppa Joe: Arte, don't quit for money. What do you need? I'll take care of it.

Arte: That's not the point. You keep hiring in people with less experience than me at more pay. There's no future here with a situation like that. I quit.

Poppa Joe: Sure sorry to see your go, Arte.

Poppa Joe sat in his office. He'd always liked Arte. What was happening? He called in Guido.

Poppa Joe: Guido, what's happening around here? Arte Jamison just quit. He's a good man.

Guido: Boss, I've tried to bring the subject up lots of times, and you're always too busy. We've got a screwed-up pay system around here.

Poppa Joe: What do you mean? I've always been fair.

Guido: You think you've been fair. But you're too busy to do all you've been doing. You hire people at one pay level and others doing the same job at another. Some get behind and never get a raise. It's a mess.

I've asked one of our vice presidents, Mary Renfro, to take a course at the University of Pittsburgh's night MBA program on personnel, especially one on compensation. She's done it. Now: Should I ask her to study the problem and talk to us about it?

Poppa Joe: O.K., let her do a study. But I'm not convinced we've got such a big problem because a few people quit.

Guido: Please boss, let's keep an open mind about this. Pay has an awfully important impact on employees.

INTRODUCTION TO COMPENSATION

At last we're going to talk about money and pay. Compensation is part of a transaction between an employee and an employer which results in an employment contract. From the employee's point of view, pay is a necessity in life. Few people are so wealthy they do not accept financial remuneration for their work. The compensation received for work is one of the chief reasons people seek employment. Pay is the means by which they provide for their own and their family's needs. For people with instrumental attitudes toward work (as discussed in Chapter 2), compensation may be the only (or certainly a major) reason why they work. Others find compensation a contributing factor to their efforts. Pay can do more than provide for the physiological needs of employees, however. It can also serve their recognition needs.

Compensation is one of the most important personnel functions for the employer, too. Compensation often equals 50 percent of the cash flow of an enterprise, and a larger percentage in service enterprises. It may be the major method used to attract the employees needed to get the work done, as well as a means to try to motivate more effective performance. A Prentice-Hall/ASPA survey of 1,400 personnel managers found that personnel executives rate compensation as their second or third most important activity.

Compensation is also significant to the economy. For the past 30 years, salaries and wages have equaled about 60 percent of the gross national product of the United States.

Compensation is the monetary reward paid by an enterprise for the work done by an employee.

Compensation or pay is only one way the employee is rewarded for work. Work also provides benefits (Chapter 13 and 14), promotions and status (Chapter 8), intrinsic rewards of the job and other rewards. The relative importance which employees attach to pay as compared to the other rewards varies with their preferences.

Objectives of compensation

The objective of a compensation system is to create a system of rewards which is equitable to the employer and employee alike, so that the employee is attracted to the work and *motivated* to do a good job for the employer. Thomas Patten suggests that in compensation policy there are seven criteria for effectiveness. The compensation should be:

Adequate. Minimum governmental, union, and managerial levels should be met.

Equitable. Each person is paid fairly, in line with his or her effort, abilities, training, and so on.

Balanced. Pay, benefits, and other rewards provide a reasonable total reward package.

Cost effective. Pay is not excessive, considering what the enterprise can afford to pay.

Secure. The extent to which the employee's security needs relative to pay and the needs which pay satisfies are met.

Incentive providing. Pay motivates effective and productive work.

Acceptable to the employee. The employee understands the pay system and feels it is a reasonable system for the enterprise and himself.

How well do you think Cardeson National Bank's pay plan is achieving these objectives?

Compensation decision makers

A number of persons are involved in making compensation decisions. Top management makes the decisions which determine the total amount of the budget that goes to pay, the pay form to be used (time pay versus incentive pay), and pay policies, such as secrecy. They also set the pay strategy (discussed below). Personnel advises them on all of these issues. As always, the operating managers at the supervisory and middle-management level also have an impact on personnel decisions, including pay. The relationships between personnel and operating managers in pay matters are given in Exhibit 11–1.

Exhibit 11–2 describes a typical modern compensation manager. This person normally is a department head in a personnel department.

At present, Cardeson National Bank has a rudimentary personnel system. It has a personnel clerk, but it does not have a personnel manager, much less a compensation manager. Poppa Joe is making almost all decisions, including personnel decisions.

Compensation is a Stage IV personnel function. It is mature in that all work organizations compensate employees, and there is a good deal of empirical data

EXHIBIT 11–1
The roles of operating and personnel managers in making pay decisions

Pay decision factor	*Operating manager (OM)*	*Personnel manager (PM)*
Compensation budgets	OM approves or adjusts PM's preliminary budget	PM prepares preliminary budget
Pay-level decisions: Pay survey design and interpretation		PM designs, implements, and makes decisions
Pay structure decisions: Job evaluation design and interpretation		PM designs, implements, and makes decisions
Pay classes, rate ranges, and classification design and interpretation		PM designs, implements, and makes decisions
Individual pay determination	Joint decision with PM	Joint decision with OM
Pay policy decisions: method of payment	OM decides after advice of PM	PM advises OM
Pay secrecy	OM decides after advice of PM	PM advises OM
Pay security	OM decides after advice of PM	PM advises OM

EXHIBIT 11–2
A typical compensation manager

Richard G. Jamison
Rockwell International

Biography

Richard G. Jamison, whose title is Director of Compensation for Rockwell International, is a graduate of Drexel University with a BS in business administration. Jamison's past experience included posts as assistant personnel manager with Vick Chemical Division of Richardson-Merrell, personnel manager of Richardson-Merrell, and director of compensation and benefits at General Mills, Inc. He has been in his present position since 1974. He has contributed a chapter to the *Handbook of Wage and Salary Administration* (McGraw-Hill) and lectured at various universities and conferences, including the University of Minneapolis, University of Wisconsin, Drexel University, the Tri-City Personnel Association, and an ASPA board of directors meeting.

Job description

The Director of Compensation for Rockwell International is responsible for development and administration of the total compensation package for salaried personnel in the corporation. This includes both direct and indirect compensation, including executive compensation, salary administration, stock options, capital accumulation plans, bonuses, and incentives.

with which to analyze the relative effectiveness of various compensation methods.

Compensation decisions

Perhaps you believe that pay can be determined by a manager and employee sitting down and talking it over, or you think the government or unions determine pay. In fact, pay is influenced by a series of internal and external factors. The diagnostic approach will be used to help you understand these factors better.

Pay can be determined absolutely or relatively. Some have argued that a pay system set by a single criterion for a whole nation or the world, an absolute control of pay, is the best procedure. However, in one of the few recorded attempts to use this approach, in Denmark, it was not a great success. Since absolute pay systems are not used, the pay for each individual is set *relative* to the pay of others.

Allen Nash and Stephen Carroll point out that pay for a particular position is set relative to three groups. These are:

- Employees working on similar jobs in other enterprises (Group A).
- Employees working on different jobs within the enterprise (Group B).
- Employees working on the same job within the enterprise (Group C).

The decision to examine pay relative to Group A is called *the pay-level decision.* The objective of the pay-level decision is to keep the enterprise competitive in the labor market. The major tool used in this decision is the pay survey. The pay decision relative to Group B is called *the pay-structure decision.* This uses an approach called job evaluation. The decision involving pay relative to Group C is called *individual pay determination.*

Consider Joe Johnson, custodian at Cardeson National Bank. Joe's pay is affected first by the pay-level policy of the bank: whether CNB is a pacesetter or a going-wage employer. Next his pay is affected by how highly ranked *his* job is relative to other jobs, such as teller. Finally, his pay depends on how good a custodian he is, how long he has been with the enterprise, and other individual factors (individual pay determination).

Chapter 11 begins with an examination of pay levels. The diagnostic approach to compensation is introduced, and the impact of external and internal factors on the pay-level decision is considered. Then pay structures in the enterprise are examined, and finally individual pay determination is explained. Chapter 12 completes the discussion on compensation and pay by describing pay methods, executive pay, and compensation policies.

A DIAGNOSTIC APPROACH TO COMPENSATION

Exhibit 11–3 highlights the diagnostic factors most important to compensation as a personnel activity. The nature of the task affects compensation primarily in the method of payment for the job, such as payment for time worked or incentive compensation, which depends on the task performed. These issues, and executive compensation, which differs in many ways from other types, are discussed in Chapter 12.

One of the most significant factors in compensation is the nature of the employee. How employee attitudes and preferences directly affect performance is discussed in the section below. Employee attitudes and preferences also affect the pay structure.

There are other factors which affect compensation. The factors external to the organization which pay are the government, unions, economic conditions, and labor market conditions, as reflected in pay or wage surveys. Organizational factors are managerial goals and pay structures and size and age of the enterprise. Discussion of these factors in the sections below illustrates why employees and managers are paid the amounts they receive and which methods are used to pay people.

COMPENSATION AND EMPLOYEE SATISFACTION

Does a well-designed pay system motivate employees to greater performance, higher quality performance, or greater employee satisfaction? The answer to this question has varied from the yes of scientific management in the early 1900s to the no of human relations theorists in the 1930s. The controversy still rages. I am not sure we can settle this age old dispute here, but the various positions will be presented.

EXHIBIT 11–3

Factors affecting compensation and organizational effectiveness

OTHER ENVIRONMENTAL INFLUENCES ZONE II

IMMEDIATE ENVIRONMENT ZONE I

WORK ORGANIZATIONS

Past work experiences

Cultural influences

SOCIETY

ABILITIES

ATTITUDES AND PREFERENCES

NATURE OF EMPLOYEE

PERSONNEL ACTIVITIES

ORGANIZATIONAL EFFECTIVENESS

ENVIRONMENT OF THE ORGANIZATION

Union requirements

Government requirements

Compensation

The organization

Goals of controlling interests

Organization style

NATURE OF THE TASK

WORK GROUP

LEADER'S STYLE AND EXPERIENCE

ECONOMIC CONDITIONS
Nature of competition
Nature of the labor market

Most important factors

Next most important factors

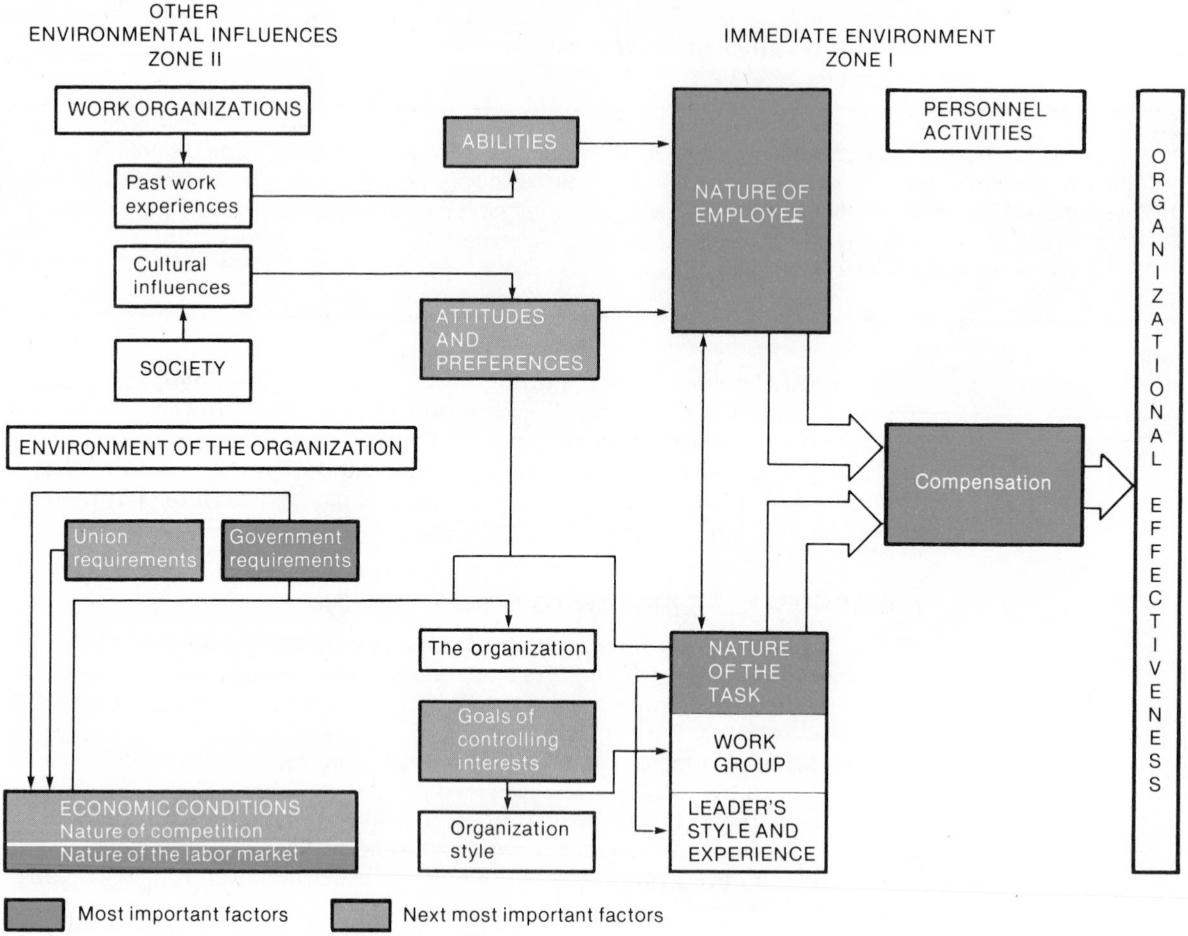

All would agree that effective compensation administration is desirable in efforts to increase employee satisfaction. And satisfaction with pay is important because, as the research summarized by Nash and Carroll shows, if pay satisfaction is low, job satisfaction is low. As a consequence, absenteeism and turnover will be higher and more costly.

Nash and Carroll have summarized much of the research on pay satisfaction. They point out that pay satisfaction varies with these factors:

Salary level. The higher the pay, the higher the pay satisfaction within an occupational group at each job level. (For example, higher paid presidents are more satisfied than lower paid presidents.)

Community cost of living. The lower the cost of living in a community, the higher the pay satisfaction.

Education. The lower the educational level, the higher the pay satisfaction.

"Oh, I've found inner peace. Now I'm seeking financial peace."

Reprinted by permission The Wall Street Journal.

Future expectations. The more optimistic the employee is about future job conditions, the higher the pay satisfaction.

Other personal characteristics. The more intelligent, self-assured, and decisive a person is, the lower the pay satisfaction.

Pay basis. The more pay is perceived to be based on merit or performance, the greater the pay satisfaction.

In sum, most people believe it is desirable to have a pay system that leads to satisfaction with pay.

COMPENSATION AND EMPLOYEE PERFORMANCE

High performance requires much more than employee motivation. Employee ability, adequate equipment, good physical working conditions, effective leadership and management, employee health, and other conditions all help raise employee performance levels. But employee motivation to work harder and better can be an important factor. And most compensation experts believe that pay can increase the motivation of employees to perform more effectively on the job. A number of studies indicate that if pay is tied to performance, the employee produces a higher quality and quantity of work.

Not everyone agrees with this. Researchers such as Herbert Meyer and Edward Deci argue that if you tie pay to performance, you will destroy the intrinsic rewards a person gets from doing the job well. These are powerful motivators too. But the research behind these concerns is in its earliest stages. There are individual differences in the importance of money to employees. And if the enterprise claims to have an incentive pay system and in fact pays for senority, the motivation effects of pay will be lost.

In sum, at present there are theorists who suggest that pay is a useful mechanism to motivate and satisfy employees. Others disagree. It seems to me that research that tries to give a yes or no answer to this question is misdirected. Because of individual differences in employees and jobs, it seems more fruitful to redirect this research to examine (1) the range of behaviors which pay may affect positively or negatively; (2) the amount of change pay can influence; (3)

"This incentive system is just an underhanded way to get us to work."

Reprinted by permission The Wall Street Journal.

the kind of employees that pay influences positively and negatively; and (4) the environmental conditions that are present when pay leads to positive and negative results.

Job desirability

As we indicated in Chapter 4 and will discuss more fully in the section on job evaluation, employees expect higher pay levels for less desirable jobs. If an enterprise has jobs in a bad neighborhood, in aged buildings, in a dirty, noisy environment, and if low status is attached to the jobs, it will have to pay higher compensation to attract competent employees. Note that lack of these instrinsic rewards, or provision of them, can have a major impact on pay levels. Of course, perceptions of what is desirable vary with individual backgrounds, expectations, and job motivations.

EXTERNAL INFLUENCES ON PAY LEVELS

Among the factors which influence pay and compensation policies are these outside the organization: the government, unions, the economy, and the labor market.

Government influences

The government directly affects compensation through wage controls and guidelines, which prohibit an increase in compensation for certain workers at certain times, and laws directed at the establishment of minimum wage rates, wage and hour regulations, and the prevention of discrimination directed at certain groups.

Wage controls and guidelines. Several times in the past quarter century or so, the United States has established wage freezes and guidelines. President Harry Truman imposed a wage and price freeze from January 1951 to 1953, and President Richard Nixon imposed freezes from 1971 to 1974, which came to be called Phases I–IV. Wage freezes are government orders which permit no wage increases. Wage controls limit the size of wage increases. Wage guidelines are similar to wage controls, but they are voluntary rather than legally required restrictions.

Economists and compensation specialists differ on the usefulness of wage and price freezes. The critics argue that the controls are an administrative nightmare, that they seriously disrupt the effective resource allocation market process and lead to frustration, strikes, and so on. Even the critics admit, however, that during times of perceived national emergencies and for relatively brief periods, the controls might help slow (but not indefinitely postpone) inflation. Those favoring them believe that controls reduce inflation. The important point is that employers must adjust their compensation policies to any governmental wage guidelines and controls. Considerable data gathering is necessary when such programs are in effect, and the employer must be prepared to justify any proposed wage increases. Even when the controls have been lifted, frequently there are wage and price advisory groups—government or quasi-government groups which some politicians use to try to "jawbone" executives into keeping price increases lower. These bodies at times might influence prices, which in turn could limit the profits needed to give wage increases. One proposed solution is TIP (Tax-based Income Policy). In TIP, when employers give employees bigger raises than government standards, the employer receives a tax increase; when the raise is below standard, he receives a tax reduction.

Wage and hour regulations. The Fair Labor Standards Act of 1938 is the basic pay act in the United States. It has been amended many times, most recently in 1974. This law has a number of provisions, including the following:

Minimum wages. All employers covered by the law (all but some small firms and some specific exemptions) must pay an employee at least a minimum wage per hour. Exempt small businesses are those whose gross sales do not exceed $325,000 in 1980, or $362,500 in 1981. In 1938 the minimum wage was 25 cents per hour. In 1979 the minimum is $2.90. Present legislation calls for it to increase to $3.10 in 1980, and $3.35 in 1981. A number of economists question the desirability of minimum wages, arguing that this law may price the marginal worker out of a job. All do not agree, however. Many experts propose a lower minimum wage for trainees to help reduce the unemployment problem.

Overtime pay. An employee covered by the law who works more than 40 hours per week must be paid one and one half times the base wage. If bonuses are also paid on a monthly or quarterly basis, the overtime pay equals one and one half the base pay and bonuses. Overtime pay tends to reduce the scheduling of longer hours of work.

Child labor prohibition. The law prohibits employing persons between 16 and 18 in hazardous jobs such as meatpacking and logging. Persons under 16 cannot be employed in jobs in interstate commerce except for nonhazardous work for a parent or guardian, and this requires a temporary permit. However, there are exceptions and limitations to the law. The Department of Labor caught 10,113 underaged persons in 1977 working in violation of the law.

Government agencies such as the Department of Labor's Wage and Hour Division enforce the wage and hour law. It has the right to examine employers' records and issue orders for back pay, get an injunction to prohibit future violations, and prosecute violators and send them to prison. For example, the department estimates that in 1976 U.S. employers underpaid employees by $89 million, in violation of minimum wage and overtime regulations. The department forced employers to pay $32 million to 293,000 employees for minimum wage violations, and 262,000 workers recovered $33 million from employers violating overtime regulations.

Other pay legislation. Employers are also subject to many other pay laws and regulations. For example, the Equal Pay Act of 1963, the Civil Rights Act of 1964, and the Age Discrimination Act of 1967 are designed to assure that all persons of similar ability, seniority, and background receive the same pay for the same work. The Equal Employment Opportunity Commission enforces the Civil Rights Act, while the Wage and Hour Division enforces the other two acts.

The Walsh-Healey Act of 1936 requires firms doing business with the federal government to pay wages at least equal to those prevailing in the area where the firm is located. It parallels the Fair Labor Standards Act on child labor and requires time-and-a-half pay for any work performed after eight hours a day. It also exempts some industries. The Davis Bacon Act of 1931 requires the payment of minimum wages to workers engaged in federally sponsored public works–construction jobs. The McNamara-O'Hara Service Contract Act requires employers that have contracts with the federal government of $2,500 per year or more or that provide services to federal agencies as contractors or subcontractors to pay prevailing wages and fringe benefits to their employees.

In addition to federal laws, 39 states have minimum wage laws covering intrastate employees and those not covered by federal laws. Some of these minimums are higher than the federal minimum. In such cases, the state minimums apply.

The government directly affects the amount of pay the employee takes home by requiring employers to deduct funds from employees' wages. For the federal government, this entails federal income taxes (withholding taxes) and social security taxes. The employer may also be required to deduct state and local income taxes.

The federal government also has other laws governing pay deductions. The Copeland Act (1934) and Anti-Kickback Law (1948) are designed to protect the employee from unlawful or unauthorized deductions. The Federal Wage Garnishment Act (1970) is designed to limit the amount deducted from a person's pay to reduce debts. It also prohibits the employer from firing an employee if the employee goes in debt only once and has his pay garnished. The employer may deduct as much from the paycheck as required by court orders for alimony or child support, debts due for taxes, or bankruptcy court requirements. Other than these, the maximum garnishment is 25 percent of take-home pay or 30 times the minimum wage per hour, whichever is smaller.

Other government influences. In addition to the laws and regulations discussed above, the government influences compensation in many other ways. For example, if the government is the employer, it may legislate pay levels by setting statutory rates. For example, for teachers, the pay scale may be set by law or by edict of the school board, and pay depends on revenues from the current tax base. If taxes decline relative to organizations' revenue streams, no matter how much the organization may wish to pay higher wages, it cannot.

The government affects compensation through its employment-level policy too. One of the goals of the government is full employment of all citizens seeking work. The government may even create jobs for certain categories of workers, which reduces the supply of workers available and affects pay rates (see Chapter 4).

Union influences on compensation

Another important external influence on an employer's compensation program is labor unionization. Unions have an effect whether or not the enterprise's employees are unionized, if it is in an area where unionized enterprises exist. For unions have tended to be pacesetters in demands for pay, benefits, and working conditions. There is reasonable evidence that unions tend to increase pay levels, although this is more likely where an industry has been organized by strong unions. If the enterprise elects to stay in an area where unions are strong, its compensation policies will be affected.

A series of legal cases has required employers to share compensation information with the unions if employees are unionized. For example, in *Shell Development* v. *Association of Industrial Scientists—Professional Employees,* Shell was required to provide the union with a written explanation of salary curves and the merit system, as well as copies of current salary curve guides, merit ratings, and so on. In *Time Incorporated* v. *Newspaper Guild, Time* was required to provide the union with a list of salaries of employees. In *General Electric* v. *International Union of Electrical Workers,* GE was required to provide the union with the pay survey information it had gathered to form compensation decisions. Thus employers would do well to communicate with and try to influence the union on compensation policy and levels.

Unions do try to bargain for higher pay and benefits, of course. The union is more likely to increase the compensation of its members when the enterprise is financially and competitively strong and the union is financially strong enough to support a strike; when the union has the support of other unions; and when general economic and labor market conditions are such that unemployment is low and the economy is strong.

Unions also bargain over working conditions and other policies that affect compensation. There is a tendency for unions to prefer fixed pay for each job category, or rate ranges that are administered to primarily reflect seniority rather than merit increases. This is true in the private and other sectors. Unions press for time pay rather than merit pay when the amount of performance expected is tied to technology (such as the assembly line).

Economic conditions and compensation

Also affecting compensation as an external factor are the economic conditions of the industry, especially the degree of competitiveness, which affects the organization's ability to pay high wages: Certain industries are more profitable than others at any one time, which is often related to the degree of competitiveness in the industry. The more competitive the situation, the less able is the enterprise to pay higher wages. Ability to pay is also a consequence of the relative productivity of the organization or industry or sector. If a firm is very productive, it can pay higher wages. Productivity can be increased by advanced technology, more efficient operating methods, a harder working and more talented work force, or a combination of these factors.

One productivity index that is used by many organizations as a criterion in the determination of a general level of wages is the Bureau of Labor Statistics' "Output per Man-Hour in Manufacturing." This productivity index is published in each issue of the *Monthly Labor Review.* Over the past 75 years, productivity has increased at an average annual rate of approximately 3 percent. The percentage increase in average weekly earnings in the United States is very closely related to the percentage change in productivity, plus the percentage change in the consumer price index.

The degree of profitability and productivity is a significant factor in determining the ability of firms in the private and third sector to pay wages. In the public sector, the limitations of the budget determine the ability to pay. If tax rates are low or the tax base is low or declining, the public-sector employer may be unable to give pay increases even if they are deserved.

Nature of the labor market and compensation

The final external factor affecting compensation to be discussed is the state of the labor market. Although many feel that human labor should not be regulated by forces such as supply and demand, in fact this happens. In times of full employment, wages and salaries may have to be higher to attract and retain enough qualified employees; in depressions, the reverse is true. Pay may be higher if few skilled employees are available in the job market. This may be because unions or accrediting associations limit the numbers certified to do the job. In certain locations, due to higher birth rates or a recent loss of a major employer, more persons may be seeking work than others. These factors lead to what is called *differential pay levels.* At any one time in a particular locale, unskilled labor rates seek a single level, and minimally skilled clerical work rates seek another. Research evidence from the labor economics field provides adequate support for the impact of labor market conditions on compensation.

Besides differences in pay levels by occupations in a locale, there are also differentials between government and private employees and exempt and nonexempt employees, as well as international differences. For example, there are differences in pay levels between the United States and Canada.

Increases in productivity are typically passed on to employees in the form of higher pay. Studies indicate that, in general, employers do not exploit employees when market conditions do not favor the employees. Employers use compensation surveys and general studies of the labor market in the area to serve as inputs to their pay-level compensation decision. The pay survey is the major pay-level decision tool.

Guido Panelli went to Mary Renfro as he had promised Poppa Joe. He told her to go ahead and prepare a report which would point out the problems in personnel, especially in compensation, that CNB was facing. Mary remembered worrying about the situation at Cardeson National Bank after learning

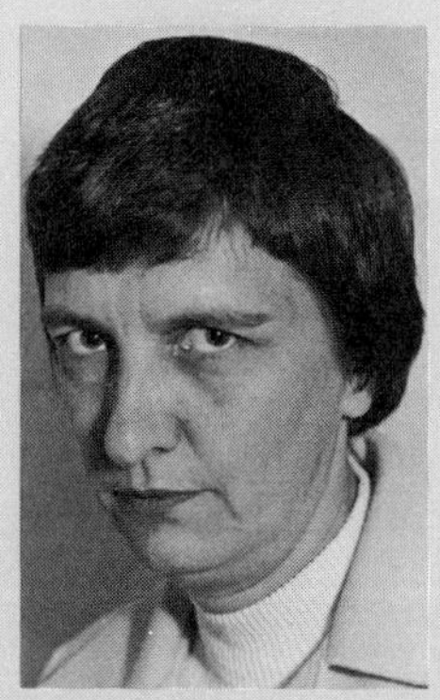
Mary

about the effect of pay on performance and satisfaction. At the bank some employees seemed to be paid for seniority, others for family need. People doing the same job at about the same performance levels received different paychecks, and they knew it. This seemed to be a bomb about to go off.

She knew the bank was following the legal requirements of compensation with regard to minimum wage and overtime. But equal-pay requirements were another situation. Often single people were paid less than married people, and married people with several children were paid more than those who were childless or had only one child. Single females were paid the least.

At present the bank was not unionized; few banks were. The labor market was good for the bank right now. There always were more applicants than needed. This has helped CNB with its problem of high turnover, for there are many eager replacements. But what would happen if the labor market should change or if the inequities in the pay rates are not corrected?

PAY SURVEYS AND COMPARABLE PAY LEVELS

Pay surveys (also called wage surveys) are surveys of the compensation paid to employees by all employers in a geographic area, an industry, or an occupational group. They are the principal tool used in the pay-level decision, as noted above.

Who conducts wage surveys?

Pay surveys are made by large employers, professional and consulting enterprises, trade associations, and the government. Some examples are described here.

Professional and trade association surveys. *American Management Association.* AMA conducts surveys of professional and managerial compensation and provides about 12 reports on U.S. executives' salaries and 16 reports on foreign executives' salaries. The *Top Management Report* shows the salaries of 31,000 top executives in 75 top positions in 3,000 firms in 53 industries. The *Middle Management Report* covers 73 key exempt jobs between supervisor and top executives. The sample includes 640 firms with 15,000 middle-level executives. The *Administrative and Technical Report* covers jobs below the middle management level. The sample is 568 firms. The *Supervisory Management Report* provides national and regional data on salaries of 55 categories of foremen and staff supervisors in 700 companies.

Administrative Management Society. This group compiles records on the compensation of clerical and data processing employees. AMS surveys 7,132 firms with 621,000 clerical and data processing employees in 132 cities. The data are gathered on 20 positions. A directory published every other year by cities and regions reports interquarterly ranges of salaries.

EXHIBIT 11–4

Typical area wage survey: Weekly earnings of office workers in Chicago, May 1976

Occupation and industry division	Number of workers	Average weekly hours (standard)	Weekly earnings (standard)		
			Mean	Median	Middle range
ALL WORKERS					
			$	$	$ $
SECRETARIES	23,101	38.5	196.00	190.00	168.00-217.50
MANUFACTURING	10,080	39.0	196.00	190.00	170.00-214.50
NONMANUFACTURING	13,021	38.0	196.00	190.00	167.00-220.00
PUBLIC UTILITIES	1,499	39.0	240.00	248.50	203.50-273.50
WHOLESALE TRADE	2,138	38.0	200.00	195.00	172.50-220.50
RETAIL TRADE	1,956	39.5	195.50	195.00	169.00-220.00
FINANCE	4,423	38.0	183.00	180.00	160.00-202.50
SERVICES	3,005	36.5	190.50	185.00	161.00-217.50
SECRETARIES, CLASS A	1,930	38.5	240.50	235.00	213.00-265.00
MANUFACTURING	834	38.5	245.50	240.00	218.50-278.50
NONMANUFACTURING	1,096	38.5	236.50	234.00	211.00-254.50
PUBLIC UTILITIES	167	39.5	271.50	264.50	242.50-305.00
WHOLESALE TRADE	189	38.5	237.00	235.00	220.50-252.00
RETAIL TRADE	247	39.0	231.50	236.00	210.00-252.00
FINANCE	271	38.0	225.00	219.50	208.00-242.50
SERVICES	222	38.0	229.50	221.00	207.00-245.00
SECRETARIES, CLASS B	5,749	38.5	210.00	207.00	185.00-230.00
MANUFACTURING	2,195	39.0	210.50	207.00	186.50-226.00
NONMANUFACTURING	3,554	38.0	210.00	207.00	184.00-231.00
PUBLIC UTILITIES	382	39.0	253.50	261.50	222.50-272.00
WHOLESALE TRADE	577	38.5	209.00	207.00	175.00-235.00
RETAIL TRADE	687	39.5	208.00	209.00	189.50-229.00
FINANCE	1,182	38.0	200.00	200.00	182.00-215.00
SERVICES	726	37.0	204.50	201.50	178.50-230.00

American Society for Personnel Administration. ASPA conducts salary surveys for personnel executives and others every other year.

International Personnel Management Association. This group surveys compensation practices for public personnel.

Surveys by other enterprises. Other enterprises which do pay surveys include Pay Data Service (Chicago), Management Compensation Services, Bureau of National Affairs, and Prentice-Hall. Many journals report on compensation, including *Compensation Review, Business Week, Dun's, Forbes, Fortune, Hospital Administration, Nation's Business,* and *Monthly Labor Review.*

Government surveys. U.S. government pay surveys include those by Federal Reserve banks, which survey private industry pay to set their employees' pay, and the Bureau of Labor Statistics. The BLS publishes three different surveys:

Area wage surveys. Annually, BLS surveys 168 areas (usually the Standard Metropolitan Statistical Areas) on the pay and benefits for white-collar, skilled blue-collar, and indirect manufacturing labor jobs (in alternate years). An excerpt of one of these is given in Exhibit 11–4.

Industry wage surveys. The BLS surveys 50 manufacturing industries, 20 service industries and public employees. Blue- and white-collar employees are covered. The surveys are done on yearly, and three- and five-year cycles. Some industries are surveyed nationally (utilities, mining, manufacturing), and others by metropolitan area (finance, service, and trade).

Number of workers receiving straight-time weekly earnings of—																				
$ 80 and under 90	$ 90 - 100	$ 100 - 110	$ 110 - 120	$ 120 - 130	$ 130 - 140	$ 140 - 150	$ 150 - 160	$ 160 - 170	$ 170 - 180	$ 180 - 200	$ 200 - 220	$ 220 - 240	$ 240 - 260	$ 260 - 280	$ 280 - 300	$ 300 - 320	$ 320 - 340	$ 340 - 360	$ 360 - 380	$ 380 and over
-	-	10	46	281	546	1200	1667	2311	2723	5097	3807	2213	1458	824	545	269	67	27	6	4
-	-	-	20	137	146	396	705	1024	1347	2466	1679	843	479	388	282	134	19	13	1	1
-	-	10	26	144	400	804	962	1287	1376	2631	2128	1370	979	436	263	135	48	14	5	3
-	-	-	-	-	9	11	50	63	72	132	168	178	259	254	158	92	40	9	2	2
-	-	-	-	5	33	126	41	203	265	516	380	304	114	61	50	26	7	3	3	1
-	-	-	3	22	54	78	158	205	135	414	395	281	155	40	10	5	1	-	-	-
-	-	10	23	72	175	362	453	485	569	1037	735	292	165	23	13	8	-	1	-	-
-	-	-	-	45	129	227	260	331	335	532	450	315	286	58	32	4	-	1	-	-
-	-	-	-	-	-	1	1	43	40	181	330	446	338	195	169	154	19	6	4	3
-	-	-	-	-	-	-	-	29	7	81	112	186	98	114	119	80	3	3	1	1
-	-	-	-	-	-	1	1	14	33	100	218	260	240	81	50	74	16	3	3	2
-	-	-	-	-	-	-	-	-	-	4	9	23	45	13	10	49	13	-	-	1
-	-	-	-	-	-	-	-	-	21	12	6	78	40	9	3	12	2	2	3	1
-	-	-	-	-	-	1	1	11	2	29	30	54	80	28	5	5	1	-	-	-
-	-	-	-	-	-	-	-	-	10	35	98	49	48	13	11	7	-	-	-	-
-	-	-	-	-	-	-	-	3	-	20	75	56	27	18	21	1	-	1	-	-
-	-	-	-	24	50	95	160	289	461	1299	1451	884	443	296	168	80	26	20	2	1
-	-	-	-	20	20	41	62	80	141	522	637	276	166	86	75	43	16	10	-	-
-	-	-	-	4	30	54	98	209	320	777	814	608	277	210	93	37	10	10	2	1
-	-	-	-	-	-	-	2	-	9	31	48	52	30	124	43	27	5	8	2	1
-	-	-	-	-	-	21	5	62	76	103	108	89	31	32	35	9	5	1	-	-
-	-	-	-	-	1	6	16	30	35	155	190	180	62	9	3	-	-	-	-	-
-	-	-	-	4	1	24	49	49	128	330	354	160	70	10	1	1	-	1	-	-
-	-	-	-	-	28	3	26	68	72	158	114	127	84	35	11	-	-	-	-	-

Professional, administrative, technical, and clerical surveys. BLS also annually surveys 80 occupational work-level positions on a nationwide basis. Although the BLS studies tend to follow the most sophisticated survey methods, they too need improvement, and BLS constantly tries to achieve this.

How pay surveys are conducted and used

How are these surveys done? One method is the personal interview, which develops the most accurate responses but is also the most expensive one. Mailed questionnaires are probably the most frequently used method, and one of the cheapest. The jobs being surveyed by mail must be clearly defined, or the data may not be reliable. Telephone inquiries are used to follow up the mail questionnaires or to gather data. This procedure is quick, but it is also difficult to get a great deal of detailed data over the phone.

There are a number of critical issues determining the usefulness of the surveys: the jobs to be covered, the employers to be contacted, and the method to be used in gathering the data. Other employers cannot be expected to complete endless data requests for all the organization's jobs, so the jobs that are surveyed should be the 2 to 20 most crucial ones. If the point method of job evaluation is used (see below), the key jobs might be selected for surveying, since they cover all ranges. The jobs which most employees hold should also be on the list (clerk-typists, underwriters, and keypunch operators for an insurance company, for example).

The second issue concerns who will be surveyed. Most organizations tend to compare themselves with similar competitors in their industry. American Airlines may compare its pay rates to those of United Airlines, for example. It has been shown that employees may not compare their pay to that offered by competitors at all. Their basis of comparison might be friends' employers, or employers that they worked for previously. If the survey is to be useful, employees should be involved in choosing the organizations to be surveyed. The employers to be surveyed should include the most dominant ones in the area and a small sample of those suggested by employees.

Government agencies use pay surveys of comparable private-sector jobs to set their pay levels. In private-sector enterprises, the evidence suggests their own pay surveys are used more than those provided by the government or other services. And they use the surveys primarily as general guidelines, as only one of several factors considered in pay-level decisions. In fact, there is some evidence that enterprises weigh job evaluation and individual pay determination more heavily than external pay comparisons. This makes sense because pay surveys are not taken often (perhaps yearly). They also average many differences into single numbers and are sometimes hard to interpret meaningfully.

At the start of this section, I suspect you thought that design and use of pay surveys was a simple matter. Now you understand why they can be difficult. An employer never knows, if there is a pay differential between the job he offers and others, how much of the difference is due to differences in the job or other fringe benefits provided, the time of the survey, the pay level of the two areas, or other factors.

Remember too that there are many surveys an employer can use. And there are many enterprises and locales it can survey. This can give the employer a great deal of maneuvering room to handle problems like relative ability or inability to pay certain wages or to deal with cost of living problems, and similar pay bargaining issues.

ORGANIZATIONAL INFLUENCES ON PAY LEVELS

In addition to the external influences on compensation discussed above, several internal factors affect pay levels: size and age of the organization and the goals of its controlling interests.

We don't know a great deal about size and pay. Generally speaking, it appears that larger enterprises tend to have higher pay levels. Little is known about age of the enterprise and pay, too, but some theorists contend that newer enterprises tend to pay more than older ones.

Goals of controlling interests and managerial pay strategies

Managers differ as much as employees do. Some believe their employees should be compensated at high pay levels because they deserve it, for example. They also accept or reject the idea that high pay or merit pay leads to greater performance or employee satisfaction. These attitudes are reflected in the pay-level strategy chosen by the managers of the enterprise. This is a major strategic choice top managers must make.

Essentially, three pay level strategies can be chosen: high, low, or comparable.

The high-pay-level strategy. In this strategy, the manager choses to pay higher than average pay levels. The assumption behind this strategy is that you get what you pay for. Paying higher wages and salaries, these managers believe, will attract and hold the best employees, and this is the most effective long-range policy. This strategy is sometimes called the pacesetter. It may be influenced by pay criteria such as paying a living wage or paying on the basis of productivity.

The low-pay-level strategy. At the opposite extreme is the low-pay strategy. In this case, the manager may choose to pay at the minimum level needed to hire enough employees. This strategy may be used because this is all the enterprise can pay—the ability to pay is restricted by other internal or external factors. (In the public or third sector, the comparable problem is a tight budget.) Or the manager may be trying to maximize short-run profits or to live with a tight budget.

The comparable-pay-level strategy. The most frequently used strategy is to set the pay level at the going-wage level. The wage criteria are comparable wages, perhaps modified by cost of living or purchasing power adjustments. For example, the Federal Pay Comparability Act of 1970 limits federal government compensation to the comparable pay paid in the private sector at the time. This going wage is determined from pay surveys (discussed above). Thus the policy of a manager of this type is to pay the current market rate in the community or industry, ±5 percent or so.

These three strategies are usually set for the total enterprise, although the strategy might have to be modified for a few hard-to-fill jobs from time to time.

The choice of strategy in part reflects the motivation and attitude set of the manager. If the manager has a high need for recognition, the high-pay strategy might be chosen; otherwise, the low-pay strategy might be chosen. Another factor is the ethical and moral attitude of the manager. If the manager is ethically oriented, then a low pay strategy is not likely to be chosen willingly. In equity, the manager tries to pay more. One study showed that even in depressions, managers tried not to cut salaries, and another found a strong ethical theme in managers' pay-level decisions.

THE PAY-LEVEL DECISION

The pay-level decision is made by managers, who compare the pay of persons working inside the enterprise with those outside it. This decision is affected by multiple factors in interaction with one another, as shown in Exhibit 11–5. These factors affect pay levels laterally, upward, or downward. Most employees' unions and minimim wage laws push the level up. Wage controls steady the level or tend to hold it down. More competition and older enterprises hold it down. Managerial attitudes toward prevailing wages would steady the level. Larger size of the enterprise would tend to increase pay level, as would a smaller supply of employees in the labor market.

This is an example of how some of the factors in the compensation activity affect the pay-level decision. When factors such as managerial attitudes, the labor market, and competition change, the pressures on pay level shift.

But remember: The many external factors affecting the process, such as gov-

EXHIBIT 11–5
Factors affecting the pay-level decision

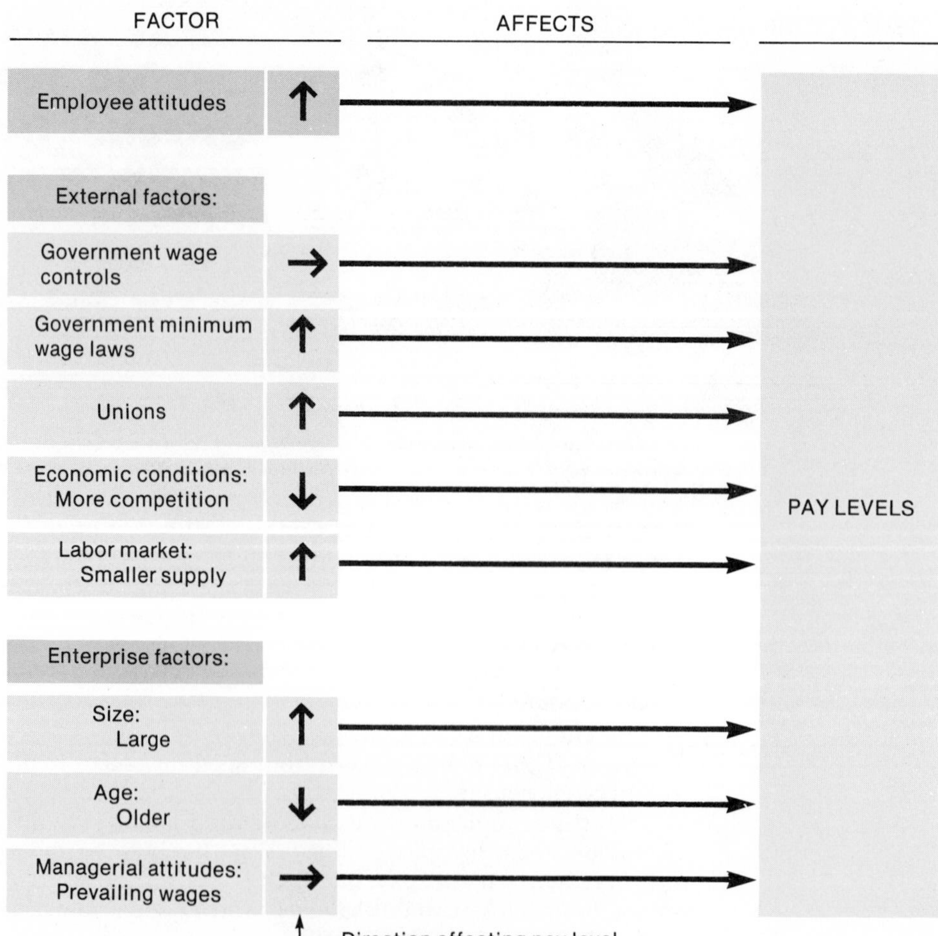

ernment and unions, are compounded by employees' job preferences which include pay and nonpay aspects. And many employees do not have a sophisticated or comprehensive knowledge of all these factors. So you can see that the enterprise has a great deal of maneuvering room in the pay-level decision.

PAY STRUCTURES

In addition to relating pay to pay levels paid for comparable jobs in other enterprises, the enterprise must also determine pay structures for its employees having different jobs *within* the organization. Factors similar to those affecting pay levels affect these pay structures too.

Managers can cope with the attempt to provide equal pay for positions of approximately equal worth by arbitrary management decisions, collective bargaining, or job evaluation. If managers try to make these decisions without help from tools such as job evaluation, unsystematic decision making is likely to lead to perceived inequities. Bargaining alone can lead to decisions based solely on relative power. Therefore, most management experts suggest that managerial decisions should be influenced both by the results of collective bargaining and job evaluation.

Job evaluation

Job evaluation is the formal process by which the relative worth of various jobs in the organization is determined for pay purposes. Essentially, it attempts to relate the amount of the employee's pay to the extent that her or his job contributes to organizational effectiveness.

It is not always easy to evaluate the worth of all the jobs in an enterprise. It may be obvious that the effective physician will contribute more to the goals of patient care in the hospital than the nurse's aid. The point at issue is *how much* the differential is worth.

Since computing exactly how much a particular job contributes to organizational effectiveness is difficult, proxies for effectiveness are used. These proxies include skills required to do the job, amount and significance of responsibility involved, effort required, and working conditions. Compensation must vary with the differing demands of various jobs if employees are to be satisfied and if the organization is to be able to attract the personnel it wants.

Job evaluation is widely used. At least two thirds of all jobs have been evaluated. Surveys indicate that most enterprises using it regard it as successful.

Once an enterprise decides to use job evaluation, a series of decisions must be made to ensure its effectiveness. Part of the decision to use job evaluation, or the first step in using it effectively, is for management to involve employees (and, where appropriate, the union) in the system and its implementation. Most experts emphasize that job evaluation is a difficult task which is more likely to be successful if the employees whose jobs are being evaluated are involved in the process by being allowed to express their perceptions of the relative merits of their jobs compared to others. This participation affords an opportunity to explain the fairly complicated process of job evaluation to those most directly affected by it, and it will usually lead to better communication and improved employee understanding.

After the program is off to a cooperative start, usually a committee of about five members evaluates the jobs. Ideally, the committee includes employees, managers, and personnel specialists. All members should be familiar with the jobs to be evaluated.

Job evaluation is usually performed by analyzing job descriptions and occasionally job specifications. Early in the process, it is imperative that job evaluators check the availability and accuracy of the job descriptions and specifications (see Chapter 4). It is usually suggested that job descriptions be split into several series, such as managerial, professional/technical, clerical, and operative. It makes sense in writing job descriptions to use the words that are keyed to the job evaluation factors.

Another essential step in effective job evaluation is to select and weight the criteria used to evaluate the job. Although there is not a lot of research in this area, it appears that only a few factors will do as good a job as many factors, especially if they are carefully designed and scaled. Typical of the most frequently used factors for job evaluation are education, experience, amount of responsibility, job knowledge, work hazards and working conditions. It is important that the factors used be accepted as valid for the job by those being evaluated.

Once the method of evaluating the job (to be discussed below) is chosen, the evaluators make the job evaluations. Basically, those familiar with the jobs tend to rate them higher, especially if they supervise the jobs. It seems useful for each committee member to evaluate each job individually. Then the evaluators should discuss each job on which the ratings differ significantly, factor by factor, until agreement is reached.

Job evaluation methods. The four most frequently used job evaluation methods are:

Job ranking.
Factor comparison.
Classification.
The point system.

The four methods do about an equally reliable job of evaluation. Job evaluation systems can be related as shown in Exhibit 11–6.

Ranking of jobs. The system, used primarily in smaller, simpler organizations, is job ranking. Instead of analyzing the full complexity of jobs by evaluating parts of jobs, the job-ranking method has the evaluator rank order *whole* jobs, from the simplest to the most challenging.

EXHIBIT 11–6
Job evaluation system compared

	Scope of comparison	
Comparison basis	*Quantitative comparison of parts or factors of job*	*Nonquantitative comparison, whole job*
A job compared to another job	Classification or grading	Point system
A job compared to a scale	Job ranking	Factor comparison

Sometimes this is done by providing the evaluator with the information on cards. The evaluator sorts the jobs into ranks, allowing for the possibility of ties. If the list of jobs is large, the paired-comparison method, whereby each job is compared to every other job being evaluated, can be used. The evaluator counts the number of times a particular job is ranked above another, and the one with the largest number of highest rankings is the highest ranked. There is no assurance that the ranking thus provided is composed of equal-interval ranks. The differential between the highest job and next highest may not be exactly the same as that between the lowest and next lowest. If the system is used in an enterprise with many jobs to be rated, it is clumsy to use, and the reliability of the ratings is not good. Because of these problems, ranking is probably the least frequently used method of job evaluation.

Classification or grading system. The classification or grading system groups a set of jobs together into a grade or classification. Then these sets of jobs are ranked in levels of difficulty or sophistication. For example, the least challenging jobs in the federal service are grouped into GS–1, the next more challenging into GS–2, and so on.

The classification approach is more sophisticated than ranking but less so than the point system or factor comparison. It can work reasonably well if the classifications are well defined. It is the second most frequently used system. It is used widely in the public sector, as well as in the private and third sectors.

The point system. The greatest number of job evaluation plans use the point system. It is the most frequently used because it is more sophisticated than ranking and classification systems, but it is relatively easy to use.

Essentially, the point system requires evaluators to quantify the value of the elements of a job. On the basis of the job description or interviews with job occupants, points are assigned to the degree of various factors required to do the job. For example, skill required, physical and mental effort needed, degree of dangerous or unpleasant working conditions involved, and amount of responsibility involved in the job. When these are summed, the job has been evaluated.

Many point systems evaluate as many as ten aspects or subaspects of each job. The aspects chosen should not overlap, should distinguish real differences between jobs, should be as objectively defined as possible, and should be understood and acceptable to both management and employees. Because all aspects are not of equal importance in all jobs, different weights reflecting the differential importance of these aspects to a job must be set. These weights are assigned by summing the judgments of several independent but knowledgeable evaluators. Thus a clerical job might result in the following weightings (according to Robert Kelly) education required, 20 percent; experience required, 25 percent; complexity of job, 35 percent; responsibility for relationships with others, 15 percent; working conditions and physical requirements, 5 percent.

Once the weights are agreed upon, reference to a point manual is appropriate. Experience required by jobs varies, as does education. The point manual carefully defines degrees of points from first (lowest) to sixth, for example. Experience might be defined in this way:

First degree, up to and including three months	25 points
Second degree, more than three months but less than six	50 points
Third degree, more than six months to one year	75 points
Fourth degree, more than one year and up to three years	100 points
Fifth degree, more than three years and up to five years	125 points
Sixth degree, over five years	150 points

EXHIBIT 11–7
Evaluation points for clerical jobs

Factor	Degree points 1st	2d	3d	4th	5th	6th
Education required	20	40	60	80	100	120
Experience required	25	50	75	100	125	150
Complexity of job	35	70	105	140		
Responsibility for relationships with others	15	30	45	60		
Working conditions	5	10	15	20		

Note: Weights assigned fit Kelly's weights of job aspects referred to above: e.g., education = 20 percent, experience = 25 percent, complexity = 35 percent, responsibility = 15 percent; working conditions = 5 percent.

Source: Robert Kelly, "Job Evaluation and Pay Plans: Office Personnel," in Joseph Famularo (ed.), *Handbook of Modern Personnel Administration* (New York: McGraw-Hill Book Co., 1972).

These definitions must be clearly defined and measurable to ensure consistency in ratings of requirements from the job description to the job evaluation. The preliminary point manuals must be pretested prior to widespread use.

Exhibit 11–7 lists Kelly's points and factors for evaluating clerical jobs. The maximum point total for any job is often a number such as 500, although this is arbitrary. Using the point system, the evaluator compares the job description by job aspect and by degree. Points are assigned and totaled to a point score; total points up to 135 could be assigned to Grade 1, 136–60 to Grade 2, 161–85 to Grade 3, and so on. The time and cost of development work against acceptance of the point system.

Factor comparison. A complex and costly system is the factor comparison method. It is probably slightly more reliable than the other methods. The factor comparison method requires five steps.

Steps in factor comparison:

1. Choose the key jobs to be evaluated. These jobs are well known in the enterprise and, in the opinion of the evaluators, are properly paid at present.
2. Rank the key jobs on important factors of job evaluation. These factors usually are mental requirements, skill requirements, physical requirements, responsibility, and working conditions.
3. Divide up the current pay among the factors. Thus, the rater is asked: If the jobs pays $2.75 per hour, how much of the $2.75 is for mental requirements? And so on.
4. Reconcile the differences in rankings found in Steps 1 and 2 by the committee members.
5. Place the key jobs on a scale for each factor. This becomes the basis for evaluating nonkey jobs in the structure.

Factor comparison is not widely used.

Pay classes, rate ranges, and classifications

After completion of job evaluation, the pay-structure process is completed by establishing pay classes, rate ranges, and job classifications for ease of administration. If an enterprise uses the factor comparison or point system of job evaluation, this is accomplished by use of pay-class graphs or point conversion tables. An example of a pay-class graph is given in Exhibit 11–8.

At intervals of say 50 points, a new pay class is marked off. The pay curve illustrated in Exhibit 11–8 is based on information obtained from wage and salary surveys and modified as necessary to reflect the enterprise's policy to pay at, above, or below prevailing rates. This exhibit shows a single-rate pay system rather than a rate-range system in that all jobs within a given labor class will receive the same rate of pay. In this example, pay classes are determined by the point value determined through a point system method of job evaluation.

Exhibit 11–9, another pay-class graph, demonstrates how wage and salary survey data are combined with job evaluation information to determine the pay structure for an organization. A compensation trend line is derived by first establishing the general pay pattern, plotting the surveyed rates of key jobs against the point value of these jobs. The trend line can then be determined by a variety of methods, ranging from a simple eyeball estimate of the pay trend to a formalized statistical formulation of a regression line based on the sum of the least squares method. The appropriate pay rate for any job can then be ascertained by calculating the point value of the job and observing the pay level for that value as shown by the trend line. By taking a set percentage (e.g., 15 percent) above and below the trend line, minimum and maximum limit lines can be established. These limit lines can be used to help set the minimum and maximum rates if a pay range is used instead of a single rate for each job. The limit lines can also be used in place of the trend line for those enterprises

EXHIBIT 11–8
Pay classes and pay curve

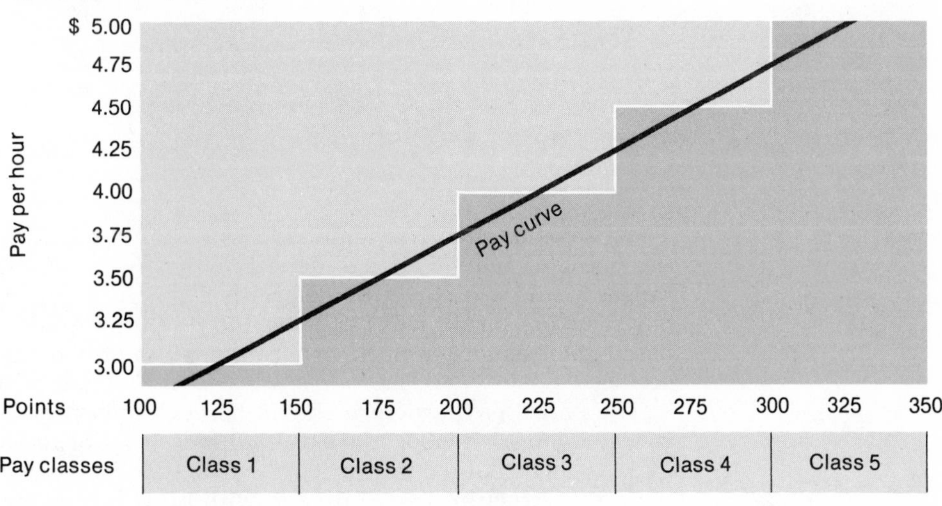

EXHIBIT 11–9
Pay-class graph with range of pay

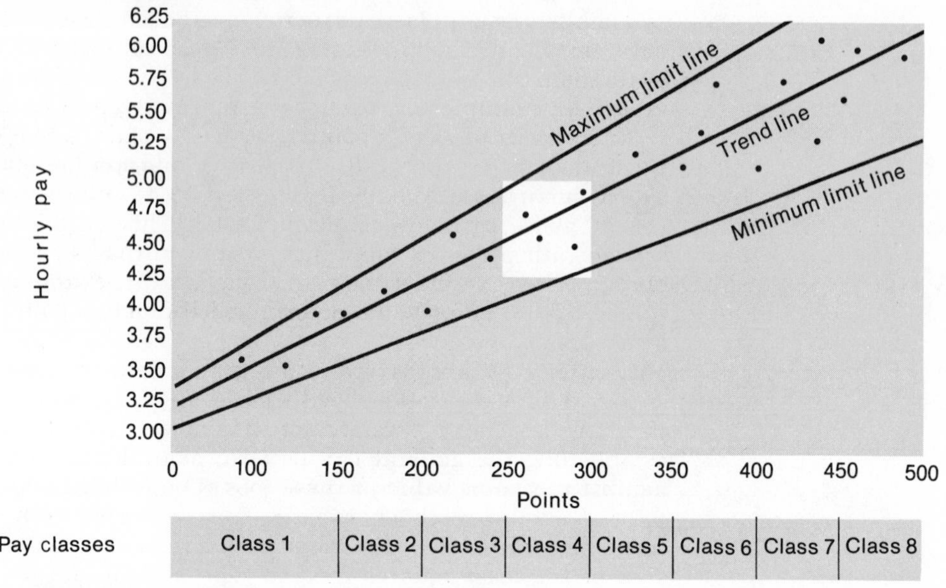

that wish to establish pay levels above market—the pay leaders—or those that want to pay slightly under the prevailing rates.

Although it is possible for a pay class to have a single pay rate (as in Exhibit 11–8), the more likely condition is a range of pays. These ranges can have the same spread, or the spread can be increased as the pay rate increases. An example of a pay structure with increasing rate ranges is given in Exhibit 11–9. The ranges are usually divided into a series of steps. Thus, within Class 4 (250–300 points), there might be four steps:

	Pay range
Step 1	$4.20–4.40
Step 2	4.40–4.60
Step 3	4.60–4.85
Step 4	4.85–5.10

These steps in effect are money raises within a pay range to help take care of the needs of individual pay determination (to be discussed shortly). Similar ranges would ordinarily be determined for all other classes to illustrate the pay structure for all jobs in the pay plan. Within-grade increases are typically based upon seniority, merit, or a combination of both, as described in the next section.

The entire pay structure should be evaluated periodically and adjusted to reflect changes in labor market conditions, level of inflation, and other factors affecting pay. Although the typical structure is shown as linear, generally a more fair structure is curvilinear, with rates increasing exponentially as pay increases.

Mary sat at her desk a few days later. She thought over the problems the bank was facing again. She had spent weeks learning about pay surveys, job evaluation, pay classifications, rate ranges—all the aspects of pay-level and pay-structure decisions. CNB had done nothing about any of these issues. How could they keep employees without much attention to pay practices?

As Mary wondered about these issues, she had the report she'd prepared for her personnel class before her. It compared the turnover and absenteeism rates at CNB to those of other banks like it in the Pittsburgh area. CNB was clearly in the worst shape.

She had interviewed supervisors and others who had talked with employees leaving CNB. A large number gave better pay as the reason for leaving. And even more often, fairness in treatment of pay was the reason given. She'd passed her report on to Guido. But would anything happen—other than receiving a grade in class for her report?

INDIVIDUAL PAY DETERMINATION

The final group used to establish pay for an employee is the employees working on the *same* job in an enterprise. This comparison leads to setting the pay of each individual, within the pay ranges that have been established. This is called individual pay determination. It is done first when the employee is hired. Then it takes place each year (or more frequently in some cases) when the employee's pay is reconsidered, often tied to performance evaluation (Chapter 8). It also is closely tied to raises (see pay administration in Chapter 12). Essentially the issue is: Given that a job can pay varying amounts within a range, which pay rate should this individual receive?

A *crucial* aspect of setting pay is individual pay determination. The persons most employees know and can compare their own pay to are other employees doing similar jobs *within the enterprise.*

Compensation specialists say that individual pay determination should be based on differences in current performance. Thus if welder 1 makes 10 percent more welds than welder 2, and if the quality of all the welds is similar, welder 1 ought to be paid higher in the rate range, according to most compensation specialists. Most white-collar employees, managers, and professional employees agree with compensation specialists in this regard.

But many other employees (perhaps a majority) believe that seniority, age, and therefore *past* performance and loyalty should have equal or greater weight in individual pay determination. And managers may claim they have merit or performance-based pay systems, but many studies indicate they are more accurately based on current performance plus seniority, or seniority alone. This can have the effect of reducing the motivations of higher performing, younger employees. It also has been shown that sex, race, personal appearance, and lifestyle influence individual pay, although many believe that this should not be.

Thus the final compensation decision is to place the employee within the pay range based on performance and other factors—individual pay determination.

SUMMARY, CONCLUSIONS, AND RECOMMENDATIONS

Chapter 11 has begun the discussion of compensation and pay structures which will be concluded in Chapter 12. The objectives of compensation have been stated, and premises dealing with the multiple meanings of pay at work, pay level, external and internal factors influencing pay level, and pay structures and their determination have been covered. Some summarizing statements follow:

1. Pay is the monetary reward paid by an enterprise for the work done by an employee.
2. To promote employee satisfaction, compensation should be adequate, equitable, balanced, cost effective, secure, incentive providing, and acceptable to the employee.
3. Compensation decisions are the joint responsibility of operating executives and personnel.
4. Because of individual employee preferences and jobs, research on motivation and compensation should be directed to examine:
   a. The range of behaviors which pay may affect positively or negatively.
   b. The amount of change pay can influence.
   c. The kind of employee pay influences positively and negatively.
   d. The environmental conditions that are present when pay leads to positive and negative results.
5. External influences on pay levels include government influences, union influences, economic conditions, and the nature of the labor market.
6. The pay-level decision involves the pay of employees working on similar jobs in other enterprises: high, medium, or low pay?
7. The pay-structure decision involves employees working on different jobs within the enterprise: Which job is worth the most, which the least, which is in between?
8. Individual pay determination involves employees working on the same job within the enterprise: How much experience, education, seniority, etc., is necessary for each pay range?
9. Pay surveys are the principal tool used in the pay-level decision.
10. Job evaluation is the formal process by which the relative worth of various jobs in the organization is determined for pay purposes.
11. After job evaluation is completed, rate ranges and pay classes are developed for each job category as the basis for individual pay determination decisions.

From the principles regarding the compensation function of personnel, the following propositions can be derived.

Proposition 11.1. The more complex and volatile the organization and its environment, the more frequently must pay surveys be run, and the more difficult they are to use.

Proposition 11.2. The most significant influence on pay level is the management pay-level strategy pursued by the enterprise.

Proposition 11.3. The more involved the employees are in their job evaluation, the more effective will formal job evaluation be.

Proposition 11.4. The more complex and volatile the organization, the more likely is it to use a more sophisticated job evaluation system such as the point method.

Chapter 12 will complete our discussion of compensation.

Guido called Mary into his office the next day to go over her findings. She decided to use her term report to illustrate possible solutions for CNB's dilemma.

Guido: I've read your paper. I like the way it deals with the personnel problem here at CNB. It was a good idea to calculate how much turnover costs the bank. This may have an impact on Poppa Joe. You've also prepared recommendations for changes in our pay program, as I asked you to do. Let me see if I understand your plan. Basically, you propose setting up a point system of job evaluation and establishing standardized pay classes and ranges which would allow for pay variations based on individual pay factors. You also recommend that we set up a pay policy according to going wages. In view of our profit picture, that seems reasonable. I'll present this plan to Poppa Joe tomorrow, with my endorsement.

Mary: What you say is exactly what I have in mind. I'll be interested to see if it has any impact.

The next day Guido gave the report to Poppa Joe to read and comment on.

Questions:

1. Do you think Poppa Joe will approve changing the pay system at CNB? Why or why not?
2. If Guido were president of the bank and he accepted the report, how long would it take to implement the new program?
3. What problems would you anticipate, especially with those employees who are "overpaid" according to the job evaluation program?

(This case will be continued in Chapter 12.)

QUESTIONS

1. What is compensation? How does it fit into the total reward system of the enterprise?
2. Distinguish pay-level decisions, pay-structure decisions, and individual pay determination decisions.
3. Does compensation affect employee satisfaction? Performance?
4. What are the external factors affecting pay-level decisions? How do they do so?
5. Discuss the major laws affecting compensation. How do they affect the enterprise's pay level?
6. What is a pay survey? What is the best way to run one?
7. What are the enterprise factors affecting pay level?
8. How does management's pay strategy affect pay level? Give an example of the most typical pay strategy. Which strategy would you pursue?
9. What is a pay structure?
10. What is job evaluation? What are the techniques for performing it?
11. Distinguish and describe the interrelationships among pay classes, rate changes, and pay classifications.
12. How are individual pay determination decisions made?

12

Compensation: Methods and policy issues

Chapter objectives

- To show how to develop methods of payment.
- To demonstrate that executive compensation is similar yet different from operative, clerical, and professional/technical compensation.
- To help you become cognizant of current crucial pay policy issues.

Chapter outline

I. Methods of Payment
   A. Payment for time worked
   B. Incentive plans
   C. Individual incentives
   D. Group incentives
   E. Enterprise incentive schemes
II. Executive Compensation
   A. Executive salaries
   B. Bonuses
   C. Stock options, performance shares, and book-value devices
   D. Executive perquisites
   E. Executive compensation policy
III. Compensation Administration Issues
   A. Pay secrecy or openness
   B. Security in pay
   C. Pay raises
IV. Summary, Conclusions, and Recommendations

Case continued from Chapter 11

Poppa Joe Paderewski is sitting in his big office in the rear of the Cardeson National Bank. Guido Panelli, his executive vice president, has just been in and dropped off the report on compensation from Mary Renfro. He also talked about some more problems with their people and pay. Several of the cases Guido and Mary have brought to his attention are going through his mind.

For one thing, CNB's executive turnover has been increasing. Mary wonders if the executive compensation package is contributing to this problem. Those leaving have given this as the main reason, but Mary realizes that compensation is the most acceptable reason to give an employer for leaving. That's why she's brought the problem to Poppa Joe. Is pay really a problem?

CNB pays the going rate for salaries and has a bonus system when profits allow it. But some of those leaving said their new employers would have performance-share programs. Poppa Joe is wondering if he should hire a consultant to advise him on the executive compensation program.

Guido had told Poppa Joe about a meeting Tom Nichols, the manager at Branch 1, had with the tellers' supervisors. Tom hadn't wanted to attend this meeting, but then, he never did want to go to meetings. He had anticipated that this one in particular would be bad, though. The tellers were never satisfied with their pay. Back in school, Tom had learned that one thing that never was settled in personnel was pay; people were almost always griping about it.

Tom told Guido the supervisors' meeting went like this:

Chet: Tom, we're here because the troops are unhappy.

Tom: The troops are always unhappy.

Chet: Sure. But this time it sounds serious. My people are tired of punching time clocks and getting paid by the hour. Everyone else here at the bank gets salaries—52 weeks a year. Why don't my tellers?

Tom: Well, you know, it's always been that way. Besides. . . .

Chet: Don't give me that it's-always-been-that-way stuff. You can do something about it. Talk to Poppa Joe. My people want the security of a regular paycheck and the dignity of no time clock. You know the union's been around. This is the kind of issue that gets a union into a bank. What are we going to do about it?

The other supervisors shook their heads and Tom had wondered what to say.

Mary had also told Poppa Joe about an incident at Branch 2. The incident involved two tellers and a supervisor. As the branch manager remembered it, the following dialogue took place:

Martha: Did you hear that Joanne makes $1.50 more an hour than me? I've been here longer, too. What is this?

Sandra: Why not go to June about it? She's the boss.

Martha (to June): How come Joanne makes $1.50 more than me? I've been here longer.

June: How do you know that's true? We don't reveal wages around here, and it's company policy not to discuss others' pay.

Martha: Never mind how I found out about it. And let's cut out that company policy stuff. Why is Joanne paid more than me?

Poppa Joe is also up against raise time. He believes he can afford about 10 percent for raises. Who should get them?

Some deserve no raise, really; others deserve something; a few deserve a lot. How should he divide the money? Should Poppa Joe really give no money at all to some? With inflation what it is, that's really a pay cut. Do they really deserve a cut? And how much should the average employee get? The cost of living has gone up 7 percent. If Poppa Joe gives them much more than that, there won't be enough to give big raises to those who really deserve them. And that says nothing about people who deserve raises because their base pay is too low, or who are being promoted. How does Poppa Joe allocate the raise money?

These are some of the issues Poppa Joe is wondering about. He's decided to talk to Mary about the problems and her report. He asks her to come in and give him a brief summary of some of the major points about compensation she learned at the college course on personnel she took.

Poppa Joe: Mary, I'm having problems with pay again, as you know. Will you give me a rundown on some of the highlights of that course you took? I don't have a lot of time, though. That's why I'd rather have you tell me than read your report.

Mary: I know you don't have much time. Let's cover some basics that we haven't discussed already.

With that, Mary briefed Poppa Joe on pay methods, executive compensation, and some key compensation issues raised in the incidents she and Guido had told him about.

Let's pick up where we ended in Chapter 11 and complete the discussion of the seven criteria for effective compensation introduced there. A compensation system which meets all these criteria will accomplish the objective of providing a system of rewards which is equitable to employer and employee alike, so that the employee's satisfaction and production are both heightened. Three of the criteria for an effective compensation system are that it should be:

Adequate. Chapter 11 gave the legal definition of adequacy as set forth in minimum-wage and other legislation. The managerial definition of adequacy, or pay-level policies designed to pay the going wage, was also described.

Equitable. Chapter 11 discussed job evaluation as one technique to be used to attain equity. Chapter 12 will touch upon the related policy issue of whether all employees should be paid salaries.

Incentive providing. Chapter 11 discussed the theory behind the merit or incentive pay system. This chapter will discuss how incentive pay systems are designed and how raises are used as a form of incentive.

The other four criteria, which will be discussed primarily in this chapter, state that the compensation plan should be:

Secure. The extent to which the employee's pay seems secure to him or her.

Balanced. The extent to which pay is a reasonable part of the total reward package, which includes benefits, promotions, and so on. Chapters 13 and 14 discuss benefits.

Cost effective. The extent to which the pay system is cost effective for the organization.

Acceptable to the employee. Whether employees think the pay system makes sense. Three aspects of this will be discussed in Chapter 12: whether pay should be secret; compensation communication to achieve acceptability; and employee participation in pay decision making.

METHODS OF PAYMENT

Employees can be paid for the time they work, the output they produce, or a combination of these two factors.

Payment for time worked

The great majority of employees are paid for time worked, in the form of wages or salaries. Paying for time worked and establishing compensation systems based on time were the compensation methods discussed in Chapter 11. Pay surveys are used to establish competitive pay for the industry, and job evaluation is the principal method for setting time-pay schedules. Then pay ranges, pay classifications, and similar tools are developed for individual pay determination, the final step in a time-based pay system.

Salaries for everyone? Typically, most employees are paid salaries. Exceptions are blue-collar and some clerical employees, who are paid hourly wages. One issue in the time-pay system is whether everyone should be paid a salary. (Tom Nichols's dilemma in dealing with hourly-paid employees is an example.) Would you rather be paid strictly by the hour and not know your income week to week, month to month, or be paid a salary so you could plan your life? In general, most blue-collar employees are given hourly pay, but there has been a movement to place all employees on salaries and give them the same benefits and working conditions others have. Firms such as IBM, Texas Instruments, Polaroid, and Avon have experimented with this plan.

The advantage claimed for this move is that blue-collar workers become more integrated into the enterprise, and this improves the climate of employee relations. No study claims that it improves productivity, and the reports of its effects on absenteeism are mixed. Some studies claim absenteeism decreases. Others have found that it increases, but management controls and peer pressure later bring it down to acceptable levels.

But if everyone goes on salaries, it is possible that the long-run security of positions will be diminished. With hourly workers, if business is down it is relatively easy for an enterprise to reduce the hours worked daily or weekly, save the labor costs, and adjust to the realities of the marketplace. If everyone is on salary, management tends to look toward full layoffs or reduction in the labor force by attrition or terminations. *Providing salaries for everyone changes labor costs from variable to fixed, and this can have serious employment security implications.*

The success of a total-salaries program requires stable, mature, responsible employees, a cooperative union, willing supervisors, and a work load that allows continuous employment. Caution is urged in adopting this approach until more studies have been done on this issue.

Incentive plans

The methods for paying employees on the basis of output are usually referred to as incentive forms of compensation. Incentives can be paid individually, to the work group, or on an enterprisewide basis. Incentive compensation assumes it is possible and useful to tie performance directly to pay, an issue discussed in detail in Chapter 11.

Individual incentives

Perhaps the oldest form of compensation is the individual incentive plan, in which the employee is paid for units produced. Today the individual incentive plan takes several forms: piecework, production bonus, and commissions. These methods seek to achieve the incentive goal of compensation.

Straight piecework usually works like this. An employee is guaranteed an hourly rate (probably the minimum wage) for performing an expected minimum

"Our incentive plan is quite simple. Make one mistake and you're through!"

Reprinted by permission of George Dole.

output (the standard). For production over the standard, the employer pays so much per piece produced. This is probably the most frequently used incentive pay plan. The standard is set through work measurement studies, as modified by collective bargaining. The base rate and piece rates may develop from pay surveys.

A variation of the straight piece rate is the differential piece rate. In this plan, the employer pays a smaller piece rate up to standard and then a higher piece rate above the standard. Research indicates that the differential piece rate is a more effective incentive than the straight piece rate, although it is *much less* frequently used.

Production bonus systems pay an employee an hourly rate. Then a bonus is paid when the employee exceeds standard, typically 50 percent of labor savings. This system is not widely used.

Commissions are paid to sales employees. Straight commission is the equivalent of straight piecework and is typically a percentage of the price of the item. A variation of the production bonus system for sales is to pay the salesperson a small salary and commission or bonus when she or he exceeds standard (the budgeted sales goal).

Individual incentives are used more frequently in some industries (clothing, steel, textiles) than others (lumber, beverage, bakery), and more in some jobs (sales, production) than others (maintenance, clerical).

Are individual incentives effective? The research results are mixed. Most studies indicate they do increase output. Although production increases, other aspects can decline. For example, in sales, straight commission can lead to less attention being paid to servicing accounts. There is also evidence that there are individual differences in the effect of incentives on performance. Some employees are more inclined to perform better than others. This should not surprise you, since we know that people have varying motivations to work.

Incentive systems may be designed to affect outputs other than performance. For example, employers may use them to try to lower absenteeism and turnover. At least for some employees, incentive pay may lower satisfaction, however. Employees may be dissatisfied if they have to work harder or if they feel manipulated by the system.

For incentive plans to work, they must be well designed and administered. After reviewing the incentive compensation research, Allan Nash and Stephen Carroll concluded that the incentive plan is likely to be more effective under certain circumstances. These are when:

- The task is liked.
- The task is not boring.
- The supervisor reinforces and supports the system.
- The plan is acceptable to employees and managers and probably includes them in plan design.
- The standards are carefully designed.
- The incentive is financially sufficient to induce increased output.
- Quality of work is not especially important.
- Most delays in work are under the employees' control.

Group incentives

Piecework, production bonuses, commissions, and other individual incentives can also be paid to groups of individuals. This might be done when it is difficult to measure individual output, when cooperation is needed to get production, and when management feels this is a more appropriate measure on which to base incentives. Group incentive plans also reduce administrative costs.

Group incentive plans are used less frequently than individual incentive plans are. The amount of research on group incentives is less than on individual or enterprisewide incentive plans. Some studies suggest that group incentives are less effective than other incentive plans but more effective than straight-time wages or salaries. Perhaps the group does not work well together, or less-well-motivated members decide to coast along on the work of others.

One problem incentive compensation schemes face is restriction of output. The Supreme Court recently ruled (*Schofield et al.* v. *National Labor Relations Board et al.*) that a union can discipline a member who exceeds the piecework norm. This legitimizes restriction of output and makes it more difficult to install group incentive plans.

Enterprise incentive schemes

Four approaches to incentive plans are used at the enterprise level: suggestion systems; company group incentive plans; profit sharing; and stock ownership plans.

Suggestion systems. Most large and medium-size enterprises have suggestion systems designed to encourage employee input for improvements in enterprise effectiveness. Typically, the employee submits the suggestion in writing, perhaps placing it in a suggestion box. If, after being screened by a committee, the idea is tried and proven useful, the employee receives a financial reward. If the savings due to the idea are hard to compute, the employee is given a standard reward, such as $25 or $100. If they are measurable, the employee receives a percentage of the first year's savings, typically 10 to 20 percent.

Effective administration of the suggestion program is essential to its success. The reasons for rejecting a suggestion must be carefully explained to the submitter. If a group idea is successful it is useful to reward the whole group rather than an individual. In general, suggestion systems seem to be useful incentive plans. But this is not always true.

"Dear Sir: Here are two thousand suggestions for the betterment and efficiency of the corporation. One . . ."

Drawing by Herbert Goldberg; © 1974 The New Yorker Magazine, Inc.

Company group incentive plans. Several companies have developed elaborate group incentive and participation schemes which generally have been quite successful. The most successful group incentive scheme at a single company is the Lincoln Electric Plan. The benefits of the plan are impressive: stable prices for customers, good employee-management relations, and large financial rewards to employees. Individual workers have received huge bonuses year in and out, into the thousands of dollars, in addition to competitive wages. From 1933 to 1951, the bonuses per worker averaged $40,000! The employee's share in the bonus is based on a merit rating three times a year.

Lincoln Electric, with $120,000,000 yearly in sales of welding and similar equipment, has multiple incentives for its workers tied to a participation scheme. An advisory board of several executives and about 30 employees reviews and makes suggestions for company improvements. The suggestion system pays 50 percent of savings in the first year. The base rate of wages is a piece rate. The firm also has a stock-purchase plan in which about two thirds of the employees participate; they now own about one third of the total stock. The stock is privately traded and not sold on any exchange.

Lincoln Electric has been extraordinarily successful in mobilizing employee energies. Employees hire the replacements for the work group. The company basically subcontracts the work to the work group, using its past performance and time studies as standards. When these standards are beaten, the employees share generously. This bonus is not used as a substitute for adquate wages and benefits, either. Needless to say, workers bid to go to work for Lincoln Electric.

Scanlon Plan companies. The Scanlon Plan is a combination group incentive, suggestion, and employee participation scheme that has been adopted by about 100 smaller and medium-sized manufacturing firms and at least one large firm, Midland Ross. It is named after Joseph Scanlon, its designer. The Scanlon Plan avoids many of the problems of the other group incentive schemes. Here is how it works. Each department of the firm has a production committee composed of the foreman and employee representatives elected by the members or appointed by the union. The committee screens the suggestions for improvements made by employees and management. The number of suggestions that come from workers in these plans is about double the normal suggestion-plan rate, and about 80 percent of them are usable. If accepted, the cost savings is paid to the work group, not just to the person suggesting it.

The plan also involves a wage formula. Gains from increased productivity are paid in bonus form to all employees: operative workers, supervisors, indirect workers such as typists, and salesmen. They receive bonuses in proportional shares. Management receives its share of productivity gains in increased profits.

Scanlon Plan advocates contend that there are positive results for everyone. These include increased participation by employees, better acceptance of change on everyone's part, greater efficiency for the company, and improved union-management relations. Most of the research studies are positive.

This plan is a most promising incentive scheme. For the plan to succeed, management must be willing to encourage and work with participating workers. All employers must provide their fair shares of suggestions and work. The union must develop a new degree of cooperation. It is likely to be more successful in organizations that are less than gigantic. It also has worked well in troubled companies that provide the necessary conditions of participation, communication, and identification.

Profit-sharing plans. Essentially, profit sharing is the payment of a regular share of company profits to employees as a supplement to their normal compensation. About 100,000 enterprises do this today. The plans must be approved by the Internal Revenue Service, which issued a "model plan" in late 1976 to fit the 1976 tax revision law in the United States.

The number of plans is growing in smaller firms and declining in larger ones. Profit-sharing plans divide a set percentage of net profit among employees. The percentage varies, but 25 percent is about normal. The funds can be divided equally based on the base salary or job grade, or in several other ways. The profit share can be paid often (such as quarterly) or less frequently (such as yearly), or deferred until retirement. The latter plan has tax advantages for the recipient.

Advocates of profit sharing contend that the plans successfully motivate greater performance by employees. Many firms also see profit sharing as a way to increase employee satisfaction and quality workmanship and to reduce absenteeism and turnover. Essentially, they contend that employees who have profit-sharing plans identify more closely with the company and its profit goal, and thus they reduce waste and increase productivity.

But there are problems with profit sharing. First, an enterprise cannot share what it does not have. And in bad years, there are no profits to share. The employees may have cut costs and worked hard, but perhaps a recession slowed sales and thus profits, or management chose an expensive but ineffective marketing program. After several bad years the employee no longer links his extra efforts to increased financial rewards. Often, even in good years, it is difficult for the employee to see the significance of extra work to profit sharing a year away, or worse, at retirement 40 years later.

Profit sharing has had limited success because of the difficulty of tying individual rewards to effort and the problems raised when there are no profits to share. The plans probably are more successful in smaller firms because the employees can identify with a smaller organization more closely and can see the relation between their productivity and company profits more easily. Plans restricted to executives have been more successful, as will be discussed later in the chapter.

In the United States, the passage of the Employee Retirement Income Security Act of 1974 (ERISA; see Chapter 14) may induce more companies to set up profit-sharing plans. The payment of annual profit-sharing funds are not subject to ERISA's requirements, and some employers may choose to use the profit-sharing mechanism to avoid the financial and paperwork problems associated with ERISA. But the Tax Reform Act of 1976 created disadvantages for profit-sharing plans.

Stock ownership plans. Many companies encourage employee purchase of company stock (often at advantageous prices), to increase employees' incentives to work, satisfaction, and work quality, and to reduce absenteeism and turnover. Purchase plans often allow for payroll deductions or company financing of the stock. Sometimes the company will agree to buy the stock back at a guaranteed rate if it appears that the employee would take a significant loss. Companies use these plans for the same reasons as they do profit-sharing plans; when employees become partners in the business, they work harder.

Some of these plans (such as Procter & Gamble's) are very successful. In general, stock purchase plans have most of the disadvantages of profit sharing. It is hard for the truck driver to identify his working harder with an increase in the value of his stock. It is more difficult when the stock drops in price. Many of these plans were terminated in the 1930s because of big drops in stock prices.

A major change in U.S. laws may have increased the usage of stock ownership plans. Recently, Congress authorized setting up an employee stock ownership plan (ESOP) through the mechanism of an employee stock ownership trust (ESOT). Firms have a number of incentives for setting up an ESOT. ERISA views an ESOT as an employee benefit plan. The Tax Reduction Act of 1975 allows firms with an ESOT to take an extra 1 percent investment tax credit in addition to the 10 percent investment tax credit. The Trade Reform Act gives a company with an ESOT preference in receiving government expansion funds for growth in areas where foreign competition has hurt. And the recent DeCouper Industries ruling by the Securities Exchange Commission (SEC) appears to allow a firm to convert a standard profit-sharing fund into an ESOT.

The ESOT has been popularized by Louis Kelso. Essentially the firm setting up an ESOT puts into the trust unissued stock or stock held by a dominant stockholder. The shares are sold to the trust, and the trust uses the stock as collateral and borrows the value of the stock from a bank. The trust then turns the cash over to the company and pays the trust back by making tax-deductible contributions to the ESOT (a maximum of 15 percent of eligible payroll of pretax income). This allows the company to borrow at half the normal cost (it pays back principal only, not the interest) and creates a market for the shares of smaller and middle-sized firms. The retiring employee (or the family of an accidentally killed employee) is given his share of the ESOT.

It is clear that for the corporation an ESOT improves liquidity and cash flow, can help the firm acquire life insurance for key stockholders, and can be useful in effecting divestitures and mergers. One expert maintains that the ESOT is best for an enterprise that is doing well financially, is in the full corporate income tax bracket, is a domestic corporation (not a subchapter S corporation or partnership), and is labor intensive, that is, has a minimum "covered" payroll of at least $500,000 annually. Compensation specialists foresee the spread of ESOTs and ESOPs. There were about 240 in existence on January 1, 1977.

Not everyone has a positive opinion on ESOPs. Some critics feel it is a loophole in ERISA and can endanger employee pension funds. The problems with profit-sharing plans (stocks decline in value, and so will retirement funds) could be worse for ESOPs if all the funds are invested in the company stock. ESOPs also have the effect of diluting earnings per share and thus stockholder equity.

The proponents of ESOPs usually devote 1 percent of their arguments to the probable motivational effects of ESOPs on employees, and 99 percent to their corporate financial advantages. It appears that tax and other financial advantages will encourage enterprises to convert profit-sharing plans to ESOPs. But the motivational effects of profit sharing (which are mixed) are also likely to be true of ESOPs. It is a long time until retirement for most employees, so they are not likely to work much harder for an ESOP. In the end, the ESOP is likely to have effects similar to pensions and profit sharing—slightly reduced turnover and absenteeism and increased employee satisfaction.

Mary and Poppa Joe's conversation on compensation continues:

Mary: In summary, Poppa Joe, one of our problems is that we pay some people salaries, and pay others by the hour. That was the problem Chet brought to Tom Nichols at Branch 1. Of course, lots of banks do this, but we could change it.

We also have not tried incentive pay here. Most banks don't offer it, but we might consider it. At least we probably ought to have a suggestion system. We might even consider a Scanlon Plan or profit sharing.

Poppa Joe: Well, I don't know. What about our executive compensation problem?

Mary: I'm going to get to that next.

EXECUTIVE COMPENSATION

Executives in the public and third sectors are normally compensated by salaries. In the private sector, business executives receive salaries too, but many of them also receive incentive compensation such as bonuses. In addition, executives in all sectors receive benefits and special treatment which are usually called perqusites (perks).

A fundamental question in executive compensation is why business executives should be paid incentives as well as salaries. A number of answers can be given. First, it is argued that these incentives improve performance, and this is good for stockholders and employees. The research on incentive compensation indicates that, in general, business executives are ideal employees for incentive compensation. A second reason is that incentive compensation is a way of retaining talented executives. Many have alternative employment opportunities with other corporations or as entrepreneurs. The third reason is that business executives are more likely to control their own compensation in the private sector than in the public sector, where legislative bodies determine it, or in the third sector, where boards, normally from outside the enterprise, have a great deal of control. For these and other reasons, the compensation of buiness executives tends to be lucrative and innovative enough to sidestep the ever-changing tax laws.

Executive salaries

Salaries of executives in the public sector are generally known to the public. Salaries of executives in the third sector have not been widely studied. In general, the highest salaries are paid in the private sector. There are many studies of this form of compensation.

To give you an idea of the salaries of some top executives, the presidents or chief executive officers (CEOs) of corporations received the following salaries (and, in some cases, bonuses) in 1977: Rapid American, $916,000; IT&T, $776,000; Exxon, $518,000. The total cash remuneration of others include: Halliburton $1,593,000; J. Roy McDermott Corp. $1,223,000; White Consolidated, $706,000.

Some studies have been done on the relationship of size and kind of business, to salary size. With regard to size, in general, as the firm increases in size, the top executive's salary increases. Several studies have examined the relative salaries of executives in different industries. For example, one study found that in companies with sales larger than $10 billion, motor vehicle companies paid the highest, followed (in order) by conglomerates and firms in office machines and oils. In the $5 billion category the order was motor vehicles, office machines, conglomerates, and oils. In the $2.5 billion sales category, the order was pharmaceuticals, packaged goods, forest products, chemicals, and food processors. In the $500 million sales category, the order was packaged goods, pharmaceuticals, chemicals, office machines, and forest products.

Various experts have tried to explain industry differences in executive compensation. Arch Patton suggested that industries that pay higher salaries are dynamic, decentralized, and result oriented. Industries that pay poorly tend to be static, centralized, seniority oriented, and monopolies with a great deal of regulation. In a later study, he added that high-paying companies tend to have stock that is widely held.

Most studies also find that the salaries below the CEO level fit a percentage pattern by industry grouping. For example, the second highest executive is usually paid about 71 percent of the CEO's salary in all except retail trade, where it is 84 percent. The third highest executive tends to be paid 55–60 percent of the CEO's salary.

If top managers believe that pay is a motivator to higher performance, it follows that they will pay themselves in a way that rewards performance. And if performance is defined as more profits, pay should be correlated with profits. Some studies indicate that this is done. Other studies show that top executive pay is correlated with sales, a proxy for size.

More sophisticated studies point out that simple correlations such as these are not likely to explain very much. The factors which influence executive pay are ownership and market concentration. Marc Wallace found that in closely held firms, executive pay was correlated with profitability. Other studies agree with this, and it makes sense. In firms where the owners can put pressure, executives are likely to encourage higher profitability. In firms with no strong ownership interest, executives can set their salaries similar to those of executives in equal-size firms, regardless of profitability. Wallace also found that in firms in competitive industries, pay was correlated with profitability. In quasi-monopolistic industries, size was the predictor of pay.

Bonuses

A bonus is a compensation payment that supplements salary and can be paid in the present or in the future. In the latter case, it is called a deferred bonus.

Exhibit 12–1 gives the salary and bonuses paid to the 15 highest paid business executives of publicly held companies. Exhibit 12–2, which shows the total compensation of the average top executives of large U.S. corporations, indicates how this compensation is related to the size of the firm. The size of bonuses and long-term payments relative to salary clearly changes with the size of the chief executive officer's company. The larger the company, the greater is the proportion of incentive awards making up total annual compensation.

A majority of large firms pay bonuses, in the belief that this leads to better profitability and other advantages for enterprises. Bonuses involve large expenditures of funds. They vary from 80 percent of top executives' salaries to 20 percent of the salaries of lowest-level participants. In spite of wide usage and

EXHIBIT 12–1
The 15 highest paid U.S. executives in 1976

	Salary and bonus (thousands)	*Gains from options exercised (thousands)*	*Total compensation (thousands)*	*Sales (millions)*	*Corporate profits (millions)*
1. Harry J. Gray, chairman and president, United Technologies	$650	$1,012	$1,662	$ 5,166	$ 157
2. C. B. Branch, chairman, Dow Chemical	453	1,195	1,648	5,652	613
3. David S. Lewis, chairman and president, General Dynamics	438	862	1,300	2,550	100
4. Zoltan Merszei, president, Dow Chemical	326	909	1,235	5,652	613
5. Elton H. Rule, president, American Broadcasting	649	584	1,233	1,342	72
6. Michel C. Bergerac, chairman and president, Revlon	694	469	1,163	956	82
7. Leonard H. Goldenson, chairman, American Broadcasting	747	313	1,060	1,342	72
8. Henry Ford II, chairman, Ford	970	—	970	28,840	983
9. Lee A. Iacocca, president, Ford	970	—	970	28,840	983
10. Thomas A. Murphy, chairman, General Motors	950	—	950	47,181	2,903
11. George H. Weyerhaeuser, president, Weyerhaeuser	364	580	944	2,868	306
12. J. W. McSwiney, chairman, Mead	364	528	892	1,599	89
13. Elliott M. Estes, president, General Motors	885	—	885	47,181	2,903
14. James P. McFarland, chairman, General Mills	450	414	864	2,645	101
15. Richard L. Terrell, vice-chairman, General Motors	860	—	860	47,181	2,903

Source: "A Year for Stock Options and Big Bonuses." Reprinted from the May 23, 1977 issue of *Business Week* by special permission.

EXHIBIT 12–2
Total compensation of chief executive officers (in thousands)

Salary	*Bonus*	*Average long-term income**	*Total annual income*
$ 50	$ 15	$ 20	$ 85
75	26	33	134
100	38	48	186
125	53	66	244
150	71	86	307
175	91	109	375
200	116	132	448
225	144	158	527
250	170	185	605
275	195	215	685
300	225	249	774

* Includes only executives who actually realized gains from stock options or long-term bonus plans.

Source: Robert Sibson, "The Outlook for Executive Pay," *Nation's Business*, November–December 1975, pp. 26–27.

high costs, there is little research support for their effectiveness. Unless more research does support bonuses, many may conclude they are an example of management's power to pay itself what it wants, passing the bill on to the public in price increases whether it performs well or not. Boards of directors are shirking their duties in such cases, and this can lead to legal problems.

John Dearden suggests a more rational approach to bonuses. His plan has these features:

- The total bonus for top executives is based on percentage of net profits after a reasonable earnings per share for the stockholder.
- The standard bonus per executive is based on number of bonus points assigned to the job, based on the position's potential impact on company profitability.
- The actual bonus payments are spread over a three- to five-year period.
- A limit (cutoff level) is put on the total of the bonus to be paid in one year. The excess funds are reserved for leaner years.

As far as bonuses for division managers are concerned, Robert Pitts suggests it makes sense to pay higher bonuses to division managers who have greater autonomy and responsibility. Pitts found systematic differences on bonus payments depending on whether the firm grew primarily internally or externally and the amount of autonomy and responsibility held by managers.

Stock options, performance shares, and book-value devices

Another form of executive compensation used in the private sector is a set of devices tied to the firm's stock. The oldest form is the stock option, which gives executives the right to purchase company stock at a fixed price for a certain period of time. The option's price usually is close to the market price of the stock at the time the option is issued. The executive gains if the price rises above the option price during the option period enough to cover the capital gains tax on the stock should it be purchased.

The popularity of stock options has risen and fallen with the tax laws (especially the 1969 and 1976 bills), the level of interest rates, the state of the stock market, and the feelings of stockholders about them. At present, because of tax law changes and these other factors, the use of stock options as incentive compensation is decreasing. For all practical purposes, the Tax Reform Act took the incentive out of new stock option plans after May 20, 1976, and all incentive stock options must be exercised by May 20, 1981.

Is this a great loss? Probably not. There was little research to indicate that stock options led to better performance; what evidence there was tended to indicate that they did not. But one implication of the research is that as management's income from ownership-related sources (dividends and capital gain) increases, these instruments can serve to improve performance.

Innovative tax lawyers and tax accountants have worked up some new compensation forms to replace the stock option and still provide ownership and incentive compensation. Several variations are primarily incentive compensation oriented, others ownership oriented, and still others a mix of the two. The ownership-oriented devices are:

Market-value purchases. The company lends the executive funds at low interest rates to buy company stock at current market value. The executive repays the loan by direct payment or receives credits on the loan payments for staying with the company and/or achieving a performance level.

Book-value purchases. The executive is offered a chance to buy the company stock at book value (or some similar nonmarket value measure) but can resell it to the company later, using the same formula price.

Exercise bonuses. Payment to an executive when he exercises a stock option that is equal to or proportionate to the option gain is called an exercise bonus. This helps the executive keep the stock rather than sell it to pay the taxes on the gain.

One device appears to be primarily a form of compensation that is linked to stocks. This is *performance shares and performance units,* used by such companies as General Motors, Gulf, Texaco, Pepsico, and International Nickel. Performance shares grant stock units due the executive in the future (such as five years later) if performance targets are met. These units appreciate or depreciate as the stock does. Performance units are performance shares paid in cash instead of stock. The units are compensation unless they are to be used to buy stock. Both are viewed as compensation by the IRS.

Another device, *stock appreciation rights,* can be either compensation or ownership oriented. This device, attached to a stock option, allows the executive to accept appreciation in value in either stock or cash.

Most of these devices are very new and are rarely used. All could have performance implications for the enterprise, but there is inadequate research at this stage to determine under what conditions they do so. The key to their success is the definition of performance.

Executive perquisites

All over the world and in all sectors of the economy, executives receive special perquisites and extras called perks. These tend to be larger in Europe than in the United States. The European executive can receive free housing and other niceties in lieu of or in addition to higher salaries. The differences can be easily explained. Some perks are taxed as income in the United States, but are not taxed elsewhere.

In 1975, the American Management Association studied perks in 742 companies; 34 perks were examined, but only 7 were regularly available in more than half of the companies studied. These include better office decor, choice office location, a company car, reserved parking, a car for personal use, and first-class air tickets.

Robert Sbarra's list of executive perks is given as Exhibit 12–3. Some of what he calls perks are also called benefits; these are discussed in Chapter 13 and 14, as noted in the exhibit. Sbarra indicates that executives prefer the following perks the most: insurance (96 percent), company car (87 percent), club memberships (84 percent), financial counseling (77 percent), travel (66 percent), company airplane (56 percent), loans (57 percent).

Perks have not been widely studied. In terms of Abraham Maslow's hierarchy of needs, however, they are likely to fulfill the physiological and especially the recognition needs of the executive. Obviously, a big office provides for recognition needs. But a company car, club membership, financial counseling, and so on provide the executive with nontaxable income—something many of them prefer to taxable income.

The SEC and other government agencies are pressing for more disclosure and taxation of executive perks at present.

EXHIBIT 12–3
Executive perquisites: A selected list

Insured or Internal Revenue Service Qualified Benefits:
Voluntary supplementary retirement benefits*
Voluntary supplementary life insurance and disability insurance†
Officers and directors liability insurance
Profit sharing, thrift saving, stock pruchase plans

Special Privileges:
Financial counseling services†
Company loans for stock option exercise, stock purchase, home purchase, education, personal investment, and so forth
Company cars
Paid memberships (initiation and dues) to country clubs, athletic clubs, luncheon clubs, dinner clubs, professional associations
Liberal expense accounts
Extra time off from work, sabbatical leaves
Company housing, hotel suites
Income deferral
Employment or termination contracts
Combined business and vacation trips
Second office in-home or near-home location
Executive medical examinations
Executive dining room privilege
Unique investment opportunities
Special office decorating allowance

Expense Assumptions:
Educational assistance (tuition, dependent scholarships or loans)
Discounts on company products, services, or use of company facilities
Uncovered family medical and dental expenses

* A benefit discussed in Chapter 14.
† A benefit discussed in Chapter 13.
Source: Robert Sbarra, "The New Language of Executive Compensation," *Personnel,* November–December 1975, p. 12. Reprinted by permission of AMACOM, a division of American Management Associations. All rights reserved.

Executive compensation policy

How does an enterprise choose the compensation package for its executives? Effective executive compensation must meet the needs of both the enterprise and the individual executive.

With regard to the enterprise, the total compensation must be competitive with that of similar enterprises. Thus it makes no sense to look at total compensation of executives, or averages. The effective enterprise determines the compensation of executives in similar-sized enterprises, in the same industry group, and with the same degree of competitiveness. Executive compensation must also be directly tied to the enterprise's strategy and objectives, so executive rewards will further achievement of the goals of the enterprise.

One way enterprises try to satisfy the needs and desires of their executives is to adjust compensation methods to changing tax laws, as was done in 1976. This often leads to the use of more deferred compensation methods.

Another way is to study the preferences and attitudes of executives toward the various compensation approaches. However, as Chapter 2 should have made you aware, since each executive is different and has differing needs for compensation, studies of pay preferences are only partly indicative of what an enterprise should do. In one study of the pay preferences of 300 executives in seven large companies, it was found that executives' compensation preferences vary widely. One consistency was a preference for 75 percent of total compensation in cash and 25 percent in benefits and deferred items, which would mean a shift from the present 85/15 percent division to include more benefits.

A way to deal with these differences is to set up a cafeteria compensation system. The cafeteria approach permits executives to determine the range of their compensation between present pay, deferred compensation, and benefits and services. This approach is described in more detail in the next chapter, where the cafeteria approach to benefits is considered for all employees. It does not change the total compensation (that could lead to perceived inequities), but the mix of how the compensation is received. Although there are administrative hurdles to be overcome, this approach fits compensation theories and makes sense. We await research to see if, in fact, the cafeteria approach does lead to increased satisfaction and performance.

At present the cafeteria system is not feasible in the public sector because of the usual rigid pay classifications and the system of a single salary plus fixed benefits. But it is possible in the private and third sectors.

Mary: So you see, boss, we've really only scratched the surface on compensation at CNB. Our executive compensation system consists of salaries (and not high ones at that), and a few perks like free memberships. We haven't tried bonuses or stock options, performance shares, or anything else. Our executive turnover is probably related to our executive compensation system.

Poppa Joe: Yeah, But high turnover also could be happening because we've hired a great group of executives. Now we're a likely target for others to pirate executives from.

Mary: I doubt it, boss.

Poppa Joe: O.K. What's left?

Mary: What's left are some key compensation administration issues.

COMPENSATION ADMINISTRATION ISSUES

Managers must make policy decisions on three issues in compensation administration for employees and executives. These issues involve the extent to which (1) compensation will be secret, (2) compensation will be secure, and (3) raises will vary with performance.

Pay secrecy or openness

The first compensation issue to be discussed is the extent to which the pay of employees is known by others in the enterprise. (This is the issue Martha raised in the beginning of the chapter.) How would you feel if your creditors, your ex-spouse, or your worst enemy could find out what you make? Would you care? Maybe you would be proud to let them see.

There are varieties of secretness and openness on pay information. In many institutions and enterprises, pay ranges and even an individual's pay are open to the public and fellow employees. Examples are public-sector salaries (federal, state, and local governments), some universities, and unionized wage employees. This is called the open system.

The opposite is the secret system, in which pay is regarded as privileged information known only to the employee, her or his superior, and such staff employees as personnel and payroll. In the most secrecy-oriented enterprises, employees are told they cannot discuss pay matters and specifically their own pay. Recently, the National Labor Relations Board ruled that this is not a legitimate policy.

In the private and third sectors, secrecy is clearly the predominant pattern. For example, a BNA study found that only 18 percent of personnel officials felt pay should be an open matter. In only a minority of enterprises is even general pay information, such as pay rates, provided, much less data on individual's pay.

Should this be changed? Research is mixed. Some findings favor the open system, others the secret system. Before an open system is tried, the individual's performance must be objectively measurable, and the measurable aspects of the jobs to be rewarded must be the significant ones. There should be little need for cooperation among jobs, and employees in the system should have a direct causal relationship on performance. The employees must also prefer the open system. Although more research needs to be done to specify the conditions under which individuals and enterprises might benefit from openness on pay, it appears that the majority of managers and enterprises oriented toward secret pay systems are not irrational in their policies.

Security in pay

Current compensation can be a motivator of performance. But the belief that there will be future security in compensation may also affect it. Various schemes for providing this security have been developed: the guaranteed annual wage, supplementary unemployment benefits, severance pay, seniority rules, and the employment contract.

A few companies provide a guaranteed annual wage to employees who meet certain characteristics. For this type of plan to work, general employee-management relations must be good. Demand for the product or service must be steady or developable into a stable situation. The best known such plans are those of Procter & Gamble, Hormel Meats, and the Nunn-Bush Shoe Company. In one plan, the employer guarantees the employee a certain number of weeks of work at a certain wage after the worker has passed a probation period (say, two years). Morton Salt Company guarantees 80 percent of full-time work to all employees after one year of standard employment. Procter & Gamble has invoked its emergency clause only once since 1923—in 1933 for a brief period at three plants. In the Hormel and Spiegel plans and others, a minimum income is guaranteed.

In the supplementary unemployment benefits approach, the employer adds to unemployment compensation payments to help the employee achieve income security if not job security (as in the GAW). The auto, steel, rubber, garment, and glass industries, among others, contribute to a fund from which laid-off employees are paid. In the 1973–74 recession, many of these funds in the auto industry went bankrupt. They provided less income security than was thought. Studies on plans where unemployment was less severe than in autos show the system has helped in employment security.

In many enterprises, the employer provides some income bridge from employment to unemployment and back to employment. This is severance pay. Typically, it amounts to one week's pay for each year of service. About 25 percent of union contracts require such severance pay. This doesn't guarantee a job, but it helps the employee when a job is lost.

In times of layoff the basic security for most employees is their seniority. If an organization is unionized, the contract normally specifies how seniority is to be computed. Seniority guarantees the jobs (and thus the compensation) to the employees with the longest continuous employment in the organization or work unit. Even in nonunionized situations, a strong seniority norm prevails which gives some security to senior employees.

The employment contract guarantees that the employee will receive compensation of a minimum of *X* dollars and *Y* years. This form of security is rarely offered, however.

Pay raises

The issues involved in pay increases, or raises, are the main ones bothering Poppa Joe. The first issue is timing of raises. If the enterprise accepts the position that pay affects performance favorably, raises should be closely tied to performance. Employees generally prefer raises to be as frequent and as large as possible (except possibly for executives with tax problems), but there may be individual differences in timing preferences. However, administrative costs for personnel and supervisory evaluation usually limit pay raises to annual events. Annual raises can be given to everyone at the same time or tied to annual performance reviews dating from the date of hire.

One problem with the current timing of raises is that raises tend to get "buried." A raise usually is given on an annual basis, so it is divided into 12 parts and mixed up with increases in taxes and insurance deductions. The take-home paycheck often looks the same after the raise. A new attempt to deal with this problem is the lump-sum raise. This allows the employee to elect to spread the raise over as many as 12 paychecks as desired or to take it at one time—in a lump sum. If the employee elects the lump-sum raise for the entire year at the start of the year, the employer deducts the interest that would otherwise accrue to the sum and pays it out. If the employee leaves before the full year is over, the proportion of the raise not earned is deducted from the last paycheck. Time will tell whether this system will increase pay satisfaction or performance.

The second aspect of raises is the use of the cost of living as a criterion. Most pay experts believe that an enterprise must adjust its pay scale to reflect the amount of inflation in the economy to some degree, so employees will not perceive a growing inequity as compared to those who receive cost-of-living adjustments. There are several ways to adjust for cost-of-living increases. Pay can be adjusted yearly or at regular intervals, or by automatic cost-of-living adjustment (COLA). In COLA plans, when the Bureau of Labor Statistics's Cost-of-Living Index increases by a rounded percentage, the wages and salaries are automatically increased by that percentage. COLA adjustments are not made each time an increase takes place, to help reduce the costs of administration. Typically the employer informs employees of the adjustment, how it was calculated, and how it affects them as wages or salaries are adjusted.

The third issue is what criteria should be used to allocate raises, other than cost-of-living factors. This takes us back to the issue of pay for performance or for merit or seniority. The negative impact on employees who do not receive merit raises can be a problem in merit pay systems. Many employees feel a fair pay raise system includes merit pay for current and past performance (seniority, etc.).

The final issue is: How large must a raise be for it to affect satisfaction and performance? Not much research has been done in this area. Several theories have been advanced to suggest that pay increases should be related to current pay, past pay increases, current consumption, or some combination of these if they are to influence the employee's satisfaction or performance. In the most sophisticated recent study, Linda Krefting and Thomas Mahoney found large individual differences in regard to an effective pay increase policy. The authors studied two groups of employees: those who perceived the increase as primarily a form of recognition for their performance, and those who saw it as satisfying physiological needs through money. The best predictors of a satisfactory increase for those who saw the raise in terms of recognition were *anticipated changes in the cost of living and expected pay increases.* For those who valued the money increase itself, the best predictors were *expected changes in the cost of living, the last pay increase, and current pay satisfaction.* Either these groups were influenced by different factors, or all individuals were influenced by more than one factor. The researchers recommend against flat percentage increases in view of their findings, because current pay was not a significant factor in predicting meaningful pay increases.

This research shows how preceding studies oversimplified the specification of raises. More research is needed to provide better guidelines on the size of effective pay raises, given these individual differences. Perhaps a cafeteria approach to pay and benefits, including pay raises, might help with this problem. Obviously the enterprise's ability to pay and other factors are important, in addition to the perceptions of employees of what a good raise is.

In summing up what she had told Poppa Joe about compensation, Mary Renfro said, "Poppa Joe, That's it. We've discussed a lot of personnel problems." Then she summarized the situation at Cardeson National Bank for him, as follows:

- You are making all the pay decisions. You hire people and pay them what you think they are worth, based on their experience (as you see it), their potential (as you see it), and their needs (as you see them). This has caused us a lot of inequity problems. Remember Arte Jamison. He was really underpaid and we lost him. You don't use pay surveys. You don't use job evaluation. You don't have pay classifications—nothing. It's all in your head, and it varies with your feelings at the moment. You have ignored the equal pay laws.
- You give raises similarly and throw in some factor for seniority—how, we don't know.
- Our turnover and absenteeism are high. I think that's largely because of pay problems. Turnover and absenteeism are complex factors, like profit. But you have been hearing a lot of complaints about pay lately, haven't you? Where there's smoke. . . . I've shown you the cost figures on turnover and absenteeism. It's a real cost. And that doesn't count morale problems directly—surly tellers, and so on.
- Executive turnover is high, too. It appears low pay and few incentives are one cause.
- There is pressure to put everyone on salary—as Tom Nichols knows.
- In spite of our pay secrecy policy, word about the differential pay situation is getting out. Remember Martha.
- We don't have a raise policy. We don't have a pay strategy. The results are all around us.
- Should we continue time pay only, or go to an incentive plan like a suggestion system or profit sharing?

While Poppa Joe is pondering these points, Guido stops by the office to help Mary make her points.

Guido: Boss, Mary has some specific suggestions for you. They're all in her report that I've given you. I've discussed them with some of the other VPs and they generally agree. . . .

Poppa Joe: Oh, they do, do they? I'll bet it'll all cost a lot of money. How can you build a bank like I'm trying to do and give away all the profits? I've been fair with everybody. And what do I get—complaints!

Well, Mary, show me where your specific suggestions for our personnel needs are in your report and I'll read them. I'll let you know.

Poppa Joe

Mary's report contained the following recommendations:

1. That one of the vice presidents be delegated to handle day-to-day personnel matters. Poppa Joe would deal only with policy decisions.
2. That a job evaluation point system be set up to determine proper pay. No person would have his or her pay lowered. But some people being paid below the suggested pay level should be raised as soon as possible. Those overpaid should be held at the same level until they are in the right category.
3. That area wage surveys be consulted in making pay decisions.
4. That a pay structure be set up.
5. That a pay strategy of paying going wages be approved.
6. That a systematic raise policy be established as soon as possible, fixing timing, amount, and criteria for raises.
7. That the pay secrecy policy be continued. The ways Martha and others were hearing about salaries should be investigated.
8. That current use of hourly pay and salaries be continued.
9. That the possibility of incentive pay for executives and other employees be investigated.

Question:

1. Which (if any) of these suggestions do you believe Poppa Joe accepted? Explain your answer.

SUMMARY, CONCLUSIONS, AND RECOMMENDATIONS

Chapter 12 has continued the discussion of compensation by adding some very important concepts: methods of payment, executive compensation, and compensation administration issues. These statements will highlight the concepts introduced:

1. Methods of payment are:
   a. Payment for time worked
      (1) Hourly wage.
      (2) Salary.
   b. Incentive plans
      (1) Individual incentives.
      (2) Group incentives.
      (3) Enterprise incentives.
2. Most employees are paid salaries; exceptions are blue-collar and some clerical employees.
3. Individual incentive plans are the most effective methods to tie pay to performance; group incentive plans are the next most effective; organization-wide schemes the least effective.
4. Group and enterprise incentive schemes provide more nonpay rewards (such as social acceptance, esteem) than individual incentive plans.
5. The least effective plans for tying pay to performance are across-the-board raises and seniority increases.
6. Executives are the most likely to think that pay should be tied to performance.
7. The more executive compensation is tied directly to performance for executives, the greater the performance effects.
8. Managers make policy decisions on three issues in compensation involving the extent to which:
   a. Compensation will be secret.
   b. Compensation will be secure.
   c. Raises will vary with performance.

Instead of presenting a chart which suggests uses of compensation in the model organizations or propositions based on the material, this chapter will close with a few predictions on the future of this crucial personnel concept. According to one researcher, there will be:

- Greater emphasis on indexing compensation and pay programs to a nationally recognized barometer of inflation.
- Smaller differentials in pay between satisfactory and top performers.
- Continual movement in the direction of a uniclass payroll system.
- More legislation that will make it increasingly difficult to pay for individual performance because of the burden of proving that no discrimination has occurred.
- More time required to disclose pay policies to employees and governmental agencies.
- The demise of individual incentive plans at all organizational levels because no plan can operate without the use of subjective judgments in any evaluation for determining incentive awards.

Another trend that appears to be developing is to give employees bonuses or travel for achieving performance. Used mostly for salespersons at present, it is spreading to other employee groups.

When dealing with the compensation issue in personnel two more factors should be kept in mind. It is vital for the employer to get feedback from employees on the effectiveness of the pay system. And, for a pay system to be effective, it must be *well designed, well administered,* and *understood* by employees.

In the next two chapters we will discuss benefits and pensions.

A week later, Mary and Guido caught Poppa Joe in his office. He'd spent much of the time since their last meeting at the branch offices—very unusual behavior for him.

Guido: Boss, are you free?

Poppa Joe

Poppa Joe: I'm very busy. But come in for a moment.

Guido: Mary and I have been wondering if you've had a chance to decide on those pay policy issues.

Poppa Joe: Yes, I have. I believe we are a small bank. We don't need a lot of paperwork and bureaucracy. So I decided to chuck the whole report in the wastebasket.

Then I thought it over and decided I ought to compromise. So I accept suggestions 5, 7, and 8. I've already put John Bolts onto an investigtion of who is letting out the salaries around here. Now, I'm very busy. So please excuse me.

Six months later, Mary Renfro left the bank. Executive and employee turnover had continued to increase. Guido Panelli took early retirement at age 55, about six months after Mary left. The bank still has two branches and about the same number of employees. Profitability has declined some, but the bank is still profitable.

Mary

QUESTIONS

1. What is the most typical payment method: time based or output based? Why?
2. Are individual incentive pay schemes effective? Which of the individual incentive pay schemes are used most frequently?
3. Are group incentive pay schemes effective? Why or why not?
4. Compare and contrast the positive and negative aspects of suggestion plans, company group incentive plans, profit-sharing plans, the Scanlon Plan, and the stock ownership plan.
5. Business executive compensation is excessive today. Comment.
6. Are executive salaries effective in increasing performance? Are perks? Bonuses? Stock options and performance shares?
7. Should compensation be kept secret? Why or why not?
8. Should compensation be made more secure? Why or why not? How?
9. When should raises be given? Should raises be given for cost-of-living changes?
10. How big should raises be to have a performance impact?

13

Employee benefits and services

Chapter objectives

- To discuss employee benefits and services.
- To suggest why they are offered, to whom, and what the results in satisfaction and performance might be.
- To show you how to manage a benefit and service program effectively.

Chapter outline

I. Introduction
   A. Why do employers offer benefits?
   B. Who is involved in benefit decisions?

II. A Diagnostic Approach to Benefits and Services

III. Mandated Benefit Programs
   A. Unemployment insurance

IV. Voluntary Benefit and Service Plans
   A. Compensation for time off
   B. Employer-purchased insurance
   C. Employee services
   D. Emerging services

V. Cost/Benefit Analysis of Benefits and Services

VI. Managing an Effective Benefit Program
   A. Step 1: Set objectives and strategy for benefits
   B. Step 2: Involve participants and unions in benefit decisions
   C. Step 3: Communicate benefits effectively
   D. Step 4: Monitor the costs closely

VII. Summary, Conclusions, and Recommendations

Harvey

Harvey Fletcher is responsible for personnel for a state in the South. As an official in the state government, he has a problem. State Senator Roger McAreavy has made a fiery speech on the floor of the Senate, attacking inefficient and ineffective government. In part his speech, which was widely covered in the media throughout the state, charged:

> I suppose that a simple businessman like myself just can't comprehend really complex matters like state government. But I'll tell you that any business which had the record this administration does would be bankrupt by now. If I were running the state, it would be on a business-like basis. Instead we have the wholesale incompetence and waste of this Shaw administration. I'm sure when the people wake up it will be thrown unceremoniously out the front door of the statehouse and the governor's mansion. Until that happy day, I guess the people will have to swallow hard and pay higher taxes for the incompetence in Capital City.

Even the TV picked up the speech. Rarely do the electronic media give much play to state government administration.

The senator cited facts to support his charge from a recently published report by the Good Government League. Normally, these reports are filed in libraries and sent to government clubs without much comment. But this is an election year—three months from the primaries and six months from the election. Governor Shaw has announced that he will run for reelection. Senator McAreavy is running against him in the primary.

The Good Government League's report covered many aspects of the state administration. The part the senator cited criticized the state for having the worst employee turnover rate in the area. The report showed that turnover for state employees was higher than in any other southern state. It compared the state *overall* and in each category of employment as well. The report said:

> It is distressing to learn that our state finishes absolute last in every category of employment turnover. Turnover is important because it is expensive and leads to gross ineffectiveness. It is expensive because every time an employee leaves, the state must incur recruiting costs, selection costs, and training costs. It is ineffective because everyone knows that there is a period during which all new employees have not reached their peak effectiveness. During that time, the employee makes mistakes. He also slows down the wheels of justice or the hospital. Something *must* be done to stop this waste of the taxpayer's money!

About an hour after the speech was on TV, the governor's office called. Sally Eure, the governor's administrative assistant, requested that Harvey be in the governor's office at 7:30 the next day to brief the governor prior to his regular Wednesday press conference. Governor Shaw knows he will get a question about McAreavy's speech, and he wants to be ready.

That's why Harvey is still at his desk at 10 P.M. Tuesday trying to prepare a briefing for the governor.

The trouble is that the figures are true. The state has had terrible employee turnover. Why? Well, the pay the state government offers has been poor for years. Often what happens is that the government winds up with employees who cannot get employment elsewhere. This may be so because they have a bad work record or because they are not adequately trained. Once they are trained, though, they leave for better jobs. And the less desirable employees get fired.

One supervisor in the conservation department has characterized Harvey's plight this way: "They send us people who come into my office and say 'Oh! What is that machine there?' I reply that it is a typewriter. As soon as they are adequately trained for clerk-typists, they go crosstown to the textile company or the lumber company at a 33⅓ percent raise."

The state has always had this problem, but it has gotten worse in the last few years. For one thing, more industry has come into Capital City. Second, the older industry has expanded. Since the population hasn't increased much, the salary structure of private industry has risen to attract the people. The legislature has been made aware of this, but in the spirit of "economy in government," it did not raise the salary scale enough.

What the state does have is a very generous benefit plan. Most of the items in the plan are nontaxable income. In fact, the state's plan is more generous than that offered in most of the industry in the area. Often, state employees have left for more money in industry but with fewer benefits, so they are really behind after taxes. But that is a hard message to get across to large numbers of employees.

The benefit program had not been well thought through. Senators have added items over the years until it has become quite expensive to maintain. Harvey is aware that in the United States typical benefits and services equal one third (and can be as much as 50 percent) of compensation costs. And benefits have been increasing at double the rate of pay increases. As a result, employers may try to reduce benefits, but the result often is that employees are unhappy or may even strike. In the state government, benefits are running 50 percent of payroll. On average, private employers are paying 25 percent of payroll.

Harvey has run a series of articles about the matter in the house organ, *The Stater,* but readership studies of the magazine are depressing. Most people don't read it. He has encouraged supervisors to discuss it, but his follow-up studies find that most supervisors don't. Their excuse is that the benefits are so complicated it's hard to explain them to employees, and many of them are not interested in the first place.

Typical problems of misunderstanding the complicated benefits are compounded by the attitudes of some of the department's employees. Recently, Harvey overheard this conversation in the department:

Joan Black (benefits clerk): Yes the state does have a health insurance plan. What kind of claim do you have?

Arlene Smith: My son has to have an operation.

Joan: Does your son live with you? How old is he?

Arlene: Yes, he lives with me, although he is 20.

Joan: Are you his sole source of support? Does he have a job? Does he have insurance there?

Arlene: Yes, I support him. He has a part-time job, but I don't know if they have a medical plan.

Joan: How long have you worked here? I must determine eligibility, you see.

Arlene: Three years.

Joan: Which medical plan do you have? Plan A, Plan B, or Plan C? Do you have the major medical plan? What's the deductible?

Arlene: I'm not sure. Why don't you get out my file?

Joan: But you should know that.

Arlene: I forget.

Joan (irritated): When you go to the hospital, be sure to bring your ID card. Fill out these forms in triplicate before you file the claim, and we'll process it as fast as we can.

Harvey believes he has administration problems too. But right now he wonders what to tell Governor Shaw in the morning.

INTRODUCTION

Employee benefits and services are a part of the rewards (including pay and promotion) which reinforce loyal service to the employer. Major benefits and services programs include pay for time not worked, insurance, and services.

This definition is a bit vague because the term "benefits and services" is applied to hundreds of programs, as we shall see. Some programs that are sometimes called benefits or services have already been discussed (for example stock-purchase plans). One benefit is so important to most employees that a separate chapter will be devoted to it. This is pensions, Chapter 14.

Why do employers offer benefits?

The programs offered in work organizations today are the product of efforts in this area for the past 30 years. Before World War II employers offered a few pensions and services because they had the employees' welfare at heart, or they wanted to keep out the union. But most benefit programs began in earnest during the war, when wages were strictly regulated.

The unions pushed for nonwage compensation increases, and they got them. Court cases in the late forties confirmed the right of unions to bargain for benefits: *Inland Steel* v. *National Labor Relations Board* (1948), over pensions, and *W. W. Cross* v. *National Labor Relations Board,* over insurance. The growth of these programs indicates the extent to which unions have used this right: In 1929, benefits cost the employer 3 percent of total wages and salaries; by 1949, the cost was up to 16 percent; and in the seventies, it has been nearly 30 percent, sometimes 50 percent or more.

Some employers provide these programs for labor market reasons; that is, to keep the enterprise competitive in recruiting and retaining employees in relation to other employers. Or they may provide them to keep a union out, or because the unions have won them.

Another reason often given is that benefits are provided because they increase employee performance. Is this reason valid?

In the most sophisticated study of benefits, Robert Ashall and John Child found that none of these reasons explained the degree to which benefits and services were provided. They found that only *size* of enterprise explained this factor. Thus, under Parkinson's law as enterprises grow in size, they offer more benefits. The move to provide employee benefit and services is just another manifestation of bureaucratization according to these researchers. *Do you believe that is why Harvey Fletcher has such a big benefits program to administer?*

Benefits and services are important because of their cost, obviously. But in an ASPA/Prentice-Hall survey, 1,400 personnel executives rated benefits and services as their third most significant duty.

Who is involved in benefit decisions?

How the benefit decision is made is discussed later in the chapter. Exhibit 13–1 shows who is involved in benefit decisions within the private enterprise.

EXHIBIT 13–1
The role of operating and personnel managers in benefits

Benefits function	*Operating manager (OM)*	*Personnel manager (PM)*
Benefits budget	Preliminary budget approved or adjusted by top management	Preliminary budget developed by PM
Voluntary benefits and services	Programs approved by OM (top management)	Programs recommended by PM
Communication of benefits	OM cooperates with PM	Primary duty of PM
Evaluation of benefits		Done by PM
Administration of benefit programs		Done by PM

Ernest J. E. Griffes
Levi Strauss & Company

Biography

Ernest J. E. Griffes is director of employee benefits with Levi Strauss & Company in San Francisco. A graduate of Grand Valley State College, Allendale, Michigan, with a BA in economics, Griffes has previously held positions as a bank operations manager, an office manager–personnel officer, a consultant (employee benefit plans), and a personnel and financial officer. Over the past several years, he has achieved a highly respected national reputation through his frequently published articles, his participation in seminars and workshops, and his lectures on the subjects of pension planning and legislation. He serves as Chairman of the American Society for Personnel Administration National Committee on Retirement Income Systems. Griffes prepared ASPA's position paper to the U.S. Congress on the subject, "Providing Adequate Retirement Income for the American People," in which he outlined ASPA's position on pension legislation.

Job description

The primary responsibility of this position is dynamic, results-oriented management of employee benefit plans to maximize the cost effectiveness of benefit expenditures for both company and employee. The incumbent develops and installs new or modified plans, administers existing plans, assures compliance with all laws, determines whether "to make or buy" group insurance, and also develops and implements corporate benefit policies, alerting management to trends.

Personnel executives often seek professional advice from specialists like a member of the Society of Professional Benefit Administrators. These persons are independent consultants or are employed by benefit carriers like insurance companies. Of course, in the public sector it is more complicated, with a legislature involved, as Harvey Fletcher knows.

In very large enterprises, the compensation department may have a specialist in benefits, usually called a manager of employee benefits, like Ernest J. E. Griffes of Levi Strauss & Company.

Benefits are still primarily a Stage I function. Many authorities argue that all organizations should have benefits and services, but there is little concrete evidence that they affect employee productivity or satisfaction.

A DIAGNOSTIC APPROACH TO BENEFITS AND SERVICES

Exhibit 13–2 highlights the most important factors in the diagnostic model of the personnel function which affect the administration of employee benefits and services.

Unions have had a major impact on benefits. In the 1940s and 1950s, a major thrust of their bargaining was for increased or innovative benefits. Union pressure for additional holidays is being followed by demands for such benefits as group auto insurance, dental care, and prepaid legal fees. Union leaders have varied the strategy and tactics they use to get "more." The long-run goal is

EXHIBIT 13–2

Factors affecting employee benefits, services, and pensions and organizational effectiveness

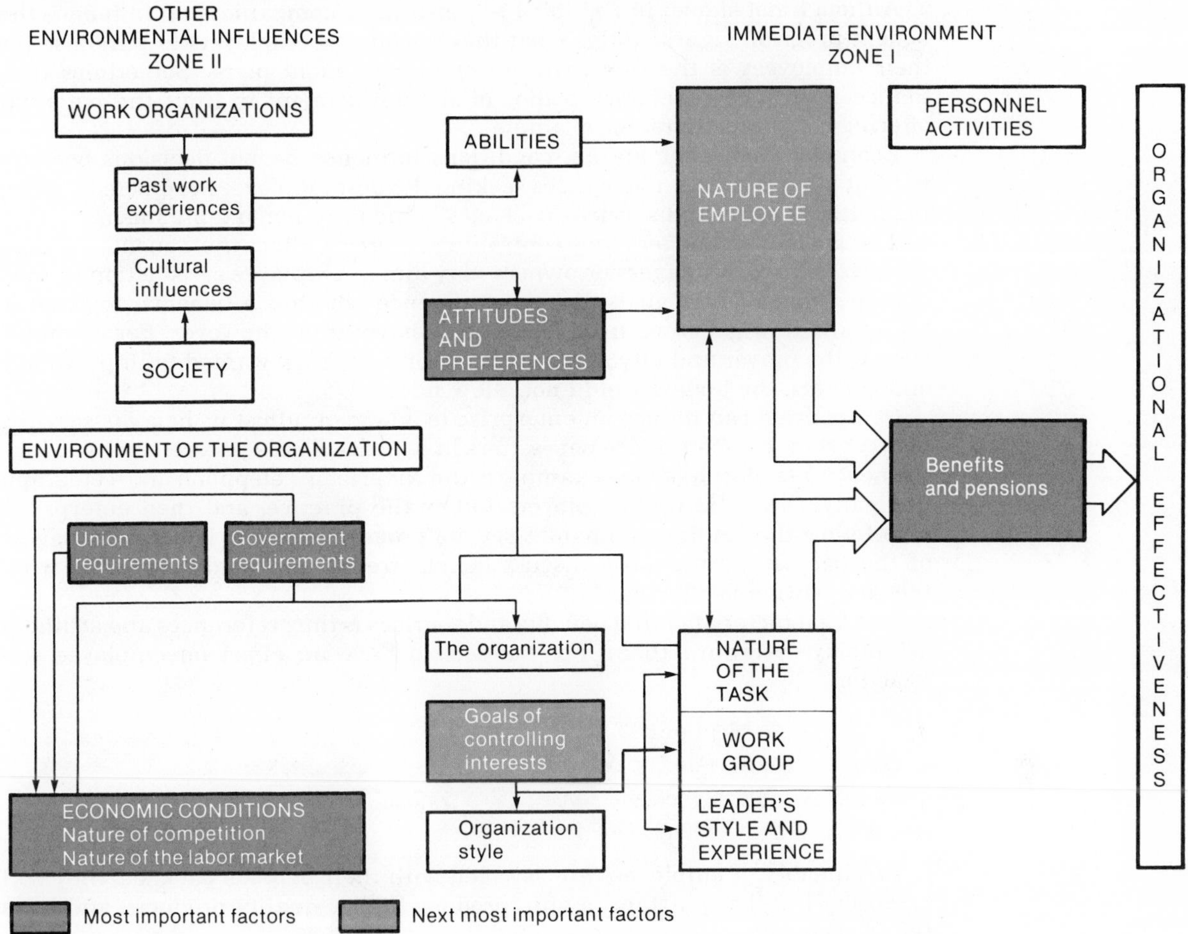

getting employers to perceive benefits not as compensation but as part of their own social responsibility.

Government requirements have affected the benefits area significantly. Three major benefits are legally required: workers' compensation (see Chapter 15), unemployment compensation, and social security (see Chapter 14). Progressive income taxes and the policy of the Internal Revenue Service to allow deductions of benefits costs as expenses have encouraged their development. In 1971, the federal government mandated four long holiday weekends. Passage of the Welfare Fund Disclosure Act requires descriptions and reports of benefits plans, and the government is considering national health insurance as a required worker benefit. The National Labor Relations Board and the courts have stringent rules on eligibility for benefits and the employer's ability to change an established benefits plan. Finally, the government's tax policy influences benefits. At present, benefits are tax free. But some agencies appear interested in taxing benefits as income, as in Canada.

Although not shown in Exhibit 13–2, insurance companies can influence the benefit program significantly. What they encourage employers to purchase for their employees is the raw material of many benefit plans. Sometimes they induce insurance regulatory bodies of the government to limit the potential offerings of competitors, for example.

Economic and labor market conditions influence benefit decisions because in tight labor markets, enterprises seeking the best employees compete by offering better benefits and services packages, which are nontaxable income.

The goals of managers and controlling interests affect the benefits-services package offered. Managers or owners may aim at employee satisfaction or may oppose unions. Other goals also can influence whether a benefits program is set up and how generous it is. These goals have limits, however. For example, even if the mayor and city administrators of New York wanted to improve pay and benefits, the budget would not allow it.

Competition can induce an enterprise to add to or adjust its benefits-services plan. Certain companies are pacesetters in benefits. These pacesetters introduce the newer benefits first. One example is the American Telephone and Telegraph Company. Other leading employers follow the practice, and then enterprises who follow the leading companies set the program up. The benefits managers of the pacesetters regularly discuss benefit trends and read surveys of what the competition is offering.

The final factor affecting benefits and services is the preferences and attitudes of employees toward them. For benefits to have an effect on employee satisfaction:

Employees must know about their benefits.

Employees must prefer the enterprise's benefits to those offered by other enterprises.

Employees must perceive the enterprise's benefits as satisfying more of their needs than competing employers' benefits would.

Presumably, if employees are satisfied with their benefits package, they will be absent less, be reluctant to quit, produce higher quality products, and have fewer accidents.

For benefits to affect employee performance:

Employees must see them as a strongly preferred end.

Employees must perceive that by performing better they can increase their benefits.

These statements fit the beliefs of expectancy theory (see Chapter 2). They make it clear that employee preferences for benefits are a significant factor in their satisfaction and performance. Studies of benefit preferences have been done, but too few. Some of the tentative conclusions follow.

As far as preference for benefits relative to other rewards is concerned, there are no studies on whether employees prefer more benefits or a promotion; more perks or more benefits; or enlarged jobs or benefits, for example. There are a few studies on whether the employee would rather have a pay raise or more benefits. In general, more educated, older, higher status people prefer more benefits to more pay, but the majority of employees prefer pay raises.

With regard to preferences between sets of benefits, some preference patterns seem rather stable. For example, medical insurance is a preferred benefit, and shorter hours are not; stock plans are preferred, and early retirement is not. But most preferences vary widely (such as those concerning holidays, vacations, and pensions), although the results may be due to differences in the research methods of the studies which reported them. And preferences have changed from the 1950s and 1960s to the present.

While the costs of benefits are increasing, there is very little evidence that the employee cares about benefits, is satisfied by them, or lets his behavior be positively influenced by the program. This poses the decision problems for the chapter:

- What benefits and services should the enterprise offer?
- How does the enterprise cope with the apparently serious preference differences among employees?

Most decisions concerning new benefit and service programs start with what is presently offered. This chapter discusses current programs, examines the relative costs of the benefits, and shows how to make competent benefit decisions.

MANDATED BENEFIT PROGRAMS

For three benefit programs, the private- and third-sector employer has no choice but to offer the programs to employees. An employer who wishes to change these programs or to stop offering them must get involved in the political process and change the laws. These three programs, as noted above, are unemployment insurance and two discussed in later chapters: social security (Chapter 14) and workers' compensation (Chapter 15).

Unemployment insurance

In the 1930s, when unemployment was very high, the government was pressured to create programs to keep people who were out of work through no fault of their own from starving. Unemployment insurance (UI) was set up in the United States as part of the Social Security Act of 1935.

Unemployment insurance is designed to provide a subsistence payment for employees between jobs. The employer pays in to the UI fund (in Alabama, Alaska, and New Jersey, so do employees). The base payment is increased if there is more than an average number of employees from an enterprise drawing from the fund (this is called the experience rating.) Unemployment insurance and allied systems for railroad and federal government and military employees covers about 65,000,000 employees. Major groups excluded are self-employed workers, employees of small firms with less than four employees, domestics, farm employees, state and local government employees, and nonprofit employers such as hospitals.

To be eligible for compensation, the employee must have worked a minimum number of weeks, be without a job, and be willing to accept a suitable position offered through a state Unemployment Compensation Commission. Recent court decisions support an Ohio law which denies compensation to employees on strike.

To fund UI the employer pays a tax to the state and federal government on total wages paid. Both the percentage of tax paid and the base wage level paid

A typical state agency which administers UI

have been raised recently. For example, the federal tax was raised from 0.5 to 0.7 percent as of January 1977. State taxes vary. They used to average round 2.9 percent. In Illinois, for example, the state tax for an employer with 25 employees recently went from $1,995 to $3,565, and the base wage level is being raised to $6,000 per employee.

The employee receives compensation for a limited period. Typically the maximum is 26 weeks, although a few states extend the term beyond this in emergency situations. The payment is intended to be about 50 percent of a typical wage and varies from a few dollars up to about $88 a week in some states. The average payment nationwide in 1976 was $60 per week.

The unemployment insurance program is jointly run by the federal and state governments and is administered by the states. Each state has its own set of interpretations and payments. Payments by employers and to employees vary because the benefits paid vary, the experience ratings of enterprises vary, and some states are much more efficient in administering the program than others.

At present there are serious problems with UI funding, due to increased benefits, recent high unemployment, extended length of benefits, poor administration, and cheating by claimants. The options are to reverse the effects of these factors or to increase the taxes, perhaps by as much as double.

Various proposals have been made to improve unemployment insurance. Congress recently proposed to extend coverage to 10,000,000 local government employees, but a Supreme Court ruling may negate this possibility. Others have proposed federalizing the benefit in order to standardize procedures and payments. This would no doubt substantially raise costs, since Congress would not standardize it at the lowest rate. I believe this is the wrong way to go. What is needed is a plan that would prevent persons unemployed in economic recessions from starving yet would not encourage unemployment. One way to do this is to relate the size of benefits and length of payment (and other conditions) to the reasons for unemployment. If an area has almost full employment (as determined by the Department of Labor), low payments for short periods would be available. High unemployment areas would offer higher payments for longer periods of time, but not high enough to encourage movement to the geographic area, as happened in welfare programs. A flexible approach appears the best way to try to improve administration of this benefit.

What can the employer do about UI cost increases? Responsible employers want to pay their fair share but do not want to support abusers. They also do not want their experience ratings to increase costs. Much expert advice has been offered on how to cut costs of the program by stabilizing employment, keeping good records, challenging fraudulent claims, and issuing effective claims control procedures. Careful hiring and separation procedures, and claims verification and control can also cut costs. Effective managers try to control the costs of unemployment insurance just as much as inventory, advertising, or other costs.

VOLUNTARY BENEFIT AND SERVICE PLANS

In addition to the benefits required by the law, many employers also provide three kinds of benefits voluntarily: compensation for time not worked, insurance protection, and employee services. There are many differences in employers' practices regarding these benefits.

Compensation for time off

Can you imagine a life in which you went to work six days a week, 12 hours a day, 52 weeks a year for life? That's what life used to be like, although it has been shown that employees did not always work hard all that time. The concepts of a paid holiday or vacation with pay did not exist. Now most employers compensate employees for some time that they have not worked: break time, get-ready time, washup time, clothes change time, paid lunch and rest periods, coffee breaks, and so on. Employers also pay employees when they are not actually at work—holidays, vacations, sick leave, funeral leave, jury duty, and other personal leaves, such as to fulfill military obligations.

Studies of employee preference indicate that work breaks are not strongly preferred; they are just expected. Vacations are generally a highly preferred benefit. Preferences for holidays vary, and lower paid and women employees have stronger preferences for sick leave. Unions have negotiated hard for added time off to give their members more leisure and to create jobs.

Paid holidays. Probably the most frequently offered of these time-off-with-pay items is paid holidays. At one time, every employee was paid only for actual days worked. In the past 25 years, more and more employers have been giving holidays off with pay. The typical number of paid holidays has been increasing. In 1970, it appeared to be between six and seven, but some recent surveys showed that this has shifted upward to about nine or more. The most typical holidays are New Year's Day, Good Friday, Memorial Day, July 4, Labor Day, Thanksgiving Day, Christmas, President's Day, Friday after Thanksgiving, December 24 and January 2. The new minivacation dates created by Congress through the federal Monday-holiday law allow for three-day weekends in February for President's Day, in May for Memorial Day, in October for Columbus Day, and in November for Veteran's Day.

Paid vacations. Another example of voluntary compensation offered for time not worked is paid vacations. This is the most expensive benefit for American employers. Most organizations offer vacations with pay after a certain minimum period of service. The theory behind vacations is that they provide an opportunity for employees to rest and refresh themselves; when they return, hopefully, they

"Let me see that vacation schedule again, Hawkins."

Jack Markow, from True *Magazine.*

will be more effective employees. Employees have pressed for more leisure to enjoy the fruit of their labors.

Government and military employers traditionally have given 30 days' vacation. Some universities give sabbatical years after six years of service. The typical vacation is one week of paid vacation for an employee of less than a year's service, and two weeks for 1–10 years' service. Three weeks of vacation are offered annually to veterans of 10–20 years, and four weeks to the over-20-year tenured. Over one fourth of the companies studied by the Conference Board now offer five- and six-week vacations, usually for 25-year employees. The trend in paid vacations for unionized employees is upward. As you can see from the accompanying cartoon, vacations need to be well planned to allow the firm to continue to operate effectively.

Personal time off. Many employers pay employees for time off for funerals, medical/dental appointments, sickness in the family, religious observances, marriage, personal-choice holidays, and birthdays as holidays. If an enterprise uses flexitime scheduling (see Chapter 4), the need for time off is minimized. The BNA survey found that 9 out of 10 firms provide paid jury duty, 9 out of 10 provide paid leave for funerals of close relatives, and 7 out of 10 provide paid leave for military duty time. Typically, the pay is the difference between normal pay and military pays. A variety of policies apply to leaves for personal reasons, such as sickness in the family or marriage. A typical policy is to allow no more than five days per year personal time.

Employer-purchased insurance

The many risks encountered throughout life—illness, accident, and early death, among others—can be offset by buying insurance. Many employers can buy insurance cheaper than their employees can, and insurance is frequently offered as a benefit. The employer may provide it free to the employee or pay part of it, and the employee "participates" by paying a share. Three major forms of insurance are involved: health, disability-accident, and life.

Health insurance. One of the most costly kinds of insurance, health or medical insurance, is financed at least partially by employers as a benefit for employees. What studies have been done indicate that employees prefer it over most other benefits. Health insurance includes hospitalization (room and board and hospital service charges), surgical (actual surgical fees or maximum limits), major medical (maximum benefits, typically $5,000–10,000 beyond hospitalization and surgical payments.) Recently increased coverage has been provided in major medical and comprehensive health insurance plans. Surveys report that almost all enterprises have hospitalization plans, almost all non–blue-collar workers are provided with surgical and major medical plans, and about three fourths of blue-collar employees have major medical insurance.

Typically, all employees get basic coverage. Beyond this, plans differ. Plans for salaried employees typically are of the major medical variety and provide "last-dollar coverage." This means that the employee must pay the first $50 of the cost or a similar deductible. The benefits may be based on either a specified cash allowance for various procedures or a service benefit which pays the full amount of all reasonable charges.

Negotiated plans for time-pay workers generally have expanded coverage which provides specific benefits rather than comprehensive major medical cov-

"Don't worry, we'll have you out of here in no time–your hospital insurance just ran out."

Reprinted by permission of Orlando Busino.

erage. This approach is preferred by union leaders because they feel individual benefits which can be clearly labeled will impress members. And these benefits can be obtained with no deductible payments by employees. Also, until recently, coverage of some desired services was not available under major medical plans. Some of the more rapidly expanding benefits of the negotiated plans are prescription drugs, vision care, mental health services, and dental care. For example, typical dental care ranges from $1,000 to $2,000 yearly. About one employer in eight provides this insurance now.

Life insurance. Group life insurance is one of the oldest and most widely available employee benefits. The employer purchases life insurance for the employee, to benefit the employee's family. Group life insurance plans provide coverage to all employees without physical examinations, with premiums based on the characteristics of the group as a whole.

Employee preference for group life insurance is not high. Surveys indicate that almost all employers offer group life insurance. In a typical program for a large company, the amount of insurance provided by the plan increases as salary increases, the typical amount being twice the salary in life insurance. But about a third of the companies surveyed have different plans for blue-collar employees, who usually get a flat amount (usually $5,000). Initially, the enterprise pays part of the premium, the employee the rest (contributory plan). The trend is to noncontributory plans in which the company pays it all. But 34 percent of blue-collar, 38 percent of white-collar, and 40 percent of managerial plans are still contributory. In view of employee preferences, it probably should stay that way. Continued life insurance coverage after retirement, usually one third the coverage while working, is provided by 72 percent of large American companies.

Long-term sickness and accident disability insurance. What happens to employees who have accidents at work which leave them unable to work, temporarily

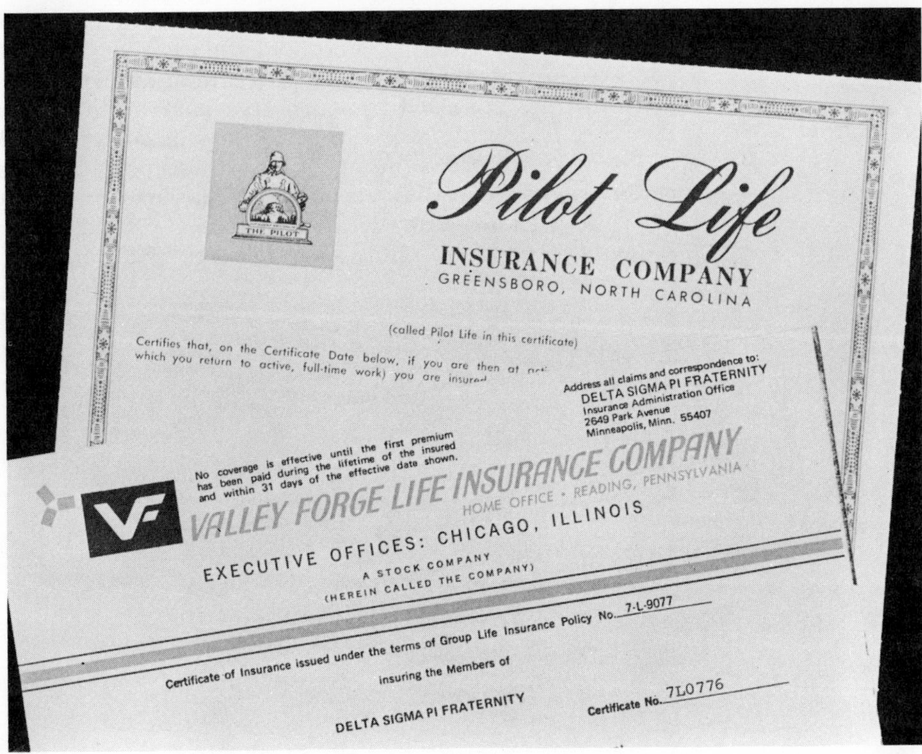

Typical insurance policies provided as employee benefits

or permanently? Workers' compensation pays a very small part of these costs, since it was designed primarily to take care of short-term disability problems (see Chapter 15). Employer-funded long-term disability insurance is designed to cover these cases, with payments supplementing benefits from workers' compensation, social security, and other agencies.

Some disability payments are very large. Recently a roofer who fell off a roof received over $5,000,000. About 75 percent of larger firms have this kind of insurance. Usually blue-collar workers are covered by flat-amount coverage (usually $5,000–10,000). For other employees, coverage is tied to salary level. Usually, there is noncontributory coverage for all employees. The goal is to provide employees with at least half pay until pension time, but the primary recipients have been non–blue-collar employees.

The majority of long-term sickness and accident disability insurance plans provide benefits for up to 26 weeks. But about 20 percent provide these benefits for a year. About 75 percent of enterprises provide such sickness and accident coverage.

Employee services

Services is something of a catchall category of voluntary benefits. It includes all other benefits or services provided by employers. These are such varied programs as cafeterias; saunas and gyms, free parking lots; commuter vans; infirmaries; ability to purchase company products at a discount; and death, personal, and financial counseling. The BNA reports that almost half of the companies surveyed provided subsidized food in cafeterias on their premises, and 82 percent of companies surveyed provided free parking to their employees. Several of the more frequently provided services will be discussed here.

Education programs. Many organizations provide for off-the-job general educational support for their employees. This varies from teaching basic skills such as reading to illiterate workers, to tuition-refund programs for managers, to scholarship and loan plans for employees' children.

Employees attending educational programs financed by their employers

Where employers provide for tuition refunds for courses, they usually place some restrictions on them. The courses must be relevant to the work being done, and a minimum grade level must be achieved. One study of some 620 U.S. firms found some form of educational assistance at 96 percent of the companies. A large majority required the course of study to be either directly or indirectly related to the employee's present job in order to qualify for reimbursement. Approximately half of the companies paid 100 percent of the tuition costs. A few firms based the degree of remuneration on the grade attained in the course. More than 75 percent of the firms made refunds only upon completion of the course.

Financial services. Some organizations give their employees help and encouragement to save funds through employee savings plans, credit unions, and thrift plans. Essentially, savings plans encourage employee thrift by matching all or part of an employee's contribution, up to, say, 5 percent of the wage or salary.

Credit unions help employees avoid loan sharks and wage garnishments; BNA found that 61 percent of the firms it surveyed provided credit unions for employees.

In the thrift plans, most funds are often invested for distribution at retirement. When companies have thrift plans, 85 percent of employees participate. As with many other services, it is difficult to tie performance or even employee satisfaction to such plans. However, they may contribute to the perception of the organization as a good place to work and thus attract better employees.

One benefit provided employees, usually executives, is financial counseling and estate planning. The other benefits and perks executives receive were discussed in Chapter 12.

Social and recreational programs. Many organizations provide recreation facilities for employees, on or off the job. Some experts foresee a growing trend to release employees from work time to participate in company-sponsored sports activities, which are intended to keep employees physically fit and tie them to employers. In one survey, three fourths of companies responding said they sponsored recreation programs, and half of them sponsored atheletic teams. The median expenditure is $6 per employee per year.

There are no available studies of the value, if any, of such benefits to the employer. These plans could be extensions of the paternalistic antiunion activities of some employers in the 1920s and later. Studies of the preferences of employees indicate that recreational services are *the least preferred* of all benefits and services offered by enterprises.

Emerging services

There are an unlimited number of services that could be provided employees. At present, four seem the most likely to emerge in the future. They are child care centers, prepaid legal services, group auto insurance, and counseling services. Time will tell if they become widely available, however.

COST/BENEFIT ANALYSIS OF BENEFITS

Conrad Fiorello tells the story about a gunman who suddenly appeared at the paymaster's window at a large plant and demanded: "Never mind the payroll, Bud. Just hand over the welfare and pension funds, the group insurance premiums, and the withholding taxes." As indicated earlier, costs of benefits are going up twice as fast as pay. That would make a good haul.

When benefit costs increase the price of products and services, they are less competitive with other products, especially those from countries where the government pays for benefits. Higher benefits can reduce permanent employment, too, since it is cheaper to pay overtime or to hire part-time employees than to pay full-time wages and benefits. It may also reduce employee mobility, but most evidence thus far is that it does not affect turnover at all.

It is rational for employees to want additional benefits, since they are tax-free income. For example, in 1977, the typical United Auto Workers member received $7,000 in fringe benefits—tax free. The costs of such benefits, however, have been rising substantially, and many enterprises cannot afford to offer endless benefits and high wages too. Just what does it cost employers to provide these benefits for their employees?

EXHIBIT 13–3
Weekly employee benefits, per employee, 1975 and 1965

	1975	*1965*	*Percent change*
Old-age, survivors, disability and health insurance taxes	$ 12.23	$ 3.13	+291%
Private pensions (nongovernment)	11.92	4.35	+174
Insurance (life, accident, hospitalization, etc.)	11.19	3.54	+216
Paid vacations	11.15	4.85	+130
Paid rest periods, lunch periods, wash-up time, etc.	7.85	2.88	+173
Paid holidays	7.23	3.10	+133
Workers' compensation	2.71	0.87	+211
Paid sick leave	2.58	0.83	+211
Profit-sharing payments	2.37	1.29	+84
Unemployment compensation taxes	2.19	1.58	+39
Christmas or other special bonuses	0.90	0.52	+73
Contributions to employee thrift plans	0.60	0.12	+400
Salary continuation or long-term disability	0.44	N.A.	N.A.
Employee meals furnished free	0.40	0.33	+21
Discounts on goods and services purchased from company by employees	0.35	0.25	+40
Other employee benefits	2.51	1.24	+102
Total employee benefits	$ 76.62	$ 28.88	+165%
Average weekly earnings	$216.42	$116.94	+85%

N.A. = Data not available.
Source: *Nation's Business,* October 1976, p. 37.

Various groups, including the Department of Labor and the U.S. Chamber of Commerce, report on the costs of benefits. Exhibits 13–3 and 13–4 present some of the latest Chamber figures, by industry and per employee. These studies indicate that benefits (not including services) cost 14 to 60 percent of payroll, although they vary by size of employer and industry. The most typical figures are 20 to 30 percent. For example, retailers and textile firms offer low benefits. Petroleum and chemical and public utilities offer a high level of benefits. The most costly benefits are time off with pay (holidays, rest periods, vacations), insurance (especially health insurance), and pensions. In sum, benefits are very costly and getting more so.

In addition to the direct costs of benefits, there are added burdens, or indirect costs. One is the administration of these plans. They can become complicated, and paperwork proliferates. Because administrative costs at smaller organizations are especially high, some smaller organizations get together in joint benefit plans for their employees.

Financing benefits can also be complicated. Some companies have found that they can save money by creating tax-exempt trusts for such benefit funds as disability pay. Examples include Westvaco, General Electric, TRW, and FMC Corporation.

An enterprise can compare its costs to those of other firms with the aid of data from an industry or professional group or published sources such as the Chamber of Commerce. Some other examples of such sources are the Conference Board, Bureau of Labor Statistics, *Nation's Business,* and *Business Week.*

Costs can be compared on four bases:

EXHIBIT 13–4
Weekly employee benefits cost, by industry, 1975

	Per employee, per week
All industries	$ 76.62
Manufacturers	
Petroleum industries	101.54
Chemicals and allied industries	96.31
Primary metal industries	92.00
Transportation equipment	88.12
Machinery (excluding electrical)	80.04
Rubber, leather, and plastic products	75.29
Electrical machinery, equipment, and supplies	73.73
Food, beverages, and tobacco	73.50
Fabricated metal products (excluding machinery and transportation equipment)	71.60
Stone, clay, and glass products	71.04
Printing and publishing	69.87
Instruments and miscellaneous products	69.04
Pulp, paper, lumber, and furniture	66.29
Textile products and apparel	41.98
Nonmanufacturing industries	
Public utilities	96.21
Miscellaneous nonmanufacturing industries (mining, transportation, research, hotels, etc.)	84.31
Banks, finance and trust companies	72.02
Insurance companies	71.48
Wholesale and retail trade	53.75
Hospitals	42.38
Department stores	41.17

Source: *Nation's Business,* October 1976, p. 37.

1. Total cost of benefits annually for all employees.
2. Cost per employee per year—Basis 1 divided by number of employee hours worked.
3. Percentage of payroll—Basis 1 divided by annual payroll.
4. Cost per employee per hour—Basis 2 divided by employee hours worked.

Costs of benefits can be calculated fairly easily. The benefits side of the equation is another issue, however. There has been little significant empirical research on the effects of benefits on productivity. In one of the few studies touching on the subject, Ashall and Child found no relationship between financial success of a sample of British firms and generous benefits and services programs. To be truly effective, managers must match the costs with benefits *prior to* making benefit decisions. Let's discuss this decision making next.

MANAGING AN EFFECTIVE BENEFIT PROGRAM

When top managers make benefit and services decisions such as the cost decision discussed above, they must consider the following facts:

- At present, there is little evidence that benefits and services really motivate performance. Nor do they necessarily increase satisfaction.
- The costs are escalating dramatically.

- As regards mandated programs, managers have no choice but to offer them.
- With regard to voluntary programs, unions, competitors, and industry trends put pressures on the manager to provide or increase benefits.

To manage the benefit program effectively, certain steps are necessary. Four of these are discussed in this section.

Steps in managing a benefit program:

1. Develop objectives and a benefit strategy.
2. Involve participants and unions in the benefit programs.
3. Communicate the benefits effectively.
4. Monitor the costs closely.

Step 1: Set objectives and strategy for benefits

There are three strategies for benefits:

1. *Pacesetter strategy.* Be first with the newest benefits employees desire.
2. *Comparable benefit strategy.* Match the benefit programs similar enterprises offer.
3. *Minimum benefits strategy.* Offer the mandatory benefits and those which are most desired and least costly to offer.

The decision about which strategy to use is made on the basis of management's goals, as discussed early in the chapter. The third strategy may be chosen because of inability to pay more benefits, or because management believes the employees want more pay and fewer benefits. Before these costly benefits and services are offered, management must set objectives that fit its benefit strategy.

Step 2: Involve participants and unions in benefit decisions

Whatever strategy is chosen, it makes sense to find out what those involved desire in benefits and services. Yet in most enterprises, top managers *alone* judge which benefits the employees prefer. Without getting some participant input, it is impossible to make these decisions intelligently. It is similar to a marketing manager trying to decide on consumer preferences with no market research input.

Therefore it is wise to permit (and encourage) employee participation in decision making or benefits and services. When employees share in benefits decisions, they show more interest in them. One way for employees to participate in the decision is to poll them with attitude surveys and similar instruments. Another is to set up employee benefits advisory committees.

Will these devices work? Many believe so, but others think employees are not well enough informed to be of much help. Others oppose asking employees about benefits because this might raise their expectations so that they expect more. Instead, supervisors and union leaders might be asked about workers' preferences; most research shows they are good predictors of employee preferences.

A more direct way of allowing employee participation in benefit decisions and dealing with the problem of major preference differences is called the cafeteria approach to benefits. This idea was introduced in the discussion of executive compensation policy in Chapter 12. Each employee is told how much money the employer has set aside for benefits plans, after provision for mandated programs and minimal health insurance. Then the employee can choose to receive the funds in cash in lieu of benefits, or decide which benefits are wanted. This approach lets employees know how much the employer is spending on the programs. Because they pick the benefits they want for themselves, their performance and satisfaction are more likely to be affected favorably. But until the cafeteria approach is tried more or more research is done on it, it will have to be considered as an interesting approach that could help with benefit decisions.

When the enterprise is unionized, it is vital that the union leadership be involved. Many times the leadership knows what employees want in benefits. Sometimes, the leadership tries to maximize benefits without having determined what employees want. It is useful to involve the union leadership in preference studies so that all parties are seeking benefits desired by the employees.

Step 3: Communicate benefits effectively

Another method for improving the effectiveness of benefits and services is to develop an effective communication program. How can benefits and services affect the satisfaction and performance of employees if they do not know about the benefits or understand them? Yet most studies of employees and executives indicate they are unaware of the benefits or significantly undervalue their cost and usefulness.

It has always been desirable to improve benefit communications for this reason. But now there is another reason. For pensions, ERISA (see Chapter 14) requires employers to communicate with employees by sending them an annual report on the pension plan and basic information on their pensions in language they can understand.

Many communication media can be used: employee handbooks; company newspapers, magazines, or newsletters; booklets; bulletin boards; annual reports; payroll stuffers; and employee reports. Other communication methods include filmstrips, cassettes, open houses, and meetings with supervisors and personnel. A typical employee report is Exhibit 13–5, which spells out the value of the benefits to each employee. How much the employee would need to save to provide this coverage himself should be stressed. Another direct means of communication is to send employees copies of bills paid by the company for medical expenses on their behalf.

The problem (as most learning psychologists would tell you) is retention of the message and learning it in its entirety. Most effective enterprises handle these problems by using multiple media and sending the message many times. For example, when the First National Bank of Chicago changed its benefits package, it told about the plan with a range of communications. These included, from first to last, the following:

A letter from the president was sent to each employee's home to explain the purpose and general nature of the changes. This letter was tested out on 15 "typical" employees for readability prior to sending it.

EXHIBIT 13–5
Summary page from a typical benefit-audit statement

YOUR TOTAL PAY PACKAGE

	Your yearly contributions		*Estimated cost if you bought it all*
Basic and major medical	$138		$1,101
Salary continuation and disability insurance	none		2,261
Life and accident insurance	none		535
Pension plan	none		3,021
Social security	632		1,264
Total	$770		$8,182
Net value of benefits		$ 7,412	
Annual salary		$35,000	
Total pay package value		$42,412	

This report tells you what your company-provided benefits can mean to you and your family at retirement or in case of illness, disability, or death. There is no way of knowing how many dollars you will actually receive. The table above, however, shows your yearly contributions and the estimated cost in annual individual insurance and benefit policy premiums if you were to buy this protection and income yourself. The company pays the full cost of your basic and major medical insurance, salary continuation, long-term coverage, and your pension. You and the company together share the cost of social security and the medical insurance program.

The company newsletter carried several articles per week for weeks after.

Employee handouts were distributed to explain the plan.

Meetings of 40 employees each were held.

Each employee was exposed to easy-to-read loose-leaf binders explaining the benefits.

Finally, employees received their individual annual benefits reports explaining what the benefits meant to them.

In sum, enterprises are spending billions on benefits and very little on benefit communications. To make these billions pay off, they need to increase the quantity and improve the quality of their communications about the benefits they represent.

Step 4: Monitor the costs closely

In addition to considering costs in choice of benefits, it is vital that managers make sure the programs are administered correctly. Especially important is the review of insurance claims. Alan Miller has shown how Rockwell International and Goodyear Tire and Rubber have lowered insurance costs by studying claims to make sure they are covered by the policy and reasonable. Large savings resulted. More efficient administration procedures using computerized methods also can lead to greater savings and more satisfied employees.

Together, these four steps will make any benefit program more effective.

SUMMARY, CONCLUSIONS AND RECOMMENDATIONS

Chapter 13 has described benefits and services as part of the rewards which reinforce loyal service to the employer. The chapter described mandated and voluntary employee benefits and some critical benefits decisions such as communication, administration, and employee participation. Let's sum up the major points:

1. Mandated benefit programs in the private and third sectors include:
   a. Unemployment insurance.
   b. Social security (Chapter 14).
   c. Workers' compensation (Chapter 15).

EXHIBIT 13–6

Recommendations on benefit and service programs for model organizations

	Benefits						
Type of organization	*Legally required benefits*	*Vacation plans*	*Paid holidays*	*Group life insurance*	*Hospital-medical insurance*	*Accident-disability insurance*	*Services*
1. Large size, low complexity, high stability	X	*	*	*	X	X	*
2. Medium size, low complexity, high stability	X	*	*	*	X	X	*
3. Small size, low complexity, high stability	X	*	*	*	X	X	*
4. Medium size, moderate complexity, moderate stability	X	*	*	*	X	X	*
5. Large size, high complexity, low stability	X	*	*	*	X	X	*
6. Medium size, high complexity, low stability	X	*	*	*	X	X	*
7. Small size, high complexity, low stability	X	*	*	*	X	X	*

* Minimized.

2. To be eligible for unemployment insurance, an employee must have worked a minimum number of weeks, be without a job, and be willing to accept a position offered through a state Unemployment Compensation Commission.
3. Three kinds of benefits many employers provide voluntarily are:
   a. Compensation for time not worked (break time, coffee breaks, clothes change time, holidays, sick leave, vacations, etc.).
   b. Insurance protection (health, disability-accident, and life).
   c. Employee services (various benefits which can include cafeterias, gyms, free parking lots, discounts, etc.).
4. To manage the benefit program effectively, follow these steps:
   a. Develop objectives and a benefit strategy.
   b. Involve participants and unions in the benefit programs.
   c. Communicate the benefits effectively.
   d. Monitor the costs closely.
5. To avoid administrative nightmares, employers should concentrate on fewer benefit plans, those preferred by most employees.

The benefit plans recommended for the model organizations are given in Exhibit 13–6.

Remember, for the benefits and services program to be effective, the operating manager and personnel manager must work together. The operating manager helps the personnel manager know what the employees prefer in benefits and asks for help in explaining the benefits and getting administrative problems cleared up. The personnel manager helps the operating manager communicate the benefits to employees and administer the program.

Chapter 14 completes the discussion of compensation with an analysis of pensions and retirement systems.

Harvey Fletcher has given the problem a lot of thought. He knows what the state should have done in regard to its employee benefit program:

- Developed a benefits strategy.
- Involved employees in benefits decisions.
- Communicated the benefits effectively.
- Monitored the costs and trained the administrators well.

He has written the governor's answer to the nasty issue raised by Senator McAreavy. It reads:

> It is true out turnover figures are high. Out studies thus far show that this is because state pay is low. Our total compensation is competitive though, because our benefit program is so generous. We give four more paid holidays than private industry does. Our people can retire after 25 years of service. Vacations are more generous than competitors' are. Our insurance program offers twice what private industry does. And so on.
>
> This state of affairs has developed because over the years the legislature has added benefits one at a time, without considering total costs. Thus there is not enough money left to pay competitive salaries.
>
> I am directing Harvey Fletcher—the state's chief personnel officer—to begin a study *today* to determine if our employees want and use the benefits, or if they'd rather have more pay than benefits. The most likely result is that we'll set up a cafeteria compensation program which will allow the employees to shift some benefit money to pay rather than benefits. This should cut our turnover and make our employees more satisfied. And it should not cost the taxpayers a penny more. The plan

will require legislation, which I'm sure the legislature will provide.

When Governor Shaw delivered this answer, the criticism was muted. Harvey began his study, and it did show that the only way to satisfy the preferences of employees of different age groups, family situations, and so on was with a cafeteria plan.

The governor proposed the plan. But Senator McAreavy was able to bottle it up in long hearings in his committee. It died in that committee in the legislative session.

Harvey retrained his benefits administrators to be more helpful. He put close cost controls on benefits. He communicated benefits more effectively. Turnover dropped by a third. But it still was very high, because the legislature had not set up the cafeteria plan of compensation. Governor Shaw planned to try again at the next legislative session.

Harvey

QUESTIONS

1. What are employee benefits and services?
2. Why do employers have benefit and service programs?
3. Which benefits and services do employees prefer? Which do you prefer? Why are these preferences significant?
4. Describe government-mandated benefits and services. Should these programs exist? How can they be improved?
5. What is a typical time-off-with-pay benefit program?
6. What is a typical voluntary insurance program?
7. If you could compare just two or three benefits and services between two potential employers, which would these be? Why?
8. Which of the benefits and services are the most costly?
9. How can managers make better benefits decisions?
10. How can managers communicate about benefits better?

14

Pensions and retirement

Chapter objectives

- To show what pensions are and how pension plans are funded and regulated.
- To investigate the significant problems with social security and public pensions.
- To discuss preretirement, early retirement, and retirement policies and programs.

Chapter outline

I. Pensions, Retirement, and Employee Preferences
II. Income in Retirement
  A. Retirement income from savings and work
  B. Social security
III. Private Pensions
  A. Criticisms of private pensions
  B. Status of private pensions
IV. Government Regulation of Private Pensions
  A. Eligibility requirements
  B. Vesting practices
  C. Portability practices
  D. Funding
  E. Fiduciary responsibility
  F. Other provisions
V. The Impact of ERISA
VI. Public Pensions
VII. Preretirement and Retirement
  A. Compulsory or flexible retirement
  B. Early retirement
  C. Employers' preretirement programs
VIII. Summary, Conclusions, and Recommendations

David

In Cleveland, Ohio, there is a small chain of food stores which operates in the black section. The stores are owned and operated by David Jefferson. He and almost all of his employees are black.

David worked for a number of years for a large grocery chain, first as a stockman and then as manager of the dairy section in a small store. He volunteered for the Navy in 1941, and, because of his experience, was assigned to handle grocery supplies throughout World War II. He was discharged in 1945 as a petty officer.

Over the years, Jefferson had saved his money. When he went back to Cleveland after being discharged, he and a friend borrowed money wherever they could and opened their first store in their own neighborhood. After the friend died in 1953, David continued to do well. He added his second store in 1956, third in 1960, fourth in 1967, and fifth in 1976. The chain is known as the Cleveland Food Markets.

Now he employs some 100 full-time employees and some part-time employees. David is 64 years old. The age distribution of his employees is as follows:

Over 60	16
59–50	28
49–40	18
39–30	19
29–20	17
Under 20	8
	106

Until now, Cleveland Markets has not had a pension plan. David has started to read up about pensions, but he is not familiar with the terms used in the literature.

He has asked some friends at the Chamber of Commerce for advice. They have recommended that he see a pension consultant, and they have supplied several names of consultants.

David invites the consultants to visit him. Over the next month, he learns a lot about pensions and retirement that will be useful. This chapter is a summary of the major items he learns about pensions in today's world.

Chapter 14 completes the four chapters in Part Five on compensation and benefits. The diagnostic factors discussed in Chapter 13 apply to pensions too, except that the government regulations are different. Pensions are now so important they deserve separate treatment. A few years ago, personnel managers rated pensions as a duty that was about fourth or so in importance. In the recent Prentice-Hall/ASPA survey of 1,400 personnel managers, pensions were named as one of the three fastest growing challenges they face. (The others were safety, Chapter 15, and equal employment opportunities, Chapter 16.)

In addition to personnel managers' perceptions, certain facts about pensions and retirement are significant. What do the facts and pension situations described in the accompanying box mean to operating, personnel, and top managers? Everyone who gets older and stops working needs money to survive. Since many people live 10–20 years in retirement, this takes a great deal of money. Enterprises set up pension plans as a form of deferred compensation to help finance employees' retirement years.

- Private pension funds were worth about $350 billion in 1977. If their rate of growth continues as at present, they will equal $700 billion in 1985. That's more than the value of the total stock market in 1977.

• Many experts believe that social security is bankrupt or seriously underfunded, and pensions for military and government employees are leading to a tax system like the one in Sweden, which recently taxed an author 102 percent of her royalties. To fund social security, your take-home pay will likely be reduced.

• Many experts believe that New York City, which is almost bankrupt, will have to increase taxes to keep up payments out of its pension plans to former employees. New Yorkers will be paying more taxes as a result.

• Some experts believe that because of shifts in age distribution, pensions everywhere will cost the enterprise much more to maintain payments. Therefore pensions will increase the cost of goods and services, and again your payroll deductions will increase.

• Inflation is so great that many people on retirement can't make it financially. Your parents may have to move in with you, and eventually you might have to move in with your children.

• The ERISA law (a new U.S. pension regulation) has caused so much paperwork that the operating or personnel manager must take time from regular duties to fill out forms such as EBS–1, which seem to change every year.

PENSIONS, RETIREMENT, AND EMPLOYEE PREFERENCES

In most of the developed world, a specific period in life can be described as the work period. It begins after full-time schooling is completed and ends when full-time working ceases. The period following the work period is called retirement.

Some words and constructs evoke positive or negative responses in almost everyone: love, hate; friends, enemies. Others bring forth significantly different responses from various individuals. Retirement is such a construct. Some look forward for years to retirement as a wonderful period during which many good experiences can take place: One can sleep late, vacation, visit friends, develop hobbies, and so on. It is seen as a release from burdens. Studies indicate that those who have held less responsible jobs but who are financially secure in their own eyes view retirement in this way. To others, retirement evokes negative feelings. It is seen as a period of uselessness, filled with empty make-work projects. This may be because many relate the concepts of retirement and death closely. This is frequently the response of professional and managerial personnel, to whom work and life are almost synonymous. To still others, retirement has both negative and positive aspects. Although employees are free, they also are close to the end of life and therefore close to death.

Retirement also means a period in which the paycheck stops. Some employers provide income in the form of deferred wages and salaries, or pensions. Retired persons may receive their incomes from this source of income, their savings, and government pensions (social security). Enterprises provide pensions so they can retire less productive employees, as a reward for loyal service, and because unions have negotiated them.

Employees do not exhibit strong preferences for pensions. Preference for this type of compensation is quite weak among young employees.

"My ultimate goal? Retirement."

Reprinted by permission The Wall Street Journal.

"They didn't give me a gold watch. They gave me a corduroy leisure suit."

Drawing by Weber; © 1974 The New Yorker Magazine, Inc.

INCOME IN RETIREMENT

Retired employees receive their income from three principal sources: (1) savings and investments and part-time work, (2) a government pension program, (3) private pension plans provided by employers. The first two are discussed in this section; private pensions are the topic of the next two sections; and public pensions provided by government are discussed separately.

Retirement income from savings and work

One source of income for retirees is postretirement work and savings. One study of 5,000 families found that 52 percent of persons expected to earn money by part-time employment after retirement. The percentage who expected to work declined somewhat as current income increased. Most who intended to work expected to earn about 20 percent of their current salaries in this way.

Another source of income is from savings. Studies find that persons save more (percentagewise and absolutely), the higher their income, and those with private pensions are more likely to save money for retirement than those without them.

Until the mid–1970s, little change in savings took place after social security started. As people were forced to pay social security taxes, their private savings for retirement tended to decline. But social security does not allow much work after retirement, and people are living longer, thanks to medical science. So they have seen the need to save more during their working years and have begun to do so. More persons will have to work to supplement social security payments in view of inflation, but if social security benefits increase substantially, people will save less during their work years.

The government has encouraged people without private pensions to save for retirement. The Keogh plan allows a self-employed person to set aside up to $7,500 yearly for retirement, tax free. People working for others can set up tax-free independent retirement accounts (IRA), and a 1976 law allows workers to include their spouses in these plans. Under proposed legislation, employees are allowed to set aside $1,500 yearly for their spouse-homemakers.

Social security

In 1935, the pension portion of the social security system was established under the Old-Age, Survivors and Disability Insurance (OASDI) program (see Chapter 15 for disability and other provisions). The goal of the pension portion was to provide *some* income to retired persons to *supplement* savings, private pensions, and part-time work. It was created at a time when the wealthy continued to live alone, the average person moved in with relatives, and the poor with no one to help them were put in a "poor house," or government-supported retirement home.

The basic concept was that the employee and employer were to pay taxes that would cover the retirement payments each employee would later receive in a self-funding insurance program. Initially, two goals were sought: adequate payments for all, and individual equity, which means that each employee was to receive what he or she and the employer had put into the fund. In the past 15 years, however, individual equity has lost out.

The program has a worthwhile objective. No one wants older people to live out their last years in crushing poverty and with little or no dignity. Anyone whose grandparents had to live with their children because they could not survive any other way (as both my grandmothers did) knows how hard this can be on everyone involved.

Until recently, the system worked pretty well. The Social Security Administration is a rather efficient government agency which has provided innovative administrative procedures such as direct deposit of checks in banks. At present, one person in seven is receiving a social security pension check monthly, and between a third and a half of the working population gets a check from social security (under the disability and medical programs, as well as pensions). The average pension check is $205 per month, adjusted for inflation.

Social security taxes are paid by *both* employers and employees. Both pay a percentage of the employee's pay to the government. The percentage, the maximum income the percentage is paid on, and maximum tax to be paid are 6.13 percent, $22,900, and $1,404 in 1979, and 6.13 percent, $25,000, and $1,588 in 1980. The percentage will continue to rise, to 7.65 percent for employee and employer in 1990. The maximum tax will rise to $3,046 in 1987 for an employee earning $42,600. How much is paid by employee and employer is calculated on the average monthly wage (weighted toward the later years).

Those receiving social security pensions can work part time, up to a maximum amount which is increased each year to reflect inflation. The maximum a person aged 65 to 70 can earn before loss of social security benefits is $4,500 in 1979 and $5,000 in 1980, rising to $6,000 in 1982 and thereafter. Just about all employ-

Reprinted by permission of the Chicago Tribune-New York News Syndicate, Inc.

ees except civilian federal government employees are eligible for social security coverage. Self-employed persons can join the system. They will pay 10.75 percent in 1990, a tax of $4,579 for a person earning $42,600.

Employees become eligible to receive full benefits at age 65, or for lower benefits at age 62. If an employee dies, a family with children under 18 receives survivor benefits, regardless of the employee's age. An employee who is totally disabled before age 65 becomes eligible to receive insurance benefits. Under Medicare provisions of the social security system, eligible individuals 65 and older receive payments for doctor and hospital bills, as well as other related benefits and services.

The reason the system stopped working well a few years ago, as noted above, is that the trust fund set up to pay the pensions was being rapidly depleted. This was happening for a number of reasons, including:

- Unrealistic inflation rate assumptions by the system's actuaries.
- Inaccurate assumptions of the birth rate.
- Unrealistic assumptions of the productivity increases by employees.
- Addition by Congress of beneficiaries who did not pay into the system fully.
- Withdrawal of many government employees from the system.

Another reason the social security system is in trouble is that many people continue to believe that social security is not just a supplement but should provide full support in retirement, at almost the same standard of living they had when they were working. "Gray power" voters reward congressmen and senators who vote their way. This goal simply cannot be reached without a dramatic increase in taxes.

Public Law 95–216, "Social Security Amendments of 1977," tried to deal with these problems. These amendments raised taxes by $277 billion between 1977 and 1987, and tripled them for the highest paid employees. By 1987 these taxes will dictate that for a person earning just over $20,000, out of every dollar received as a pay increase, more than 50 percent will go to federal income and social security taxes. They also readjusted the wage indexing formula to reduce inflationary add-ons to social security benefits.

The politicians are beginning to get some feedback on these taxes, and some are talking of cutting them. If they do that, they will bankrupt the system.

Probably the best way to "save" social security is to create a significant *communication* program to tell people the facts about retirement and social security. Everyone must understand these facts and comprehend their applicability to their own situations.

FACTS ABOUT SOCIAL SECURITY

Social security is a *supplement.* You cannot live on it alone. And if population trends for the foreseeable future prevail, the country will be unwilling to tax wage earners enough so that social security could cover all expenses.

You must expect to save during your lifetime to supplement social security payments in retirement.

If possible, you should try to get a job with a private pension to supplement social security.

You probably will have to lower your standard of living when you retire in order to pay your expenses, even if you have savings, social security, and a private pension. You may have to work part time in retirement or even live with relatives to make ends meet.

PRIVATE PENSIONS

As we shall see shortly, ERISA requires that all persons participating in pensions must be notified about them in writing and in language *they can understand.* The U.S. Department of Labor set out a six-page notification form in "laymen's language" which employers could use to notify retirees about their pensions. One firm sent this report, littered with pension terms like "vested benefits" and "fiduciary," to its retirees. "The reaction of retired employees who received the letters was near hysteria," according to Mr. Donnelly, personnel director at Vulcan, and the company's pension-plan administrator. "Nearly half of them called the company, desperate to learn whether the gobbledygook meant their pensions were going to be raised or cut." We will translate the gobbledygook into "pension terms" to help you follow the rest of the chapter.

A pension is a fixed amount paid by an employer or its representatives at regular intervals to a former employee or the employee's surviving dependents, for past services performed.

Portability Nonfunded
Vesting
Uninsured
Pension payments
Funded
Noncontributory
Insured
Benefit formula
Fiduciary
Contributory

Vesting. This is the right to participate in a pension plan. Pension plans state how long a person must be employed before he has a right to a pension or a portion of it should he quit. When the employee has completed the minimum time after which he has a right to a pension, he is said to be vested in the pension.

Portability. This is the right to transfer pension credits accrued from one employer to another. It becomes possible when several employers pool their pensions through reciprocal agreements.

Contributory or noncontributory. Some pension plans require employees to pay some of the costs of the pensions during employment (contributory). Other employers pay all the pension costs (noncontributory).

Funded or nonfunded. Some pension plans finance future payments by setting money aside in special funds. These are called funded pension plans. Nonfunded or pay-as-you-go plans make pension payments out of current funds.

Insured or uninsured. Funded plans can be administered by insurance companies. Under the insured method, the payments made for each employee buy him an annuity for the retirement years. An uninsured or trustee plan is usually administered by a bank or trust company. In these cases, the administrators invest the pension funds in securities, real estate, and so on, from which pension payments are generated.

Pension payments. Pensions can be paid in one of two ways: a flat or defined dollar payment, or an annuity. The defined benefit approach uses a benefit formula, as described below. In an annuity, the payments vary according to the value of the investment trust used to pay the pensions. If the value increases, the payment increases, and *the reverse* is also true. In the stock market decline of the mid–1970s, some pensioners learned that valuable annuities vary downward as well as upward.

Fiduciary. Fiduciaries are persons responsible for pension trust funds, such as pension trustees, officers or directors of the company, controlling shareholders, and attorneys.

Benefit formula. A benefit formula is used to calculate the size of a pension payment. It expresses the relationship between wages and salaries earned while employed and the pension paid.

The first step in determining the formula is to indicate which earning figure should be used as a base in this computation. Some experts have noted a trend toward using the average of the final several years of employment as the base earnings figure. An earlier approach was to average career earnings, but this is not fair in an inflationary period.

Once average earnings are determined, by whichever formula approach is used, the actual pension benefit is determined by multiplying the average earnings times the number of years of service times the stipulated percentage, generally between 1 and 3 percent. Some firms offset this figure to some degree by social security benefits. This approach is generally designed to yield a monthly benefit, including social security, that is approximately 50 percent of the individual's projected salary during the final year of employment.

Criticisms of private pensions

In the late 1960s and early 1970s, there was much criticism of the private pension system. The major criticism was that they were a hoax. Many people who thought they were covered were not because of complicated rules, insufficient funding, irresponsible financial management, and employer bankruptcies. Some pension funds, including both employer-managed and union-managed funds, were accused of mismanagement, and others required what the critics considered unusually long vesting periods. Over the years, therefore, pension regulation laws were regularly debated. ERISA was passed in 1974 to respond to these kinds of criticisms.

Status of private pensions

About half the nonagricultural employees in the United States (about 30,000,000 people) now expect a private pension. Like many other benefits, private pensions are relatively new; the private pension plans in existence prior to 1950 covered less than one sixth of the nonagricultural work force. In the decade of the fifties many new plans were introduced and coverage doubled, so that by 1960 about 15 million workers were covered. Coverage during the sixties remained rather stable, and the percentage participating had also stabilized. Studies have found that the kinds of employees covered vary greatly. Certain industries (mining; manufacturing, especially nondurable goods; construction; transportation; communication; and public utilities) are more likely to provide pensions than others (retailing and services). Larger firms are more likely than smaller firms to have pensions. And the higher the employee's income, the more likely it is that a pension exists. Unionized employees are more likely to be covered than nonunion employees. And everyone working for employers with pension plans is not covered by them; the Treasury Department estimates that 35 to 45 percent of employees of companies with pension plans are not covered. Part-time employees, for example, are rarely included in pension plans.

GOVERNMENT REGULATION OF PRIVATE PENSIONS

The law regulating private pensions is the Employee Retirement Income Security Act of 1974. As noted above, ERISA was designed to cover practically all employee benefit plans of private employers, including multiemployer plans. Basically, the legislation was developed to ensure that employees covered under pension plans would receive the benefits promised.

Existing regulations were tightened in ERISA, but the major impact of the law is in the minimum standards established, which all plans are required to meet. ERISA *does not require an employer to have a private pension plan.* Indeed, many existing private pension plans were terminated rather than meet ERISA's requirements. The major provisions of the law are as follows.

Eligibility requirements

Enterprises were prohibited from establishing requirements of more than one year of service, or an age greater than 25, whichever is later. An employee hired before the age of 22 who continues unbroken service must at age 25 be given at least three years' service credit for vesting purposes. An exception is allowed employers who provide immediate 100 percent vesting in that they may require a three-year eligibility period.

Vesting practices

The employer may choose from three vesting alternatives: (1) the 10-year service rule, whereby the employee receives 100 percent vesting after ten years of service; (2) the graded 15-year service rule, whereby the employee receives 25 percent vesting after five years of service, graded up to 100 percent after 15 years; and (3) the rule of 45, which provides 50 percent vesting when age and service equal 45 (if the employee has at least five years of service), graded up to 100 percent vesting five years later.

The new vesting standards appear to provide a major advantage to employees. Previously, those who changed employment after 10 or 15 years of service did not receive benefits; now they will. Although small, the benefits received will increase the total income at retirement.

Portability practices

From the employee's point of view, it is desirable for pensions to be transferable or portable. Employers, however, find portability an expensive provision. Under ERISA, portability becomes a voluntary option of the employee and his employer. If the employer agrees, a vested employee leaving a company is permitted to transfer (tax free) the assets attributable to his vested pension benefits or his vested profit-sharing or savings plan funds to an individual retirement account (IRA). The benefit to employees is in the opportunity to defer the payment of taxes on the funds.

Funding

Many employers have been funding their pension plans at a rate equivalent to or faster than that required under ERISA. Those who have not, must accelerate funding of pension costs. The funding provision has two sections: (1) the employer operating a new plan is required to pay annually the full cost of current benefit accruals *and* amortize past service liabilities over 30 years; and (2) plans in existence as of January 1, 1976, must make the annual payments but are allowed 40 years to amortize costs.

Fiduciary responsibility

Because of the need to provide more effective safeguards for pension funds, the law imposes new standards for fiduciaries and parties-in-interest, such as trustees, officers or directors of the company, controlling shareholders, or attorneys. The "prudent man" rule is established as the standard for handling and investing pension plan funds.

A fiduciary is prohibited from engaging in certain activities. He may not: (1) deal with the fund for his own account; (2) receive personal consideration from any party dealing with the fund in connection with a transaction involving the fund; (3) make loans between the fund and a party-in-interest; and (4) invest more than 10 percent of the assets of the pension plan in securities of the employer. These prohibitions have caused a great deal of concern, and it is expected that Congress will amend the standards.

Other provisions

ERISA provides for plan termination insurance to ensure vested pension benefits (similar to FDIC provisions at banks). The Pension Benefit Guaranty Corporation was set up to pay pensions to employees of firms whose pension plans become bankrupt.

Reporting and disclosure provisions of the law require the employer to provide employees with a comprehensive booklet describing major plan provisions, and to report annually to the Secretary of Labor detailed information concerning the operation and financing of the plan. The act also imposes limits on contributions and benefits and changes the tax rules related to lump-sum distributions to employees. As discussed in Chapter 12, ERISA and other laws created the conditions for setting up ESOPs.

What about those who have no employer-sponsored pension plan or who are self-employed? Persons having an employer but without a pension plan can set aside 15 percent of their compensation or $1,500, whichever is less, and pay no taxes on this income until they are 70.5 years old. IRAs (individual retirement accounts) are managed by banks and other financial institutions. ERISA limits the investment of these funds to specific choices: savings accounts, certificates of deposit, retirement annuities, endowment or retirement income policies, mutual funds, trust accounts, individual retirement bonds, and others. The money cannot be withdrawn before age 59.5 without tax penalty. Firms without pensions plans can set up IRAs for their employees. Self-employed persons can set up IRAs or Keogh plans. Legislation allows a self-employed person to set aside up to 15 percent (or $7,500) in tax-deferred trusts. There is more flexibility for investment of Keogh funds than IRA funds, and the withdrawal provisions are the same. About $2.5 billion is invested in about 7 million Keogh plans.

THE IMPACT OF ERISA

What has ERISA done since 1974? Are American employees better off? Are American employers? It is a mixed blessing. Evaluation depends on which set of facts you accept. In general, it appears to involve a lot of government regulations for very little added protection. To review what has happened in pensions as a consequence of ERISA's passage in 1974, consider the following:

A flood of employees and employers have been to Washington to complain about the law and its administration. More than 5,000 pension plans had to be rewritten to meet the legal requirements. The Internal Revenue Service is enforcing the letter of the law. The Securities and Exchange Commission may get involved in enforcement, too. With this many government agencies involved, conflict over enforcement was almost inevitable.

In the first full year of operation 5,035 pension plans were terminated by employers: four times the number expected by the bill's sponsors. In 1976, 8,000 were terminated. Some say the terminations were due to costly and complicated regulations. Others contend that the economy was bad, or they cite other reasons. Some experts claim the law will cause older workers who are laid off or let go to be permanently unemployed. Only time will tell on this charge.

Pension plan consultant fees tripled. CPAs required firms to tell stockholders in annual reports ERISA's cost to the firm. Lower corporate profits were expected because of funding requirements of ERISA. One expert predicted $3 to 7 billion more per year would be necessary. Trust fund costs by banks went up 90 percent. Others contended the costs would not be as high.

EXHIBIT 14–1
ERISA information requirements to be communicated to employees

Item	*Benefit plans affected*	*Deadline*	*Related information*
1. Communications required for all employees Summary plan description	All welfare and pension plans	August 31, 1975 (except for pension plans using alternate)	EBS-1 form may be substituted
Announcement of material modifications	All welfare and pension plans	120 days after end of plan year in which changes were made	Except for pension plans using alternate, modifications will be included in the summary plan descriptions this year; when future changes are made, they will be reported separately
Summary annual report	All plans with funds controlled by a bank, insurance carrier, or similar institution; certain plans with under 100 participants are exempt	Calendar year plans: July 28, 1976; non-calendar year plans: 210 days after 1975 plan year ends	Includes assets and liabilities; receipts and disbursements; other information necessary for an accurate summary
Interim summary plan description	Pension plans using alternate	August 31, 1975	Existing booklet or other description with a supplement of new information required, such as names and addresses of administrator and trustees
Updated summary plan description	Pension plans using alternate	120 days after end of plan year	New plan description of amended pension plan and incorporating information required, such as names and addresses of administrator and trustees
2. Information available for examination Plan document	All welfare and pension plans	January 1, 1975	Clearly identified copies must exist at each geographic location of employer at reasonable times for viewing
Annual report	(Same as summary annual report above)	(Same as summary annual report above)	(Same as plan document above)
3. Information to be furnished on request Annual report	(Same as summary annual report above)	(Same as summary annual report above)	Employee may be charged up to 20 cents per page
Plan document	All welfare and pension plans	January 1, 1975	Employee may be charged up to 20 cents per page
Vesting statement	Pension plans	January 1, 1975	Employee may request one statement during each 12-month period

Source: Sandra Fleming, "Getting Your Money's Worth from ERISA," *Personnel,* May–June 1975. Reprinted by permission of AMACOM a division of American Management Associations.

The law limited per-person pensions a year to $75,000, to cut the level of executive pensions. Companies have reacted by designing deferred bonuses and other forms of alternative compensation.

Since pension managers or firms are liable for losses, many now must buy $1 million liability insurance policies. The law's requirement that pension fund managers be "prudent men" has had a major impact on their investment decisions and on the securities markets.

Paperwork is a real problem. Partly this is a consequence of the law being administered by several federal agencies (Department of Labor and Treasury), as well as IRS and SEC influence.

On the positive side, ERISA's disclosure requirements have focused needed attention on benefits communications. The items which must be disclosed to employees about the pension plan are listed in Exhibit 14–1. In the process of fulfilling the law's disclosure requirements, employers can improve benefits communications in general, and this is useful.

Another positive aspect is that the Pension Benefit Guaranty Corporation began paying out $225,000 *per month* to 1,700 people whose pensions collapsed in 1975. The total assets of the PBGC at the time were $28 million, but by mid-1978 it had taken over 194 pension plans covering 18,522 employees and $90,000,000 in unfunded liability.

In 1977, the House passed a bill raising the per-employee payment from $1 to $2.25. A Senate bill raised it to $2.60. At the time of this writing, the two bills must be reconciled and then signed by the President. Of course, the former employees receiving pensions are glad there is ERISA and PBGC.

Another positive result is that ERISA has focused the attention of managers on the unfunded pension liabilities of their companies. It is difficult to determine the actual size of these liabilities because accountants have not developed uniform accounting rules for them yet. But a survey in 1977 by Standard and Poor's estimated that these liabilities were huge. ERISA allows the government to take over up to 30 percent of the net worth of a company's assets if the pension plan is underfunded. Samples of unfunded vested benefits as a percent of net worth are the following: Lockheed, 166 percent; LTV, 108 percent; Uniroyal, 89 percent; Pan American Airways, 59 percent; Bethlehem Steel, 48 percent.

In sum, the results of ERISA are mixed so far. Some employees are getting pensions that would have been lost without the Pension Benefit Guaranty Corporation. But employers are unhappy with administration and costs, and many more than expected are terminating plans.

PUBLIC PENSIONS

Employees in the public sector also receive pensions. The Tax Foundation estimates that pensions are now almost universally available at the state and local levels. Federal employees are covered by civilian or military pension plans, and about two thirds of state and local government employees are also covered by social security. Typically, public pensions are contributory. The bulk of the costs is paid by the government and investment income. The employee usually contributes about 7 percent of wages or salary.

Exhibit 14–2 compares private to public pensions. One study comparing private with public pensions found that the benefit levels of the latter are approximately *twice* the level of those in private industry. Even adjusting for the portion paid for by the employees themselves, public pensions are still one third larger

EXHIBIT 14–2
Private versus public pensions at a glance

	Private sector	Public sector
Number of plans	Over 32,000 (excluding 10,000 profit-sharing plans)	2,100 state and local
Covered participants	30 million	9.5 million
Retired beneficiaries	6 million	1.4 million
Retirement payments annually	$10 billion	$4 billion
Asset value (book)	$133 billion	$93 billion
Contributions	1972–$14 billion (with $1.2 billion contributed by employees)	$9.6 billion in 1973 (with $3.5 billion contributed by employees)

Source: John Sweeney, "More Like the Private System Every Day," *Pension World,* August 1975.

than industry's. The plans are not coordinated with social security. Since public pension and social security payments have been rising dramatically, a number of public servants now retire at *greater* net income than they had when working. Needless to say, this is a strong inducement to retire and has helped lead to the crisis in public pensions.

The crisis is this: As public pensions rose (often because politicians gave public employees greater pensions than wage increases and left the bill for their successors to pay), funding did not. All the studies show a consistent pattern: a rising spread between funds and payouts. Exhibit 14–3 illustrates how, as benefits rose, contributions did not.

EXHIBIT 14–3
Public pensions and funding

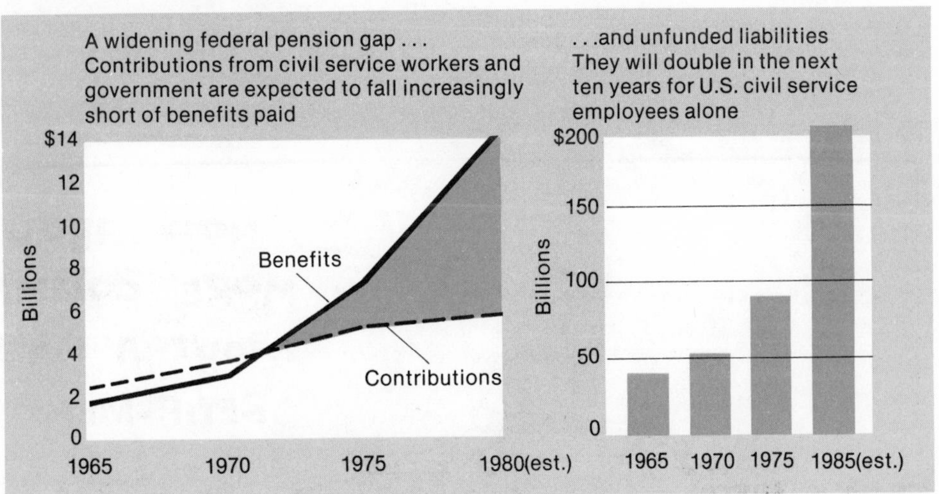

Source: John Perham, "The Mess in Public Pensions." Reprinted with the special permission of *Dun's Review,* March 1976. Copyright, 1976, Dun & Bradstreet Publications Corporation.

There are only two ways to take care of this: raise taxes *dramatically,* or lower pension checks. A third answer, to place the public plans under ERISA, is not helpful. A better solution is to reform the public pensions so that benefit payouts are coordinated with social security and total no more than private industry's payout of about 55 percent of final salary. The length of service required to receive full pensions should be more like that in private industry, too. Taxes must rise or benefits must fall, or the total government budget could be going to pensions. Citizens have a responsibility to be heard on this issue.

PRERETIREMENT AND RETIREMENT

As indicated earlier, retirement has mixed meanings for people: some look forward to it, others dread it. Various policies affect the way people will live in retirement. These include compulsory or flexible retirement policies, early retirement policies, and employer preretirement programs.

Compulsory or flexible retirement

A major issue regarding retirement has been whether it should be compulsory or flexible. There are advantages to both of these policies. Flexible retirement policies take account of individual differences but can cause difficulty in administration, especially as regards favoritism. Compulsory retirement assures a predictable turnover of older employees, opening up positions for younger ones, and equality of treatment for all employees. When new job openings come up, EEO requirements can be fulfilled more easily. Those closest to retirement age favor flexible retirement policies, not compulsory ones.

Nevertheless, new legislation has stipulated that effective January 1, 1979, the private and third sectors cannot have mandatory retirement policies that specify less than 70 years of age. The only exception is that firms may retire top executives and policymakers who at age 65 have employer-financed pension or retirement benefits of at least $27,000 per year (exclusive of social security). College professors with tenure can be retired at 65 until July 1, 1982, when the minimum age will be 70. Prior to this new legislation, federal employees could be forced to retire at age 70. There now is no maximum age limit for federal employment.

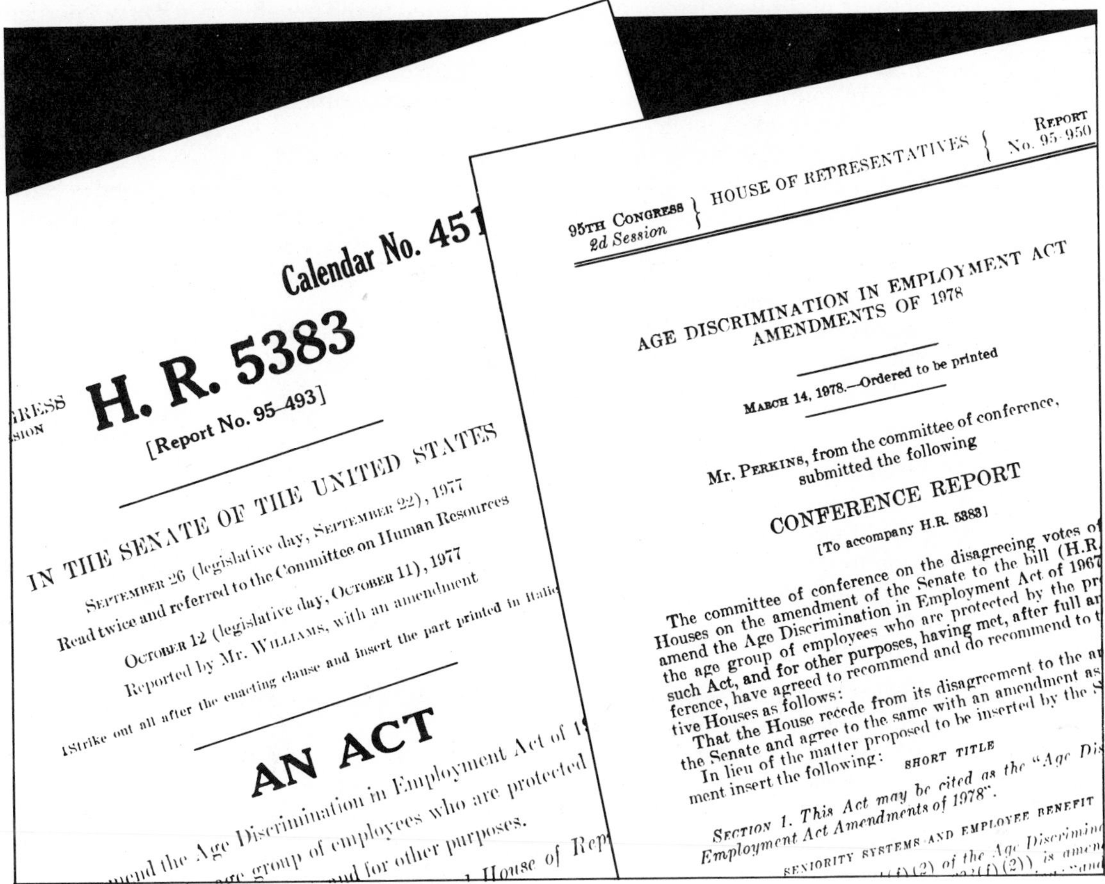

Recent government legislation affecting retirement

The Congress enacted this legislation by amending The Age Discrimination Act of 1967. The proponents of the bill contend that they will introduce legislation soon to eliminate mandatory retirement entirely. This legislation is likely to have a significant impact on pension funding, since present pensions are built on those actuarial assumptions. It could also have a major impact on unemployment and many other factors.

Early retirement

The opposite of the movement to keep older employees working is early retirement. Some employees prefer not to work up until normal retirement age. In recent years, more than 90 percent of pension plans studied have made provision for early retirement.

Typically, the minimum age for early retirement is 55; others call for a minimum age of 60. Most early retirement plans require a minimum number of years of work (typically 10 or 15 years) before the employee is eligible for early retirement. As far as benefits are concerned, all plans will pay the actuarial equivalent of the normal retirement benefits, but 30 percent of the plans pay more than that. One study found that in a typical year an average of 10 percent of those eligible retire early, but this is related to the benefits paid. Only 5 percent of those with nonliberalized payments retire early, whereas 30 percent of those eligible for early retirement with liberalized benefits do so. The U.S. Census Bureau found that more men retire early than women.

Several studies have examined which employees take early retirement. They have found that black men have a lower propensity to retire early than white men. Their study also found that the employee is more likely to retire early the higher the pension benefits, the smaller the number of dependents, the higher the assets, and the poorer the health. Blue-collar workers are more likely to retire early than white-collar workers. Executives are especially averse to early retirement. Government workers retire early more frequently than private-sector employees. People generally are reluctant to retire early in times of raging inflation. One expert argues that at those times, management must take positive steps to make early retirement more attractive.

Employers' preretirement programs

In the early 1970s there were over 20 million retirees. By 1980 there will be 25 million, and 50 million people will be over 50. What have American employers done to smooth the way for these potential retirees? Until recently, very little.

In more recent years, many enterprises have begun providing preretirement counseling. A comprehensive preretirement program that includes these topics is recommended:

First meeting: Developing a healthy attitude for a happy retirement. This session emphasizes the positive steps society has taken to ease the financial burdens on senior citizens by reducing the costs of recreation, housing, and taxes. The potential retirees are encouraged to keep mentally and physically active, and programs designed to help, such as adult education, are discussed.

Second meeting: Leisure time converted to happiness. Potential retirees are acquainted with the variety of leisuretime activities, and they are encouraged to choose specific goals and to take steps to develop plans that will bring them to fruition.

Third meeting: Is working in retirement for me? Retirees are given lectures on service projects and part-time job experiences that may provide variety in the retirement period.

Fourth meeting: Money matters. This session discusses the sources of funds available to retirees: social security, pensions, and supplementary jobs. Personal budgeting is developed for each retiree to help him adjust to his new income level more smoothly.

Fifth meeting: Relocation in retirement. The advantages and disadvantages of living in retirement communities, staying in present quarters (if possible), or moving in with children are discussed.

Sixth meeting: Other subjects. Rights under Medicare are discussed. Retirement publications such as *Harvest Years* and *Modern Maturity* are analyzed. The preparation of wills is encouraged. Social and marital adjustment problems during retirement are covered.

At present, the great majority of firms do the counseling when employees are 64 or 65 years old. About a third counsel employees between the ages of

60 to 65. Very few do so prior to age 60. The ages may now change in view of the 1978 law. Preretirement counseling is an inexpensive benefit which can help the employee a great deal.

SUMMARY, CONCLUSIONS, AND RECOMMENDATIONS

Pensions are so important that this entire chapter has been devoted to them. As you have seen, there are many regulations governing pension plans. An employer must be ready to assimilate these when funding a pension plan. Some statements which summarize the major points are:

1. Retirement is the period following the work period. This can be a rewarding time of life or a frustrating experience, depending on the individual and his or her values, assets, and attitudes.

EXHIBIT 14–4
Recommendations on retirement and pension programs for model organizations

Type of organization	*Joint employer preretirement program*	*Employer preretirement program*	*Postretirement program*	*Joint employer pension*	*Employer pension program*
1. Large size, low complexity, high stability		X	X		X
2. Medium size, low complexity, high stability	X				X
3. Small size, low complexity, high stability				X	
4. Medium size, moderate complexity, moderate stability	X				X
5. Large size, high complexity, low stability		X	X		X
6. Medium size, high complexity, low stability	X				X
7. Small size, high complexity, low stability				X	

2. Retirement income is received from three principal sources:
   a. Savings and investments and part-time work.
   b. A government pension program.
   c. Private pension plans provided by employers.
3. *Social security is a supplement* to the other sources of retirement income.
4. The Employee Retirement Income Security Act of 1974 is the law regulating private pensions. It was developed to ensure that employees covered under pension plans would receive the benefits promised.
5. The more liberal the early retirement pension, the larger will be the percentage of employees who retire early.
6. Top managers must make a series of strategic decisions on retirement and pensions such as enterprise policies on mandatory retirement, whether to have a private pension plan, and whether to provide preretirement programs.

Exhibit 14–4 lists the recommendations on pensions for the model organizations.

In Chapter 15 we turn to another important concern, safety and health.

David Jefferson is sitting in his office wondering about pensions and a retirement plan for his Cleveland Food Markets chain. He feels his business is much too small to conduct retirement counseling sessions. But several of the pension carriers offer this service to firms like his, and he intends to take advantage of it.

The ERISA regulations scare him. So much paperwork! Yet he's convinced that social security benefits won't be enough for his retired employees. He has polled them informally and found that those over 45 years old are interested in a pension. They are the people who helped him build his business. The younger ones don't stay. But maybe they would if he had a pension plan.

The pension consultants have been a big help. They know their business like he knows food retailing. David decides that the pension plan that seems most efficient would have these characteristics:

Eligibility: Age 25.
Vesting: Graded 15-year service rule.
Nonportability.
Fully funded.
Contributory: The firm pays half, the employees half.
Insured.

He chooses a well-known insurance firm recommended by one of the consultants. The consultant will help him complete government paperwork and communicate with his employees.

David

David is satisfied. He feels he's done a good thing for his employees in these inflationary times. He has asked them what they wanted and considered their desires and his ability to pay in the design of the plan. He'll keep an eye on the results to see if it pays off in employee satisfaction and loyalty. Right now, he feels he has helped provide a better benefit package for his employees at Cleveland Food Markets.

QUESTIONS

1. Why do enterprises have pensions and retirement plans?
2. How do retired people support themselves?
3. What is social security? Is it a viable program? How does it work? How can it be improved?
4. What is meant by vesting, portability, contributory, funded, insured, fiduciary, and benefit formula in reference to pensions?
5. What are the criticisms of private pensions that led to ERISA? Are these criticisms more or less severe than those of social security?
6. How many people are covered by private pensions in the United States?
7. What are the major provisions of ERISA regarding vesting, funding, fiduciary, responsibility, and portability?
8. What have been the major impacts of ERISA? Have they been negative or positive?
9. Are public pensions sound? How do they compare to Social Security? Private pensions?
10. Are early retirement programs a good idea? Have they been successful?

equal employment opportunity is the law

igualdad de oportunidad en el empleo es la ley

Private Industry, State, and Local Government

Title VII of the Civil Rights Act of 1964, as amended, prohibits job discrimination because of race, color, religion, sex or national origin.

Applicants to and employees of private employers, state/local governments, and public/private educational institutions are protected. Also covered are employment agencies, labor unions and apprenticeship programs. Any person who believes he or she has been discriminated against should contact immediately

The U. S. Equal Employment Opportunity Commission (EEOC)
2401 E St., N.W.
Washington, D. C. 20506

or an EEOC District Office, listed in most telephone directories under U. S. Government.

Federal Contract Employment

Executive Order 11246, as amended, prohibits job discrimination because of race, color, religion, sex or national origin and requires affirmative action to ensure equality of opportunity in all aspects of employment.

Section 503 of the Rehabilitation Act of 1973 prohibits job discrimination because of handicap and requires affirmative action to employ and advance in employment qualified handicapped workers.

Section 402 of the Vietnam Era Veterans' Readjustment Assistance Act of 1974 prohibits job discrimination and requires affirmative action to employ and advance in employment (1) qualified Vietnam era veterans during the first four years after their discharge and (2) qualified disabled veterans throughout their working life if they have a 30 percent or more disability.

Applicants to and employees of any company with

Industrias Privadas, Gobiernos Locales y Estatales

El Título VII de la Ley de Derechos Civiles de 1964, enmendado, prohibe la discriminación en el empleo por razón de raza, color, religión, sexo o nacionalidad de origen.

La ley protege a los empleados y solicitantes de empleo en empresas privadas, gobiernos estatales y locales e instituciones educacionales publicas y privadas. También abarca las agencias de empleo, sindicatos de trabajadores y programas de aprendizaje. Cualquier persona, tanto hombre como mujer, que crea que ha sido objeto de discriminación debe escribir inmediatamente a

The U. S. Equal Employment Opportunity Commission (EEOC)
2401 E St., N.W.
Washington, D. C. 20506

o a cualquier oficina regional de EEOC, las que se encuentran en las guías telefónicas locales bajo el nombre de: U. S. Government.

Empleos En Compañías Con Contratos Federales

La Orden Ejecutiva Número 11246, enmendada, prohibe la discriminación en el empleo por razón de raza, color, religión, sexo o nacionalidad de origen y exige acción positiva para garantizar la igualdad de oportunidad en todos los aspectos del empleo.

Las Sección 503 de la Ley de Rehabilitación de 1973, prohibe la discriminación en el empleo contra personas que sufran de impedimentos físicos o mentales y exige acción positiva en el empleo y promoción de personas que sufran de impedimentos físicos o mentales, siempre que reúnan las condiciones indispensables para el desempeño del empleo.

La Sección 402 de la Ley de 1974 de Asistencia para el Reajuste de los Veteranos de la Era de Vietnam, prohibe la discriminación en el empleo y exige acción positiva en el empleo y promoción de (1) veteranos de la era de Vietnam, durante los primeros cuatro años después de haber sido

part six

Safety and health, equal employment opportunity, and labor relations

Part Six is comprised of chapters that focus on three of the most significant personnel activities. All are closely regulated by the government, and all directly affect most employees today.

Chapter 15 describes safety and health programs. These programs, operated by personnel departments, are designed to minimize, if not eliminate, the accidents, occupational illnesses, and work-related deaths that threaten the physical security of most employees.

Chapter 16 focuses on equal employment opportunity programs. These programs are designed to assure all employees, regardless of sex, race, ethnic background, religion, and, in some cases, age, a fair chance to be hired and to have worthwhile careers.

Chapter 17 discusses formal and informal mechanics for processing employee grievances. It also describes how some employees join unions and associations and how these unions negotiate and help administer contracts for their members.

15

Employee safety and health

Chapter objectives

- To demonstrate why enterprises and the government have safety and health programs.
- To show how enterprises have tried to create healthy and safe workplaces for their employees.
- To discuss government requirements and programs designed to assure the health and safety of employees.

Chapter outline

I. A Diagnostic Approach to Safety and Health
II. Who Is Involved with Safety and Health?
III. Causes of Work Accidents and Work-Related Illnesses
IV. Organizational Responses to Health and Safety Challenges
    A. Safety design and preventive approaches
    B. Inspection, reporting, and accident research
    C. Safety training and motivation programs
    D. Auditing safety programs
    E. Health programs for employees
V. Government Responses to Health and Safety Problems
    A. OSHA safety standards
    B. OSHA inspections
    C. OSHA record keeping and reporting
    D. Some consequences of OSHA
    E. Overall evaluation of OSHA
VI. Workers' Compensation and Disability Programs
VII. Evaluation of Safety and Health Programs
VIII. Summary, Conclusions, and Recommendations

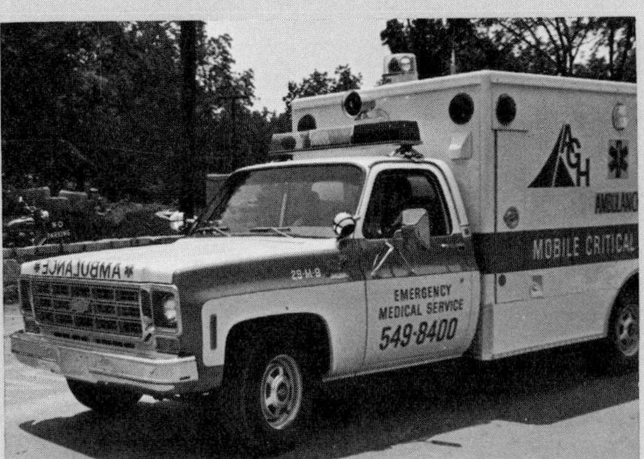

Clint

The ambulance has just pulled away from Lysander Manufacturing. It is headed for a Denver hospital, carrying Dale Silas. Dale has been badly hurt; he might be disabled for the rest of his life.

Clint Woodley, the plant manager, wonders if there is anything he could have done to prevent Dale's injury. It was not the first injury this year at Lysander. What could he do to make it the last? Clint decides that he'll visit his friend Bob Undine, who operates a similar plant in a nearby town. He calls Bob and arranges to have lunch the next day.

At lunch, Clint explains how upset he is about Dale's injury. Dale had been with Lysander for 15 years—longer than Clint had been. He has a wife and five children to support. The word from the hospital is not very good.

Bob: Well, Clint, sometimes accidents happen. You know our business is dangerous. And sometimes the men are not following the safety rules. What is your safety record over the last ten years?

Clint: I don't really know. We've only got records since that damn OSHA (Occupational Safety and Health Act) came in. But the personnel guy, Otto Richmond, handles that paperwork. When our people are hired, we tell them to be safe. The supervisors are supposed to handle that.

Bob: You mean you don't have a safety unit?

Clint: No.

Bob: Then you probably don't do accident research, safety design and prevention, safety inspections, or safety training either, do you?

Clint: No. We do fill out the OSHA paperwork. Luckily, we've never been inspected by OSHA.

Bob: Well, then, maybe you ought to be upset about Dale. You aren't doing all you could to protect your employees. And if you don't do it, maybe OSHA will make you.

Clint: I don't want that. Can I come back with you and see what happens at your plant?

Bob: Sure.

This chapter covers some of the main points that Bob and his safety executive, Mary Lou Vaugh, explained to Clint.

Safety hazards are those aspects of the work environment which have the potential of immediate and sometimes violent harm to an employee. Examples are loss of hearing, eyesight, or body parts; cuts, sprains, bruises, broken bones; burns and electric shock.

Health hazards are those aspects of the work environment which slowly and cumulatively (and often irreversibly) lead to deterioration of an employee's health. Examples are cancer, poisoning, and respiratory diseases. Typical causes include physical and biological hazards, toxic and cancer-causing dusts and chemicals, and stressful working conditions.

How many safety and health hazards exist in workplaces today? On the average, 1 employee in 10 is killed or injured at work *each year.* But some occupations (such as dock workers) have many more injuries per year than others (e.g., file clerks), so the odds for some workers are worse than 1 in 10 each year.

Statistics on safety and health hazards are debated. The official statistics indicate that about 400,000 persons per year contract an occupational disease, and deaths from this cause average 100,000 per year. But Nicholas Ashford cites data to indicate this figure is too low and argues that many occupationally contracted diseases are not reported as being caused by work.

The National Safety Council reports about 13,000 accidental deaths at work in a recent year (and about 6,000,000 reported accidents). The Occupational Safety and Health Administration (OSHA) places work-related deaths at about 9,000 per year. All agencies do not report the same figures. Note the use of the verb "reported." A number of studies indicate that perhaps as few as half of all occupational accidents are reported.

Accidents and illnesses are not evenly distributed among employers in the United States. Employees facing serious health and safety dangers include fire fighters, miners, construction and transportation workers, roofing and sheet metal workers, recreational vehicle manufacturers, lumber and wood workers, and blue-collar and first-line supervisors in manufacturing and agriculture. A few white-collar jobs are relatively dangerous: dentists and hospital operating room personnel, beauticians, and X-ray technicians.

All accidents and diseases are tragic to the employees involved, of course. There is pain at the time of the accident, and there can be psychological problems later. In addition to pain, suffering, and death, there are also direct measurable costs to both employee and employer. About 30,000,000 work days were lost in the United States because of health-related absenteeism in a recent year. This may mean direct costs of workers' compensation and indirect costs of lost productivity for the enterprise. The average company's workers' compensation for disability payments is 1 percent of payroll, and the indirect costs are estimated to be five times greater. These indirect costs include cost of wages paid the injured employee, damage to plant and equipment, costs of replacement employees, and time costs for supervisors and personnel people investigating and reporting the accident or illness. Both because of the humanitarian desire of management to reduce suffering and because of the huge direct and indirect costs of accidents, deaths, and illnesses, the effective enterprise tries hard to create safe and healthy conditions at work.

An unsafe or unhealthy work environment can also affect an employee's ability and motivation to work. As noted in Chapter 2, security/self-preservation is one of the most fundamental needs people have. Poor safety and health conditions are likely to endanger fulfillment of the security needs of employees.

Until recently, the typical response to concern about health and safety was to compensate the victims of job-related accidents with worker's compensation and similar insurance schemes. This chapter will discuss both the compensation approaches and the programs designed to prevent accidents, health hazards, and deaths at work.

A DIAGNOSTIC APPROACH TO SAFETY AND HEALTH

The environmental factors important to health and safety are highlighted in Exhibit 15–1. Probably the most crucial one is the nature of the task, especially

EXHIBIT 15–1
Factors affecting health and safety and organizational effectiveness

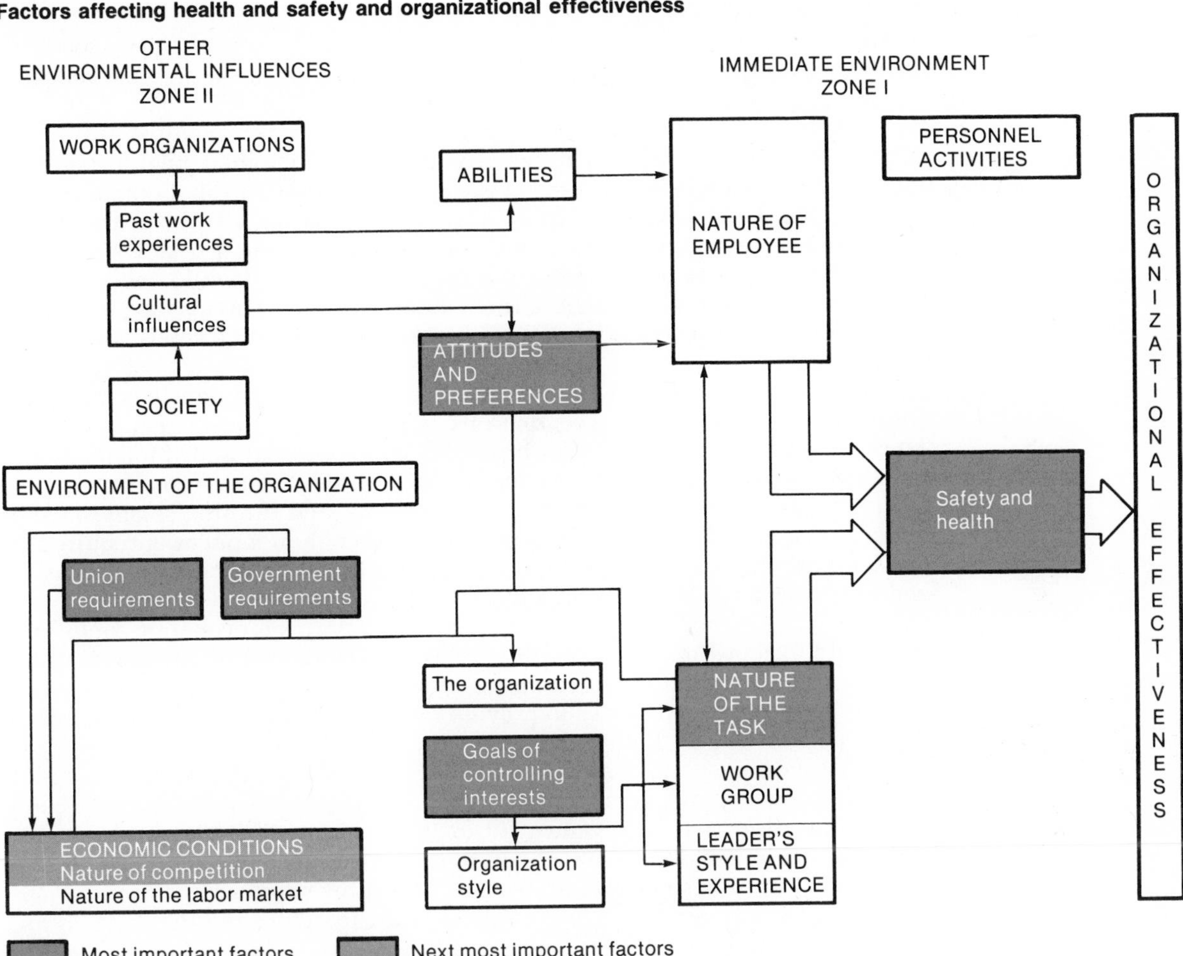

as it is affected by the technology and working conditions of the organizational environment. Health and safety problems are a lot more serious for coal miners, whose working conditions entail coal dust in the air, than for typists in the Social Security Administration. An X-ray technician has a much greater chance of getting cancer as a result of working conditions than does an elementary school teacher.

A second vital factor is employee attitudes toward health and safety; they can vary from concern for safety and cooperation regarding safety programs, to apathy. If employees are apathetic about it, the best employer safety program and the most stringent safety inspection by the government or the safety specialists in the personnel department will not be successful in improving safety and health conditions.

A third factor affecting health and safety on the job is government. Federal and state governments have attempted to legislate conditions to improve safety and health for some years. The government programs currently in operation will be discussed later.

A fourth factor is the trade unions. Many unions have been very concerned about the safety and health of their employees and have pressured employers in collective bargaining for better programs. Some unions have taken extraordinary steps to protect their members' health and safety. For example, the Teamsters Union recently hired a nationally known occupational health expert to investigate unexplained illnesses at the Robert Shaw Controls Company plant in Ohio. The United Rubber Workers' contract calls for a study of the effects of benzene on employees. The Oil, Chemical and Atomic Workers Union has been subsidizing medical student interns and residents to study occupational health conditions in plants where their members work. Unions also have used their political power to get legislation passed to improve the safety and health of members.

A fifth factor is management's goals. Some socially responsible managers and owners had active safety programs long before the laws required them. They made safety and health an important strategic goal and implemented it with significant safety considerations designed into the enterprise's layout. The safety program included safety statistics, contests, and training sessions. Other managers, not so safety conscious, did little other than what was required by law. Thus managerial attitudes play a large part in the significance of the health and safety program of the enterprise.

The final factor affecting health and safety programs is economic conditions. We would accept the worst possible assumptions about human nature if we believed that any employer *knowingly* would choose to provide dangerous working conditions or would refuse to provide reasonable safeguards for employees. But there is a lack of knowledge about the consequences of some dangerous working conditions, and even when there is such knowledge, economic conditions can prevent employers from doing all they might wish. The risks of being a uranium miner are well known: 10 to 11 percent will die of cancer within ten years. As long as there are no alternative methods and as long as there is a need for uranium, some employees will be risking shorter lives in these jobs. Engineers and scientists are constantly at work to determine the dangers and to prevent or mitigate the consequences. But the costs of some of the prevention programs are such that the enterprise may find them prohibitive, and may consider the programs economically infeasible.

WHO IS INVOLVED WITH SAFETY AND HEALTH?

As with other personnel functions, the success of a safety and health program requires the support and cooperation of operating and personnel managers. But it is more complicated than that. In some enterprises, safety is a separate function of its own. Exhibit 15–2 makes that clear. But it is still true that both operating and staff (either personnel or safety) have their parts to play to protect the employees.

Top management must support safety and health with an adequate budget. They must give it psychological support too. Acting on safety reports is another way top managers can be involved in these efforts. Without this support, the safety and health effort is hampered. Some enterprises have responded to the environmental problems which can increase accidents, deaths, and disabilities by placing the responsibility for employee health and safety with the chief exec-

William J. Danos
New Wales Chemicals, Inc.

Biography

William J. Danos, Safety Engineer of New Wales Chemicals, Inc., was graduated from Louisiana State University, Baton Rouge, with a degree in chemical engineering. He has had extensive training in the safety field, including the Industrial Hygiene Training Course (National Safety Council) and the Industrial Facilities Protection Program (Ft. Gordon, Georgia). Danos entered the safety field in 1959 as safety supervisor at Allied Chemical Corporation, Baton Rouge Works. Since that time he has held positions such as safety engineer for Boh Brothers Construction Company and safety supervisor for Uniroyal, Inc. He joined New Wales Chemicals in 1974.

In addition, Danos was editor of "The Chemical Treat," a magazine at Allied Chemical. He is a certified safety trainer and has served as National Safety and Health Chairman for ASPA.

Job description

As Safety Engineer at New Wales Chemicals, William J. Danos is responsible for total loss-control programs. This includes such areas as safety on the job, security, fire prevention, medical attention, and workers' compensation.

utive officer of the organization: the hospital administrator, the agency administrator, the company president. This is the approach taken by most smaller organizations that have health and safety threats, or middle-sized organizations with few health or safety threats. Operating managers also are responsible, since accidents and injuries will take place, and health hazards will exist, in the work unit. They must be aware of health and safety considerations and cooperate with the specialists who can help them reduce accidents and occupational illnesses.

In larger and some medium-sized enterprises, there is a safety unit in personnel. In some enterprises with 2,000 or more employees, safety can be an independent department. This chapter will illustrate what a safety and health specialist does.

EXHIBIT 15–2
Responsibility for compliance with OSHA

	Person assigned responsibility			
Function	*Safety specialist*	*Medical staffer*	*Personnel generalist*	*First-line supervisors*
Self-inspection for OSHA compliance	43.1%	1.4%	27.9%	28.9%
Recordkeeping and posting notices	25.6	9.6	61.9	6.8
Monitoring working environment	37.9	4.8	35.6	37.7
Safety training	38.7	3.3	36.6	30.8
First aid	14.4	35.9	26.0	25.5
Periodic medical testing	8.4	37.1	21.0	3.7
Communicating and enforcing safety and health rules	31.5	7.5	52.6	41.4

Source: Adapted from "The Personnel Executive's Job," *P-H Personnel Management: Policies and Practices,* December 14, 1976; published by Prentice-Hall, Inc., Englewood Cliffs, N.J. Reprinted with permission.

The success of the safety program rests primarily on how well employees and supervisors cooperate with safety rules and regulations. Often this relationship is formalized in the creation of a safety committee consisting of the safety specialist, representative employees, and managers.

Usually there are two levels of safety committees. At the policy level is the committee made up of major division heads; this committee sets safety policy and rules, investigates major hazards, and has budget responsibility. At the departmental level, both supervisors and managers are members. Safety committees are concerned with the organization's entire safety program: inspection, design, record keeping, training, and motivation programs. The more people who can be involved through the committees, the more likely is the program to be successful. Finally, the government inspector plays a role in keeping the enterprise on its toes regarding the safety of the employees.

Employee health and safety is a mature personnel function—Stage IV, as described in Exhibit 1–6 (Chapter 1). Many studies have been made of it, especially by engineers and psychologists.

CAUSES OF WORK ACCIDENTS AND WORK-RELATED ILLNESSES

Work accidents and work-related illnesses have many causes. The major causes of occupational accidents are:

- The task to be done.
- The working conditions.
- The nature of the employees.

Some examples of causes in the task and working conditions area include poorly designed or inadequately repaired machines, lack of protective equipment, and the presence of dangerous chemicals or gases. Other working conditions that contribute to accidents include excessive work hours leading to employee fatigue, noise, lack of proper lighting, boredom, and horseplay and fighting at work. The new National Institute for Occupational Safety and Health should find out more about the causes of accidents and occupational health hazards.

There are data to indicate that some employees have more accidents than the average. Such a person is said to be an accident repeater. These studies indicate that employees who (1) are under 30 years of age, (2) lack psychomotor and perceptual skills, (3) are impulsive, and (4) are easily bored are more likely to have accidents than others. Although some believe accident proneness can be measured by a set of attitude or motivational instruments, most experts who have examined the data carefully do not believe that attitudinal-motivational "causes" of accidents are a significant influence on accident rates. We need to know much more about accident proneness before such serious actions as attempting to screen out the "accident prone" person.

The rest of the chapter will describe what organizations and governments have done and are doing to decrease work-related accidents and illnesses.

ORGANIZATIONAL RESPONSES TO HEALTH AND SAFETY CHALLENGES

The safety department or unit and the safety committee can take three approaches to improving the safety of working conditions:

- Prevention and design.
- Inspection and research.
- Training and motivation.

Bob Undine's plant took all three approaches.

Safety design and preventive approaches

Numerous preventive measures have been adopted by organizations in attempts to improve their safety records. One is to design more safety into the workplace through safety engineering. Engineers have helped through the study of human-factors engineering, which seeks to make jobs more comfortable, less confusing and less fatiguing. This can keep employees more alert and less open to accidents.

Safety engineers design safety into the workplace with the analytical design approach. This total design approach analyzes all factors involved in the job. Included are such factors as speed of the assembly line, stresses in the work, and job design. On the basis of this analysis, steps are taken to improve safety precautions. Protective guards are designed for machinery and equipment. Color coding warns of dangerous areas. Standard safety colors, which should be taught in safety classes, include gray for machinery and red where the area presents danger of fire. Other dangers are highlighted by orange paint.

Examples of safety equipment

Protective clothing and devices are also supplied for employees working in hazardous job situations. These can include:

Head protection, principally with helmets.

Eye and face protection, with goggles, face shields, and spectacles.

Hearing protection, with muffs and inserts.

Respiratory protection, with air-purifying devices such as filter respirators and gas masks, and air-supplying devices.

Hand protection, with gloves.

Foot and leg protection, with safety shoes, boots, guards, and leggings.

Body protection, with garments such as suits, aprons, jackets, and coveralls.

Belts and lifelines to prevent those working in high places from falling.

The few studies on the effectiveness of these preventive design measures indicate that they do reduce accidents.

Well-designed rest periods increase safety and productivity, as do clearly understood rules and regulations. These rules should be developed from analyses of equipment and conditions such as flammability. No-smoking areas and hard hat areas where safety helmets are required for all employees and visitors are examples. Effective selection and placement of employees can also improve safety. It makes sense, for example, to assign the physically handicapped where their handicaps cannot add to the possibility of accidents.

Inspection, reporting, and accident research

A second activity of safety departments or specialists is to inspect the workplace with the goal of reducing accidents and illnesses. The safety specialist is looking for a number of things, including answers to these questions:

Are safety rules being observed? How many near misses were there?

Are safety guards, protective equipment, and so on being used?

Are there potential hazards in the workplace that safety redesign could improve?

Are there potential occupational health hazards?

A related activity is to investigate accidents or "close calls" to determine the facts for insurance purposes. More important, such investigations also can determine preventive measures that should be taken in the future. Following an accident requiring more than first aid treatment, the safety specialist, personnel specialist, or manager must *investigate* and report the facts to the government and insurance companies. These data are also used to analyze the causes of accidents, with a view to preventing possible recurrences.

Reporting of accidents and occupational illnesses is an important part of the safety specialist's job. Usually, the report is filled out by the injured employee's supervisor and checked by the safety specialist. The supervisor compiles the report because he or she usually is present when the accident occurs. And doing so requires the supervisor to think about safety in the unit and what can be done to prevent similar accidents.

At regular intervals during the work year, safety and personnel specialists carry out *accident research,* that is, systematic evaluation of the evidence concerning accidents and health hazards. Data for this research should be gathered from both external and internal sources. Safety and health journals point out recent findings which should stimulate the safety specialist to look for hazardous conditions at the workplace. Reports from the National Institute of Occupational Safety and Health, a research organization created by OSHA legislation, also provide important data inputs for research. Data developed at the workplace will include accident reports, inspection reports by government and the organization's safety specialists, and recommendations of the safety committees.

Accident research often involves computation of organizational accident rates. These are compared to industry and national figures to determine the organization's relative safety performance. Several statistics are computed. Accident frequency rate is computed as follows:

$$\text{Frequency rate} = \frac{\text{Number of accidents} \times 200{,}000}{\text{Number of work hours in the period}}.$$

The accidents used in this computation are those causing the worker to lose work time.

The second statistic is the accident severity rate. This is computed as follows:

$$\text{Accident severity rate} = \frac{\text{Number of work days lost} \times 200{,}000}{\text{Number of work hours in the period}}.$$

OSHA suggests reporting accidents as number of injuries per 100 full-time employees per year, as a simpler approach. The formula is:

$$\frac{\text{Number of illnesses and injuries}}{\text{Total hours worked by all employees for the year}} \times 200{,}000.$$

The base equals the number of workers employed (full-time equivalent) working full time (for example 40 hours per week and for 49 weeks if vacation is three weeks).

The enterprise's statistics should be compared with the industry's statistics and government statistics (from the Department of Labor and OSHA). Most studies find that although effective accident research should be very complex, in reality it is unsophisticated and unscientific.

Safety training and motivation programs

The third approach organizations take to safety is training and motivation programs. Safety training usually is part of the orientation program. It also takes place during the employee's career. This training is usually voluntary, but some is required by government agencies.

The techniques used vary (Chapter 9 described most of them). Studies of the effectiveness of such training are mixed. Some studies indicate that some methods, such as job instruction training (JIT) and accident simulations, are more effective than others. Others contend that the employees' perception that management really believes in safety training accounts for its success. Negative studies find that the programs make employees more *aware* of safety, but not necessarily more safe in their behavior. Effectively developed safety training programs can help provide a safer environment for all employees.

Safety specialists have also tried to improve safety conditions and accident statistics by various motivation devices such as contests and communication

A safety training class

programs. These are intended to reinforce safety training. One device is to place posters around the workplace with slogans such as "A Safe Worker Is a Happy Worker." Posters are available from the National Safety Council or can be prepared for the enterprise. Communication programs also include items in company publications and safety booklets, and billboards. The billboard in front of Bob Undine's plant, for example, read:

> Welcome to American Manufacturing Company
>
> A Good Place to Work
> A Safe Place to Work
>
> We have had no accidents for
> 182 days

Sometimes safety communications are tied into a safety contest. If lower accidents result over a period, an award is given. The little research that has been done on safety communications and contests is mixed. Some believe they are useful. Others contend they have no effect or produce undesirable side effects, such as failure to report accidents or a large number of accidents once the contest is over or has been lost.

In general, too little is known scientifically at this point to recommend use or reduction of safety motivation programs. One example of the needed research is a study which examined the conditions under which safety motivation and education programs were effective in a shelving manufacturing company. It found that:

- There are safety-conscious people and others who are unaware of safety. The safety-conscious people were influenced by safety posters.
- Safety booklets were influential to the safety-conscious employees when their work group was also safety-conscious.
- Five-minute safety talks by supervisors were effective when the work group was safety-conscious and when the supervisor was safety-conscious.
- Safety training was effective on the safety-conscious employee when the supervisor and top management were safety-conscious.
- Safety inspections were effective when the work group and supervisor were safety-conscious.

Auditing safety programs

It is all very well to design organization safety programs. But to assure that the program is put into effect, most enterprises need to audit the program while it is underway. One expert suggests an audit committee composed of the safety professional, the supervisor, and the supervisor's superior. Others propose that nonaccident measures be used to supplement accident measures as standards for the audits.

Health programs for employees

Some larger enterprises maintain their own medical and health facilities. Bernard Burbank notes that these facilities provide various kinds of services for employees and employers. Their responsibilities can include such matters as:

- Treating accidents and medical emergencies at work.
- Performing physical examinations in conjunction with the selection of employees.
- Evaluating possible health hazards involved in transfers of employees to different regions or countries.
- Advising management on health hazards associated with the use of materials, chemicals in manufacture, or consumer usage of products.
- Advising management on health-related problems of employees, such as drug addiction, alcoholism, and emotional problems.
- Undertaking preventive medicine through periodic examinations and immunization and group surveys for diabetes, cancer, TB, and heart disease.

Many of these functions are more important now than in the past because of government regulations (to be discussed shortly). To the list of activities Burbank provides, two more can be added which have received more emphasis recently:

- Supervising physical fitness programs for executives and other employees.
- Supervising mental health counseling and stress-reduction programs.

Equipment to check for hearing problems

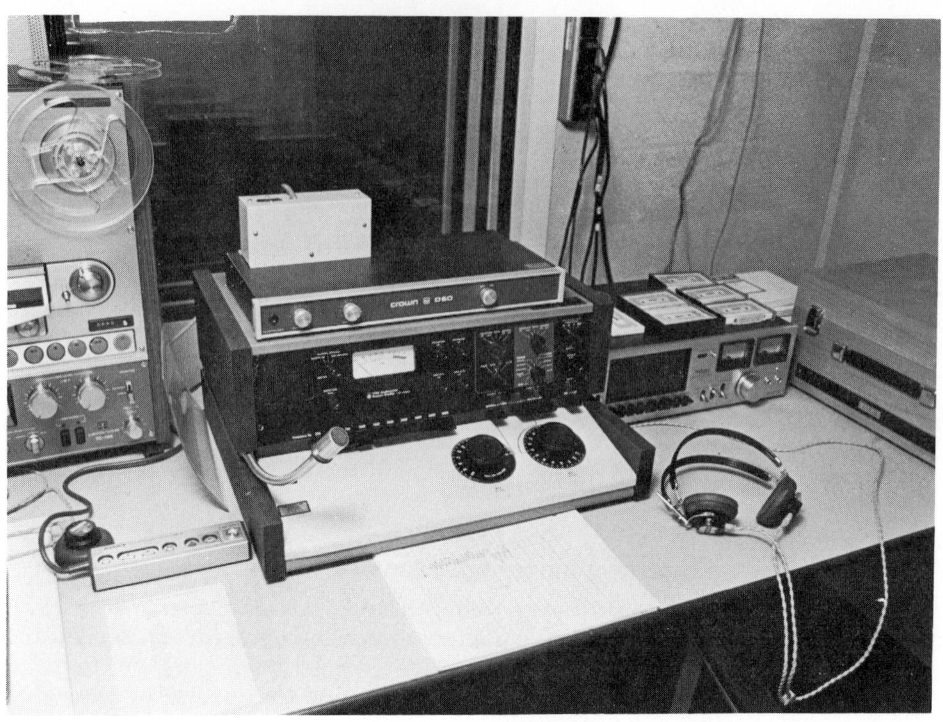

The type of programs available depends on two crucial variables: organization size and degree of health hazards on the job. The larger the company and the more hazardous the jobs, the more likely it is that on-site health programs will be available. Burbank maintains that small (under 500 employees), nonhazardous organizations near medical facilities do not need their own health programs. Organizations from 500 to 1,500 employees should have a nurse, physician on retainer, and health facilities consisting of several rooms. Larger enterprises (with more than 1,500 employees) will need two nurses and one additional nurse per thousand employees; a full-time physician should be hired when there are 2,500 employees.

Health programs are much less widespread than safety programs, and there are considerable differences between industries and enterprises on their use.

GOVERNMENT RESPONSES TO HEALTH AND SAFETY PROBLEMS

Although many enterprises (like Bob Undine's) have done a good job of safeguarding the safety and health of their employees, with little or no supervision from government sources, others (like Clint Woodley's) have not. This has led governments to become involved in holding the enterprise responsible for prevention of accidents, disabilities, illnesses, and deaths related to the tasks workers perform and the conditions under which they work.

Prior to passage of the Occupational Safety and Health Act (OSHA) in 1970, the feeling was that private enterprise had not done enough to assure safe and healthy working conditions. The federal law in effect, the Walsh-Healy Act, was thought to be too weak or inadequately enforced, and state programs were incomplete, diverse, and lacked authority.

Lobbying by unions and employees led to the passage of several federal laws related to specific occupations, such as the Coal Mine Health and Safety Act of 1969 and the related Black Lung Benefits Act of 1972. The movement for federal supervision of health and safety programs culminated in passage of the Occupational Safety and Health Act.

OSHA, the product of three years of bitter legislative lobbying, was designed to remedy safety problems on the job. The compromise law that was enacted initially received wide support. Its purpose was to provide employment "free from recognized hazards" to employees. OSHA provisions originally applied to 4.1 million businesses and 57 million employees in almost every enterprise engaged in interstate commerce.

OSHA has been enforced by federal inspectors or in partnership with state safety and health agencies. It encourages the states to assume responsibility for developing and administering occupational and health laws and carrying out their own statistical programs. Before being granted full authority for its programs, a state must go through three steps. First, the state plan must have the preliminary approval of OSHA. Second, the state promises to take "developmental steps" to do certain things at certain times, such as adjusting legislation, hiring inspectors, and providing for an industrial hygiene laboratory. OSHA monitors the state plan for three years, and if the state fulfills these obligations, the third step is a trial period at full-enforcement levels for at least a year. At the end of this intensive evaluation period, a final decision is made by OSHA on the qualifications of the state program.

If OSHA and the employer fail to provide safe working conditions, employees as individuals or their unions can seek injunctions against the employer to force it to do so or submit to an inspection of the workplace. The employer cannot discriminate against an employee who takes these actions. OSHA has many requirements, but the three that most directly affect most employers are:

- Meeting safety standards set by OSHA.
- Submiting to OSHA inspections.
- Keeping records and reporting accidents and illnesses.

OSHA safety standards

OSHA has established safety standards, defined as those "practices, means, operations, or processes, reasonably necessary to provide safe . . . employment." The standards can affect any aspect of the workplace; new standards were established or proposed, for example, for such factors as lead, mercury, silica, benzene, talc dust, cotton dust, noise, and general health hazards. The standards may be industrywide or apply only to a specific enterprise.

OSHA safety standards

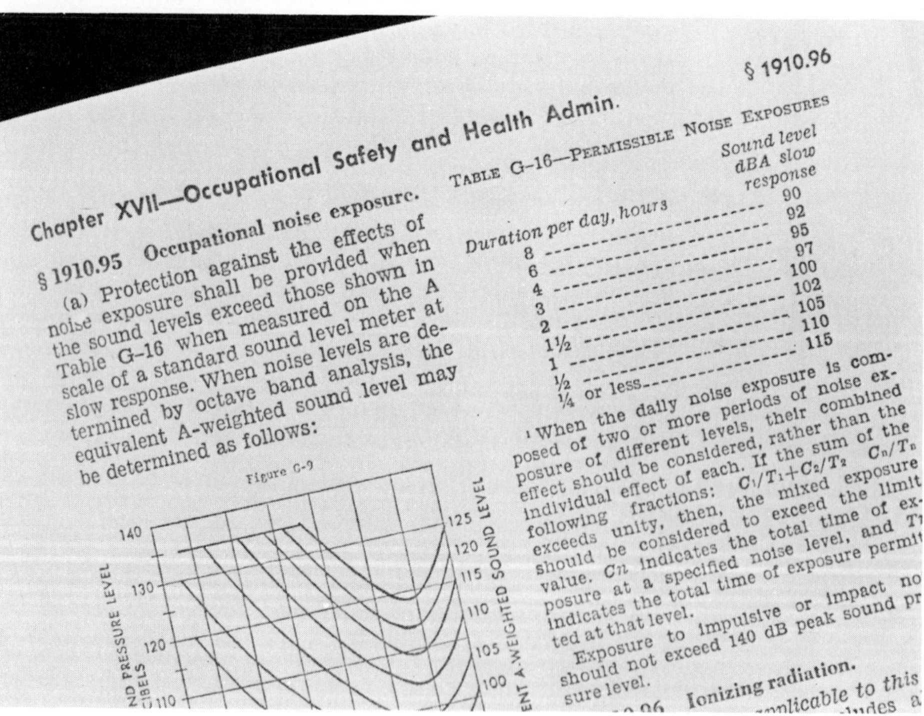

§ 1910.96

Chapter XVII—Occupational Safety and Health Admin.

§ 1910.95 Occupational noise exposure.

(a) Protection against the effects of noise exposure shall be provided when the sound levels exceed those shown in Table G-16 when measured on the A scale of a standard sound level meter at slow response. When noise levels are determined by octave band analysis, the equivalent A-weighted sound level may be determined as follows:

Figure G-9

TABLE G-16—PERMISSIBLE NOISE EXPOSURES

Duration per day, hours	Sound level dBA slow response
8	90
6	92
4	95
3	97
2	100
1½	102
1	105
½	110
¼ or less	115

[1] When the daily noise exposure is composed of two or more periods of noise exposure of different levels, their combined effect should be considered, rather than the individual effect of each. If the sum of the following fractions: $C_1/T_1+C_2/T_2$ C_n/T_n exceeds unity, then, the mixed exposure should be considered to exceed the limit value. Cn indicates the total time of exposure at a specified noise level, and Tn indicates the total time of exposure permitted at that level.

Exposure to impulsive or impact noise should not exceed 140 dB peak sound pr[illegible] sure level.

Ionizing radiation.

The Secretary of Labor revises, modifies, or revokes existing standards or creates new ones on his own initiative or on the basis of petitions from interested parties (employees or unions). The National Institute of Occupational Safety and Health in the Department of Health, Education, and Welfare is responsible for doing research from which standards are developed and for training those involved to implement them. OSHA, an agency of the Department of Labor, administers the act. Federal or national consensus standards (such as those of the National Fire Protection Association) have also become OSHA standards. And temporary emergency standards can be created for imminent danger. Employers may be granted temporary variances by showing inability to comply with a standard within the time allowed, if they have a plan to protect employees against the hazard.

The employer is responsible for knowing what these standards are and abiding by them. This is not easy. The *initial* standards were published in *The Federal Register* in 350 pages of small print, and interpretations of the standards are issued yearly *by volume.* One recent annual volume was 780 pages long! OSHA officers work with compliance operations manuals two inches thick. Even the *checklist* which summarizes the general industry standards is 11 pages long and lists 80 items. The responsible manager is subject to thousands of pages of such standards. If they are not met, an enterprise can be shut down, and the responsible manager can be fined or jailed for not meeting them.

OSHA inspections

To make sure the law is obeyed, OSHA inspectors visit places of employment, on their own schedules or on invitation of an employer, union, or employee. An employee who requests an inspection need not be identified to the employer. If the employer is found guilty of a violation, the penalties include (1) willful or repeated violations, $10,000 per violation; (2) citation for serious violation, $1,000 each; (3) citation for less serious violation, up to $1,000 discretionary; (4) failure to correct cited violation, $1,000 per day; (5) willful violation causing death, up to $10,000 or up to six months in jail; (6) falsification of statements or records, up to $10,000 and/or six months in jail. For example, in 1977, OSHA fined Dawes Laboratories a record $34,100 for allegedly unsafe conditions.

A recent Supreme Court decision ruled that employers can bar OSHA job safety inspectors from their workplaces if the inspectors don't have a search warrant. But these warrants have been made easier to obtain. They can be issued by a court in advance without notifying the employer, so the surprise element of the inspection can be maintained.

If you think this is bad, France has started jailing its plant managers for safety violations. American managers ought to be pleased they don't have to comply with Hammurabi's safety code, which was quite severe even by present standards.

OSHA inspectors examine the premises for compliance and the records for

accuracy. They categorize a violation as imminent danger (in which case they can close the place down), serious (which calls for a major fine), nonserious (fine up to $1,000), or de minimus (small—a notification is given, but no fine.) In 1977, Atlas Roofing (Georgia) and Frank Irey (Pennsylvania) argued that fining without court action violated the Seventh Amendment, but the Supreme Court supported OSHA unanimously. The employer has the right to appeal fines or citations within OSHA (up to the level of the OSHA Review Commission) or in the courts.

OSHA tries to portray their inspectors as helpful to employees and employers, but employers seldom see it that way. Frank & Ernest (in the cartoon agree) with these employers.

OSHA record keeping and reporting

The third major OSHA requirement is that the employer keep standardized records of illnesses and injuries and calculate accident ratios. These shown to

EXHIBIT 15–3

OSHA injury and illness reporting form

VIII. Injury and Illness Summary (covering calendar year 1977)

Instructions:
- This section may be completed by copying data from OSHA Form No. 102 "Summary, Occupational Injuries and Illnesses," which you are required to complete and post in your establishment.
- Leave Section VIII blank if there were no recordable injuries or illnesses during 1977.
- Code 30 – Add all occupational illnesses (Code 21 + 22 + 23 + 24 + 25 + 26 + 29) and enter on this line for each column (3) through (8).
- Code 31 – Add occupational injuries (Code 10) and the sum of all occupational illnesses (Code 30) and enter on this line for each column (3) through (8).

			Fatalities (deaths)	Lost workday cases			Nonfatal cases without lost workdays*	
Code (1)		Category (2)	(3)	Number of cases (4)	Number of cases involving permanent transfer to another job or termination of employment (5)	Number of lost workdays (6)	Number of cases (7)	Number of cases involving transfer to another job or termination of employment (8)
10		Occupational injuries						
21	Occupational illnesses	Occupational skin diseases or disorders						
22		Dust diseases of the lungs (pneumoconioses)						
23		Respiratory conditions due to toxic agents						
24		Poisoning (systemic effects of toxic materials)						
25		Disorders due to physical agents (other than toxic materials)						
26		Disorders due to repeated trauma						
29		All other occupational illnesses						
30		Sum of all occupational illnesses (Add Codes 21 through 29)						
31		Total of all occupational injuries and illnesses (Add Codes 10 + 30)						

*Nonfatal cases without lost workdays—Cases resulting in: Medical treatment beyond first aid, diagnosis of occupational illness, loss of consciousness, restriction of work or motion, or transfer to another job (without lost workdays).

Comments: __________

IX. Report prepared by: __________ Date: __________

Title: __________ Area code and phone: __________

EXHIBIT 15–4
Guide for reporting and recording accidents, illnesses, and deaths

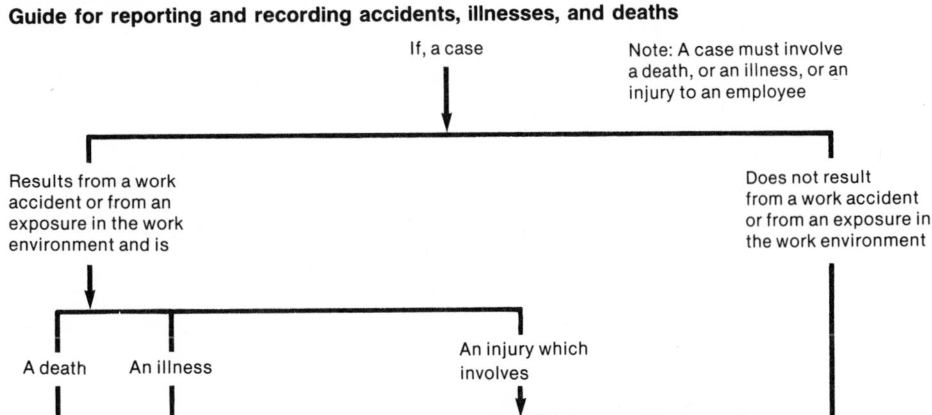

Source: U.S. Department of Labor, Bureau of Labor Statistics, *Occupational Safety and Health Statistics: Concepts and Methods,* BLS Report 438 (Washington, D.C., 1975).

OSHA compliance officers who ask to see them. The form used is shown in Exhibit 15–3. In 1979, a new form will be issued. Accidents and illnesses that must be reported are those that result in deaths, disabilities that cause the employee to miss work, and medical-care injuries that require treatment by a physician.

An OSHA guide to when to report and record an illness, injury, or death is shown in Exhibit 15–4. Injuries or illnesses that require only first aid and involve no loss of work time need not be reported. Employers go to great lengths to categorize incidents as "minor injuries," trying to treat them through first aid and keeping the employee on the job (even a make-work job), to avoid reporting them. To do so might lead to an OSHA inspection or raise their workers' compensation insurance rates. The employer must also report accident frequency and severity rates. The firm must also post OSHA Form 102 in a prominent place at work. It is a summary of the injuries and illnesses report.

Some consequences of OSHA

It is generally agreed that OSHA has had a very rocky hisory thus far. Most experts believe it has fallen far short of its promise. Let's examine each of the responsibilities to make that criticism clear.

Safety standards six years later. The general conclusion of most experts is that the agency's standards are unreadable, arbitrary, overly specific, too oriented toward trivia, too costly to implement, and unworkable. As an example of the trivia in the OSHA standards in circulation, in a publication on ranch safety it suggested to ranchers that "since dangerous gases come from manure pits, you should be careful not to fall into manure pits." I don't suppose many ranchers willingly fall into them, with or without dangerous gases.

A more critical condition than the poor quality of the standards is the fact that many of them originally were not in written form. In the first five years, only three new sets of standards were written. Many others are still in the process. OSHA has difficulty writing standards for existing technology, but it *really* has problems with new technologies where no standards exist. It is very difficult to adjust old standards to new technologies.

OSHA is under attack from many directions and is giving way on some standards. For example, it is not going to enforce the standards for small businesses. In 1978, OSHA responded to criticism of its standards. It revoked 928 rules that account for 10 percent of the 1977 standards and would try to eliminate more which are trivial or outdated. Further progress like this would be appreciated by most enterprises. OSHA is also trying to rewrite its standards to make them more readable. And it has been required by the courts to justify some of its standards, as in *AFL–CIO* v. *Brennan.*

What is needed is a whole new strategy for standard setting and enforcement. In the same way OSHA did not try to inspect all industries equally but created priorities based upon known hazardous occupations, all standards should not have equal emphasis. In the standards already set, the readability should be improved. More importantly, the agency should categorize the subparts of the standards into categories based on likelihood of accident or illness. These categories might be:

Most important. To be enforced at once and fully.

Of average importance. To be enforced later and in the spirit, not the letter, of the regulation.

Desirable. To be enforced when the most important standards and those of average importance are in full compliance.

If the standards were publicized to highlight these weights, employers could live with OSHA a bit more easily.

Consequences of inspections. To enforce the law, on-site inspections are required. The records of the first several years of enforcement show:

1970–71 . . . 29,255 locations inspected; 45 percent penalized.
1972 . . . . . . 36,100 inspections, with 125,400 violations and fines of $3,121,000.
1970–73 . . . 95 percent of all sites *not* inspected.
1973 . . . . . . 98 percent of violations were nonserious; average fine $18.
1974 . . . . . . 150,000 inspections by state officials; 54,461 federal inspections.
1975 . . . . . . From January to August; 42,791 citations issued, with fines of $6,121,638, an average of $743.

OSHA does not inspect each industry with equal frequency. Initially, they set up five target industries to be inspected often because of their high rates of accidents: longshoring; roof and sheet metal work; meat packing; miscellaneous transportation (mobile homes), and lumber and wood products. Later foundries and casting and metal-stamping industries were added to the target industries list. Target health hazard industries are those involving asbestos, carbon monoxide, cotton dust, lead, and silica. The ten areas where violations were found most frequently are given in Exhibit 15–5.

An employer who wishes to appeal a violation citation can do so within OSHA, through the Occupational Safety and Health Review Commission, or through the federal courts.

Generally speaking, neither management nor labor has been happy with the inspections, one side claiming too few, the other too many. The recent Supreme Court decision regarding the need for search warrants is a result. Because of a shortage of inspectors and this court ruling and because OSHA recognizes that it cannot enforce the law without the employers' help, the agency has begun to emphasize voluntary compliance. This consists of educational programs and "dry run" inspections in which the employer is advised of hazards but is given a chance to correct them before a citation is issued. Current OSHA administration would like to shift to a service or advisory approach rather than fines and citations. Congress appears ready to approve a program in which OSHA will advise employers if a visit is desired and will not issue citations on that visit.

Consequences of record keeping and reporting. Few people would quarrel with the need to keep adequate records on accidents and health and to calculate accident ratios. It seems reasonable for them to be recorded and reported in a standardized way, for ease in summarizing. But OSHA has been severely criticized for the amount of paperwork required and the frequent changes in it.

The Commission on Federal Paperwork was especially critical of OSHA in 1976, when it issued a complex study of job-safety paperwork which made 26 separate recommendations to the Secretary of Labor. The commission suggested that employers with fewer than 100 workers be exempt from keeping logs of

EXHIBIT 15–5
OSHA's terrible 10

Area of violation	*Violations in fiscal year 1975*	*Penalties levied (in thousands)*
National Electrical Code requirements (from loose wires to ungrounded equipment)	37,273	$493.3
Safety of abrasive wheel machinery	6,662	37.1
Construction and placement of compressed gas containers	6,196	59.0
Marking of exits	6,121	14.1
Safety of pulleys in mechanical power-transmission gear	6,037	75.6
Maintaining portable fire extinguishers	5,965	29.6
Safety of drives in mechanical power-transmission gear	5,431	53.2
Guarding floor and wall openings, platforms, and runways	5,321	140.2
General housekeeping requirements (from unmopped puddles to flammable rubbish piles)	5,204	74.8
Effectiveness of machinery guards	4,779	157.3

Data: OSHA.
Source: "Why Nobody Wants to Listen to OSHA." Reprinted from the June 14, 1976 issue of *Business Week* by special permission.

injuries and illnesses, that the government assume the cost of monitoring the medical condition of workers in hazardous plants, and that certain duplicate reports required of companies and state governments be dropped. OSHA needs to act soon to improve its paperwork procedures.

Overall evaluation of OSHA

How can we evaluate a program which in 1975 cost enterprises $3.2 billion to implement, not counting the costs of wages and salaries? So far, there is only impressionistic evidence on the "It's doing a great job" versus "It's a failure" issue. Ashford, who had great hopes for OSHA, concluded his Ford Foundation report in 1976 by saying "The OSHA Act has failed thus far to live up to its potential for reducing job injury and disease." General Motors pointed out that although it was spending $15 per car to implement OSHA, and although up to 1975 GM had been inspected 614 times, received 258 citations, and spent $29,000,000 to fulfill the requirements (and 11,000,000 *worker-years* to get in compliance) "there was no correlation between meeting OSHA's regulations and reduction of accidents."

On the positive side, one study reported a 30 percent drop in meat-packing accidents (one of OSHA's target industries) since the agency came into being and attributes this to OSHA regulations. Another study reports decreased accidents in utilities since OSHA regulations took effect. OSHA claims that in 1975 injuries were down 16 percent and deaths down 10 percent from 1974. How much of this was due to unemployment and non–OSHA causes is not known. One expert says workers like OSHA three times better than the state plans, and in general, OSHA does seem to be making progress in research through the National Institute of Occupational Safety and Health. It has begun to build a strategy for safety research and a systematic way to set target-industry strategies.

Ultimately, whether OSHA succeeds or fails depends on a decrease in the number and severity of accidents and the incidence of occupational disease in the working population. OSHA's annual reports are phrased in bureaucratic "success" terms such as increases in numbers of inspections, pamphlets printed, and dollars of research spent. Until it can show that the *costs* of enforcement are exceeded by *benefits* in terms of reduced accidents and fewer disease victims, we shall have to wait and see whether the program should be called a success or a bureaucratic nightmare.

Management feels that an important factor is not presently covered in OSHA's approach: the worker's responsibility for his or her own health and safety. All the responsibility is placed on *management*. For example, if employees wish to skip medical tests to determine if they are developing an occupational disease, OSHA has ruled they can. If an employee refuses to cooperate in safety matters and an OSHA inspector finds a violation, the *company* is held responsible. For example, there are many instances of employees refusing to wear the safety equipment recommended by OSHA. If the inspector sees this, he *fines the company*. All the company can do is discipline (or possibly fire) the employee.

What can the operating manager or personnel specialist do to help keep the enterprise in compliance with OSHA? The personnel specialist should know the standards that apply to the enterprise and check to see that they are being met. Personnel is also responsible for keeping OSHA records up to date and filing them on time. The operating manager must know the standards that apply to her or his unit or department and see that the unit meets the standards.

As citizens, all managers should see to it that OSHA is effective at the enterprise. But they can also write their representatives to improve it so that:

Standards are understandable and focus on important items.
Advisory inspections are permitted.
Records and reports are minimized and efficient.

Together, managers and OSHA can make safety and health at work a reality.

WORKERS' COMPENSATION AND DISABILITY PROGRAMS

Disability programs are designed to help workers who are ill or injured and cannot work (see Chapters 13 and 14). Employees show little preference for them. Although before his accident Dale Silas was probably not too interested in workers' compensation, he is now. He's also interested in Lysander's health insurance plan.

There are three programs in the United States for private- and third-sector employees. One is federal. The social security system is called OASDI, and the

Workers' compensation form

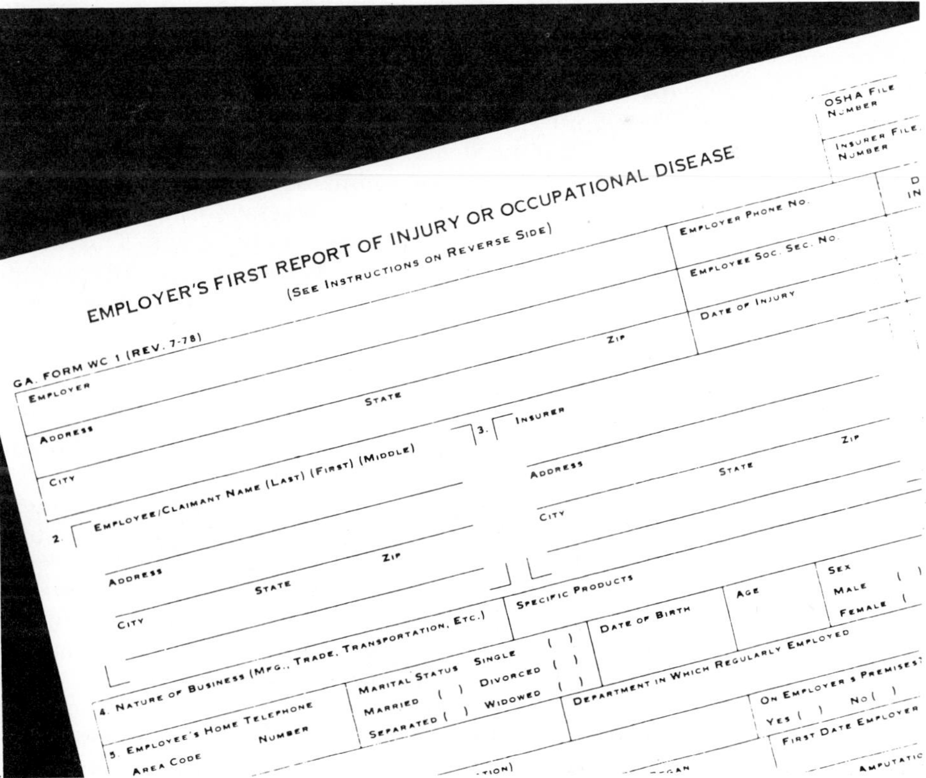

OSHA File Number
Insurer File Number

EMPLOYER'S FIRST REPORT OF INJURY OR OCCUPATIONAL DISEASE
(See Instructions on Reverse Side)

GA. FORM WC 1 (REV. 7-78)

Employer
Address
City
State
Zip
Employer Phone No.
Employee Soc. Sec. No.
Date of Injury

2. Employee/Claimant Name (Last) (First) (Middle)
Address
City
State
Zip

3. Insurer
Address
City
State
Zip

4. Nature of Business (Mfg., Trade, Transportation, Etc.)
Specific Products
Date of Birth
Age
Sex Male ( ) Female (

5. Employee's Home Telephone Area Code Number
Marital Status Single ( ) Married ( ) Divorced ( ) Separated ( ) Widowed ( )
Department in Which Regularly Employed
On Employer's Premises? Yes ( ) No ( )
First Date Employer

"DI" stands for disability insurance. A person who is totally disabled and unable to work can receive a small payment, perhaps $60 a week, from social security until age 65. As with other social security programs, this is financed by employer and employee payroll contributions.

The second program is the state-run workers' compensation, financed by employer payments. It pays for permanent partial, total partial, or total disability arising out of the employment situation. Requirements, payments, and procedures vary somewhat from state to state. Workers' compensation systems are compulsory in most states. For federal government employees, the Federal Employees Compensation Act of 1949 (last amended in 1974) provides for payments for accidents and injuries paralleling workers' compensation.

The compensation comes in two forms: monetary reimbursement, and payment of medical expenses. The amount of compensation is based on fixed schedules of minimum and maximum payments. Disability payments are often based on formulas of the employee's earnings, modified by economic conditions such as the number of dependents. There is usually a week's waiting period prior to the payment of the compensation and fixed compensation for permanent losses (such as $200 for loss of a finger).

The employee receives workers' compensation no matter whose fault an accident is. Payment is made for physical impairments and for neuroses which may result from a physical loss. The employer must also pay compensation for diseases which result from occupations (such as black lung disease in mining) and for the results of undue stress laid on employees, such as hernias resulting from lifting heavy materials. Both workers' compensation laws and OSHA require the employer to keep detailed accident and death records.

The employer pays the entire cost of workers' compensation, usually by participating in private insurance plans or state-run schemes or by self-insurance. The improvement of safety conditions at the work site can lead to lower insurance costs if accidents decline as a result.

The cost of workers' compensation varies by industry and type of work. For example, in a recent year, the average firm devoted less than 1 percent of its total compensation to workers' compensation. This varied from 1.5 percent for nonoffice, nonmanufacturing jobs to a low of 0.03 percent for office employees. But workers' compensation claims went from $3.9 to $7.8 billion from 1972 to 1977. Industry claims that the proposed Williams Javits Bill would triple the cost of workers' compensation insurance and that many insurance companies would withdraw from participation.

In some states, if the employee will receive social security disability payments, workers' compensation is adjusted so that a joint maximum (for example, $80 per week) is not exceeded.

Criticism of workers' compensation programs centers on the fact that the systems were designed to prevent hardship but not to discourage return to work or rehabilitation of the injured worker. The National Commission on State Workers' Compensation was very critical of state workers' compensation plans. It found that the benefits are too low, and too many employers have inadequate accident prevention programs. The commission made 80 specific recommendations to the states which, if not actuated, should be legislated by Congress.

The third program under which employees receive workers' compensation is private disability insurance provided by employers. About two thirds of the companies surveyed provide accident and sickness insurance to their employees (usually for blue-collar workers). A variation for white-collar workers is sick pay–salary continuance insurance. About 85 percent of the companies surveyed have this. These plans pay wages or salaries to employees with short-term disabilities. Generally they supplement workers' compensation. Long-term disability pay or pensions for employees was also being offered by 74 percent of companies surveyed for managers, 62 percent for white-collar employees, and 28 percent for blue-collar workers. This insurance is designed to supplement government programs and bring total compensation up to a more livable level. Luckily for Dale Silas, Lysander does have disability coverage.

EVALUATION OF SAFETY AND HEALTH PROGRAMS

Health and (especially) safety programs have begun to receive more attention in recent years. The consequences of inadequate programs are measurable: increased workers' compensation payments, larger insurance costs, fines from OSHA, and union pressures. A safety management program requires these steps.

Establishment of indicator systems (for example, accident statistics).

Development of effective reporting systems.

Development of rules and procedures.

Rewarding supervisors for effective management of the safety function.

Top management support is needed, and proper design of jobs and man-machine interactions is necessary, but probably the key is participation by employees.

A health and safety program can be evaluated fairly directly in a cost/benefits sense. The costs of safety specialists, new safety devices, and other measures can be calculated. Reductions in accidents, lowered insurance costs, and lowered fines can be weighed against these costs. Studies evaluating safety and health programs show that safety is cost effective.

In a very sophisticated study, Foster Rinefort interviewed 54 respondents and received questionnaires from 86 more in the chemical, paper, and wood-product industries in Texas. Rinefort found that the most cost-effective safety programs were *not* the most expensive ones. They were programs which combined a number of safety approaches: safety rules, off-the-job safety, safety training, safety orientation, safety meetings, medical facilities and staff, and strong top-management participation and support of the safety program. Engineering and nonengineering approaches were used, but the emphasis was on the engineering aspects of safety. Cost/benefits studies for health and safety programs can be very helpful in analyzing and improving them.

SUMMARY, CONCLUSIONS, AND RECOMMENDATIONS

Effective safety and health programs can exist in all enterprises. The nature of the safety program varies, of course, as the diagnostic approach emphasizes. Some clues to this are given in the statements below:

1. Safety hazards are those aspects of the work environment which have the potential of immediate and sometimes violent harm to an employee.

2. Health hazards are those aspects of the work environment which slowly and cumulatively lead to deterioration of an employee's health.
3. Support from top management and unions for health and safety programs helps assure their effectiveness.
4. The major causes of occupational accidents are the task to be done, the working conditions, and the employee.
5. Organizational responses to health and safety challenges include:
   a. Safety design and preventive approaches.
   b. Inspection, reporting, and accident research.
   c. Safety training and motivation programs.
   d. Auditing safety programs.
   e. Health programs for employees.
6. The Occupational Safety and Health Act was the culmination of the movement for federal supervision of health and safety programs. It has requirements such as:
   a. Meeting safety standards set by OSHA.
   b. Submitting to OSHA inspections.
   c. Keeping records and reporting accidents and illnesses.
7. Workers' compensation and disability programs are designed to help workers who are ill or injured and cannot work.

Exhibit 15–6 gives the recommendations on health and safety for the model organizations described in Exhibit 1–7 (Chapter 1).

The next chapter develops a topic which is often discussed in the newspapers and other media these days; equal employment opportunity.

EXHIBIT 15–6

Recommendations on health and safety for model organizations

Type of organization	*Formal safety department*	*Safety as duty of personnel specialist*	*Formal health department*	*Arrangement with health team*
1. Large size, low complexity, high stability	X		X	
2. Medium size, low complexity, high stability	X			X
3. Small size, low complexity, high stability		X		X
4. Medium size, moderate complexity, moderate stability	X			X
5. Large size, high complexity, low stability	X		X	
6. Medium size, high complexity, low stability	X			X
7. Small size, high complexity, low stability				X

After the visit to Bob's plant, Clint returns to his own. He does not feel good, thinking that maybe a safety unit could have prevented Dale's accident. That night, he drives to Denver to visit Dale in the hospital. He gets good news: Dale would not be totally disabled. He would be handicapped, but he would be able to work about half time after his recuperation.

Clint had taken the time to check with Otto Richmond of personnel about the company's disability plan and workers' compensation. So he could tell Dale that between the two plans his compensation would be kept up at its normal level.

Clint: I feel very upset though, Dale. Maybe, just maybe, your accident needn't have happened. So I'm hiring a safety specialist as soon as possible to try to avoid similar accidents in the future.

Dale: I'm glad you are. But it was my fault too. I've been at Lysander a long time. I know I shouldn't have done that with the machine. I just got sloppy.

Clint: The best news I've gotten in a long time is that you'll be back. Will you help me with the safety program?

Dale: I'm a living witness of what can happen if you're not safety conscious. You can bet I'll be behind the safety program.

In the years that followed, Lysander's safety record improved. The improvement was at least partly due to the new safety program Clint installed.

QUESTIONS

1. How do top managers, operating executives, employees, union officials, safety committees, and safety specialists interact to make the workplace healthy and safe?
2. Why do enterprises set up safety and health programs?
3. What are safety hazards? Health hazards?
4. How dangerous is it to work in the United States? Which places are the most risky?
5. What causes accidents and work-related illnesses?
6. Describe the programs enterprises have to prevent accidents and illnesses. Which are most effective? Least effective?
7. Why did the U.S. government legislate in the occupational safety and health area? What are the major laws affecting work safety?
8. What legal requirements must an enterprise follow in the health and safety area?
9. Evaluate the relative success or failure of OSHA, the U.S. health and safety agency. What can be done to improve its future operations?
10. What is workers' compensation? Why does it exist? What does it do?

Chapter objectives

- To demonstrate what equal employment opportunity is and why it is important.
- To discuss how to run an effective EEO program.
- To describe how to meet the legal requirements for equal employment opportunity.

Chapter outline

16

Equal employment opportunity programs

Hugo

Gregory

Hugo Gerbold, the personnel manager at Reliable Insurance, is sitting in his office, thinking. The problem is equal employment opportunity. Reliable is a middle-sized company in the Midwest which specializes in homeowners', auto, and, to a lesser extent, life and health insurance. As is typical of firms of this type, the top management team members are all white, in their sixties, and have been with the firm all their careers. The work force is mainly composed of:

- Salespersons—98% white males, the rest white females and black males.
- Underwriters—98% white males, 2% white females.
- Claims agents—90% white males, 8% white females, 2% black males.
- Clerical staff—90% white females, 10% black females.
- Other administrative personnel: Computer programmers, marketing staff, security, etc.—95% white males, 5% white females.

Reliable is located in an area where at least 35 percent of the labor force is black.

Hugo knows many firms just like Reliable have been fined back-pay differentials and been ordered to set up affirmative action plans. At a recent conference, Reliable's lawyers had devoted much time to discussing the laws and recent cases. This had prompted Hugo to visit the company president, Gregory Inness. Gregory, 64 years old and a lawyer by training, did not give Hugo much hope that things were going to change at Reliable as regards equal employment opportunities.

It is a few days after this meeting. Hugo has just received a call from a professor at one of the local universities. The professor had encouraged a competent black female, Osanna Kenley, to apply at Reliable for a management trainee position which had been advertised. She had been discouraged by the personnel department, because, they said, she was a liberal arts major. She'd also been told there were no positions. In fact, the company had just hired a white male for a trainee position. Somehow she'd found out about this.

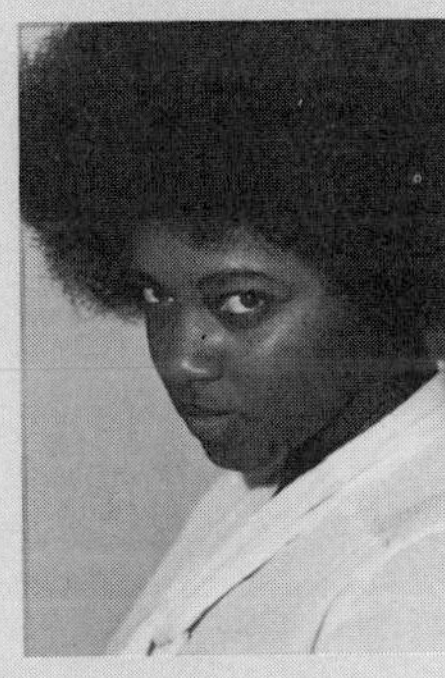

Osanna

The professor said Osanna was going to file a complaint against the firm with the EEOC. He suggested Hugo talk with her before she went to the EEOC. In fact, she is on her way over to see Hugo right now.

Hugo and Osanna have a pleasant talk, but it is clear that she means to open up Reliable to all applicants, even if she personally does not get a job there. He arranges to see Gregory right after Osanna leaves.

Hugo: Gregory, remember how I was just talking about EEO? Well, we may have a case on our hands. And remember the insurance company that just paid out $15,000,000 in back pay and must hire their fair share of minorities as a result?

Gregory: Well, maybe we should hire this young woman. That ought to take care of the problem, won't it?

Hugo: No, it won't. We better get going on an EEO program now.

Gregory: Tell me more about what's behind all this EEO.

Hugo gave Gregory the following summary of what EEO is all about.

INTRODUCTION

Equal employment opportunity programs are operated by employers to prevent employment discrimination in the workplace or to take remedial action to offset past employment discrimination.

Equal employment opportunities is one of the most significant activities in the personnel function today. In the recent Prentice-Hall/ASPA survey of 1,400 personnel executives, the respondents labeled it as one of the big three of such activities. Personnel managers and specialists are spending 14.2 percent of their time on EEO—not just compliance, but full EEO implementation.

Of the 1,400 company representatives surveyed, 18 percent reported they had established full-time EEO offices, and 15 percent had hired new employees to handle EEO.

EEO cuts across a number of personnel activities, and various personnel officials and others are involved. Top managers must get involved in EEO issues and programs to make sure that the enterprise is in compliance with the law, to avoid fines, and to establish a discrimination-free workplace. Operating managers must help by changing their attitudes about protected-category employees and helping all employees to adjust to the changes EEO is bringing to the workplace.

EEO is in an early stage of development, probably between Stage II and Stage III as defined in Exhibit 1–7 Chapter 1. The effectiveness of EEO depends on the strength of top management's commitment to it. This can be either reinforced or countered by the influence of the unions.

A DIAGNOSTIC APPROACH TO EQUAL EMPLOYMENT OPPORTUNITIES

Exhibit 16–1 highlights the key factors in the diagnostic model of the personnel function which affect equal employment opportunities. Some of these were noted in the introduction above: union requirements, goals of controlling interests, and personnel activities involved. Others are discussed below: societal values, attitudes and preferences of workers as reflected in economic status of minorities and women, and government regulations. Knowledge of these factors can contribute to an understanding of why EEO developed and how it operates. To be effective, EEO must influence the whole personnel process.

This chapter was co-authored by James Ledvinka of the University of Georgia.

Jeanne Buchmeier Cornish
Economics Laboratory, Inc.

Biography

Jeanne Cornish has been Supervisor, EEO/Affirmative Action at Economics Laboratory, Inc. since 1977. Her varied personnel experience has included positions as senior clerk in the personnel records division and principal clerk at the Student Employment Service of the University of Minnesota; graduate research assistant in the Industrial Relations Center at the University of Minnesota; Manager, EEO at Donaldson Company, Inc.; and Manager, Program Development at Cargill, Inc.

Cornish is a member of the Twin Cities Personnel Association. She served on its board of directors from 1975 to 1977 and as chairperson of the University Relations Committee in 1978. Other professional associations she has membership in are the American Society for Personnel Administration, Minnesota State Affirmative Action Association, and the National Alliance of Business/Plans for Progress EEO Coordinating Committee.

Job description

As Supervisor, EEO/Affirmative Action for Economics Laboratory, Inc., Jeanne Cornish has responsibility for development, updating, and implementation of affirmative action programs nationwide. This includes corporate headquarters, research and development facilities, nine production facilities, distribution centers, and four major sales divisions. This position reports to the Director of Human Resources with periodic reports to the management and senior management committees. Responsibilities include handling government audits and reports, investigating discrimination complaints, development and presentation of training programs, and maintaining college and community contacts to facilitate recruiting. Current concerns have been the development of an EEO fact sheet for distribution to all employees, editing a monthly management letter, and working with the vice president of administration to develop a minority vendor program.

HOW EEO EMERGED

The three main influences on the development of EEO were: (1) changes in societal values, (2) the economic status of women and minorities, and (3) the emerging role of government regulation. The first two are discussed below; information on the third factor is so detailed it is considered in a separate section.

Societal values and EEO

For over 2,000 years, Western society has accepted the principle that people should be rewarded according to the worth of their contributions. When the United States became a nation, that principle was embodied in the American dream: the idea that any individual, through hard work, could advance from the most humble origins to the highest station, according to the worth of her or his contributions. In America, success did not depend on being born into a privileged family; equal opportunity was everyone's birthright. To this day, the American dream, with its emphasis on merit rather than privilege, is widely accepted by the American public.

EXHIBIT 16–1

Factors affecting equal employment opportunities and organizational effectiveness

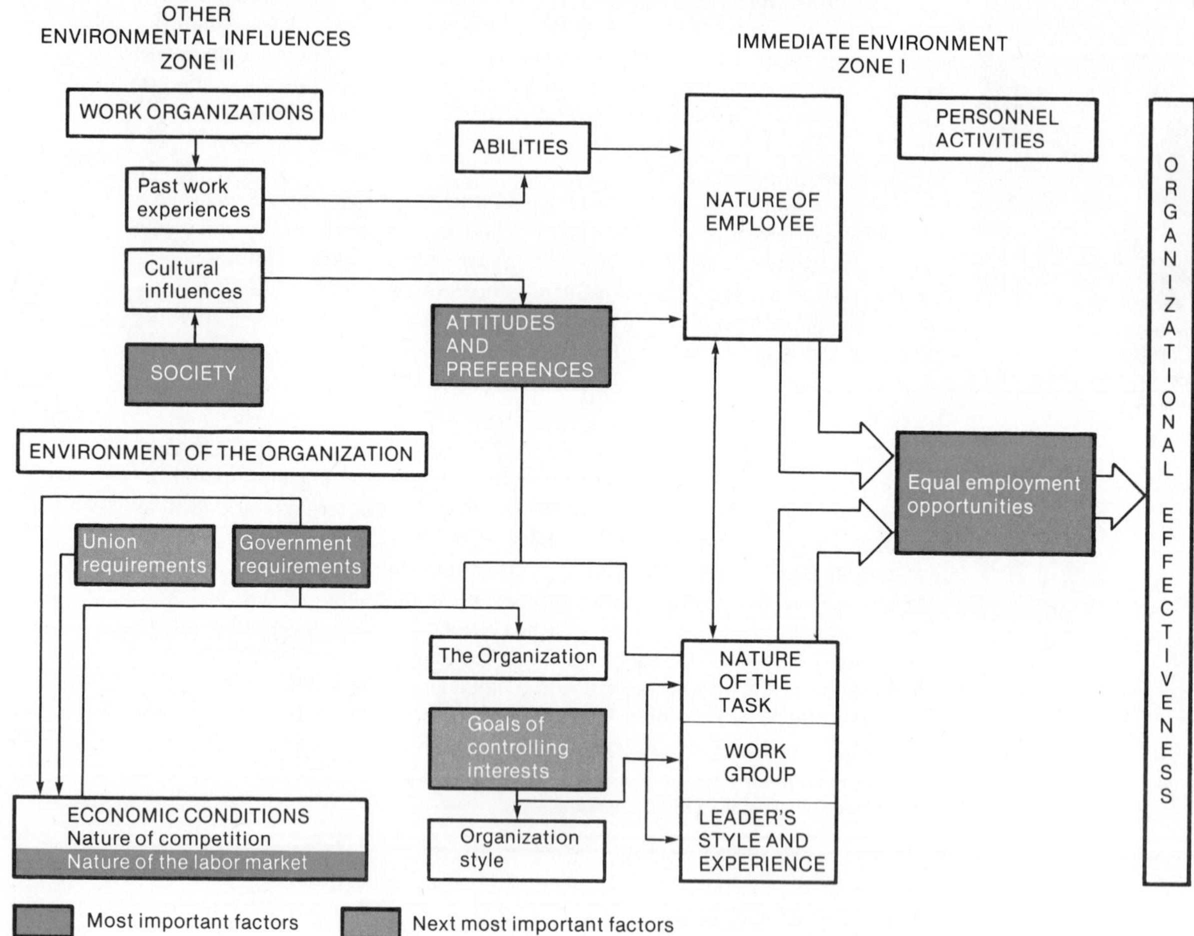

Another value that has encouraged equal opportunity is the profit motive. Nondiscrimination makes good business sense. If a company limits opportunities to white males, it cuts itself off from the vast reservoir of human talent comprised of women and minorities. Moreover, it adds to such societal problems as poverty, crime, high taxes, and civic disorder, which also hurt the business community.

Up to the early sixties it was not unusual for people, while believing in the American dream of rewards based on merit, to also believe that blacks (and other minorities) had their "place"—a place largely cut off from the rewards that the majority received. This apparent contradiction in beliefs was the American dilemma observed by the distinguished Swedish economist Gunnar Myrdal in his studies of American race relations for the Carnegie Corporation. Blacks were often excluded from schools, public accommodations, jobs, and voting, and economic realities for blacks belied the ideals of the American dream.

The differences between American ideals and American realities lent special significance to the civil rights conflict of the 1960s. The conflict began in Montgomery, Alabama, on December 1, 1955, when Mrs. Rosa Parks, a black department store worker in her fifties, was arrested for refusing to give up her bus seat to a white man. Out of that single act of protest emerged a previously unthinkable act—a bus boycott by blacks. At the center of the boycott was a loosely knit group called the Montgomery Improvement Association, which chose as its leader a new young minister in town, Dr. Martin Luther King, Jr.

Then came years of demonstrations, marches, and battles with the police which captured headlines throughout most of the early 1960s. Television accounts included scenes of civil rights demonstrators being attacked with cattle prods, dogs, and fire hoses. These events shocked the public into recognition that civil rights was the most critical social problem of the time in the United States. Gradually, overt discrimination declined and recognition of the problems faced by minorities grew. The business community shared in this attitude change, voluntarily supporting such EEO–related efforts as the National Alliance of Bussinessmen.

As the U.S. Congress turned its attention to civil rights, laws were passed prohibiting discrimination in education, voting, public accommodations, and the administration of federal programs, as well as discrimination in employment. The civil rights movement was instrumental in raising congressional concern and stimulating the passage of this legislation.

Economic status of women and minorities

Undeniable economic inequality helped focus national attention on employment as a specific area of discrimination. Unemployment figures for blacks were twice as high as for whites, and higher still among nonwhite youth. While blacks accounted for only 10 percent of the labor force, they represented 20 percent of total unemployment and nearly 30 percent of *long-term* unemployment. Moreover, in 1961, only one half of black men worked steadily at full-time jobs, while two thirds of white men did so. Blacks were three times as likely as whites to work less than full time. Similar statistical differences existed for other minorities, such as Hispanics and Indians.

When they did find work, minorities were relegated to lower status jobs, and consequently their income was far below that of whites. Minorities such as blacks were over three times as likely as whites to be unskilled laborers. Whites were over three times as likely as blacks to be in professional or managerial positions. While only 9 percent of black men were skilled craftsworkers, 20 percent of white men were. In the tobacco, paper, and trucking industries, blacks were ordinarily segregated into less desirable lines of progression or sections of the company. In the building trades, they were concentrated in the lower paying "trowel trades," such as plastering and bricklaying. Some unions excluded blacks entirely, and others organized separate locals for them. In carpentry, blacks actually *lost* ground between 1910 and 1969.

The inequalities are especially striking in the income comparisons between blacks and whites. In 1962, the average family income for blacks was $3,000, compared with nearly $6,000 for whites. More importantly, the relative position of blacks had been worsening during the preceding ten years. While black family income was only 52 percent of white family income in 1962, it was 57 percent of white family income in 1952. These inequalities could not be attributed entirely to differences in educational level between blacks and whites. The average income of a black high school graduate was lower than the average income of a white elementary school graduate.

Facts and events such as these led to the passage of laws designed to bring about economic equality. Recent evidence that things have not improved much since then is prompting Congress, the courts, and the presidency to strengthen those laws.

A related influence is the changing aspirations of women and minorities. One of the biggest changes has been the increasing need and desire of women to be fully employed. Often two incomes are needed, and many young women today seek to free themselves from the kinds of family ties that interfere with outside work, and may choose not to have children or not to marry. The number of family units with two workers or more (normally male and female adults) grew from 36 to 49 percent of the total, from 1970 to 1975. Moreover, large numbers of unmarried women are now heads of families with children. And, as societal attitudes have changed, larger numbers of blacks, Hispanics, and other minorities are attempting to enter the labor force, while older Americans are seeking to reenter it. All these persons trying more actively to find work constitute another pressure on the EEO effort.

GOVERNMENT REGULATION OF EEO PROGRAMS

There are many laws and executive orders prohibiting employment discrimination. Since it would be impossible to discuss all of them in a single chapter, this chapter will consider Title VII of the 1964 Civil Rights Act and Executive Order 11246. Considerable understanding of the entire legal framework can be gained by considering how these operate.

Title VII of the 1964 Civil Rights Act

Employers, unions, employment agencies, and joint labor-managment committees controlling apprenticeship or training programs are prohibited from discriminating on the basis of race, color, religion, sex, or national origin by Title VII of the 1964 Civil Rights Act. Other laws protect the aged, the handicapped, and special classes of veterans. Title VII prohibits discrimination with regard to any employment condition, including hiring, firing, promotion, transfer, compensation, and admission to training programs. The Equal Employment Opportunity Act of 1972 amended Title VII by strengthening its enforcement and expanding its coverage to include employees of state and local governments and of educational institutions, as well as private employment of more than 15 persons. However, Indian tribes and private membership clubs are not covered, and religious organizations may discriminate on the basis of religion in some cases. Federal government employees are also covered by Title VII, but enforcement is carried out by the Civil Service Commission with procedures that are unique to federal employees.

The EEO coverage of government employees is noteworthy. While discrimination has been illegal in government employment since the end of the spoils system and the advent of open competitive examinations in the public service, race and sex inequalities have persisted in the public service. The "merit system" in government employment has had a mixed record. Some of its features have held back minorities over the years. Now, with the 1972 amendments to Title VII, public administrators are finding themselves subject to the same sorts of EEO burdens that managers in private enterprise have shouldered since the passage of Title VII in 1964.

One clause of Title VII permits employers to discriminate based on sex, religion, or national origin if these attributes are a "bona fide occupational qualification." This seems like a loophole, but it is a small one indeed. For instance, courts have said that the clause does not allow an employer to discriminate against women simply because they feel that the work is "inappropriate" for them, or because customers might object. The best example of this reasoning was the decision in *Diaz* v. *Pan American Airways* that an airline could not limit its employment of flight attendants to women. At the time, the idea of a male flight attendant was unusual, but that was not a legal justification for Pan American's refusal to hire Diaz in that position.

When is sex a bona fide occupational qualification? One obvious but unusual situation is when one sex is by definition unequipped to do the work—as in the case of a wet nurse. Another is when the position demands one sex for believability—as in the case of a fashion model. A third instance is when one sex is required for a position in order to satisfy basic social mores about modesty—as in the case of a locker room attendant. And that is about all. Clearly, the bona fide occupational qualification clause is virtually useless as a defense against charges of discrimination for most employers.

Executive Order 11246 was issued by President Lyndon B. Johnson in 1965, superseding President John F. Kennedy's Executive Order 10925. Employment discrimination by federal government contractors, subcontractors, and federally assisted construction contracts is prohibited. While Executive Order 11246 prohibits the same actions as Title VII does, it carries the additional requirement that contractors must develop a written plan of affirmative action and establish numerical integration goals and timetables to achieve equal opportunity. The affirmative action planning requirement is discussed in greater detail later in this chapter.

Virtually every state also has some form of equal employment law. In 41 states, plus the District of Columbia and Puerto Rico, there are comprehensive state "fair employment" laws similar in operation to Title VII. In fact, some of these state laws antedate Title VII. If a state's law is strong enough, charges of discrimination brought under Title VII are turned over by the federal government to the state fair employment practices agency, which has the first chance at investigating it.

Discrimination: A legal definition

All the laws discussed above are designed to eliminate discrimination. Would you believe the laws never defined it? It's true; the courts have had to do this when they interpret the laws. The courts arrive at definitions by looking at the history behind a statute, examining the *Congressional Record* to gain insight into the social problems Congress hoped it would solve. Then they define terms like "discrimination" in a way to help solve these problems. For Title VII, the history of the civil rights conflict clearly identifies the problems: economic inequality and the denial of employment opportunities to blacks and other minorities.

The courts have defined discrimination in three different ways since the first days of federal involvement in employment practices. Initially, during World War II, discrimination was defined as *prejudiced treatment:* harmful actions motivated by personal animosity toward the group of which the target person was a member. However, that definition was ineffective as a means of solving the problem of economic inequality because it is difficult to prove harmful motives, and that made it difficult to take action against many employment practices that perpetuated inequality.

Then the courts redefined discrimination to mean *unequal treatment.* Under this definition, a practice was unlawful if it applied different standards or different treatment to different groups of employees or applicants. This definition outlawed the practice of keeping minorities in less desirable departments (different treatment), and it also outlawed the practice of rejecting women applicants with preschool-aged children (different standards). The employer was allowed to impose any requirements, so long as they were imposed *on all groups alike.*

To enable Title VII to solve the social problems that Congress wanted it to, the U.S. Supreme Court arrived at the third definition of employment discrimination: *unequal impact.* In the case of *Griggs* v. *Duke Power Co.,* the Court struck down employment tests and educational requirements that screened out a greater proportion of blacks than whites. These practices were prohibited because they had the *consequence* of excluding blacks disproportionately, *and* because they were not *related* to the jobs in question. The practices were apparently not motivated by prejudice against blacks. And they certainly were applied equally: both whites and blacks had to pass the requirements. But they did have an adverse impact on blacks. Today both unequal treatment and unequal impact are considered discrimination.

A two-question criterion. By way of a summary, the criterion for EEO and affirmative action compliance or noncompliance can theoretically be reduced to two questions:

Does an employment practice have unequal impact on the groups covered by the law? (Race, color, sex, religious, or national origin groups.)

Is that practice job-related or otherwise necessary to the organization?

A practice is prohibited *only* if the answers to *both* questions are unfavorable. Even practices that are unnecessary and irrelevant to the job are legal if they have equal impact on the groups covered by the law. This means that employers do not have to validate tests or follow the employee selection regulations if their tests do not exclude one group disproportionately.

This two-question approach does have some exceptions, and getting a straight answer to the second question is especially difficult because of the stringent guidelines that employers must follow. Nevertheless, the two questions are a good place to begin in understanding EEO and affirmative action.

Some believe that, because new cases are constantly being decided and guidelines are undergoing important changes, EEO programs are in a period of total uncertainty. Nevertheless, these two basic questions remain as underlying principles through all the changes.

EXHIBIT 16–2
Partial summary of major employment discrimination laws and orders, enforcement agencies, and regulations

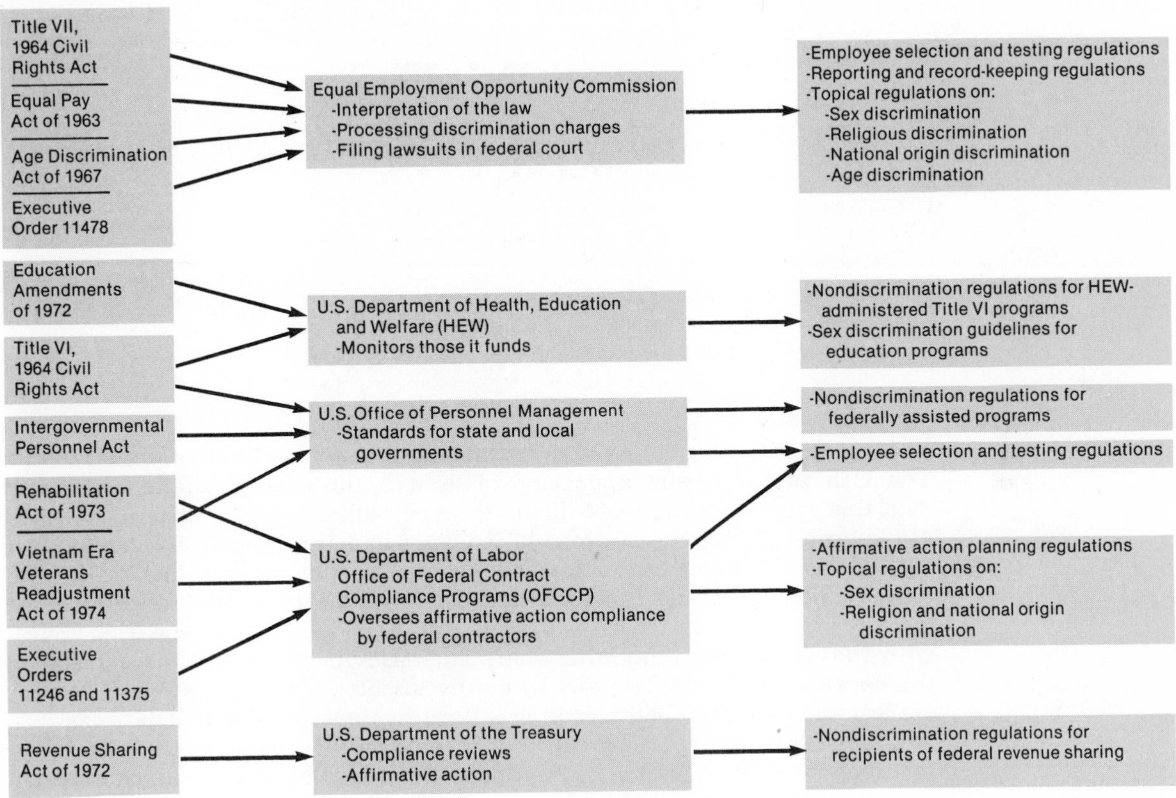

Enforcement agencies and regulations

Most employment discrimination laws provide for enforcement agencies, which issue the regulations that affect personnel administrators most directly. Exhibit 16–2 provides an overview of the complex agency scene, showing some of the principal laws, the agencies that enforce them, and the guidelines issued by these agencies. The units of government *most* responsible for enforcing the regulations considered here are the U.S. Equal Employment Opportunity Commission (EEOC) and the federal courts, which enforce Title VII; and the Office of Federal Contract Compliance Programs (OFCCP), which enforces Executive Order 11246.

Equal Employment Opportunity Commission. Title VII originally gave EEOC the rather limited powers of resolving charges of discrimination and interpreting the meaning of Title VII. Later, in 1972, Congress gave EEOC the power to bring lawsuits against employers in the federal courts, but the agency still does not have the power to issue directly enforceable orders, as many other federal agencies have. Thus EEOC cannot order an employer to discontinue a discriminatory practice, nor can it direct an employer to give back pay to victims of discrimination. However, EEOC has won these things in out-of-court settlements, and it has made effective use of the limited powers it does have.

EEOC has the power to:

Require employers to report employment statistics. Typically, they do so by completing a form called EEO–1 each year.

Process charges of discrimination, as follows:

- The preinvestigation division interviews the complainants.
- The investigation division collects facts from all parties concerned.
- If there seems to be substance to the charge, the EEOC tries to work out an out-of-court settlement through conciliation.
- If conciliation fails, the EEOC can sue the employer.

Is the EEOC effective? One way to find out is to review EEOC's annual report. The 11th annual report, appearing in January 1978, for example, reports on data that were two years old at the time of publication. In 1976, EEOC filed 414 lawsuits—up about 100 from 1975. One year later, it had a backlog of over 150,000 cases. When EEOC sought to clear away some of the blacklog, its employee union complained this was a speed-up and forced employees to violate the law in processing the cases too hastily. Each year, the agency tries to deal with the backlog by requesting sharp increases in its budget. As a result of the backlog, charges take years to be investigated. During that time, records get lost and memories fade, making it hard for investigators to determine how justifiable the original charge was. Besides that problem, critics claim that investigations are often not conducted competently enough to uncover all the information that is available. This leads to selective enforcement of the law.

The result of these problems is that only a very small percentage of charges ever get resolved by EEOC or the courts. Consequently civil rights advocates are not happy with the agency, and of course, many employers are less than enthusiastic about it (or any regulatory agency, for that matter).

On top of all this, internal audits of the agency have led to charges of fraud, illegal use of federal property, failure to submit contracts to competitive bidding, and chaos in the accounting system. The FBI investigated, as did congressional committees. This led to proposals for restructuring of the federal government's EEO work.

In spite of this, EEOC has made legal history, and its combativeness has probably helped to exact favorable settlements from employers. The agency has done much to fulfill the objectives Congress set for it, but it may have to change drastically in order to survive. The current chairperson is making some progress in solving some of the EEOC's problems.

Office of Federal Contract Compliance Programs. This office was originally established to enforce Executive Order 11246. Now it also enforces laws covering employment of veterans and the handicapped. OFCCP has the power to remove a federal contractor's privileges of doing business with the government, but it seldom exercises that power. OFCCP regulations require that all contractors with over $50,000 in contracts and over 50 employees have a written affirmative action plan on file.

OFCCP has the power to order an employer to:

Survey the labor market and determine the availability of minorities.

Prepare an affirmative action plan to show the jobs minorities are underrepresented in.

Set goals and timetables for making the work force representative of the labor market.

Audit the affirmative action plan to see if the goals are being met.

If the investigator decides that the contractor is not in compliance with Executive Order 11246, he may have a "show cause" order issued against the contractor. This triggers a lengthy sequence of administrative decisions and appeals, which can culminate in the contractor being debarred from government contract work.

Is the OFCCP effective? Most studies have found that OFCCP is administratively inept, and a cost/benefit analysis would show submarginal yields for the agency's efforts. Some data have indicated small positive effects on employment gains for black males, a smaller gain for white males, zero or negative effect for other minorities and women, and zero effects on wage and occupational gains on all minority groups. Some experts doubt that OFCCP can alter employment distributions of minorities.

One reason for the ineffectiveness was that OFCCP used to delegate its compliance review authority to 13 other agencies. It was no surprise, then, that contractors complained of conflicting agency regulations. Moreover, the 13 agencies were principally in business for some reason other than equal employment. For instance, the Department of Defense had an EEO operation housed in the bureau that was principally responsible for making sure that defense contracting was carried out well, with the right goods and services delivered at the right time. Undue concern with EEO, however, could be seen as impeding contract fulfillment. Thus, EEO was not an overriding concern in some of these agencies. President Carter has recently consolidated these compliance functions as shown in Exhibit 16–2. Perhaps this will allow OFCCP to become more effective.

The courts

Besides the agencies (federal and state), the courts are constantly interpreting the laws, and these rulings can conflict. Appellate courts then reconcile any conflicts. All the employment discrimination laws provide for court enforcement, often as a last resort if agency enforcement fails. With regard to Title VII, the federal courts are frequently involved in two ways: settling disputes between EEOC and employers over such things as access to company records, and deciding the merits of discrimination charges when out-of-court conciliation efforts fail.

The legal maneuvering often makes the court enforcement picture confusing, largely because every step of the process is appealable. And with three parties involved—EEOC, the charging party, and the employer—appeals are commonplace. All these possibilities for trial, appeal, retrial, and even appeal of the retrial can cause several years' delay before the issue is settled. When that delay is added to EEOC's charge-processing delay, the result is discouraging to anyone who wants to see justice served.

Once a final court decision is reached in a Title VII case, it can provide for drastic remedies: back pay, hiring quotas, reinstatement of employees, immediate promotion of employees, abolition of testing programs, creation of special recruitment or training programs, and others. In a class action suit against Georgia Power Company which sought back pay and jobs for black employees and applicants, the court ordered the company to set aside $1.75 million for back pay, and another $388,925 for other purposes. Moreover, the court imposed numerical goals and timetables for black employment in various job classes. If Georgia Power failed to meet the goals, then the court order provided for mandatory hiring ratios: one black was to be hired for each white until the goal percentages were reached. Other courts have ordered companies to give employees seniority credit for the time they have been discriminatorily denied employment.

Many court orders are not so drastic, however. Much depends, of course, on the facts surrounding the case. One important factor is whether the employer is making any voluntary efforts to comply with employment discrimination laws. If the company shows evidence of successfully pursuing an affirmative action plan, the court may decide to impose less stringent measures. This is discussed further in the section on costs and benefits of affirmative action plans, later in this chapter.

EEO PROGRAMS: A PREVENTIVE APPROACH

Many employers face the legal enforcement of EEO regulations with a mixture of resignation and despair, feeling little can be done to minimize the threat of legal action. But a preventive strategy is possible which can reduce the likelihood of employment discrimination charges and assure equal employment opportunities for applicants and employees. Perhaps the best way to gain an initial understanding of such a program, however, is to consider an example: AT&T's program for women in outside crafts.

AT&T's program for women outside-crafts workers

Of all employers in the United States, probably none has received more attention for its affirmative action program than the American Telephone and Telegraph Company. AT&T was involved in the largest back-pay settlement in the history of equal employment. As part of that settlement, the company was required to make significant strides in increasing employment opportunities for women and minorities. The program that resulted from that settlement exemplifies some of the more advanced EEO efforts in American industry.

The scope of AT&T's affirmative action program is so vast that it is impractical to focus on more than a small segment here. One particularly interesting segment of AT&T's program is its provisions for increasing the employment of women in outside-crafts positions: the various lineworkers, telephone installers, and repair workers whose work is mostly done outdoors. These components are an integral part of affirmative action for any job at any company.

Step 1: Analyzing underrepresentation and availability. AT&T found a problem simply by examining the sex composition of their job classes: There were almost no women in outside-crafts positions. But how great was the extent of underrepresentation? Many enterprises find the answer to this question in the statistics

Outside-craft worker

compiled for affirmative action plans by state labor departments in every state, which show the number of women and minorities in each of 10 or 20 broad occuptional groups. Others use the overall population figures compiled by the U.S. Census. Both sets of data are readily available from the appropriate government agencies. In addition, some larger firms are investing in sophisticated labor market studies to arrive at a more accurate estimate of availability. All availability statistics are open to criticism. Many employers strive to collect those that put them in the best light. While some may argue that such a strategy is manipulative, it often does succeed in reducing enforcement pressures. Employers are likely to continue using it until such time as there emerges a generally accepted statistical definition of availability.

Step 2: Goal setting. Once the statistics are agreed upon, the enterprise sets goals to help achieve greater minority representation in the job in question. EEO goals must be realistic, and they must be attainable without discriminating against those in the majority. Nevertheless, while good availability statistics help make goals realistic, there is no way to be sure that goals will not discriminate in reverse, unless the means by which the company seeks to attain them are carefully planned.

Step 3: Specifying how goals are to be attained. If the means to goal attainment are to be nondiscriminatory against white males, management should find out the causes of underrepresentation of women and minorities in the company's work force. Otherwise, it will not know what discriminatory employment practices must be changed in order to increase representation without preferential treatment of women and minorities. For example, the underrepresentation of women in a certain job class may be caused by a company's reputation for being rough on women, or by a policy that unnecessarily schedules work shifts so that women workers cannot get home in time to meet their children coming back from school. If management knows the cause, it can attempt to increase the representation of women by working on its public image and by exploring the possibility of retiming the shifts. But if management doesn't know it, it may attempt to increase the representation of women by lowering the requirements for women applying from the outside, or by granting transfers to women employees while refusing to grant them to more qualified men employees. This would not only increase the risk of discrimination charges from white males, it would also contribute to morale problems and foster resentment against women in the company.

Identifying discriminatory employment practices calls for a full-scale audit of personnel administration in the organization. This audit reviews each step of the personnel function, from recruitment to retirement. Ideally, it also examines supervisory practices that might have an unfavorable impact on women or minority employees. If the audit uncovers barriers to the employment of women or minorities, action could be taken to reduce or remove those barriers.

In AT&T's case, the company took the following steps:

- Tried to change the image of craft employees from male to neutral by advertising, public relations, and relationships with guidance counselors.
- Redesigned the jobs so that women could perform them more easily.

Other examples of EEO programs

As indicated earlier in the chapter, EEO permeates the personnel process. It can require changes in employment planning, recruiting, selecting, evaluation, career planning, training, and other functions. Rather than discuss each personnel function, we will focus on some special features of EEO programs for various groups.

Women. In many companies, EEO for women is more a matter of career design than job design. Women often find themselves locked into their positions with no career path upward; this is especially true of clerical positions. Typists and secretaries usually have little likelihood of promotion to supervisory or managerial positions.

Sometimes the solution to that problem involves training or job rotation for clerical workers. Management training can give them the specific skills they need to assume higher level positions, and job rotation can give them the breadth of experience they need to become effective managers. In other cases, the problem is that the employees of the enterprise, women included, are unaware of the promotion and transfer opportunities it offers. Larger companies often establish very thorough and elaborate systems to inform employees of job openings in the company. Among other things, these systems may include individual career counseling for employees, which helps identify promising talent at the same time it keeps employees informed.

A second problem area is management attitudes. Ten years ago, resistance to placing blacks in management positions was widespread. Today that resistance seems to have dissipated somewhat. But resistance to women in management positions remains. These attitudes can be changed, too.

A third problem area for women is policies that single them out for unfavorable treatment. For instance, married women may be denied opportunities because the company fears they will leave if their husbands change jobs. This can become a self-fulfilling prophecy. What is the incentive for a couple to remain in an area for the sake of the wife's career if the wife's employer denies her career opportunities?

In sum, to prevent EEO problems with women employees, the employer must examine the total personnel program to see that personnel policies encourage equal employment opportunity and do not restrict the employment potential of females.

Older employees. The Age Discrimination Employment Act protects workers between the ages of 40 and 70 against job discrimination. In the past, the enforcement agencies did not press too hard on discrimination against older persons, but recent actions suggest this will no longer be true. The law prevents employers from replacing their staffs with younger workers, whether the purpose be to give the company a more youthful image or to save money in the pension program. While age requirements are illegal in most jobs, the law does not cover all of them. For example, a bus company was allowed to refuse bus driver jobs to applicants over age 35 with the justification that aging brings on slower reaction times, which can adversely affect safety.

A number of barriers face older workers in many enterprises. Some are a matter of company economics, others a matter of management attitudes. The economic reasons include the added expense of funding pensions for older workers and the increased premiums necessary for health and life insurance benefit plans. The attitude problems are more difficult to pin down. Sometimes managers feel that older workers lose their faculties, making them less effective on the job. Yet there is evidence that the intelligence levels of many older employees increase as they near retirement age. Besides, there are other advantages to hiring older workers: lower turnover, greater consciousness of safety matters, and longer work experience.

When an enterprise determines it has an EEO problem with older employees, it should follow a pattern similar to the three-step approach described above for AT&T.

Racial and ethnic minorities. The laws prohibit discrimination against a person because of race, color, and national origin. The specific protected minorities are blacks, Hispanics, American Indians, Asian–Pacific Islanders, and Alaskan natives. These groups historically have had higher unemployment and underemployment and have held the lowest level jobs.

While every ethnic and racial minority is unique, one problem facing them all is adverse personnel policies. Examples of such practices are numerous. Height and weight requirements, which have an adverse impact on Asian Americans and Hispanic Americans, were, until recently, commonplace among police departments in the United States. Seniority and experience requirements based on time in a department tend to lock in blacks who move out of segregated departments. They find themselves at the bottom of the seniority lists in their new departments, even though they have had many years with the company. Vague, subjective performance evaluations by supervisors are so subject to bias that many minority group members find they cannot attain high enough ratings to get promotions or merit pay increases. All these practices, along with others, are prime targets for change in the EEO program.

Some barriers are more difficult to change, even though they have an adverse impact on minorities. College degree requirements are common for some jobs, although one study found that 65 percent of the jobs reserved for college graduates could be performed by workers with no more than a high school education. Employers should examine their own job specifications to see if educational requirements can be reduced without sacrificing job performance. Where the requirements cannot be reduced, the organization might consider redesigning or breaking down the job so that people with less education could perform satisfactorily. While job redesign is usually a big step, the resulting increase in opportunitites for minorities may make it worthwhile for the enterprise.

Employers would do well to go through the three-part program designed by AT&T to improve equal employment opportunity for minorities. There are many examples of successful minority programs.

Religious minorities. The EEO–type laws prohibit discrimination in employment based on religious preference, but there have been few cases thus far charging that employers have discriminated against religious groups in employment and promotion. This is surprising, given the reality that certain employers have had a policy of limited or no hiring of persons who are Jewish, Orthodox Christian, or Roman Catholic, at least for the managerial class. Catholics, for example, are seriously underrepresented in managerial and professional groups in the United States.

The focus of religious discrimination cases has been on hours of work and working conditions. The cases largely concern employers telling employees to work on days or times that conflict with their religious beliefs—at regular times or on overtime. For example, employees who are Orthodox Jews, Seventh-Day Adventists, or Worldwide Church of God members cannot work from sunset Friday through sundown Saturday.

Again, the enterprise can take the steps AT&T did to make sure it is not discriminating against the employment rights of particular religious groups. It must make a reasonable attempt to accommodate the working hours and days of its employees to avoid charges of religious discrimination.

Physically and mentally handicapped workers. Section 503 of the Vocational Rehabilitation Act of 1973, which is enforced by OFCCP, requires that all employers with government contracts of $2,500 or more must set up affirmative action programs for the handicapped. At present these programs require no numerical goals. They do call for special efforts in recruiting handicapped persons, such as outreach programs; communication of the obligation to hire and promote the handicapped; the development of procedures to seek out and promote handicapped persons presently on the payroll; and making physical changes which allow the handicapped to be employed (e.g., ramps). Employers who are dedicated to improving the handicapped's chances also will set up training programs and partially redesign jobs so the handicapped can perform them effectively.

The biggest hurdle that handicapped persons must face is not their physical (or mental) handicap, but myths and negative attitudes about their ability to do the job. It has been demonstrated that they are myths, and the handicapped can do the job. Affirmative action may help give them the chance to use their abilities.

Veterans. The Vietnam era Veterans Readjustment Act of 1972 requires federal contractors to take affirmative action for the employment of disabled veterans and veterans of the Vietnam era. This act imposes fewer obligations than the other employment discrimination laws. No numerical goals are required, but the enterprise must show it makes special efforts to recruit them. In determining a veteran's qualifications, the employer cannot consider any part of the military record that is not directly relevant to the specific qualifications of the job in question.

White males. If you are a white male, you probably are thinking about now: Women and minorities are getting a better chance for employment and promotion than they used to. But what does this do for me? Will I get a job? Will I get promoted to a better job? Or is *reverse discrimination* likely in my future? This concern is natural. White males are filing charges of discrimination against employers. At present, the Supreme Court is reviewing *Kaiser Aluminum and Chemical* v. *Weber.* This case could have a significant impact on EEO programs. Title VII prohibits discrimination based on race and sex, *and that includes* discrimination against white males. The laws that were originally passed to give better opportunities to women and minorities are now being interpreted as protecting the rights of the majority as well.

The obligations of the enterprise to white males are the same as its obligations to other groups: It must not discriminate for or against any race, sex, religion, or minority group. This presents a problem to employers with numerical affirmative action goals. How are goals to be attained without favoring the disadvantaged groups? The answer is to seek *other* means of satisfying goals which do not in turn discriminate against the advantaged groups. For example, employers could undertake more intensive recruiting efforts for women and minorities, as well as eliminating those employment practices that inhibit their hiring and promotion.

Employers should *never* set numerical goals so high that they can be attained *only* through reverse discrimination. If the goals are already too high, action should be taken to lower them. The courts are increasingly saying that employers cannot use their numerical affirmative action goals as an excuse to discriminate against white males.

At present there appear to be problems in interpreting these rulings. Recently the New York Bell division of AT&T promoted a woman rather than a white male who had greater seniority and better performance evaluation ratings. The judge ruled that the company should have promoted the woman to meet its EEO goals, but the male was discriminated against. The judge ordered the promotion to go through but also ordered the company to pay the white male $100,000 in damages.

The courts themselves may still impose goals that discriminate against white males. But federal agencies may not impose such goals on employers, and employers may not impose them on themselves.

The conclusion that emerges is that employment discrimination laws were passed for the benefit of those groups that have historically been the victims of discrimination; nevertheless, these laws do not allow the employer to bestow such benefits voluntarily by depriving white males of their rights.

MANDATED ACTIONS IN EEO–AFFIRMATIVE ACTION PROGRAMS

EEO programs have been presented as a "preventive" approach aimed at ensuring equality of employment opportunity and avoiding charges of discrimination. What happens if charges are made anyway? What requirements are likely to be imposed on an employer if the charging party wins?

Most cases do not proceed further than an EEOC investigation. When EEOC investigates a charge of discrimination, all it can force the employer to do is provide information. But this power is more threatening to employers than one might guess. EEOC's request for information almost inevitably goes beyond the facts and incidents surrounding the original charge. It involves a very extensive investigation into the company's employment practices in an effort to uncover evidence of more systematic discrimination. This evidence might support a more ambitious lawsuit, possibly a class action suit involving a large group of employees or applicants.

As a consequence of EEOC's demand for extensive information, companies that are the subject of discrimination charges often face demands for information that require hundreds of hours of staff time to assemble. Imagine, for instance, a demand that the employer produce information on every applicant interviewed, including the reasons for accepting or rejecting each applicant! This may be but one of dozens of items requested.

In the legal steps beyond investigation, the employer may also be faced with mandates that are part of the settlement of the charges. In the first step beyond investigation (conciliation), EEOC will attempt to gain a voluntary settlement of any charge that the agency's investigation has found. If a voluntary settlement is not forthcoming and the case goes to court, a settlement will come either through mutual agreement among the parties to the suit, or through the judgment of the court if the parties cannot agree.

At a minimum, the employer in these settlements will usually be required to eliminate any practice that evidence indicates is discriminatory. For example, the company could be required to give up its testing program, revise its seniority system, stop using subjective supervisory evaluations as a basis for promotions, or cease doing whatever else is deemed to be illegal. Also, the employer may be required to give back pay or other monetary compensation. If the back pay is awarded to a *class* of people (such as all black employees in certain labor grades during a certain period), it can get expensive. This was certainly true in the AT&T and Georgia Power cases discussed above.

A third requirement of some settlements is mandatory hiring ratios. The logic is that since discrimination operates against a group (for example, blacks), the relief should be given in a way that restores the group to where it *would be* if the discrimination *had not* occurred. While employers cannot adopt a quota system of hiring blacks and whites as a method for satisfying affirmative action plans, a court can order a company do do so. Usually courts do not do this unless they have reason to believe that an employer will not increase the employment of underutilized groups voluntarily. Nevertheless, the fact is that quotas have become commonplace in court orders. This fuels the fires of resentment by white males over what they regard as widespread reverse discrimination.

COST/BENEFIT ANALYSIS OF EEO PROGRAMS

The costs of an equal employment opportunity plan can be calculated for an employer. They include the added expense of recruitment, special training programs, test validation, job-posting systems, equipment redesign, and whatever other programs the organization includes in its plan. An added cost is for the preparation of reports. The personnel manager or specialist may have to compute these costs and justify the expense of such a plan to higher management by citing the benefits to be derived.

Unfortunately, the benefits are difficult to compute. Even if they are computed, they may not outweigh the costs in the short run. Consequently, some top managers may tend to view EEO as a necessary evil, something that must be done because the government requires it, not because of any benefits to be derived by the organization. This can do much to destroy the personnel manager's position as the person responsible for the plan, because top management attitudes are contagious. If higher management does not provide the necessary support and resources, then lower levels of management may be reluctant to cooperate.

Therefore, it is important for managers to be aware of the benefits of EEO programs, even if they are long-range ones that are difficult to quantify. One immediate benefit is that EEO increases the likelihood that the company will stay eligible for government contracts. Another benefit is an increase in the pool of eligible employees that results from providing opportunities to women and minorities. Then there is the obvious benefit of better public relations and increased goodwill among employees that comes from a properly administered EEO program.

One benefit that EEO does not provide is insulation from liability in discrimination court cases. While a good EEO plan may make employees more satisfied and less likely to file charges of discrimination, it provides no presumption of innocence if an employee does take a charge to court. For instance, one General Motors plant had a good record of hiring minorities, but that did not keep a court from finding that it was guilty of discrimination in promoting them. Still, EEO programs can help an employer in court. Some courts have been less stringent when companies seem to be making progress with their affirmative action plans. This alone may make the costs of EEO worth it.

SUMMARY, CONCLUSIONS, AND RECOMMENDATIONS

This chapter has focused on EEO programs designed to eliminate bias in personnel programs. In 1976, Library of Congress researchers attempted to estimate the cost of job discrimination. Their conclusions were that, assuming the nation could absorb the additional workers without job discrimination, 638,000 minority employees would have jobs and millions more would have better skills and earnings. The nation would gain $55.8 billion (3.7 percent) in gross national product, reflecting $22.3 billion in increased wages and salaries. With this kind of potential achievement for the minorities and the nation, a better understanding of the EEO legislation and programs is well worthwhile.

To summarize this chapter on EEO, the following statements are listed:

1. Equal employment opportunity is one of the most significant activities in the personnel function today.
2. The three main influences on the development of EEO were (1) changes in societal values, (2) the economic status of women and minorities, and (3) the emerging role of government regulation.
3. Two laws prohibiting employment discrimination which were discussed in Chapter 16 are:

   a. *Title VII of the 1964 Civil Rights Act.*
   b. *Executive Order 11246.*
4. Three different definitions of discrimination have been arrived at by the courts over the years:
   a. Prejudiced treatment.
   b. Unequal treatment.
   c. Unequal impact.
5. The criterion for EEO and affirmative action compliance can theoretically be reduced to two questions:
   a. Does an employment practice have unequal impact on the groups covered by the law? (Race, color, sex, religious, or national origin groups.)
   b. Is that practice job-related or otherwise necessary to the organization?
6. The government units *most* responsible for enforcing EEO regulations are
   a. U.S. Equal Employment Opportunity Commission (EEOC)—Title VII.
   b. Office of Federal Contract Compliance Programs (OFCCP)—Executive Order 11246.
7. Courts are constantly interpreting the laws governing EEO. Due to numerous appeals, an EEO compliant can be years in reaching ultimate settlement.
8. EEO planning can be used as a preventive action to reduce the likelihood of employment discrimination charges and assure equal employment opportunities for applicants and employees.

EXHIBIT 16–3
EEO programs for model organizations

	Staff responsibility for EEO program			*Recruiting methods for EEO program*			*Training and facilitating*			
Type of organization	*Separate department*	*Separate program director*	*Part of manager's job*	*State employment service*	*Liaison with community groups*	*Separate offices, etc.*	*Longer training*	*Buddy system*	*Transportation*	*Financial counseling*
1. Large size, low complexity, high stability	X			X	X	X	X	X	X	X
2. Medium size, low complexity, high stability		X		X	X	X	X	X		X
3. Small size, low complexity, high stability			X	X	X		X	X		
4. Medium size, moderate complexity, moderate stability		X		X	X		X	X		X
5. Large size, high complexity, low stability	X			X	X	X	X	X	X	X
6. Medium size, high complexity, low stability		X		X	X		X	X		X
7. Small size, high complexity, low stability			X	X			X	X		

9. There are special aspects of EEO planning for each of the groups listed below:
   a. Women.
   b. Older employees.
   c. Racial and ethnic minorities.
   d. Physically and mentally handicapped workers.
   e. Veterans.
   f. White males.
10. A good EEO program is not a guarantee that an employer will not face charges of discrimination.

Exhibit 16–3 lists some recommendations for effective EEO programs.

Although minority employees were the major focus of EEO programs in the past, the major emphasis of these programs is shifting to female employees presently. In the future, protection of older employees and reemployment of older employees who have lost their jobs through no fault of their own will continue to gain emphasis in EEO programs.

Chapter 17 discusses how enterprises deal with another group of employees: unionized employees.

Hugo Gerbold, personnel manager, has just returned from his discussion with Gregory Inness, company president. Gregory seemed impressed with Hugo's presentation. But he still was doubtful that more women and minorities would "fit in" at Reliable. Hugo had pointed out that EEOC and the courts wouldn't think much of this reasoning. He wondered if Gregory would take the next step in instituting an EEO plan at Reliable Insurance.

Hugo decided to be ready, just in case. He prepared an EEO program designed to focus on the areas where he felt Reliable was in the worst shape. He prepared a list of current employees, primarily in the clerical ranks, who could be promoted to underwriters and claims agents. This could increase female representation in better jobs fairly quickly. It would require training, but it could be done.

To get minorities represented fairly in all categories would require special recruiting efforts. Hugo prepared a plan to increase their recruiting efforts in all categories of employment. The plan was drawn up to protect the position of current white male employees and applicants. In no case would a person be hired with fewer qualifications than white male applicants.

Luckily, Reliable was growing and was hiring more people as it expanded. Attrition would also help in most lower managerial, professional, and sales positions.

After spending quite a bit of time on development of the plan, Hugo waited. When he didn't hear from Gregory, he made an appointment to see the president.

Hugo: Gregory, you recall we discussed the EEO issue. We hired Osanna, but that's as far as our effort went. I've prepared an EEO. . . .

Gregory: Hugo, after we discussed it, I checked with the rest of the management team. We feel we're OK as is. We don't want to upset our loyal work force with an EEO plan. Now, about the pay plan for next year. . . .

And that was that. Hugo took his EEO plan and placed it in a folder in his desk drawer.

Six months later, a female employee filed a complaint. The EEOC came to investigate, and the investigation is still going on at Reliable.

QUESTIONS

1. What are the crucial factors in the diagnostic model affecting EEO programs?
2. How did societal values affect EEO efforts?
3. What are the major laws affecting EEO?
4. What is discrimination?
5. What government agencies enforce the EEO laws?
6. Are the enforcement agencies effective?
7. What can the agencies and courts do if an enterprise violates EEO regulations?
8. Describe a preventive-approach EEO program.
9. Compare and contrast the present position of women, minorities, and other protected categories in our society. Who is better off? Worse off?

17

Labor relations

Chapter objectives

- To describe the labor relations process.
- To show you how to become an effective manager of the labor relations process at the unit and division levels.
- To demonstrate why grievances arise and how to manage them effectively.

Chapter outline

Hardisty Manufacturing Company is a fairly new firm which has grown substantially in its short history. Hardisty is located in the Boston area and is a manufacturer of consumer goods. It has a volatile technology and employs about 750 persons.

Tom

Stan

The president of the company is Tom Hardisty. He used to work for the largest firm in the industry, until he had a fight with his boss, quit, and went into competition with his former employer. Several of the key executives of Hardisty were recruited from the same firm.

The last year or two have seen increases in sales for HMC. But because of extreme competitive pressures, profits have been low or nonexistent. At times, HMC has had to layoff employees. And pay and benefit increases have not kept up with inflation. Tom has been too busy trying to keep sales up and financing available to notice the lack of positive change in his own paycheck. That isn't necessarily true for all the others at HMC. Stan Goebel, the personnel VP, has tried to bring this up with Tom from time to time. But Tom always seems to be too busy to talk about the problem.

Then one day, Stan came rushing into Tom's office.

Stan: Tom, there are union organizers on the parking lot trying to get our employees to sign authorization cards.

Tom: Authorization cards? What are they? We engineers don't know much about unions and don't like them much either.

Stan: An authorization card is the form the organizers use to get enough people to sign up to hold an election that can unionize us.

Tom: Stan, calm down. You're shaking! We have nothing to worry about. It's one happy family here. Our employees won't join a union.

Stan: Oh yeah? Then why are many of them signing the cards?

Tom: You saw some signing?

Stan: Yeah. Lots of them.

There was a pause while Tom thought for awhile.

Tom: What can we do?

Stan: Well for one thing, we can't throw them off the parking lot. We allowed charities to solicit there. Remember, I warned you!

Tom: No. I meant, what should we do to keep the union out?

Stan: The union must get 30 percent of the employees to sign the cards. . . .

Tom: They'll never get that many. The few malcontents will sign and the rest. . . .

Stan: I've talked to enough personnel people who've been through this. You *can't* assume that. You gotta do something.

Tom: Let's talk about unions and labor relations and decide what we should do. . . .

Stan then discussed some facts of life with Tom: About labor relations, unions, contracts, law, grievances, and similar issues affecting Hardisty Manufacturing Company.

In a nonunionized enterprise, management has flexibility in paying and promoting people, establishing work rules, handling disciplinary situations, administering benefits, and other personnel matters. This can change when the employees join a union. Then, the union and the enterprise draw up a contract which spells out how things will be done. Strikes, slowdowns, secondary boycotts, and other pressures to accept the union's proposals may face the enterprise.

This chapter examines how operating and personnel managers proceed to manage labor relations. It also discusses the employee grievance process in unionized and nonunionized enterprises.

Labor relations is a continuous relationship between a defined group of employees (represented by a union or association) and an employer. The relationship includes the negotiation of a written contract concerning pay, hours, and other conditions of employment and the interpretation and administration of this contract over its period of coverage.

Labor relations is an emotionally charged personnel activity. Few employers or employees get as emotionally involved over recruiting methods or career development plans, for example, as they do over this aspect of the personnel function. The reason is that collective bargaining goes to the heart of employee relations problems: power. Whoever has the power to fire an employee has power over whether that employee and his or her family can survive. Whoever has the power to discipline an employee in performance evaluation has the power to affect significant human needs negatively, as noted in Chapter 2. Underlying the concept of leadership in management is the need for power, as David McClelland describes it. People thirst for the power to affect others' destinies, if only for eight hours a day.

Most employers have used their power fairly. They have hired employees, given them reasonable jobs, compensated them well, respected their dignity, and retired them after rewarding careers. Others have not dealt with their employees as well. They have exploited them economically and dealt many a blow to their human dignity.

When employers have behaved inequitably toward their employees, some employees have reacted by entering the political process. In extreme circumstances, revolutions are mounted and labor and socialist governments, pledged to protect employee rights and dignity, are elected. In the United States, conditions considered unfair or exploitative have led to the development of the collective bargaining process. Employees have joined together so that, as individuals, they do not have to stand alone against the power of a General Electric, a Department of Defense, a Wayne State University, or a Barnes Hospital.

In considering collective bargaining, one focus is the big picture: national and international unions all locked in major struggles with industry or in Congress. As interesting as this is, the focus of this chapter is primarily on the effects of labor relations activities on the personnel function of the employer. National contracts, and especially national contracts for a multiunit enterprise, are the business of a few top managers, a few top union officials, some staff lawyers and support persons, and a few government officials. Very few individuals are involved in these interactions. This chapter is concerned with how the collective bargaining process affects the *day-to-day operations* of an employer and its employees.

Labor relations is a Stage III personnel activity as outlined in Exhibit 1–6 in Chapter 1. Studies about unions have conflicting results. As noted above, labor relations elicits a more emotional response than perhaps any other function considered in this text.

A DIAGNOSTIC APPROACH TO LABOR RELATIONS

Exhibit 17–1 highlights the diagnostic factors important in labor relations. The attitudes of employees toward unions influence whether they will join or support a union in the workplace. Managerial attitudes toward unions in general and the union officials they deal with in particular also affect labor relations.

The goals of the controlling interests influence managerial attitudes and behavior toward labor relations. If management is very antiunion, the negotiation

EXHIBIT 17–1
Factors affecting labor relations and organizational effectiveness

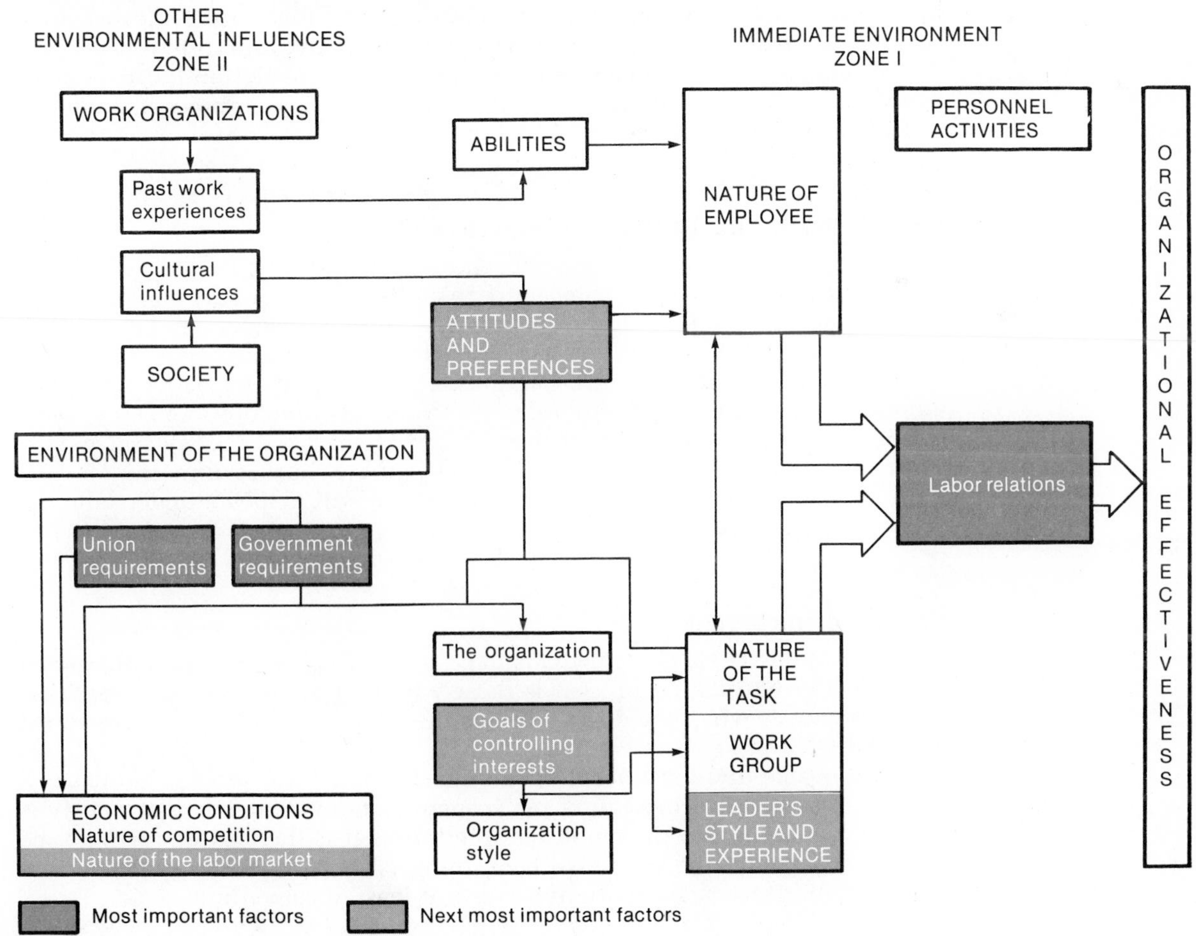

and administration process will not proceed smoothly. The union is the other focal organization in effective collective bargaining relationships. Union officials face management daily and at contract time. Union and managerial attitudes toward each other affect the degree of peace and effectiveness that can exist in labor management relations.

In addition to union requirements, two other environmental factors influence the nature of collective bargaining. Labor market conditions influence both management and the unions in their relationships. If the labor market is tight and demand for goods is strong, the union can hurt management by striking. If the demand for goods is soft and the labor market has a surplus, management has an advantage. It can sustain a strike, and perhaps even benefit economically from one. The other factor is government, which creates the legal environment within which labor relations take place. Government boards adjudicate legal differences in the system, and government mediators and conciliators often help settle disputes.

Labor relations varies by the sector in which the enterprise operates. As will be described shortly, unions relate to managers in the business world (private sector), in government settings (public sector), and in other settings such as health, education, and voluntary organizations (third sector). Differing labor relations among the sectors are due to institutional and legal differences.

This chapter discusses how each of these factors impacts on labor-management relationships. Each also affects how the labor relations process, including collective bargaining, works.

WHO IS INVOLVED IN LABOR RELATIONS?

To understand labor-management relations, it must first be understood that people act; organizations respond to people's decisions. Unions do not do this and corporations do that; rather, spokesmen and role occupiers make decisions and attempt to mobilize their organizations to action. The people and groups of people involved in collective bargaining are, to a greater or lesser extent, unionized and ununionized employees, union officials, employers and employers' officials, government officials, customers and clients, and the general public. The motivations and perceptions of these persons are the most important factors in the collective bargaining process. This section will help you understand the actions a little better.

Unionized employees

One of the first sets of individuals to be understood in order to comprehend the collective bargaining process is those who join unions. Perhaps the most crucial factor is why they do so. Various theorists and researchers have tried to explain this process.

It is probable that most people join unions as much for protection, security, and self-respect as to increase their economic status. Better pay obviously is one of the reasons, but the employer who thinks it is the only one will not be able to understand the collective bargaining process. There is evidence that noneconomic reasons are more important, at least at some times.

Employees not presently unionized

All employees have not accepted the rationale for unions. Attitudes develop out of the individual's experience and the experiences of others. Thus new workers in heavily unionized areas such as the East, Midwest, and Far West are more likely to know about and accept the rationale and operations of unions than rural workers in the Southeast. Many of the reasons employees have for joining unions could be modified if the employer provided the benefits voluntarily, as some do. They may provide company-run camps and country clubs, try to maintain good jobs supervised by well-trained managers, and communicate with employees often and effectively.

Generally there are three reasons people do *not* join unions.

They identify with management. Those who work with or are close to management tend to identify with it and consider the union as an adversary. If they experience job dissatisfaction, however, they will lose this identification and consider joining a union.

They do not agree with the goals of unions. Other employees may disagree with the objectives of unions politically and organizationally. For example, they may prefer merit to seniority rules, may fear union social or political power, may resent dues paying, and may feel unions interfere in free enterprise and individual initiative.

They see themselves as professionals and unions as inappropriate for professionals. For years, many employees, such as engineers, nurses, teachers, and others, saw themselves as independent professionals working for an organization. The concepts of union member and independent professional were viewed as opposites. These perceptions may be breaking down.

Union officials and union organizations

The people most directly involved in collective bargaining are the parties sitting across the table from each other: union leaders and employers (or labor relations managers). Their job is to come to an agreement on future conditions of work at contract time or interpretation of the contract between contracts. Most such agreements require the two parties to assess the data involved in the decision and decide the set of conditions with which they can live. The key officials are those of the local union.

The local union members elect officials such as president, secretary-treasurer, business representative, and committee chairmen. If the local is large enough, the business representatives and secretary-treasurer are full-time employees. The business representative plays a crucial role in contract negotiations and grievances. He usually administers the local office and handles such duties as public relations. The president and other officials, such as committee chairmen, hold full-time jobs in the trade or industry. Typically, they get some released time for union duties and are paid several hundred dollars a year in expenses.

Another local unit personality is the shop steward or job steward. The steward has a position equivalent to foreman. He represents the union on the job site and is charged with handling grievances and disciplinary matters. Normally the steward is elected by members in the unit for a one-year term. In fact, the effectiveness of the local is usually judged in terms of effective grievance handling.

A union meeting

Union leaders, especially local union leaders, have much less power than their managerial equivalents. They are always subject to reelection, and the contracts they negotiate must be ratified by union members. Members can also keep union leaders in line by voting their union out or by engaging in wildcat strikes. But the union member is typically apathetic about union affairs except in times of crisis, such as the decision to strike. Usually only 10 to 15 percent of the members attend an ordinary union meeting. This gives more freedom and power to the union leader during "normal" times.

The union leader often has a strong personality and can mobilize the members against the "enemy"—the employer. The effective union leader realizes, however, that the demands made by the union must not put the employer out of business. Good union leaders help employers by policing the contract and keeping maverick members in line. Leonard Sayles shows how union leaders' personalities vary by the type of work done. More highly skilled workers choose quiet, competent, senior leaders. Semiskilled workers choose aggressive, vocal leaders. Union leaders are as different as managers are. Some of the difficulties in collective bargaining arise because management and union leaders' personalities conflict.

Despite union leaders' control efforts, union members have a lot to say. The union leader's job should be to locate, reconcile, and finally represent the diverse, conflicting demands and interests of the union membership. This is a significant point—the membership is frequently divided on what it wants. Managers usually exaggerate the power of the local union leader and overlook the pressures members and union subordinates can apply.

In addition to internal pressures, unions compete with each other for members. Unions have trouble deciding what personnel functions they should provide, whether they should allow their own employees to unionize (most do not allow this), and when to be militant or amenable.

Local and national or international unions. To become a union member, a person joins one of the 70,000 or so local unions. The local is a subunit of one of the 173 national unions, of which 110 belong to the American Federation of Labor–Congress of Industrial Organizations (AFL–CIO). In general, the local union has little legal autonomy. The national can charter or disband a local as well as suspend it or put it under national trusteeship. In many unions, the local must get permission from the national union before it can strike.

There is great variety in the size and power of nationals. Local unions also vary greatly. In size, they range from 8 or so members up to the approximately 40,000 members in Local 32–B (New York City) of the Service Employees International Union.

The AFL–CIO represents about 80 percent of all unionized employees. Its method of organization is shown in Exhibit 17–2.

EXHIBIT 17–2
Structural organization of the American Federation of Labor and Congress of Industrial Organizations

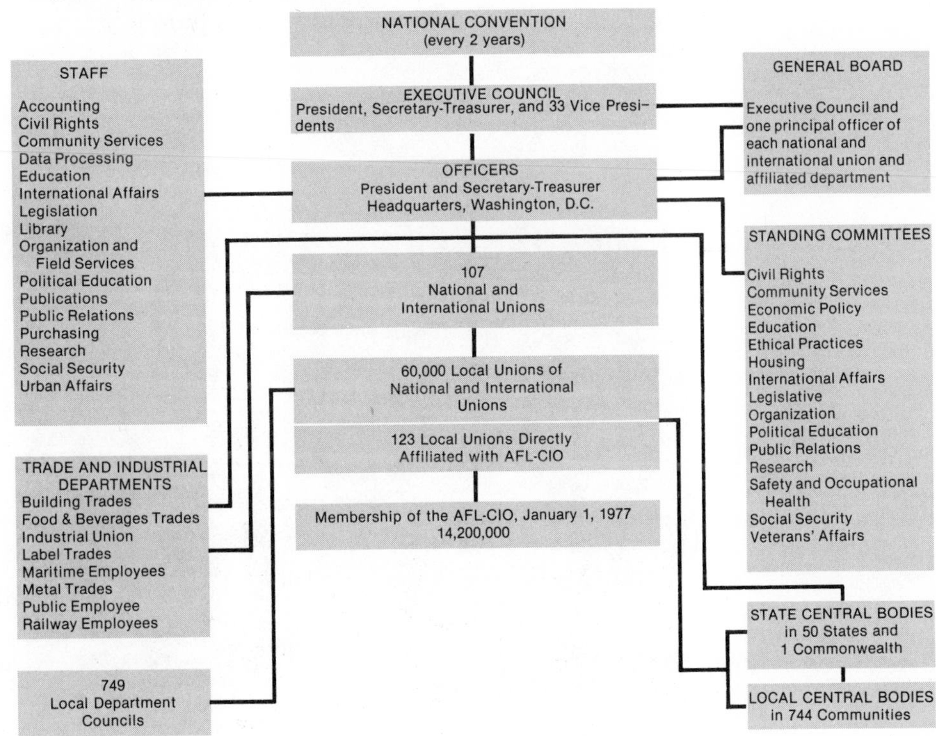

How does the AFL–CIO work? It's chief governing body is the biennial convention, which sets policy. Between conventions, the executive officers, assisted by the Executive Council and the General Board, run the AFL–CIO. Executive officers are the president, who interprets the constitution between meetings of the executive council and heads the union staff, and the secretary-treasurer, who is responsible for financial affairs. The Executive Council also has 33 vice presidents. It meets three times a year and sets policy between conventions. The General Board consists of the Executive Council and the head of each affiliated national union and department.

National headquarters provides many services to subsidiary union bodies: training for regional and local union leaders, organizing help, strike funds, and data to be used in negotiating contracts. Specialists available for consultation include lawyers, public relations specialists, and research personnel. Under the national union are regional groups of local unions which may provide office space and facilities for local unions.

Very large unions which are members of the AFL–CIO are those of the steel workers, electrical workers, carpenters, machinists, and hotel and restaurant workers. The smallest national union, a unit in the printing trade, has 18 members. A number of the larger unions are independent of the AFL–CIO. These include those of the teamsters, auto workers, and mine workers.

About 21 million people belonged to trade unions and employee organizations in 1977. This is about 33 percent of the *eligible nonagricultural* civilian labor force. Essentially, union membership has been stable in the private sector. In the public sector, union membership is growing rapidly. Membership in public unions grew from approximately 1.5 million to 5.5 million from 1964 to 1974.

AFL–CIO national headquarters

Photo of AFL–CIO Building by Steve Yarmola, AFL–CIO News.

H. W. Stadtlander
Morton Salt Company

Biography

The current Labor Relations Manager for Morton Salt Company, H. W. Stadtlander, earned his BS in management from the University of Illinois, following three years' service in the U.S. Army. He earned his masters in labor and industrial relations at the same university in 1967. Prior to joining Morton Salt in 1972, Stadtlander was employed by Union Carbide Corporation in three different positions: administrative assistant for labor relations; personnel manager; and industrial relations manager.

Job description

As Morton's Labor Relations Manager, Stadtlander is responsible for providing counsel and guidance to the department on matters pertaining to industrial and labor relations. His accountabilities include:

1. Recommend and achieve approval and changes in industrial relations philosophies, programs, and objectives; audit implementation by operating and staff managements at assigned locations.
2. Achieve satisfactory settlements of labor agreements at assigned locations within authorized limits in a manner which will assure efficient operations and sound relationships, and which will protect the company's competitive position.
3. Provide counsel and guidance and supervise outside legal counsel on matters relating to the National Labor Relations Board; and other allied responsibilities.

Labor relations managers

The role of labor relations manager is a very important one on the personnel team. In the recent Prentice-Hall/ASPA study of 1,400 personnel executives, labor relations were rated as the most important issue to be faced in unionized firms.

Both personnel and operating managers are involved in labor relations. Personnel managers or specialists are of necessity technical experts on labor relations who train and advise operating managers on the contract provisions. They also bargain with the union on the contract and serve as a step in the grievance process. But operating managers are the persons who make the contract work. They advise personnel on problem areas in the contract so they can try to improve them during the next negotiations, and they face grievances first. An overall vital influence in labor relations is exerted by top management. Top managers' attitudes toward unions strongly influence the attitudes of personnel and operating managers and help determine whether union-management relations will be amiable or combative. Top managers also strongly influence the negotiating process. The bargaining philosophy and strategy they assume at the time of negotiations will help determine whether a contract will be signed, and how soon, or whether impasses such as strikes, lockouts, and arbitration will occur.

Labor-management stereotypes

The facts and opinions considered in collective bargaining and their interpretation are filtered by the attitudes and motivations of labor relations managers and union officials. There have been a number of studies of the attitudes of these two groups toward one another in the private sector which show the unflattering, dysfunctional stereotypes they have developed of one another. These stereotypes can distort the data presented during the collective bargaining process. The typical union official's stereotype of a labor relations manager is a "pretty boy," snobbish, country-club type, fawning over his boss, who could not find his way to the bathroom without a map and never worked a real day's work in his life. His job is only to cheat honest workers out of a few cents an hour to get a big bonus. The labor relations manager, on the other hand, may stereotype the union official as a loud-mouth, uneducated goon who probably is stealing pension funds and no doubt beats up uncooperative workers. He will ruin the company because he does not understand the dog-eat-dog marketplace it must compete in.

These differences in perceptions between the two groups are compounded by major differences in such factors as age, education, and social class background. And the employer organizations are hierarchical: The labor relations manager has a boss to report to. The union is peer oriented: The agreement must be approved by a vote of the members.

In sum, one of the challenges of labor relations is that on the union side of the bargaining table the representatives have more conflicts and usually less power than those on the employer's side. There are conflicts within the management side, too, but usually there is an official, such as the president of the enterprise, who can "settle" these conflicts by a decision. This is not so on the union side.

In spite of these differences, there are many examples where the two groups are compatible and get along well. This results when both sides work hard at developing rapport. Or in some cases it is because one side has corrupted the other.

Government officials and others

The major actors and actresses in labor relations are the employees, unions and union officers, and labor relations executives. But others do have an impact. The first is the government regulatory bodies that administer the labor laws. In the United States, the National Labor Relations Board (NLRB) administers the laws and regulations in the private and third sectors. Many states also have state boards to administer state labor laws.

Labor relations administrators have two major duties:

- To supervise representation elections and certify unions as bargaining agents.
- To hear appeals of alleged violations of the laws.

Most experts believe the boards do a satisfactory job with elections. Some contend they are too slow in processing violations appeals. However, they receive a large number of complaints, and it is not an easy job. For example, in the month of March 1977, 5,273 new cases were filed with the NLRB. Some who favor the union side contend that these delays benefit management, and management deliberately takes its time and regularly appeals violation decisions. For example, cases where management is charged with firing prounion employees might take two years (with appeals and delays) to decide. By then the fired employees have other jobs or are tired of the process. Management disputes this, and the NLRB and other boards have attempted to expedite these cases.

At present, there is a law before Congress which would increase the size of the NLRB to speed the processing of cases. The laws administered by these government officials are discussed in the next section.

Others with a possible impact on labor relations include customers and the general public. Customers and clients of the enterprise may mobilize to move the negotiation process along faster. Customers who need goods or services may exert pressure on the employer directly to settle or lose the business. They also do this indirectly by buying elsewhere and letting the home office know it.

The general public tends to be neutral or uninterested in most collective bargaining incidents. Both sides try to mobilize public support through the media, however, because if the public is denied service it can bring political or other pressures to bear on the settlement. This normally happens when the public is severely affected by loss of the goods or services.

LABOR LAWS AND REGULATIONS

The laws affecting collective bargaining are complicated, and most employers and unions have lawyers to advise them on the details. The laws change all the time, it seems. Only the general characteristics of the laws will be outlined here.

The major law affecting collective bargaining in the United States is the National Labor Relations Act (Wagner Act) as amended by the Labor-Management Relations Act of 1947 (Taft-Hartley Act), and the Landrum-Griffin Act of 1959. These acts cover many aspects of labor relations, including the procedure by which unions come to represent employees in the private sector.

The private sector: Union organizing law

Union organizing goes through several phases to reach fruition. The first is the preliminary phase, in which employees invite union representatives to come to the workplace, or the union representatives come on their own.

Union organizers try to get the employees to sign cards authorizing their union to represent the employees in collective bargaining with the enterprise. These cards must be signed by 30 percent of the employees before the union can call for a representation election.

It is illegal for employers:

- To interfere with, threaten, or do violence to organizers.
- To install listening or similar surveillance devices to stop unionization, although management may observe what is going on in person.
- To discharge employees for prounion activity. Management must be careful to document discharges for inadequate performance during organizing efforts:

It is also illegal for *either* employers or union organizers to threaten employees during the unionization campaign.

Unions can picket the organization if the employees are not already unionized, if a petition for election procedures has been filed within 30 days with the National Labor Relations Board (NLRB), and if there has *not* been a recognition election in the preceding 12 months.

Union organizers can solicit employees for membership as long as this does not endanger the safety or performance of the employee. It can take place at lunch, at break time, and even during work time *if* the employer has allowed other groups such as United Appeal to solicit contributions during work time. If the employer has not allowed solicitations of any kind, it can refuse to allow union organizers on the property (including parking lots). The employer also will usually refuse the union a list of employees. Thus it is in the employer's interest to prohibit soliciting at work and in the parking lot.

The role of the NLRB

The National Labor Relations Board plays a specific role during the preliminary union organizing period. It sends a hearing officer or examiner to investigate the situation, upon notice by the union or employer.

The examiner determines if 30 percent of the employees have signed authorization cards. The examiner also decides what the bargaining unit will be: the organization (exclusive of managerial personnel), or a series of subunits.

If there appears to be enough evidence and if the examiner's decision to schedule an election is approved by superiors at NLRB, the employees are notified of the election and the employer is apprised of its rights (NLRB form 666). If the union gets 50 percent plus one employee to sign the cards and can prove the employer has committed a serious unfair labor practice, the NLRB will often declare the union the bargaining agent *without* an election. The employer cannot even challenge the conditions under which the cards were signed.

There are two types of elections: consent elections and stipulation for certification upon consent elections. The latter is preferable to management, since it allows appeals. Within 30 to 60 days, an election is held by the NLRB, which provides secret ballots and ballot boxes, counts the votes, and certifies the election. The union becomes the employees' representative if it wins the election.

The NLRB and equivalent governing boards go to great lengths to enforce the law at organizing time. Many of the cases it accepts arise over alleged "illegal" practices during the campaign. Yet a landmark study of the campaigns and elections drew the conclusion that this was misplaced effort. Julius Getman et al. studied 31 elections and found that the board implicitly assumes that honest campaign speeches and printed material are crucial to fair elections. Getman and his associates suggest the NLRB should stop enforcing its honest-speech rules and similar campaign regulations. This would release about 25 percent of the board's time, which it could use to enforce more significant violations of the law. The board should also develop and enforce regulations for real threats such as the firings of prounion employees at organizing time, the authors conclude.

At the present time there are bills in Congress to speed up organization elections. The outcome of the bill is not known at this writing.

Other private-sector labor relations laws

The specific rights of the parties involved in collective bargaining have been defined by law. The Wagner Act protects "employee rights" by prohibiting employers from:

Interfering with, restraining, or coercing employees in the exercise of their rights to join unions and bargain collectively.

Dominating or interfering with the formation or administration of any labor organization or contributing financial or other support to it.

Encouraging or discouraging membership in any labor organization, by discrimination in regard to hiring or tenure or any term or condition of employment. Section 8(3), however, includes a proviso removing union security agreements from the general prohibition of encouragement or discouragement of labor organizations.

Discharging or otherwise discriminating against an employee for filing charges or giving testimony under the act.

Refusing to bargain collectively with the representatives of the employees.

The Taft-Hartley Act prohibits unions from engaging in six specific unfair labor practices:

To coerce employees in the exercise of their rights or to coerce employers in the selection of their representatives for purposes of collective bargaining or adjustment of grievances.

To cause an employer under a union shop agreement to discriminate against employees denied admission to the union or expelled from the unions for reasons other than nonpayment of dues and initiation fees.

To refuse to bargain collectively.

To engage in a jurisdictional strike or secondary boycott.

To charge excessive or discriminatory initiation fees to employees covered by a union shop agreement.

To cause an employer "in the nature of an exaction" to pay for services not performed.

The Taft-Hartley Law also includes the controversial Section 14.b, which allowed states to pass right-to-work laws which prohibit union shops and other union security agreements.

The third sector

In rulings in 1970 and 1974, the National Labor Relations Board and the courts ruled that third-sector enterprises were subject to private-sector labor relations laws. Although the laws are the same, there are differences in how labor relations takes place in the third sector. There is a good deal of labor relations action in this sector today—in health care, universities and colleges, and the performing arts. Essentially, however, the structure and legal environment are similar to those in the private sector.

The public sector

The second largest group of unionized employees is in the public sector. One third of all unionized public employees work for the federal government. The rest are employed primarily by local government.

There are major differences between labor law and regulations in the private and public sectors. In the private sector, the law tries to get management and labor to the table as equals. In the public sector, the government defines itself as the superior through the use of the sovereignty doctrine. In addition, responsibility for negotiating with employees is complicated by the separation-of-powers doctrine. Some managerial responsibility lies with the executive branch, others with the legislative.

Public-sector collective bargaining is relatively new in the United States and has not been developed definitively. There is more clarity for federal employees than others. In the public sector, federal labor relations are regulated by executive orders issued by the president alone. Each new order rescinds previous orders on the same topic. In 1962, President John Kennedy issued Executive Order 10988, designed to parallel federal bargaining to private bargaining. It included a strong management-rights clause and banned strikes and the union shop.

Executive Order 11491, issued by President Richard Nixon to update 10988, was designed to bring public bargaining even closer to that in the private sector. Under this order, the Secretary of Labor has the authority to determine bargaining units, to supervise procedures for union recognition, and to examine standards for unfair labor practices and rule on them.

Order 11491 also created the Federal Labor Relations Council (FLRC), which reviews decisions of the Department of Labor and interprets the executive order implementation. It is composed of the Secretary of Labor, chairman of the Civil Service Commission, and director of the Office of Management and Budget. The FLRC supervises the Federal Service Impasse Panel, comprised of seven neutral members appointed by the president from outside the federal service to settle labor disputes in that sector. Executive Order 11491 also required a simple majority of employees to choose an exclusive representative union and stipulated criteria for determining the bargaining unit.

Executive Order 11838, issued by President Gerald Ford in 1975, required federal agencies to bargain with their employees on all issues unless the agency could show *compelling need* not to negotiate. All personnel policies became subject to negotiation. And the FLRC was appointed the final arbitrator on these issues and what constitutes compelling need. Subjects for grievances were also broadened. But this order still bans union-agency shops and has a strong management-rights clause.

Labor relations regulations for public employees at state and local levels are diverse and complicated. For example, 12 states have no applicable labor law at all for public employees. Another 20 states have such laws, and the other 18 have laws that cover certain aspects of labor relations for these employees.

For a time it was thought the answer to this confusion might be a federal law applicable to state and local employees. But the Supreme Court and other federal courts have made it clear that the federal government cannot interfere with state and local employees. These rulings have also said that these government employers do not have to bargain with their employees. So the degree of public bargaining practiced and the methods used vary from state to state and city to city.

State labor relations laws

In addition to federal law, the states have passed labor laws affecting certain aspects of labor relations. Normally, these laws affect strikes, picketing, and boycotts, and collective bargaining by public employees. Two fifths of the states also have right-to-work laws.

UNION ORGANIZING CAMPAIGNS

When employees are not represented by a union, three groups can initiate unionization: the employees themselves, a union, or management (the latter rarely does so). In some cases, when employees are quite dissatisfied, they can take the initiative and invite a union in to begin the organizing of an employer.

The ability of a union to organize the workers in an enterprise or an industry depends first on its own financial support for the initial organizing of employees. This varies by union and from time to time. Generally speaking, better financed unions attempt to organize employees more frequently. Organizing is also a function of the unions' motivation to organize. Some unions organize because they wish to grow larger. Growth motivation is present in unions as it is in businesses. Or they may wish to unionize an enterprise if similar enterprises are union affiliated, because nonunionized enterprises could harm the success of the unionized enterprises. Some unions will selectively organize those employees who have strategic market or technological positions.

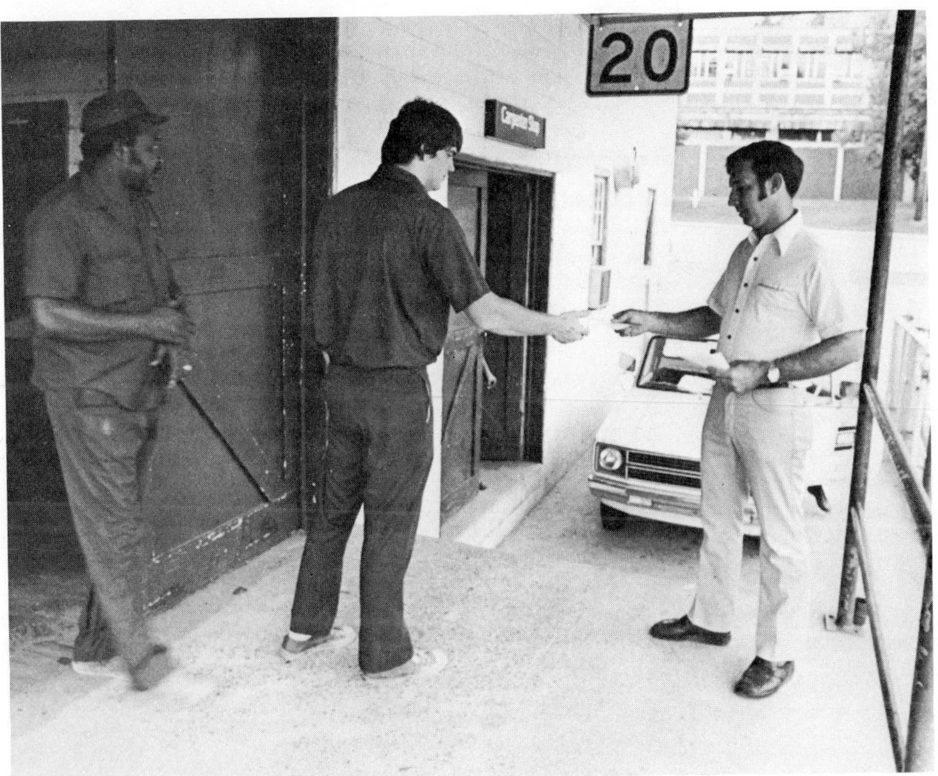

A union organizing campaign

The organizing campaign

Whether the employees or the union take the initiative, next comes a time of high drama: the organizing campaign itself. From the union's point of view, the object is to get 30 percent of the employees to sign authorization cards and then to get a majority vote in the election. The union tries to keep the initial stages secret so it can get up momentum before management can mount a counteroffensive. During the organizing period, unions and management pursue campaigns to affect employee attitudes toward unionization. Typically the union stresses how it can improve the workers' lot in terms of compensation, benefits, and employee protection. Management mounts a countercampaign stressing how well off the employees are already and the costs of union membership in dollars and "loss of freedom." It is illegal for either side, in mass meetings, literature, or individual meetings, to threaten employees with discharge or violence. Both sides must be truthful, or the procedure can be set aside. It is probably unlawful for management to interrogate employees individually about their feelings toward unions, but secret polls are allowed.

Who wins these elections? Why do people sign these cards? They sign when they are dissatisfied with working conditions and feel the union can satisfy their needs. Unions are also likely to win when the work unit is large.

> Analyses of the results of NLRB elections since 1936 indicate that about 80 percent of employees vote in the elections. Prounion votes are registered by about 60 percent of those who vote yearly. But each year, about 12,000 employees vote to throw the union out in a decertification election.

Some studies of management successes in representation elections have found that when management communicates with employees early in the process and consistently during it, management wins. In the most successful campaigns management holds meetings with employees and distributes letters and memorandums stating its case. Some employers send their managers outside the firm to be trained in these techniques. However, it has been found that issues and communication techniques by themselves do not win elections.

The structure of negotiations

How the 150,000 or so labor contracts are negotiated yearly in the United States varies a great deal, depending on the size and importance of the agreement. There are several possible structures for the negotiations.

> **Union negotiation structures:**
>
> A single union negotiates with a single employer (Type A).
> A single union negotiates with more than one employer (Type B).
> Several unions negotiate simultaneously with a single employer (Type C).
> Several unions negotiate simultaneously with several employers (Type D).

Most contract negotiations are Type A bargaining structures. Multiple-employer bargaining (Type B) allows all the employers to get the same wage rates and prevents some employers from settling for higher wages and becoming uncompetitive. Multiple-employer bargaining is common in construction, retailing, local trucking, and service industries such as hotels.

Coordinated bargaining (Type C) takes place when several unions coordinate their contract demands and strategies. It appears to be increasing in the private and public sectors, although some experts doubt its long-run viability. There are few examples of Type D bargaining at present.

These bargaining structures develop as a consequence of the changing ways enterprises do business; that is, as the technology and markets change, their structures change. Unions adjust the bargaining structure accordingly. One study found that the greater the seller concentration in an industry (monopoly, oligopoly), the more pattern there is to bargaining in the industry. One company settles; the others follow suit with the same terms. He also found that the greater the seller concentration, the less likely there was to be multiple-employer bargaining. Company size also was an important factor. The smaller the company, the more likely it was to try multiple-employer bargaining. This approach has cost savings and gives the smaller firm more power in the negotiations. Multiple-employer bargaining is also fostered if it is a labor-intensive industry, the firms are closely located spatially, and the union hires and recruits the workers for the employers.

NEGOTIATING CONTRACTS WITH UNIONS

Once a union is recognized as the bargaining representative for a group of employees, its officials are authorized to negotiate an employment contract. There are usually three phases to this: preparation for negotiations, negotiation, and settlement. The negotiations often are very businesslike. Sometimes they are exciting, with strikes and publicity involved. But this is a rarity.

Preparations for contract negotiations

Prior to the actual negotiations, both management and the union prepare for them. There are major differences in the degree of preparations, with smaller unions and employers preparing less thoroughly or more informally than larger ones. The more complex the bargaining, *the further ahead* preparations begin. Typical time requirements are three to four months of preparation prior to negotiations for a small firm that bargains through employer bargining associations, and nine months for large, multiplant firms.

The preparation process for management consists of five steps.

1. ***Determine contract changes.*** The beginning part of the preparation concerns problems in contract administration and changes in contract language. Probably since the signing of the last contract, both sides have been compiling a list of issues to be brought up the next time. Management has asked its supervisors how they would like the contract modified to avoid problem areas. The personnel department has been studying patterns in grievances to see where problems to be remedied lie. The contract has been examined to identify undesirable sections, especially those that management feels restrict its rights. Both offensive and defensive strategies regarding contract changes are prepared.

If management or the union wishes to make changes in a contract, it must notify the other party in writing of desire to terminate or modify the contract at least 60 days before the contract expires. This notification also should include an offer to meet the other side to discuss the issue.

2. *Gather statistical information.* For example, management seeks information on economic conditions affecting the job (such as pay or productivity) from its staff, industry data, and published sources. An attempt is made to determine the cost of each likely union demand. Preliminary tradeoffs are thought through. The union tends to ask for more than it knows it can get, so management tries to calculate the best strategy.

3. *Prepare detailed studies of the union leadership and membership personalities.* This helps the enterprise develop the bargaining strategy.

"I say we throw a good scare into the union -- offer to sell them the plant."

Reprinted by permission The Wall Street Journal.

4. *Undertake intercompany efforts.* This step is necessary if the organizing effort is industrywide. Enterprises in the industry exchange information at many levels.

5. *Arrange preliminary meeting with the union.* Management may meet with the union to try to narrow the bargaining scope and get a feel of the other's priorities.

The union also prepares for negotiations by preparing lists of problems with the contract. It too gathers statistical information, studies the opponent closely, and coordinates with other unions involved. Unions may also have internal differences, usually over what the bargaining objectives are. For example, younger workers may want a pay increase, while older workers prefer better pensions. Increasingly, unions poll their members on their preferred objectives for negotiation.

After these five steps have been completed, both sides will have prepared their bargaining books and visual displays. They will be ready to negotiate.

Negotiating the contract

Negotiations at the local union and single-operation level usually take place between two teams of negotiators. The union team is large. Typically it has about seven members, including local officers, several stewards and committeemen, and a representative from the regional or national union. Management fields a team of three or four from personnel and line management. They usually operate within guidelines set by their top management officers.

Benjamin Selekman contends that nine types of bargaining strategies can be used. Four of these are rather *rarely* found in the United States. These include:

Racketeering. Corrupt union leaders have relationships with "cooperating" managements.

Ideological. The bargaining process is viewed as part of a class struggle, to reach ends other than just short-run improvement in working conditions.

Collusion. Management and labor combine to get an advantage over the public or competitors by illegal or quasi-illegal means.

Deal. Management and labor negotiate secretly, with little involvement of employees.

The five most frequently used strategies are:

Containment-agression. The union aggressively tries to take over management rights, and management aggressively tries to keep the union down.

Conflict. The employer tries hard to get rid of a union, and the union resists.

Power. Union and management try to get all possible advantages from each other.

Accommodation. Both sides live and let live.

Cooperation. Both sides are concerned about the total work environment and try hard to improve bargaining and the work environment.

The predominant strategy in union negotiations in this country appears to be the power strategy. Typically, power bargaining follows several stages of development.

1. ***Each side presents its demands.*** Usually the two parties are far apart on some issues.

2. ***Reduction of demands.*** After the postures have been taken, each side trades off some of the demands they were not too serious about. These demands were included for trading purposes. Pressure is received from the public, customers, union members, and others regarding the bargaining terms.

3. ***Subcommittee studies.*** Getting down to business, the two parties form joint subcommittees which try to work out reasonable alternatives.

4. ***Informal settlement.*** The two sides go back to their reference groups. The management team determines if top management will accept the terms, and union leaders take soundings of the memberships to see their reaction. If management is agreeable, the process develops into the formal settlement stage.

Reverse collective bargaining. A final stage which has appeared recently is renegotiations, or what Peter Henle calls reverse collective bargaining. This is his description for cases where, in the middle of a contract, the union asks to reopen negotiations to increase wages in a time of inflation. This is less likely if cost-of-living allowances are included in wage contracts. But Henle also describes 12 cases in 1971–72 where contracts were renegotiated to *lower* wages or fringe benefits. These occurred when larger multiplant corporations an-

A contract negotiation session

nounced that because wages were too high, they would have to close a plant or greatly scale down employment. The unions agreed to lower wages in these cases to save jobs, because the companies could demonstrate the wage disparities. Henle argues they also did so because the two parties had a history of mutual trust and confidence in bargaining.

Reed Richardson recommends these procedures to make negotiations effective:

Keep your real objectives confidential.

Don't hurry; when in doubt, caucus.

Be flexible, and remember bargaining is by nature compromise.

Try to understand why the other side is taking its position. Respect their need for face-saving.

Build a reputation of firm but fair negotiation.

Control your emotions.

Measure each move against your objectives.

Remember, the impact of present concessions affects the future.

Contract issues

Any labor contract can have a large number of clauses, and there are numerous issues over which the two parties can bargain. The number of items an employer must bargain over has increased greatly in the last 30 years. The issues can be categorized into the five groups named below.

1. ***Compensation and working conditions.*** All contracts stipulate compensation and working conditions, such as direct compensation rates, benefits, and hours of work. Two examples of compensation and working conditions being negotiated in the late 1970s are shorter work weeks and less rigorous work rules.

2. *Employee security.* Seniority is a special concern in this bargaining category. Seniority is continuous service in a work unit, plant, or organization. Unions feel that seniority should be the determining factor in promotions, layoffs, and recalls. Management contends that it is its right to make these decisions on the basis of job performance, or efficiency will suffer. The clause many contracts have stipulates that in cases of promotion and layoff, when efficiency and ability are substantially equal, the most senior employee shall be favored. In the late 1970s unions are negotiating for lifetime job security, especially in steel and higher education.

3. *Union security.* To have as much influence over members as possible, the union tries to write a requirement for a union shop into the contract. A union shop is an employment location at which all employees must join the union after a brief introductory period. Failing this, the union tries to get a modified union shop: all employees except a few exempted groups must joint the union. If the union shop clause cannot be won, an agency shop may be acceptable to the union. In this, those who do not join the union must pay the equivalent of union dues to the union.

4. *Management rights.* This issue usually presents an especially difficult set of problems. Management lists certain areas or decisions as management rights or prerogatives which are excluded from bargaining. Management tries to make these lists long, and unions have chipped away at them. Recently the United Auto Workers argued that handling health and safety problems should be a joint union-management area. This union also disputes a foreman's right to suspend a worker without pay over issues other than violence, drunkenness, and illegal refusal to work.

5. *Contract duration.* This issue is of special concern to the enterprise Companies tend to prefer longer contracts to avoid the turmoil of frequent negotiation. Over 90 percent of U.S. contracts now cover two- or three-year periods.

To increase the effectiveness of the bargaining process, one suggestion is for both sides to make a list of the bargaining items and rank order them. An example of how this is done is shown in Exhibit 17–3.

EXHIBIT 17–3

Collective bargaining by objectives—a guide for data preparation, strategy, and evaluation of bargaining results (blank form)

Bargaining items*	Priorities†	Range of bargaining objectives			Initial bargaining position‡	Evaluation results		
		Pessimistic	Realistic	Optimistic		P	R	O

* Classify items in two groups: financial and nonfinancial.

† Relative priority of each bargaining item to all bargaining items.

‡ Actual visible position taken by parties at opening of negotiation (union initial proposal or company response or counteroffer).

Source: Reed Richardson, "Positive Collective Bargaining," in H. Heneman, Jr., and D. Yoder (eds.), *Employee and Labor Relations,* vol. 3 (Washington, D.C.: Bureau of National Affairs, 1976), pp. 7-111–7-143.

Agreeing upon, ratifying, and formalizing the contract

An agreement comes about when both sides feel they have produced the best contract they can. Their perceptions are influenced by the negotiations, the relative power of the two at the time, and other factors. Power factors such as a weak union or a strong employer are very important in the settlement of the contract. If the economy is slack, the union may be under more pressure to settle than in times of full employment. If the employer's business has certain crucial times (e.g., new-model time for autos, harvesttime for food, Christmastime for the post office), the union may choose that time for negotiations to give it an advantage. If the government is committed to few strikes, it may intervene. All of these external factors and more enter the bargaining process.

To create a formal settlement, a memorandum of agreement is prepared for the negotiating committee's assent. Both sides sign this memorandum. In most unions, the contract does not become official until the union membership ratifies it. The members must believe the contract is the best the union could get. At one time membership ratification was mostly a rubber stamp. Union locals now refuse to ratify contracts sometimes. In one year in the midseventies, for example, 12.3 percent were rejected by members, and the statistics on rejections have been increasing. If the membership refuses ratification, the union negotiating team must try to achieve more concessions from management.

The agreement or contract sets out the rules of the job for the contract period. It restricts some behavior and requires other behavior. Proper wording of the agreement can prevent future difficulties in interpretation. Both sides should thoroughly discuss the meaning of each clause to prevent misunderstanding, if possible. A typical format for the sections normally covered in the contract or agreement is given in Exhibit 17–4.

Even if the contract is accepted at one level, it may require adjustments at other levels. For example, when Ford signs a contract with the UAW at the national level, local plants must then settle disputes on work rules and other issues at each plant. Only when these are settled is the contract negotiation process over for a while.

EXHIBIT 17–4
Standard labor contract format

Section no.	*Subject*
1	Purpose of the parties (union and management)
2	Management rights
3	Union security and dues checkoff
4	Grievance procedures
5	Arbitration of grievances
6	Disciplinary procedures
7	Compensation rates
8	Hours of work and overtime
9	Benefits: Vacations Holidays Insurance Pensions
10	Health and safety provisions
11	Employee security-seniority provisions
12	Contract expiration date

IMPASSES IN COLLECTIVE BARGAINING

The description of contract negotiation above suggests a smooth flow, from presentation of demands to settlement. This flow is not always so smooth, and impasses may develop at which one or both sides cannot keep the process moving. Three things can happen when an impasse develops:

- Conciliation or mediation.
- A strike or lockout.
- Arbitration.

Conciliation and mediation

Conciliation or mediation is the process by which a professional, neutral third party is invited in by both parties to help remove an impasse to the negotiations.

All experts agree that it is better for the two parties to negotiate alone. When it appears this process has broken down, however, a mediator, usually a govern-

"Well, at least he's got them agreeing on something!"

ment mediator such as those provided by the Federal Mediation and Conciliation Service (FMCS), can be invited in. Some states also offer mediation services to both sides. The 250 men and women of FMCS offer such services as developing factual data if the two sides disagree, setting up joint study committees on difficult points, or trying to help the two sides find common grounds for further bilateral negotiations. Instead of waiting until an impasse, the FMCS also offers preventative mediation—when the two parties anticipate serious problems prior to deadlines for strikes, and so on.

By U.S. federal law, both parties must notify FMCS of unresolved disputes not later than 30 days before the contract expires. One of the most frequent uses of mediation and conciliation is in public-sector disputes, where strikes are prohibited.

Are fact-finding, mediation, and conciliation helpful in breaking impasses? In general, the evidence is that conciliation required *by law* is not effective. Some research finds the evidence mixed: sometimes it helps, sometimes not. Too little evidence is available to specify the conditions when it is effective.

Strikes and lockouts

If an impasse in negotiations is quite serious, a strike or a lockout can take place.

A strike is a refusal by employees to work.

A lockout is a refusal by management to allow employees to work.

Strikes can be categorized by the objectives they seek. A *contract strike* occurs when management and the union cannot agree on terms of a new contract. More than 90 percent of strikes are contract strikes.

A *grievance strike* occurs when the union disagrees on how management is interpreting the contract or handling day-to-day problems such as discipline. Strikes over grievances are prohibited in about 95 percent of contracts, but they occur fairly frequently in mining, transportation, and construction industries.

A *jurisdictional strike* takes place when two or more unions disagree on which jobs should be organized by each union. About 2.5 percent of strikers are involved in these strikes, although the Taft-Hartley law gives the NLRB the power to settle these issues, and unions also have internal methods for settling them.

About 1 percent of strikes are *recognition strikes.* These occur as a strategy to force an employer to accept the union. *Political strikes* take place to influence government policy and are extremely rare in the United States.

Strikes differ too in the percentage of employees who refuse to work. A *total strike* takes place when all unionized employees walk out. If only a percentage of the workers does so, the result may be a partial strike, semistrike or slowdown. In a *slowdown,* all employees come to work, but they do little work. The union insists on all work rules being followed to the letter, with the result that output slows down. In a *partial strike* many employees strike but others come to work.

A picket line during a strike

This type is especially prevalent in the public sector so essential services can be continued.

Some researchers suggest that a partial strike is a solution to no-strike provisions in public employment. All employees could do some work and withhold some services. Both employers and employees would be hurt and thus pressured to settle, but the public's essential interest would be preserved. Other researchers suggest a graduated partial strike as a solution. If an impasse exists, the workers would reduce services two hours per week and get three fourths of their regular pay for hours not worked. The next week, they would work four hours less but get only five-eighths regular pay for hours not worked, and so on. This idea puts financial pressures on both sides, but it is less costly than a total strike.

In Europe, a much more destructive type of partial strike is used—the *ratchet strike.* Employees deliberately slow down, or what appears to be random absenteeism and sick calls take place. The ratchet or rotating type of strike has been used very effectively in Italy. Workers 1, 3, 5, 7, 9, etc., on an assembly line call in sick for the morning. Workers 2, 4, 6, 8, etc., become sick for the afternoon. This causes havoc for production and cuts the costs to the strikers from loss of pay. This method also was apparently used by striking Canadian rail workers in 1973.

Strikes in the private sector. The Bureau of Labor Statistics estimates that fewer than 4 percent of contract negotiations result in strikes, and less than 0.4 percent of working time was lost to strikes in recent years. It is instructive to examine the trends of these and similar data. According to the International Labour Office, in the decade 1965–74 the number of strikes increased from 3,963 to 6,074; the number of workers involved in strikes increased from 1,550,000 to 2,778,000; and the number of work days lost from strikes increased from 23,-300,000 to 48,044,660. In some industries, such as mining and longshore work, the probability of strikes is high; in others, such as agriculture and trade, it is low.

Strikes or the threat of strikes do put added pressures on both sides to settle their differences. Most strikes do not seriously affect the public welfare, but if it appears this is the case, the Taft-Hartley Act allows the President to appoint a board of inquiry and issue an injunction for an 80-day cooling-off period. During this period, the employees are polled by secret ballot to see if they will accept the employer's latest offer.

Strikes in the public sector. In the United States, most states have antistrike laws, but they are generally ineffective. One study of these laws found that after no-strike laws were passed in eight states, in one the number of strikes *increased,* in three they decreased, and in four they stayed the same.

Strikes in the public sector are shorter than in the private sector and involve fewer employees. The public employees most likely to strike are sanitation employees, utility and transportation workers, and teachers. However, strikes in the public sector are increasing.

Anatomy of a strike. For a strike to take place, three actors must make decisions. *Management* must decide it can afford to "take a strike." If this is the case, it has built its inventories up, has sufficient financial resources, feels it will not lose too many customers during a strike, and believes it can win. *The union* must believe it will win more than it loses, that the enterprise will not go out of business, and that management will not replace the union employees with strikebreakers. *The union members* must be willing to live with hardships and worries about no paychecks. They must also be willing to give the union a strike vote. When members give the union the authority to strike, its bargaining hand is strengthened, and it can time the strike to occur when it will hurt management the most.

During the strike, the union sets up the legally allowed number of pickets at the plants. Union headquarters becomes strike headquarters, and the union tries to mobilize support among allies in other unions and the public. It also might try to get them to boycott use of the enterprise's goods and services. A strike is a very emotional experience, and violence can occur if management tries to bring in strikebreakers. Union officials build the morale of the strikers, especially on the picket line.

What does management do if there is a strike? Lockouts are rarely used. In general, it tries to encourage the workers to return to work by advertising circulars, phone calls, and so on. The longer the strike, the harder it is on the strikers. If the union has only limited strike funds and workers' savings run out, a back-to-work movement can cause the strike to collapse. This is what management wants. In recent years, management has tended to play a defensive "wait them out" game and to keep the enterprise operating during a strike. Nonunionized employees such as white-collar workers and managers may try to keep things going. If management goes on the offensive, it can hire strikebreakers or threaten to close the plant. It is difficult to calculate when to operate and when to close down; there are many imponderables and unknowns in the conditions. The advantages of continued operations include teaching the union a lesson, continuance of vital services, and an improved bargaining position. The disadvantages

"The N.L.R.B. will hear of this, Mr. Dexter!"

Joe Mirachi in True. *Copyright © 1967; used by permission.*

include increased bitterness during and after the strike, property damage and violence, and public relations defeats. A strike ends when both sides return to the bargaining table, or the weaker side gives in.

Arbitration

> Arbitration is the process by which two parties to a dispute agree to settle the dispute by accepting the decision of an independent quasijudge called an arbitrator. Arbitration can be used to settle issues at contract time or to settle grievance issues during the contract's period.

Arbitration can settle all kinds of dispute issues. The most frequent issues to be sent to arbitration are (in order of importance) discharge and disciplinary actions, seniority, job evaluation; and overtime. If an issue is decided by an arbitrator, that ends it. It cannot be appealed to the courts.

Arbitration can be modeled as shown in Exhibit 17–5. The six steps in the process are also described here.

EXHIBIT 17–5
The arbitration process

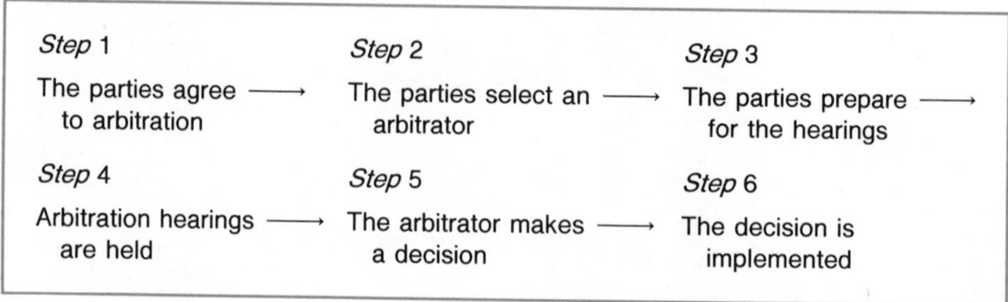

Step 1: The parties agree to arbitration. This is done by providing for arbitration in the contract or agreeing on it at the time of the issue. The subject of the hearing is stipulated in the submission agreement, which also states that the arbitrator has final authority to settle the issue.

Step 2: The parties select an arbitrator. Both parties seek an individual who is fair and knowledgeable. The typical arbitrator is a lawyer or professor who is paid expenses plus a fee of about $250 per day. Some parties agree ahead of time to use a specific arbitrator should they need one. Others select one from a list provided by the American Arbitration Association or Federal Mediation and Conciliation Service.

Step 3: The parties prepare for the hearing. Both sides prepare their cases carefully in advance. Although precedences need not hold, they are accumulated. Both sides develop the evidence, reduce witnesses to a minimum by getting stipulations to facts, and use documents instead of witnesses where possible for efficiency puproses.

Step 4: Arbitration hearings are held. The hearings vary in formality from sessions similar to those in court, with the swearing in of witnesses and so forth, to quite informal hearings. The case presentation begins with an opening statement by both sides. Witnesses are presented and cross examined. In arbitrating contracts, both sides must present their evidence. In arbitrating grievances or deciding disciplinary cases, the arbitrator tries to see if there is guilt beyond a reasonable doubt, something like in criminal court cases. In grievance cases, he examines the contract and precedents in the case, as well as how long the precedents have been in existence. Most arbitrators stipulate that the burden of proof is on the party who filed the grievance or disciplined the employee in these types of cases.

The arbitrator seeks to assure a fair hearing to both sides. He can admit relevant hearsay evidence, question witnesses, and ask for more information from one or both parties. The arbitrator wishes to have all the facts available before the decision is made. Once the arbitrator has heard all the evidence, the hearing is adjourned.

Step 5: The arbitrator makes a decision. How do arbitrators decide cases? Research found that it is easier to say how arbitrators did *not* decide than how they did. They do not flip coins, decide on the basis of the power involved, ignore the record, or decide on personalities rather than the record. The process used varies from informal to formal. Some write up the facts, and in the process the decision comes. Others research the issues further after the case presentation is completed.

So the arbitrator makes a decision. Then he proceeds to write the arbitration award, which is binding on both parties. The award normally reviews the facts in the case prior to stating the decision. It usually is presented within 30 days of the hearing. The arbitrator attempts to write the award in language that is understandable to all parties concerned, including the employee involved in a grievance. It should clarify the situation so as to prevent future problems from arising.

Step* 6: *The decision is implemented. Once the decision is known, both parties implement it. For example, the decision might call for the reinstatement of a discharged employee.

Is compulsory arbitration an alternative to striking? Those not familiar with labor relations often try to substitute compulsory arbitration for allowing strikes. Is this effective as an alternative to strikes? The answer is, sometimes. Some positive results have been found for use of a variation of compulsory arbitration called final-offer arbitration, and compulsory arbitration itself. But most of the evidence is negative. Some question its constitutionality. In general, compulsory arbitration is used in the public sector. In the most extensive usage so far—in Australia, where 90 percent of the work force is covered—the number of days lost due to strikes has *increased* under arbitration, not decreased. It appears to be a possible alternative only if both sides *willingly* submit the issue. This is not so if they are *forced* to use it. After it was used during World War II, it was the *unamimous opinion* of the arbitrators that the best thing that happened to the United States was the return to free collective bargaining, strikes and all.

GRIEVANCES

A grievance is a formal dispute between an employee and management on the conditions of employment.

Grievances arise because of:

- Differing interpretations of the contract by employees, stewards, and management.
- A violation of a contract provision.
- Violation of law.
- A violation of work procedures or other precedents.
- Perceived unfair treatment of an employee by management.

The rate of grievances may increase when employees are dissatisfied or frustrated on their jobs or they resent the supervisory style, or because the union is using grievances as a tactic against management. Grievances may also be due to unclear contractual language or employees with personal problems or who are otherwise "difficult."

The U.S. Department of Labor has found that the most frequent incidents leading to the filing of a grievance are employee discipline, seniority decisions at promotion or layoff time, work assignment, management rights, and compensation and benefits. As will be discussed in Chapter 19, some enterprises use grievance and complaint statistics as a measure of the personnel department's effectiveness.

The grievance-processing system

The employee grievance process involves a systematic set of steps for handling an employee complaint. Most union contracts provide the channels and mechanisms for processing these grievances. The grievance process has at least three purposes and consequences. First, by settling smaller problems early, it may prevent larger problems (like strikes) from occurring in the future. Second, properly analyzed, grievances serve as a source of data to focus the attention of the two parties on ambiguities in the contract for negotiation at a future date. Finally, the grievance process is an effective communication channel from employees to management.

The method by which formal grievances are processed varies with the labor contract. Exhibit 17–6 diagrams the grievance process. On the left side of the exhibit are the steps followed in many, if not most, smaller enterprises. The larger organization (shown on the right side of the exhibit) adds two intervening steps.

EXHIBIT 17–6
Steps in processing a grievance

	SMALLER ENTERPRISE	LARGER ENTERPRISE
1st step	Employee and steward meet with supervisor and employee files a grievance orally or in writing	
	If not settled, go to 2d step	
2d step	Employee files grievance in writing. It is reviewed by:	
	Head of local work unit and shop committee	Personnel office and chief steward or business agent
	If not settled, go to last step	If not settled, go to intervening steps
		Reviewed by personnel director or plant manager; union represented by plant committee
		If not settled, go to next step
		Top corporate management and national union representatives review it.
		If not settled, go to last step
Last step	Arbitration	Arbitration

Step 1: Initiation of the formal grievance. An employee who feels that she or he has been mistreated or that some action or application of policy violates his rights in the contract may file a grievance with his supervisor. He can do

this orally or in writing. If he wishes, he can formulate the grievance with the help and support of the union steward.

The supervisor may let the employee blow off steam and cool down before attempting to deal with the grievance. But the supervisor must take it seriously and attempt to determine accurately the reason for it. The grievance should be attended to as soon as possible after making sure the facts are accurate. The effective approach is to try to solve the problem, not to assess blame or find excuses. The supervisor should consider what the contract says as modified by the employer's policies and past precedents in such cases. If the supervisor has a good working relationship with the steward, they can work together to settle the problem at that level. Supervisors should be trained in how to handle grievances with the use of effective counseling techniques. Seventy-five percent of grievances are settled at Step 1.

Step 2: Department head or unit manager. If the steward, supervisor, and employee together cannot solve the grievance, it goes to the next level in the hierarchy. At this point, the grievance must be presented in writing and both sides must document their cases. What this level consists of depends on the size of the organization. In small organizations, it could be the head of the local employment unit—general manager, or administrator. The union may be represented by a shop committee. In larger enterprises, there may be an intermediate level, such as department head. In the largest enterprises, the personnel department and union business agent may be the second step, followed by a third step of unit manager and local union president (see Exhibit 17–6). One fifth of all grievances are settled at this step.

Step 3: Arbitration. If the grievance cannot be settled at this intervening step (or steps), an independent arbitrator may be called in to settle the issue. Only about 1 percent go to arbitration. The other 4 percent, primarily in larger enterprises, are taken care of in the intervening steps.

Grievances in the public and third sectors. Executive Order 11491 governs the grievance process for federal employees. The first two steps are in the private sector. Then conciliation and mediation are tried. If no solution is found, the grievance goes to the Federal Service Impasses Panel and finally to arbitration. The incidence of grievance systems for state and local government employees is also increasing.

Grievances in nonunionized enterprises. As described in more detail in Chapter 18, nonunionized enterprises offer alternatives to the grievance system to give employees justice. Approaches used include counseling; the open-door policy whereby the grievant can go over the supervisor's head; and use of an ombudsman, or a quasi-grievance process in which the personnel specialist or a third party represents the employee.

Reducing grievances and improving the process

Various approaches have been suggested for reducing grievances. One is to reduce the causes of the grievances, such as bad working conditions or an employer-oriented supervisory style. Educating managers on contract provisions and effective, human relations–oriented grievance processing helps. Quick and efficient processing will ultimately reduce grievance rates. It is also suggested that supervisors should consult personnel and other supervisors before processing grievances to get the best advice and improve their effectiveness in the grievance process.

SUMMARY, CONCLUSIONS, AND RECOMMENDATIONS

This chapter has introduced you to labor relations, an emotionally charged personnel activity. It has discussed the mechanisms used in collective bargaining and group negotiations, labor unions, federal laws, grievances, and the participation of various enterprise employees in the labor relations process. To summarize some of the most important points:

1. Conditions considered unfair or exploitative have led to the development of the collective bargaining process.
2. The people and groups of people involved in collective bargaining are unionized employees, union officials, employers and employers' officials, government officials, customers and clients, and the general public.
3. Collective bargaining is a technical area requiring experience and legal knowledge.
4. Personnel managers or specialists are of necessity technical experts on labor relations who train and advise operating managers on the contract provisions.
5. The National Labor Relations Board (NLRB) administers the laws and regulations in the private and third sector; many states have state boards to administer state labor laws.
6. The major law affecting collecting bargaining in the United States is the National Labor Relations Act (Wagner Act) as ammended by the labor-Management Relations Act of 1947 (Taft-Hartly Act), and the Landrum-Griffin Act of 1959.
7. In general, less than 1 percent of work days is lost due to work stoppages such as strikes.

It is impossible to detail the various stages in organizing a union, the steps in arbitration, and so here without repeating much of the chapter. Please refer to the appropriate sections to review this material. Remember, when there are difficulties, the grievance system provides an outlet to handle them.

No propositions or recommendations for model organizations will be given in this chapter because more detailed data would be required to do so.

Chapter 18 discusses the employee disciplinary process in unionized and nonunionized enterprises.

Tom Hardisty and Stan Goebel had lunch after their discussion about labor relations. After lunch, Stan said: "We could follow a strategy of fighting the union to keep it out. Or we could let nature take its course and live with them."

Tom replied, "That's what you think! I'm *not* running a unionized place. I'll sell out first. You are to figure out how to keep that #*& union out of HMC!"

Stan then prepared a communication program and proposed increases in pay and benefits as part of the "keep the union out" strategy. He costed out the proposed changes in pay and benefits and took these to Tom.

Tom: The communication program looks good, Stan. We'll have personal visits with the employees to talk about the union problem. The supervisors will run some of the meetings. You and I will split up and attend as many as we can. You'll train the supervisors on why the employees shouldn't join the union. But we can't afford to add these pay and benefit increases at this time.

Stan: You know the union will exploit that. Our money situation, together with the lack of security because of layoffs, puts us at a big disadvantage.

Tom: I know it. But its your job to keep the union out.

In the next days and weeks, Stan did his best. Lots of personal meetings were held. They mailed letters to the employees' homes. But the union got 30 percent of the employees to sign the authorization cards. And the NLRB got involved, to schedule the unionization election. Shortly after the NLRB examiner left, Tom called Stan into his office.

Tom: How could we lose this election? What do I have a personnel manager for if he can't beat the union?

Stan: It's not over yet. They have to get a majority. But Tom, we're being hurt by the pay item. You told me we had to lay off people to cut costs, and the layoffs came in the middle of the organizing campaign. A lot of people felt threatened. When people get threatened, they join unions.

Tom: See here, I'm tired of excuses. We're going to get the job done. I promise you, we'll have no more layoffs. But we had to keep ourselves above water, and we needed those layoffs. I'll help with the communication program again.

Between then and the election, both sides campaigned. The vote looked close. When the votes were counted, the union had won. HMC challenged the votes of several persons, but the NLRB declared the union as the bargaining agent.

One week later, Stan quit. Tom didn't fire him. He hadn't spoken to Stan since the results of the election, though. Stan's replacement, Ed Shermans, has had a good deal of experience negotiating contracts and handling grievances. But the contract negotiations look like they will be difficult, because Tom is quite bitter.

QUESTIONS

1. What is labor relations? What diagnostic factors affect it?
2. Why do people join unions?
3. How do union officials and labor relations experts perceive each other? Why?
4. Describe the major unions in the United States. How are they organized? Are unions growing in strength?
5. Describe the major provisions of the most important labor laws and regulations.
6. How do labor relations differ among the public, private, and third sectors?
7. Describe what a union organizing campaign is like. What are managers allowed to do? What should managers do if they wish to prevent unionization?
8. Describe how contracts are negotiated.
9. When are mediators helpful to negotiations?
10. When do strikes take place?
11. Under what conditions would you use arbitrators in labor relations?
12. What is a grievance? How do enterprises process them?

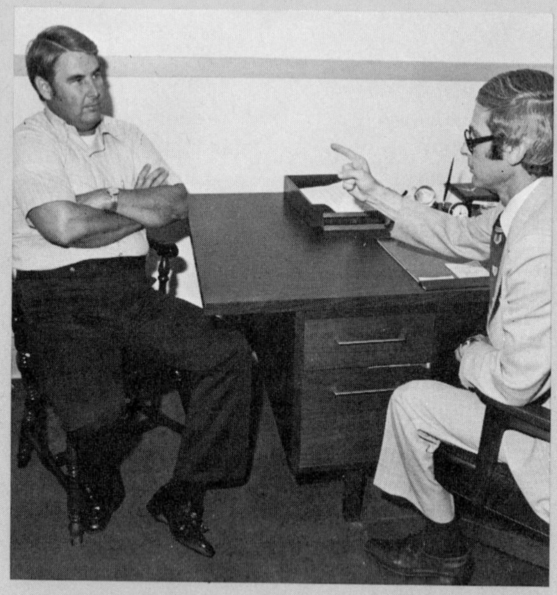

ALCOHOL
ABUSE
CLINIC

part seven

Discipline, control, and evaluation

Efforts to control and evaluate the human resource in the enterprise take various forms.

Chapter 18 discusses the symptoms indicating that an employee is difficult to deal with and the systems available to attempt to modify his or her behavior.

In Chapter 19 the emphasis is not on the individual employee but on methods used to evaluate and measure the overall effectiveness of the human resources and the personnel function of an enterprise. It also looks at the future of the personnel function.

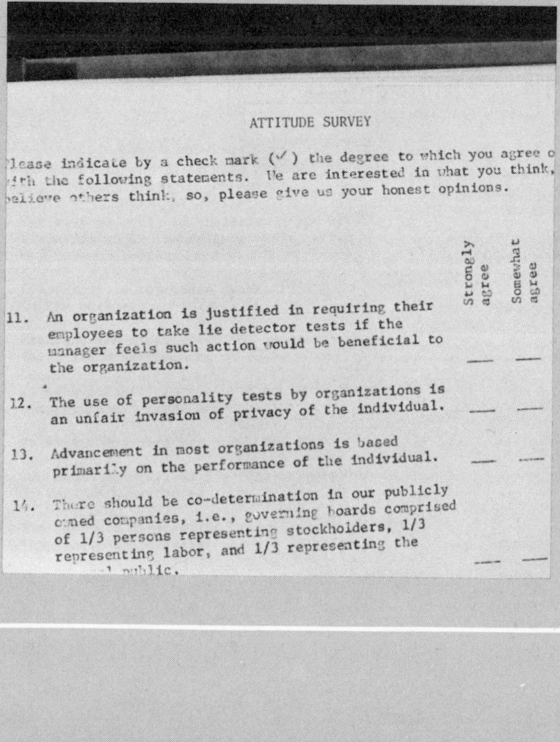
ATTITUDE SURVEY

lease indicate by a check mark (✓) the degree to which you agree o
ith the following statements. We are interested in what you think,
elieve others think, so, please give us your honest opinions.

	Strongly agree	Somewhat agree
11. An organization is justified in requiring their employees to take lie detector tests if the manager feels such action would be beneficial to the organization.	___	___
12. The use of personality tests by organizations is an unfair invasion of privacy of the individual.	___	___
13. Advancement in most organizations is based primarily on the performance of the individual.	___	___
14. There should be co-determination in our publicly owned companies, i.e., governing boards comprised of 1/3 persons representing stockholders, 1/3 representing labor, and 1/3 representing the general public.	___	___

18

Discipline and the difficult employee

Chapter objectives

- To show why disciplinary systems are necessary in an enterprise.
- To examine the characteristics of different types of difficult employees.
- To discuss the variety of disciplinary philosophies, methods, and systems available for use in managing difficult employees.

Chapter outline

I. A Diagnostic Approach to Discipline
II. Categories of Difficult Employees
   A. Category 1: The ineffective employee
   B. Category 2: Alcoholic and addicted employees
   C. Category 3: Participants in theft, crime, and illegal acts
   D. Category 4: The rule violators
   E. Are certain types of employees likely to be difficult?
III. The Discipline Process
IV. Administration of Discipline
   A. Hierarchical discipline systems
   B. Other discipline and appeal systems
V. Summary, Conclusions, and Recommendations

Managers supervise a variety of types of employees as part of their work. Most employees perform effectively most of the time. But any management development session eventually comes around to a discussion of employees like Al, Susan, Joyce, or Tom. These four employees are employed by a small conglomerate in the Boston area, Judge Incorporated. Judge owns manufacturing and retailing units.

- Al is the salesman who had the largest sales increases of any of the sales force just after he was hired. Later, his sales dropped off. When his supervisor checked, Al was found to be making just enough sales calls to reach his quota.
- Susan is often a good worker. Then there are days when all the forms she types have serious errors on them. These are the days Susan is drinking.
- Joyce seems to do good work. She is courteous to the customers. She puts the stock up quickly and marks the prices accurately. But Joyce takes more than her paycheck home every week.
- Tom is a pretty good employee. But John, his supervisor, is driven up the wall by him. Tom just can't seem to follow the company rules. And when John tries to talk to him about it, Tom gives him a hard time and may even seem to threaten him if he tries to do anything about the problem.

At present, Judge Incorporated has no well-organized discipline system.

These examples illustrate a time-consuming and worrisome aspect of the personnel job: dealing fairly with the difficult employee. The seriousness of the problem is shown by the fact that the largest number of cases going to arbitration involves disciplinary matters. Unionized organizations have ways of dealing with these incidents, but most employees do not work in a unionized situation.

This chapter is concerned with the characteristics of difficult employees and some of the reasons they are the way they are. It also considers systems of discipline and appropriate means for rehabilitating difficult employees. Too often discipline has been oriented toward punishment for past misdeeds. This is required in Joyce's case, but more important for the others is behavioral change to improve employee productivity.

The emphasis of the chapter will be on *on-the-job behavior*. Enterprises such as the military and the church have tried to control the total behavior of the employee; the military often will court-martial and punish soldiers for civilian offenses such as speeding, whether or not civilian authorities prosecute. The work organization, however, should be concerned with off-the-job behavior only when it affects work behavior. Thus if Susan drinks before work so that she cannot do her job, this is of concern to her employer. If she has a few drinks after work and this in no way affects her job, it is none of her employer's business, even if the boss happens to be a teetotaler.

Generally, the operating supervisor is the person primarily involved in disciplining employees. Personnel specialists may be involved as advisers if they are asked to do so by the operating manager. Sometimes the personnel manager serves as a second step in investigation and appeal of a disciplinary case. Or, when the union is involved, the personnel manager may advise the operating manager on contract interpretation for a specific case.

Discipline is a Stage III personnel activity as defined in Exhibit 1–6 (Chapter 1). Some studies have been performed on the topic, but there is a wide divergence in the disciplinary practices applied in various enterprises.

A DIAGNOSTIC APPROACH TO DISCIPLINE

Exhibit 18–1 highlights the factors affecting the discipline process in an enterprise. The employee is the crucial factor, especially insofar as his or her attitude toward work is concerned. Discipline problems are not as likely with work-oriented people as with those who have an instrumental orientation (see Chapter 2). These work attitudes probably were developed from the employee's past work experiences and cultural heritage.

The kind of discipline system used is normally related to the enterprise. It will be more formal in larger enterprises, especially those that are unionized. It is quite informal in smaller enterprises.

How strict discipline is depends on the nature of the prevailing labor markets. In times of high unemployment, for example, it can be quite strict. It also is related to the supportiveness of the work group (if the work group "covers"

EXHIBIT 18–1

Factors affecting discipline and organizational effectiveness

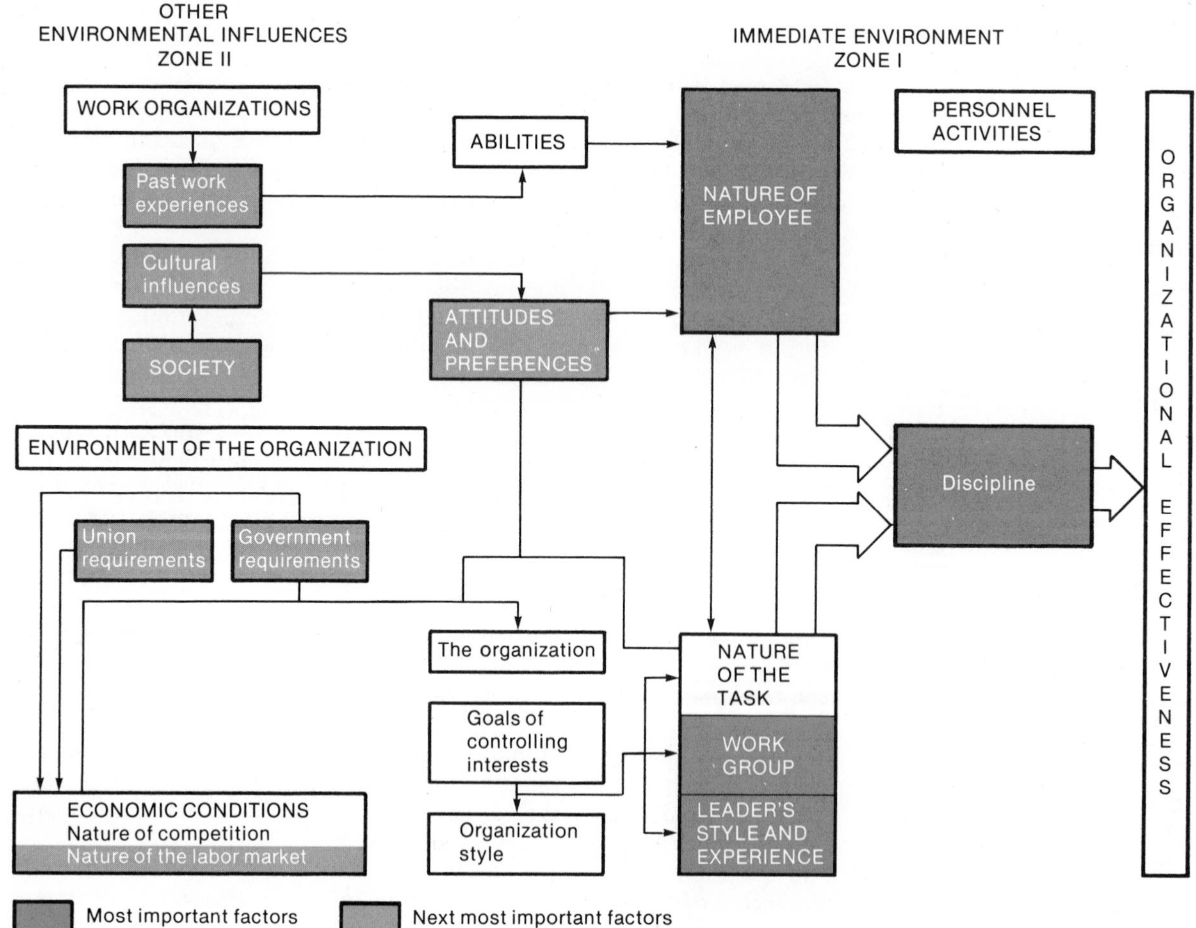

for the employee and feels the issue is unimportant, management's ability to discipline will be limited), and to the nature of the leader or supervisor (a liberal leader's approach to discipline will be quite different from a conservative leader's). The government and the legal system may provide support for employer or employee.

The effective operating or personnel manager will try to diagnose each of these factors in the discipline situation. For example, the supervisor may try to diagnose the difficult employee's motivation, with a view to improving performance. This is not always easy to do. If the manager does not know the employee well, because there are many employees or for other reasons, it may be virtually impossible. Discipline is one of the most challenging areas in the personnel function. The diagnostic approach has many advantages over the "give her a fair trial before you hang her" approach in dealing with the difficult employee.

CATEGORIES OF DIFFICULT EMPLOYEES

This chapter will focus on discipline and behavior modification of four kinds of employees whose behavior can be described as difficult.

Categories of difficult employees:

Category 1. Those whose quality or quantity of work is unsatisfactory due to lack of abilities, training, or job motivation. (Al is an example.)

Category 2. Those whose personal problems off the job begin to affect job productivity. These problems can include alcoholism, drugs, or family relationships. (Susan is an example.)

Category 3. Those who violate laws while on the job by such behavior as stealing from the organization or its employees or physical abuse of employees or property. (Joyce is an example.)

Category 4. Those who consistently break company rules and do not respond to supervisory reactions. (Tom is an example.)

The difficulty of determining the causes of any human behavior pattern was noted in Chapter 2. It is especially difficult to assess the causes of undesired behavior, but John Miner has devised a scheme for analyzing deficient behavior which provides a checklist of possible causes:

I. Problems of Intelligence and Job Knowledge
II. Emotional Problems
III. Motivational Problems
IV. Physical Problems
V. Family Problems
VI. Problems Caused by the Work Group
VII. Problems Originating in Company Policies
VIII. Problems Stemming from Society and its Values
IX. Problems from the Work Context (e.g., Economic Forces) and the Work Itself

Many of these causes can influence deficient behavior, which can result from behavior of the employee alone, behavior of the employer alone, or interaction of the employee and the employer. Al's behavior (Category 1), which is directly related to the work situation, could be caused by Miner's Factors II, III, and VII. Susan could drink (Category 2) because of Miner's Factors II, IV, V, and others; the primary cause of her behavior is outside the control of the employer. Or she could drink because of Miner's Factor VII, which the employer could remedy. Frequently, difficult behavior is caused by personal and employment conditions which feed one another. Joyce's behavior—theft and other illegal activities (Category 3)—is normally dealt with by security departments and usually results in termination and possibly prosecution of the employee. Tom's behavior (Category 4) is often caused by Miner's Factors III, VII, VIII, and IX.

Category 1: The ineffective employee

Employees who are performing ineffectively may do so because of factors which are directly related to the work situation and are theoretically the easiest to work with and to adjust. Robert Mager and Peter Pipe have systematized this pattern of undesirable behavior and have designed a conceptual model of questions by which management can deal with it. Their model is presented as a flow diagram in Exhibit 18–2.

Mager and Pipe indicate that there are four key issues with which managers must cope. The first (I on the diagram) is: The employee is not performing well; the manager thinks there is a training problem. They suggest three general questions and follow-up questions to analyze the problem:

1. *What is the performance discrepancy?* Why do I think there is a training problem? What is the difference between what is being done and what is supposed to be done? What is the event that causes me to say that things aren't right? Why am I dissatisfied?
2. *Is it important?* Why is the discrepancy important? What would happen if I left the discrepancy alone? Could doing something to resolve the discrepancy have any worthwhile result?
3. *Is it a skill deficiency?* Could he do it if he really had to? Could he do it if his life depended on it? Are his present skills adequate for the desired performance?

Question 3 leads to II on the diagram. Key issue I is solved: Yes, it is a skill deficiency. To check this further, Mager and Pipe suggest general questions 4–7:

4. *Could he do it in the past?* Did he once know how to perform as desired? Has he forgotten how to do what I want him to do?
5. *Is the skill used often?* How often is the skill or performance used? Does he get regular feedback about how well he performs? Exactly how does he find out how well he is doing?
6. *Is there a simpler solution?* Can I change the job by providing some kind of job aid? Can I store the needed information some way (written instructions, checklists) other than in someone's head? Can I show rather than train? Would informal (i.e., on-the-job) training be sufficient?
7. *Does he have what it takes?* Could he learn the job? Does he have the physical and mental potential to perform as desired? Is he overqualified for the job?

EXHIBIT 18–2
Analyzing undesirable employee behavior

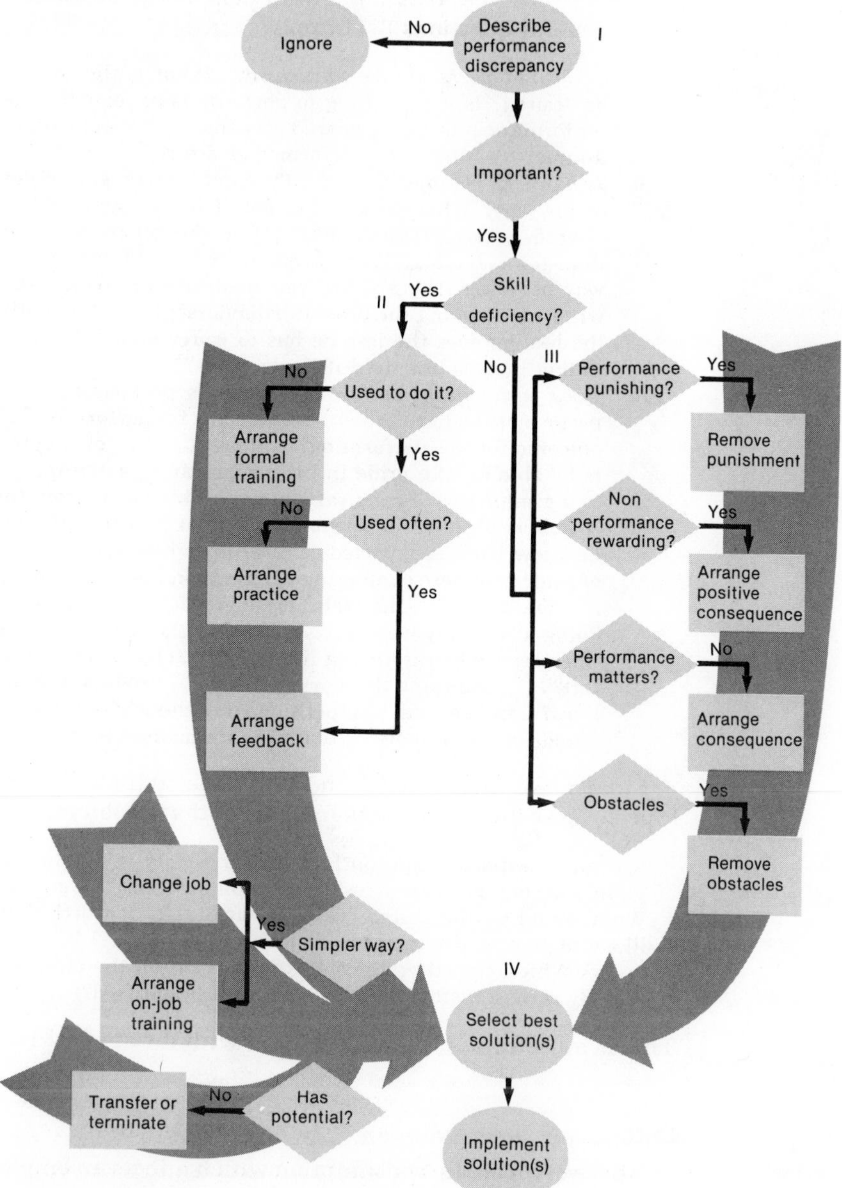

Source: Robert Mager and Peter Pipe, *Analyzing Performance Problems.* Copyright © 1970 by Fearon-Pitman Publishers, Inc., 6 Davis Drive, Belmont, California. Reprinted by permission.

At this point it might appear that the conclusion to II was not correct, or the question may have been answered no in the first place. In this case the key issue would be: It is not a skill deficiency; he could do it if he wanted to. At III, general questions 8–11 apply:

8. *Is desired performance punishing?* What is the consequence of performing as desired? Is it punishing to perform as expected? Does he perceive desired performance as being geared to penalties? Would his world become a little dimmer (to him) if he performed as desired?
9. *Is nonperformance rewarding?* What is the result of doing it his way instead of my way? What does he get out of his present performance in the way of reward, prestige, status, jollies? Does he get more attention for misbehaving than for behaving? What event in the world supports (rewards) his present way of doing things? (Are you inadvertently rewarding irrelevant behavior while overlooking the crucial behaviors?) Is he "mentally inadequate," so that the less he does the less he has to worry about? Is he physically inadequate, so that he gets less tired if he does less?
10. *Does performing really matter?* Does performing as desired matter to the performer? Is there a favorable outcome for performing? Is there an undesirable outcome for not performing? Is there a source of satisfaction for performing? Is he able to take pride in his performance, as an individual or as a member of a group? Does he get satisfaction of his needs from the job?
11. *Are there obstacles to performing?* What prevents him from performing? Does he know what is expected of him? Does he know when to do what is expected of him? Are there conflicting demands on his time? Does he lack the authority? . . . the time? . . . the tools? Is he restricted by policies or by a "right way of doing it" or "way we've always done it" that ought to be changed? Can I reduce interference by improving lighting? . . . changing colors? . . . increasing comfort? . . . modifying the work position? . . . reducing visual or auditory distractions? Can I reduce "competition from the job"—phone calls, "brush fires," demands of less important but more immediate problems?

Finally, we arrive at IV, the key issue: Which solution is best? Mager and Pipe suggest these questions to analyze that problem:

> Are any solutions inappropriate or impossible to implement? Are any solutions plainly beyond our resources? What would it "cost" to go ahead with the solution? What would be the added "value" if it did? Is it worth doing? Which remedy is likely to give us the most result for the least effort? Which are we best equipped to try? Which remedy interests us most? (Or, on the other side of the coin, which remedy is most visible to those who must be pleased?)

This is a useful approach to dealing with a Category 1 employee.

Category 2: Alcoholic and addicted employees

Abuse of alcoholic consumption which affects an employee's job performance is a serious problem with effects on enterprises everywhere throughout the world. More and more, alcoholism is being viewed by the courts and by therapists as an illness, a *treatable* illness. More often than not it is treated as humorous, as in the Frank and Ernest cartoon. Those who know and love people who are alcoholics don't think it is funny at all!

Estimates of the number of alcoholics employed in America vary, but about 10 percent of the labor force are alcoholics and another 10 percent are borderline alcoholics. The greatest incidence of alcoholism is in people aged 35–55 who

© 1978 by NEA, Inc. Reprinted by permission of NEA.

have been employed at the same enterprise 14–20 years. The direct cost to industry alone is estimated at $8 billion a year in lost productivity and allied expenses. This estimate may be low because alcoholics often are sent home as "sick" rather than as drunk.

Of course, alcoholic consumption does not affect all employees the same at work, nor does it affect performance of tasks equally. Studies indicate that alcoholic intake tends to reduce some ability performance levels (for example cognitive and perceptual-sensory skills) more than others (psychomotor skills). For many persons, it takes about an hour for the alcohol to affect performance negatively. About a third of America's largest employers had set up alcoholism control programs. Many medical plans now cover the costs of treatment for alcoholism if the employee will take it, and if they refuse, many companies fire them.

Generally the successful program for alcoholics includes a conference between supervisor and employee. These points are covered:

- The supervisor documents the effects at work of the employee's alcoholism to the employee.
- The supervisor offers to help.
- The supervisor *requires* the employee to participate in a rehabilitation program such as Alcoholics Anonymous (which has been evaluated as by far the best program).
- The supervisor notifies the employee that the consequence of not participating in rehabilitation is loss of the job.

Many unions are now participating in joint employer-union programs designed to deal with alcoholism.

In larger enterprises, the health department helps alcoholics. In medium-sized and smaller enterprises, personnel refers them to consultants and to treatment programs. Personnel and the supervisor cooperate to help the employee to become well again or, alternatively, to be terminated. If the decision is to terminate; personnel and operating managers need documentation to support their decision, in arbitration hearings if necessary.

The addicted employee. Employers also are finding more employees addicted to drugs such as cocaine and heroin and are becoming more aware of this problem area. Drug addiction manifests itself in ways similar to alcoholism. The problem may be less well known to employers because of laws against possession and use of drugs, which causes employees to hide their habit.

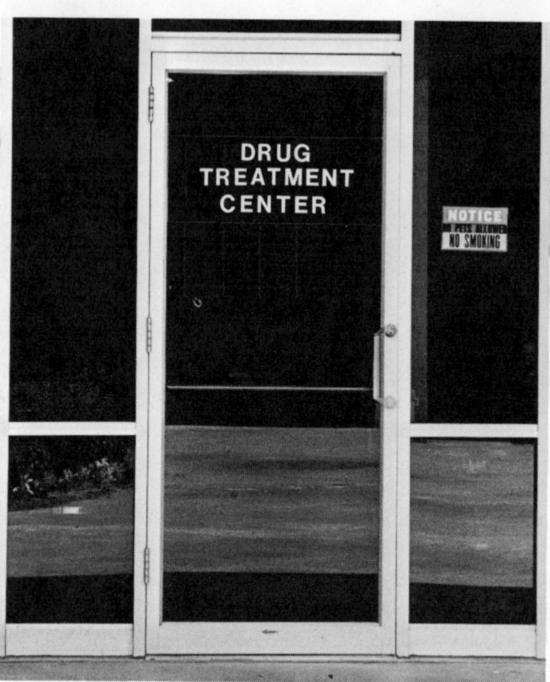

Rehabilitation is encouraged for drug-using employees

How many drug addicts there are in the employment situation is not known precisely. In 1971 the American Management Association studied 23 companies. More than half of the companies surveyed said they had dealt with problems of employee drug abuse during the preceding year. The drugs involved were marijuana (29 percent), amphetamines (18 percent), heroin (17 percent), cocaine (2 percent), and other (10 percent).

Companies believe that absenteeism, turnover, accidents, and lower productivity are caused by drug addiction, and some thievery is due to the need for addicts to support their habit. What have they done about it? One survey of 108 companies on employees' use of drugs found that 81 percent tried to find out if the employee had used drugs prior to hiring, and 51 percent have company policies against drug use by employees. Their responses to the problem include detection methods to determine the extent of the problem, more careful recruitment and selection, educational programs for supervisors, policy statements, and counseling programs which refer addicts to rehabilitation programs.

Companies follow similar control programs for drugs as they do for alcohol, although treatment methods vary more in the drug area. Drug usage is illegal, and public attitudes are much more negative on drugs than on alcohol. In industry, the company health department can try to rehabilitate drug users. Often, however, the ultimate decision is discharge and discipline, although this may lead to arbitration. A summary of arbitration rulings on the subject and a survey of members of the National Academy of Arbitrators by Edward Levin and Tia Denenberg found that because of the legal implications and the difficulty drug users would have in getting future jobs, arbitrators demand full and complete proof of drug usage. This is sometimes difficult for employers to provide. Employers can help protect themselves by asking the employee to certify previous drug experiences. If it can be shown this record is falsified, arbitrators view this as grounds for discharge or discipline. If company policy is to discipline or discharge employees who use drugs, company rules and employment controls should be explicit about this prohibition. Evidence must also be given that these prohibitions have been communicated clearly to all employees.

Arbitrators have discharged drug-using employees if their habit ruins a firm's reputation or causes it to lose business. They are more likely to uphold discharges for drug usage after conviction than after arrest alone, and they discipline drug pushers more severely than drug users. In general, according to Levin and Denenberg, arbitrators tend to urge employers to give drug-using employees a second chance if they agree to rehabilitation programs.

Category 3: Participants in theft, crime, and illegal acts

Employers often have to deal with employees who engage in various illegal acts. Employers may steal (remember Joyce), misuse company facilities or property, disclose trade secrets, embezzle, or kidnap executives for terrorist purposes. They may sabotage products, or use company telephones and credit cards for personal purposes, or pirate company materials or labor to repair their own homes. One source estimates that 75 percent of stolen goods is taken by employees and suppliers. Yet some arbitrators have recently ruled that employee property (such as their cars in the parking lot) cannot be searched without a warrant. The enterprise must also be concerned with thefts and similar crimes by visitors and guests.

Enterprises try to deal with employee theft and similar problems in a number of ways. One is to try to screen out likely thieves. For example, a weighted application blank has been developed to help with this.

Other enterprises try to prevent thefts by training and preventative measures. Ten ways to prevent theft are given in the accompanying box.

Ways to prevent employee theft:

1. The employee should be made to feel that the job is worth keeping and it would not be easy to earn more elsewhere.
2. Normal good housekeeping practices—no piles of rubbish or rejects or boxes, no disused machines with tarpaulins on them, and no unlocked, empty drawers—will help assure that there are no places where stolen goods can be hidden. The first act of the thief is to divert merchandise from the normal traffic flow.
3. Paperwork must be carefully examined and checked at all stages so invoices cannot be stolen or altered.
4. Employees' cars should not be parked close to their places of work. There should be no usable cover between the plant doors and the cars.
5. Women employees must not be allowed to keep their handbags next to them at work. Lockers that lock must be provided for handbags. Merchandise has a way of disappearing into a handbag, and once the bag is closed a search warrant is needed to get it open again.

6. Whether the plant is open or closed at night, bright lights should blaze all around the perimeter so no one can enter or leave without being seen.
7. There should be adequate measures to control issuance of keys. There have been cases where a manager or supervisor would come back at night for a tryst with a girlfriend and would give her an armload of merchandise to take home with her. Key control is very important.
8. As far as possible, everyone entering or leaving should have an identification card.
9. Unneeded doors should be kept locked. If only two must be open to handle the normal flow of traffic, the rest should be bolted.
10. Everything of value that thieves could possibly remove, not just obvious items, must be safeguarded.

A method enterprises can use to oversee these procedures is to set up a security department or program. Often this responsibility is assigned to the personnel department. The protection program typically is called industrial security and includes security education, employment screening, physical security, theft and fraud control, and fire prevention.

Most companies engage in at least minimal industrial security operations such as identification or "badge" systems, prior employment screening, special safeguards for or destruction of sensitive documents, and escort services for visitors.

Jerry Wall believes an enterprise is of sufficient size to have a security program when it has about 100 employees. It can approach this program in two ways, by hiring a technically skilled person to serve at least part time as a security manager, or by leasing this service from a local security agency. In many cases, these agencies will provide both security consulting services and a guard force. Wall found that the larger the enterprise, the greater the likelihood that security measures would be used. Most enterprises also attempt at least some industrial security planning in selecting sites and designs for remodeling or construction of facilities. Security vulnerabilities are assessed and structural barriers such as fences, lighting, and the building itself are designed to reduce security hazards. Wall's study of 1,200 enterprises found them much more security conscious today.

Operating and personnel managers may both be involved in disciplinary matters involving Category 3 employees. Often firings and legal action are considered. Visitors involved in illegal acts may also face the law.

Category 4: The rule violators

Difficult employees of the fourth category consistently violate company rules, such as those prohibiting sleeping on the job, having weapons at work, fighting at work, coming in late, or abusing the supervisor. An especially difficult issue is verbal and physical abuse of supervisors. It is useful (though not necessary) for the enterprise to have an established rule prohibiting verbal and physical abuse. Disputes charging abuse often go to arbitration. Ken Jennings has reviewed the decisions of arbitrators in such cases. In general, arbitrators take the position that the decisions of supervisors deserve respect. Their rulings have been influenced by several facets of the cases:

The nature of the verbal abuse. If the shop talk is usually obscene, unless the employee personally applies the obscenities to the supervisor ("God damn you"), arbitrators are not likely to uphold disciplinary measures for use of obscene words.

The nature of the threat. Discipline will be upheld if an employee ***personally*** threatens a supervisor, not if the employee talks vaguely about threats.

The facts in physical abuse cases. If the employee directly attacks the supervisor personally or indirectly (e.g., abusive phone calls) ***and if*** the employee was not provoked, the disciplinary decision will be upheld by arbitrators.

Jennings found that in 54 percent of the cases studied, arbitrators have reduced disciplinary penalties given by supervisors. They take into account mitigating circumstances like prior excellent work records and how fairly the management has treated the employee prior to and at the time of the incident. They also check to make sure that management has consistently disciplined other employees in similar cases and that the disciplinary decisions have been consistent. Arbitrators have treated altercations between supervisors and union stewards differently from those between supervisors and other employees. They view the supervisor and steward as equal and feel the steward need not be as "respectful" as other employees.

It is more difficult to establish rules about other infractions. Many enterprises

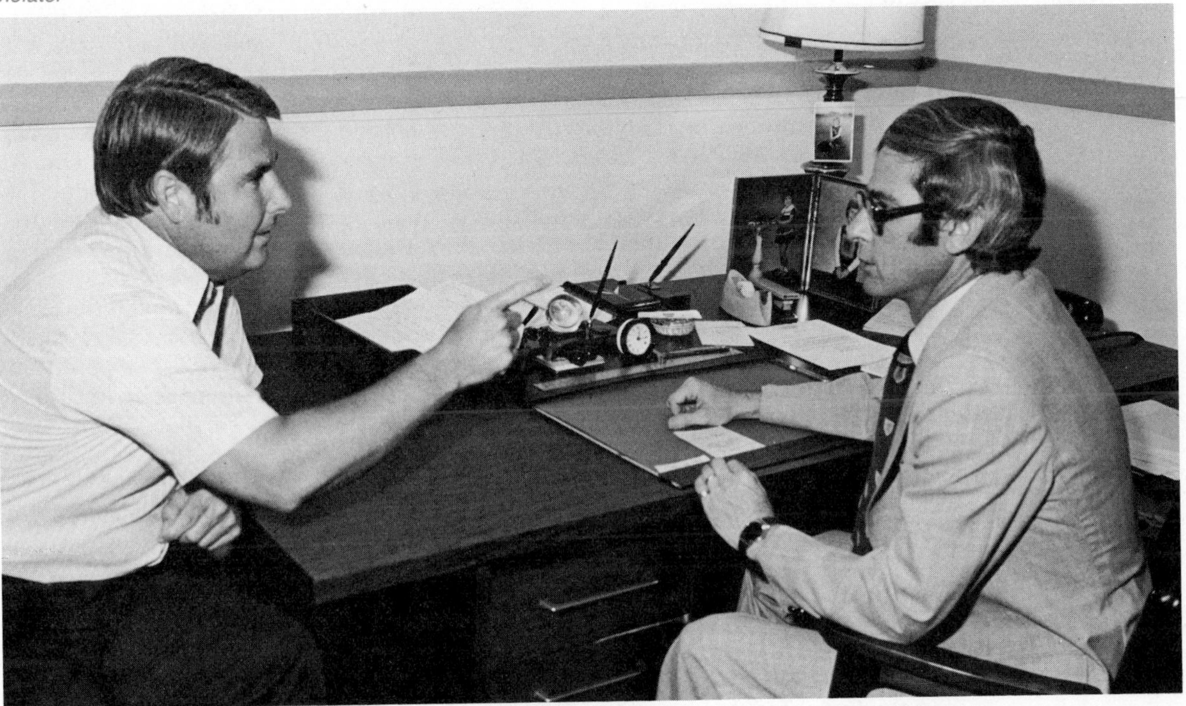

A supervisor discussing a rule violation with the violator

prohibit gambling on company grounds, to avoid lowering productivity and losing time from fights over gambling losses. Yet few want to prohibit nickel-dime poker at lunch.

Enterprises usually have rules prohibiting employees from making decisions when there is a conflict of interest (such as a purchasing agent who has an interest in a supplier) or when they are indebted to others. Many enterprises prohibit their employees from accepting gifts over some nominal value or from being guests at lavish entertaining. Conflict-of-interest dealings are usually specifically prohibited.

The enterprise probably should have a rule prohibiting sexual harassment, but this may be difficult to investigate or enforce. Women who have had to submit to sexual relations with the boss (or clients) to hold a job are turning to the EEOC and the courts to resolve this issue. This is a difficult problem for management. Not too long ago, it was criticized for rules prohibiting fraternization between employees as constituting an invasion of privacy.

The problem of the ex-convict as an employee is a long-standing one. Many can become excellent employees, others will not. Personnel must be especially careful in the supervision and discipline of ex-convicts if they are to be developed as good employees.

Are certain types of employees likely to be difficult?

Various experts have tried to identify the personality characteristics of the difficult employee. This search may be as illusive as trying to find the personality characteristics of good leaders.

One who has tried to isolate these characteristics is Claire Anderson, who studied 1,635 hourly workers in two plants of a manufacturing company in the eastern United States. She was searching for the "marginal worker"—the one who consistently and frequently is difficult, as measured by more frequent absences, turnover, firings, discipline cases, grievances, and accidents. She reviewed the literature *thoroughly* prior to testing hypotheses and found that the marginal worker was most likely to be one of a *few* employees who caused the most problems. Characteristically, this type of employee was a production worker in a large production department, working on a late shift and receiving high overtime or incentive pay rather than the day rate. The marginal worker was also most likely to be young, male, U.S.–born, and black.

Anderson's study is carefully qualified—it is a one-company study in the East, and so on. But the probability is that some of these characteristics are likely to be universal, in view of many collaborating studies on age, sex, type of job, shift, and pay. Whether the race and native-born factors would hold up in studies of locales such as El Paso, Chicago, or Los Angeles needs further testing. It is possible that socioeconomic class rather than race is the deciding variable.

In any event, it is possible, from Anderson's and similar studies, to identify a group of marginal employees and carefully watch this group. Whether all marginal employees would have the same characteristics as those described above is yet to be determined.

THE DISCIPLINE PROCESS

Exhibit 18–3 is a model of the discipline process. The employer establishes goals and rules and communicates them to employees. Employee behavior is

EXHIBIT 18–3
Elements in a disciplinary system

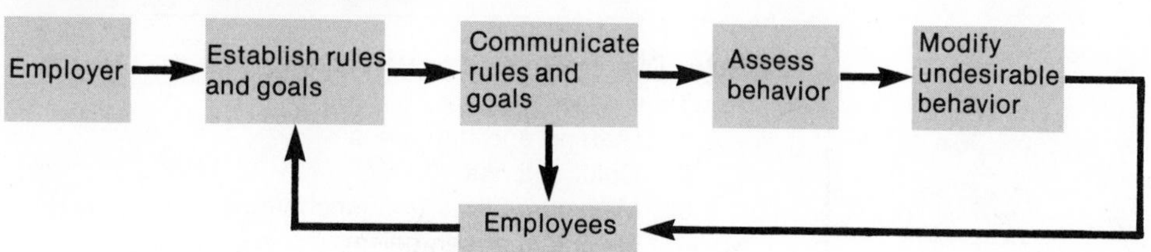

then assessed, and modification may be found desirable. This process is an attempt to prevent difficulties and is positive in nature. It is designed to help employees succeed.

The first element in the process is the establishment of *work and behavior rules.* Work goals and standards were discussed as part of performance evaluation (Chapter 8). Through whatever method is used (time and motion study, examination of past performance or performances by others, management by objectives), a set of minimally acceptable work goals is established. Behavior rules cover many facets of on-the-job behavior. They can be categorized as concerning behavior that is directly or indirectly related to work productivity. Both types are often negatively described as prohibited behavior. Exhibit 18–4 lists some examples of employee behavior rules.

The second important element in the disciplinary process is the *communication* of the rules to all employees. Unless employees are aware of the rules, they can hardly be expected to follow them. Closely related is a willingness to accept the rules and their enforceability. If employees or their representatives participate in the formation of the rules, their cooperation is more likely to be assured. Employees must be convinced that the rule is *fair and related to job effectiveness.*

It is useful for management to seek employee advice on periodic revision of rules. The objective is to reduce the number of rules to the minimum and enforce those that are important. Customs and conditions change. Rules, like laws, need regular updating to achieve the respect and acceptance necessary for order in the workplace.

The third element of the disciplinary process is an *assessment mechanism.* In most organizations, performance evaluation is the mechanism for assessing work behavior deficiency. Rule-breaking behavior usually comes to the attention of management when it is observed or when difficulties arise and investigation reveals certain behavior as the cause.

Finally, the disciplinary process consists of a system of *administering punishment or attempting to motivate change.* This varies from supervisory administration of discipline to formal systems somewhat like courts or grievance procedures.

ADMINISTRATION OF DISCIPLINE

Another important issue in discipline is how it is accomplished so as to protect employees' rights. In unionized organizations, the employee has a formalized procedure which provides adequate protection: the grievance procedure dis-

EXHIBIT 18–4
Examples of employee behavior rules

I. Rules Directly Related to Productivity
   A. Time rules
      1. Starting and late times
      2. Quitting times
      3. Maximum break and lunch times
      4. Maximum absenteeism
   B. Prohibited-behavior rules
      1. No sleeping on the job
      2. No leaving workplace without permission
      3. No drinking on the job
      4. No drug taking on the job
      5. Limited nonemployer activities during work hours
   C. Insubordination rules
      1. Penalties for refusal to obey supervisors
      2. Rules against slowdowns and sit-downs
   D. Rules emphasizing laws
      1. Theft rules
      2. Falsification rules
   E. Safety rules
      1. No-smoking rules
      2. Safety regulations
      3. Sanitation requirements
      4. Rules prohibiting fighting
      5. Rules prohibiting dangerous weapons

II. Rules Indirectly Related to Productivity
   A. Prevention of moonlighting
   B. Prohibition of gambling
   C. Prohibition of selling or soliciting at work
   D. Clothing and uniform regulations
   E. Rules about fraternization with other employees at work or off the job

cussed in Chapter 17. In nonunionized situations, the hierarchical system is the most prevalent.

Hierarchical discipline systems

Discipline is administered to most nonunion employees by the supervisor, who also evaluates the employee. When the employee is found to be ineffective, the supervisor decides what needs to be done. In this hierarchical system, the conditions allow a supervisor who might be arbitrary, wrong, or ineffective himself to be policeman, judge, and jury over the employee.

A person accused of a crime such as speeding in many of our courts can have counsel, the judge is not the arresting officer, and the penalty may be a $50 fine. In the employment situation, where the employee has none of these

The open door policy in action

safeguards, the penalty for an infraction of work rules may be his job and salary. Even if the employee is convicted of speeding, he can appeal to a higher court. What can the employee do if he is unfairly fired by his supervisor? There is, of course, the *open-door policy:* he could appeal to the supervisor's superior. But this is usually no help at all. The whole value system of the hierarchy is based on support of the supervisors to build a good management team. Of course, the informal open-door policy can lead to a quasi-legal form of justice such as that developed by IBM, in which the employee's case is recorded and systematically reviewed at several levels. A strictly hierarchical justice system is more prevalent in businesses than in other work organizations.

A feeling of helplessness and lack of due process for employees can become a *powerful* force leading to the unionization of enterprises. To work at all, hierarchical systems must be considered fair by employees. There must be adequate proof of any deviance. Employees will support discipline only if they feel that the disciplined employee was treated fairly and consistently compared to other past offenders. Mitigating circumstances must be considered if disciplinary procedures are taken. The minimal safeguard to prevent serious injustice in the hierarchical system is the mandated right to job transfer in disputes with less than overwhelming evidence against the employee.

If hierarchical systems are to be effective and fair, operating and personnel managers must administer discipline equitably. There have been a few studies of the extent to which this is so. The best study on the subject found that even in companies with a well-developed discipline system, discipline was unevenly administered. Other studies have found that prejudice against minorities or union members has led to unequal discipline. The data on differences in degree of discipline provide reasons for having systems of appeal besides the open-door policy to supplement or supplant the hierarchical approach.

If discipline is called for, the manager can apply a series of sanctions to improve future performance or behavior. These vary from the brief fatherly or motherly chat to locking up the violator, as the military does on occasion.

The first technique the manager can use is *counseling.* This is the most frequent method of disciplinary action. The supervisor determines if in fact a violation took place, explains to the employee why the violation significantly affects productivity, and suggests that it should not happen again. Sometimes the supervisor pushes counseling to the "chewing out" stage. This approach works for most violations. Counseling will probably be more effective if the supervisor applies the behavior modeling–interaction management technique (see Chapter 10).

If a second or more serious violation takes place, the supervisor again counsels the employee, this time noting that the incident will be entered in the employee's personnel file. If the violation was sufficiently serious, the employee may also be given an oral or written warning of the consequences of a future recurrence.

If the incident concerns ineffective productivity, the employee may request transfer or be asked to transfer to another job. The employee may have been placed in the wrong job, there may be a personality conflict between the employee and the supervisor, or more training might help. In some rare cases, demotions or downward transfers are used.

If counseling and warnings do not result in changed behavior, and if a transfer is not appropriate, the next step is normally a *disciplinary layoff.* If damage resulted from the deviant behavior, the deductions may be made from employee's pay over a period of time to pay for the damage. Most disciplinary action will not require this severe a step. The layoff is usually of short duration, perhaps a few days up to a week.

The next most severe form of punishment is what Lawrence Steinmetz calls *dehiring,* and most people call getting an employee to quit. Getting the unsatisfactory employee to quit has many advantages over termination, for both employee and employer. Both save face. The employee finds another job and then quits, telling the peer group how much better off he is at the new location. The employer is happy because he has rid himself of an ineffective employee without having to fire him or her. Dehiring is not a forthright approach to discipline. Many supervisors find it unethical. It should be used only if the supervisor prefers it to the next step: discharge.

The ultimate punishment is *discharge.* To many inexperienced managers, discharge is the solution to any problem with a difficult employee. Often discharge is not possible, because of seniority rules, union rules, too few replacements in the labor market, or a number of other reasons. Discharge has many costs, both direct and indirect. Directly, it leads to a loss of all the personnel investments already made, for recruiting, selection, evaluation, and training; many organizations also pay severance pay. Then these same personnel investments must be made again for the replacement, and frequently there is a period during which the new employee is not as productive as the former employee was. The indirect costs are the effect on other employees of firing one of their numbers. If it is a blatant case of severe inability or deviant behavior, there is not too much problem with peer group resentment. But too often, the facts are not clear, and other employees may feel the employer acted arbitrarily. Some employees may seek employment elsewhere to prevent an arbitrary action happening to them. Others may reduce productivity in protest.

Thus discharge is the *last alternative* to be tried—when all else fails or in very serious cases, such as discovery of fraud or massive theft. One subtle reason restrains many supervisors from suggesting discharges. If the supervisor has had the employee a long time, management may begin to ask: "If this employee is so bad, why wasn't he downgraded sooner? Why didn't he get rid of him sooner? Why did he hire him in the first place? Do you think he's a good judge of employees? Is he supervisory timber?" Many discharges are reversed by arbitrators. For these reasons, actual discharges are rare.

Most employers pay severance allowances to all discharged employees except to those in Category 3. They differ on whether severance pay should be offered to Category 1 employees and the most blatant cases of laziness and so forth in Category 4 employees.

Other discipline and appeal systems

Although the hierarchical discipline and grievance system is *by far* the most used in industry, other employing organizations use different models more often. A few business organizations have also taken steps to design systems which may protect the employee from arbitrary supervisory action more effectively than the hierarchical model does. The alternatives to the hierarchical models are peer, quasijudicial, and modified hierarchical approaches. In the peer system, a jury of peers evaluates and punishes. The quasijudicial approach uses an independent arbitrator or ombudsman to resolve disputes. Modified hierarchical systems are regular appeals channels *inside* the organization, but including someone other than the supervisor's superior. One mechanism is to have all disputed dismissals or behavior modification plans submitted to specified personnel specialists for conciliation and assessment. Another is to have a top management executive or executives far removed from the scene hear the facts and judge whether proper action was taken.

Nonhierarchical systems are used by such varied organizations as unions like the United Auto Workers, the Civil Service Commission in the U.S. government, and the American military. The private sector almost never uses nonhierarchical systems.

It must be noted that there is little or no empirical evidence that providing nonhierarchical systems necessarily provides fairer treatment of employees. But a study of the history of justice under various systems in the public domain would indicate justice is much more likely under systems that provide for independent assessment of evidence and judgments than one in which the superior is prosecutor, judge, and jury.

SUMMARY, CONCLUSIONS, AND RECOMMENDATIONS

Some of the most difficult human and personnel problems involve handling the difficult or ineffective employee. Guidelines for assessing the causes and how to deal with this situation follow:

1. Most deviant or difficult employees' problems probably have multiple causes. Some of these are listed below:
   a. Problems of intelligence and job knowledge.
   b. Emotional problems.
   c. Motivational problems.
   d. Physical problems.
   e. Family problems.
   f. Problems caused by the work group.
   g. Problems originating in company policies.
   h. Problems stemming from society and its values.
   i. Problems from the work context (e.g., economic forces) and the work itself.
2. Categories of employees which cause discipline problems include:
   a. The ineffective employee.
   b. Alcoholic and addicted employees.
   c. Participants in theft, crime, and illegal acts.
   d. The rule violators.
3. The discipline process involves:
   a. Employer establishes rules and goals.
   b. These rules and goals are communicated to the employees.
   c. Employee behavior is assessed.
   d. Undesirable behavior is modified, punished, etc.
   e. Depending on the behavior, its severity, and the number of offenses, continued violation might result in termination.

EXHIBIT 18–5
Recommendations for model organizations on difficult employees and discipline

Type of organization	Hierarchical justice systems	*Reinforce hierarchical justice systems with:* Peer committees	Ombudsmen	Outside committees
1. Large size, low complexity, high stability	X		X	X
2. Medium size, low complexity, high stability	X		X	
3. Small size, low complexity, high stability	X	X		
4. Medium size, moderate complexity, moderate stability	X		X	
5. Large size, high complexity, low stability	X		X	X
6. Medium size, high complexity, low stability				
7. Small size, high complexity, low stability	X	X		

4. Employers should concentrate on trying to modify the effects and advise rehabilitation and counseling for such problems as alcoholism and drug addiction.
5. For discipline systems to be effective, the disciplinary review must take place as soon after the action as possible. It must be applied consistently and impersonally.

Exhibit 18–5 gives the recommendations for the use of different kinds of justice systems in the model organizations defined in Chapter 1.

It is important to remember that discipline is an area in which help is needed from many areas: supervisors, personnel, the work group, arbitrators, and top management. Each has a crucial role to play if the discipline system is to be effective.

Chapter 19 will conclude the discussion of the personnel function by outlining the evaluation process and providing a glance into the future of personnel.

Jeremy Schultz, the personnel vice president at Judge Incorporated, is reflecting on the results of his interviews with four supervisors this week. These supervisors are responsible for Al, Susan, Joyce, and Tom.

Because of these four and many similar employees, Jeremy decides to set up a formal disciplinary system. In conjunction with supervisors and a sample of employees, he sets up in written form the rules of working at Judge. The performance evaluation system is strengthened to make the goals clearer.

Jeremy runs some training sessions and communicates the new system to the employees. The new discipline system sets up a step-by-step process and a set of "costs":

1st violation or problem: Counseling by supervisor

2nd violation or problem: Counseling by supervisor and recording in personnel file

3rd violation or problem: Disciplinary layoff

4th violation or problem: Discharge

For alcohol or drug problems, mandatory counseling at counseling centers is required, or discharge will result. Legal violations result in discharge and prosecution.

In all cases of disciplinary layoff, the employee will receive counseling from personnel. If there appear to be problems between supervisor and employee, Jeremy will serve as an ombudsman.

With regard to Al, Susan, Joyce, and Tom, Jeremy recommends the following actions:

Al. Transfer to a new supervisor. There appeared to be a personality conflict between Al and his supervisor. (The transfer did not help. Eventually Al received a disciplinary layoff and was terminated, in spite of much counseling.)

Susan. Ask her to join Alcoholics Anonymous. (She did, and got her drinking problem under control, at least at work.)

Joyce. Watch for evidence that she is stealing. (When the evidence was clear, she was terminated and prosecuted. The judge gave her a suspended sentence.)

Tom. Give him counseling about his behavior. (The supervisor reported later that Tom was a better employee.)

All in all, Jeremy felt the new disciplinary system would work rather well.

QUESTIONS

1. What is discipline?
2. What are the four categories of difficult employees?
3. What are the major causes of difficult job behavior?
4. Describe the ineffective employee. How do Mager and Pipe suggest analyzing undesirable behavior?
5. How serious a problem is the alcoholic employee at work? How should the alcoholic employee be handled?
6. How serious a problem is the addicted employee? How should the addict be dealt with?
7. How serious is the employee who violates laws? How should this employee be dealt with?
8. Describe the discipline process.
9. Contrast various discipline philosophies. Which one do you accept?
10. Describe the disciplinary methods available and when you would use each.

ersonnel

the

for the
ager

e

ation of the Personnel
Function

III. Evaluation by Checklist or Copying Others
IV. Statistical Approaches to Evaluation
   A. Evaluation of turnover
   B. Evaluation of absences
   C. Evaluation of complaints and grievances
   D. Evaluation using attitude and opinion surveys
V. Compliance Methods of Evaluation
VI. Evaluation of the Personnel Function Using Management by Objectives
VII. Personnel Research
VIII. Summary, Conclusions, and Recommendations
IX. The New Personnel Manager and Personnel's Future

19

Evaluation of the personnel function and the future of personnel

The setting is a massive conference room. The top managers of General Products, a large manufacturing company in Seattle, are participating in the annual planning meeting. Each functional vice president presents the department's budget for next year, after a review of the past year's accomplishments.

Denton

Emily

After Emily Park, vice president for marketing, completes her budget request, her advertising budget for the next year is cut. Last year, profits were down at the plant.

Denton Major, vice president for personnel and organization planning, speaks next.

Denton: Well, folks, I'm not going to take much of your time. It's been a long day. You know what we do for the company. We hire, train, and pay the employees, provide benefits, counsel, help with discipline, EEO, and so on. Personnel is not asking for any major increases. My budget is simply last year's budget adjusted upward 7 percent for inflation. Any questions?

Emily: Wait a minute, Denton. My budget just got cut. Here you come asking for 7 percent more than last year. I suppose we have to have a personnel department. But why shouldn't my advertising budget be increased and your budget cut? After all, advertising brings in customers and helps us make money. What *specifically* does personnel do for our profit and loss statement? How *specifically* does personnel help us reach our goals of growth and profitability?

Emily has unknowingly pointed out what purpose a personnel audit serves. If Denton had been systematically evaluating the personnel department, he would have some answers ready. And it looks like he will need some good ones, or personnel's budget and activities could well be cut.

Evaluation of the personnel function (the personnel audit) is a systematic, formal experience designed to measure the costs and benefits of the total personnel program and to compare its efficiency and effectiveness with the enterprise's past performance, the performance of comparable effective enterprises, and the enterprise's objectives.

Evaluation of personnel is performed:

- To justify personnel's existence and budget.
- To improve the personnel function by providing a means to decide when to drop activities and when to add them.
- To provide feedback from employees and operating managers on personnel's effectiveness.
- To help personnel do its part to achieve the enterprise's objectives.

Top management's part in the personnel audit is to insist that all aspects of the enterprise be evaluated and to establish the general philosophy of evaluation. Personnel's job is to design the audit. In part the data for the audit arise from the cost/benefit studies of the personnel activities as described in Chapters 4–17. The operating manager's role is to help gather the data and to help evaluate the personnel function in the same way it evaluates other functions and uses of resources in the enterprise.

Evaluation of the personnel function is a Stage II activity—many researchers have advocated its implementation, but only a few good empirical studies of effective and ineffective ways of evaluating or auditing the activity have been done.

A DIAGNOSTIC APPROACH TO EVALUATION OF THE PERSONNEL FUNCTION

Exhibit 19–1 shows the factors in the diagnostic model which affect evaluation of the personnel function in an enterprise. The major factors in determining whether evaluation takes place are the orientation or attitudes of the controlling interests toward evaluation and the organization's style.

Some managers feel formal evaluations of the function are very useful. Others do not favor them. Formal evaluation programs of functions are more likely to be conducted in some types of enterprises than others. Larger organizations that are labor intensive and geographically dispersed probably have some type of evaluation for most functional departments, including personnel. Such programs are also more likely when economic conditions are bad, particularly for economically oriented organizations, because they can establish the cost effectiveness of such functions.

APPROACHES TO EVALUATION OF THE PERSONNEL FUNCTION

Once it has been decided that it is useful to evaluate the effectiveness of the personnel function and the organization's use of human resources, the next issue is how it should be done and what measures or criteria of effectiveness should be used. The criteria can be grouped as follows:

1. Performance measures.
   a. Overall personnel performance; for example, the unit labor costs per unit of output.
   b. Personnel department costs and performance—the cost per employee of personnel programs.
2. Employee satisfaction measures.
   a. Employees' satisfaction with their jobs.
   b. Employees' satisfaction with personnel activities such as training, pay, benefits, and career development.
3. Indirect measures of personnel performance.
   a. Employee turnover—rate of quits as a percentage of the labor force and by units over time.
   b. Absenteeism—rate of voluntary absences of the labor force and by units over time.
   c. Scrap rates.

EXHIBIT 19–1
Factors affecting evaluation of the personnel function in an enterprise

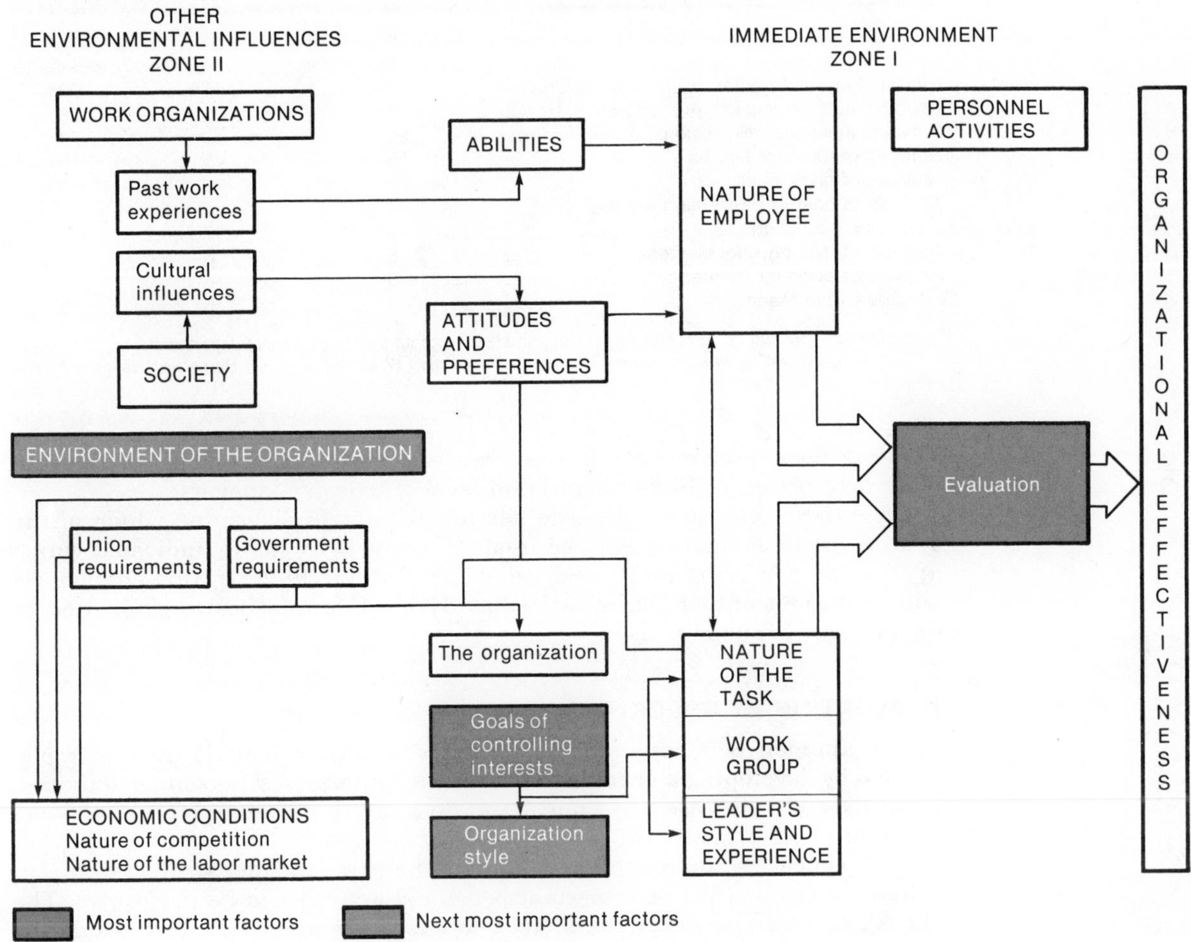

d. Other measures of quality.
e. Rates of employee request for transfer.
f. Number of grievances per unit and in total labor force over time.
g. Safety and accident rates.
h. Number of improvement suggestions per employee over time.

Each of these measures or some combination of them measures the efficiency and/or effectiveness of the personnel effort. To make personnel worthwhile, it is necessary for the enterprise to measure its achievements against specific goals, such as:

Reduce labor costs by 3 percent.
Reduce absenteeism by 2 persent.
Increase the satisfaction index recorded on the attitude survey.

EXHIBIT 19–2
Personnel evaluation methods used

	All companies	*Larger*	*Smaller*
Evaluating departmental results against goals	33%*	37%	23%
Periodic audit of policies, procedures	25	25	26
Surveys, meetings, discussions, and interviews	20	19	23
Analysis of turnover figures	16	15	19
Analysis of grievances	8	9	10
Analysis of cost of performing various personnel functions	6	7	5
Analysis of training effectiveness	5	5	5
Analysis of accident frequency	5	6	4
Feedback from managers	5	5	5

* Includes 7 percent of companies specifying an MBO program for the personnel department.
Source: *Labor Policy and Practice—Personnel Management* (Washington, D.C.: Bureau of National Affairs, 1975).

These goals are set relative to past trends, current achievements of relevant other enterprises, or higher aspiration level of today's managers.

Once these criteria are set, the next decision is to determine which of the approaches to evaluation is to be used. A recent BNA survey indicated which approaches are being most used today (see Exhibit 19–2). In this chapter we will examine some of the most frequently used approaches to evaluation of the personnel function.

EVALUATION BY CHECKLIST OR COPYING OTHERS

One approch is to copy other enterprises' practices. This is usually implemented by developing a checklist of the model enterprises' personnel activities. Checklists are also used by consultants to analyze an enterprise's personnel function.

In the checklist approach to evaluation, the personnel department or a consultant prepares a list of important personnel activities to be performed. The checklist usually requires the analyst to check yes or no columns beside the listed activity. The checklist may also include items designed to determine if existing personnel policies are being followed. The items on the checklist are usually grouped by personnel activity area, such as employment planning or safety and health.

Although a checklist is better than a totally informal approach, it still is a rather simple approach to evaluation. And even though checklists provide a format that is relatively easy to record and prepare, scoring interpretation is quite difficult. Three nos in one group of items may not equal three others. Some of the policies are more important than others. Ignoring EEOC or OSHA rules is a lot more negative than the absence of a Christmas party, for example. About 20 percent of enterprises with formal audits use the checklist approach.

STATISTICAL APPROACHES TO EVALUATION

The most frequently used formal evaluation methods are those that examine the work organization's employment statistics and analyze them. The statistical approach can be much more sophisticated than checklists. The statistics gathered are compared to the unit's own past performance or to some other yardstick of measurement. Of course, quantitative factors alone never explain or evaluate anything by themselves. The *reasons* for the statistics are the important thing; statistics only indicate where to begin to look for evaluation problems.

EXHIBIT 19–3
Personnel evaluation ratios

Effectiveness ratios
- Ratio of number of employees to total output—in general.
- Sales in dollars per employee for the whole company or by organizational unit (business).
- Output in units per employee hour worked for the entire enterprise or organizational unit.
- Scrap loss per unit of the enterprise.
- Payroll costs by unit per employee grade.

Accident ratios
- Frequency of accident rate for the enterprise as a whole or by organizational unit.
- Number of lost-time accidents
- Compensation paid per 1,000 hours worked for accidents.
- Accidents by type.
- Accidents classified by type of injury to each part of the body.
- Average cost of accident by part of the body involved.

Organizational health ratios
- Number of grievances filed.
- Number of arbitration awards lost.

Turnover and absenteeism ratios
- Attendance, tardiness, and overtime comparisons by organizational unit as a measure of how well an operation is handling manpower loading.
- Employee turnover by unit and for the organization.

Employment ratios
- Vacations granted as a percentage of employees eligible.
- Sick-leave days granted as a percentage of man-days worked.
- Military leaves granted per 100 employees.
- Jury duty leaves granted per 100 employees.
- Maternity leaves granted per 100 employees.
- Educational leaves granted per 100 employees.
- Personal leaves granted per 100 employees.
- Employment distribution by chronological age.
- Employment distribution by length of service with organization.
- Employment distribution by sex, race, national origin, religion.
- Managerial distribution by chronological age, sex, race, national origin, religion.
- Average age of work force.
- Average age of managerial work force.

The raw data of such reports are interesting themselves, and they can provide some input to evaluation. Most organizations that perform evaluation, however, analyze these data by the use of ratios and similar comparative methods. Exhibit 19–3 provides a list of such ratios and similar analytical methods. Once these and similar ratios are computed for an organization, they can be compared to similar organizations' ratios.

The statistical approaches used most frequently consider turnover, absenteeism, grievances, attitude surveys and other measures of effectiveness, and statistical analysis of the personnel department itself.

Evaluation of turnover

Turnover is the net result of the exit of some employees and entrance of others to the work organization. Turnover can be quite costly to an employer. One estimate is that it costs American industry $11 billion a year. The costs of turnover include: increased costs for social security and unemployment compensation; terminal vacations; severance pay; underutilized facilities until the replacement is hired; employment costs, such as recruiting ads and expenses, interview time, test costs, computer record costs, and moving expenses; and administration costs of notification and payroll changes. Obviously there is also a loss of productivity until the new employee reaches the performance level of the one who left the job.

All turnover is not a net loss, however. Employees who are not contributing to organizational effectiveness should be retrained or dehired. And the employer has no control over some turnover: A student's wife, for example, works as a typist until he graduates and they move away.

There are several quantitative methods for computing turnover. Some of the traditional formulations are:

$$\text{Separation rate} = \frac{\text{Number of separations during the month}}{\text{Total number of employees at midmonth}} \times 100 \quad (1)$$

$$\text{Quit rate} = \frac{\text{Total quits}}{\text{Average working force}} \times 100 \quad (2)$$

$$\text{Avoidable turnover} = \frac{\text{Total separations} - \text{Unavoidables}}{\text{Average work force}} \times 100 \quad (3)$$

Formula (1) is the most general and is the one recommended by the Department of Labor. Formula (2) tries to isolate a difficult type of turnover, and Formula (3) is the most refined. It eliminates quits by those groups that can be expected to leave: part-timers and women leaving for maternity reasons. These data can be refined further by computing turnover per 100 employees by length of employment, by job classification, by job category, and by each organizational unit.

In a BNA study of absenteeism and turnover in 136 companies, it was found that 53 percent used Formula (1), and most others used slight variations of this if they calculated turnover rates. Usually the variations used as the divisor either total number of employees at the beginning (or end) of the month or average number of employees for the month.

In the BNA study, about two thirds of companies reported computing turnover;

73 percent of new businesses calculated it, and more large businesses than small ones did so. Almost 70 percent computed the rate monthly, and most of the others calculated it annually.

The BNA study also found that 57 percent of the enterprises surveyed computed the data in such a way as to analyze turnover by department or division. This is more likely to be done in large businesses and nonmanufacturing firms than in other types of enterprises. Enterprises which include all employees in the calculation (67 percent) could calculate the differences in turnover by employee groups. In one recent year, the average turnover was 4.2 percent, but the range was as high as 38 percent.

One way employers analyze the tunover rate is to compare the enterprise's rate with those of other enterprises. Various sources publish average turnover rates quarterly or yearly. These include agencies such as the government labor departments, the Administrative Management Society, and BNA's quarterly reports on turnover and absenteeism. Another approach is to analyze the enterprise's turnover by comparing the differences in rates by employee classifications or departments.

Most theories of turnover maintain that employees leave their jobs when their needs are not being satisfied at their present place of work *and* an alternative job becomes available which the employees believe will satisfy more of their needs. These theories have not received a great deal of support, but they seem plausible.

Analysis of a large number of studies examining the interrelationships between turnover and absenteeism shows that, in general, these factors are intercorrelated. That is, if turnover is high, absenteeism is also likely to be high. These studies also found that both were caused by the same factors. In general, employees first exhibited high absenteeism, and this led to high turnover. Thus absenteeism and turnover are not alternative methods of showing dissatisfaction. Rather, high absenteeism is a sign that high turnover is likely in the future.

Overall, enterprises try to reduce turnover by a number of methods: better employee selection, orientation, communication, supervisor training, incentive awards, and data analyses. In addition, many enterprises have tried to determine why their turnover takes place. One method is to interview employees just before they leave the enterprise to try to determine why they are leaving. This is the exit interview. Some find exit interviews unreliable and not useful. Others contend that, properly done, they are reliable enough for these purposes. Problems can arise when exiting employees give partial reasons for leaving because they need references from the employer or might want to be reemployed at a future date.

Other methods which have been tried to reduce turnover, besides exit interviews, include telephone or in-person interviews a few weeks after termination. These would seem to have the same flaws as exit interviews, but little data are available on the reliability of these methods. Another approach being tried is to give employees a questionnaire as they are exiting and ask them to complete it and mail it back a month or so later. This gives the employee some protection and would appear to be a much better approach than the others. Organizations using this method find a rather low percentage of employees complete the questionnaires, however. No reliability data appear to be available on these questionnaires.

Evaluation of absences

A second measure used to evaluate the personnel function is absenteeism rates.

Absenteeism is the failure of employees to report for work when they are scheduled to work.

Tardiness is partial absenteeism, in that employees report late to work.

Absenteeism is undesirable because of its costs and the operating problems it causes. Absenteeism's costs to the enterprise include the costs of benefits, which continue even when workers are absent, so benefit costs are higher per unit of output. Overtime pay also may be necessary for the worker who is doing the job for the missing worker. Facilities may be underutilized and productivity may drop because of reduced output due to understaffing. There also may be increased break-in costs for replacements, substandard production, the need for more help from supervisors and peers, and increased inspection costs.

How is absenteeism computed? According to a BNA study, the standard formula recommended by government bodies and used by over 70 percent of those who compute absenteeism is:

$$\frac{\text{Number of employee days lost through job absence in the period}}{\text{Average number of employees} \times \text{Number of work days}} \times 100.$$

Most others use a variation of this formula, such as

$$\frac{\text{Total hours of absence}}{\text{Total hours worked (or scheduled)}} \times 100.$$

Of the 136 enterprises surveyed by BNA, about 40 percent calculated absenteeism rates, usually for all employees, and most often monthly (54 percent) or annually (40 percent). Of those calculating absenteeism, 70 percent did so by department or division. Most also separated out long-term absences from short-term ones.

Current research raises questions about the use of absence rates, especially aggregate measures of absenteeism, to evaluate the personal function. Some observers suggest abandoning the measure. It appears that it is more useful to pursue research designed to identify absence-prone persons, work groups, working conditions, and communities with a view to designing strategies to reduce absenteeism.

One good example is a study by Hilde Behrend and Stuart Pocock of 1,200 men employed at a General Motors Plant in Scotland from 1969 to 1974. One of the major conclusions of this study was that overall absence ratios, although of some use, are open to serious misinterpretation. For example, the "average" employee in their study experienced three absences per year, totaling about 18 days. But the range was from employees who were not absent one day in six years to several who were absent 600 days over the six-year period. The authors convincingly demonstrate that it makes much more sense to classify employees into categories of absence proneness. When this approach is used, management can focus on workers with higher absence rates. Remedial action can then be taken to improve health if the cause appears to be illness, or by counseling, discipline, and so on if health is not a factor.

Evaluation of complaints and grievances

A complaint is a statement (in written or oral form) of dissatisfaction or criticism by an employee to a manager.

A grievance is a complaint which has been presented formally and in writing to a management or union official.

Chapter 17 discussed what grievances are and how they are processed. The complaint-grievance rate and the severity of the grievances is another way to evaluate the personnel function. Of course, not all complaints or grievances relate to personnel issues. They can be about equipment, machinery, and other matters, too. And the grievance rate can be related to the militancy of the union or the imminence to contract negotiations. Nevertheless, an increase in the rate and severity of complaints and grievances can indicate dissatisfaction, which in turn might lead to increases in absenteeism and turnover. Both factors indicate how successful the personnel department is in securing productivity and satisfaction for the employee. Statistical analyses of complaints and grievances have not been done as scientifically as for turnover and absenteeism.

Evaluation using attitude and opinion surveys

Another indicator of employee and managerial evaluation of the personnel program is obtained through the use of attitude or opinion surveys.

An attitude or opinion survey is a set of written instruments completed by employees (usually anonymously) expressing their reactions to employer policies and practices.

Effective attitude surveys are designed with precise goals in mind. The questions and items used are designed professionally and are tested on a sample of employees for reliability and validity prior to administration. Several other administrative factors may affect the validity. One is whether the employees feel that the employer is sincerely interested in knowing the truth and will act wherever possible to follow up on their suggestions.

The survey may include many personnel activities, job satisfaction, and other aspects of the enterprise's operations. Usually, after the results of the survey are in they are analyzed and fed back to the employee units. About a third of the large employers surveyed used attitude surveys to help evaluate the effectiveness of the total personnel program or parts of it, such as pay, benefits, or training. Attitude surveys were described in more detail in Chapter 3.

COMPLIANCE METHODS OF EVALUATION

In the compliance approach to evaluation of the personnel function, the main concern is the extent to which personnel procedures reflecting the law or company policy are being followed in the enterprise. Attempts are then made to determine where changes are needed.

One study describes how First National City Bank (New York), one of America's largest banks, performs this audit. The first step is to identify 18 crucial personnel areas it wishes to audit. Then the bank randomly chooses branch banks (eliminating recently reorganized banks) to be studied. The audit procedure followed is diagrammed in Exhibit 19–4. The review is conducted by the

EXHIBIT 19–4

Personnel compliance audit process at Citibank

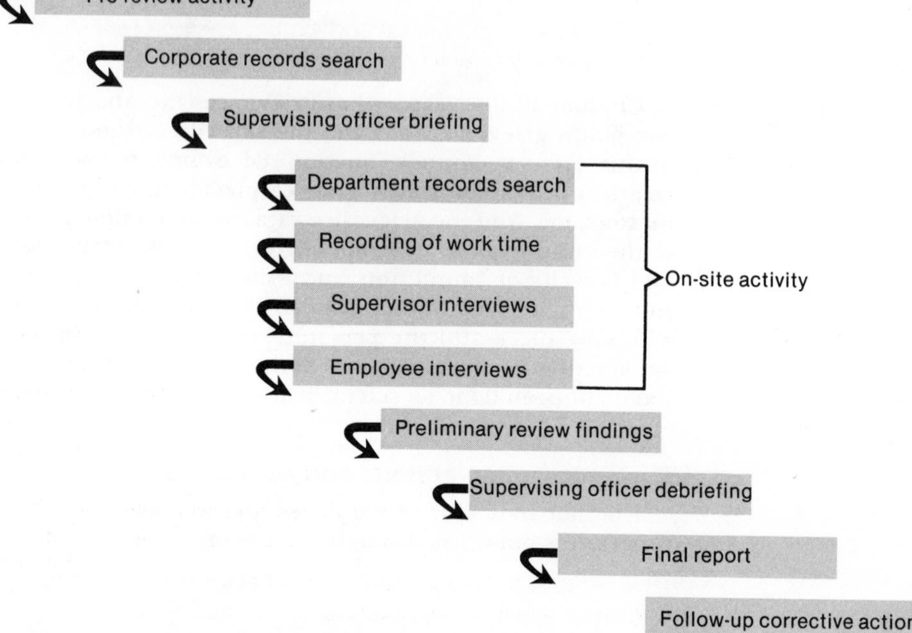

Source: Paul Sheibar, "Personnel Practices Review: A Personnel Audit Activity," *Personnel Journal,* March 1974, p. 213. Reprinted with permission *Personnel Journal* copyright March 1974.

Personnel Practices Review Unit (six personnel reviewers, an operations manager, and clerical support), which reviews all branches every other year. The bank believes that this audit has substantially improved its personnel effectiveness.

EVALUATION OF THE PERSONNEL FUNCTION USING MANAGEMENT BY OBJECTIVES

Management by objectives is the system of relating activities to goals or objectives of the enterprise or unit. Without systematic goals or objectives, the personnel department may fall into the trap of being activity instead of objectives oriented. Thus it may list as progress the running of 12 training programs as compared with 10 the year before, forgetting that the criteria of effectiveness are productivity and satisfaction, not activities alone. MBO was described in Chapters 8 and 10. It is not known how many enterprises follow the MBO approach, but it is probably not a large number at present. MBO shows promise of being one of the best approaches to evaluation of the personnel function, however.

One related activity: personnel research can help the enterprise with evaluation.

PERSONNEL RESEARCH

The purposes of personnel research are to find solutions for personnel problems for the employer, to aid in evaluation of the personnel function, and to extend the knowledge of personnel to all those concerned. This activity is performed by universities, consultants, independent research institutes, and a few employers. The 150 or so employers who perform their own personnel research are invariably large, such as AT&T. One expert estimates that as few as 15 corporations actually use their research fully. These studies also indicate that personnel research does not have a significant impact on top management. The best departments are staffed by persons with Ph.D.'s, mainly in psychology or personnel. Sometimes personnel research is attached to units other than personnel departments, such as research and development groups. One study asked personnel researchers to estimate how they spent their time. They reported that they spent 20 percent consulting with line managers, 15 percent running their department, 9 percent on self-development, and 55 percent on research. Of this, 13 percent was spent analyzing personnel statistics, 15 percent studying improved means of employment, 16 percent on improving the organization climate, and 11 percent studying training and development.

Much of the research the personnel department does is descriptive. Studies show that most departments use surveys, historical studies, and case studies. Few have tried experimenting with various approaches to personnel.

One researcher who surveyed personnel research departments to see which aspects of personnel were studied in personnel research found that most of them followed the problems emphasized in industrial psychology. Thus 98 percent studied selection and placement, 75 percent ran attitude and communication studies, 30 percent studied training and development; 20 percent studied evaluation methods and motivation; and 16 percent studied overall effectiveness. Less than 10 percent spent any time on supervisory style, accident prevention, stress, managerial obsolescence, counseling, recruitment, or any basic research that did not directly affect the employer at the time.

SUMMARY, CONCLUSIONS, AND RECOMMENDATIONS

Any function as important as the effective use of human resources needs to be evaluated. The difficulty in evaluating the results of the personnel function is that effectiveness has multiple causes, and it is difficult to separate out how much of the effectiveness results from each cause. Here is a list of some of the major statements in the evaluation section of Chapter 19 to use as a guideline.

1. Evaluation of the personnel function is a systematic, formal experience designed to measure the costs and benefits of the total personnel program and to compare its efficiency and effectiveness with the enterprise's past performance, the performance of comparable effective enterprises, and the enterprise's objectives.
2. This evaluation is performed to
   a. Justify personnel's existence and budget.
   b. Improve the personnel function by providing a means to decide when to drop activities and when to add them.
   c. Provide feedback from employees and operating managers on personnel's effectiveness.

d. Help personnel to do its part to achieve the objectives of the enterprise.
3. Evaluation of the personnel function can be done by one or a combination of the following means:
   a. Checklist.
   b. Statistical approaches, including evaluation of turnover, absenteeism, and complaints and grievances, and the use of attitude and opinion surveys.
   c. Compliance methods of evaluation.
   d. Evaluation using MBO.

Exhibit 19–5 provides recommendations for the model organizations on personnel audits and evaluation and research.

Some propositions which can be derived from the text also sum up the evaluation of the personnel function:

Proposition 19.1. The larger the organization, the more likely it is to evaluate its personnel program formally.

Proposition 19.2. As the task gets more repetitive, absenteeism has a tendency to rise.

Proposition 19.3. If employees are dissatisfied with pay and promotion policies, turnover will increase.

Proposition 19.4. The more satisfied the employees are with supervisory style and their co-workers, the lower the turnover rate.

EXHIBIT 19–5
Recommendations for model organizations on personnel research and evaluation of the personnel function

					Performed by			
Type of organization	*Checklist*	*Statistical*	*Compliance*	*MBO*	*Organization*	*Consultant*	*Organization and consultant*	*Personnel research department*
1. Large size, low complexity, high stability			X	X	X			X
2. Medium size, low complexity, high stability		X	X				X	
3. Small size, low complexity, high stability	X					X		
4. Medium size, moderate complexity, moderate stability		X	X				X	
5. Large size, high complexity, low stability			X	X	X			X
6. Medium size, high complexity, low stability	X						X	
7. Small size, high complexity, low stability								

The setting is again the conference room at General Products. The time is the next annual planning meeeting. Last year, because Denton Major was not in a position to justify his budget for personnel, he was not awarded the 7 percent increase he asked for. In fact, personnel was cut by the same percentage figure as the marketing department was. If he could help it, that wouldn't happen again. Emily Park, vice president for marketing, had struck at his weak flank. In the past year, he had examined the personnel audit approaches.

In evaluation, use of a checklist or copying other enterprises appeared useful and easy. Compliance methods appeared useful, as did attitude surveys. Statistical approaches, especially evaluation of turnover, also appeared to be helpful. But the best approach seemed to be an MBO system of evaluation. This was an especially good idea because Henry Wolcott, the company president, had had an MBO system put in about 18 months previously.

As Denton waited, he was confident of the results of his budget request this year. Eventually, his time came to present his request.

Denton: The Personnel Department has a report that is included in your packet of materials. You'll note that we have the results of our compliance audit. The company is substantially in compliance with government regulations. This was not true a year ago. But we set that as an objective and reached it.

You'll also note a checklist audit. The checklist was used to set preliminary objectives for our MBO program. It was developed from an analysis of the personnel program at Acme Company, San Francisco. We checked around, and this company was recommended as having the best personnel program in the West.

A copy of the attitude survey is also included: Again, we used this as a method for identifying problem areas for our MBO program.

From the checklist, attitude survey, and compliance items, we came up with qualitative and quantitative targets for our MBO program. Our major targets were to reduce costly turnover and improve the cost effectiveness of our compensation program.

Next year's MBO targets are given on page 10 of the report. You'll also note our cost/benefit studies justify the shift of funds among our personnel programs and the justification for an 8 percent increase in our budget.

Henry: The budget for personnel is well documented and appears reasonable.

Emily: A big improvement from last year's presentation, Denton.

Denton's budget was approved that year.

The chapter concludes with a brief glimpse of the future of the personnel function.

THE NEW PERSONNEL MANAGER AND PERSONNEL'S FUTURE

This book has been designed to help you develop as a successful manager of the personnel function, either as a personnel professional or as an operating manager with people to manage. It has used a series of mechanisms to advance the necessary knowledge:

The diagnostic approach. It was shown that the effective new personnel manager is a diagnostician who observes the various aspects of the organization's environment. She or he considers the size, structure, goals, and style of the organization, and the nature of the employee, the task, the work group, and the leader. The diagnostic manager realizes that the personnel policies of the enterprise must be congruent with all these factors, and others, if personnel is to do its part to contribute to enterprise effectiveness.

Model organizations. This mechanism was used to focus attention specifically on how personnel activities are performed differently in different types of organizations. This is certainly true of the many different kinds of enterprises in the private, public, and third sectors.

The role of the top manager and operating manager. Top managers and operating managers have important parts to play in the personnel process. Successful personnel managers know how to relate to these persons and to present personnel programs to them in the language and thought processes of operating and top managers. How is this done?

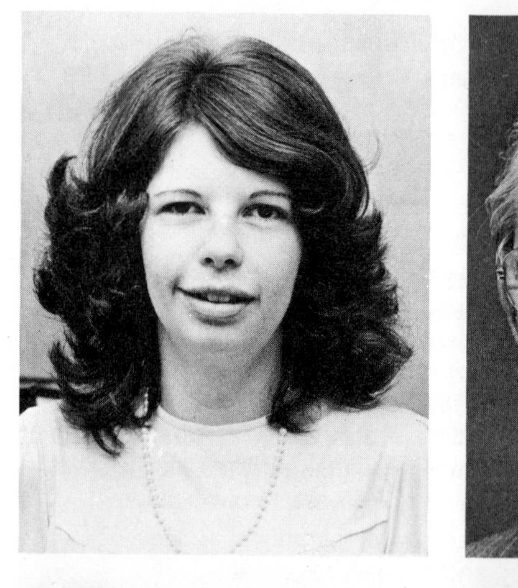

Some future personnel executives

The new personnel manager

The new personnel manager manages by objectives and shows how personnel has helped achieve enterprise goals. Few enterprises exist to hire and develop people. They exist to reach goals such as producing goods to satisfy customers while achieving a profit, or curing patients at reasonable cost, or improving the education of teen-age children in a community.

The new personnel manager can show how, through the careful performance evaluation of employees, their satisfaction will be increased, absenteeism and turnover will be decreased, and their performance will be improved. Thus both quality and quantity of output improve, and enterprise goals are achieved. This requires a cost/benefits comparison emphasis.

The new personnel manager is part of the team that makes the key decisions, the strategic decisions such as: Are we going to grow? In what direction are we going to grow? Are we going to merge with another enterprise? What's the future going to be if our plans work out?

Each of these strategic decisions has important implications for personnel. And the personnel department can provide important counsel about the human resources affecting these decisions. Personnel can only have the impact it should have if its leadership is well trained to do the job and if it can convey to top management a goal-oriented attitude when seeking additional funds to do its job.

The new personnel manager who is part of the top-management team will be reporting what programs have been phased out, with appropriate savings, and what programs have been kept, and the savings and improvments resulting from them. Specific budget justifications will be made for proposed additons and specific measurable results that will help the enterprise reach its goals will be proposed. Further, the personnel manager will be able to show how to achieve these results. Managers who are used to making decisions this way will know that this executive team makes the *real* decisions that affect personnel.

In the smaller enterprise, the new executive responsible for personnel and other functions should begin to consider personnel decisions in the same hard-nosed way he or she does other decisions. Resources are scarce, and human resources are the most precious to conserve and develop.

The new personnel manager must do her or his part to help top management face some future threats and opportunities. Some of these may include:

- Shortage of resources. Consider the impact of the lack of energy on work schedules in 1977, for example.
- Declining population of younger employees.
- Outdated manufacturing facilities in many industries.
- Fewer manufacturing jobs, more service jobs.
- Low-growth strategies for some industries.
- The possibility of more employees working at home some of the time.
- New privacy legislation affecting many aspects of personnel.
- Improving the quality of work life.

Better training and new attitudes will equip the new personnel executive to handle all the challenges the environment and the enterprise can present—EEOC, OFCCP, OSHA, and others we don't even know about yet.

If the book has provided the data to improve decision making and has made clear these attitudinal emphases—in short, if it has helped develop the new personnel manager—it has satisfied my own goals.

QUESTIONS

1. What is evaluation of personnel?
2. Why do we evaluate personnel activities and functions?
3. Compare and contrast the checklist, compliance, and MBO evaluation methods. Which is best?
4. Compare and contrast the statistical indicators of personnel evaluation. Which are the best indicators? How are they measured?
5. What significant future events are likely to affect personnel practices?
6. How will the new personnel executive help achieve the enterprise's goals? Personnel's goals?

341
352

Cases

1. Mark Whitcomb*

Mark Whitcomb had been at Harkon I
with substantial organizational and fidu
comb had a visitor, Mr. Greylock.

Greylock's visit had been a matter
ten days since the appointment had be
smoothly.

"I know other areas of the organization have personnel problems, but I have my finger on it here," Whitcomb said. "I really know my people and what bothers them."

As Whitcomb and Greylock entered the foyer they passed an older, distinguished-looking man, Harry Winslow, who had been with Harkon for many years.

"Hello Harry! How's the wife?" Whitcomb called out in a friendly way.

"Still dead, sir," was Harry's reply.

Discussion questions:

1. How do you think Mr. Greylock reacted to Whitcomb's encounter with Harry Winslow?
2. How could an awareness of human behavior and the uniqueness of the individual help Mark Whitcomb to become a better manager?

2. Kenrac†

Kenrac is a medium-size ($100 million per annum sales) manufacturing firm supplying tools to automotive servicemen. Kenrac carries a prestige line of hand tools and sells and services its customers directly through salespersons operating as independent agents. Each salesperson has a territory, the size of which depends on number of accounts to be serviced. Products are distributed nationally. Advertising is through trade journals. Salespersons are hired by the corporation from persons completing a battery of tests and an interview.

The number of personnel engaged in sales is 870. The turnover rate is approximately 30 a year. This turnover figure is in the lower third of the industry.

Salespeople once hired are required to make a $25,000 investment for inventory and a step-up van. Eighty percent of the investment is financed by the company. A training program, paid for by the company, is required of each trainee. The duration of the program is six months, and it includes classroom and on-job training.

Once past probation, salespersons receive a commission. A $10,000 per annum salary guaranteed against draw is provided each person. Commission is 6.5 percent of orders booked.

Six lines, with different return margins to the firm on each, are carried by each of the salespersons.

---

† This case was prepared by Benjamin Lowenberg, University of Wisconsin—Parkside.

Line	*Return on Investment*
A	21%
B	15
C	26
D	17
E	23

For ten territories that, in terms of number and type of accounts, are substantially similar, the following data were collected:

Product Line	*A*	*B*	*C*	*D*	*E*
1	85,000	120,000	44,000	115,000	65,000
2	78,000	57,000	95,000	62,000	54,000
3	58,000	105,000	58,000	117,000	48,000
4	60,000	62,000	59,000	47,000	68,000
5	54,000	68,000	72,000	71,000	64,000
6	57,000	40,000	120,000	48,000	54,000
7	84,000	58,000	91,000	46,000	78,000
8	92,000	68,000	73,000	60,000	58,000
9	105,000	98,000	80,000	46,000	75,000
10	67,000	72,000	68,000	59,000	43,000

The characteristics of the persons selling in each of the territories were as follows:

Territory	*Age*	*Education*	*Performance Rating (Range 1–10 with 10 as maximum)*
1	27	16	6
2	35	14	7
3	26	18	5
4	39	13	7
5	48	12	7
6	43	13	8
7	55	12	9
8	38	14	6
9	62	13	7
10	52	12	7

How can the organization maximize its return for each salesman? A reduction in manpower, i.e., two people are to be fired. Indicate the two people you would replace.

3. West Coast Chemicals

West Coast Chemicals is a small producer of organic chemicals located in the Los Angeles area. It has been in business since 1945 and has prospered. At present, it employs 250 persons. The marketing department is headed by Arthur Gonzalez, age 54. The salesmen report to him, and he has had two assistants who do sales planning, sales analysis, and, to some extent, market research work.

He has been contemplating whom he should select to replace one of his assistants who left to go back East. Through his own analysis and from the personnel department, he has three persons from whom he is likely to choose. The candidates' vitas provide the following information.

Candidate 1: Jose Raminez. Age: 34. Education: completed high school. Jose has also supplemented this with additional correspondence courses. Experience: after four years in Air Force, ten years' selling experience in machinery and manufacturing goods areas. For the past two years, sold somewhat related product to the company's, but not to West Coast's customers. Sales performance adequate to good, depending on whether you believe written recommendations or reference checks by phone. Health: good, according to physical exam. Intelligence test scores indicate above-average brainpower. Preliminary screening interviewer comments that Jose was "a live wire."

Candidate 2: Nancy Wentworth. Age: 38. Education: high school graduate. Mother of two children, ages 18, 16. Husband employed by City of Los Angeles. Experience includes ten years as executive secretary to marketing director, Arthur Gonzalez. Nancy has done the usual secretarial work and has helped out on many sales planning and sales analysis projects when assistants were overburdened. Personality: moderately lively, is very competent and reliable person. Test score: about same as Jose's. Health: good.

Candidate 3: Douglas Newsom. Age: 22. Education: BS in Business Administration, California State at Los Angeles, A− average, marketing major. Many courses and projects in marketing. Excellent recommendation letters. Member of honoraries, business fraternities, etc. Originally from farm in Utah. Doug worked his way through college with such odd jobs as waiter in pizza parlor several nights a week and weekends, construction and farm work in summer. Personality as indicated by screening interviewer: quiet, determined. Test score: higher than Jose's. Health: good.

Arthur is pondering which one of these he should hire. He is planning the kinds of additional information he wants to acquire in the interview and what criteria he will use to select the best assistant.

Discussion questions:

1. How should Gonzalez prepare for the interview?
2. What are some of the criteria Gonzalez can use to help make an effective selection decision based on the candidates' vitas and the interviews?

4. Frankfurt Insurance

Frankfurt is a medium-sized insurance company with headquarters in New York City. It specializes in health and auto insurance. The company employs about 1,275 persons. It has been in business since the mid–1920s, but most of the growth has come since 1950. The organization chart describing some of the relations at Frankfurt Insurance is given in Exhibit 1. The two branches are organized identically. The staff support units, such as personnel and accounting, report to the branch managers. But the home office vice presidents have functional advisory authority over these units as well.

EXHIBIT 1
Organization chart: Frankfurt Insurance

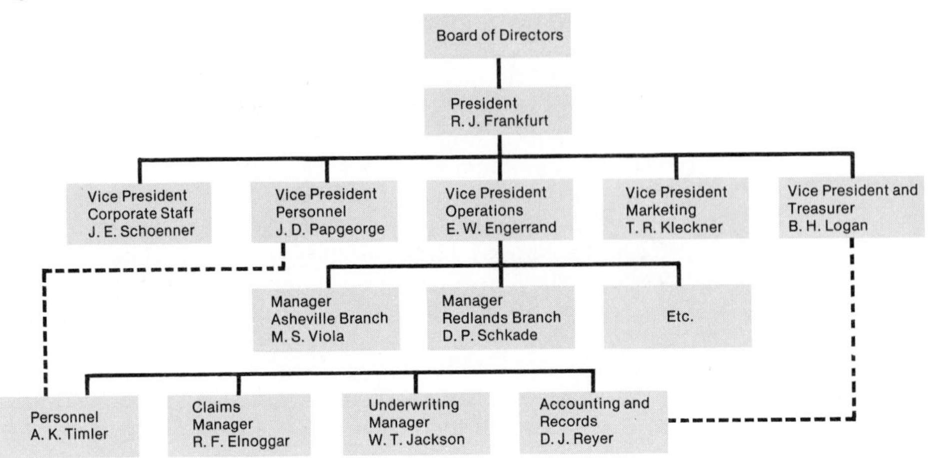

Vice President–Personnel John Papgeorge is 54 years old. He is a graduate of the New York University's school of business. In the past ten years he has taken short courses in personnel offered by NYU and two other universities.

Art Timler is 31 years old. He was a personnel major at Wake Forest University where he received his BS–BA. He had six years' personnel experience with a large firm in North Carolina before joining Frankfurt two years ago. He likes his job at Asheville. He gets along well with Mitch Viola and Reggie Elnaggar, who are also at Asheville. His relations with Wilbur Jackson are correct and a bit distant, but he has tried to improve them ever since he's been there. Early in his tenure there, he didn't hire Jackson's cousin for a job because he didn't appear qualified. Ever since then, there have been strained relations between Jackson and Timler.

Papgeorge has been trying to improve the quality of employee evaluation at Frankfurt, and Timler has cooperated. In his recent classes for supervisors, Timler has discussed effective use of performance evaluation. The firm uses a graphic rating scale. Timler has emphasized the importance of the evaluation interview. He has stressed the discussion of positive points first, then negative points. He suggested that the supervisors not dwell on the negative points too much. Rather, they should be mentioned in reference to how the supervisor could help the employee improve in the future.

To determine if his training was taking, he secretly taped some of the evaluation meetings of some of the supervisors. A summary of the data on these tapes is given in Table 1. An excerpt from an interview by Frank Jones (a supervisor) with Claude Kelly (an employee) follows:

JONES: Well, Claude, you've seen the sheet I turned in on you. You do a good job about three-and-a-half to four days out of five. I guess I'm really thankful for that. But just about every week I have a Friday or Monday problem with you.

KELLY: What do you mean, a problem?

JONES: Well, you procrastinate a lot. I tell you to do something one way and you go your own way.

TABLE 1
Distribution of time in a sample of employee evaluations

			Evaluation score (100 = perfect)	Supervisor's comments		Employee responses	
				Positive (%)	Negative (%)	Positive (%)	Negative (%)
Supervisor	1	Joe Kishkoones					
Employee	2	Bill Morey	85	20%	60%	5%	15%
	7	Hank Sheffieck	90	30	60	5	5
	9	Carl Burns	70	10	65	5	20
Supervisor	3	Dick Camealy					
Employee	4	Pete Smith	68	10	80	0	10
	6	Jake Collons	92	15	70	5	10
	8	Stan Osterhaus	87	12	80	3	5
Supervisor	5	Frank Jones					
Employee	5	Ken Ipade	74	5	80	0	15
	6	Claude Kelly	78	10	70	0	20
	10	Sherwin Chew	76	5	85	0	10
Supervisor	8	Paul Justis					
Employee		Vern Swanda	88	50	20	20	10
		Curt Graybard	90	60	10	25	5
		Mario Carrabino	93	70	7	20	3

KELLY: I've been here about as long as you. Doesn't a person have anything to say about his work?

JONES: I didn't say that. Besides, I'm the supervisor here. I don't care if you've been here a hundred years, you'll take your orders from me. So if you want to get your ratings up, you'll watch it on Mondays and Fridays from now on. But as I said, you do a pretty good job.

Later, Jones was heard to say that Kelly was driving him crazy. "He won't do anything on his own before asking me what to do. I can't get my own work done."

Requirement:

You are Art Timler. Evaluate the status of performance evaluation at Asheville. Design a program to improve the shortcomings you've detected.

5. Karpenter Foods, Inc.

Karpenter Foods is a small manufacturer of snack foods in Chicago. Karpenter employs about 240 persons and manufactures a line of snacks in tins, bags, and boxes. It was started by Winston Karpenter in 1925. The firm has the organization plan shown in Exhibit 1.

Rumors are that there are serious inequities in the base pay of the retail salesmen. These persons call on grocery stores, sell the product, and stock the shelves with the products from their trucks. They receive base pay plus incentive compensation if they exceed previous period sales by certain amounts. The rumors are that some of the best salesmen are not being paid as high as the average salesmen, or even some of the poor ones.

Ted Pfeffer was told during a recent exit interview by a departing salesmen

EXHIBIT 1
Organization chart: Karpenter Foods

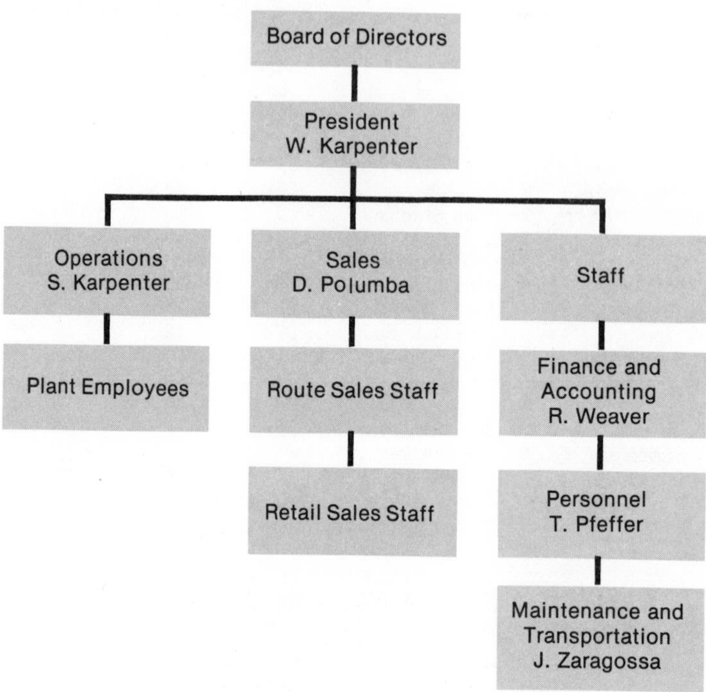

that he was leaving because he felt others less qualified than he were paid more. He has heard this before. Dave Polumba has examined the salaries of the employees in his department and feels that they are equitable and that the rumors are unjustified. he has decided that the way to handle this is to have a department meeting and discuss everyone's compensation openly. The Karpenters suggest that he does not do this because "it will all bow over if you just forget about it." But he has full authority to go ahead if he wishes.

The salesmen's turnover has been especially high this year, and Dave is pondering what he should do.

Discussion questions:

1. What is individual pay determination? How can Karpenter apply the system to their salespersons?
2. What is the open pay system? Should Polumba institute this approach in the sales department?

6. The Community College

The Community College is a state-supported institution located in California. Its compensation package traditionally has included salaries which were about the same as other colleges of its type in the area. It also has included a more than generous benefits program.

In addition to the legally mandated programs such as social security, the college offers the following benefits:

1. State-paid state pension system. The College pays 10 percent of the faculty member's salary into this fund. The professor does not contribute to the pension. He or she is vested after ten years' service.

2. Life insurance. The college pays for life insurance equivalent to the professor's nine-month salary, up to $20,000 per year free life insurance.

3. Hospitalization insurance. The college pays three fourths of the group rate for faculty members and their families.

4. Disability insurance. The college also provides for 75 percent of the cost of disability insurance under a salary continuance plan.

5. Free tuition for the faculty member's family is also provided.

There are other small benefits. The usual one month's vacation is also provided.

George Paul, department chairman of the college's journalism department, has a problem. Herman Pascucci, one of his best young faculty members, is threatening to leave. He has a family to support, and a competing college is offering him $2,500 more on a nine-month salary scale. George cannot meet this salary. He knows, however, that the competing school has a poor benefit program. In fact, that is one of the reasons it offers more salary. It does not pay for family tuition, disability insurance, hospitalization plans, or life insurance. It contributes only 4 percent of the faculty member's salary to a pension fund TIAA–CREF.

Herman is 33 years old. His three children are eight, six, and two years old. George is wondering how he can convince Herman that tax-free income from benefits is worth more than a few dollars in pay.

Discussion question:

1. What facts should George use to convince Herman that the benefits which Community College offers offset a small salary increment from the competitor?

7. Hartley Conglomerate (A)*

The Hartley Conglomerate is composed of ten autonomous divisions and corporate headquarters, as Exhibit 1 indicates. The case focuses on the Bien Works. Its organization is given in Exhibit 2.

Bien Works is housed in a building erected in 1904. The building is five stories high. The top two are not used, since the floors are too dangerous. The second and third floors have holes and rotted places in them.

The third floor holds the rack shop, lab, and marketing departments. The second floor contains the office, some warehousing, and some buffing compound production lines. The first floor contains the warehousing for heavier materials and the rest of the manufacturing lines. The main operation is manufacturing. The rack shop is a support unit to make racks for drying chemicals. The works is nonunion.

Jesse Fuller, the plant manager, has been with Hartley for 20 years, all of it in conjunction with the Bien Works. He holds a BS in chemistry from City

* This is a disguised case—for obvious reasons.

EXHIBIT 1
Organization chart: Hartley Conglomerate

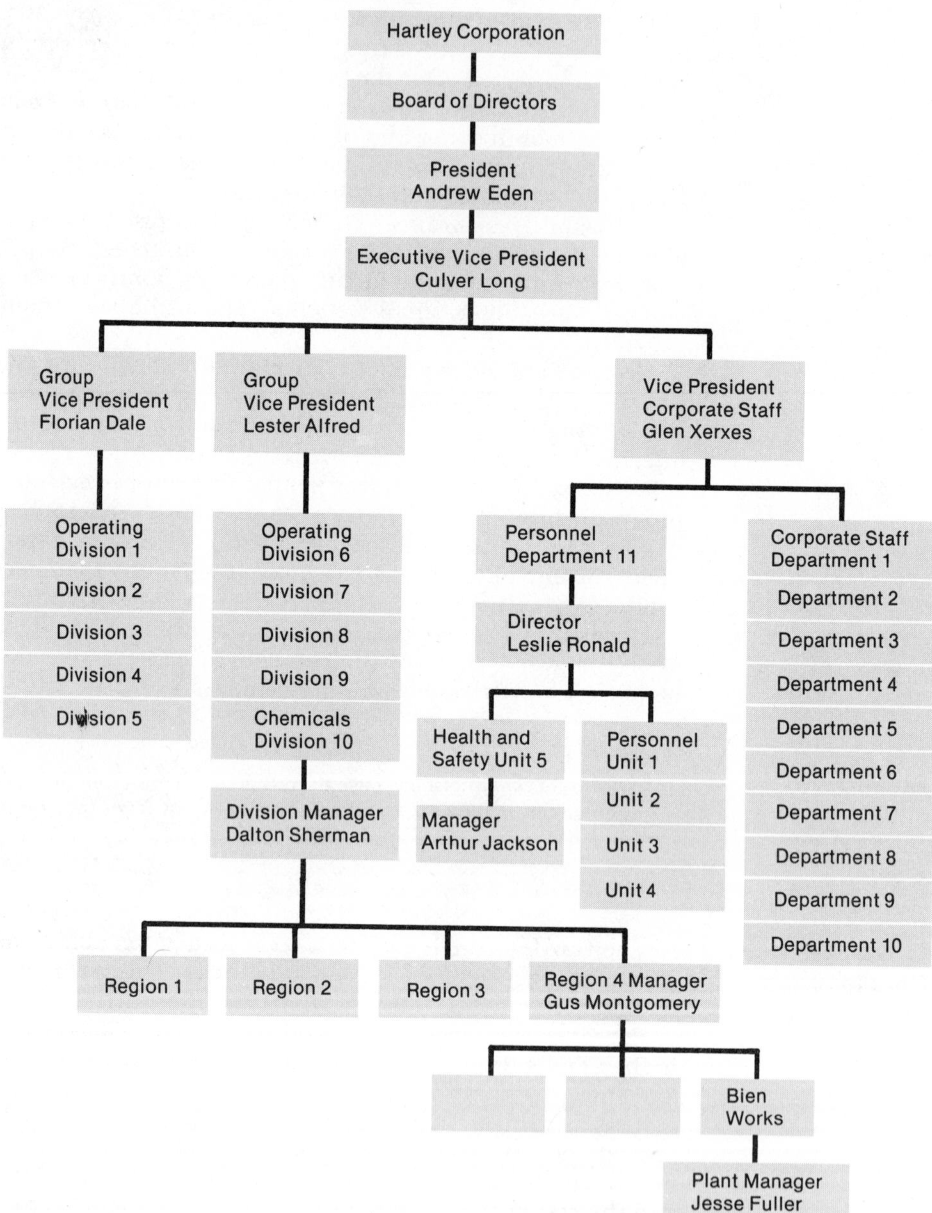

University of New York. He worked his way through college. He's done almost everything at Bien. He started as a foreman in the manufacturing unit. He's run the rack shop, supervised the warehouse for two years, sold the compounds. The office and lab are white-collar or technical jobs, so he's not worked there. His employees like him, although they are a bit afraid of him, too. He has a

EXHIBIT 2
Organization chart: Bien Works

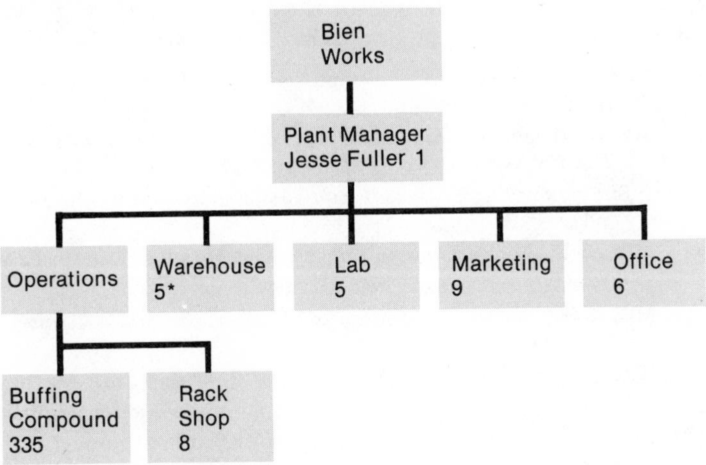

* Indicates number of employees in the unit.

terrible temper which he loses about once a month. When that happens, everyone tries to get out of the way.

Jesse is now 53 years old. He's happy with the Bien Works. He likes the town and wouldn't move. Bien is like his own firm, since he's isolated geographically from Hartley. Bien makes more money for Hartley than the budget calls for, so they let Jess alone. He has a lower turnover than expected. Absenteeism is also low. His safety and health record is about average. All in all, Hartley and Jess are happy with the Bien Works.

Then the OSHA legislation was passed. For some reason, the OSHA inspector came around Bien often. The local inspector was James Munsey. In April, James came to Bien when Jesse was at a meeting at Hartley. He determined that the buffing manufacturing was producing unsafe gases. As is his right, he shut the plant down that day. Jesse flew back and modified the gas filters. James passed the filters, and Bien started production again.

In May, James came back and shut the plant again when Jesse was at a Rotary meeting. Again, the filters were cleaned and modified. This time Jesse was really angry. After the plant was reopened and James had gone, Jesse held a meeting of all employees. At the meeting, he said:

> Look, this OSHA guy is killing us. This is an old works. We can't afford to be shut down. At my recent meeting at corporate headquarters, I tried to make the case that we needed a new building here. The sharp-pencil boys pointed out that we are profitable now, but not if we have to build a new plant. The industry is overcrowded, and Hartley will close this plant rather than spend money on it. If we get shut down or have to buy a lot of antipollution crap, Hartley could shut us down. That OSHA guy is the enemy—just like a traffic cop. We've got to pull together, or we could all sink together.

The employees had never seen Jesse so angry before, and they feared for their jobs now more than ever. There was a lot of unemployment in the area.

Hartley Conglomerate (B)

It is July now and James Munsey has appeared again at the Bien Works office. When the office girls saw James coming, they headed for the powder room. Melanie Smith, one of the lab technicians, greeted him. Melanie had just been hired in June and didn't know James.

JAMES: I'm the OSHA inspector. I need to talk to Mr. Fuller. He should accompany me on my inspection.

MELANIE: Just a moment, sir. I'll get him. *(Melanie goes to Jesse's office and says):* The OSHA inspector is here to see you.

JESSE: Oh my God! *(pause).* You go out there and tell him I'm too busy to see him today.

MELANIE (back in office): I'm sorry sir. He's too busy to see you today.

JAMES: Ask your boss if he's too busy tomorrow.

MELANIE (on the intercom): Mr. Fuller, are you too busy tomorrow to see the inspector?

JESSE (on the intercom): What do you want this time, Munsey?

JAMES: Because of previous violations, you're due for another inspection.

JESSE: Look, I'm busy. But come and inspect first thing in the morning.

JAMES: I'll be here at 8:30.

The rest of the day was a red alert.

No work was done. The whole plant was cleaned up. The lab was put in order. Bottles which leaked were secured. Shelves were straightened. The rack shop was cleaned up. Machine guards were put on—they weren't used otherwise. Machines without guards were moved and covered up as if they were no longer used. Machines too heavy for the third floor were moved.

The filters were cleaned. The water bath was cleaned. The slippery flood made of metal that was supposed to be neutralized and *scrubbed* daily (though it usually got it monthly) was neutralized and scrubbed. Everyone helped. Even the secretaries and lab technicians helped clean.

The next day, the inspector came back. The prettiest secretary was assigned to get him coffee and "chat him up." James and Jesse toured the plant and the inspector passed Bien Works. But the employees wondered if the inspector didn't have to realize what had happened.

Hartley Conglomerate (C)

On August 15, James Munsey returned to Bien Works. This time Melanie knew who he was. She got him a cup of coffee and then went to Jesse Fuller's office.

JESSE: Tell him I'm out—that you can't find me. Stall!

MELANIE: Mr. Fuller seems to be out. As soon as he returns, I'll tell him you're here.

While James was drinking coffee, Jesse called all departments and told them to clean up in a hurry. They started to. Forty-five minutes later, James said to Melanie, "Miss, I can't wait any longer. Let me talk to whoever is here."

Melanie got one of the foremen. Together James and the foreman did the inspection. The foreman took the inspector to the warehouse first to give the other areas more time to clean up. It didn't help, James issued four warnings and gave Bien 24 hours to comply.

Jesse was so angry that this time he set up a plan. One of his foremen, Harry Coat, was moving to another division because of his wife's health problems. Jesse said, "Harry, I want you to do me a favor. You're moving to Arizona anyway. That SOB inspector is bound to be back before you go. When he comes back, it's worth $500 to me to pick a fight with him and cold cock him. Don't worry, I'll cover for you." Harry said it sounded like fun.

Hartley Conglomerate (D)

On October 13, James Munsey appeared for another inspection. Jesse called Harry and said, "Harry, it's D-Day. Get ready for the assault." Harry said, "I'm ready."

As James walked through Harry's work area, Harry came up to him and started a fight and knocked James cold. James went back to OSHA to report the incident. Jesse called the OSHA office.

JESSE: This is Jesse Fuller at Bien Works. Let me talk to the boss.

ART: This is Art Grubb. I'm in charge of this office.

JESSE: Listen, this fellow Munsey has been giving us fits. Now he's picked a fight with one of my managers. I fired my manager. I assume you'll do the same.

James Munsey was transferred to another OSHA unit shortly thereafter.

Discussion questions:

1. Are the OSHA inspectors too strict on the Bien Works? Is Jesse reasonable in his attitude towards OSHA inspections?
2. What constructive steps should Jesse take to improve conditions at the Bien Works and move toward compliance?
3. You are Mr. Grubb at OSHA. Outline how you will deal with Bien Works next year.

Hartley Conglomerate (E)

In January, the new OSHA inspector, Pamela Morton, appeared at the Bien Works. After her inspection, she ordered it closed and issued five warnings.

8. Age Discrimination at National Oil Company*

James Brunson had worked for National Oil Company for 29 years. An intelligent man, although possessing only an eighth-grade education, he had worked his way up in the organization from laborer to the position of staff assistant. In this capacity he trained and supervised subordinates and had a number of specific duties to perform. (See Exhibit 1 for a job description.)

Brunson had trained 25 of the 33 employees who were presently in the administrative section headed by Charles Grimsley, even though by 1974 all of the young men coming into this section had earned college degrees. He got along well with colleagues and subordinates alike and was proud of the fact that he had trained so many of the younger employees.

* This case was prepared by Gerald Hart and Roland B. Cousins, both of the University of Southwestern Louisiana.

EXHIBIT 1

Job description: Staff assistant (SG)

1. Group Head—Invoices, account distribution and vouchering, rate schedules, contractors' insurance and master contracts in General Accounting Section.
2. Coordinate, direct, and assist personnel in performance of their duties in my group.
3. Process invoices for payment.
4. Handle all qualifications for contractors' insurance in accordance with provisions of Master Contracts. (Forms 212, 406, 1024, 1320, and 1020.)
5. Maintain a file on current contractors' rate schedules.
6. Maintain and furnish a list to all supervisory personnel of contractors who are approved to perform contract services.
7. Handle correspondence with vendors pertaining to errors or discrepancies between delivery tickets, contract, rate schedules, bids, and invoices.
8. Check with Field Foremen by correspondence, radio, or telephone for any information needed to verify correctness of invoices or charges.
9. Post and maintain control on recurring services, such as telephone, utility, and contracts.
10. Post and maintain control on returnable items.
11. Perform other duties as assigned.

In March 1976, after returning from an early morning doctor's appointment, James Brunson was amazed to find one of his young subordinates sitting at his desk. When questioned, the subordinate replied that Charles Grimsley, Brunson's boss, would explain the situation to him. After a lengthy discussion during which Grimsley, as was his usual practice, evaded the question as much as possible, it began to dawn on Brunson that he had been demoted and his job had been given to his former subordinate. Brunson was handed a job description (see Exhibit 2) outlining his new duties. To this point Brunson had been proud of the progress that he had made with National Oil and thought that even at the age of 61 he was still performing well. Although his recent performance evaluations had only rated him as an average employee, his boss had never

EXHIBIT 2

New job description: James Brunson

1. Process invoices for payment.
2. Maintain a file on current contractors' rate schedules.
3. Handle correspondence with vendors pertaining to errors or discrepancies between delivery tickets, contract, rate schedules, bids, and invoices.
4. Check with Field Foremen by correspondence, radio, or telephone for any information needed to verify correctness of invoices or charges.
5. Post and maintain control on recurring services such as telephone, utility, and contracts.
6. Post and maintain control on returnable items.
7. Perform other duties as assigned.

indicated any specific weaknesses in his performance. Nor had he given even the slightest indication to Brunson that his job was in jeopardy.

As Brunson sat back and reflected on his new situation, he became more aggravated with recent trends which suddenly began to become apparent. Over the last five years, or so it seemed, every employee in the regional office was to some extent shuffled aside as the age of 60 was reached. Brunson had noticed this happening but had assumed that these employees were no longer productive and, consequently, had deserved the demotions received. He had never dreamed that he too would receive the same treatment.

During the weeks that followed, Brunson's anger and feelings of betrayal grew as he realized that he was spending almost three hours a day answering the questions of his young replacement. He had been training the young men moving into his department for years, but he had never found himself in the position of training his boss before.

For several years Brunson's subordinates had been receiving above-average performance evaluations by Grimsley, while Brunson's own were only average. Although company policy stated that only those employees receiving above-average ratings would be eligible for merit raises, Brunson had never been particularly concerned with his stable pay, as his needs were modest. Recently though, with the pressures of inflation, he could vividly see the declining purchasing power of his salary. As he reflected on his new situation he decided to go back through his section's records and look at the one measurable index of performance available—invoices processed. The primary responsibility of Brunson and his three direct subordinates was the processing of invoices. Last year, the records showed that 41 percent of all invoices processed by these four individuals were handled by Brunson.

Several months after Brunson's demotion one of his former subordinates, a young man with whom Brunson was particularly close, told Brunson that he was quitting his job to go with another oil company. When asked why, the former subordinate responded that it was obvious to him how the older employees were being mistreated. He stated that he had no desire to spend his career in a firm which rewarded loyalty in such a way. In concluding their conversation, he advised Brunson to look into the age discrimination laws and see if any action could be taken against the firm. This idea intrigued Brunson, although with only two and one-half years before retirement, he wondered if such action, even if possible, would jeopardize his pension.

Brunson did feel that he should make his feelings known to someone. The question, however, was to whom. There was no personnel manager for the entire division. All personnel matters were handled wherever possible by each individual's superior in the chain of command. Brunson felt that he could not go to Grimsley and state his feelings, as Grimsley might take offense and make his position even more difficult in the future. He wondered how and to whom he should express his concerns.

Discussion questions:

1. Does the company's treatment of Brunson constitute an infringement of the present definition of discrimination?
2. On what can Brunson base his action against the firm?
3. What are Brunson's chances if he decides to file action against the firm? What problems will he face?

9. Kimball Brick Works

Kimball Refractories Company is one of the largest producers of ceramic materials and refractory bricks in the world. Its home office is in New York City. About two thirds of its operations are outside the United States. Its largest plant, the Kimball Brick Works, is located in North Carolina. Kimball is a centralized firm. Most job specifications, purchases, product decisions, and so forth come out of New York.

The North Carolina Works was founded in the 19th century. At that time it consisted of the works and the housing owned and operated by the company. After the firm deducted rent and utilities, there wasn't much left for the employees. Most production employees were blacks. The homes are now privately owned, but the neighborhood is quite run down.

The operation includes the works, a distribution center, and the sales office. The latter is located downtown in an office building and includes a sales manager and six salesmen for the region. The works organization is shown in Exhibit 1.

The plant employs 160 persons. The tunnel kiln and special-cements departments are the crucial elements of the operations. They are in different buildings, but these two units have to work together for plant efficiency. However, they compete with each other for equipment and materials.

The special-cements division is located in a large five-story building. Its output is wet and dry mortars, hand-molded bricks, and ramming compound. This unit is the most profitable. The tunnel kiln produces refractory bricks and is unprofitable. It continues because the cement customers also require these bricks.

Production facilities are old. The same whistle which told employees of the 19th century when to start and finish lunch and work still is blown. The plant dates mostly from the 1930s, if not earlier, and uses the same processes it has used for years. Most of the work is still done by hand. The operation requires extensive maintenance to keep things patched together. Many machines must be completely overhauled every other week.

At the tunnel kiln, bricks are pressed out by three large presses, placed on carts, and moved into the kiln. The kiln-drying process takes three days, then the bricks are banded on pallets, ready for shipment. In the special cements unit there are four or five processes. Each requires three- to four-man crews. For example, the mortar-mixer crew consists of a batch mixer, a mortar mixer,

EXHIBIT 1

Organization chart: Kimball's North Carolina Works

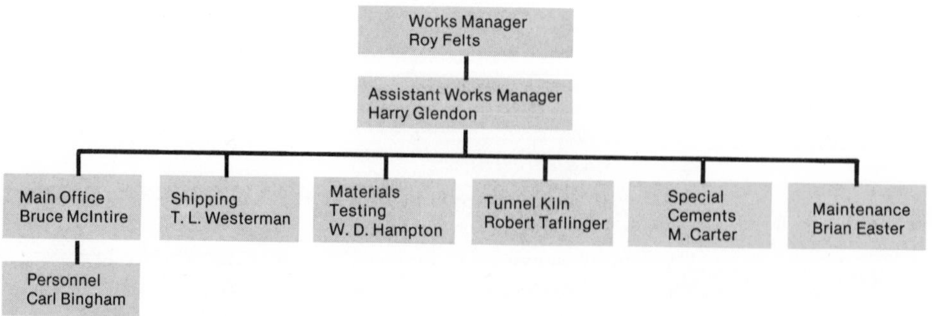

and a man to seal and stack drums. There are no easy jobs. Nearly every process requires a great deal of physical labor. The plant is extremely noisy and constantly filled with silicate dust. Most workers wear dust masks supplied by the company. Many develop silicosis of the lungs, a condition similar to emphysema. Many workers die quite young.

All jobs are defined in great detail in the job specifications and job descriptions. There is a carefully defined set of duties and relationships, but they are not always followed. The home office even has a requirement that all employees, from work manager on down, will be called by their first names.

Because of the marginal profits of the works, there is great pressure for efficiency. The tunnel kiln and special-cements departments are rated on cost per ton per day. Thus the foremen often run the machines continuously, whether there are orders for the product or not. The plant's aisles and warehouse are full of stock, often unneeded for years to come.

Robert Taflinger was given his current job when his older brother, who previously held it, was transferred. Taflinger is 42, with an eighth-grade education. He is a heavy drinker.

Roy Felts is from the old school. He is 55, with some high school education. He began his work career as a miner and is intolerant of any inefficiency or disobedience. He is feared by the other employees. He is married to Harriet Johnson. Her brother is executive vice president of Kimball in New York.

Harry Glendon has just been appointed to his job. In fact, the job was created for him after he married the daughter of the vice president and treasurer in New York.

T. L. Westerman received his job because he is a close personal friend of Felts from school days. He attends the same church as Felts.

Mel Carter has been at the North Carolina plant for two years. He has long tenure in that job. There have been six special-cement foremen in the previous eight years. He himself is talking about leaving. Mel is a college graduate, majoring in romance languages. He is a laissez-faire leader. Most workers have liked his style.

Another crucial department is maintenance. Brian Easter, maintenance supervisor, has five heavy-equipment mechanics, two carpenters, an electrician, and two machinists.

The 118 production workers consist of the following:

Special cements, day shift	40	
Special cements, night shift	15	
Special cements, third shift in busy season	5	(skeleton shift)
Tunnel kiln, day shift	40	
Tunnel kiln, night shift	18	

To give the reader an idea of the quality of supervision at the plant, the second shift supervisor of the tunnel kiln is a moonlighting high school biology teacher. The second shift special-cements supervisor is paid only hourly wages and has an eighth-grade education. But he has little trouble supervising.

All but 2 of the 118 production workers are black. The two whites are over 60. They have the two best jobs in the tunnel kiln department. The maintenance men are white and are members of their respective craft unions. Most of the maintenance people moonlight to increase their income.

All of management is white. Of the 116 black production employees, three distinct groups can be delineated:

1. Forty-one employees, mostly in their late 50s and early 60s. All have been with the firm all their careers. Some of them started out living in company housing. Most attended school only about six to seven years. Many of them cannot read or write.
2. Thirty-six employees, middle aged. They were hired during a major expansion of the works in the late 1940s.
3. Thirty-nine young employees, in their 20s and 30s. These men are reasonably well educated. Many were graduated from high school.

Pay is relatively good in North Carolina for blacks with their education and training. Typical base salaries are $2.95 per hour. Better jobs with piece-rate incentives could pay up to $55 per day. The average wage is about $6,000 per year. Employees bid for the better jobs when they come open. Normally they are awarded on the basis of seniority, at the union's insistence. This pay has put many of the blacks in middle-income groups for their community. But often they have large families, for example, 10–12 children. Large families often mean some bills don't get paid, so this leads to garnishment of wages. After four garnishments, a worker is dismissed because of the bookkeeping costs involved.

Although Kimball prohibits drinking and drugs on the job and smoking in some areas, these have been constant problems. Normally, an employee is given three warnings about drinking on the job before dismissal. However, few are dismissed. The union often has "saved" them. Fifteen of the men have serious alcoholic problems. Often employees have been found sleeping on the job as a result of alcoholism. Absenteeism and tardiness are regular problems.

The production employees belong to a local of the United Brick and Clay Workers of America. AFL–CIO. This union is not a powerhouse such as the Teamsters or UAW. But it does a good job in its day-to-day work of processing grievances, which occur about once every other week. Few of these have gone to arbitration. The men are loyal to the union, for they know how much of their security is derived from its protection.

Like almost all of its members, the union leadership is black. The shop steward, Jessie Hawkins, is 62 years old. He tends toward a "live and let live" policy. The union president, Oscar Bishop, is 48 and a rigid labor leader. So at Kimball there exists a white management and a black union. This problem is compounded by having separate restroom and shower facilities for blacks and whites, a holdover from the past. But the separation is still there. The whites' restroom is in a nice part of the building. The blacks' is in the back, behind the tunnel kiln building.

The Kimball works has a history of long and sometimes bitter strikes. Usually there has been a strike when the contract was up every other year. The last strike lasted six months and was made even more bitter for the members when it was discovered that the union treasurer had embezzled half the strike funds.

The management obviously does not trust the men. Whenever there is racial trouble in nearby cities, management closes the plant for three days, even though no racial incident has taken place there. This has embittered the men since they need the money, and they resent the implications of this act.

One day recently there was a confrontation between Taflinger and Bishop. Taflinger had accused one of the men of being drunk on the job. Bishop said:

"Listen, I've seen a dozen foremen come and go, and I'll be here long after you're gone. That's a laugh! Your accusing one of the men of being drunk! That's a laugh."

Taflinger put out the word that he wanted to get rid of Bishop. "I don't care how we do it. We're going by the book. If you see him doing any union business on company time, we'll get him. If he takes a drink, we'll get him. If he sits down a minute, we'll get him. Do you hear me?"

One week later, a foreman claimed that Bishop had talked to one of his men and it was union business. Bishop and the men denied it. Taflinger fired Bishop over the incident. The men walked out in a wildcat strike. Their strike funds are low. The union headquarters is demanding that the incident go to arbitration. Taflinger and Felts have vowed to fight to the finish over this one.

Requirement:

You are Carl Bingham, the newly transferred personnel manager at the North Carolina works. You have just gathered the information in this case. Felts wants you to get the men back to work without rehiring Bishop or going to arbitration. Plan your strategy.

10. Midwest Electric Company*

Midwest Electric Company did business nationally in the field of communications. One major activity of the company was the rebuilding and/or repairing of communication equipment for other companies in the industry. Midwest operated field repair units in 20 different metropolitan locations of the United States. High standards of workmanship and promptness of deliveries were of primary importance to Midwest and its customers, for, as Barry Neponset, manager of Unit I, said, "If one item of a multiitem order does not measure up or is not delivered on time, I fry for the whole order."

The management of Midwest believed that its industry was highly competitive. As one manager commented, "If you will permit me to editorialize, we see it this way. We are competing with other companies in the same market. The record of my unit is being appraised against the record of all other units in our company. As a major company in the field of communications we are under constant scrutiny by government. If we are to remain successful and private, we must have a record of advancing technology and reducing cost and prices. We are proud of our record, but we do not feel that we can relax for a minute."

For many years Midwest had used a wage incentive system for its nonsupervisory production employees. Management stated that, in its opinion, the system functioned to the benefit of both the company and its employees, as the company benefited from reduced cost and the employees by increased income. The union officials, with whom the company had bargained since 1937, did not share management's enthusiasm for incentive systems. In 1957, basic incentive wage levels of the system were a critical issue in bargaining, and a strike occurred. The strike lasted several weeks before management finally agreed to abandon incentives and to use a straight hourly rate of pay for several pay grades.

---

* This case was developed and prepared by Professor L. Curtise Wood, College of Business and Industry, Wichita State University, Wichita, Kan. Reprinted by permission.

Seniority, technology, and "High Ball Red"

Prior to the events of this case, Midwest had long recognized seniority as an important factor in promoting and upgrading personnel. However, company policy had always emphasized that other essential factors had to be weighed before seniority became the determining factor. The union, on the other hand, interpreted the labor contract to mean that if a man met the minimum qualifications, seniority prevailed. (See Exhibit 1 for provisions of union contract dealing with seniority and upgrading.) According to Neponset the company never formally accepted the union position; however, the union presented so many grievance cases that management informally adapted to the union positions, and the number of grievances dropped.[1]

New discoveries and developments in the field of electronics in the post–World War II period convinced Midwest management that one of its future problems would be an adequate supply of trained personnel, at field-service locations, to service new types of communications equipment. With this idea in mind, management approached the international union, with which it bargained on companywide standards, and proposed that the company give free schooling for new jobs. The company also proposed that selection for and place-

EXHIBIT 1

Selected provisions of union contract: Midwest Electric Company

Upgrading

1. GENERAL

   1.1 It is mutually recognized by the International and the Company that Seniority (term of employment) shall receive the fullest weighing consistent with the efficient operation of the business, when employees are to be selected for upgrading. The parties further recognize that the work of the hourly rated, nonsupervisory employees falls into four distinct occupational groups—production, warehouse, shop trades, and nontrades occupations, and that efficiency of operation and employee satisfaction ordinarily are best served by progressing an employee within his own occupational group.

2. SELECTION OF EMPLOYEES

   2.1 In filling job openings above Grade 1, employees considered for upgrading shall ordinarily be those within the same occupational group in the next lower grade, on the basis of Seniority and Qualification for the job to be filled. Qualification for the job to be filled shall be determined by the company and shall be based upon the employee's experience, transferable skill and demonstrated productive efficiency. Where no employee in the next lower grade is qualified for the job to be filled, the upgrading shall be made from the successively lower grades observing the same occupational group, Seniority and Qualification principles. The parties recognize that there may at times be exceptional cases in which upgradings which cross occupational group lines will be justified.

[1] The labor contract stated that the union reserved the right to challenge any action taken by the company in job grading. While the company had agreed that a challenge must be procured through the grievance procedure, such matters could not be taken to arbitration.

ment in new jobs should be on the basis of tests. The union's officials agreed in principle with Midwest's proposal, but insisted that the company sell its program to each local chapter of the union before putting it into effect. Several months later, union officers requested that their regular convention sanction the action taken relative to the Midwest proposal. Although opposed by a number of locals, the convention approved the action of its national officers.

Shortly after the meeting with union officials, Midwest managers were approached by their largest customer, United Communications, with a request that Midwest's services be expanded to include the servicing of new electronic equipment that United intended to put into use rapidly, as existing mechanical equipment was in need of replacement. United representatives stated that this change in equipment was but the first of a series of programs designed to replace much of their mechanical equipment. They also stated that previous Midwest standards for workmanship and delivery would not be satisfactory, as the equipment was to be in operation on a 24-hour basis and they intended to have but two pieces of each kind—one in use and one in reserve.

Midwest's management believed that United's proposal offered an opportunity to move into a new field and that, if the company could successfully complete this contract, it would be in a good position to compete for many other large contracts. Terms were agreed upon and the contract was labeled "High Ball Red."

After a series of conferences Midwest management made the following decisions: (1) Unit I would be in charge of training for, and the servicing of, "High Ball Red." (2) The new work was so complex that qualifications for training would be primary. (3) A group should be selected from Grade 4 (highest grade of production group) for a review program of 25 hours devoted to electrical and magnetic principles, after which a test would be given to select the six best qualified to enter training for work on electronic equipment. (4) All personnel would be paid their regular wages while in training. (5) The hourly wage to be paid on the new job would be 20 cents higher than that paid to the top production grade.

The hourly paid production employees in Unit I numbered slightly over 300 men and women. The average length of employment of 51 percent of the group was in excess of 20 years, with the remainder having an average service of 5 years. Many of the older people were employees of the company when Unit I was organized by the union in 1937, and it was common knowledge that the older people dominated the union organization.

When the Midwest proposal for training was brought before the national convention, delegates from Unit I had spoken and voted against the proposal. Again and again through the years union representatives of Unit I had made concessions at the bargaining table on other issues of working conditions at Unit I in order to maintain the seniority principle in their contract.

For several years prior to the acceptance of "High Ball Red," the management of Unit I had informally discussed the importance of skill development and the problem of seniority with local union officials. Local officials had consistently refused to make any concessions to subordinate seniority to skill, and, when management insisted that the day was coming when changes would have to be made if the company was to survive, union officers had responded with, "We'll cross that bridge when we come to it. You are just trying to get your foot in the door."

One cold, bleak, Wednesday morning in November, Colin Hunington, manager of Shop Trades, arrived late for work. On his desk was a notice which said:

> Colin:
>
> We received notice this morning to start the training programs for "High Ball Red" two weeks from today. You are in charge. However, may I suggest that you develop a course of action which recognizes that the union may decide to meet us head on and talk with me late Friday afternoon.
>
> (Signed) *Barry*
> Barry Neponset
> Unit Manager

Discussion question:

1. What strategy should Colin Hunington develop to get the local to accept skill as the basis for selecting trainees?

11. The Fight*

Richard Casey, foreman in the mechanical department, had his hands full keeping on top of all the work he had to get done. And, to make matters worse, he wasn't having much luck in quieting the heated feelings which had been brewing between Hal Wilson and Dave Larson, who were both on the same crew.

Less than a month ago Larson had requested to be transferred to either a different crew or to a different part of the operation of the same crew. His request was not granted.

The company policy on fighting was quite clear, and Casey had no doubt that everyone understood it. Unfortunately, it didn't seem to deter what everyone knew would eventually happen. Just after lunch Casey heard some loud shouting and swearing. When he got to where the ruckus was coming from, he saw several men standing between Wilson and Larson.

Larson had a big red mark on the side of his face, and it was fairly obvious that he had been struck.

None of the bystanders, however, would admit that they had seen the alleged blow being struck. So Casey sent Wilson home for the remainder of the shift and told Larson to get back to work and keep busy.

Larson then told Casey that if the situation were not corrected, he would quit his job.

Not knowing what to do and being too busy with his own work, Richard Casey did nothing.

Two days later Dave Larson quit.

Discussion questions:

1. What did this cost the company?
2. What could the foreman have done to prevent this situation?
3. Why do you think Casey did nothing and let Larson quit?

* This case was prepared by Professor Charles E. Watson of Miami University.

12. Pollock, Incorporated

Pollock, Inc., is a firm which offers computer software to computer users. Its home office is Miami, Florida. This case involves the Tampa sales office. Don Bowin is a regional sales manager who operates out of Tampa. He supervises eight sales agents. These individuals are independent businessmen who represent several companies such as Pollock in the office supplies and computer area.

Don's job is to work with the manufacturer's reps to help them reach the company's sales goals by product line. Some of Pollock's products are more profitable than others. If he isn't careful, the reps will sell their entire quotas in the easy-to-sell and less profitable items. This doesn't help Pollock or Don.

Two of his reps are giving him special problems. They are Dalmar Fitzpatrick and Henry Lokey. These men barely reach quota or sell only the easy products. This pulls Don's results down. Last year he lost his incentive bonus because of these two. He made it clear that this had happened. Both Dalmar and Henry expressed their sorrow and said they would redouble their efforts so it wouldn't happen this year. But nothing had really changed. It looked like he would lose his bonus again.

Don went to the sales manager, Harold Brecht with the proposal that he terminate these agents.

HAROLD: It always looks easiest to terminate a rep. But it took a long time to train these guys. They know their trade too. What guarantee have we got that their replacements won't be worse?

DON: They're bound to be better. Both of these guys have it made. They aren't hungry enough for the business. Fitz is 62, with lots of money. Why he only works 3 days a week! Lokey is only 45 and I know he's been with Pollock for 20 years, but he's not tapping the territory's potential. Why, Bill Schuman just took over the territory next to his, with no experience or knowledge of the trade. That territory has half the potential of Lokey's. And he's already outselling Lokey by 20 percent.

HAROLD: Well, Don, you may have some good points there. Why don't you make them to Fitz and Lokey. After guys have been with us that long, we can't just let them go because they've slipped a bit for a year or two. Here's a real challenge to your managerial abilities—to motivate guys like that. We'll find out how good a salesman you really are now.

Discussion questions:

1. What category of discipline problem do Dolman Fitzpatrick and Henry Lokey fit into?
2. What tactics should Don Casey take to motivate Fitz and Lokey?

13. Eco-Control Systems, Inc.*

Eco-Control Systems, Inc., is a moderate-size manufacturing firm whose 1978 sales exceeded $30 million. The firm manufactures, distributes, and sells environmental control systems nationally.

The company president, Mr. Burdette, is also chairman of the board and the largest stockholer in the family-owned firm. He refers collectively to his employees as "the Burdette family." Now in his advancing years, Mr. Burdette

* This case was prepared by Professor K. Mark Weaver of Bradley University.

EXHIBIT 1

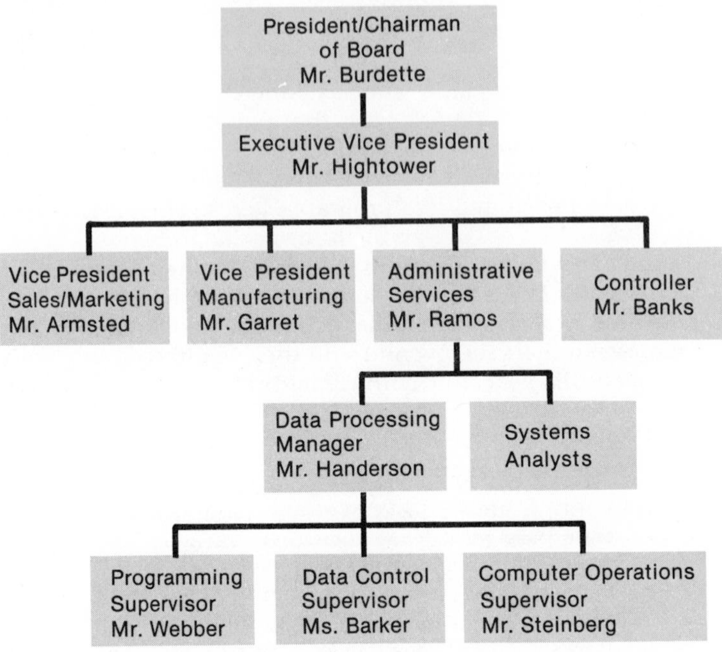

has left the management of the company to the Executive Vice-President, Mr. Hightower. This allows Mr. Burdette to devote more of his time to civic activities and to promote the community image of the corporation.

The vice-president of sales and marketing, Mr. Armsted, the vice-president of manufacturing, Mr. Garret, and the manager of administrative services, Mr. Ramos, all report to Mr. Hightower, as does Mr. Banks, the controller. Mr. Ramos is the immediate superior to the data processing manager, Mr. Handerson. Mr. Handerson, in turn, has three department heads under him, including Mr. Webber, the programming supervisor, Ms. Barker, the data control supervisor, and Mr. Steinberg, the computer operations supervisor. Mr. Ramos also supervises the two systems analysts. Exhibit 1 depicts these organizational relationships.

It had come to the attention of Mr. Hightower that the data processing division, in particular the programming department, had problems with morale and productivity. To investigate this matter, Mr. Hightower appointed a special assistant to research the problem and investigate the numerous complaints from the programmers. The assistant spent several weeks in the programming department under the pretense of another project and submitted the following report:

Attention: Mr. Hightower

Subject: Special report concerning the Programming Department

As previously recognized, both morale and efficiency within the programming department are low. The programmers make a game out of being clever at avoiding work. Jokes about the lack of ability of Mr. Webber, Mr. Handerson, and Mr. Ramos are numerous. Mr. Ramos in particular is viewed as insincere due to the phoney social comments he makes during his infrequent encounters with the programmers. In the absence of proper supervision, bedlam breaks loose in the programming department. "Snoopy" calendars and "computer art" are common projects. Although there are only eight programmers, it is quite evident that definite cabals and cliques exist. In some cases the benefits are positive, since the individuals compensate for the programming supervisor's weaknesses. At the other extreme, however, it tends to divide the department and create dissension. Petty quarreling among programmers is commonplace.

A frequent complaint from the programmers is the lack of a productive atmosphere. Schedules are constantly being disrupted by priority projects which have inadequate lead times, according to the programmers. Mr. Webber may ask for more time, but Mr. Ramos may refuse. Many times Mr. Handerson accepts projects and pushes them through without any apparent purpose, yet at the expense of other projects. Even on regular projects, Mr. Webber often establishes arbitrary time limits. The programmers complain that these deadlines do not correspond to the time needed to accomplish the task. Another complaint is that the programmers have to rely on the grapevine to receive information about matters directly affecting their work.

Programmers also feel that their jobs require creativity, and that when they are "in the mood" to work, they should not be restricted to a mandatory lunch hour or coffee break. Instead, they feel that they should be allowed more flexibility and responsibility in allocating their time. Mr. Webber overemphasizes the enforcement of company regulations instead of showing concern for accomplishing the project at hand.

The programmers complain of being blamed when something goes wrong, but not having the authority to take preventative measures or make decisions. Also, there are many times when the entire supervisory staff is absent, as in the case of a seminar, and authorized decision-making personnel are unavailable for important on-the-spot decisions. Even when the supervisors are present, they are often too busy doing "their own work" to discuss problems. In many cases, the programmers are not certain what their responsibilities and authority are.

The programmers feel that salary reviews are cursory and are not related to performance. The main reason for this, they feel, is that Mr. Webber is "too busy" to have any factual knowledge of an individual's actual abilities and performance. Also, confusion exists because some programmers are salaried and some are paid hourly.

The programmers see Mr. Webber as a "yes man" who is afraid to make a decision which may be contrary to that of Mr. Handerson. They jokingly refer to him as "Handerson's Echo."

Mr. Handerson is viewed as having long ago verified the "Peter Principle," but he is still generally recognized as the most qualified man in the organization to fill the job of data processing manager.

The programmers are generally frustrated in achieving their own goals. Often their assignments are in areas where they have no interest or which concern repetitive projects. Promotions are nearly nonexistent except for the "in" groups.

After receiving this report, Mr. Hightower began questioning some of his employees concerning their views of the current situation.

The controller, Mr. Banks, stated that he felt a reorganization was needed to place the data processing divisions under his office, since "data processing affects and is affected by almost every other department within the organization."

Mr. Ramos suggested that the programmers were being pampered and "have too much of a good thing. New job descriptions and productivity requirements would solve the whole problem."

In conversations with some of the programmers, Mr. Hightower found them quite vocal. One senior programmer stated, "Programmers are not like machines that can be turned on and off by the flick of a switch. Programming is a creative process. A good deal of thought is involved in each step to maximize efficiency and still solve the problem. Ideas that we incorporate into their programs have saved the company thousands of dollars in computer time. We should be given authority comensurate with our responsibilities."

Mr. Hightower was concerned about these conversations and was undecided about his course of action. He realized a decision must be made soon, or the data processing department would altogether lose its effectiveness.

Discussion question:

1. What approach should Mr. Hightower take to solve his problem with the programming department?

14. Personnel Manager's Time Problem*

At 7:30 A.M. on Monday, Sam Lennox, personnel manager of the Lakeview plant of Supreme Textile Corporation, pulled out of the driveway of his suburban home and headed for work. It was a beautiful day; the sun was shining in a bright blue sky, and a cool breeze was blowing. The plant was about nine miles away, and the 15-minute ride gave Sam an opportunity to think about business problems without interruption.

Supreme Textile Corporation owned and operated five plants: one yarn-spinning operation, two knitting plants, and two apparel-making operations. Supreme enjoyed a national reputation for quality products, specializing in men's sports shirts. Corporate headquarters was located in Twin-Cities adjacent to two of the plant operations. The Hillsville, Eastern, and Lakeview Plants were 100–200 miles distant. Each employed 70–100 people. About 250 employees were located in Twin-Cities.

Sam had started with Supreme's Eastern plant after college. He progressed rapidly through several staff positions. He then served two years as a night foreman. He became known for his ability to organize a "smooth team," never having a grievance procedure brought against him. While his productivity figures were not outstanding, he was given credit by many people in the company for being the person who prevented the union from successfully organizing the Eastern plant. As a result he was promoted to assistant personnel manager.

Sam's progress was noted by Glen Johnson, corporate vice president of personnel. Glen transferred Sam to the Lakeview plant, which was having some personnel problems, as a special staff assistant. Six months later he was made personnel manager when the incumbent suddenly resigned. Sam had been able to work out most of the problems and was beginning to think about how to put together a first-rate personnel program.

Sam was in fine spirits as his car picked up speed and the hum of the tires on the newly paved highway faded into the background. He said to himself, "This is the day I'm really going to get things done."

* This case was prepared by Jack D. Ferner, Lecturer in Management, Babcock Graduate School of Management, Wake Forest University, Winston-Salem, N.C.

He began to run through the day's work, first one project, then another, trying to establish priorities. After a few minutes, he decided that the MBO program was probably the most important. He frowned for a moment as he recalled that, on Friday, Glenn Johnson had asked him if he had given the project any further thought. He had been meaning to get to work on this idea for over three months, but something else always seemed to crop up. "I haven't had much time to sit down and really work it out," he said to himself. "I'd better hit this one today for sure." With that, he began to break down the objectives, procedures, and installation steps. "It's about time," he told himself. "This idea should have been followed up long ago." Sam remembered that he and Johnson had discussed it over a year ago when they had both attended a seminar on MBO. They had agreed it was a good idea, and when Sam moved to the Lakeview plant it was decided to try to install it here. They both realized it would be met with resistance by some of the plant managers.

A blast from a passing horn startled him, but his thoughts quickly returned to other projects he was determined to get underway. He started to think about ideas he had for supervisory training programs. He also needed to simplify the employee record system. The present system not only was awkward, but key information was often lacking. There were also a number of carryover and nagging employee grievance problems. Some of this involved weak supervisors, some poor working conditions, and some just poor communication and morale. There were a few other projects he couldn't recall offhand, but he could tend to them after lunch, if not before. "Yes, sir," he said to himself, "this is the day to really get rolling."

Sam's thoughts were interrupted as he pulled into the parking lot. He knew something was wrong as Al Noren, the stockroom foreman, met him by the loading dock. "A great morning, Al," Sam greeted him cheerfully.

"Not so good, Sam; my new man isn't in this morning," Al growled.

"Have you heard from him?" asked Sam.

"No, I haven't," replied Al.

Sam frowned as he commented, "These stock handlers assume you take it for granted that if they're not here, they're not here, and they don't have to call in and verify it. Better call him."

Al hesitated for a moment before replying. "Okay, Sam, but can you find me a man? I have two cars to unload today."

As Sam turned to leave, he said, "I'll call you in half an hour, Al," and headed for his office.

When he walked into the personnel office there were several plant employees huddled around his secretary, Terry. They were complaining that there was an error in their paychecks. After checking their files and calling payroll twice he found an automatic pay increase had not been picked up properly. He finally got everyone settled down.

He sat down at his desk, which was opposite Terry's and two other clerks. One of the girls brought him a big pile of mail. He asked her to get him a cup of coffee and started to open the mail. The phone rang; it was the plant manager asking him about finding a new secretary. As Sam hung on the phone listening to all the problems the "old man" had with secretaries, he thought, "Fussbudget." When he finished he took a swallow of the coffee, which had gotten cold. He started to call a couple of foremen to see if they had someone to fill in for Al in the stockroom when he was interrupted by one of his clerks asking him to check over several termination reports. He was trying to decide whether any of these represented trouble spots when the phone rang again. Glen Johnson was on the other end. With an obvious edge in his voice, he asked, "I've heard rumblings about some of the grievances we can't seem to solve. What about it?" Sam responded that he hadn't had time, but would. There followed a series of questions. The conversation ended with, "Sam, you really need to get after those problems." Sam sighed. Terry was at his desk asking him to approve a couple of rate changes.

Several job applicants came into the office as a result of want ads the company had run over the weekend. There was a buzz as the applications and interviews progressed. Sam started to help out. Sam was talking with one applicant when Cecil Hardy came in. Cecil was the plant engineer, who liked to stop by to chat and have a cup of coffee. He was approaching retirement and today wanted to talk about the company's pension benefits. He also described in detail a round of golf he had played Saturday afternoon. Sam had played a lot when he was in school and enjoyed an occasional game with Cecil.

It was suddenly 10:45 and time to go to a staff meeting. They were going to discuss something about quality control and Sam wasn't awfully interested, but the plant manager wanted all the department heads at staff meetings. "They always drag on so long and we get off on things that don't seem real important to all of us," Sam reflected as he headed toward the conference room.

Sam went to lunch with a friend who owned a plastics fabrication business. He called an hour ahead to say he wanted to discuss a major medical package which had been proposed by an insurance company. They drove across town to a new restaurant.

When Sam returned at about 2:00 P.M. the office was busy again with job applicants. He suddenly remembered the replacement stock clerk. "Too late now," he mused. He sat down and began to assemble the files relating to the grievances. The production superintendent called to discuss his need for several production people. He wanted experienced people and wasn't happy with some of the prospects Sam's department had sent him. Sam took a break to get a coke from the storage room. He noticed some of the confidential employee files had been pulled out and not returned. As he straightened them out he thought, "I wonder who the hell did this?"

Sam returned to his desk to find a Boy Scout troop selling advertisements in a program for a rally they were putting on. This was one of the odd tasks Sam had been assigned by the plant manager. As the afternoon wore on, Sam became increasingly irritated at not being able to make much progress with the grievances. "Trouble is, I'm not sure what should be done about the Sally Foster and Curt Davis cases."

At 4:45 the personnel manager at the Eastern plant called to ask about some employee matters Sam had handled when he was there. When he finished, it was 5:30 and he was the only one left in the office. Sam was tired. He put on his coat and headed toward the parking lot. He almost ran into Al Noren who was also heading for his car. "Thanks for the stock clerk," Al grumbled as he drove off.

With both eyes on the traffic, Sam reviewed the day he had just completed. "Busy?" he asked himself. "Too much so—but did I accomplish anything?" His mind raced over the day's activities. "Yes and no" seemed to be the answer. "There was the usual routine, the same as any other day. The personnel function kept going, and we must have hired several new people. Any creative or special project work done?" Sam grimaced as he reluctantly answered, "No."

With a feeling of guilt, he probed further. "Am I a manager? I'm paid like one, respected like one, and have a responsible assignment with the necessary authority to carry it out. Yet, one of the greatest values a company derives from a manager is his creative thinking and accomplishments. You need some time for thinking. Today was like most other days; I did little, if any, creative work. The projects that I so enthusiastically planned to work on this morning are exactly as they were last week. What's more, I have no guarantee that tomorrow will bring me any closer to their completion. There must be an answer."

Sam continued, "Night work? Yes, occasionally. This is understood. But I've been doing too much of this lately. I owe my wife and family some of my time. When you come down to it, they are the people for whom I'm really working. If I am forced to spend much more time away from them, I'm not meeting my own personal objectives. What about church work? Should I eliminate that? I spend a lot of time on it, but I feel I owe God some time, too. Besides, I believe I'm making a worthwhile contribution. Perhaps I can squeeze a little time from my fraternal activities. But where does recreation fit in?"

Sam groped for the solution. By this time, he had turned off the highway onto the side street leading to his home—the problem still uppermost in his mind. "I guess I really don't know the answer," he told himself as he pulled into his driveway. "This morning, everything seemed so simple, but now. . . ." His son ran toward the car, calling out, "Mommy, Daddy's home."

Discussion questions:

1. Personnel consists of numerous activities. What areas were illustrated by Sam's schedule on this particular day?
2. List the areas of ineffective management and time robbers.
3. Discuss Sam's career progress. Is he now promotable?

References

Chapter 1

Babcock, David, and Boyd, John. "PAIR Department Policy and Organization." In Dale Yoder and Herbert Heneman, Jr. (eds.), *PAIR Policy and Program Management.* Washington, D.C.: Bureau of National Affairs, 1978.

Benedict, Clyde. "A Personnel Perspective—Today." *The Personnel Administrator,* November 1975, pp. 27–30.

De Spelder, Bruce. *Ratios of Staff to Line Personnel.* Columbus: Bureau of Business Research, Ohio State University, 1962.

Foulkes, Fred. "The Expanding Role of the Personnel Function." *Harvard Business Review,* March–April 1975, pp. 71–84.

Henderson, James. "What the Chief Executive Expects of the Personnel Function." *The Personnel Administrator,* May 1977, pp. 40–45.

Howes, Marshall, and Yates, Bennie. "How to Control Personnel Costs in Overhead Functions." *Personnel,* July–August 1976, pp. 22–29.

Meyer, Herbert. "Personnel Directors Are the New Corporate Heroes." *Fortune,* February 1976, pp. 84–88.

Miner, John, and Miner, Mary. "Managerial Characteristics of Personnel Managers." *Industrial Relations,* May 1976, pp. 225–34.

Myers, Charles, and Turnbull, John. "Line and Staff in Industrial Relations." *Harvard Business Review,* October–November 1969, pp. 1–12.

"Personnel: Fast Track to the Top." *Duns Review,* April 1975, pp. 74–77.

"The Personnel Executive's Job." *Personnel Management: Policies and Practices,* 1977, published by Prentice-Hall, Inc., Englewood Cliffs, N.J.

"Walton Burdick: A Look at Corporate and Personnel Philosophy." *The Personnel Administrator,* July 1976, pp. 21–26.

White, H., and Boynton, R. "The Role of Personnel: A Management View." *Arizona Business,* vol. 21, no. 8 (1974), pp. 17–21.

Chapter 2

Atkinson, J. W., *An Introduction to Motivation.* New York: American Book Co., 1964.

Dunlop, John. "The Limits of Legal Compulsion." *Labor Law Journal,* February 1976, pp. 67–74.

Emshwiller, John. "Change in Attitudes." *The Wall Street Journal,* February 3, 1977.

Freud, Sigmund. *The Basic Writings of S. Freud.* Trans. A. Brill. New York: Modern Library, 1938.

Gilroy, Edwin, et al., "Personnel Administration in the Multinational/Transnational Corporation." In Dale Yoder and Herbert Heneman, Jr. (eds.), *PAIR Policy and Program Management.* Washington, D.C.: Bureau of National Affairs, 1978.

Hackman, J. Richard. "Work Design." In J. Richard Hackman and J. Lloyd Suttle (eds.), *Improving Life at Work.* Santa Monica, Calif.: Goodyear Publishing Co., 1977.

Herzberg, Frederick; Mausner, Bernard; and Snyderman, Barbara. *The Motivation to Work.* New York: John Wiley & Sons, 1959.

Hodgson, James. "Public Policy in PAIR." In Dale Yoder and Herbert Heneman, Jr. (eds.), *PAIR Policy and Program Management.* Washington, D.C.: Bureau of National Affairs, 1978.

Jung, Carl. *Personality Types.* New York: Harcourt Brace, 1923.

Lewin, Kurt. *Dynamic Theory of Per-*

sonality. New York: McGraw-Hill Book Co., 1935.

McClelland, David. *The Personality.* New York: Dryden Press, 1951.

Maslow, Abraham. *Motivation and Personality.* New York: Harper and Row, 1954.

Morgenthaler, Eric. "Dropouts Revisited." *The Wall Street Journal,* December 29, 1976.

Chapter 3

Allen, Fred. "Ways to Improve Employee Communication." *Nation's Business,* September 1975, pp. 54–56.

Barnard, Chester. *Functions of the Executive.* Cambridge: Harvard University Press, 1938.

Bassett, Glen. "PAIR Records and Information Systems." In Dale Yoder and Herbert Heneman, Jr. (eds.), *Planning and Auditing PAIR.* Washington, D.C.: Bureau of National Affairs, 1976.

Berrien F., and Angoff, W. "The Sensitivity of Employee Attitude Questionnaires." *Personnel Psychology,* vol. 13, no. 3 (1960), pp. 317–27.

Bureau of National Affairs. *Employee Communications.* Personnel Policies Forum Survey no. 110. Washington, D.C., 1975.

Cowan, Paula. "Establishing a Communication Chain: The Development and Distribution of an Employee Handbook." *Personnel Journal,* June 1975, pp. 342–49.

Dahle, T. L. "An Objective and Comparative Study of Five Methods of Transmitting Information to Business and Industrial Employees." *Speech Monograph* 21 (1954), pp, 21–28.

Davis, Keith. *Human Behavior at Work.* 5th ed. New York: McGraw-Hill Book Co., 1977. Pp. 261–73.

Davis, Keith. "Readability Changes in Employee Handbooks of Identical Companies during a 15-Year Period." *Personnel Psychology,* Winter 1968, pp. 413–20.

Gelfand, L. I. "Communicate through Your Supervisor." *Harvard Business Review,* November–December 1970, pp. 101–4.

Glueck, William F. *Management.* Hinsdale, Ill.: Dryden Press, 1977. Chap. 9.

Habbe, Stephen. *Following Up Attitude Survey Findings.* Studies in Personnel Policy no. 181. New York: National Industrial Conference Board, 1961.

Hare, Von Court, Jr. "Communication and Information Systems." In Joseph McGuire (ed.), *Contemporary Management.* Englewood Cliffs, N.J.: Prentice-Hall, 1974.

International Association of Business Communicators. *Readership Surveys.* Akron, 1970.

Jones, D. E. "The Employee Handbook." *Personnel Journal,* vol. 52 (1973), pp. 136–41.

Kindre, Thomas. "Corporate Policy, Programs and Communications Media." In Joseph Famularo (ed.), *Handbook of Modern Personnel Administration.* New York: McGraw-Hill Book Co., 1972. Chap. 72.

Knippen, Jay. "Grapevine Communication: Management Employees." *Journal of Business Research,* January 1974, pp. 47–58.

LeBreton, Preston. *Administrative Intelligence-Information Systems.* Boston: Houghton Mifflin Co., 1969.

Level, Dale. "Communication Effectiveness." *Journal of Business Communications,* Fall 1972, pp. 19–25.

Lublin, Joanne. "Underground Papers." *The Wall Street Journal,* November 3, 1971, p. 8.

Seamans, Lyman, Jr. "Establishing the Human Resource Data Base System." *The Personnel Administrator,* November 1977, pp. 44–49.

Silverman, Robert. "The Cross Fertilization Concept: An Employee Publication That Communicates." *Personnel Journal,* September 1973, pp. 819–22.

Sweets, Clarence. "Role of Employment Communications." In Dale Yoder and Herbert Heneman, Jr., *Administration and Organization: PAIR Handbook.* Washington, D.C.: Bureau of National Affairs, 1977.

Wilkesberg, Albert. "Communication Networks in Business Organization Structure." *Academy of Management Journal,* vol. 11 (1968), pp. 253–62.

Walker, James. "Evaluating the Practical Effectiveness of Human Resource Planning Applications." *Human Resource Management,* Spring 1974, pp. 19–27.

Chapter 4

Coleman, Bruce. "An Integrated System for Manpower Planning." *Business Horizons,* October 1970, pp. 89–95.

Glueck, William. "Changing Hours of Work: A Review of the Literature." *Proceedings,* Academy of Management, 1977.

Grey, James, and Waas, Robert. "A Mini Human Resources Inventory System." *Personnel,* November–December 1974, pp. 59–64.

McCormick, Ernest. "Job and Task Analysis." In Marvin Dunnette (ed.), *Handbook of Industrial and Organizational Psychology.* Chicago: Rand McNally & Co., 1976.

McCormick, Ernest. "Job Information: Its Development and Applications." In Dale Yoder and Herbert Heneman, Jr. (eds.), *Staffing Policies and Strategies: PAIR Handbook.* Washington, D.C.: Bureau of National Affairs, 1974.

Magoon, Warren, and Schnicker, Larry. "Flexible Hours at State Street Bank of Boston." *The Personnel Administrator,* October 1976, pp. 34–37.

Mahoney, Thomas; Milkovich, George; and Weiner, Nan. "A Stock and Flow Model for Improved Human Resources Measurement." *Personnel,* May–June 1977, pp. 57–66.

Mendelson, Jack. "What's Fair Treatment for Terminated Employees?" *Supervisory Management,* November 1974, pp. 25–34.

Milkovich, George, and Mahoney, Thomas. "Human Resources Planning and PAIR Policy." In Dale Yoder and Herbert Heneman, Jr. (eds.), *PAIR Handbook,* vol. 4. Berea, Ohio: American Society of Personnel Administrators, 1976.

Traum, Richard. "Reducing Headcount through Attrition and/or Termination." *Personnel,* January–February 1975, pp. 19–25.

Chapter 5

Behling, Orlando, and Rodkin, Henry. "How College Students Find Jobs." *Personnel Administration,* September–October 1969, pp. 35–42.

Dahl, Dave, and Pinto, Patrick. "Job Posting: An Industry Survey." *Personnel Journal,* January 1977, pp. 40–42. Material reprinted with permission of *Personnel Journal* copyright January 1977.

Field, Hubert, and Holley, William. "Resume Preparation: An Empirical Study of Personnel Managers' Perceptions." *Vocational Guidance Quarterly,* March 1976, pp. 229–37.

Glueck, William. "Decision Making: Organization Choice." *Personnel Psychology,* Spring 1974, pp. 77–93.

Greco, B. *How to Get a Job That's Right for You.* Chicago: Dow Jones–Irwin, 1975.

Ornstein, Michael. *Entry into the American Labor Force.* New York: Academic Press, 1976.

"The Personnel Executive's Job." *Personnel Management: Policies and Practices,* 1977, published by Prentice-Hall, Inc., Englewood Cliffs, N.J.

Sibson, Robert. "The High Cost of Hiring." *Nation's Business,* February 1975, pp. 85–88.

Simison, Robert. "Sifting Seniors." *The Wall Street Journal,* March 30, 1977.

Wernimont, Paul. "Recruitment Policies and Practices." In Dale Yoder and Herbert Heneman, Jr. (eds.), *Staffing Policies and Strategies: ASPA Handbook.* Washington, D.C.: Bureau of National Affairs, 1974.

Chapter 6

Bureau of National Affairs. Personnel Policies Forum, Survey 114, September 1976.

Campbell, John P., et al., *Managerial Behavior, Performance, and Effectiveness.* New York: McGraw-Hill Book Co., 1970.

Chase, Richard. "Working Physiology." *Personnel Administration,* November 1969, pp. 47–53.

Jauch, Lawrence. "Systemizing the Selection Decision." *Personnel Journal,* November 1976, pp. 564–66. Material reprinted with permission of *Personnel Journal* copyright November, 1976.

Kessler, Clemm C., III, and Gibbs, Georgia J. "Getting the Most from Application Blanks and References." *Personnel,* January–February 1975, pp. 53–62. Material reprinted by permission of AMACOM, a division of American Management Associations. All rights reserved.

Owens, William. "Background Data." In Marvin Dunnette (ed.), *Handbook of Industrial and Organizational Psychology.* Chicago: Rand McNally & Co., 1976.

"The Personnel Executive's Job." *Personnel Management: Policies and Practices,* December 14, 1976, published by Prentice-Hall, Inc., Englewood Cliffs, N.J. Material reprinted with permission.

Reid, John E., and Inbau, Fred E. *Truth and Deception: The Polygraph Technique.* Baltimore, Md.: Williams & Wilkins Co., 1966.

Schmidt, Frank, et al., "Job Sample vs Paper and Pencil Trades and Technical Tests: Adverse Impact and Examinee Attitudes." *Personnel Psychology,* Summer 1977, pp. 123–31.

Sibson, Robert. "The High Cost of Hiring." *Nation's Business,* February 1975, pp. 85–88.

Siegel, Laurence. *Industrial Psychology.* Homewood, Ill.: Richard D. Irwin, 1969.

Wilson, W. "Toward Better Use of Psychological Testing." *Personnel,* May–June, 1962, pp. 55–62.

Chapter 7

Boe, Warren, and Stone, Thomas. "A Comparison of Three Placement Methods." *Proceedings,* Academy of Management 1973. Pp. 372–77.

Gomersall, Earl R., and Myers, M. Scott. "Breakthrough in On-the-Job Training." *Harvard Business Review,* July–August 1966, pp. 62–71.

Holland, Joan, and Curtis, Theodore. "Orientation of New Employees. "In Joseph Famularo *Handbook of Modern Personnel Administration.* New York: McGraw-Hill Book Co., 1972. Chap. 23.

Ilgen, Daniel, and Seeley, William. "Realistic Expectations as an Aid in Reducing Voluntary Resignations." *Journal of Applied Psychology,* vol. 59, no. 4 (1974), p. 452.

Jones, Don. "The Employee Handbook." *Personnel Journal,* February 1973, pp. 136–41.

McClintock, Marian, et al., "Orienting the New Employee with Programmed Instruction." *Training and Development Journal,* May 1967, pp. 18–22.

"The Personnel Executive's Job." *Personnel Management: Policies and Practices,* 1977, published by Prentice-Hall, Inc., Englewood Cliffs, N.J.

Pilengo, Ronald. "Placement by Objectives." *Personnel Journal,* September 1973, pp. 804–10.

Schein, Edgar H. "How to Break in the College Graduate." *Harvard Business Review,* November–December 1964, pp. 68–76.

Sibson, Robert. "The High Cost of Hiring." *Nation's Business,* February 1975, pp. 85–86.

Van Maanen, John. "Breaking In: Socialization to Work." In Robert Dubin (ed.), *Handbook of Work, Organization, and Society.* Chicago: Rand McNally & Co., 1976.

Wanous, John. "Organizational Entry: From Naive Expectations to Realistic Belief." *Journal of Applied Psychology,* February 1976, pp. 22–29.

Chapter 8

Blanz, Fritz, and Ghiselli, Edwin. "The Mixed Standard Scale: A New Rating System." *Personnel Psychology,* vol. 25 (1972), pp. 185–99.

Bureau of National Affairs. *Employee Performance: Evaluation and Control.* Personnel Policies Forum, Survey 108. Washington, D.C., February 1975.

Bureau of National Affairs. *Labor Policy and Practice—Personnel Management.* Washington, D.C., 1974.

Cummings, Larry, and Schwab, Donald. *Performance in Organizations.* Glenview, Ill.: Scott Foresman & Co., 1973.

Downs, Cal, and Spohn, David. "Case Study of an Appraisal System in an Airline." *Proceedings,* Academy of Management, 1976.

Duffey, Kirt, and Webber, Robert. "On 'Relative' Rating Systems." *Personnel Psychology,* vol. 27 (1974), pp. 307–11.

Goodale, James, and Burke, Ronald. "BARS Need Not Be Job Specific." *Journal of Applied Psychology,* vol. 60, no. 3 (1975), pp. 389–91.

Grey, Ronald, and Kipnis, David. "Untangling the Performance Appraisal Dilemma: The Influence of Perceived Organizational Context on Evaluative Processes." *Journal of Applied Psychology,* vol. 61, no. 3 (1976), pp. 329–35.

Kelley, Michael. "Subjective Performance Evaluation and Person-Role Conflict under Conditions of Uncertainty." *Academy of Management Journal,* vol. 20, no. 2 (1977), pp. 301–14.

Kircher, W. K., and Dunnette, Marvin. "Using Critical Incidents to Measure Job Proficiency Factors." *Personnel,* vol. 34 (1957), pp. 54–59.

Locher, Alan, and Teel, Kenneth. "Performance Appraisal—A Survey of Current Practices." *Personnel Journal,* May 1977, pp. 345–54.e

McGregor, Douglas. "An Uneasy Look at Performance Appraisal." *Harvard Business Review,* May–June 1975, pp. 89–94.

Moses, Joseph, et al., *Standards and Ethical Considerations for Assessment Center Operations.* Quebec: Third International Congress on the Assessment Center Method, May 1975.

Shrauger, J. Sidney. "Responses to Evaluation as a Function of Initial Self-Perceptions." *Psychological Bulletin,* vol. 82, no. 4 (1975), pp. 581–96.

Smith, Patricia. "Behaviors, Results, and Organizational Effectiveness." In Marvin Dunnette (ed.), *Handbook of Industrial and Organizational Psychology.* Chicago: Rand McNally & Co., 1976.

Thompson, Paul H., and Dalton, Gene W. "Performance Appraisal: Managers Beware." *Harvard Business Review,* January–February 1970, pp. 149–57.

Tornow, Walter, and Pinto, Patrick. "The Development of a Managerial Job Taxonomy: A System for Describing, Classifying and Evaluating Executive Positions." *Journal of Applied Psychology* vol. 61, no. 4 (1976), pp. 410–18.

Zawacki, Robert, and Taylor, Robert. "A View of Performance Appraisal from Organizations Using It." *Personnel Journal,* June 1976, pp. 290–92, 299 ff.

Chapter 9

Bass, Bernard, and Vaughn, James. *Training in Industry: The Management of Learning.* Belmont, Cal.: Wadsworth Publishing Co., 1966.

Bureau of National Affairs. *Training Employees.* Personnel Policies Forum, Survey 88. Washington, D.C., 1969.

Curry, Theodore, II. "Why Not Use Your Line Managers as Management Trainers?" *Training and Development Journal,* November 1977, pp. 43–47.

Franklin, William. "A Comparison of Formally and Informally Trained Journeymen in Construction." *Industrial and Labor Relations Review,* July 1973, pp. 1086–94.

Goldstein, Irwin. *Training: Program Development and Evaluation.* Monterey, Cal.: Brooks/Cole Publishing Co., 1974.

Kepner, Charles, and Tregoe, Benjamin. *The Rational Manager.* New York: McGraw-Hill Book Co., 1965.

Kirkpatrick, Donald. "Determining Training Needs." *Training and Development Journal,* February 1977, pp. 22–25.

McGehee, W., and Thayer, P. *Training in Business and Industry.* New York: John Wiley & Sons, 1961.

Murray, William. "The Role of Training at Harris Bank of Chicago." *Training and Development Journal,* December 1976, pp. 16–18.

Roderick, Roger, and Yaney, Joseph. "Developing Younger Workers: A Look at Who Gets Trained." *Journal of Management,* Spring 1976, pp. 19–26.

Rundquist, Edward. "Designing and Improving Job Training Courses." *Personnel Psychology,* Spring 1972, pp. 41–52.

Silvern, Leonard. "Training: Man-Man and Man-Machine Communications." In Kenyon De Greene (ed.), *Systems Psychology.* New York: McGraw-Hill Book Co., 1970. Pp. 383–405.

Speer, Edgar. "The Role of Training at United States Steel." *Training and Development Journal,* June 1976, pp. 18–21.

Utgaard, S. B., and Davis, R. V. "The Most Frequently Used Training Techniques." *Training and Development Journal,* February 1970, pp. 40–43.

Yoder, Dale, and Heneman, Herbert, Jr., *Training and Development: PAIR Handbook,* Washington, D.C.: Bureau of National Affairs, 1977.

Chapter 10

Berne, Eric. *Games People Play.* New York: Ballantine Books, 1964.

Berne, Eric. *Transactional Analysis in Psychotherapy* New York: Ballatine Books, 1961.

Blake, Robert, and Mouton, Jane. *Critiqube.* Austin, Tex.: Scientific Methods, 1976.

Burnaska, Robert. "The Effects of Behavior Modeling Training upon Manager's Behaviors and Employee's Perceptions." *Personnel Psychology,* vol. 29 (1976), pp. 329–35.

Campbell, John P., et al. *Managerial Behavior, Performance, and Effectiveness.* New York: McGraw-Hill Book Co., 1970.

Ely, Donald, and Morse, John. "TA and Reinforcement Theory." *Personnel,* March–April 1974, pp. 38–41.

Goldstein, A. P., and Sorcher, M. *Changing Supervisory Behavior.* New York: Pergamon Press, 1974.

Gould, M. "Counseling for Self-Development." *Personnel Journal,* March 1970, pp. 226–34. Material reprinted with permission of *Personnel Journal,* copyright March 1970.

Holland, John. *Making Vocational Choices: A Theory of Careers.* Englewood Cliffs, N.J.: Prentice-Hall, 1973.

Kepner, Charles H., and Tregoe, Benjamin B. *The Rational Manager.* New York: McGraw-Hill Book Co., 1965.

Kirkpatrick, D. L. "Techniques for Evaluating Training Programs." *Journal of the American Society of Training Directors* vol. 13, no. 14, 1969–1970.

Margulies, Newton, and Raia, Anthony. *Conceptual Foundations of Organization Development.* New York: McGraw-Hill Book Co., 1978.

Moses, Joseph, and Ritchie, Richard. "Supervisory Relationships Training: A Behavioral Evaluation of a Behavior Modeling Program." *Personnel Psychology,* vol. 29 (1976), pp. 337–43.

"Plotting a Route to the Top." *Business Week,* October 12, 1974.

Rettig, Jack, and Amano, Matt. "A Survey of ASPA Experience with Management by Objectives, Sensitivity Training and Transactional Analysis." *Personnel Journal,* January 1976, pp. 26–29.

Steelman, H. Stanley. "Is There a Payoff to OD?" *Training and Development Journal,* April 1976, pp. 18–23.

Strauss, George. "Organization Development." In Robert Dubin (ed.), *Handbook of Work, Organization and Society.* Chicago: Rand McNally & Co., 1976.

U.S. Air Force, *Air Force Manual,* pp. 36–43.

Chapter 11

Crandall, N. Fredric. "Personnel and Human Resource Decisions in Organizations: An Empirical Study of Compensation Administration." *Proceedings,* Academy of Management, 1978.

Deci, Edward. *Intrinsic Motivation.* New York: Plenum Publishing Corp., 1975.

Engelke, Glenn. "Conducting Surveys." In Milton Rock (ed.), *Handbook of Wage and Salary Administration.* New York: McGraw-Hill Book Co., 1972.

Hyatt, James. "Merit Money." *The Wall Street Journal,* March 7, 1977.

Kelly, Robert. "Job Evaluation and Pay Plans: Office Personnel." In Joseph Famularo (ed.), *Handbook of Modern Personnel Administration.* New York: McGraw-Hill Book Co., 1972.

Lawler, E. E., Jr. *Pay and Organizational Effectiveness.* New York: McGraw-Hill Book Co., 1971.

Livernash, E. R. "Wages and Benefits." In Woodrow Ginsberg et al. (eds.), *Review of Industrial Relations Research.* Madison, Wis.: Industrial Relations Research Association, 1970.

Meyer, Herbert. "The Pay for Performance Dilemma." *Organizational Dynamics,* Winter 1975, pp. 39–50.

Nash, Allen, and Carroll, Stephen. *The Management of Compensation.* Monterey, Cal.: Brooks/Cole Publishing Co., 1975.

Patten, Thomas. *Pay.* Glencoe, Ill.: The Free Press. © 1977 by The Free Press, a division of Macmillan Publishing Co., Inc.

"The Personnel Executive's Job." *Personnel Management: Policies and Practices, 1977,* published by Prentice-Hall, Inc., Englewood Cliffs, N.J.

Chapter 12

Bureau of National Affairs, Personnel Policies Forum, Survey 97. Washington, D.C., 1972.

Deardon, John. "How to Make Incentive Plans Work." *Harvard Business Review,* July–August 1972, pp. 117–24.

Deci, Edward. *Intrinsic Motivation.* New York: Plenum Publishing Corp., 1975.

Geare, A. J. "Productivity from Scanlon-type Plans." *Academy of Management Review,* July 1976, pp. 99–108.

Hearst, Peter. "Employee Stock Ownership Trusts and Their Uses." *Personnel Journal,* February 1975, pp. 104–6.

Krefting, Linda, and Mahoney, Thomas. "Determining the Size of a Meaningful Pay Increase." *Industrial Relations,* February 1977, pp. 83–93.

Lawler, E. E., Jr. *Pay and Organizational Effectiveness.* New York: McGraw-Hill Book Co., 1971.

Lincoln, James. *Incentive Management.* Cleveland, Ohio: Lincoln Electric Co., 1969.

Meyer, Herbert. "The Pay for Performance Dilemma." *Organization Dynamics,* Winter 1975, pp. 39–50.

Nash, Alan, and Carroll, Stephen. *Management of Compensation.* Monterey, Calif.: Brooks/Cole Publishing Co., 1975.

Patton, Arch. *Men, Money and Motivation.* New York: McGraw-Hill Book Co., 1961.

Pitts, Robert. "Incentive Compensation and Organization Design." *Personnel Journal,* May 1974, pp. 338–44; 348 ff.

Sbarra, Robert. "The New Language of Executive Compensation." *Personnel,* November–December 1975, pp. 10–18.

"Special Privileges," *The Wall Street Journal,* September 18, 1975.

Uly, Bruce R. "Compensation Management: Its Past and Its Future." *Personnel,* May–June 1977, pp. 30–40.

Wallace, Marc. "Type of Control, Industrial Concentration and Executive Pay." *Proceedings,* Academy of Management, 1976.

Chapter 13

Administrative Management Society. "Going Back Means Moving Up." *Administrative Management,* May 1971, pp. 61–62.

Ashall, Robert, and Child, John. "Employee Services: People, Profits, or Parkinson?" *Personnel Management,* Fall 1972, pp. 18–22.

Bailenson, Stewart. *How to Control the Cost of Unemployment Compensation Claims and Taxes on Your Business.* Homewood, Ill.: Dow Jones–Irwin, 1976.

Bureau of National Affairs. *Services for Employees.* Personnel Policies Forum, Survey 105. Washington, D.C., 1974.

Bureau of National Affairs. *Employee Health and Welfare Benefits.* Personnel Policies Forum, Survey 107. Washington, D.C., 1974.

Bureau of National Affairs. *Paid Leave and Leave of Absence Policies.* Personnel Policies Forum, Survey 111. Washington, D.C., November 1975.

Bureau of National Affairs. *Social, Recreational, and Holiday Program.* Personnel Policies Forum, Survey 109. Washington, D.C., 1975.

Meyer, Mitchell, and Fox, Harland. "Profile of Employee Benefits." In Bureau of National Affairs, *Basic Patterns in Union Contracts.* Washington, D.C., 1975.

Miller, Alan. "How Companies Can Trim Employee Health Benefit Claims." *Harvard Business Review,* January–February, 1978, p. 608.

Nealey, Stanley. "Compensation Fungibility." *Proceedings,* Industrial Relations Research Association, 1977. Pp. 154–59.

Paul, Robert. *Employee Benefits Factbook.* New York: Martin Segal Co., 1976.

"The Personnel Executive's Job." *Personnel Management: Policies and Practices,* 1977, published by Prentice-Hall, Inc., Englewood Cliffs, N.J.

Shott, Gerald, and Schulz, Richard. "A Communication Road Map." *The Personnel Administrator,* May–June 1972, pp. 18–20.

U.S. Chamber of Commerce, annual surveys on fringe benefits. Published in *Nation's Business,* U.S. Department of Labor Statistics.

Werther, William. "A New Direction in Rethinking Fringe Benefits." *MSU Business Topics,* Winter 1974, pp. 35–40.

Chapter 14

Carlson, Donald. "Responding to the Pension Reform Law." *Harvard Business Review,* November–December 1974, pp. 133–44.

Hopkins, Mary, and Wood, Marcia. "Who Wants to Retire?" *The Personnel Administrator,* October 1976, pp. 38–41.

Ignatius, David. "Paper Weight." *The Wall Street Journal,* July 16, 1976.

Katona, George. *Private Pensions and Individual Savings.* Monograph 40, Ann Arbor: Survey Research Center, University of Michigan, 1965.

Meyer, Mitchell, and Fox, Harland. *Early Retirement Programs.* New York: National Industrial Conference Board, 1971.

Myers, Robert. *Social Security.* Homewood, Ill.: Richard D. Irwin, 1975.

Pension Benefit Guaranty Corporation. *Annual Report to the President and Congress.* Washington, D.C., June 30, 1978.

"The Personnel Executive's Job." *Personnel Management: Policies and Practices,* 1977, published by Prentice-Hall, Inc., Englewood Cliffs, N.J.

Pyron, H. C. "Preparing Employees for Retirement." *Personnel Journal,* September 1969, pp. 722–27. Material reprinted with permission of *Personnel Journal,* copyright September 1969.

Chapter 15

Ashford, Nicholas. *Crisis in the Workplace: Occupational Disease and Injury: A Report to the Ford Foundation.* Cambridge, Mass.: MIT Press, 1976. Chap. 1, 3.

Burbank, Bernard. "Employee Health." In Joseph Famularo (ed.), *Handbook of Modern Personnel Administration.* New York: McGraw-Hill Book Co., 1972.

Bureau of Labor Statistics. *Injury Rates by Industry.* Washington, D.C.: U.S. Department of Labor, 1978.

Ettkin, Lawrence, and Chapman, J. Brad. "Is OSHA Effective in Reducing Industrial Injuries?" *Labor Law Journal,* July 1975, pp. 236–49.

Gardner, James. "Employee Safety." In Joseph Famularo (ed.), *Handbook of Modern Personnel Administration.* New York: McGraw-Hill Book Co., 1972.

National Safety Council. *Accident Facts.* 1978 edition.

Occupational Safety and Health Administration, *Annual Report to the President.* Washington, D.C.: U.S. Department of Labor, yearly.

Occupational Safety and Health Administration. *Occupational Safety and Health Statistics of the Federal Government.* Washington, D.C.: U.S. Department of Labor, 1978.

Peterson, Dan. "The Future of Safety Management." Material reprinted with permission from the January, 1976 issue of *Professional Safety* magazine, official publication of the American Society of Safety Engineers.

Rinefort, Foster. "A New Look at Occupational Safety." *Personnel Administrator,* November 1977, pp. 29–36.

Van Namee, James. "Occupational Safety and Health." In Dale Yoder and Herbert Heneman, Jr. (eds.), *PAIR Policy and*

Program Management. Washington, D.C.: Bureau of National Affairs, 1978.

Yaney, Joseph, et al., "Environmental Changes in the Workplace." In *Proceedings,* Midwest Academy of Management, 1974.

Chapter 16

Affirmative Action Book. Reading, Mass.: Addison-Wesley Publishing Co., 1976.

Equal Employment Opportunity Agreement between American Telephone and Telegraph Co. and Equal Employment Opportunity Commission and U.S. Department of Labor, January 18, 1973." *Commerce Clearing House Labor Law Reports,* no. 373, 1973.

Equal Employment Opportunity Commission. *Annual Report.* Washington, D.C.: U.S. Government Printing Office, yearly.

Gallese, Liz. "Battle over Bias." *The Wall Street Journal,* February 17, 1978.

Glazer, Nathan. *Affirmative Discrimination.* New York: Basic Books, 1976.

Herwegh, Virginia. "Compliance in the Real World of Business." Paper presented at the Equal Employment Opportunity Seminar of the American Society for Personnel Administration, June 29, 1976.

Milkovich, George. "A Few Overlooked Research Issues on the Way to Equal Opportunity." *Proceedings,* Academy of Management, 1976.

Myrdal, Gunnar. *An American Dilemma: The Negro Problem and American Democracy.* New York: Harper & Row, 1944.

"The Personnel Executive's Job." *Personnel Management: Policies and Practices,* 1977, published by Prentice-Hall, Inc., Englewood Cliffs, N.J.

Purcell, Theodore. "How G.E. Measures in Fair Employment." *Harvard Business Review,* November–December 1974, pp. 99–104.

Chapter 17

Bok, Derek, and Dunlop, John. *Collective Bargaining in the United States: An Overview.* New York: Simon & Schuster, 1970.

Chickpring, Lawrence. *Public Employee Unions.* San Francisco: Institute of Contemporary Studies, 1977.

Davey, Harold. "How Arbitrators Decide Cases." *Labor Law Journal,* April 1974, pp. 200–209.

Dworkin, James B., and De Nisi, Angelo. "Empirical Research on Labor Relations Law: A Review, Some Problems and Some Directions for Future Research." *Labor Law Journal,* September 1977, pp. 563–71.

Getman, Julius, et al. *Union Representation Elections: Law and Reality.* New York: Russell Sage Foundation, 1976.

Greenberg, David. "The Structure of Collective Bargaining and Some of its Determinants." *Proceedings,* Industrial Relations Research Association, December 1966. Albany, N.Y., 1966.

Henle, Peter. "Reverse Collective Bargaining? A Look at Some Union Concession Situations." *Industrial and Labor Relations,* January 1973, pp. 956–68.

Kassem, Sami, and Mitterer, Marcia. "A Critique of Public Policy toward Teacher Strikes and Some Alternatives." *Public Personnel Review,* April 1971, pp. 82–86.

McClelland, David. *Power.* New York: Irvington Publishers, distributed by Halsted Press, 1975.

"The Personnel Executive's Job" *Personnel Management: Policies and Practices,* December 14, 1976, published by Prentice-Hall, Inc., Englewood Cliffs, N.J. Material reprinted with permission.

Richardson, Reed. *Collective Bargaining by Objectives: A Positive Approach,* © 1977, p. 107. Englewood Cliffs, N.J.: Prentice-Hall. Reprinted by permission.

Sayles, Leonard. *Behavior of Industrial Work Groups.* New York: McGraw-Hill Book Co., 1958.

Selekman, Benjamin. "Varieties of Labor Relations." *Harvard Business Review,* March 1949, pp. 177–85.

Stagner, Ross, and Rosen, Hjalmar. *Psychology of Union-Management Relations.* Belmont, Calif.: Wadsworth Publishing Co., 1965.

Walton, Richard E., and McKersie, Robert.

A Behavior Theory of Labor Negotiations. New York: McGraw-Hill Book Co., 1967.

Yearbook of Labour Statistics. Geneva: International Labour Office, 1978.

Yoder, Dale, and Heneman, Herbert, Jr. (eds.). *Employee and Labor Relations.* Washington, D.C.: Bureau of National Affairs, 1976.

Chapter 18

Anderson, Claire. *The Marginal Worker: A Search for Correlates.* Unpublished doctoral dissertation, University of Massachusetts, 1976.

Bureau of National Affairs. *Employee Conduct and Discipline.* Personnel Policies Forum, Survey 102. Washington, D.C., 1973.

Chambers, Carl, and Heckman, Richard. *Employee Drug Abuse.* Boston: Cahners Books, 1972.

Halpern, Susan. *Drug Abuse and Your Company.* New York: American Management Association, 1972.

Healey, Richard, and Walsh, Timothy. "Security Policies, Programs, and Problems." In Dale Yoder and Herbert Heneman, Jr. (eds.), *PAIR Policy and Program Management.* Washington, D.C.: Bureau of National Affairs, 1978.

Jennings, Ken. "The Problem of Employee Drug Use and Remedial Alternatives." *Personnel Journal,* November 1977, pp. 554–60.

Jennings, Ken. "Verbal and Physical Abuse toward Supervision." *Arbitration Journal,* December 1974, pp. 258–71.

Levin, Edward, and Denenberg, Tia. "How Arbitrators View Drug Abuse." *The Arbitration Journal,* vol. 31, no. 2 (1976), pp. 97–108.

Lipman, Mark. "What You Can Do About Employee Theft." *Nation's Business,* May 1976, pp. 63–65.

Mager, Roger, and Pipe, Peter. *Analyzing Performance Problems.* Palto Alto, Calif.: Fearon Publishers, 1970. Copyright © 1970 by Fearon-Pitman Publishers, Inc., 6 Davis Drive, Belmont, California. Reprinted by permission.

Miner, John. *The Challenge of Managing.* Philadelphia: W. B. Saunders Co., 1975.

Scott, William G. *The Management of Conflict: Appeal Systems in Organizations.* Homewood, Ill.: Richard D. Irwin, 1965.

Shaak, Phillip, and Schwartz, Milton. "Uniformity of Policy Interpretation among Managers in American Industry." *Academy of Management Journal,* March 1973, pp. 77–83.

Steinmetz, Lawrence. *Managing the Marginal and Unsatisfactory Performer.* Reading, Mass.: Addison-Wesley Publishing Co., 1969.

Wall, Jerry L. *Industrial Espionage in American Firms.* Unpublished doctoral dissertation, University of Missouri—Columbia, 1974.

Chapter 19

Behrend, Hilde, and Pocock, Stuart. "Absence and the Individual: A Six-Year Study in One Organization." *International Labour Review,* November–December 1976, pp. 311–27.

Bureau of National Affairs. *Employee Absenteeism and Turnover.* Personnel Policies Forum, Survey 106. Washington, D.C., May 1974.

Byham, W. *The Uses of Personnel Research.* AMA Research Study 91. New York: American Management Association, 1968.

Habbe, Stephen. *Following Up Attitude Survey Findings.* Studies in Personnel Policy 181. New York: National Industrial Conference Board, 1961. *Personnel Audits and Reports.*

Hinnrichs, John. "Characteristics of Personnel Research Functions." *Personnel Journal,* August 1969, pp. 597–604.

Mahler, Walter. "Auditing PAIR." In Dale Yoder and Herbert Heneman, Jr. (eds.), *Planning and Auditing PAIR.* Washington, D.C.: Bureau of National Affairs, 1976.

Meyer, Herbert. "PAIR Research." In Dale Yoder and Herbert Heneman, Jr. (eds.), *Planning and Auditing PAIR.* Washington, D.C.: Bureau of National Affairs, 1976.

Odiorne, George. "Evaluating the Personnel Program." In Joseph Famularo (ed.), *Handbook of Modern Personnel Administration.* New York: McGraw-Hill Book Co., 1972.

Odiorne, George. "Personnel Management for the 1980's." In Dale Yoder and Herbert Heneman, Jr. (eds.), *PAIR Policy and Program Management.* Washington, D.C.: Bureau of National Affairs, 1978.

Seybold, Geneva. *Personnel Audits and Reports to Top Management.* Studies in Personnel Policy 191, New York: National Industrial Conference Board, 1964.

Index

This book has been set Videocomp in 9 point and 8 point Primer, leaded 2 points. Part numbers are in 36 point Vanguard Medium and part titles are in 30 point Vanguard Light. Chapter numbers are in Avant Garde and chapter titles are in 24 point Vanguard Light. The maximum size of the type page is 38 picas x 48 picas.

DATE DUE

OC 17 '80			
NO 10 '81			
NOV 29 '83			
MR 6 '84			
MAR 27 '84			
APR 17 '84			
MAY 8 '84			
NOV 2 '84			
NOV 20 '84			
MR 1 5 '85			
MAY 1 4 '85			
MR 22 '91			
AP 19 '91			
MY 3 '91			